CW01499775

ACKNOWLEDGMENTS

My thanks to all who have helped in any way, particularly to

STAFF: Miss Bayard, Mrs Bebb, Miss Bidwell, Miss Crombie, Miss Eastaugh, Mrs M. Edwards, Miss Law, Miss Moore, Miss Pagan, Mrs J. Phillips, Miss Rudkin, Miss M.C. Sharp.

STUDENTS: W. Baker, M. Ball, E. Barsham, O. Bunting, B. and L. Butler, S. Butler, G. Cardy, L. Clarke, M. Cock, D. Coker, S. Coombs, M. Gallyer, M. Gayler, K. Gibberd, P. Gibson, F. Gregory, L. Guttridge, J. Heskell, E. Howson, M. Jarrett, D. King, H. Lott, C. Masters, A Morrison, M. Read, P. Scott, J. Spriggs, L. Tanner, H. Thorrington, C. Trotter, O. Watts, P. Wheeler, H. Whitfield, E. Wickens, W. Wragg, B. Young.

Colin Pointer, Graham Dalling, Stephen Sellick

Especial thanks to all who lent their precious photgraphs, and to Valerie Carter for all her kindness and practical help.

FOREWORD

Surely, you say, the story of a twentieth century Grammar School appeals only to the ten thousand and more girls who attended it, to their parents, husbands, children and grandchildren, to the nine hundred or so teachers, to Governors and to local people? Even if that were so, it would still interest many. Admittedly, what individual students actually did concerns them primarily, although the lives of the originals before the Great War would fascinate anyone. Who could fail to be amused by the doughty, often eccentric, Mistresses who stayed a lifetime? The general reader can skip or wallow without losing the thread of the narrative.

Boys' schools have histories of several centuries, ECS of barely six decades. The differences over that short period are sometimes comically unbelievable, the similarities occasionally surprising. This one school reflects not only its times but all such schools. Unique in its qualities, personalities, absurdities, it is yet like so many others in so many aspects. It has undoubted social importance; we see its reactions to great events and movements of the century, to economic good and bad times, to fashion, even to names. Its story might help to counteract the present myth that grammar schools were over-privileged places.

School's greatest value lies in the opportunities it has offered to all, especially to intelligent girls from modest homes. Someone might even be inspired by the range of careers in many different countries, perhaps to become a carnival queen, or enter a gorgeous female competition, to restore Old Masters, to represent county or country in any one of countless sports, to raise money for good works, to discover an unknown species, to provide meals for Royalty, to run a poultry farm on the most scientific lines, to clip poodles, to become a priest or a member of the Stock Exchange or a sorter of industrial diamonds. Whereas a few former pupils are magistrates, School is understandably reticent about one tried on deception charges.

Anyone teaching or involved with change in educational theory and practice might be encouraged to know how ECS sprang from a Pupil Teacher Training establishment. Our story tells which activities worked well and which failed, as one institution tried to come to terms with the Great War, the slump of the Thirties, the Second World War, its aftermath of greater freedom and questioning, and how it was finally overtaken in 1967.

ONWARD EVER

The story of Enfield County School for Girls,
1909-1967

JOAN HART

First published 1999 by Joan Hart,
Enfield, UK

ISBN 0 9536687 0 3

Produced in Great Britain by
Axxent Ltd,
The Short Run Book Company,
St Stephen's House, Arthur Road,
Windsor, Berkshire SL4 1RY

CONTENTS

HEAD MISTRESSES

Miss E.R. Broome, MA, 1909-1937
Miss M.C. Sharp, MA, 1937-1962
Miss I.K. Hogg, BSc, 1962-1974

DEPUTY HEAD MISTRESSES (Senior Mistresses)

1909-1911	Miss M.G. Buckeridge, BA
1911-1939	Miss I.C. Florence, MA
1939-1946	Miss F.M. Forrest, BA
1947-1959	Miss F. Sharp, BA
1959-1963	Miss D.V. Cox, BA
1963-1966	Miss G.V. Morley, MA
1966-1980	Mrs J.H. Hart, MA

STAFF ABBREVIATIONS

Miss Barker = Barkie
Miss Broome = E.R.B.
Miss Hodgson = Hoddie, Hodge
Miss Rudkin = O.D.R.
Miss M.C. Sharp = M.C.S.

Miss Bidwell = Biddy
Miss Forrest= F.M.F.
Miss Hogg = I.K.H.
Miss F.Sharp = F.S., Effie
Mr Whitehead = Charlie

* = Colours or Distinctions

PART ONE

THE FIRST DAYS

CHAPTER ONE

IN THE BEGINNING

The Setting

Charles Lamb had thought it a little teasing image of a town, with shops two yards square, but became disenchanted with "this country village, dull and totally lacking in interest"; that *was* after his sister had in a fit of madness, killed their mother.

The Enfield in which the first Enfield County (ECS) students grew up was still a pleasant old market town with wooden shops and houses, although it was no longer "the solitarie desert for those who are studious and lovers of privacy". Indeed, a pupil was lamenting the fast disappearance of the old Enfield as new houses were springing up. What would she think of the borough now? Yet golf courses and riding schools, country pubs and Hilly Fields, Maiden's Bridge and Gentleman's Row recall its past peace.

The town has a long history, confirmed by Stone Age implements, Roman burial ground, Saxon hamlets, Domesday Book, Norman moats. Medieval manors gave their names to Durants and Suffolks schools, a Constable of the Tower to Mandeville, Elizabethan nobility to Cecil, Sydney, Raleigh and Essex Roads. Less attractive were the burning of two witches and the arrival of the Black Death. The market has survived for nearly seven centuries; its central open house was new to the first ECS girls as it commemorated the coronation of Edward VII. As children,they would have seen the windmill at the top of Windmill Hill.

Schools? As so often happens, the Boys' Grammar and the Girls' County are next-door neighbours, although segregation of pupils was long the aim of authority. A chantry school was set up in the churchyard of the Parish church. By 1507, a priest received £6:13:4 a year " to teach children within the towne to know and reade their alphabet, to reade Latin and English, and to understand grammar, and to wright their latines according to the use and trade of the grammar schools". Even with this modest curriculum, for children, read boys.

Founders' Day for Enfield Grammar School (EGS) was May 25, 1558, although it had but one large schoolroom for nearly two hundred years. One master, celebrated botanist Dr Uvedale, introduced rhubarb and sweet peas into this country. Lawsuits led to its closure in 1873, but it was reopened two years later as a day school, "under entirely new management, after being thoroughly cleansed, renovated and improved", with 19 pupils.

In 1900, it adopted its badge and motto of *Tant que je puis*. The Head for forty years, Mr Eagles, " known as Beak for his thin face and nose", had a house in the school and is said to have patrolled each evening wearing his gown and mortarboard and carrying a lantern.

And the girls, poor relations in the shadow of such traditions? Education for girls just 'growed', despite hostility from State and Church.

The Opening

"The Enfield County School for Girls was opened on September 25, 1909, by Mr. County Alderman Colonel Bowles, JP, Chairman of the Middlesex Education Committee and of the Board of Governors of the School. A short service was conducted by the Rev. E.A.E. Saunders, M.A., JP, rural Dean of Enfield, and the hymn "O God, our help in ages past", was sung. Colonel Bowles gave an interesting address, dealing with the educational work of the Middlesex County Council, and then Mr. Regester formally declared the School open. A vote of thanks to Mr. Regester was moved by Mr. Councillor Engel, Chairman of the Enfield Education Committee. A vote of thanks to the Chairman was moved by Mr. County Councillor Penny and seconded by Mr. County Councillor Weston. The pupils of the School sang the anthem " Except the Lord build the house, their labour is lost that built it". The ceremony concluded with the National Anthem."

Thus the first school magazine, with its nice blend of Church and State, of regional and local, its formality and use of capital letters, in what one Mistress called those gracious and carefree days. The report continues:

"We were interested to learn from our programmes that the site upon which the School stood was five acres in extent and cost £4,776, while the building itself cost £12,329, and was designed to accommodate 250 girls. The architect was Mr. H.G. Crothall. Everything possible seemed to have been done to enable School life to be carried on in the best and most pleasant manner. Those members of the School who had previously suffered many things in

12

the little iron building now used as a Gymnasium rejoiced greatly to see the end of their trials".

Our hard-hearted predecessors wanted value for money while at the same time they used almost Biblical language to express common emotions. This pious approach continues.

"A tennis court and a court for basketball have been laid out on the asphalt playground, and we also have two tennis lawns and a hockey field. A delightful new feature of our School life in the present term is the Gymnasium. We hope that all girls will make full use of the many opportunities which the school affords for physical exercise. Success at examinations is useless without health and strength".

Thus formally launched, School had, in fact, opened its doors a year earlier to 111 pupils. By July, 1910, numbers had grown to 137 and to 153 by the end of that year.

From the four-page, deckle-edged programme, covered in whorls, scrolls and fancy lettering, we learn that "the Opening of the Enfield County School and Technical Institute" took place at "Three o'clock, pm" on a Saturday , and began with prayers for forgiveness of sins, blessings on this place and a request to become as little children.

An impressive beginning, indeed, which suggested glories to come.

Facing page
Top: The County School and Institute
Bottom: The Laboratory

Above: The Cookery Room

Opposite:
Empire Day at
Enfield Grammar School, 1911
Centre Mr Eagles, Colonel
Bowles, Miss Broome, Miss
Buckeridge, Miss Gale

Left: Sir Henry and Lady
Bowles in their Daimler

16

Above: *Staff 1910,* l to r
Back Row *Miss Hunter, Mr Crofts, Miss Forrest, Miss Gale*
Seated *Miss Bidwell, Miss Murphy, Miss Broome, Miss Buckeridge, Miss Florence*
On ground *Miss Garside*

School and Staff 1911

CHAPTER TWO

Woe betide anyone whose table manners were not respectable.

Aiming to extend opportunities for girls, an Act of 1902 created an urgent demand for teachers. To prepare students for Training Colleges at the age of 16, Pupil-Teacher Centres, most attached to a Grammar school, were established.

For most girls, anything beyond elementary schooling had been a pipe-dream; boys had priority in the family to stay until the qualifying age. Money was the major headache and improvements were slow; grants remained inadequate, although free meals for the needy became available from 1906, and free places up to a quarter of the intake the following year.

The first local centre was in the old British Hall in Chase Side. A temporary school, nicknamed the Tin Tabernacle, was then built, in which "we froze or sweltered, according to the Calendar".

Some 24 students, four of them male, assembled in the Old Hall in 1906, a year after the Head had been appointed. Miss Broome, Miss Buckeridge and Miss Garside were joined by Miss Florence, Mr Crofts and Mr Greenfield, the gentlemen on a visiting basis. The Head presided over dinners sent in from a neighbouring restaurant. Daring spirits who indulged in tea and buns from Painter's Tea Shop were caught and reprimanded.

One large room was available for lessons; the back row was in front of a roaring fire, well suited to roasting chestnuts. Pencil sketches of white models, mostly cones and cylinders, were produced in Mr Greenfield's weekly class. Students filed along to Enfield Grammar School to use its laboratory – the first, but by no means the last, example of sharing premises. The litmus paper and smell were remembered fifty years later. Girls had to wear gym tunics and long black woollen stockings for Physical Training (PT), although no apparatus existed.

Who would grumble at present-day bus services if they faced a journey of three or four miles each way, as students did, in the first decade of this century, with no public transport for most and no private transport for any? When it was too wet to walk or to struggle on a heavy bicycle, a student from Freezywater or Enfield Lock had to walk to Forty Hill station, take one train to Edmonton, then a second to the Town. One year, a sort of Black Maria, its windows suitably darkened, was provided. The driver sat at the front of the horse-drawn box on wheels; steps at the back led to wooden benches seating eight on each side – an early version of a mini-bus. Services did improve sporadically; school's opening coincided with the start of the double-decker, open-topped tram , greeted with flags, from the Town to Wood Green, but many girls still depended on their own two feet.

The Board of Education sent the names of candidates to be instructed; the then solitary male headed the list of ten. More were added before the Centre closed. The two, three or four year course was now free and sometimes supplemented by maintenance bursaries until the teacher began to earn. Students over 16 had to pass an examination to achieve acceptance at a Training College. Four grades of teachers were then recognised in Elementary schools: Pupil, Provisional Assistant, Uncertificated and Certificated, these last being the only ones who could expect promotion.

Most of the Pupil Teachers transferred to ECS for at least one year; after 1910, the system was abolished as it was felt that it undoubtedly led to considerable overstrain, and that a more thorough Secondary school education would present great advantages.

Instead, on favourable report from the Head, the County awarded bursaries, which meant that, as well as free tuition, students enjoyed not only a higher regard but also maintenance and travelling allowances.

During their last year, each spent one day a week at ECS and four as teachers at a local school, which " sorted out those who were unsuitable as teachers and saved a lot of heartbreak". After all this effort, a trained woman teacher could expect £85pa certificated (a man, £150) and uncertificated £75 (£140), and a head mistress £119-£250 ,according to the size of the school.

Preliminary Prospectus: Enfield County School

This tells us that the Enfield County Secondary School for Girls was erected jointly by Middlesex County Council (M.C.C.) and the Enfield Urban District Council and maintained by the former.

The Governing Body under the Chairmanship of County Alderman Colonel Bowles, JP, MA, was listed first. His Deputy was G. Spicer, Esq., JP, who gave his name to an Enfield school

Eight were appointed by Middlesex Education Committee, seven by Enfield District Council. In addition to Chairman and Vice-Chairman, they were:

Mr County Cllr. Penny	Mrs County Alderman Ford, JP
Rev R.H. Brown	N. Hepworth,Esq.
G. Fitch, Esq., JP	Mr County Cllr. Weston
Miss Webster, MA	Mrs Bernard Roth
E.A. Stearns, Esq., JP	Mr County Cllr. Engel
W. H. Middleton, Esq.	W. F. Field, Esq.

S. Beaven, Esq.

The Clerk to the Governors was Mr B.S. Gott, MA, at Westminster Guildhall, S.W.

An assurance was given that additional Mistresses would be appointed before the opening.

The prospectus continues with *Objects of the School:*

The School is to be conducted as a Public Secondary Day School for Girls, under the regulations and inspection of the Board of Education. Pupils will be admitted from the age of 10 years and upwards. The course of instruction includes:

Holy Scripture, Reading, Writing, English Literature, Composition and Grammar, History, Geography, French, German, Latin, Mathematics, Botany, Physics, Nature Study, Art, Needlework, Singing and Physical Exercises, with such others as may be arranged from time to time.

Next, *Buildings*:

The buildings, which provide accommodation for about 250 girls, are situated in Holly Walk, Enfield. The following provision is made for the Secondary School:

Central Hall, Nine Classrooms, Art Room, Science Laboratories, Preparation Room, Domestic Room, Lavatories, Cloakrooms, etc.

Fees:

The School Fees, payable in advance to the Enfield Branch of Lloyds Bank, are £2:2s:6d per term, including the use of books and stationery. All pupils, other than new pupils and scholars, who have not paid their fees before the first Monday of each term, and new pupils whose fees are unpaid upon the second Monday after admission, will be excluded from the School. Parents and Guardians will be requested to notify the Head Mistress before Mid-term of their intention to remove a pupil at the end of that term, or, in the alternative, to pay half a term's fees.

General Regulations: The School Hours (subject to alteration) are from 9 to 12-15, and 1-15 to 3-55.

Saturday is a whole holiday.

The year is divided into three terms of about 13 weeks each, with about 7 weeks holiday in the Summer, 3 weeks at Christmas and 3 weeks in the Spring.

Applications for admission must be filled in and signed by the Parent or Guardian and sent to the Head Mistress.

No pupil will be allowed to attend the School from a house in which there is a case of infectious disease; and if the pupil has suffered or been in contact with such a disease, a Doctor's Certificate is required before the pupil can return to School.

All ordinary books and stationery will be provided, but the books remain the property of the School, and therefore care must be taken of them.

Any careless treatment or wilful damage of School property by a pupil must be paid for by the Parent or Guardian of the pupil.

There is a playing field attached to the School.

Provision is made for the following games: Hockey, Tennis and Net Ball.

A report on the work of each Pupil will be sent to the Parent or Guardian at the end of every term.

Pupils will be required to wear the School hat-band when going to and from School, and to keep a pair of shoes for use therein; and are also requested to provide a School Gymnasium Dress.

Prospectuses and Forms of Application may be obtained from the Clerk to the Governors, Mr. B. S. Gott, M.A., Guildhall, Westminster,S.W.; Mr. N. Hepworth, Public Offices, Enfield; the Head Mistress, Holly Walk, Enfield; and Mr. E.M. Andrews, "Glenlyn", Enfield.

There are two handwritten additions. The first is the list of Form Mistresses:

I, Miss Murphy, BA	II, Miss Hunter,BSc
III, Miss Forrest, BA	IV, Miss Florence, MA
V, Miss Buckeridge, BA	VIA and VIB, Miss Broome, MA

The second, a notice to parents and guardians, was clearly intended for those whose daughters had already been accepted.

Homework. It is requested that the Head Mistress may be notified at once if any student exceeds the daily time allotted for Home Work, viz, in Forms I and II, 1 hour; in Forms III and IV, 1½ hours; in Forms V and VIA, 2 hours. Form VIB [second year Sixth] are allowed to arrange their own study time, but must not work after 10pm.

Dinners. A hot dinner of two courses is supplied for 6d at the school. Hot milk, tea or cocoa can be obtained for 1d.

Dancing. It has been suggested that the drill costume would make a very suitable and inexpensive dress for the younger girls, and that a modification of the same costume, with a lengthened tunic, would be very neat and pretty for the older students. The costume allows free movement and unrestrained development, and is therefore admirable for growing girls. The Head Mistress will be very pleased if any parents care to adopt this suggestion.

Jewellery, intended for ornament only, should not be worn at school.

Visitors. The Head Mistress will be very pleased to see any parents, or friends of the students, who wish to consult her or to inspect the working of the school. The most convenient time for visitors is on Wednesday morning, between 9:30 and 12:o'clock, but other times can be arranged, if notice of an intended visit is given.

This delightful document, dated 10:11:09, is signed by Miss Broome, MA, Head Mistress.

The Site, yes, But the Building....

The girls naturally wanted ECS to be a success. The new school concentrated on establishing itself, its magazine, clubs and sports, and on beautifying itself, largely by students' own efforts. The first sports and drill display (tea and programme, 6d), the first little bazaar, raised £19.

"Although our school is still young", it was possible to list the pictures in the formrooms. Almost all had uplifting or instructional purpose, nothing being bought for merely intrinsic beauty.

Form I had, appropriately, *The Age of Innocence* (Reynolds). Lady Murphy, mother of a Mistress, presented two copies of "very fine etchings" – *St. Paul's* and *Greenwich* for the Second's formroom. IIIA, boasting *The Light of the World* (" the best religious picture ever painted by an Englishman") won Meissonier's *1814*, kindly presented by Miss Broome at Sports Day. IIIA were edified by a Corot and *The Gleaners*, IVA favoured with Constable's *Crossing the Ford*, *The Pool* (Cole), a painting by Hobbema and portraits of Dickens and Thackeray. VA, in addition to *The Fighting Temeraire* (prize for Decoration), received two large Coronation portraits. VB saw Clay's *Dutch Boats*, *Returning to the Fold* and a splendid picture of the Victoria Falls. The room shared by VIB and VIA was as yet unadorned.

The hope was expressed that "some kind friends will be so good as to help us by presenting us with some other framed copies of famous pictures. Such gifts will be most acceptable".

More had been secured by 1912. Miss Bidwell gave three coloured historical cartoons to Form I – *St George and the Dragon, King Arthur and his Knights* and *Joan of Arc*. A bazaar provided Van Dyke's *Charles I* for IIIB, IIIA had *Christ blessing little children*, in memory of a child who had died, IIIA and IVB gazed on two fine views of Swiss scenery donated by the Murphy ladies. IVA had the extra joy of winning Millais' *The Boyhood of Raleigh* in the Team Race. Mr Goodwin, later a Governor, presented *Persephone* and *Captive Andromache*, and Miss Forrest, Whistler's *Carlyle*. The Sixth Forms received from another Governor a colour print of an engraving. Portraits of George V and Queen Mary adorned the Hall.

The following year, "School was heartily in agreement in expressing thanks to Mr Fraser for the generous gift of a sketch of a block of [his daughter's] pretty and artistic drawing. .. A word of thanks is also due to Mr Quilter for the trouble he has taken to get the drawing ready for us".

Girls twenty-five years later lamented that the same pictures were still on the walls.

One Mistress, received kindly by Miss Broome, remembered "a dear little school, perhaps about a hundred pupils. Classes were a heavenly size, and one could always migrate to an empty classroom if such a course seemed convenient". Another recalled the building as "new and clean, with that fascinating Sixth Form Study with a open fireplace". Yet pressure on space began early; that study soon became a classroom. There was nowhere to house the books being collected.

The main building remains familiar as little changed for over 35 years. A long corridor divided the ground and first floors unequally. All three entrances had ill-fitting doors. Beyond the unimposing main one were two large classrooms, one on each side. With enormous windows, rooms were exceptionally cold. In winter, they were soon dark as gas lamps hung from an extremely high ceiling. Only in 1983 were false ceilings installed to conserve heat and reduce costs. Teaching was difficult when a Mistress had to clamber on to a rickety platform of upturned hollow boxes if she wished to reach her desk or the blackboard, whilst anyone with a ladylike voice could hardly be heard beyond the front row.

Along the downstairs corridor, matters were worse. To the left, under a lavishly decorated arch, was the Hall; glimpsed at the far end was the platform, the Middlesex crest on the wall behind it. It functioned also as music room, second drill hall and shelter for any dispossessed class. On the other side were four formrooms, the Head's study, one small and two full-size classrooms.

Building went on in 1913; girls were "planted out in such classrooms as were ready for use to do some kind of entrance exam to the accompaniment of the hammering of the builders". Such noises, workmen swarming all over, the smell of sawdust, all became more well-known with the years.

A few years later, there were five entrances as the archway at the far end led to a formroom, Staff cloakrooms and toilets with "hateful" lavatories, "so un-private ... very much a masculine idea of what would do for girls". For many years, the Head, to everyone's embarrassment, used them if she wished to avoid a long trek. Is that why she is so often remembered with her right hand outstretched as if to clear her passage?

Stairs at each end led to the first floor. The Mistresses' Room, a large dank cloakroom and a tiny prep. room were half-way up, as was a room which was variously the secretary's office and a prefects' sanctum. It faced a larger cloakroom, which, even when electric light was finally installed, remained obstinately gloomy. Above the main entrance, a huge laboratory, virtually unchanged until the Fifties, with a prep. room or museum, faced the cookery room, which housed a water-heater, tables and an open crockery stand – and nothing else. Off the corridor on the wider side were two formrooms and another laboratory. On the narrower side was the Art room; an early photograph shows desks and chairs along three walls so that all could see the blackboard on its easel. It was backed by a walk-in cupboard which would become the library.

The floors were – are – noisily and coldly stony. It was – is – easy to be confused with the two mezzanine floors.

The gymnasium pavillion (as it was spelt) was on the far side of the field.

CHAPTER THREE

Their interest and kindly help were unfailing

The Governing Body easily outnumbered the staff of six Assistant Mistresses and three Visiting Teachers. Listed above them in each magazine, they received considerable publicity; greater participation, especially with donations, was expected of them than became true later. Although some remain names only at this distance of time, they were important people in both town and school. Service ranged from one year to twenty-five.

Eight of them donated prizes for Botany 5, Drawing 6, Drill, English 2, French 4, General Knowledge, General Progress 2, History, Languages, Mathematics 2, Junior 1 and Senior 2 Tennis and 100 yards.

As well as prizes, Mr Fitch presented a colour print, *Mrs Lister*, to Form VI, Mrs Roth, as Vice-Chairman, twice distributed Sports Day awards. Another Vice-Chairman, Mr Vernon Gibberd, JP, actually a Parent Governor although not appointed as such, seconded the vote of thanks to the Head at the first Prize Giving, once proposed it to the speaker and twice took the Chair himself. His wife also distributed Sports Day prizes. Their interest continued long after their daughter had left. Mr McEwen, husband of a Governor, became deeply involved, funding 31 prizes altogether for his General Knowledge examinations, and lecturing on Norway and on Geography, his main interest. Members of the Geography and History Society (GHS) later visited him at his Surrey home. Mrs Nicholson graciously presented Sports Certificates and "some fine specimens of Roman pottery from St Paul's Churchyard and some interesting fossils". One trusts that these artifacts were not simply picked up.

Over and above these encouragers of the new school, two gentlemen command attention.

The 200-year old parish church of St Andrew overlooking the Market Square was inevitably closely connected with ECS, particularly in the person of the Reverend Richard Howel Brown, twice Vice-Chairman, twice Chairman and proposer of thanks at the first Prize Giving. He encouraged the study of Scripture by funding the valuable Hodson Memorial Prize. His predecessor, the crafty Rev. George Hewitt Hodson, MA, thus commemorated, Vicar of Enfield 1870-1904, Rural Dean and prebendary of St Paul's, stopped at little to secure church schools and thus was at battle stations with both national educational authorities and other denominations, once even barring the way to a Congregational coffin. A strange man to remember thus in a State School.

Rev. Howel Brown gave VB "a most interesting lecture" on, and conducted a tour of, the church, instructing others similarly fifteen years later. Characteristically of his period, he involved himself with the celebration of Armistice Day, giving a fine address to boys and girls; his short and impressive service was an annual event until 1922. Perhaps as a gesture of thanks and/or remorse, girls spent a dinner-hour cleaning the churchyard which abuts part of the school grounds – removing soil and weeds rather than litter or graffiti.

His successor, Rev. William Daisley, MA, and his wife were heartily welcomed. He too conducted an inspiring service for 1930's Empire Day; his wife did her duty at Sports Days. The close, friendly sense of belonging is, however, never the same with anyone who is not one of the pioneers. In 1939, Rev. James Bruce Harrington Evans, MA, took over, in 1955, Rev. Graham Buston, MA, and in 1965, Rev. Eric Franklin Tinker.

It was a tremendous help that the local bigwig, Enfield's MP 1889-1905, was a Governor for 29 years and Chairman for 19. School's link with the outside world was able to make his presence felt in the community. He lived in the Big House, his father having bought Forty Hall for him. As Chairman of Middlesex Education Committee (MEC), old Harrovian Colonel Henry Ferryman Bowles had urged School's foundation. He fostered traditions, especially with sporting or patriotic connections; this was in tune with Miss Broome's aspirations.

Apparently giving an address on the slightest provocation, Col. Bowles took the chair on many occasions, thus being in the happily popular position of acceding to each speaker's request for an extra holiday. This old-time gentleman presided over the first Sports and Drill Display. Almost as familiar figure as her husband, Mrs Bowles donated prizes for Drill for four years and one for Domestic Science (Home Making).

In 1912, "with his usual sportsmanlike interest, [he] very kindly presented" a Silver Challenge Hockey Cup, for which four North Middlesex schools competed. He specified two matches against each other, two points for a win, one for a draw. Although ECS clearly felt that Colonel Bowles belonged to ECS, they lost their heads and it was two years before the fledgling school managed to win the trophy – as a result of improved team work. He too sent fossils and rocks, promising more, to the newly formed GHS. Still in accord with Miss Broome, he gave a prize for an essay on New Zealand. One Old Girl (OG) remembers him as genial and encouraging, although a member of Staff remembers him as no gentleman.

His wife's sudden death in 1935 meant to ECS "the loss of one of its kindest of friends, dear Lady Bowles. Again and again her gracious presence and kindly words have added to our happiness". The magazine tribute is within the black framework customary at the time, but a sense of genuine sorrow comes through the formal words. At Prize Giving six weeks later, the Head lamented: "The gift of bestowing happiness was hers in full measure. I never met her but I felt this beautiful and precious gift and we shall always treasure her dear memory. How very much we all appreciate Sir Henry's kindness in coming to preside tonight: we have felt with him in both joy and sorrow".

One of the great values of the contemporary English educational system was the scope it allowed to the gifted, concerned and well-to-do amateur. "School has not looked upon his like again".

They don't make them like this any more, dignified and benevolent

What of the Staff who had to make this new establishment into a going concern? Some were symbolic in that their counterparts could be found almost anywhere in almost comparable schools. Others would have been significant in any school, one would have remarkable in any walk of life.

The first surprise is that full-time and visiting members were simply transferred from the Centre, as training teachers and teaching girls do not require the same knowledge or the same expertise. Nevertheless, transferred they were. This doubtless contributed to the early concentration on teaching as a choice of career.

Miss Emily Rose Broome (E.R.B.) became the first Head Mistress. It is difficult to convey fairly someone who, although a stranger, was known to many acquaintances and of whom many words and actions are recorded. For some, her position and views were unquestioned: "A Tartar, an autocrat, ruthless in the exercise of her authority". For most, she was too remote and unreal to have any impact, so was ignored as far as possible. She was Head and that was that. This contrasts sharply with the awe and respect growing into a sense of privileged affection which first Heads often attract. Her reproduced likenesses are unhelpful; the portrait on the Library stairs suggests a superior washerwoman, the 1937 magazine photograph a sophisticated maiden aunt. She was nicknamed "Poke, short for poke nose".

While it is clear, and indeed accepted by pupils and Staff, that she could not cope with the demands of the mid-Thirties, by which time school was running on its own momentum, she was a Head of immensely long experience – at the Centre from 1905 and from 1909 at ECS – eventually a total of 32 years, most in ever-changing circumstances which included the difficulties of the Great War. She understood the need for good public relations and instituted interesting traditions, although here again, we face a problem. Vividly remembered by her pupils, virtually all of these ceremonies sank without trace on her departure. At times, it appears that School flourished independently of her. Perhaps this explains why an educational dignitary could say on a public occasion, from the platform to a packed Hall:" Of course, we did not know what the school was to become when we appointed the present Head". A long-serving Mistress once told me: "She was weighed up and found wanting".

Her own schooldays and training were fully Victorian, which may explain why she seems almost a caricature. Her actions, the events and charities which she sponsored, the opinions which she expressed publicly and the tone which permeates all, suggest three priorities: patriotism, especially in regard to the British Empire: the Navy, which, among other manifestations, forced the hymn *Eternal Father, strong to save* on wearying Staff and students: and Domestic Science, her constant reference to this subject upsetting pupils with academic and feminist aspirations. "Some of my happiest hours have been spent in trying out new recipes for my family. The better educated a woman is, the more able she should be to undertake that most difficult and delightful of tasks – that of making a perfect home. Some thorough instruction in household matters is really necessary. I once knew a gifted woman with the highest university honours who tried to buy butter by the yard".

These themes derive from her family and upbringing. One uncle, Sir Frederick Napier Broome, KCMG, was Governor first of Western Australia then of Trinidad. Another, the Hon. William, became Judge and Master of the Natal Supreme Court. Her father, a Naval Lieutenant, retiring early because of ill-health, commuted his pension and lost. Brought up in New Zealand from the age of 12, she and her two sisters were poor, with no woollen gloves for winter and no proper school books. The first editor of her school magazine, she took an external degree at almost the earliest possible age whilst teaching at an elementary school. She proclaimed that she owed all her education and professional training to New Zealand where she taught for eight years. She looked back with nostalgia to "all the happy life, the beauty of that delightful country, the Land of Loveliness", never ceasing to be glad that she had the interesting experience of seeing something of the growth of that wonderful Dominion. She wistfully suggested that pupils should write to girls out there, an idea not received with any enthusiasm. One girl who did initiate a correspondence felt defeated by the distance. "I should very much like to go on a trip, but there is little chance of our summer holidays being sufficiently long to permit such a visit".

When the family returned home in 1901, she had short-lived teaching posts in grammar schools and at St Leonard's Ladies' College. Eventually, Colonel Bowles, connected in some way with her father, secured her appointment as Head of the two-class Centre. A senior Mistress never forgot how thankful Miss Broome was at being thus rescued from poverty. Her salary of £200 increased to £510 by 1919; receiving £1 for every additional pupil above the first hundred, she was by the following year earning £740.

Miss Florence ("goodness itself in her treatment of Miss Broome and little thanks was she given") and the redoubtable Miss Forrest ran the school, the latter bullying the Head right, left and centre. She received little better from her erstwhile benefactor, the Colonel not only bullying her but sometimes refusing requests however sensible, such as a sink in the Art room or a school wireless; he refused the latter saying that the Staff would be listening to it instead of teaching. Her main counter weapon was weeping.

Either she, or the Governors, who had a major say, or both together, had the ability to attract good teachers. Mr Quilter commented that she allowed perfect freedom in the choice of subject and the method of treatment while giving practical help and encouragement in every way. She was aware of the intellectual superiority of many. She herself had taught English, French, Science, Botany, Arithmetic and Latin at the Centre. At ECS, besides giving classes in Roman History and Civics to the Sixth, she took Scripture/Religious Instruction (RI) throughout, as was the custom then and later. She generally set Bible verses to be learned for homework and end-of-term tests. At one time, she carried a market basket full of souvenirs from the Holy Land; a bottle of Jordan water was remembered seventy years later. "She would come into the room punctually, draw a diagram of Mt Sinai on the blackboard, ask us to open our books at a certain chapter and then be called away. Never did we get to the top of Mt Sinai, but caught up on our homework". Staff had to reserve a free period for Scripture supervision. "She told of a woman reading a newspaper under an umbrella on the Dead Sea": this confirmed her silliness until a student saw this phenomenon for herself.

She referred to girls, whatever their ages, as students, which was advanced for the times. Sentimental over sinners, always trying to help with her " innate courtesy and kindness", she did all she could to prevent a thief (yes, such did exist in those far-off days) from being traced; she gave money more than once to another whose lack of it caused her crime. One father refused to allow his daughter to stay on to prepare for college entry after Miss Broome had blamed her for letting form subscriptions be taken from her case. Yet, despite genuine concern for the less fortunate and practical, unobtrusive help for parent or daughter, she was snobbishly unkind. Scholarship girls were paraded at the end of term in front of the whole school for public rebuke if she felt that they were not living up to the public money invested in them.

With a phobia about sex, she refused to allow a book by Mary Webb into school, considering it unsuitable for a girl of sixteen. Luckily, she was unaware of the choice selection of literature assembled by the wily Miss Forrest, who managed to extract money for her subject, despite E.R.B's expressed wish to be the most economical Head in Middlesex. She never understood that *her* savings were simply reallocated.

Every day, on the platform at Prayers, she raised one hand and announced either "Those who have seats may sit" or "Seats may sit". She became President of the Geographical and Botanical Society (GBS), presented the Hockey Cup at a Fancy Dress Dance, acted for a time as treasurer of School Fund, gave a prize to the best individual performer on Sports Day and donated books on miscellaneous subjects to the Library on its formation and on her retirement. Her attempt to form a Girl Guide Company after the Great War was less successful: "I shall always be grateful to the Mistresses who have carried on the work that I should probably have found increasingly difficult in view of my many other duties".

Ex-pupils fill in bizarre details. "I can't be sure whether she actually DID make my form practise earthquake drill or just tell us how to do it. But I do remember that she made us eat school-dinner jelly with a fork, which is why I refused ever to go again after mis-managing an over-liquid mess". Another student shudders to this day at her hacking horribly at a half-shoulder of mutton to be divided adequately and equally between 14 or 15 girls. She regularly served the pudding, handing it over to senior staff only after the war.

"I was a self-righteous pacifist when the 1914 war came and went to see Miss Broome with a friend to ask if we need sing the second verse of the National Anthem. 'Oh', said Miss Broome, 'You object to the word

Confound. You must not think it is a bad word; here it simply means put to confusion'".

During the war, she qualified as a VAD, taking on hospital and air-raid tasks as well as factory canteen work and served on the committee responsible for Belgian refugees. At various times a member of the National Council for Domestic Studies, the Students' Careers' and local Girl Guides' Associations, the British Empire, Shaftesbury and the Royal Empire Societies, the Victoria League, the Enfield Emergency Employment Council and the Juvenile Organisations' Committee, she was President of the local branch of the Girls' Friendly Society, Secretary of school's Dr Barnardo's Young Helpers' League and active in the Head Mistresses' Association.

Even post-war, she remained suspicious of EGS. Girls were staggered when the first tennis match between the two schools took place. "I don't know how Miss Broome was persuaded to allow such a thing". Victory was generally attributed to the forceful approach of the games Mistress. The Sixth form Civics class was not allowed even in the early Twenties to go to the Magistrates' Courts. Previously unable to steer the girls outside before the sordid details of a paternity case emerged, she was not willing to risk that again. Strangely, one old student felt that they were well prepared for their future life.

Others portray her vividly as she tripped and skipped. "She always carried a bunch of keys and clinked a little. ...When I was an Old Girl and came back to reunions, I was greatly impressed by her manner of greeting us as she had obviously forgotten who we were. 'So nice to see all these old faces again' she would say, 'are you still happily working where you were, dear?'". Her concern for social training is repeatedly mentioned, be it the way panama hats were worn, the type of summer dress, the length of skirt or behaviour at dinner. Girls were instructed that it was impolite, when given Christmas or New Year greetings, to say "The same to you". The long envelopes for Reports must be sealed with the flaps on the right.

Anyone who felt sorry for this short, plump, dingily-clad but basically kind person, her hair in a Victorian bun, found it difficult to help her with friendliness. She rebuffed with petty jealousy or suspicion or embarrassed with obvious attention at a wrong moment. Eventually, the poor soul took refuge in increasing lethargy, spending ever longer in her basket-chair by the office fire.

To be more charitable, she did encourage Staff professionally, she eagerly arranged visits. All agree that this lonely person had high ideals of public service for herself and the girls. "I feel sure that behind the façade put up by the schoolmistress, there was a likeable person".

Totally committed to ECS and its high standards

A photograph taken outside the Hall tells it all: gowns and mortar-boards for the graduates, a gown only for the gentleman (impolite to wear a board in the presence of ladies?). His stiff-collared shirt and high-waisted suit match the ladies' white high-necked, often tucked, blouses and long skirts. Three have bar pins whilst four wear ties, including the PE Instructress in her yoked gymslip, sitting demurely on the ground. All have upswept long hair. The Domestic Science (DSc) teacher, in her cooking cap, looks only too aware of her lowly status. The aspidistra flourishes, the other plant's foliage droops.

Miss Mabel Grace Buckeridge, a wise, efficient and forceful Second Mistress, would now be called Deputy Head. Appointed ten days after Miss Broome and eight years younger, with a degree in English and her Teacher's Certificate, she had taught for one year. She offered History, Geography, Music, Needlework and Arithmetic. Her salary was virtually half that of the Head, £110. After three annual increments of £10, any further increase depended on recommendation.

Popular and attractive, she led the Juniors on geography expeditions to study rivers, took charge of tennis and attended the Debating Society, once suggesting an impromptu subject which apparently proved very amusing. But she committed the sin unforgivable in those days: after two short years, she married, therefore had to leave, a loss keenly felt by both older girls and Staff. The girls gave her a picture (yet another example of their astonishing importance), the former pupils, at an evening party, a silver cream jug and sugar basin, whilst the Staff presented the almost inevitable silver teapot. Over twenty years later, she wrote:"I still use and appreciate the bit of Enfield I carried away with me in the shape of a silver teaset". School was informed of her new name, her address and the arrival of a son and daughter.

Number 3 on the register and another of the founder Staff is Miss Isa Craig Florence. Educated in school and university in Aberdeen and teaching for three years in Elgin, this thorough Scot joined the Centre in February, 1906. When Miss Buckeridge married, she became Second Mistress, carrying out for twenty-eight years that arduous task with "dignity and steadfastness, seldom outwardly ruffled, often inwardly troubled". Nearly twenty years on, a pupil described her as a good-humoured but firm mistress, patient with those not mathematically minded. Another remembered vividly over sixty years later this "relentless teacher [who] could paralyse one with a glance and as I could never do any arithmetic, I was regarded as a hopeless case", although she did acquire a respect for exactness. By 1914, Miss Florence was, in effect, Head of Mathematics.

When the Singing Master could not keep control, Miss Florence "was sent to sit on the platform with a desk in front of her piled with books to mark. The moment there was any noise, she would look over her glasses at the offender, and quiet reigned at once". Her astigmatism helped, as girls were unsure where the quelling glance actually fell.

At first, her pronounced accent made her difficult to understand; she, in turn, found English names hard to recall. She travelled to Cuffley when two girls invited her for a walk in the holidays. They remained tongue-tied, so she had to do all the talking: "It felt like finding ourselves with someone from another world". Intensely committed to the betterment of mankind, whether by encouraging young teachers or strongly supporting the Suffrage movement, she always addressed Pupil Teachers as Girls and Boys; most put the males first. Blue-eyed, silver-haired, a strict disciplinarian with "a nice sense of humour, a kindly soul who mellowed", she was highly amused when told of her regular saying:" look at the board and I'll go through it".

Sadly, the period of development and scholarship ushered in by Miss Broome's successor came too late for her. Although privately confessing that her last year at ECS was the happiest, she could no longer stand the pace, having had an awkward position to maintain between the Head on the one hand and the forceful ebullience of Miss Forrest on the other. The latter remembered her as no less wise and efficient than her predecessor, albeit somewhat less forceful, but enhanced this grudging compliment by adding that her steadiness of outlook endeared her to everyone. She had the gift of making pupils feel ashamed of their misdeeds.

She involved herself in most aspects of school life, inevitably in that day and age, and especially in a small establishment with few Staff, but she seems to have done so willingly: Treasurer of School Fund for thirteen years, committee member of the Old Girls' Association for at least nine, donor of library books, some reflecting her own interests such as *London* and Scott's *Last Expedition*. Presumably she organised public events, although references remain few; maybe some were left to, or probably taken over by, Miss Forrest.

Number 4 was Mr Arthur James Crofts, whose own education and career illustrate the struggles of those lacking private means. After three years at a Higher Grade School, he achieved 1st Class in a scholarship examination at the age of 17. For the next seven years, he worked for South Kensington Certificates: Ist Class in the Advanced Stage in Inorganic Chemistry, Sound and Light, Mechanics of Solids and Fluids and part I of the Honours Stage in Magnetism and Electricity. For two years during this period, he was at Cheltenham Training College before becoming an assistant teacher. In 1899, as First Assistant at Blackburn Day School of Science, he followed classes at the local Technical School. Appointed in 1902 to a similar post for three years, he studied at Birmingham University for one year, gaining his BSc external London degree at the age of 26. A triumph of persistence.

Appointed originally for 1h25 weekly at the Centre, then for Tuesday and Wednesday mornings for Elementary Science at the new School, he also taught at the Technical College and was a temporary assistant at Ponders End Trade School. His wife later recalled that Miss Broome was her first social caller. His salary rose from £150 by recommendation to £200, then annually by £10 to a maximum of £250. One student, later teaching at ECS, recalled being turned out into a corridor for the abominable offence of giggling in class. He eventually became the first Principal of Ponders End Technical School.

In January, 1915, "we were all very sorry to part with Mr. Crofts who had so long been a valuable member of Staff".

Eight years younger, Miss Dorothy Fox Hunter ("a most stable person") was appointed at a salary of £120. Her life had been much easier; educated privately, she graduated after four years at Royal Holloway College (RHC), London. With experience in a private school, she offered Pure and Applied Mathematics, Botany and Physics. She accompanied girls to the Selbourne Natural History lectures, took several rambles, and stimulated collections of dried fruit and flowers. In hockey, "she spared no pains; the successes are due to her excellent coaching", and returned for a Social after her departure, when she was much missed after her hard work. So popular was she that, on her last day, one girl, normally reserved, failed to control her misery and was quietly sobbing. The inspired Miss Hunter thereupon invited her to help with her packing. She later became Head of a new Public School – 4 Mistresses, 4 maids, 4 pupils – and married when she was 47.

Of the remaining Centre Staff, three stayed on register, although, as the two gentlemen did not join ECS, it is unclear why. Monsieur Henri Gédéon Le Bas could not have coexisted with Miss Forrest. Instructor in five other areas before taking evening classes for MCC and teaching privately, he was already 51 when he came to take French Conversation and Reading for 4h20 each week at a salary of £175, by recommendation to £190.

Mr Albert Henry Greenfield spent three years at the Centre. He too had to teach while gaining first his Art Master's, then various Advanced, certificates from South Kensington. Joining MCC in 1906, he took Art classes at three local Grammar schools, evening classes at Enfield

Technical Institute and visited the Centre for 2h55 weekly, teaching Freehand and Model Drawing to all students for a total annual salary of £150. A tiring life. Five decades later, his pencil sketches were still remembered.

Continuing duties as a Visiting Teacher, Miss Nellie Garside completed the Staff, becoming Drill Instructress in October, 1905, first for 1h20, later for two mornings and one afternoon, before being transferred in 1911 to another district. After training and private teaching, she became Instructress to two authorities. She instituted the Drill Display, then Sports Day, the pattern of which varied little for half a century, and donated prizes out of her salary of £120. She used much of her own leisure in coaching the girls in hockey and giving them swimming lessons; her help in these sports was invaluable and her pupils would remember it gratefully. She clearly had an eye for equipment, courts, the new gymnasium. School indeed owed her much. Former pupils, at her evening party, gave her a pair of silver photograph frames, girls presented her with a silver buckle and the Staff's gift was an attaché case.

The five originals were joined in September, 1909, by four others.

Volcano in frequent eruption

Perhaps the most gifted, certainly the most eccentric, teacher, enjoyed and feared by girls and Staff according to their temperaments and social standing, Miss Frances Marion Forrest dominates the memories of all who came into contact with her. Her vitality was overwhelming; so was her vanity. Woe betide any unwarned newcomer who sat in *her* chair in the Staff Room, or touched *her* cup and saucer, or who served herself with coffee before F.M.F. had been *given* hers. No-one was allowed to sit at her table "piled to the roof and bursting at the seams with paraphernalia of various kinds". To her credit, her vanity was professional rather than personal, as anyone familiar with her longish dark skirts and insecure dentures would agree; every possible care was taken to avoid sitting in the front row. An early photograph, however, does show a stylish black bow on the back of her head. One pupil felt that the word dynamic was invented for her, as her form not only carried off all the prizes but also invariably won the hockey, netball and tennis championships. Needless to say, she was socially and academically choosey about which form she had.

Her phenomenal ability as a pioneer teacher of Modern Languages, primarily French, especially in pronunciation, was recognised throughout the country and in France itself. A member of the Modern Languages Association (MLA) from 1910, several times its chairman, she participated in international congresses in France, Belgium, Switzerland and Latvia. She spoke the official thanks to Mussolini at the reception given to delegates. As an experienced examiner for London University, she helped to institute its oral and written examinations for schools.

Miss Forrest built up the work in a not highly regarded subject, taught hitherto in *la plume de ma tante* fashion, and did so by her own example, her personality and her pride in her task. For her achievements in classroom, in school travel and for her many books, now dated in subject matter but less so in presentation, she was made in 1933 Officier de l'Académie Française, the first English woman to receive this *distinction rarement offerte aux Anglais* from the Ambassador himself.

It is astonishing that she became so early, and remained, *une grande dame*. The transition from a school in Paris (1889-1893) to one in Llandaff must have been daunting. Apart from a year's unexplained absence, she was there until 1901, gaining certificates unknown to modern times: Senior and Honours of the Welsh Board, Mathematics (Stages 1 and 2), Botany (Elementary, Advanced), Drawing (Freehand, Model), from the B. of E. After graduating in French from Cardiff, she acquired the Cambridge Secondary Teacher's Certificate and taught for four years in Camarthen.

She then displaced herself to Enfield for the rest of her life. Appointed at a salary of £130 which, by the end of the war, had reached the dizzy height of £350, she arrived in an antedeluvian growler, bringing her academic gown with her as instructed by telegram. A year later, she acquired a 1st Class Certificate in French Phonetics from London University as well as the Diplôme de l'Académie Phonétique Internationale. Another keen Suffragist, she walked in the university section of the procession from the Embankment to the Albert Hall.

F.M.F. retained until the last pathetic year of her life the power to terrify. One pupil, having rashly said that she had 'done' French before, remembered seventy years later her first lesson as the most humiliating moment of her whole life. Another recalled that if F.M.F's hair was standing on end and she was ringing a handbell vigorously, you had to be especially polite and even give her a pretty flower when she came into the room. Students were learning how to deal with the phenomenon.

She did not teach the Free Place or Scholarship girls on their arrival; for some, a slight social stigma, although a relief for one who was glad to be the pupil of a human being. By year IV, as she always, but always, had the top set, that same girl found that she acquired a good accent, and, surprisingly, a liking for French. Not so surprisingly, she also acquired an ability to walk the tightrope of accepted behaviour and to keep a weather eye out for storms.

This remarkable teacher kept, so it is said, a list of women who gained 1st Class Honours at Oxbridge: partly snobbery, but mainly because she could not bear the idea of any inferior being teaching her beloved language. In the late Fifties, she allowed two of us to bring up-to-date *Apprenons le Français* which she had devised with the delightful Irish Miss Forde, but retracted this honour in floods of tears, unable to tolerate the thought of such desecration – which spurred us on to write *Travaillons Ensemble.*

My last memory is not untypical. She invited three guests to a French Embassy Reception, an expensive and exhausting evening by the time we had paid for our own new clothes, her taxis hither and yon, a day-room where she could change, a corsage of flowers and a meal afterwards as well as retrieving personal articles which she scattered like confetti. Wearing her new 'gong' as Chevalier dans l'Ordre des Palmes Académiques, she sailed in, incredulous that His Excellency, newly *en poste* did not immediately recognise her.

Back now to 1912. She formed, and was permanent President of, Le Cercle Français for older girls. Fortnightly meetings included lectures, talks, games, debates, papers, readings and plays. She wrote in violet ink on any handy bits of paper the programme for *La Grammaire* and an invitation card to Fourths and Fifths.

Ecole du Comté ENFIELD
Les membres du Cercle Français prient Mademoiselle X
de leur faire l'honneur d'assister à la représentation de
la comédie LA GRAMMAIRE qui aura lieu le 28 mars à sept
heures et demie.

A formal reply in French was requested and expected. The evening ended with all singing *La Marseillaise*, "un succès fou malgré l'ignorance de quelques-unes parmi l'assistance"

Girls attending Conférences Françaises in London thanked "Mademoiselle Forrest de tout ce qu'elle fait pour que nous aimions le plus que (sic) possible le français". They mounted a debate: Qu'il vaut mieux faire une étude particulière des langues que des mathématiques: in which Science students participated. The motion, to be debated several times with scientists in the future, was well and truly won, 18 to 5. She actively encouraged all French or, during both wars, pro-French activities.

School journeys abroad were almost unknown in areas such as Enfield and uncommon in comparable schools. After arranging visits for two girls (required to give *un récit* on their return), she began official travel in 1913. Very much weighed down by their luggage, probably heavy leather, a hand-picked group of five ("she was very good to take such unruly people with her"), accompanied her with much trepidation to Paris.

"With what subdued feelings we at last took leave of our parents". It is hard now to realise the prevailing insularity; Customs provoked fear, seasickness (always called Mal-De-Mer) long remained a terror. Yet after less than a week, English food compared very unfavourably with the delicate fare of the Parisian restaurants. F.M.F. took her portable tea-making apparatus; as there were not enough cups, a butterdish and a glass were used. She showed the girls where she had been to school, but absolutely refused to go in with them to buy stamps. Some activities would amaze their successors: spending the afternoons in their rooms or the garden writing letters or reading Mr Quilter's book on the pictures in the Louvre, playing *Consequences* until bedtime. The sole mishap was the loss of F.M.F's umbrella, which surprised no-one. Six more girls went in 1914, again enjoying tea, this time from a Thermos flask, in their reserved railway carriage. They all dressed for dinner: remember, no drip-dries.

Sightseeing was, as it would always be, strenuous and comprehensive, the magazine account filling nearly four pages. The Madeleine was so closely packed for the 11am service that once inside, they could hardly move. They took a train to Versailles. Small things fascinated: a bullock cart: high steps to the train: gong for breakfast: the waiter's striped waistcoat: croissants ("a delicious kind of roll which cannot be made in England"). "When we reached Newhaven, we were absolutely overjoyed at seeing a real English policeman. The French specimens are not nearly as substantial and reliable-looking".

More than any other person, Miss Forrest put her stamp on the School.

No Drawing is ever Perfect

No man was appointed to the permanent Staff for over fifty years. A visiting teacher for Art and Music, Mr Harry Charles Quilter joined at the opening and survived for ten years, spending, as he himself said, three happy days a week.

His qualifications read oddly nowadays. Educated at an elementary school before St Mark's College, Chelsea, he gained many certificates over a nine-year period: Teacher's, Art Class Teacher's (no. 5858), School Teacher's Music in Tonic Solfa and the Association of Tonic Solfa's, before becoming an Examiner in the Rudiments of Music with the Royal Society for the Encouragement of Arts, Manufacture and Commerce (RSA). He taught in West Ham for nine years, then, while part-time at Tottenham P-T Centre, he was also visiting master at Edmonton Latymer (to which he later went full-time) and Tottenham Grammar Schools. His two weekly sessions at ECS increased to six in 1912. His starting salary of £170 rose to £400 by the time he left.

He did not long teach Art beyond the First Forms; never giving 10 out of 10, he remained always interested. He kindly took Seniors to see the Wallace Collection in order to study the works of various Masters. Girls drew and painted flowers and objects, but nothing from life. He sent sinners to tell the Head that they were silly, but never checked that they went.

As Singing teacher, "he was really quite good, but some noisy elements interrupted"; the 1913 magazine simply records that he no longer took Singing. Earlier, he had selected Fifth- and Sixth-formers to form a Mendelssohn Choir. After his very interesting account of the life and work of the composer, a concert of 14 items – unison, solo, duet, three-part, piano – was given to School, then to a very appreciative audience of boys and girls at Edmonton Latymer to raise funds to buy new music. Much enjoyed by all was his most interesting lantern lecture on his European travels. Interesting – already an overworked adjective.

He returned to judge, with the Head, the best decorated room for Trafalgar Day and to attend the Silver Jubilee Reunion, when he recalled lessons in Drawing and the pleasure of teaching Singing during the first three years.

A strange, lonely and, at times, humiliating professional life.

The Utmost for the Highest

Finally, Miss Ellen Muriel Emma Murphy, for whom life seems to have been much easier, with private education, first in London, then in a fashionable suburb of Paris, and subsequently at Le Lycée Molière. More private tuition preceded her entry to Newnham College, Cambridge, followed by Cambridge Training College. She sat the Medieval and Modern Languages tripos (ordinary degree standard), English and French sections, gaining BA and three years later MA, both Dublin degrees, Cambridge not recognising women until 1925.

Her first post was Junior Mistress and Assistant to French and German Mistress at a Girls' Public Day School Trust establishment. Despite her qualifications, her salary was but £110 rising to £300. A local Councillor, at the Opening, referred to all these highly priced teachers. One twelve-year old thought this disrespectful; it was also clearly inaccurate.

After a year's absence before the war, girls welcomed her back especially after her experiences in Germany which were anything but pleasant. On leaving, she donated a special prize for German.

How much time and trouble

Appointed in October, 1909, Miss Grace Annie Cook left after a year of excellent work owing to the arrival of a Domestic Science teacher who taught Cookery as well as Needlework. Poor Miss Cook: privately educated, with City and Guilds certificates for Needlework, she seemed doomed to be peripatetic, teaching at no fewer than ten Centres when employed by MCC in 1892. She received £70 for six months of Technical classes and 5/- to 10/6 for each school lesson.

Her replacement, Miss Hilda Constance Gale, fared better, visiting fewer schools and spending three days each week at ECS for an annual salary of £110. After tuition privately and at a public secondary boarding school, she attended the National Teachers' School of Cookery, gaining 1st Class Diplomas in Cookery, Needlework, Elementary Science of Common Life, anf a certificate for Chemistry, and had varied teaching experience. Miss Broome supported her enthusiastically: "Cookery classes form a most valuable addition to the School course and we are glad to say that most girls regard them as pleasures rather than as tasks".

She left in mid-war to marry and live in an ancient cottage on a Wiltshire hilltop "replete with every medieval inconvenience and all the things that really matter". Twenty years on, she recalled having been most kindly received by the Head "who made me feel at home and helped me in many ways".

The great influence of her inspired teaching

Appointed in 1910 after six years' experience and retiring in 1944, Miss Margaret Evelyn Bidwell was inevitably known as Biddy. Despite increasing deafness, she lived until she was 103, alone in London after the death of Miss Woods, her inseparable companion. Overwhelmed by the Queen's telegram, flowers, gifts and cake from friends, former students and the Crown Commissioners on her 100th birthday, she was lively, in good health and enjoying herself. She remembered seeing *Die Valkyre* in Berlin, having to miss the last Act in order to catch the last train back to Potsdam – in 1898! She attended painting classes in her nineties, as befitted a great-granddaughter of the water colourist Cotman, and practised her skills on Italian holidays. She was sailing in an open boat when 96.

Educated privately, she gained both the Cambridge Higher Local and Teacher's certificates after one year in Bedford College. I first met her when she was a delicately built lady of 66 and last saw her as a fragile but determined character of 99 at a January Old Girls' Association (OGA) meeting, to which she had travelled alone on Tube and bus, wearing sensible but attractive jersey and trousers. Tough, obviously, but feminine too – appropriately for one who had been a fiery Suffragette before the Great War, not afraid to accost Prime Minister Asquith in the fight to obtain votes for women.

Appointed to take charge of about 20 pre-free place girls, she offered Junior and English subjects (English, History, Geography, Scripture), Elementary Arithmetic, Drawing and Needlework. By the end of the war, her salary had risen to £300. For 34 years, every First Former passed through her "wise hands and owed to her the firm foundation of good work [and] discipline laid in that important first year". Her good taste and encouragement to develop their personalities are praised. Her fame lives on: a 1979 pupil remarked that her grandmother remembered being taught by her.

The 1913 magazine paid the first of many tributes. That netball had improved very much during the year was greatly due to Miss Bidwell, who coached both teams, that is Junior and Senior. A contributory stimulus was the acquisition of a full-size court. She inspired personal devotion: "It is the wish of both teams to prove really worthy of her by doing something great. If girls realised how much time and trouble Miss Bidwell and those members of Staff who interest themselves in netball spend in coaching and refereeing, I am sure that slackness would disappear". She instituted the Criticism (Crit.) Book; girls must have been tough, as some remarks were distinctly shaming. Playing Attacking Centre in the Mistresses' Team, helping on Sports Day, originating Inter-House matches – all were "a perennial labour of love".

These were not her only activities. Many "lively but well-behaved lambs" of the First forms have recollections of exciting journeys to see the wonders of the British Museum, to study Greek statues and especially to inspect the Elgin Marbles. This became an annual outing. She took IV Upper to see *Henry V*. She herself remembered occasional concerts and annual trips to Kew Gardens and the cinema.

Her chief interest for many years was dramatic work, mainly with the small performers of Year I. For such a robust character, her choice of plays now seems decidedly twee: for example, *Paddly Pools*, "a charming play", performed for a wartime bazaar and later by the Junior Dramatic Society. Yet its appeal was still felt over ten years later: "I can still see those sunset fairies". Her Verse Speech Choir gained 1st Prize and a Challenge Cup at the Enfield Musical Festival (EMF), gave a demonstration and entered outside competitions. She later trained girls in Choral Verse-Speaking for an Open Day.

Another pleasure was travel. One year Vice-President of le Cercle, she accompanied Miss Forrest and 13 girls to Paris, where they spent a giddy week, but returned none the worse for it. Seven years elapsed before she went again; visits with F.M.F. were not rest cures. This second one proved enjoyably hectic.

During the Second War, she was an Air Raid Warden. Shrewd business woman and difficult landlord, she, typically practical, requested no funeral flowers but donations to Save the Children Fund.

Heartiest thanks for help so willingly given

Miss Helen Robertson Baxter took her MA at Aberdeen in English Literature and British History (Hons.), Latin, Logic, Natural Philosophy and Botany. Appointed in 1911 with seven years' experience, she stayed 29 years. Her initial salary of £120 with annual increments, first of £10, then of £20, leapt to £350 in 1918, which princely sum was reduced the following year to £277:10:0.

Her interests were literary and Scottish. Recognised as the English specialist (there being then no such post as Departmental Head) and involved in Senior plays, she never sought to see her name in print. She was largely responsible for the magazine's literary content, and, more interestingly to us now, its tone. Contributions indicate that Scott was a well-taught novelist and that Lamb and Keats were on the syllabus. She took part in readings (once from Drinkwater), talked to the GBS on *Whaling* and gave books to the library.

In the Twenties, she gained confidence, perhaps after acting as First Assistant during Miss Florence's Grace Term of absence. She took girls and Staff to Oxford, having greatly helped the competitors with their recitations. Inspectors found her lessons on Composition sound and stimulating. Staff and pupils remember her sterling Scottish character and accent, her deep knowledge of literature, her keen sense of humour and the fact that she was not over-patient. Indeed, she had a reputation for throwing things. A rare personal note on her retirement thanked all the "good and faithful workers, worthy of upholding the traditions of the School to which we are all proud to belong". This enigmatic person does not come clearly down the years, yet she laid good foundations for this fundamental subject and encouraged so many to enjoy acting.

Education had been no problem either for Miss Elvira Juanita Inez Read: two private schools, Girton College, Cambridge (another Dublin degree), a portfolio of certificates and six years' experience.

Miss Elsie Bigland, another visiting instructress, stayed three years. Her sound education included two years at Dunfermline College of Hygiene and Physical Education with Diploma with Distinction in the Theory of Movement, Teaching, Games and Swimming. Her experience was also good in two high schools. I breach no confidentiality, for the magazine printed these details as did at one time the local weekly newspaper. A visiting mistress in Tottenham, she took evening classes there and in Edmonton. Her non-graduate salary was but £100 for teaching throughout the school.

Making her mark by winning the Mistresses' Potato and Spoon race, she organised the 1913 Drill Display at which parents and friends witnessed an exhibition of physical exercises, marching and country dances. "Miss Bigland must have been pleased to see the enthusiasm and evident enjoyment of both audience and pupils".

An additional Mistress came in 1912 because pupil numbers increased from 172 to 197. Educated privately, Miss Florence Mary Woolmer gained 2nd Class Honours in English at Bedford College, then her teacher's Diploma. After one year's experience, she offered English, Latin, British History and Arithmetic. She received the customary heartiest thanks for hockey coaching. She symbolises the plight of some spinsters, for, in 1915, "she left us the poorer by the loss of an enthusiastic and lively personality when her home duties called her away". A young lady of many parts who might have enjoyed a later, freer age.

More Staff were again needed the following year as numbers shot up to 238. Joining on probation was Miss Mabel Mitchell, already almost 24 years old. Her definitive appointment confirmed on the outbreak of war, she stayed three years. From Reading, then a Public University College, with Certificate and Diploma in Commerce, she offered Commercial Subjects plus Arithmetic, Algebra, Elementary Geometry and Geography. Her salary rose by two annual increments of only £5 and then three of £10 from £110 to £150 maximum. Her departure at the winter half-term of 1920 was noted somewhat ambiguously: "We wish [her] all the happiness married life ought to bring". St Winifred's House, more graciously, gave her a party.

Six more were appointed before war broke out, although their total service amounted to only 25 terms and 11 days. Miss Daisy Elizabeth Coutts achieved her degree the hard way through evening classes; she offered English, French, Latin, Greek, Arithmetic, History, Geography and Needlework (this last under the supervision of the DSc mistress). When she left in 1916, she too was thanked for hockey coaching. Miss Kathleen Balls, with a 1st Class Honours degree, took several outings for Botanical work, and, of course, coached hockey. Surely never were hockey teams so well coached, or, at least, coached by so many.

Transients are not a feature peculiar to modern times; at least, substitutes were willing and available then. It is surprising that four well-qualified and experienced women should be available and willing to fill in for absent Staff. Miss Chaney was a linguist and a singer, Miss Mare a musician and conductor of choirboys, Miss Cant a graduate who came top in University Commerce examinations, and Miss Stone another graduate who seemed willing to undertake any subject, including "correction of written work in Language and Mathematics, Scripture classes throughout the School, Geometry with IVB and Latin with VA and VI", all for a fortnight.

The first twenty-five, 1909-1914: official numbering

1 Miss Broome	2 Miss Buckeridge	3 Miss Florence
4 Mr Crofts	5 Miss Garside	6 Mr Greenfield
7 M. le Bas	8 Miss Forrest	9 Miss Hunter
10 Miss Murphy	11 Mr Quilter	12 Miss Cook
13 Miss Gale	14 Miss Bidwell	15 Miss Baxter
16 Miss Read	17 Miss Bigland	18 Miss Woolmer
19 Miss Mitchell	20 Miss Coutts	21 Miss Balls
22 Miss Chaney	23 Miss Cant	24 Miss Mare
	25 Miss Stone	

Of the full involvement in School life of these first teachers, there is no doubt, nor of their ability and willingness to tackle subjects for which their training had not prepared them. With so few Staff, such laudable adaptability was necessary; some subject teaching must have lacked specialist knowledge later taken for granted. This was especially true in Games, for which everyone was assumed to be naturally endowed. Participation in Sports Day was automatic, both as officials and as competitors in 'fun' events. The magazine commented approvingly on the keen interest both Mistresses and girls take in sports of all kinds. This was not, incidentally, limited to Staff. To meet the wishes of some parents, a Dancing Class was taken after school hours during the winter and spring terms of 1910. Perhaps this kind of extra commitment had some connection with post availability and salaries.

They travelled long distances to try for posts – they were not called jobs then. ECS benefited from the wider experience and different horizons of these women from various parts of the United Kingdom. Some came from richer, better known establishments to the new institution. Most gave freely of their time, and, often, of their own money, out of hours, on Saturday mornings, even during holidays. Many were sturdy individualists, some militant feminists.

Despite a considerable gulf between Mistresses and girls – it was not 'done' to speak to each other out of school, a constraint which persisted into the Thirties – it was the era of passionate or coy feelings on the part of the pupils. Clearsighted appreciation of their elders' faults and failings, as well as of their talents, has, however, been reached as these students have grown older and looked back with surprising and refreshing detachment.

Staff came from varied social and economic backgrounds. For some, the professional path had been smooth; others, particularly the gentlemen, had had to struggle in a way which students of the last fifty years would find incomprehensible and intolerable. There were short-stayers and long-timers who remained for life. Retirement was forced on some: a spinster needed at home, those who married, which was generally at an age earlier than is current today.

Possession of a degree was important not only for salary, permanent employment and promotion, but also for acceptance by the community. The wearing of academic dress accentuated glaring social, professional and economic distinctions between the full-time, University-educated Mistress and the part-time Visiting Instructress. Not that a degree was a guarantee of a permanent post. What is unexpected is that men taught in a Girls' school.

What can be said with confidence is that ECS was fortunate with its first Staff.

A little larger than life

Memories are predominantly of people, often of someone neither pupil nor teacher. Every school has its original, its 'character'; such a one was Mrs Hill.

She, as cook and receptionist, and her husband both attended the opening, for he was then in charge of the building. A new pupil of 1911 was impressed by three people: Miss Florence, Miss Forrest and Mrs Hill. When Mr Hill, a former sailor, died in 1913, School sent a wreath shaped as an anchor. With three children to rear on a niggardly sum, his widow became caretaker, or, as it was more accurately written, care taker. She herself was in no doubt that she was an integral, indeed central and essential, part of the establishment.

The magazine refers several times to her over the next 25 years – to her and her dog. "Our attention has been drawn to the fact that, whereas the prowess of our girls and the activities of our Staff have been set forth in no small measure of praise, there is one member of our establishment who has not received the recognition due to her long and faithful service". In 34 lines of attractive verse to Bunty, we learn of her beautiful omnipresence and her supreme self-confidence as she climbed the stone stairs to the kitchen where she curled up on a cosy, faded cushion in her own battered wicker armchair.

> Dignified of mien and graceful
> Small in size but high in station
> She for whom I wield the quill
> Bunty, dog of Mrs Hill.

Regularly recurring families of cats are also recalled.

Mrs Hill did all the shopping, her forthright manner being well-known in the Town. Most Mistresses kept their distance. She took over the kitchens which were used for DSc and Needlework classes. Not merely did she cook for Staff and girls, but at 4 o'clock, she took a tray of tea to Miss Broome in the Holy of Holies.

She is pictured standing on a chair in a classroom full of Belgian refugees to whom she was dispensing tea and cakes amid pandemonium; a mother and two children lodged with her. When School adopted an old-age pensioner for eight years, Mrs Hill was scornful when girls forgot to put soap and darning wool in the parcels.

A pupil described, seventy years later, how she hauled up the dirty plates from the dining room in a creaking lift and washed up with the gusto associated with her every action – this with a Latin lesson going on in the Cookery room adjoining. Her forceful voice, penetrating the clatter, haunts to this day. "I'm busy", or "Lor' bless you" as she launched into "a boisterous description of the little ways and sayings of our elders and betters". This large, bustling woman knew everybody and everything.

"She liked her own way, and if by any chance she told you to 'clear out', you did so to avoid a loud voice shouting at you. She would do anything for you if you treated her well. I remember her in the summer in a corner of the playground with a large wooden bucket containing ice and home-made ice-cream. She served cornets to a long queue of girls in break". The only doubt is whether this memorable feature of school life cost 1d or ½d. Kind, buxom, white-aproned and crowned with a black hat, she received Staff candidates, served them tea on a battered black tin tray, washed the Head's white cotton gloves (draping them over tennis nets to dry), and brewed reeking cough mixture on the kitchen stoves. Afraid of no-one, she once commented after a Staff meeting, "And now I suppose yer as far as yer wos".

Clearly a woman to be treated with respect, a law unto herself. In 1935, great anxiety was expressed as to the whereabouts of the kitchen curtain which had been as much a part of ECS as Mrs Hill: the lady had burnt it. Much relished was the occasion in the holidays when she took girls up a ladder through a trapdoor on a conducted tour of school under the roof. When the playing fields were shared, her vociferous efforts to clear the boys out as "they were keeping my girls waiting" matched her imperturbability on many other chaotic occasions.

When "our old friend" retired with the Head, she rated greater coverage. She had "never failed in her work for all those who are connected with the County School. We can quite understand her leaving at the same time as Miss Broome, knowing how she has always served the latter with faithfulness and greatness of heart. We miss her big hearty voice ordering the timid First Formers about, a voice which we well know and love. She is sure to miss her large family of schoolchildren, but her industrious nature will find another outlet for her energies".

Although she died before the Golden Jubilee, she was then remembered as one who moved through the School in an uninhibited manner which aroused admiration and awe.

CHAPTER FOUR

I felt very important

The early days of any institution are concerned with creating traditions, so that loyalty can be focussed on special things which belong to it and to no other. In such choices, atmosphere and aims come clearly to light.

The most obvious way of creating a sense of corporate identity seems to have caused little disquiet – then: uniform, which, for Staff as well as girls, everywhere in the country, generated more heat than light after the Great War. The newcomer's delight turns into an odd mixture of distaste and pride. Miss Bidwell's assertion that girls chose it remains uncorroborated. Old ladies, pupils before 1914, rarely mentioned it. When asked, they recalled with amused excitement kneeling before Miss Broome to ensure that the hem of the tunic just touched the floor. A photograph of 1911 shows Miss Garside indistinguishable from the girls in long black stockings, sensible lace-up shoes, long-sleeved white blouses fastened at the neck, and green tunics with velvet yokes. Half a dozen are wearing ties. Almost all have their hair long, tied with ribbons which would be frowned upon in a few years' time. All in uniform? Not quite. Seven are in mufti: six must be Pupil Teachers. The seventh, whose identity remains untraced, looks about six years old. In another contemporary photograph, all are wearing the largest of straw boaters, with a green and white band. One or two assert their independence by placing them on the back of the head to form a substantial halo. "What fun it was when they blew off and went bowling down the road".

Something special occurred a few days after the opening. Girls, assembled in the Hall, were allowed to choose their own School motto, by vote. The Head offered two. One OG, twenty-five years later, relived the occasion. "I decided passionately in favour of the alternative. Now, I can't even remember what this other motto was". They chose "the inspiring words *Onward Ever*, a call to a brave and earnest life", although F.M.F. preferred the other. This mixture of autocracy (only two to choose from) and democracy (choice , albeit limited, allowed), of heartiness and pious endeavour, is apparent throughout these early days. After the voting, graced by the Chairman of Governors and his wife, the Colonel expressed his approval and his hope that they would never forget to act upon their choice. It became sacred to E.R.B. when she discovered that it was the motto of the New Zealand Expeditionary Force " who fought so bravely for the cause of right and freedom at Gallipoli and elsewhere". She trusted "that our record shows that we have not been forgetful of this motto".

In 1912, not content with a School motto, each Form voted for one of its own:

I Stand Firm (Miss Bidwell)
II Essayez (Miss Woolmer)
IIIA Knowledge is Power (a pupil)
IIIB Nil Desperandum (two pupils)
IVB The Utmost for the Highest (Miss Murphy)
IVA Nothing without Labour (Miss Hunter)
VB Play the Game
VA Honour before Honours (a pupil)
VI Labor Omnia Vincit (A.E. Hogg)

A Head often determines particular traditions by her own interests. Instituted in 1902, Empire Day was observed from the first. "The month of May was overshadowed by the death of King Edward, but the thought of his devotion to his Empire's welfare inspires our observance of Empire Day. Mr Eagles kindly invited the girls to join the Grammar School boys in saluting the flag, after which Colonel Bowles made a short speech referring to the Empire's sorrow for the late King and to the many links uniting the Mother Country and her colonies". Seeming now a world away, this celebration long continued. For some elderly ladies, this red-letter-day remains vivid, although they suspect at least two extraneous attractions: the unique opportunity to see the boys, albeit on the far side of the field, and a holiday for the remainder of the day.

The basic ceremony remained unchanged until 1916, when the unfurling and saluting of the flag preceded a service in the parish church, at which Miss Broome, supported by Miss Buckeridge and Miss Gale, wore a long jacket, ankle-length skirt and a high hat.

1917's celebrations come to life. "We practised on the School field. Each Form was lined up in two ranks. The Form Prefect was in front. We marched forward to the Saluting Base and the Form Prefect said:'Form IVA, eyes left', and, looking left herself, saluted – none too easy when you are wearing a wide-brimmed hat. Then, when we were safely past the Flag, the Prefect said: 'Eyes front'. Before this, our hats were inspected, I think by Miss Broome herself. The Grammar School playground had an uneven and stony surface, and, as we marched, we raised clouds of dust". Dust is a recurrent complaint:"At the end of the ceremony, nobody could see anything at all for the dust which had been kicked up". After all the boys and girls had marched past, Colonel Bowles, who had been standing at the Saluting Base with various notables, said:' Boys, three cheers for Miss Broome!' The boys cheered. Then: 'Girls, three cheers for Mr Eagles!' We cheered. It was rather rare not to have one or two unfortunates who fainted. When Miss Hodgson was in charge of the marching in the Twenties, no troops could have rivalled it. The boys were completely in the shade, as the Governors proceeded to tell them ". In church, such hymns as *England Arise, O Brother Man, Mine Eyes have seen the Glory, I Vow to Thee, my Country, God of our Fathers* and *Lest We Forget*, complemented the address, the unvarying theme of which was Service. "Freely have ye received, freely give: that sort of thing. No drum banging, no glory".

Some remember happily the afternoons when the cricket match between Masters and Boys was watched by a goodly gathering.

Strangely, Miss Broome watched too, but, if the following week,

"one dawdled in the playground to watch the boys play cricket, she would tell us to go away as we might be hit by a ball".

The Choir participated in three annual festivals of Empire. A book of music for the great Crystal Palace Concert on Wednesday, June 19, 1912 at 3pm, price 2s (untinted 1/6), gives the programme of twelve songs and advertises hymns for Empire Day such as *The Union Jack* (Sixpence, Vocal Parts, Twopence). Suitable flags could be hired at ½d per week. For this formidable undertaking, full instructions were given. "Try how beautifully you can sing, not how loudly". Choir gained a certificate the following year. A junior participant, however, felt that Saturday morning rehearsals were not altogether acceptable. The war stopped such mass gatherings.

The Head's patriotism was also reflected in Prize Givings, perhaps most clearly in 1918, when the whole school sang the three-part song *Daughters of England*. Lest enunciation be less than perfect, the words were printed.

1. To the land of your birth, in a paean of joy
   Proud daughters of England, your voices employ;
   Extolling her virtues, God's beautiful dower,
   That nourish her honour, establish her power.
Chorus Daughters of England, loyal and true,
   Hear now your country, calling on you:
   Princess or peasant, or daughters of earls,
   England the service claims of England's girls.

2. By thoughts springing pure as the light from its source,
By words wing'd with truth, scattering Error's dark face,
By deeds, tho' unvaunted, in Heaven appraised,
To loftier station shall England be raised.

3. In the days yet to come may the arm of her might
Strike ever and only and surely for Right,
So on-rolling years gather round her great name,
Rich increase of honour, of glory and fame.

Although "naughtiness consisted in knocking over a bucket of water in the dining hall", Miss Broome felt otherwise. A comprehensive, but surely unrealistic, *Guide To Good Behaviour*, printed professionally, was circulated to all formrooms.

1. There must be no speaking without permission in any part of the building except the Central Hall.

2. Running on stairs or in the passages is forbidden.

3. The first bell will ring at 9:5am, when girls must be ready to go to their classrooms. Silence must be kept when in line.

4. Girls lunching in School must form in line in the Hall at 12:30pm, and pass to the Dining Room in single file with the Mistress on duty. After lunch, they must go out of doors, except when they have special permission to remain in the Hall. Visiting classrooms, or loitering in cloakrooms, lavatories, bicycle shed, passages, or in front of the school is forbidden. No girl may leave the school bounds without permission. Some exercise should be taken. Girls in the Lower School must not study during the period 12:15 to 1:55pm. Upper School girls may obtain leave to do so, but only after 1:30pm.

5. Hockey sticks, etc., must not be taken out during the interval 10:40 to 10:55am. The bell will be rung at 1:40pm., when all those playing hockey etc., must stop their games, put sticks etc., away, and if necessary prepare themselves for afternoon school.

6. Girls must not receive help with their *written* homework from anyone but their Form Mistress. The time allotted in the Home Work Time Table must not be exceeded. If too much work is set for this time, the Form Mistress must be informed.

7. Girls taking Domestic Science or Laboratory Work must not wear flannelette blouses or hair-combs other than metal ones.

8. The hair must always be plaited or tied back.

9. All schoolbooks must be neatly covered with brown paper, which may be obtained at school.

10. Hats or caps with the school colours must be worn to and from school.

11. Walking shoes must be exchanged for house shoes, or tennis shoes, before school.

12. All shoes, handkerchiefs, gloves and hats must be marked with their owners' names.

13. Lockers must not be visited except immediately before and after morning and afternoon school. All valuables must be kept in lockers. [Originally, an order mark was forfeited if a key were mislaid.]

14. Girls who have been absent, and girls unable to prepare their homework must bring written excuses from their parents or guardians to the Head Mistress before morning school. Absence for trivial reasons is contrary to the School Regulations.

15. Conduct Marks will be lost for breaking Rules 1 to 8, and for any other form of bad behaviour. Order Marks will be lost for breaking Rules 9 to 13, and for untidiness of any kind, eg., careless dressing, leaving books in the Central Hall, etc. [Five lost Order Marks meant one lost Conduct Mark and a Report to the Head.] Anyone who loses 5 Conduct Marks in the Upper School or 10 Conduct Marks in the Lower School, during the half-term, will have to return for an hour's detention on Saturday morning, and this will be notified to her parents. Unprepared lessons must be prepared before leaving school if Rule 14 is broken.

E.R. Broome, M.A.
Head Mistress

Certain points stand out: emphasis on tidiness and neatness, assumption that hair will be long, central position of the Head, importance of exact timing and of silence, separation of Juniors and Seniors, stress on a healthy body, use of etc. to cover all eventualities, intrusion of school life into the private life of pupil, parent and Mistress – Saturday morning at risk, no less – and, above all, lack of flexibility.

Clubs were gradually formed – and died – and were re-formed, as in every school. Parties were hugely enjoyed, for virtually all entertainment was self-created. Expeditions and matches also encouraged the sense of belonging.

Almost from the beginning, school had a strong and praiseworthy tradition of helping others. The earliest recorded, in 1912, concentrated characteristically on children less fortunate than themselves. The Cripples' League received money to send a local invalid child to the seaside for a fortnight; young sufferers visited ECS which adopted Dr Barnardo's, forming a branch of the Young Helpers' League. "Once a year a voluble lady came and lectured on the work of the Homes. It was always on Friday afternoons when the Vth and VIth forms missed gym". This doubtless delighted some, but annoyed the majority. A concert and afternoon tea raised money for the cause. Even the great event of the swimming season, the Gala, was held in aid of the School Self-Denial Fund, proceeds amounting to £2:8:6.

A modest beginning to which the war gave unexpected stimulus.

A large number of spectators

The new school had to be publicised, so that parents and friends could feel that it formed a part, and a flourishing part, of the community. Prize Givings, concerts, Sports and Drill Displays were all popular, although, or maybe even because, they took place either on Saturdays or in the evenings. In 1912, each form was allowed an afternoon reception. Mothers did not work outside the home, at least not mothers who could afford school fees. Parents flocked to see "the work of the school as fully as possible". Form I entertained with a little play, an adaptation of Tennyson. Who thought that Open Days were a modern invention?

Suitable contributions are earnestly requested

A magazine is assumed to reach only committed parents; in those first days, most parents *were* committed. With it, a school seeks to establish an identity and a sense of continuity. Besides giving facts, editorial and articles, consciously or unconsciously, reflect its spirit, aspects of its work, changes of attitudes and approach. Early editions resemble evangelical prayers of self-evaluation.

A school magazine communicates with former students, those in administrative authority, Heads of other schools (an unwritten law decreed exchanging copies with neighbouring establishments, although none of these have been discovered), suppliers and local shopkeepers. Even if, on occasion, the product seems inappropriate (Real Test Men's Cricket Bats in your size), the income from advertisements was helpful, often crucial; such ventures were run on a shoestring, indeed almost always at a loss. These admirable productions helped to make this story possible.

Few exist today; there is too much competition for pocket – or job – money and spare time. School's official publication ceased, regrettably, in 1966. Sporadic attempts to circulate a school-printed version demanded too much of the energy and enthusiasm of the editor and the cooperation of the secretarial department.

Number 1, Volume 1, saw the light of day in December, 1910. No price is indicated, although all other pre-war ones cost 6d. Its 18 pages of thick deckle-edged paper 9½" long by 7" wide, boast huge margins of 1½" at top, bottom and sides. Paper was not in short supply. A decrepit bound volume, weighing 4½lbs and so defying easy consultation, embossed with gold leaf, is beautifully inscribed: "Presented by the Old Girls to Miss E.R. Broome, M.A., the first Head Mistress on her retirement in 1937. At her death, given to Miss M.C. Sharp, M.A.". 1927's insertion bears jagged holes where it must have been hung in a formroom.

It began life as a chronicle, a record of the year. As expeditions, societies, matches, examinations and pupils increased in number, the booklet grew larger, as obviously its appeal required the inclusion of as much as possible. Nothing is more calculated to make you buy than the knowledge, hope or fear, that your name is in print.

Criticism of the first number is unfair, as it is filled with details of the school, its opening, building, activities and results. There are only three non-news items. M.C. contributed *Visite à Paris*, the first of many pieces on travel and of a quite remarkable number written in French; all the main buildings, unimaginatively listed, were visited in one short week. The other two came from young women who had been at the Centre. Evelyn Cole's 2½ pages told *The Story of a Mirror*, supposedly belonging to Mary, Queen of Scots. B. Hitchcock's *The Advantages and Disadvantages of Life in London*, "the heart of a mighty empire", reveals strong class consciousness; the millionaire dashing along in his motor car, the élite of fashionable society in Rotten Row on horseback are contrasted with the hundreds of starving poor leading a miserable existence. Few girls would have visited the capital; London was a world away. An almost apocalyptic vision concludes the article, confirming the gap between Enfield and London, the country being the work of God, the city of man.

> And in the future time some day
> London, with all her grand array.
> Her pomp, her pride and her display,
> Her heaving human sea,
> Shall vanish, fade and melt away
> Into eternity.

The final word came from the editor, then probably Miss Broome and another Mistress. Prose contributions were deemed preferable, an unexpected constraint, as verse floods in acceptably during the War. Letters dealing with matters of interest would be welcomed, although not one was printed. Henceforth, the magazine would be edited by senior girls, and it was hoped that the rest of the School would do their best to help them. Another democratic procedure.

The second edition of 32 still largely factual pages had two editors (the masculine form was always used) and no fewer than seven sub-editors. They gratefully acknowledged some very acceptable articles, hoped to receive still more the following year and regretted their inability to use the humorous pieces. A pity, as some light relief would have been welcome, the only original work being essayish and didactic. Lists of Governors and of Staff changes became regular features.

Although certainly not true after the Second War, when society has intruded into the workings of schools whether schools wished it or not, it is often mistakenly thought that girls' schools before 1914 were protected seminaries. Whilst references to contemporary events were few – for example, debate on Daylight Saving, 1913 –, magazines do give a limited idea of how far ECS deliberately involved itself in the world outside. As all polling in the 1910 General Election did not take place on the same day, girls, with long drawn-out excitement, affixed coloured flags to a large map of the British Isles. School had the honour of a visit of members of the Imperial Conference of Colonial Teachers. Girls were not allowed to ignore death. A thick black line frames an *In Memoriam* notice for one of the first Governors and for the Chairman's mother.

In those monarchical times, the 1911 Coronation was, of course, the great event for everyone. School was one of the many that enjoyed the holidays granted at the King's request. "On June 20, we had our own celebration. All the classrooms were decorated with flags and flowers and loyal mottos. Prizes for the best decorated rooms were awarded to Forms V and II. Then the whole School assembled in the Hall to sing patriotic songs after which Colonel Bowles gave a short address on the Coronation. School then closed for three days, the rest of our week's holiday being added to the summer vacation". A nice sense of realism. No wonder they were Royalists: a week's holiday, indeed.

Holiday in Belgium (D.E.C.) told how a girl's father made all the arrangements in July for the departure in early August from St Katherine's Dock, Tower Bridge, on board one of the Steam Navigation ships bound for the 10-hour journey to Ostend, one of the few boats sailing because of a dock strike. "As soon as the boat was moored, we were surrounded by a large number of gesticulating porters who wished to help with the luggage". Some things don't change; some really do. In their hotel, there were about 150 guests, 60 of whom were English. A potted geography lesson on the countryside, notes on the religious procession for August 15, a guided tour of towns – the article might have gone on for ever but "the serious news about the railway strike somewhat discomfited us, so we thought it wiser to return home".

Two former students, unnamed, suggest what future candidates might find at Training College. Dormitory accommodation, early rising, frantic dressing before the Roll Bell, reading, fancy work (or buttoning shoes) during Roll Call: a ½d fine for being late or "losing a chair": breakfast 7:30-8, waiting while letter monitresses sorted post, morning service 8:30: work from 8:45, with two hour-long lectures separated by five minutes' break: twenty minutes for lunch, time for a walk in summer or a nice rest in winter: two more lectures: Monday and Friday afternoons, drill lessons, otherwise students were free, but expected to go out for as long as possible on fine days: on wet, they cosily read, sewed, talked or played games: 4-30, Tea, followed at 5-15 by three hour-long lectures, supper, Evening Service, bed at 9-15, Silence Bell and Lights Out at 10. What would today's students think? It is understandable that one writer felt the need to be determined to look on the bright side of things and to see the sun shining behind the darkest cloud. Midnight feasts "seem to be highly thought of by the Juniors: girls come in their dressing gowns, with their hair streaming down their backs". A friend's birthday was toasted in clear, cold water.

Already by 1912, it had become necessary to produce a smaller magazine in order to avoid debt. Reduced to 20 pages, it still cost 6d. With little space for original contributions, it was perhaps not altogether unfortunate that only two were received. Winifred Epps' 3-page article on *Mes Expériences en France* was, indeed still is, informative, if in slightly suspect French: the sense of panic on arrival at the Paris station, the charming village with every house different, life on the river barges, carpetless floors, big wooden beds, shuttered windows, vines growing on the walls: the different ways of using cutlery, cleaning the plate with bread ready for the next course, chocolate for breakfast, excellent bread *vendu par le mètre*, people eating and drinking outside. All Frenchmen wore beards or moustaches. "Toutes les jeunes filles deviennent grandes personnes plus tôt que les Anglaises". Trains were disgusting, trams bizarre. Shopping in Paris became a headache because "tout le monde regarde et pousse. ... Les souvenirs de ma visite sont très bons et j'espère les continuer plus tard".

The hope that original articles would be a feature the following year brought more contributions than they were able to use. Miss Baxter, two joint editors and a committee of ten were learning the perversity of life. Even so, two of the 32 pages remain blank. As a literary organ, its development was slow and the attention paid to original material condescending, the results being mainly of historical interest.

An article on Covent Garden market is by a girl whose initials indicate her identity as the daughter of a Wholesale and Retail Salesman. To get there by 6am. meant the 5:10 train from the Great Northern station. She described how the flowers arrived, were arranged and their prices argued over by porteresses, "all with a great deal to say. Instead of wearing coats, they have large shawls tied across their shoulders, and little round bonnets, like small cushions, flattened out by the weight of the boxes which they carry on their heads". Their wages were twopence to go round the market and collect the flowers and plants which a man had bought. What are now called racial or ethnic distinctions were observed: foreigners all talking broken English, Frenchmen distinguishable only by their clothes and habits, Jews selling toys and ornaments to the salesman. The market closed at 9am, deserted within an hour.

No-one can accuse the magazine of being parochial. Another traveller, unidentifiably XYZ, gave a page of sweeping generalisations: "the peasants in Holland and Belgium spend their time in making lace and so do the Swiss peasants. ... The chief feature of Holland is the picturesque dress of the people, otherwise, it's very like Belgium". Would-be travellers might be confused to learn that Belgian money is French, the same as the Swiss. "Things are very dear in Holland, especially Dutch china – you pay 4/- for a very small piece".

Few attempted original work. To Helen Muriel Wylie IIIA, goes the honour of writing the first poem printed, an unpretentiously pleasing evocation of the forest harvest. Hilda Dean's first impressions of ECS are expectedly conventional. Winifred Hyde, the first known mother of a future pupil, immortalised her generation's enthusiasm in *Hurrah for Hockey.*

Although by its publication date, 1914's edition belongs to the war years, only the editorial betrays this. G. Morgan, aged 11, contributed an 11-stanza ballad on Balin and Balan, who fought over a fair damsel at Arthur's court. Another first former, Myrtle Macht, wrote of an old doll, Lily, whose mistress preferred a new china model until she realised how unhappy poor Lily was. Children were younger then.

As a chronicle, the magazine was well and truly established. The committee thanked the many girls who took the trouble to send contributions and hoped that they would not be deterred by the fact that not all had been so far included.

War made little difference to its appearance: paper was still available. Many years passed without noticeable change.

School life seems to prove pleasant to all

and we try to work together under our motto Onward Ever". Is it fanciful to feel that this gives the essence of School in its early years?

Looking after the welfare of the older girls, Miss Florence had seventeen 14-years olds, Miss Buckeridge a small group of 15- and 16-year olds. Forms I ("12 little girls") and II (12 slightly older children) were fee payers who preceded the Scholarship entry and some late transfers at 11 who went into a large Form III, the "fate" of Miss Forrest. To relieve pressure on numbers, two or three were subsequently promoted to Form IV. Staff newcomers were given lower forms. The form room was the centre of life.

The so-called Sixth, supposedly in Miss Broome's care, attended on alternate days to be taught mainly by her, Miss Florence, Miss Buckeridge and the two visiting gentlemen. As pupil teachers, they visited elementary schools to learn how to teach. Not all transferred to ECS, nor did all stay long; few institutions have Old Girls within days of opening.

Prayers were held in the Hall after registration. At the end of morning break, girls lined up to be admitted in an orderly fashion. Lunch could be brought from home and eaten outside on warm days. Later generations left too much litter for this to continue.

No timetable has come to light and little is known of actual teaching. Fourteen elected to learn Latin with the Head and two took German, Miss Murphy being much envied by those who had to deal with large numbers. For Mathematics and French, any large class was divided. VIA (then the first year Sixth) and VIB had joint lessons, so some always began the History syllabus in the middle. Looking back after only twenty years, one student remembers painting a Union Jack, staying in to rewrite an essay on camping (although lines were the usual form of punishment), and learning the order of French pronouns! A new 12-year old soon noticed the keen interest in sports of all kinds, "but that was not all, for the lessons, besides being instructive, were very interesting and engrossing". Botanists walked in the nearby countryside; many lanes and hedges, the rushes in the ditches belong to yesteryear. Many small fish swam then in the four centuries-old New River; its present and future condition concerns their great-grandchildren today. She also observed groups of merry girls standing chatting to their particular friends, all busily engaged in laughing and talking happily. Many remained life-long friends.

Holidays varied in length: 1912-1913 saw nearly 4 weeks at Christmas, 4½ days at Easter, 3 weeks at Whit, and from July 31 to September 28, whereas the following years, Easter gave 3 weeks and Whit 2 days.

Seventy years on, a student felt that the competition which permeated work and play was bad, a reinforcement of egoism, but the school needed some drive to gain standing in the world outside. From the outset, examinations were taken, soon increasing in number and broadening in scope. In the first year, 13 gained the Senior Oxford Local Certificate, essential for Training Colleges. In the second, 10 sat, 10 passed; the national average for girls was 54%. The pass rate continued high with London University School Certificate (SC), the Head being justifiably proud as six of those successful had had 2-2½years only of secondary education. Matriculation exemption rose to 5, that is 100%, by 1914. Honours and Distinctions (*) increased steadily: French Oral (O) and Written (W) and Botany gained most, then History, followed by Geography, German O, Mathematics, Latin and Drawing. Candidates had to pass in all subjects at one attempt or retake the whole examination.

Four secured Pitman's Elementary Shorthand certificates. The RSA ran French examinations, so Miss Forrest inevitably entered candidates, whatever their specialisation. In the first pre-war entry, 7 passed in French O (2*) and 3 gained 2nd Class at the Advanced level (AL).

So, if examination results are any criteria, the new school was more than holding its own academically. It was examined for two days by three Inspectors from London University, including Professor Rippman of French textbook fame. Unfortunately, the Report had not been received before the magazine was printed; no further reference to it has emerged. The teaching of certain selected subjects was further scrutinised another year.

Prizes, always donated as there was as yet no official provision, were awarded to the first three in Forms I-IV; as two girls occasionally tied, marks were probably the deciding factor. Names of donors were recorded, although one for General Progress was, in Victorian fashion, Given by A Friend.

What of the evening which, above all others, reflects aims and achievements and provides a showcase, when prizes and trophies are presented, the Head delivers her Report, Governors and local worthies are present to be inspected, and parents, and, if there is room, interested friends, can sit in judgment? Even without any reception afterwards, Prize Givings were lengthy affairs, preparation and rehearsals intruding into many lessons. Programmes, printed then as always in pale green, have survived, but no actual speeches.

The first, December 16, 1910, in the Hall was parochial in that Mrs Bowles kindly consented to distribute examination certificates and thirty-three prizes, while her husband took the chair at the surprising time of 8:30pm. The report, presentation, address and Votes of Thanks were followed by entertainment. Nine girls performed a French play in four scenes, *The Two Fairies*: a summary was thoughtfully provided. Musical items were sung by six varied groupings: *Bethlehem, The Lord's my Shepherd, On Wings of Song, Evening, Where'er You Walk, My Native Land* (Ireland): then a solo, *The Carnival* and two duets, *Joyeux Echos* and *Dreamland* before all rose for the National Anthem.

This combination of business and generous, if unbalanced, entertainment persisted. Having presented the prizes in 1911, Mrs Creighton "was so kind as to give us a most interesting and inspiring address". Performed to a crowded audience were three of La Fontaine's Fables, Folk Songs *Les Noces du Papillon* and *Les Joutes*, and a Dramatic Sketch, *L'Anglaise en France*, written by one of the actresses. The Mendelssohn Choir and senior music class each sang five items before the evening concluded with the rousing *Ye Mariners of England.*

The following year's proceedings differed slightly as the whole school opened with *Fight the Good Fight.* The very interesting and helpful address given by Mrs Bryant, Head of the superior North London Collegiate School, was followed by six three-part songs, two duets, a German contribution *Beider de Weige* and another French folk song. Eva Crane was the accompanist.

1913 brought in a real outsider, the Hon. John McCall, Agent-General for Tasmania, who, "in an amusing and instructive speech, tried to make us realise something of Colonial Life". He promoted the Victoria League, "the object of which is to unite Great Britain and her Colonies as closely as possible, and we shall certainly be able to take a much greater interest in the colony of Tasmania now that we have heard him". The varied entertainment began with *It was the Winter Wild* and continued with the 2-part song *L'Ourelet,* German and English folk songs, a recitation *L'Oreiller d'une petite fille* and *Who is Sylvia?*

The emphasis on Service is seen most notably in the institution by Colonel Bowles of the Dux medal for the Head Girl's leadership. This fearsome white and green gong, presented at Prize Giving, was received with mild aesthetic distaste until one recipient mislaid it in the Fifties. Again in emulation of Public Schools, prefects, ten in all, were chosen, first from Sixths, then from Fifths as well. Experimentation was, and has remained, a feature. Details remain hazy, but we are assured of their valuable work.

Monitresses inaugurated modest self-government. As the older girls of the Centre were overburdened with other work, this exercise of authority was felt to be beneficial to the ten girls selected, whose work was marked by increased thoroughness and a higher sense of responsibility and who greatly helped in maintaining a good tone. It becomes impossible to distinguish between prefects and monitresses; bewilderingly, the number of the latter, a more autonomous group, was one year considerably increased and prefects were not mentioned. The next years saw a slight clarification, with 15 prefects besides the monitressess from the Upper School with their special duties. It clearly took time to reach a satisfactory organisation of Senior pupils who could feel part of, and contribute to, Authority.

1909's monitresses formed the first club, a Debating Society. At the sole meeting, a serious subject was treated seriously: Cavaliers versus Roundheads, the Head and First Assistant being present by invitation. The aim still remains that girls run their own clubs, although this does not always prove successful. E.R.B. kindly took the chair later, when heated though interesting discussions ensued, some of the Mistresses also taking part on that burning topic of Women's Suffrage. Surprisingly, Suffragists carried the day by only one vote: children were natural conservatives. The club broadened its appeal; no longer the preserve of the monitresses, it was run by Miss Baxter and a committee.

This era of pious earnestness and thirst for the didactic was also one of practical jokes: moving the Head's reading desk to the edge of the platform in the vain hope that it might fall during Prayers is one recently admitted. Miss Florence decreed that the two offenders be sent to Coventry for the rest of the week – hard punishment when School had to provide almost every pleasure.

More regular practice is essential for good team work

Games were relished at first for their novelty and the means of escape which they offered, as well as the opportunity to be with an adored Mistress. Skills were minimal; the aim was steadfastness.

Hockey was and remained the most popular. The first matches, played on Saturdays, were both lost as girls were in many cases quite ignorant of the game. Unfortunately, time was limited, for, as games were not compulsory until immediately before the war, they were not timetabled and had to be played after school."It is much to be regretted that during the greater part of the hockey season, it is too dark, so that there are practically no proper practices". Apart from matches against local schools, Conservative girls played Liberals. Was this unique event the result of genuine political commitment, or did it resemble later sponsoring of the Boat Race? For the record, Liberals won 1-0.

Standards soon rose; detailed accounts, praise and criticism of named individuals were offered, with the usual swing between expected improvement and dashed hopes, between exhortation ("there is no room for a selfish player") and excuses.

One writer extols the game's compelling fascination, its heavy calls on the speed and stamina of girl athletes, its frustrations, its healthy trial to the temper. In this very pure and genuine sport, play was fast and furious. There were few funks and no shamateurs, the word then denoting someone who does not try her best, who shams. "All enthusiasts play for the love of a good game and this is second to none in the good sportsmanship which prevails on the field. The healthful exercise and excitement, and the friendly intercourse which each player enjoys before, during and after the game, more than compensate for wounded ankles and shins". One season concluded pleasantly with a social evening enjoyed by 40 girls, 4 Mistresses and the Head.

Net Ball (*sic*) had been vigorously practised, and it was hoped that matches might be arranged; it is easy to forget contemporary isolation and the need for pioneer organisation. Two teams won matches but "our girls will do better still next term if they keep more closely to their places when playing".

Netball, spelt thus by 1912, always played second fiddle to hockey; fixtures coincided and girls were in both teams. Juniors did not lack skill, but rather height and experience of tactics. Miss Bidwell's coaching soon began to pay dividends. Mistresses offered a statuette of Discobolous for the best form, so a knock-out tournament was arranged, although that harsh-sounding term was not yet used. With the pre-war season the most successful, the game was well and truly launched, girls showing greater involvement.

Two tennis matches, both lost, were played in the first summer. A singles tournament proved much, among other things the exceedingly great value of steadiness. Mr Engel earned popularity by donating a 'racquet'. With the exceptionally fine weather, they had plenty of opportunities to play in 1911. A junior championship preceded inter-form events, arranged by the indefatigable Miss Forrest. Increased successes included victories against the Staff. In 1914, matches (games won, 816, lost, 586) were played against the OGs and EGS, which the girls won, although the boys' team had improved greatly.

"It was with great joy that, one morning in the beginning of the summer term [1911], we received the longed-for news that arrangements had been made for the formation of a Swimming Club. The first day at [Edmonton] baths is a day that will not be forgotten". Most were non-swimmers but had been rehearsing the strokes at home. Eventually, one brave soul cautiously ventured down the steps leading to the water which looked terrifyingly deep. The noise apparently resembled a midnight cat concert. By the end of that summer, almost all could swim; a team of four entered outside events.

Membership increased. Medals were won for swimming half and one mile. 1913's modest gala included an inter-form race and one for learners. The first fine careless rapture was soon replaced by entreaty: "It is hoped that next year the School will take a keener interest; swimmers must encourage others to take the opportunity for becoming acquainted with one of the most useful and invigorating of sports". In short, it was "time we did something, so wake up, Enfield!" The number did increase of those who could quite comfortably keep themselves afloat.

Annual Sports Days, Drill Displays and a Gymnastic Competition were of enormous importance as events which, while publicising the new school, involved as many students as possible. Spectators received good value.

The first Sports Day, July 8, 1910, demonstrated the Lower School's Swedish Drill and Marching, VA's Scarf Drill, VIA's Morris Dancing and the Upper School's Free Movement, similar to later Keep-Fit. Forward-looking schools were beginning to move away from military-style drill with shouted commands and harsh discipline.

To encourage everyone, prizes were awarded for a bizarre mixture of achievements: 100 and 70 Yards, Long Jump (competitive athletics, but not taught as such), 3-legged, Circular Skipping (comparable with Sunday School Treats), Team and Consolation. Sheepfold is as perplexing as the much-admired Bicycle Maze. After presentations, choruses and solos provided maximum entertainment.

VIB presided over afternoon tea (6d) which, together with the sale of programmes (none of which has come to light) raised nearly £8, to which was added over £11 from another little bazaar arranged by Thirds and Fourths. The total went towards books and, yes, pictures. The regard in which the afternoon was held is indicated by the fact that Lady Somerset presided under the pavilion in the presence of a large assembly.

For the last time, 1911 opened with a display of dancing – Morris, Ribbon, Irish and minuet – after which, sporting events changed but little. More items were added and a balance kept between the athletic – High Jump – and the fun kind – Chariot, Sack, Hat trimming (very popular) and Cloakroom. For at least four decades, audience participation was enforced by competitions for Mistresses, visitors and parents. Once, the intervals between the races were made more pleasant by the rendering of musical selections by the Enfield Silver Prize Band. In the first championship, whoever amassed most points on the day received a Gold Medal.

School seemed to be having a stab at anything and everything and had yet to find consistency and professionalism.

With radio, television, video and the like so easily to hand, it is hard to put ourselves in the position of these girls and their teachers of nearly 90 years ago. Strenuous efforts were made to entertain. Reflecting the spirit and tastes both of the times and of individual Mistresses, this also had a unifying effect. All had to be homemade. Cynics might comment that everyone had hours to spare because of the lack of provided amusements. Consider, however, the extra time needed for even the simplest activity because of lack of transport, gadgets, labour-saving devices, electric light, heating, convenience foods, modern ovens and synthetic fibres. There was, on the other hand, a willingness to give up free time for a common effort.

Miss Garside's pupils gave a very successful display of drill and dancing. The breaking-up party which ended the first Autumn term passed pleasantly in dancing, music and games. An excellent supper was eaten and, after a happy time together, they concluded with *Auld Lang Syne*.

An effective dramatic recital of Tennyson's *The Victim* in February, 1910, raised 16/- towards the adornment of the Sixth form Study. Thirteen girls represented characters of their own choice, the two best receiving prizes. An award for correctly naming the greatest number encouraged audience participation. Mere pleasure was never enough. Musical items and recitations followed. A similarly organised Dickens evening took place less than a month later.

"Acting and entertainment were encouraged, which, besides proving useful to the performers, was very interesting to the girls in their respective forms". Perhaps this was why the tradition of School Plays, later so strong, was slow in establishing itself. Only in 1912 was the first, billed for 8pm., Saturday, February 17, programme 1d. The cast list of *The Princess*, a dramatised version of Tennyson's poem, contains names which recur in all aspects of school life, as pupils and as OGs. Songs, carried over from the concert (*Sweet and Low, Home They Brought her Warrior Dead, Tears, Noble Tears*) were sung during the intervals. It must have been Victorianly lachrymose. Despite good attendance, the initial stage expenses were so heavy that, although total receipts were £12:7:8, a debt of £5:19:10¾ remained, which they hoped to clear by the proceeds of the next production. A heady but worrying experience.

A trip to London being a major undertaking, seeing a Shakespeare play there caused a delight, which, albeit more quietly expressed, resembles the thrill enjoyed by today's teenagers with the latest groups. Not, incidentally, that the word teenager had been invented. Even adolescent belongs to the post-war period. They were either girls or young women. *Macbeth, The Merchant of Venice, A Midsummer Night's Dream* – not a dazzling total, but performances by all-time greats.

Seniors were taken to the Tate and National Galleries by a male teacher with none of the present-day safeguards or parental consent forms. The Thirds explored the Tower. Autumn half-term saw a group at Covent Garden Market. Students of French attended lectures at Palmers Green and at the Cosmopolis on, for example, Hugo, Mistral and Provence, Pierre Loti and Egypt:" à la fois, intéressantes et instructives".

Girls and Mistresses were beginning to look further afield, stimulated by Staff lectures, usually with lantern slides, by accounts from individuals and small groups of their European holidays, and by le Cercle Français.

CHAPTER FIVE

These very interested and stimulating girls

The complicated and often inappropriate admission registers required, not always successfully, exact dates of birth, admission and leaving, position on arrival and on departure, each term kept (surely a waste of time), fees paid or exemptions (amounts, date of receipt, length of tenure and by whom granted), father's occupation, place(s) of education during the previous two years, date of recognition as Bursar/Pupil teacher, examination results and specific activities. Time-consuming paper work is not a new chore.

Of the 110 students in 1909, 43, mainly Scholarship holders, were probationers, transferring from the Centre, some in their late teens, one born on January 1, 1890. They undoubtedly contributed to the noticeable sense of high purpose; contact with younger girls must have helped them. With little choice between teaching, clerical work, staying at home and marrying, they were serious-minded, for an independent future depended on hard work and good results. Grateful for even limited opportunities, many had a difficult time. These pioneers felt part of the new school which had not existed when they began their secondary education. With them, we see features which recur throughout.

They travelled from far and near, from the Town, Ponders End and Enfield Lock, from Palmers Green and Alexandra Park, most coming from the more congested and poorer eastern districts, some facing a journey of at least five miles. There was considerable stability; one moved two doors away (not a unique occurrence), one nearer to school; only one had several changes. One delightful address was simply Myrtle Villa, another the wealthier Mall in Southgate.

Fourteen had transferred from Upper Grade and four from neighbouring county secondary, the rest from seven local schools, Chesterfield being the most successful with 15.

One father had died, a draper had retired. Just one was "Not Known. In Canada". With great diversity of jobs, incomes must have shown considerable differences. Royal Small Arms (RSAF) employed 10, the first of over 100 in Miss Broome's time, as factory hands, foreman writer, gunmaker and Inspector of Works. Printing and manufacture each supported 4, the land and clerical work 3 each. Ordinary Artisans (OA, a description often repeated) were in engineering and railways. Individuals were: accountant, bootmaker, cab driver, commercial traveller, dentist, floorcloth fitter, house agent, insurance official and shop proprietor. A Guardian was a Master Tailor.

I include all of these first pioneers as all future students were their heirs.

Four pupils defied expectations when they left school and stayed At Home (as it was always written). The first, but by no means the last, was Olive Hill Robinson, who married a fruit rancher to live in British Columbia with her five children, the second Dorothy Wilson, winner of a General Knowledge prize. The other two were affected by ill-health, then a greater hazard. A medical certificate of fitness was required at the beginning of each term until 1944; parents signed that their daughters had neither suffered from, nor been in contact with, any infectious or contagious disease or condition during the previous four weeks. Although playing hockey, Doris Mary Walking failed her college medical and went to Clark's secretarial college. Dorothy Isabel Clark stayed at home because of rheumatic fever.

Four did not teach. Life would surely be kinder to number 3, Scholarship holder Dorothy Eugénie Cocks, whose earlier education had been at the dispiritingly-named London Orphan Asylum. This poor but intelligent girl had to give up her hoped-for career, her chance to escape, as standing was considered injurious to her health. Surviving half a term, she was the first of many secretarial trainees. Kathleen Mary Davis, despite scholarship and participation in literary events, failed to qualify; enterprisingly, she went as a governess in France. Ivy Hilda Dowsett became a nursery governess. A soloist with an extensive repertoire, the youngest entrant, Doris Amelia (Nellie) Petre chose a clerkship with the Prudential Approved Insurance Company.

Florrie Wilson did train locally, after playing hockey and winning prizes for Best Collection of Fruits, Drawing and Scripture, but she joined the eleven others who, failing to get into Training Colleges, worked locally as uncertificated teachers: Gertrude Fowler, Elizabeth Goldsmith, Mary Tuill and Maud Gladys Nicholas. Ellen Annie Howe attended classes in Holborn, Kate Hilda Minty (the eldest of three sisters) sang at Sports Displays and a French evening and became Head of an Infants' School: sisters Kathleen and Hockey-playing Mary Turl: singer Ethel Freeman, Florence Score, first recipient of the Hodson prize and Emily Singleton, of Ivy Cottage, who taught at her old school in the same road.

Twenty-three went on to nine different colleges away from home, Hockerill being easily the favourite. Most taught locally, most were active in school life. Gertrude Mary Codling (followed by her younger sister), Lilian Edith Onken and Prefect Constance Minty (the middle sister, the youngest, Frances Mary, becoming a clerk in the War Office) remain names.

A worthy first entrant on the register was Grace Louise Allen, whose sister joined her and taught before becoming a nun (Sister Mary Wilfred) and Head of a convent school. The strong tradition of sisters attending ECS, often excelling in the same subjects, began early. Grace won a prize for her representation of Mrs Gamp. She was somewhat overshadowed by the second transfer, Ida Bullen, who came top of VIB, gained a prize for Composition and distinctions in Geography and History, and was the first to matriculate, thereby qualifying for university; she struggled against thirty years of ill-health.

The others: prize-winners Annie Hilda Gooch, Doris May Bydawell, Ivy Louise Olley (with matriculation): with examination distinctions, Lucy Mary Meesson (History-cum-Geography), Maud Purdon (Geography), Nellie Alicia Peryer (Botany), future Head of a London elementary school: magazine editor Daisy Muriel Down: sporting types, Christine Telling (who also sang at the Sports and Drill display), Frances Mary Hawker, Ellen Mary (Nellie) Munday, prefect and actress Gladys Dorothy Cadman and Beatrice Ellen Mason who won the Bicycle-Egg-and-Spoon race at the ripe old age of 18: Winifred Allen Packman who recited and acted in French, and sang in a duet (*Home Dreams*)at Prize Giving. Olive Winifred Lawday and Lillie Fitchew participated in literary evenings, Lillie being joint organiser of an Old Girls' college party which was broken up by a good romp in *Sir Roger de Coverley*. What did these young teachers get up to?

Two remain, prefects, debaters, academics, sportswomen. Audrey Frances Croucher sang at Prize Givings, literary evenings and sports displays (*The Angel of Hope, The Bells of Lynn*). Pupil, teacher, mother of a pupil, Ethel Margaret Brooks was the leading light. Winner of the racquet, she played tennis for school and for the Old Girls, was an excellent centre forward and invaluable captain of hockey, her strength appreciated when she was obliged to stay away from school, when illness destroyed her chance of the Dux medal. She won the High Jump (4'3") and many prizes. She was, therefore, a most suitable person to present the OGA's retirement gifts to Miss Broome and Mrs Hill.

CHAPTER SIX

A most sporting set

Shortage of accommodation, equipment and Staff limited expansion, but the 43 Pupil Teachers were joined, if not overwhelmed, by 68 true schoolgirls in September 1909. The total pre-war intake was 363, although only 189, just over 50%, arrived at the beginning of a school year. As they also left at odd dates, with at least 87 of the 201 failing to survive until the end of a summer term, the school population was a shifting one. They stayed an extraordinary amount of time, one girl remaining 28 terms until she was over 19, whereas 13 managed fewer than three terms. Four left for private tuition. Both teaching and learning must have been exceptionally difficult. By the outbreak of war, forms had increased to 11. Five girls followed elder sisters, 13 pairs attended at the same time.

These girls, sent with such high hopes, often show their vintage by their forenames, or Christian names as they were then always called. All but a handful had at least two, a few were burdened with family surnames as well. A cursory glance suggests that most were called Nellie, actually only 7, for this was a common form of Ellen (8), and there was one Nella. Some names seem dated (Clarice), others have become more popular (Brenda). 172 different ones are registered, although this small sample proves nothing. Unique for all time are Alethea, Anastasia, Decima, Eda, Euline, Ila, Persis and Zélie. Two were called Mercia, a name which never reappears: 8 share with one other girl later (Cordelia, Ellaline, Flora, Lena/Leonora, Selina, Thirza, Vida) but the runaway favourite for these girls born between 1890 and 1903 coincides with the national choices: Dorothy/Dorothea/Dora and Mary/Marie/Maria (42).

Addresses indicate a wider social spread, with a distinction between those who have a numbered, and the many who had a named, sometimes large, residence. Until the middle Twenties, many more houses were known simply by names: Elm Cottage, Clay Hill: Maisonette, Bush Hill Park: Woodleigh, Enfield. At least 13 girls lived over the shop, hospital, pub: The Residence, GNR Station: Rectory Farm: Farm School: Pork Butcher's: The Post Office, Lancaster Road, although this father was a baker.

Greater mobility is soon reflected: 11 changed houses, one girl three times. Distances travelled remained considerable, 2 coming in from Harold Wood and Chingford, 10 from Waltham Cross, 15 from Bush Hill Park, others from Ware and the Greater London area. Proportionately fewer, about 40%, lived in Eastern Enfield, some moving from these older districts towards the Town itself,which was favoured by the majority.

In 1912, the first telephone number was notified.

As always, about 70% (285) came from Public, Higher or Upper Grade or County schools, and from 15 local ones. Chesterfield and St Andrew's each sent 52; over 20 had been in Southgate or Tottenham.

More significantly, parents had paid fees at private establishments for 74 locally and for 36 outside Enfield. Many more also transferred later from Palmers Green High. Ten others called themselves High Schools (Lynwood), were known by the name of the building (Elm and Clarendon Houses, Woodstock), or, as Dame Schools, by the names of their lady owners: Miss Bassett in Bush Hill Park, Miss Jones in Cecil Road, and, best known and most popular, Shirley Lodge run by the elderly Misses Chambers. "They gave us an excellent education and their opinions were accepted by Miss Broome". A welcome influx came from Scotland, Jersey and at least seven different counties. Three had been in Johannesburg, one at an elementary school, two sisters at a convent. There was even one from Jamaica. Another reversed custom by leaving Clark's College. This leaves ten at opposite ends of society: nine received tuition at home (the ultimate, a private governess), the tenth at the Orphan Asylum.

By this social mix, ECS pointed the way for girls to climb out of what would otherwise have been predestined status. It also opened the eyes of the well-heeled to real poverty and to genteelly concealed discomfort, especially in a large family.

Some girls had two sources of support: 125 received free tuition with Day Scholarships, Maintenance Grants were increased from £5pa (Forms I and II) to £8 or £10 (III and IV). The magazine's publication of full details suggests either insensitivity to recipients of financial aid or pride in achievement of awards. Four received £5pa for three years from Enfield Parochial Authorities, 38 had Junior, 2 Senior, County Scholarships. An Intermediate one (£5 for two years) seems to have depended partially on progress. Bursars numbered 35. One thoughtful father would not let his daughter try for a scholarship and so deprive a girl who needed financial assistance, as he could afford to pay. 140 had no assistance, yet, for some, further training, even with help, was impossible because of extra costs and because the parents needed the girl's earnings.

One student remembered over seventy years later that "when I found out that I was to be sent to the new school, I cried for a day. I could not believe that my father would be so cruel as to uproot me. I was 12, a pupil at the reputable private school which had been one of the reasons for our removal to this part of the London countryside. We lived on Slades Hill and the fields began three houses further down. It sounded drastic, because my school friends said in tones of horror that tradesmen's daughters would go there. My father snorted and pointed out that my private school would take such daughters if the fathers were rich enough. He said I could get much better teaching and have the chance to go to the University". Mr Gibberd, incredibly enlightened, was proved right. Yet fathers in the Fifties were sometimes less helpful. One refused to sign university applications as late as the Sixties. At 1983's Prize Giving, the Head was still obliged to say:" It never ceases to amaze me when a parent says that university is all right for my son, but my daughter does not need it". In fact, Mr Gibberd's daughter found the atmosphere more pleasant and more wholesome and paid tribute to the goodness and extreme kindness of these underprivileged pupils.

Fathers' occupations were, as might be expected, infinitely varied, the nuances in status being explicitly stated: Proprietor (Prop.) or OA. With the entry"No occupation. Of Independent Means", the new establishment was clearly winning social as well as educational approval.

For a short period, jobs had to be registered by a number from 1 to 15. Difficult now to assess the subtle gradations, compilers then were not always sure, some trades recurring under two, even three, numbers, some not appearing at all. The first four concern: ministers of religion: schoolteachers and professors of all grades: professionals which extended to financiers, some civil servants, motor engineers and greyhound trainers: and landowners (their workers come in group 12 – apart from a groom, who makes only number 14 – along with cemetery caretaker, chauffeur and janitor) and proprietors.

So far, so clear, but classification is now more confused and confusing, although not without antiquarian interest.Wholesale traders, proprietors (again) and manufacturers (5) are separated both from smaller owners and skilled workers such as grocers and licensed victuallers, and, oddly, hairdresser's assistant (6) and from OAs which include butcher, milk roundsman, window dresser (7). Groupings now overlap hopelessly: constructional engineers, haulage contractors and house decorators if proprietors (8) precede inspectors and superintendents on railways, in RSAF, post office, Enfield librarian and the Controller of Lighting for Tottenham Gas Company (9). Workers (10) in safe jobs (for example, timekeeper, cashier, telephonist, retail assistant) are ahead of those who might be thought to be uniformed workers (11) such as police and services, were it not for the inclusion of pensioner. Number 13 includes yet more OAs, such as hairdresser, benchhand, and labourers, a mixed bag which includes hot water fitter. The rest fit into 14; more labourers plus painter's mate, foreman fish porter and oysterman. There's no mistake about 15: retired 4, deceased 15 (five widows are described as independent), unknown or not vouchsafed 1. There were then no state pensioners with no other earnings as there are now; conversely, those without a job did not need one.

Nine mothers were in charge, five for fathers in good jobs as accountant, hotel assistant, engineers, foreman blacksmith and teacher in Canada, Australia, South Africa and Jamaica.

The largest number, 54, were in trade, mainly as Props – drapers, and furnishers (8), licensed victuallers and wholesalers 6 each, ironmongers and grocers 4 each, butchers 3 masters. Individuals had a range of unusual jobs: glove and leather makers, sellers of foreign produce, silver, jewellery, musical instruments.

Unsurprisingly, civil servants 4 (one an Indian official) and clerks of all grades (36), in insurance, tax office, Stock Exchange, came next.

Munitions provided local work for 31: RSAF employed 23 from 8 OAs, 4 foremen, and section hands to machinists, engineers and skilled artificer. Chemists worked at the Government Gunpowder Factory, a foreman at Nobel's Company Explosive, a Commissary at the Army Ordnance department and 3 individuals were gunsmiths.

Construction work took 26: 13 builders of various standards, 5 paperhangers/decorators, 3 carpenters, designer and seller of furniture, removal contractor.

Local landwork supported 25 fathers in horticulture, dairies, nurseries, stables, on farms, the 8 Props., 2 foremen, 6 labourers and one gardener at a private residence again reflecting social divisions.

Varied engineering and electrical work occupied 19, closely followed by the professions 15 (in finance 5, pharmacy 3, law 3, medicine 2, architecture and surveying) and education 14 (11 teachers, 1 Head, secretary to EEC and caretaker). Ten more were in printing, including the editor of *The Gazette*, and 10 in transport, mainly on the railways, plus a shipper's representative and motor body builders. Two were police constables, 2 Inspectors and 4 were in the post office.

The unique fathers? Scientific instrument maker and wheelwright, gas meter maker, ivory and tortoiseshell worker, tennis racket bender (all

OAs), walking-stick maker, skilled embroidery manufacturer, pianoforte tuner and dealer, film renter. The choicest, surely, are ventriloquist (retired) and butler.

Another first: a working mother, hairdresser, Prop.

With 285 jobs recorded, ECS clearly represented a cross-section of the Enfield district population. Hardly élitist, as critics of Grammar schools suggest.

HEAD GIRL (Dux)

1909 Ida Butler   1910 Margery Score
1911 Dorothy Copplestone   1912 Eva Ryder
1913 Eva Ryder (Dux medal awarded to Kathleen Gibberd)

How to choose fairly representatives of the prize and sports winners, team stalwarts, participants in activities, who, together, created School's identity? Few coasted along without any recorded mention, even if it were simply to suggest a form's motto or read a paper.

I have tried to include those who made outstanding, unusual or pioneering contributions or who made a personal appeal. Let Gladys Ethel Almond represent the many omitted. Followed by sister Elsie Lucy, she came aged almost eleven and stayed seven years before going to training college – free place, matriculation (Mathematics*) RSA French O and W, 2nd in the Potato Race, student teacher, wife of another student's brother.

For a few, life was unkind. One child left after five weeks when she became ill and her father died suddenly. What happened to her was "Unknown. No answer to enquiries". Three other fatherless short stayers were contemporary phenomena. The first, her Guardian a licensed victualler, stayed 16 months and within three months of leaving was dead, aged 13. The second stayed one term before being adopted by the Poor Law Guardians and sent to Chase Farm Schools. The third departed, aged 16, after seven months, as, although a good hockey player, she was weak academically, no doubt through constant ill-health. Two died while still on roll; 11 suffered ill-health: "No further education until health improves ... Absent for most of the year".

ECS provided a ladder. One ill-nourished scholar, bursar, student teacher, monitress and prefect, had to act as mother to her two small sisters (who followed her to ECS), listen to them saying their prayers before putting them to bed, and prepare her father's tea. She won form prizes, swam in both School and Secondary Girls' Schools Teams, spoke in French in favour of Mathematics and trained, eventually retiring from the Mathematical Staff of the International Correspondence Schools. One sister added lustre in her turn, shining in games and work before becoming Head of a Junior school. Anyone similarly placed before the opening of schools such as ECS was doomed to domestic service or, with the Great War, factory work.

What happened to over 60 is left blank. Such record keeping is not unreasonable for those early years without professional secretarial assistance. The astounding thing is that, for nearly one-third, nothing did happen, although they may have got employment later. Seventy are noted as at home, some unfitted for work, most simply because they were girls. It is not a euphemism for unknown, as five are thus described. An 11-year old coming in January, 1914, and leaving a term later, is listed as having no post at present. Thirty transferred to other establishments, mostly private and boarding, two returning to Dame schools and two going on to Upper Grade schools. Three returned abroad, two emigrated. At least 25 marriages were notified, and at least three daughters came to ECS.

Some thirty took clerical posts in Civil Service, banks, insurance and a London merchant's office (£32pa). One did bookkeeping in her father's business. Seventeen trained, ten at Clark's college; Vera Pennock later won the Ladies' Challenge Cup at the RAC Light Car Trials.

A mixed bag of individual posts included trainee dispenser, cashiers, shop assistants, public singer, apprentice to a draper, then to a milliner, who became a chiropodist. There were to be three nurses, one a VAD and one a future missionary. One trained at the Royal College of Music, four at Art schools and two at the Royal School of Needlework, one joining Liberty's as an embroideress. A firm of fine art embroiderers took another. One attended classes with a view to training as a Dancing Mistress.

Of the three daily nursery governesses, one, strangely, had been promoted to Form VB for elementary subjects only by special permission of the Head Mistress for reasons of health. Although teaching was losing its predominance, girls trying new posts and changing courses later, there were still 11 uncertificated local teachers and 53 who trained. The two most popular colleges were Hockerill and Goldsmiths. The first PT specialist went to Dartford.

On the Commercial course, Janet Brown was the first to gain a 1st class Pitman's Shorthand certificate (Speed). Dorothy Ellen Case ended her schooldays with extra studies whilst acting as laboratory assistant and Miss Broome's secretary for 5/- per week, less insurance, 3d. It is cheering to know that she became a member of Prudential Assurance's Flying Squad, speeding up methods of work and output. As a widowed grandmother in New Zealand, where there is now a sizeable colony, she became a part-time secretary again. Grace Minnie Beaton went full tilt for her career: five Pitman's certificates in Shorthand and one in Typing, as well as London University's School Commercial certificate (French*, Business Methods*, Typing*). By 1916, there was VIB Commercial, in which she won first prize.

Edith Alice Box is memorable as the first beginner to swim a width, the Head presenting a book as a reward for her efforts. Olive Goodwin, who also won the Drill competition, wrote a no-nonsense account of Sports and acted before training for kindergarten work. She taught until she married and therefore had to leave.

Hockey enthusiast Violet Hilling's strength was mainly sporting; she came mortifyingly second only once in six athletic events over three years. She became, as did Annie Emily Hogg, President of the OGA, of which Eva Lillian Crane was a long-standing official, and to which Minnie Adeline Jarrett left all her relevant personal papers. Eva and Minnie both matriculated (3* each), both examined for le Cercle. Eva taught music locally, serving on the EMF committee for over 60 years. She drew the Bowles Cup for reproduction in the magazine of which she was a committee member, and won prizes for work and for water-colour painting. Scholar Annie matriculated (4*), was *trésorier du Cercle*, tennis champion, and hockey captain until she became ineligible as a student teacher. Her report, full of wise words and inverted commas, was clearly aimed at certain unnamed individuals. "When a girl has been chosen to play in the School first XI, it is her duty to herself, as well as to the School, to make herself as efficient as possible, and deserve the place of honour to which she has been elected. It is no use going to matches with muddy boots, a hockey stick and a great deal of fuss and 'a professional air', if you cannot become 'a conquering hero', and it is impossible to become one, and decidedly unfair to girls who are keen, if a few absent themselves from practices without any good reason for doing so". A new twist: her son married an OG.

Of the 21 pairs of sisters, most were involved in all physical activities, were caught up in French events and enjoyed different lives: the hockey playing Jennings, Dorothy May and Kathleen Maude, the former distinguishing herself by her reliability in the onerous position of goalkeeper: tennis champion Nellie Josephine, hockey and sports enthusiast Marjorie, Perkins: the Barrands who swam their way to success, Ethel being the smallest competitor in the Enfield Ladies' Gala, Christiana being the first of many to gain her elementary Shorthand certificate. Of the three Williams girls, Phyllis Cordelia won a medal for swimming half a mile and third prize in the Enfield Junior Gala, tennis player Nella went on to Art school, and sports winner Kathleen Brenda achieved Recitation and Reading prizes.

Two were the first to receive the MBE, Amy (telephone operator, then bank clerk) and Sibyl Cook.

Writer of lucid games reports and secretary of the Lit. and Deb., Winifred Edith May Brooks, sister of the great Ethel, presented a bouquet at the Opening; she was successful in innumerable odd things: 2nd in Hockey Dribbling, 100 Yards and Addition races, 1st in Obstacle and Egg-and-Spoon, sharing sports championships, displaying the best collection of dried specimens.

Minnie and Nellie Biggs won sports events; Nellie read a paper on Corals, Minnie on Milton. The third ECS graduate (English, Subsidiary French), she trained and, unusually, taught in different parts of the country. Winner of French recitation prizes, Nellie, in nearly four pages, details departure, journey, sea-sickness and arrival as well as problems of communication and comprehension on an Easter visit to Paris. Lively if self-centred, she conveys the excitement of the unknown. When 17, she wrote the first of the too many pieces on Moonlight, dwelling on the revelries of Queen Mab and her fairies, her mastery of technique at odds with the innocence of the subject.

Edith Marion Fraser took up dairy farming. Marrying an eminent biologist, she joined her name to his, Mrs Fraser-Darling. They lived on a remote island, then in the Scottish highlands, without light or gas, the nearest water 50 yards, the next house 12 miles, away. Mail came fortnightly, stores monthly – but no dirt, no blackleading, a daily visit from a golden eagle, building their own wooden hut after a tented year. She became Warden of the National Association of Mixed and Girls' Clubs' hostel in Argyllshire. Sister Gladys Ellen lived up to the high reputation already gained by the Duxes (the contemporary plural). Games captain, joint first on Sports Day, arranger of the swimming races, joint editor, she passed not only RSA French and Pitman's Shorthand Theory, but also matriculated (3*). Another Birkbeck graduate, Miss Fraser returned to help during wartime Staff absence. She farmed poultry.

Swimming champion Kathleen Pickard appealed for Life Saving Classes, and had the brainwave that every capable swimmer had two pupils among the beginners for whose progress she was responsible. She won the Drill prize, acted in the first play and at Prize Giving, read papers on *Plants of the South Downs* and *Place Names* and defended Arts against Science in debate, despite prizes for best collections of both fruits and wild flowers. Another pioneer, she trained as a DSc. Instructress, returned to teach and later took up silversmith work. Dorothy won the Long Jump

(10'10½"), then broke a wrist in the High Jump ("We were all very sorry for her mishap"), so causing the event to be abandoned the following year.

The first two Willmott girls, Myra Julie and Constance Mary, were evenly matched, as Scholars and in games, Myra writing a Captain's sensible advice and criticism, Connie being Sports and Tennis Champion. Both passed RSA and matriculated, Myra with three distinctions. Both went on to St George's College, previously the Civil Service department of King's, Connie subsequently qualifying as a masseuse from Guy's – another change of career.

Staying only a year before becoming a cashier, Violet Ward Hayes was overshadowed by Ruby Ward, 18 months her junior, who was the first to win a 3-year Science (Mathematics and Biology) Scholarship (£40pa), which took her to East London College to gain BA Hons. in Mathematics. After teaching, she spent 27 years as a trained hospital nurse, but she had not finished with ECS, returning to teach from 1954 until her retirement nine years later.

Two pairs, Dorothy Emma and Mildred Mary Copplestone, Eva Gladys and Florence Elizabeth Ryder, were academic, literary and linguistic. Dorothy pioneered a Belgian holiday and French exchange, keeping in touch with her penfriend for over 40 years. She became Head of a Roman Catholic elementary school. Florence recited in French at her first Prize Giving and won French prizes. She was a chief translator in French and Spanish in the War Trade department.

Mildred won F.M.F's prize for letter-writing, and, with Eva, supported languages in debate. They both studied at Birkbeck; she went on to the Sorbonne with a grant from the International Guild (£30) and a county scholarship (£20), astonishingly remaining there during the war. Magazine editor Eva wrote in French (mistakes surely result from the unmastered art of proofreading), examined and acted for le Cercle, read a paper on *Les Misérables* for the Literary and Debating (Lit. and Deb.) Society of which she was president for two years. She achieved an entrance scholarship of the princely sum of £5 in English, French and Latin, then a final studentship of five guineas, and a senior county award.

Four setters of standards.

By 1914, no-one had actually gone to university, but soon 13 would be accepted by four colleges affiliated to London University, Charing Cross School of Medicine and Apothecaries' Hall. Two girls brought special honour to ECS.

Admitted without examination from a Dame School, Lily Clarkson Butler swam in the secondary schools' team race, won prizes, passed all examinations. Encouraged by her enlightened father, she was, in 1917, the first to enter the London School of Medicine for Women (later the Royal Free), to pursue what was still a comparatively new career for women. She did midwifery in the Pentonville Road area, armed with matchsticks to kill the bugs. In 1923, she became School's first Doctor, achieving the degrees of MRCS and LRCP in the shortest possible time since matriculation. Three years later, with the Diploma of Public Health, she worked for the London County Council, undeterred by the existing conditions: vermin, malnutrition, rickets, rheumatism, tuberculosis, diphtheria and the soup kitchens which provided a meal of soup and bread for 1d. Certifying officer for the mentally deficient, Infant Welfare worker, Deputy Divisional Medical Health Officer, she was, for 20 years, Surgeon of the local St John Ambulance Brigade. The wheel came full circle when she became an ECS Governor.

As a schoolgirl, I cribbed from *The People's Government,* never dreaming that I would know the author, then an attractive, sprightly, lucid octogenarian about to make a sane contribution to a television commentary on Old Age. A birthday insertion in *The Times* in 1987 by an old school-friend gives the flavour:" Vivat Crescat Floreat ... all-time friend".

Kathleen Gibberd enjoyed everything. She represented characters at literary evenings, wrote and acted in both English and French, was secretary of le Cercle and one of its examinateurs pour *les concours littéraires*, won prizes for Form, French, Scripture, VI English, *le meilleur costume du bal costumé* and the best collection of wild flowers, and was one of the most energetic members of the magazine committee, being joint editor. She fittingly proposed in a delightful and witty speech the toast at the first OGA Dinner, later helping to produce the Silver Jubilee magazine. Participating in hockey, tennis and sports, her forte was swimming. As captain and with a medal for swimming a mile, she reported sensibly on one of the more useful and invigorating of sports. The departure of "our fastest swimmer caused lamentation".

Lest this give a conventional impression, Miss Gale recalled 25 years later that Kathleen was a real monkey and could never resist a dare. On one occasion, she 'accidentally' kicked over a bucket of water, to the great delight of the class. "The other day, I came across a favourable criticism of a book by this same little lady on a sociological subject, and said to myself:' Dear me, Kathleen is still upsetting things!'" Kathleen retained a rich appreciation of the absurd, chuckling at such childish pranks as putting Hudson's powder into the cakes made in Cookery, climbing over the pavilion roof (spotted, if not stopped) by Mrs Hill), and letting off squibs in a most unsuitable place.

As if this were not enough, she was actually the first to go to University. What a first! Her Exhibition (£20pa) was doubled by a county scholarship (English, French, Latin) at St Hilda's Hall (which became a college only in 1926), Oxford. She remained amused by her low degree; perhaps she was too entranced by the city's beauty captured in her article on *May Morning*. As the then Prince of Wales apparently liked to bathe in the Cherwell in the nude, swimming was prohibited – the only disappointment of a happy University life. Her novel about Oxford, completed when she was unemployed, won a Bronze Medal.

Socialist and life-long pacifist, her varied career bewilders: Social Science diploma in one year at the London School of Economics, educational advisor to the National Union of Housewives, chairman of the World Disarmament group, teacher and Governor. As organiser for the National Confederation of Women Workers (£2pw), "my usual activity was to stand (preferably on a borrowed chair) outside some East End factory urging the girls to stop grumbling and join a trade union".

She found her true métier when, appalled by contemporary textbooks, she wrote and lectured on government, the League of Nations and the Independent Labour Organisation. During World War II, she was on the staff of Chatham House, assistant editor of the *British Survey*, deputy director of the British Society for International Understanding, volunteer area organiser for London refugees and Forces lecturer. When preparing her book on comprehensive schools, she returned to ECS.

As assistant editor on *The Times Educational Supplement* in the Fifties, "for the second time in my life, I was taught to write. The first time, of course, was under the ruthless blue pencil (how grateful I am) of Miss Baxter". From the educational correspondent of *The Sunday Times* and *The New Statesman* and member of the General Council of the Ockendon Venture, books flowed: *The People's English, No Place Like School, Teaching Religion in Schools*.

Despite severe arthritis, she remained busy into her nineties, writing, reviewing and working for the elderly less fortunate, physically, mentally and financially, than herself: a life with which she, and ECS, were justifiably happy.

What, then, can be said about the first five years of School's life? What had been established? In what state was ECS to face the strains of war?

Twenty-three Staff had been appointed, if we exclude the two gentlemen who did not transfer. One married, four were temporary substitutes, five had left, five remained until they retired, a total between them of 166 years. There was, therefore, both reasonable stability and more or less acceptable change.

Whilst prizes and examination successes, considerably above the national average, must never be the sole criteria by which schools are judged, stress was laid on them in these early years as the obvious justification for School's existence, as bait for parents and as the sole means of career for an intelligent girl. Fifty-nine had passed Senior Oxford, two Senior Cambridge, Locals, of whom 19 had matriculated. New examinations had been introduced: 11 had won Pitman's Elementary Shorthand certificates, the first six had passed RSA French O, and three had reached Advanced Stage in French W: 130 carefully graded Form and 72 Special prizes had been awarded.

Traditions had been created: Motto, Empire Day celebrations, Play, Open afternoons. Charity work had been encouraged. An appeal had been launched for books with which to start a library. Experiments continued to find the best system of older student responsibility; the Head Girl, or Dux, received her badge of office. Self-entertainment and self-improvement – the sheer novelty of it all helped to found societies which made an unexpected appeal to Arts and Science pupils alike, for the main thrust was to be a good all-rounder. Choir and concerts, literary evenings, Christmas parties, annual Prize Giving, all flourished. The magazine, primarily a chronicle, had been created, the Governors helping financially. A modest beginning had been made with expeditions; the first continental holiday was a success; it was a new experience to travel together.

Above all other enjoyments, those offered by PT (nowadays PE) were the most energetically promoted. With increasing facilities, Drill and Sports Days were successful, events often encouraged as a health-giving duty. The very idea of team games was absolutely new to these girls. At first, few matches had been played against at least 11 other establishments, as well as the Staff, OGs and EGS: won 78, drawn 7, lost 39. Hockey received the greatest Staff support, netball took off more slowly, tennis was always enjoyed. The swimming club was formed, although participants had to swim in out-of-school hours. Difficulties added to its popularity – at least initially.

ECS was firmly established.

A deep sense of gratitude was felt as early as 1913. Here, "we learned to work, play, and, above all, think. Dear School, thank you and Onward Ever". The wording may be off-putting, but what institution, new or established, could wish for a better testimonial?

PART TWO

THE GREAT WAR – 1919

CHAPTER SEVEN

These troublous times: they showed no signs of fear

Miss Florence's entertaining account of her thrilling German holiday brings alive pre-war tension and excitement: mobilisation orders posted on all public buildings: no apparent discontent at having to join up: Rhine bridges guarded: no traffic after dark. Hearing that Russia had declared war on Germany, crowds, huge but orderly, thronged the streets; bands played patriotic airs.

Twelve Russian spies had been shot already. Travellers had to remain on board their river steamer because of the strong feeling against foreigners. "A gorgeous and irate official, eagerly watched by the whole population, addressed the passengers on deck, shook his fist at us and told us that we would be arrested and put in a fortress if we dared set foot in Germany. He even looked behind the curtain to see if any spy was hiding". Police boats hailed them at every bridge; they were escorted to the consulate at Mannheim. Aiming to get a passport, this indomitable lady courageously determined to go to Frankfurt before troops moved, even though this meant abandoning heavy luggage. Despite no authentic news, she was pretty certain that England had declared war, so the sooner English people could get back to their own country, the better.

Eventually, along with the Vice Consul and as many English as were free, they crowded into the train for quite a merry journey until ordered out to wait in a black hole of Calcutta for 10½ hours. Then, partly on foot in the rain, crossing a bridge two by two, escorted by a file of soldiers on each side, with jeering crowds looking on, they reached Cologne and were taken to the Criminal Police Office, where any disobedience was threatened with internment. After a weekend of circumspect behaviour, they received permits to begin a stop-and-start journey up-river to Rotterdam. At the frontier, the men were removed, all aged 18-45 being detained as prisoners of war.

Miss Florence triumphantly saved her best hat from the fate of most of her belongings, which languished in durance vile until hostilities ceased. The hat was never worn again, so squashed had it been in her knapsack.

The Channel crossing was "delightful. We reached Folkestone without having been blown up by a mine or captured by a German cruiser". Stirring stuff: I wish I had met my predecessor.

"Since the summer holidays, the War has filled our thoughts. Nearly everyone has a cousin or two in the Forces, and 28 girls have a father or brother fighting for King and Country" – high involvement in a school of only 253. The emotional attitude was simple: for King and Country. Nearly 100 Old Boys of EGS were killed; some were close relatives.

Miss Broome being sure that all were anxious to do everything that girls could do to help in this great crisis, ways were found almost immediately for all to play a practical part, both financial and personal.

A weekly sum was contributed to help relieve distress. Most girls wished to support a Belgian mother and her child, but, for reasons unknown, it proved impossible to carry this out for longer than one week. The fund was then used to help local families who were suffering because of the war.

The immediate response was for the Cottage Hospital, 40lb of jam being despatched before Christmas. Over 240lb were sent altogether, some specially made (average cost, fruit and sugar, 4½d per pound), but most transferred from home cupboards. Girls remained concerned for Belgians. The Governors sanctioned the purchase from them, at one-third the price, of over 100 new garments which were added to toys and sweets for the children on St Nicholas' Day. The Hall was used for a weekly reunion of the 170 or so refugees in Enfield. "Sacrificing [our] Saturday afternoons, almost all of us have helped to entertain our guests", who presented a picture of their King Albert as a token of their appreciation of those happy interludes in their sad exile. The total spent was £6:12:0½.

This mixture of local and wider help undertaken speedily still obtains.

As befitted an educational institution, priority was given to informing the girls. Mr Maconachie gave a Victoria League lantern lecture on War and the Empire. Seniors had the pleasure of listening to a course of six lectures on the French provinces delivered in French by Madame la Comtesse de Croze; the inhabitants of Alsace, "although under German rule, were truly French in spirit. We saw three good lantern slides of the King of Belgium, the President of France and King George. We ended by singing the three National Anthems".

Florence Ryder wrote a graphic account of the destruction of Rheims cathedral, "cet outrage honteux", although she carefully pointed out that this, "le comble de vandalism du Kaiser", was "une action indigne des Allemands". In an article largely borrowed from *The Times*, Mary Callander registered surprise that soldiers appreciated Scott's poetry.

At Prize Giving, shorn of its usual festivity, the Guest, Miss Gray, MA, a Head and Secretary of the Girls' Patriotic Union, "gave an extremely interesting and inspiring address on discipline and the duty of girls as well as boys to King and Country". That phrase again. Seniors sang *Land of Hope and Glory*, as well as the National Anthems of the Allies, which now included Russia. Queen Mary Gift Books were awarded to those who came first in each form, those second and third received certificates. Sports Day prizes were similarly replaced.

Girls soon got into their wartime stride. Clothes showed wide variations in colours from dark green to a dull orange; no two people seemed to have the same shade. One octogenarian sufferer remembered green bloomers into which they tucked their handkerchiefs, and long woollen stockings. As war continued, black knickers (the 'passion-bafflers' of the Thirties) became the norm. Despite difficulties in finding the green serge, belted tunics were worn for Drill (in the Hall), for Gym (in the Gym)and for all games. Otherwise, they wore what dresses and coats they liked.

Miss Broome tried to insist that gloves were worn even during the summer, but without complete success. There remained the dreaded straw boater, with shallow crown, broad brim and green and white hatband. "They were uncomfortable if worn at right angles to the forehead, but they stayed on. If worn as a halo, they fell off". Elastic, worn chafingly under the chin, secured them. Apparently, comfort and fit improved when the creation was soaked in water before use. Bands were transferred in winter to the black felt or velours, which, as the war continued, gave way to green caps, serge, or, more often, handknitted.

Although one girl remembered only a poor affair of mostly egg and soup, Mrs Hill's wartime meals were recalled with gratitude – a rare tribute to school dinners. The redoubtable lady managed to serve herrings and rabbit: "that we had any dinners at all in those meatless, sugarless and often potatoeless days speaks highly for her untiring resourcefulness". Proud to reflect that they never failed to provide an appetising meal of two courses without ration cards, Head and Cook had many anxious consultations. Local Authorities, allowed to exceed the ½d rate laid down, could supply meals during school holidays.

Le Cercle lamented "la difficulté d'obtenir de quoi manger". Christmas parties were cancelled, as were, by common consent, Sports Day teas from 1917. At the 1918 Garden Fair, "the vegetable stall was soon sold out of fruit: we are told that people were almost fighting each other in their efforts to buy".

Activities were hit by two problems. First, "il faisait si noir le soir après l'école". In *London by Night*, Nessa Spencer stressed the horrors – accidents, getting lost, searching for a policeman, crossing the roads: it was all too much. "The chief wish of all now is to get back to the jolly ways and customs of dear old London, and to see the end of this terrible War and the 'lights of London' once again".

The second difficulty was the fear of air raids, the first time that defenceless civilians faced such problems. They imposed an unanticipated responsibility on Mistresses; for girls, they had an acceptable, as well as a frightening, side. "Often homework could not be done. Having sat up most of the night, we were too fatigued to work next day". Moonlight was no longer appreciated. Air raid drill? Ah, that was something else again. Anyone thinking this peculiar to the Forties should learn that "we used to have large, stiff-covered drawing books with the School coat of arms stamped upon them. These books were kept in readiness to serve as 'cushions' to sit on during air-raid drill. As soon as the whistle sounded, we each seized our book, the form monitress made a dash for the cupboard and took out a magnificent jar of sweets kept for such occasions". Blackboards on top of doors, or shelves in stock cupboards provided slight extra protection. One girl brought her own cushion to make a cosy corner of her nook. "At the order 'Move Over', we moved away from windows and glass partitions and sat under the desks". Each form had its 'dug-out' on the ground floor.

Many practices are remembered, but only one raid; the sweets, nevertheless, continued to disappear. "When we have been struggling with an obstinate problem in Algebra and have got frightfully cross with it, or when an explanation of a lost book is demanded, and we fear an impending conduct mark, what a relief to hear that beloved whistle. For nothing must stand in the way of air-raid drill". Another recalled being marshalled in the corridors, where the architects had been less lavish with the glass.

Miss Broome, aware of these happy breaks in tiresome lessons, encouraged them to sing together all the songs they knew and generally make as much noise as possible to cover the sound of approaching planes. They sat in the stone passages shouting *Three Blind Mice.* She agreed subsequently that it was great fun: "we can laugh now, but it would have been a sorrowful story if a bomb had hit the school".

Isa Spencer's poem shows that aerial bombardment was in its infancy:

> When once downstairs, I quietly sit,
> And watch the others read or knit;
> Then the guns begin their terrible din,
> And to our dug-out we hurry in.
> Thus we patiently wait until we hear the sound
> Of the bugle boy as he goes his round.

One raid was signalled as dinner was about to begin. E.R.B. judged it wise to continue, first moving as far as possible from the windows. "We happened to have rice pudding, a dish not always popular, but every girl came to me for a second helping that day to show she was not afraid".

The nearest bomb fell at Northaw in 1917; a botanical expedition had therefore to be abandoned. Girls hoped that raids would not continue to upset their arrangements.

The playing field was shared with the boys whose field had been dug up as part of the Dig for Victory campaign. Tennis being thus curtailed, sharing was received with mixed feelings, but it paved the way for occasional meetings, formerly frowned upon, between girls and boys. Part of the land was turned to good account, being divided into 'allotments' (the inverted commas indicate their novelty), which, during dinner hours, were each worked by two or three girls, and splendid crops raised. Artichokes flourished by the bicycle sheds. Madge Peachey grew 58lb of potatoes in a single bed. "In case this should inspire anyone, I will reveal an awful truth. The field is densely populated with wireworms".

The war was brought nearer home by the temporary loss of two people. Miss Balls answered an urgent request from her old college to replace a professor called up by the Ministry of Munitions. More seriously, the groundsman went off to fight the foe. Two girls kept the tennis courts in order; School was greatly indebted to them and thoroughly appreciated their services.

What did girls do consistently to help the outside world? The biggest single contribution was literally that – fund-raising. Charities already adopted were not forgotten. The Young Helpers' League continued to collect for Dr Barnardo's Homes, which also received the profits from *Hiawatha* (£23:1:6), IIIB's bazaar and 1918's *Pedlar's Parade* ("a very gratifying result"). Other disadvantaged children were helped; the Fresh Air Fund, Enfield Cripples' Mission and Clothes for Poor Children, names which recall the distress and attitudes of a bygone era, benefited from the weekly contributions and Carol Singing (about £20).

Money provided nourishment for an invalid woman or child, or added a weekly 22/- to the inadequate Old Age Pension. The tradition of Christmas gifts began, the magnificent sum of £67:19:1 being disbursed to the old. More than financial help was involved when School adopted one old lady. "We used to visit [her] in our own time, and take her a little something: *we* took bananas. We did a lot of listening – a good discipline". The young of ECS changed little in this regard, but maybe few realise the long history of such visits.

Five local hospitals received small amounts which added up to £36:12:0, whilst three military hospitals had a share of the £120 or so raised by the 1916 bazaar, a fourth part being reserved for Prisoners of War in Germany.

Soldiers, with a total of £55:18:11, were, rightly, School's priority. The Middlesex Regiment's Fund increased by £28:7:0, St Dunstan's Hostel by 9 guineas. Edmonton received £4:13:0 for what is called, first, a Tearoom for Soldiers' and Seamen's Wives, then a Newsroom and finally a Club.

Sailors concerned the Head more closely. King George's Fund for Sailors gained £5:4:11¾ in three small sums; oddly, no-one added a farthing to make 5 guineas. The creation of a ward at the Star and Garter Home to be named after Jack Cornwell, the 19-year old hero of the battle of Jutland, who, mortally wounded, stayed at his post and won a posthumous VC, was supported by £33:11:4. Sailors' Day raised one guinea, the British and Foreign Sailors' Society £1:10:0 and £5 were sent to provide an outfit for a boy entering the Navy from a training ship, a total of £46:7:3¾.

Miscellaneous charities included the YMCA Hut (£2:12:6), League of Empire (14/2), Mission to Deep Sea Fishermen (5 guineas), and "Our Day" with two contributions of £2:11:0.

During 1918, School Fund was registered as a War Charity. Considering other calls on the pocket money of the girls, none of whom was rich, amounts kept up steadily. Although not as inventive as their grandchildren would be, their fund-raising means included Drill Display (£18:16:6), production by student teachers and girls (£8:0:8), Swimming Gala, Sales of Work and of waste paper, special collections and Donations from Friends. At least £555:17:5¼ were forwarded by this small, relatively new school.

Money was not the sole way of helping. Eggs, to the value of £9:12:1 were sent to the Military Hospital for Wounded Soldiers, whilst in each of three July weeks four dozen were despatched to the National Egg Collection. Knitting comforts cost the large sum of £25:11:6, which made 214 pairs of mittens, 93 scarves, 10 pairs of socks, 5 helmets (presumably balaclavas) and 2 belts; material for shirts, another £1:17:3, the contents and carriage of parcels £6:11:6, three-quarters of which went on cigarettes. A concert for wounded soldiers necessitated an outlay of £1:0:4. Beekeeping was inspired by a lecture; "the bees, under the care of Miss McDermid, have done splendidly". Some 20 sections produced a net profit of £1:2:3 – and that's the last we hear of them.

Miss Broome rightly claimed that the girls had done their best to respond to the many appeals: "we have always found them ready to do all in their power, with the kind help of their parents".

Self-help, presented as a wartime duty, began in 1917. Mr McEwen's interesting address explaining War Savings certificates resulted in the formation of an Association with Miss Murphy as treasurer. From March to October, 1918, subscriptions increased from £106:19:0 to £375:9:0 and by 1919 were over £400. "This is very creditable and shows that members are doing their part nobly, but the Chancellor of the Exchequer has now started a campaign for selling 2 million certificates: therefore, we hope that the membership will be increased 50 per cent". Unfortunately, the impetus faded, although the Association did continue throughout the life of the County School.

All these activities brought the world into school, but how were the girls informed of, and involved with, the reality outside, as a deliberate policy, rather than simply because of air-raids, dark streets, inadequate food, casualty lists and appeals, none of which could be avoided by anyone? Henceforth, they were not shielded from events and ideas as their mothers and immediate predecessors had been.

Empire Day was observed with even greater fervour; they more than held their own against the khaki-clad cadets. Despite the special March Past, 1918 disappointed all as, because of the weather, they were obliged to wear mackintoshes which rather spoiled the effect. In the afternoon, a number of girls, relatives of past and present members of the fighting forces, went to a celebration in the Albert Hall. Splendid music was rendered by massed orchestras and united choirs. The King, Queen and members of the Royal Family attended. The Empire was a living and relevant concept. With his customary kindness, EGS' Head invited seniors to join the boys to hear a lecture thereon. All listened with close attention.

The Allies were remembered. A Belgian pupil, addressing le Cercle, pulled no punches. "Le lâche empereur d'Allemagne violait la neutralité de la Belgique et mettait toutes les nations en émoi". She described crowds in the streets, messenger work done by "les jeunes boy-scouts", arrests of German spies, wounded soldiers returning from the Front, the call-up, constant anxiety, impossibility of sleeping, gifts of fruit from market stall holders to volunteers, the exodus before invading troops. "Les gens se sauvaient, n'emportant que quelques menues choses. On entendait des cris et des pleurs, il y avait même des massacres, mais il paraît que pour le moment tout est calme".

Mr McEwen lectured annually on the Geography of the War. "We shall never forget that the German fleet is now in Scapa Flow, although we have never seen that wonderful harbour". The GBS heard how bombs were made. Of more immediate value, perhaps, Sister Cope from Bush Hill Park military hospital most kindly gave a series of useful lessons after school on First Aid and Home Nursing. Indefatigable in taking girls to the great picture galleries in London, Mr Quilter accompanied the Sixth to the South Kensington Exhibition of Allied War Photographs.

Girls occasionally took the initiative, in discussions new and daring: Conscription – if women share men's privileges, should they not share their labours too?: King or Republic?: Can any excuse be made for conscientious objectors? Widening of horizons led to such debates as: Is it proper for a woman to smoke? – a social rather than a medical approach: Should there be a tax on spinsters? – how did all the unmarried Mistresses react? The war would make it more difficult to find husbands.

An OG described one way of serving their country. Armed with kitbags and blankets, some 600 students aired beds, swept out their tents, washed, sorted letters and parcels, cooked, enjoyed two courses for breakfast and a good meat supper, held concerts, took long walks, formed a procession in night attire on their last night – all in the cause of flax-pulling. After 30 days, they received a green armlet, becoming a contemporary version of a Land Girl.

Another patriotic tradition began in 1916. Trafalgar Day was celebrated in many schools, but rarely with such fervour and for as long as at ECS, although it is remembered with markedly less enthusiasm than Empire Day. Advising parents that both days were used to teach true patriotism and the spirit of self-sacrifice, Miss Broome wrote with passion of her desire to do something in wartime, but what? Everyone was knitting for the troops, lectures frequently failed to cover expenses, concerts needed preparation. "It was then that I had what I still consider a happy idea: to combine Open Day with a special impromptu display". 'Impromptu' reveals a lack of realism. She fiercely repudiated the charge of glorifying war: "I have the greatest personal reasons for being unwilling to do this", and called upon George Washington, the Bible, indeed upon Christ himself, for support in her wish to combat wrong and tyranny. She flatly refused to believe that it was "an affront to the French to celebrate our victory [as] we are all taught to take defeat in games. Three times our Navy has saved us" – Armada, Napoleonic times and now.

Some Mistresses, less than enthusiastic, resolutely refused to do more than keep their charges in order. Forms decorated their rooms and put on an act, staged a tableau, sang a song, had a display of naval momentoes – a sailor's cap, a picture of Nelson, a ship's biscuit. The Form Prefect was in charge. Although the relevance remains unclear, the Latin Mistress decreed that her form dress as Romans, wearing togas made from sheets brought from home. "Much trouble we had trying to conceal the long woollen sleeves of one girl's vest. I remember climbing into the churchyard to get greenery for the decoration. Miss Broome, when she heard of it, was troubled lest the Vicar be concerned about this behaviour". This was felt, on balance, to be unlikely in view of the disgraceful state of the area. Parents and friends were invited and collections made for naval causes. As the best adorned rooms won prizes, "we stuck a sheet of brown paper over the glass pane in the door, so that no-one could pinch our idea".

The initial success owed something to novelty and to an excellent lecture on the Navy and its training ships; "we are now regarding it as an annual custom". E.R.B. proudly announced at Prize Giving that this celebration had been added to school's festivals as a tribute to the Navy's great record of courage and devotion to duty.

What most distinguishes the Great from the Second War was the nature of patriotic fervour. An example, as originally punctuated, of the jingoistic approach remains.

The Fate of Ten Zeppelins

Ten silver Zeppelins, started when 'twas fine,
But there came a sudden gale,
Then there were nine.

Nine mur'drous Zeppelins, grinding hymns of hate,
One soon got out of tune,
Then there were eight.

Eight scattered Zeppelins, keeping close to heaven,
One repeated evil deeds,
Then there were seven.

Seven shining Zeppelins, baffling searchlights fix
One fell in flames to earth,
Then there were six.

Six vengeful Zeppelins, to bomb us did contrive,
But one it met a British shell,
Then there were five.

Five harassed Zeppelins, strafed and strafed still more,
The R.F.C. strafed one of them.
And then there were four.

Four beaten Zeppelins sailing o'er the sea,
One fell down into the waves,
And then there were three.

Three straying Zeppelins, doubtful what to do,
One got lost in far-off lands,
Then there were two.

Two remaining Zeppelins, came upon a gun,
Soon the gunners claimed a Zepp.,
That left only one.

One lonely Zeppelin hadn't any fun;
Off went a dreadful bang.
Then there were NONE. (Geraldine Marshall)

The editors commented on the surprising and gratifying number of verse contributions. "Zeppelins and Gothas are responsible for awakening the poetic faculty in many youthful minds, so give the Germans one good mark for that". Did that comment cause a wince? To be fair, girls did discuss what they should feel on seeing a Zeppelin fall.

Strangely, Ruby Chambers made her first flight in 1916. Uncle casually asked mother if she would like to go for a fly. It was, literally, sick-making. "I don't think I ever want to go up in an aeroplane again". There was no suggestion that here was either a lethal war weapon or a normal means of transport.

More representative of mid-War patriotic feeling was this poem by 13-year old Gladys Black.

What have we done for England?
The land of our love and pride.
What have we done, every one,
To make ours the victor's side?

Our soldiers are giving their manhood,
To fight on the side of the right;
Our sailors are ever watching
All through the dark, cold night.

But what can we do for England
We who are weak and small?
We can help the poor and suffering,
By actions kind to all.

Although this seems but little
Towards our country's need,
Yet every little helps to win,
Peace for the world, indeed.

Alison Little's poem delighted the Head.

The Navy

No matter how stormy the weather may be,
  The waves breaking high, and the wind blowing wild,
The Navy is always patrolling the sea,
  Blessed by us, by the Germans reviled.

The men they are brave, the ships they are rare,
  They're waiting the enemy out on the deep;
The guns they will roar and shells whizz through the air,
  They are always watching and never sleep.

They have cleared the sea of the enemy ships;
  No matter how far o'er the world you may roam,
No German ships sail, and no German flag dips,
  While our Navy may go where it likes on the foam.

So thanks to our Navy, this island's still 'tight',
  And our food still comes in from far distant lands,
For since the great battle was fought in the Bight,
  The Germans won't risk a defeat at our hands.

Janet Edwards' martial ghost tells of a soldier who could not rest because he failed to die in battle. Now with his great-great-grandson coming home with the Victoria Cross, the ghost was at peace.

Daisy Wright, transferring the wartime spirit to School, conveys the exultation, the religious elation that many older people felt was characteristic.

Onward Ever

Work in the might of your love for the school,
  Work but to win her renown;
It is she who has taught and carried you on,
  And to her be the crown.
Work in the hope that you serve her,
  That those for whom schooldays are done,
May see in the school you are forming,
  The signs of the triumphs they won.

Play in the might of your love for the school,
  Play for her honour and fame;
What does it matter who shooteth the goal,
  If the school win the game?
Play on, that she may be glorious,
  That the players of all the past years
May hear in the games you are winning,
  The echoes of their mighty cheers.

Live in the might of your love for the school
Live for her bravely and long;
Keep her name pure, and her aim ever high,
And fill her with song.
Live on that she might be honoured,
That those not as happy as we,
Who have not our school for their loving,
Wish their school as honoured as she.

School was a happy place in spite of the war

One Mistress assures us that everything continued apparently more normally than during the Second War. Steadily increasing numbers brought continuing lamentations of lack of space. As building was impossible, thoughts turned to self-help.

It is easy to take for granted the splendid room in the New Building, its shelves of books well catalogued, easy to trace and reach, its bays, tables and displays. ECS established itself for five years without a library. Not that there was anywhere to house it, but in the first term of the war, one was formed.

Future teacher Grace Dear, with prizes and matriculation distinctions, was the first librarian. She found the great demand for books, especially among the younger girls, encouraging, although she often had difficulty in satisfying it. A pioneer whose cry for more books is still repeated. Emphasis shifted from pictures to books to enable girls to read good literature for pleasure and not as a task. By the end of the war, *two* libraries were being discussed: one for reference, one for enjoyment. Dreaming harms no-one.

A smaller aim arose out of the Garden Fair, when, by accident, the piano was left out, uncovered, in the rain, thus developing a permanent cough. Girls were daily reminded of its demise as they marched to and from Prayers in silence.

The young have the perennial problem of growing up, to one of this generation, one of the most disagreeable hardships that mortals have to endure. One perplexed fashion-conscious young lady agonised over the *correct* length of hair (up or down?) and of skirts which "hover perpetually between the painful extremes of the long and the short. The prospect of an old skirt too short is worse than that of a new skirt too long", for, in those days, clothes had to allow for growth. Grown-ups were shocked if she inked her leg to hide a provoking hole in a stocking.

Social behaviour mattered: she must not be a hoyden, go out gloveless, munch apples, fill the mouth with delicious lumps of toffee or climb a tree. Not for Helen Obott and her contemporaries the freedom to do their own thing. Yet she did not wish her mind to grow up, for she hoped to enjoy always a game, fairy tales, nursery rhymes, Christmas trees, wild flowers and "the little beasties of the countryside".

Authority remained the same.

Onward Ever – The Enfield County School for Girls 1909-1967

CHAPTER EIGHT

These intrepid ladies, they held the upper hand

The Governing Body, no longer outnumbering the Staff, changed somewhat: nine members were replaced, two former ones returned. Two newcomers, Mr H.A.Desborough Brown ("a wise counsellor") and Mrs Rothwell served ECS well. Continuity and normality were the responsibility of the Mistresses; 22 were appointed during this period, of whom five were long-stayers.

Miss Margaret Hodgson, with her Chelsea Diploma, had had three temporary posts for one year before becoming a visiting Physical Instructress, working half-time at both Tottenham County and ECS; her salary of £100 was subtly less than that received by the more orthodoxly scholarly.

Indefatigable, she was responsible for developing not merely physical skills, but also enjoyment and a sense of fair play. Her Drill classes and her effect on Sports Day were soon noteworthy. No fool, she insisted on white blouses so that she could see at a glance when a wash was due; indeed, full uniform was obligatory only for PE.

On joining the full-time Staff in 1919, she came into her own, receiving heartfelt thanks for untiring work in displays and dances, acting in the Staff play, playing netball, unflagging coaching of tennis and hockey, and writing brutally frankly in the Crit. Book: – a later generation would have curled up with mortification.

An infectiously happy personality, with a compassionate yet robust approach, she retained the energy, wonder and simplicity of a child; this, as she grew older, disconcerted at first, but her sincerity and sheer good nature won over the most cynical.

Straight from Edinburgh schools and university, offering Geography, Geology and History for a salary of £200, Miss Marion Crombie (nicknamed Crumbs) spent her whole career at ECS. A stimulating teacher, she was full of energy into her nineties. Inspectors praised a clear and vigorous lesson with VA, despite the serious lack of proper equipment. Upsetting Miss Broome's frugal soul, they suggested that tables might advantageously replace desks, recommended excursions for contour mapping and urged the provision of theodolites, plane tables and a large central laboratory (with water supply) for contour modelling.

Although no narrow specialist, Miss Crombie's main involvement was in activities with strong, or even marginal, connections with Geography. Even when enthusiastic members were few, tribute was paid to her unflagging help in the Geographical, Botanical and Scientific Society; the three-subject club dwindled into the Geographical in 1919, before becoming the longer-lived and popular Geographical and Historical (1925-1946).

She made all arrangements herself, down to the last bus timetable and fares. "I never went anywhere unless I had personal contacts with people in the area, as the main object, apart from the purely geographical one, was to mix with the local people". When in this country, girls wore uniform. Juniors rejoiced over her river explorations; a party visited the Museum of Practical Geology, demolished in 1932. Easter 1915 saw her, three Mistresses and girls at the YWCA at Tunbridge Wells. "We are proud to think that we can do such work. For us, education is a training of the observation and intelligence, not a cramming of the mind with mere book knowledge".

Miss Elizabeth Jane Hyslop, kind and understanding, also retired after 30 years of devoted and unselfish work. Welsh born and educated, with two years' experience, she taught Mathematics, Botany and Science; her salary of £120 rose annually by £10 to £200. She accompanied study parties, played in netball matches, audited School Fund and was treasurer of the senior dramatic society. Another tough lady, she regretted her non-attendance at an OGA function when she was 90, and enjoyed her 100th birthday celebrations.

School's musical foundations and successes were due almost entirely to Miss Ethel Woods, whose qualifications included Higher Froebel certificate and eight years' experience. Teaching also some English and History, she was also instructress at Enfield Technical Institute for Needlework and English, then for Singing. Staff were apparently most unhelpful: the cause is unlikely to have been her Lancastrian origins nor her propensity for wearing green, but doubtlessly originated in snobbery, social or so-called intellectual.

Apart from acting and coaching hockey, she, wisely and fruitfully, devoted herself to music, instituting the making of bamboo pipes and forming a small band. Although a sound tradition needs time to develop, great results came soon and were continuously spectacular. Her first and well-patronised concert in 1918 raised £13:11:0 for School Fund. She took evening classes for OGs, although her finances improved little thereby as she charged but 1/- a term. With Miss Bidwell, she organised the still-flourishing Enfield Musical Festival (EMF); they were joint secretaries for 25 years, Biddy being Guest of Honour at its Golden Jubilee.

Newcomers to the profession faced a probationary period before appointment was confirmed, as did Miss Beatrice James, one of the many forced to earn her living in order to take her degree in Botany with subsidiary Physics from Birkbeck. A good secretary for War Savings, she too audited School Fund, participated in school holidays and became president of the post-war Scientific Club. Retiring, having long been a valued member of Staff, praised as an enthusiast whose aim was to arouse the same enthusiasm in her pupils, she subsequently lectured for the Victoria League.

The hand of friendship was extended to Miss Helen Marion Evans who stayed eight years until she married. An experienced graduate, she taught English, Arithmetic, Algebra, History and French, played netball and accompanied Miss Forrest to Paris. Her departure was mourned: "Those of us who have had the happy privilege of working with [her] will always think of that time in our careers as a past joy that brings no regrets: we wish her a present and future joy as great and satisfying".

1917 saw the beginning of a tradition – the return of former pupils. Two such now found themselves playing for the Mistresses: were there problems as some girls remembered them at school? Secretary of the OGA Literary Society, Miss Dorothy Pickard had to teach half a day here, half a day there and at evening classes before being welcomed as one who had already played an important part in School's story. With diplomas in Housewifery, Laundry and Cookery from the National Training School, she received £90 plus £10 war bonus.

Miss Ethel Brooks had taught at a local elementary Infants' school. As always, she involved herself in everything besides teaching Nature Study, Arithmetic and other subjects to the lower forms. Her IIIA thoroughly deserved their first prize on a later Trafalgar Day. Despite winning the OG Race, she ran second to Miss Hodgson, some ten years her senior, in the Mistresses' Race. Although she married, she was allowed to stay on to help during Miss Broome's absence.

Miss Elizabeth Mary Macgregor had a strange history at ECS. Appointed at three guineas per week to teach junior French, although her offered subjects were Latin, Greek and Scripture, she departed after nine days for various temporary posts, but was reappointed three years later, this time staying five years before leaving to open a school of her own.

Despite ill-health which caused a term's absence, probationer Miss Winifred Maria Haugh also taught for five years. Another all-rounder who participated in games, she donated prizes for a French poetry competition and for improvement in French. Highly qualified, and "a human being", she devoted the first term to phonetics, laying great stress on the position of mouths and tongues. "We had mirrors and looked for our uvulas", to the great distress of one girl who despaired of ever learning French as she could not find hers.

Young teachers often moved on after two years, their experience and skills increased. Miss Gladys Muriel McDermid, Froebel-trained and after one year in a boarding school, took charge of the 8-9 year olds, teaching them Geography, Arithmetic, Handwork and Nature Study as well as junior Singing. Thanked notably for her valiant efforts in hockey, she was missed as she had done much for School.

The other two were adventurous. Classicist Miss Ethel Elizabeth Cooke changed direction to gain honours in Music; offering also French, English and History, she taught Singing throughout as well as doing her obligatory stint of hockey coaching. Her classes sang carols and "other appropriate songs" at Prize Giving before she was "lost" to marriage. The younger but more highly paid Miss Edith Langdon taught mainly in the middle school, offering Arithmetic, Geometry, Algebra and Science in addition to her degree subjects of Botany and Chemistry. Girls rejoiced over her tadpole fishing and flower collecting as she helped with the GBS. Uniquely so far, she left teaching for industry, as chemical assistant in a gas works.

The rest were well-qualified transients or substitutes. Two survived two weeks for six guineas, another for three (Domestic subjects, 12/6 per day), a fourth for a month; two stayed a term, one being that rarity a mathematician (£70), one for two terms (£120); Mrs Nellie Coventry taught for two days each week for five terms for 15/6 a day rising to 17/-, and took private classes. She was the first married woman; either she was a widow or rules were different for visiting teachers. Miss Goulding, for one year, had the highest linguistic qualifications from France, Belgium and Germany as well as experience, having been in five different schools during the war.

Girls expressed gratitude to those "who order the affairs of our school and strive to fit us to face the perils of life as well as to make the most of its good things".

Appointments

26 Miss Cooke 1914-1916	27 Miss Crombie 1915-1945
28 Miss Hodgson 1914-1951	29 Miss Langdon 1914-1916
30 Miss McDermid 1915-1917	31 Miss Mather 1915
32 Miss Jacoby 1916	33 Miss James 1916-1930
34 Miss Macgregor 1916, 1919-24	
35 Miss Haugh 1916-1921	36 Miss Hyslop 1916-1946
37 Miss Woods 1916-1944	38 Miss Taylor 1917
39 Miss Stevenson 1917	40 Miss Short 1917
41 Miss Pickard 1917-1923	42 Miss Evans 1917-1925
43 Miss Brooks 1917-1927	44 Mrs Coventry 1917-1919
46 Miss Foster 1919	48 Miss Bassett-Kidd 1919

50 Miss Goulding 1919-1920

CHAPTER NINE

We count ourselves very fortunate

Day-to-day matters took their normal course. Girls under 11 went as before into Forms I and II, 11-year old fee-payers, bringing with them their receipts from Lloyds Bank, into IIIA. IIIB girls said "Scholarship", some with pride and some with a sense of social stigma; they provided most of the successes and most of the interesting characters. Over 27%, 124 girls had free places from Middlesex, or, for a few transfers, from other counties. Many who came in 1917 kept in touch with ECS. and with each other all their lives. On roll at the outbreak of war were 253; numbers gradually rose until September 1919 began with 358 in 14 forms instead of 11.

Student teachers increased from 10 to a peak of 13 in 1917; there were only 3 thereafter. Fifteen prefects were still chosen, one girl from VA being uniquely privileged. There were stirrings: the Lit. and Deb. discussed whether the system should be extended or abolished. Girls still remembered their form prefect after sixty years and more. This linking lasted until split sites in 1967 made it unworkable.

Rules? No change. "We didn't run in corridors or on stairs. We didn't talk in corridors or in the cloakrooms, or in the Hall while we waited for prayers. We had Order Marks for, I suppose, Disorder – untidiness, forgetting books, mislaying locker keys – and we had Conduct Marks for bad behaviour, not that there was really much bad behaviour. We signed our names and the reason for our punishment in a book" kept by the Form Mistress. Those lockers lasted well into the Sixties, keyless, often doorless, and the wrong shape and size for modern books and equipment. Girls once debated whether the system of rewards and punishments was to be commended.

Although expeditions were curtailed for unavoidable reasons, botanical rambles, geographical excursions, the Juniors' visits to the British Museum continued. Student teachers had a delightful outing with the Selbourne Society. Pleasant afternoons were spent in Cuffley studying landscapes. 1918 saw School's first Art exhibition: "We are sure Mrs Coventry and Mr Quilter must have felt that their energy and enthusiasm were well spent, the show was so interesting and so novel".

Seniors enjoyed an interesting lantern lecture on New South Wales given by a one-time Governor, and paid a memorable visit to hear Sir Ernest Shackleton describe his Polar expedition. Muriel Hake wrote the equivalent of a lecture describing life at the Little Commonwealth, where delinquent children learned to work, play and govern themselves, in the belief that antisocial behaviour resulted from environmental mismanagement by their elders and by society. F.M.F. indefatigably kept alive interest in France and all things French. Le Cercle held social gatherings, play readings, literary competitions (with *quatre examinateurs* from *Sextus Nobilissimus*), even *le bal costumé,* for which she donated prizes. Girls presented *Le Luthier de Crémone*, copies gathering dust for over half a century.

Theatrical delight was provided by *The Merchant of Venice* and *Hamlet.* With Matheson Lang as Shylock and Martin-Harvey as the Prince, it is understandable that the playgoers thought they had seen Shakespeare under the best conditions. The Tercentenary celebrations aroused much enthusiasm, with a whole day of acting and seeing others act. Especially commended were *A Midsummer Night's Dream* (Juniors), and *King Lear* (VIB), but all did splendidly. The Birthday commemoration long continued, although scenes were not always from the Bard. The Staff helped in dressing and what was called other necessary work. Hearty applause was obligatory. "As a permanent reminder, we purchased an artistic reproduction of an authentic portrait of Shakespeare"; alas for the word permanent for it is nowhere to be found today.

Wartime conditions did not favour full-scale dramatic activity, especially as a tradition had not been firmly established. However, Miss Bidwell and Form I spared neither time nor trouble for weeks to make scenes from *Hiawatha* an unqualified success with not a single hitch; they mounted hunting expeditions after Red Indians at the British Museum. The small performers were praised for their lack of self-consciousness, for entering into their roles with zest and ease. Clear speech, understanding of the roles, involvement in all aspects of production (including the making of dresses and props), the printing of programmes – these were Biddy's hallmarks.

A successful concert was very enjoyable. Student teachers and girls produced *Dante and Beatrice*, the combination of scenes and tableaux providing a delightful effect as well as raising £8 for School Fund.

Former students, helped by girls and Miss McDermid, performed *Love's Labours Lost*, clearing 17 guineas. Alas for high hopes: after two silent years, the OG Dramatic club re-emerged – as a singing group. Their literary society, with increased numbers, held meetings at which members read an essay on their favourite book to those assembled round the table in the Head's Room. Discussion – and criticism – followed.

Wartime highlights were the Bazaar and the Garden Fair. For the first, December, 1916, everyone worked splendidly, their efforts rewarded by a great many visitors who spent freely, despite bad weather and prevailing conditions. An exhibition of art and curios, competitions, bran tubs, stalls (Fancy, Plain, Sweets, Fruit and Flowers), teas under Miss Florence's capable direction in Art and Physics rooms – it is all familiar to anyone ever involved in Sales of Work.

The Garden Fair, Wednesday, July 17, 1918, in aid of the War Supply Depot greatly in need of funds, was a day never to be forgotten by Mistresses and girls. The gratifying total was £484:10:3, of which School raised £185:12:6. Forms arranged entertainments to obtain money to start their stalls, the most important being VB's scenes from *Julius Caesar.*

It was held in the spacious and beautiful grounds of Enfield Court, kindly lent by Lady Somerset. ECS had a closer connection with the Court after the Second War. Stalls sold handkerchiefs, Soldiers' Comforts and White Elephant goods. Juniors, again under Miss Bidwell's direction, performed Christina Rossetti's *Pageant of the Months* in a charming manner, indeed to the approval of both *The Mirror* and *The Sketch.* Student teachers were waitresses; so many volunteered that a selection process was devised.

Thousands flocked from near and far. The Fair was opened by no less a personage than Mrs Lloyd George."Our hearts all thrilled with pride as we listened to our choir, in [her] honour, singing the Welsh National Anthem, *Land of my Fathers*, in Welsh". A tremendous downpour ended the fun prematurely. All made for the Riding School, where suppers were served and a concert given by Depot workers until the rain stopped about half-past eight. The only casualty was, as we know, the grand piano.

Societies provided less spectacular, more homespun entertainment. With 72 Fifth and Sixth form members initially, the GBS fulfilled admirably its objective of promoting scientific interest. At fortnightly after-school meetings in the laboratory, Staff and girls read papers on Rocks, Adaptation of animals to environment, the origin of the earth, Earthquakes, Light, the Gramophone, the Microscope, Aspects of the War. The Society sank to a low ebb in 1917-1918, when only three papers were given: Place Names (again), Whaling and Frontiers. Immediately post-war, topics were exclusively geographical: South Sea Islands, Venice, Divers, Geysers.

This ardent desire to collect and disseminate knowledge found another outlet in the Lit. and Deb. Miss Baxter contributed papers on Alfred Noyes, Modern Literature and Robert Burns. In an enjoyable Scotch evening,

Mistresses kindly gave the programme, reading poems and singing songs. Other papers touched on Milton's opinion of women, Gilbert and Sullivan, Ballads and Myths; girls gave prose, verse and dramatic readings. Impromptu discussions were many, heated and various. Some topics recurred with each generation: Homes, Phonetic Spelling. Others concerned specifically female concerns: Should women be lawyers? A standard dress for women? Should men do their own darning? Can souvenir-hunting be justified was probably sparked off by air-raids. Whatever the subject, each was thoroughly discussed with great animation.

There was no intention of slacking

Sports Days went from strength to strength. During 1915's remarkable thunderstorm, all were kept happy by Miss Hodgson's Drill classes, Miss Cooke's singers and, at short notice, Miss Woolmer's solo. The following year, in delightfully fine weather, many enthusiasts found the Obstacle and Parents' races full of excitement and amusement. Weird and wonderful non-athletic events continued, offering scope to those physically ungifted: Walking, Stilt, Circular Journey, Ball juggling, Shake and Bunny, Snake Kangaroo, Flowerpot and Ball, whilst Slow Bicycle remained a favourite for over thirty years. Competition was so keen in 1916's 35 events that two Gold Medals were awarded. Chase Farm boys supplied the music.

1917's ceremony began at 5pm, still, of course, on a Saturday, with some 500 visitors. An aeroplane flying very low several times over the field brought an extra thrill. Rain the following year caused postponement to an equally wet Monday; events were run off during the week with no lack of spirit. Gold brooches replaced medals and Colours awarded for the first time.

The Drill competition was held as usual. More enterprising was the display, before a large audience, of Swedish Drill, apparatus work on vaulting-horse and balance forms, dancing and a running maze, all the result of Miss Hodgson's untiring work.

Games became compulsory. Is that why hockey became less successful and the Bowles Cup was lost? "What we have done once we can do again", despite such hindrances as mud, snow and "the unathlete who soon develops the art of inventing plausible fiction" to escape. With the stimulus of Hoddie's coaching, seven Colours were gained. In the last war year, however, the first XI entered for the Cup and came third. This was particularly disappointing, as only three schools entered. By then, all suffered from a lack of energy. Not all results are recorded, but at least 20 matches were won, 14 lost, 7 drawn.

Inter-Form netball contests remained popular, the Sixth suffering from too few pupils. Miss Bidwell inaugurated a shooting competition, seven girls from each form being allowed two minutes each. The team was judged worthy of inclusion in the Netball Association in 1915, although 11 years passed before it survived the first round of its competition. When these matches were suspended, a professional coach was deemed necessary. "We derived much benefit from her advice, and since the whole School was allowed to watch and hear the results, netball should show great improvement". So it did. There was much public spirit shown; they proved themselves to be "a sporty lot", but the tide ebbed and flowed. Two, sometimes three, teams won 38 matches and lost 33; 8 Colours were awarded. In one year, Mistresses beat Girls three times.

As Miss Forrest still did all the arduous work of organising tennis fixtures, interest dared not flag, although courts were shared with EGS. Two teams each had three couples and two reserves. Helped by a Student teacher and one afternoon's professional coaching, a miracle was expected despite the dearth of experienced players. Of 31 matches played, 17 were lost. The whole school watched the championship final which provided one girl's first experience of intense collective emotion. "I didn't understand the game: I didn't know who won, but what a wonderfully thrilling afternoon that was".

Membership of the Swimming Club had to be refused to anyone living near any Baths. Emphasis was wisely laid less on competitive results than on individual proficiency. Twenty minutes in the water fled by all too quickly – that on Friday evenings and Saturday mornings. As soon as all the first members were able to do more than merely keep afloat, Standards (¼, ¾ and one mile) and Life-Saving classes were established. "Swimming is a healthy and delightful exercise, but if we do not learn how to make use of it as a means of saving life, we do not accomplish much". Good progress, although the Baths were distant, was soon reported. Three received Colours for all-round swimming : breast and side strokes, back swimming, diving, speed and style. A tall order!

This must be a war number

A printed magazine of between 24 and 32 pages flourished throughout 1914-1918 as it failed to do in the Second War. Its price remained constant at 6d, although the Governors were unwilling to continue their subsidy.

Whilst still primarily a chronicle and without any coherent pattern, it does reflect contemporary moods, activities and interests. Accounts were interspersed with individual articles and news of, even articles by, OGs. First came editorial comment, often coy. "We offer grateful thanks to the public-spirited who offered so many and such varied contributions, and we hope the less public-spirited will follow the example of this year's contributors another time; we feel sure there is hidden talent lying waiting". An undertone of irony, perhaps? Certainly, a patronising note. The remark bore fruit, nevertheless.

Some themes had obviously been set for homework, and the content is too often trite, repetitive or cloying, if technically above average. Rain inspired Kathleen Gudgeon's mock-heroic *Battle of the Raindrop Knights* and Eleanor Nicholson's simpler *A Rainy Day*. The favourite topic is Autumn: with personification –

> He's a spirit! he's immortal!   (Phyllis Pickard)

or literary borrowing –

> How wild and wondrous is thy sunset beauty
>> That dyes the distant west!
> Touching the boulders like dull coals of burning
>> As Phoebus sinks his steeds to rest.   (Violet Wrenn)

or the pleasingly childish –

> And mingled with the splendour
>> Of the rich autumn tones
> The juicy hips are shining
>> In lovely scarlet cones!

by Winifred Allen who also saw fairies and goblins in the glowing fireside coals, a pleasure missed by most today.

Others recorded experiences such as an Indian Christmas in Natal Barbara Ellis), Schoolgirl correspondence (Kathleen Loos), English writers and the Lake District (Faith Woolgar) and Sunny Sussex by Madge Peachey, writing after a surfeit of Kipling. A farmer's daughter, she also brought the countryside to ECS, as she told of her love for her small animals such as piglets.

On a visit to Kew, Annie Tozer found it sad that even in those beautiful peaceful gardens, the signs of war were apparent: flower-beds less well kept, a few houses closed, one lake bordered by an exceptionally fine crop of onions. An ornamental sundial in the midst of a potato patch looked incongruous. Kew, however, remained a paradise not only to botanical students but to millions of slum children. In *The essentials of Fine Art*, Agnes Osmond urges us to think of higher things. "Art constitutes the beautiful and the ideal side of life, as a complement of the practical everyday side"; it should therefore not be neglected even in war-time.

A good secondary education

Form I began to make a doll's house in woodwork for the Home for crippled children ; girls were still at it when they moved up to IIB. Otherwise, the curriculum remained unchanged.

Wars fail to halt examinations; indeed, the number of externals taken and passed rose, and not simply through increased pupil numbers. The last year of peace was impressive: all 9 candidates for Junior county scholarships and all 7 for matriculation were successful. In all, 21 won these scholarships, the annual grant rising from £5-£10 to £6-£12.

Public examinations at Fifth form level were standardised in 1917, with subjects in groups; they were now recognised by most professional bodies. Of the 24 successful candidates, 23 matriculated, with 25 distinctions in written papers and 14 in Language Orals.

Sixth form studies were stimulated by these results and by the special grants made to attract capable students to advanced courses. Thirty-seven Senior school certificates earned 4 distinctions. Intending teachers, numbering 31, still benefited from tuition fees, maintenance grants and bursarships (rising from £10 to £12). It seems unlikely that fathers' means were the sole criteria.

Commercial certificates, Public, Pitman's and RSA, over two years increased at varying levels: 39 for Shorthand, 10 for Typing as well as for French (59 passes, 13 Oral*) and German (5 with 2 Oral*).

Four won University entrance scholarships (£20 for three years), plus two scholarships (one of £40) and an Exhibition to Oxford.

Form prizes numbered 148, and Sixth form prizes 10, whilst specials decreased to 12 as actual and potential donors felt the financial pinch. Because certificates largely replaced books, Prize Giving, although remaining an occasion for patriotic fervour and self-congratulation, appeared less than its customary self.

In 1914, Miss Broome reviewed the possibilities which ECS afforded towards training commercial secretaries, general and DSc teachers. She felt that this last 2-year compulsory course was excellent preparation for family life. She sensibly advocated general studies for at least three years before any specialisation, and urged that girls should come as early as possible to take full advantage of opportunities offered; there is no evidence that those who came younger stayed longer. All but three of the pupil teacher entrants had been between 14 and 15; all but four left between 18 and 19. The age of school entry was raised from 10 to 11 in 1915; the average age was 12½.

Apart from songs, wartime Prize Givings were modest affairs with local speakers from 1915. Mrs Roth made the presentations at one afternoon ceremony. Mrs McEwen, who funded prizes and distributed Sports Day certificates, "made some interesting remarks", – alas, unrecorded. Honours lists were clipped into the 1916 and 1918 magazines, but no programmes have surfaced. Taking place unusually on a Monday, 1917's was to have been more elevated. However, owing to indisposition, Lady French was unfortunately unable to present the certificates, but Mrs Bowles kindly undertook the duty at very short notice.

1919's ceremony, held in the spring because of the Election before Christmas, honoured the previous year's excellent results of 49 passes and 17 distinctions. Five prizes were won in the Navy League Southern Counties essay competition; internally, Scripture, Improvement (Forms I and II), German, French and Dried Flowers gained awards. The Head reviewed four years of steady work and growth in spite of all war difficulties. Miss Drayton, known to older girls as secretary of the Victoria League, spoke, thus ensuring another patriotic occasion.

CHAPTER TEN

Because of family circumstances

The total intake over the five years was 448, annual entry ranging between 71 and 107. Over half came on the proper September date, the proportion rising steadily to 71% by 1918. Others still wandered in, 66 during term-time. Four enrolling in the spring of 1915 and one in January 1916 were hardly at fault: they were Belgian refugees.

With those who joined by 1920, whose birth dates fell between 1898 and 1909, the year of school's foundation, was there much change in the popularity of forenames? 158 are recorded, with 50 new ones, some to appear more frequently (Beryl, Joan, Joyce, Patricia): others sagged for a while (Jean, Caroline, Clarice). Three are the only ones to be called Queenie. Five have names which will recur once: Annella, Elfrida, Letitia, Maggie, Myfanwy. Eleven remain unique: Chrystabel, Isa, Laurence, Leal, Lizzie, Mariella, Naomi, Sadie, Salome, Sophia, Tryphena. The runaway favourites were Winifred/Winnie 30, May 38, Marjorie/Margery/Margaret 51, and, again top, Mary (with Marie 2 and Maria 1) 60. The initials of one unfortunate spelt GOD.

A few had been at local secondary establishments, but, as usual, the majority came from 16 local publicly maintained schools, the major contributors being Chase Side 47, Chesterfield Road 46 and George Spicer 41. About half lived within a mile of the Town, one over the shop at *The Crown and Horses*. Fewer than ten reported moving house. Twenty-four travelled from the limits of Enfield, 9 from neighbouring areas, 30 from the countryside , some from Greater London, whilst the rest transferred from apparently all round the South and East coasts from Torquay to Lowestoft.

Those privately educated, 108, had been at an even greater number of schools , 36 in all, including the still popular Dame and self-styled High Schools: Elmcroft 9, Roanoake 5, the Misses Chambers 5, Gardner (Woodstock) 5, and Lee-Jones (Ingleby)2. Apart from Palmers Green High 4, no fewer than 13 others within a radius of five miles are named; not one exists today. A religious element is noticeable. Besides Enfield Convent 6, girls had been at six others in England, one in Belgium and one in Durban; she left for boarding school after four terms. Others had attended the

Friends' School at Saffron Walden, the Old Palace at Mayfield and Miss Bertram's Private Training College (Commercial), Glasgow. One girl's previous school was, uniquely, left blank. Another had had no school for the previous two years, because of travelling – odd, as father was a retail pastrycook and confectioner. Several had been taught privately by a governess.

In short, 448 girls from 77 different institutions.

Parental occupations were equally varied. Two fathers had retired, no fewer than 22 had died, and six were unrecorded. Maybe one unknown had simply vanished, for one-parent families are not a recent phenomenon. Two widows were left with independent means, their spouses having had no occupation, then, not as now, a sign of affluence. The indefatigable Mrs Roth was guardian of the South African. The first step-father, a contractor's carman, appears.

The war soon made itself felt. RSAF employed 28 in at least 10 different trades, the Waltham Abbey Gunpowder factory another two. By 1917, seven more were in munitions as shell examiners and gunbarrel driller (OA), two more were in the Army, one in the RNVR and a fourth a Lieutenant in the Royal Army Medical Corps, whose daughter stayed a term only. By 1918, a bank messenger was an Air Force Sergeant, a machinist became a wartime floor cloth printer, a silk merchant had enlisted and a wholesale tea merchant was serving in the Royal Naval Volunteer Reserve.

Increasing numbers, 34, were engineers, aeronautical, mechanical, electrical, sanitary, of all grades. Assuming greater importance were directors, managers, manufacturers, of their own companies, of wholesale firms and factories, producing a wide range of items and employing such as iron turner, moulder, thermometer toolmaker, metal hardener, stoker. The solid core of proprietors (whole or partly), masters and assistants remained in small retail businesses, some 150 in all: – food, drink, hotels 31: building and allied trades (one Master plumber) 29: newsagents, tobacconist 32: photographers, printers 22: clothing 18: motor industry, coal merchants 3 each: hairdressers, jewellers, opticians, warehousemen 2 each.

The land supported 32, Props. and men, with 11 on farms, 10 as nurserymen (one tomato grower, glass), 5 as gardeners, 2 as estate managers, with individuals as cowkeeper, market salesman, saddler, and, comprehensively, fruit grower/market gardener/farmer.

Officials included Superintendent of the Poor Law schools, School attendance officer, Enfield's assistant surveyor, and, further afield, chief bailiff for Waltham Abbey Crown Court, LCC Referencer and Clerk of

Works, chief clerk at Lambeth police court and chief bill clerk of the City Corporation engineering department. One Council labourer paid fees for his daughter throughout. Seven were policemen, three with the Metropolitan force, with one CID Inspector. Railways, then the steadiest of jobs, employed 15, manual and clerical, with one Great Eastern station master. Four more were in the Post Office.

Over 100 white-collared men worked as secretaries, clerks, bank officials, schoolmasters, commercial travellers, in accountancy, insurance and publishing, as Civil Servants (one in the Gold Coast, now Ghana), as Stock Exchange callers, as dealers (stamps, antiquarian books, art), in law, dental surgery, pharmacy and the churches.

Almost 200 different jobs are listed. Unusual are literary advisor for Selfridge's, foreman clockmaker, furniture japanner, Theatre Proprietor/ Manager, Tobacco-Pipe Mounter and Gold and Silver Stick Mounter (Prop.).

The war was brought closer by refugees from Antwerp and Brussels, daughters of an accountant, a clerk, the manager of a furniture business and a Government clerical officer on the railways. Béatrice Andrée Marthe and Henriette Fernanda Adam, aged 15 and 13, and Marthe Joanne Marie Claessens stayed one term on scholarships giving Béatrice time to gain a distinction in RSA French (O). Not quite ten years old, convent-educated Irène Van Trappen won a form prize and a Sports race before returning home at the age of 13.

Yvonne Van Der Elst became part of ECS for over three years, returning home after teaching French and Dancing at Miss Bagshaw's preparatory school. She wrote a powerful account of her country's invasion and a charming piece on traditional family celebrations. Prefect and committee member of both magazine and Cercle, she took Ist Class in RSA Advanced French (O).

School's summer fête of 1936 included a balloon distance race.

"Dear Sir,

Walking along the beach this morning, I was fortunate enough to find the enclosed balloon". The writer told of her pleasure at the happy days spent at Enfield County School. "I do wish I could go back to the happy days in your country". The finder was none other than Yvonne.

Excluding the Belgians, 440 left between autumn 1914 and summer 1919. Over a third, 36%, continued to leave at unorthodox times, although ever-increasing numbers stayed long enough to pursue worthwhile studies. Six stayed just one term, one stayed 10 years, the average being only 11 terms.

Of pre-war entrants, 42 had left before they were 14, most, but unfortunately not all, going to other places of education because parents had moved. In contrast, only 23 wartime students departed before that age. Seven left because of ill-health, two dying within a year or so, one left because mother required her companionship, although there was a father and the family means were good. The raising of the school leaving age in 1918 to 14, much needed legislation in many areas to protect children and especially girls, made little difference to ECS; perhaps it helped a few individuals.

Forty changed to other schools as far apart as York and Hastings. Astonishingly, in the middle of the war, two transferred to Belgium and Switzerland. In 1918, one went to an establishment in Germany, and yet another enrolled at a Belgian convent. One family moved to the country with no secondary school near; no official transport or subsidies then.

It is disheartening that the immediate whereabouts of 139 remain unknown, despite often reasonable qualifications. This may be partly because of wartime problems as well as reserve about what were still felt to be personal concerns. Matters improved as the figures for 1918 and 1919 are creditably low at six and eight respectively.

Numbers pursuing higher education remained high, 67 in all, with an ever-increasing quota, 17, studying for degrees, including medicine, one gaining both BA and BSc. University College proved the most popular. Training colleges claimed 49, Hockerill taking the largest number, the remaining one being the first horticultural student at Swanley. One was a student teacher under the LCC, six were uncertificated.

Clerical workers displaced teachers, several changing careers after the war; 87 went directly into posts which were offering variety as men joined the Forces. Four had temporary war work in Government departments, four gained permanent Civil Service posts, four had clerkships in Lincoln House (the Post Office), three worked in banks. Thirteen trained first, including six at the prestigious St George's College, one at Clark's College, and one, for family reasons, at Edmonton Polytechnic. They too began to consider retraining, especially if clerical work, even with increasing responsibilities, proved unattractive, or if posts were lost to returning Servicemen. One became a part-time nurse, another a secretary in Holland.

Odd jobs? These were few: three milliners, three shopworkers (one a draper's assistant), nursery governess who became a missionary, VAD worker, two private piano teachers, two hairdressers (one surely the best qualified *coiffeuse*, with School Certificate, RSA French (O), prizes for Improvement in French and Form work), factory hand. Two emigrated, one becoming secretary to the Professor of Anthropology in Australia. At least 82 married (one twice) and at least 10 daughters and one granddaughter followed on at ECS

I am glad that I can look back with laughter

... at my schooldays". "I cannot honestly say that I should like to live [them] over again, for that would mean living through the War once more, but I should like to be one of the new girls who have entered IIIUpper this term" – yes, these 1934 entrants would, mostly, escape Second War schooling.

It seems increasingly unfair to omit so many whose solid achievements in examinations, sports, games, in writing papers and magazine contributions, and who, as office-holders, maintained School's consistently high levels and who, then and subsequently, provided a standard by which those able and willing and those less able and unwilling could and can judge themselves. Girls who have left no mark can be counted on the fingers of one hand. An arbitrary choice, therefore, of schoolgirls typical through the years and of the times, of the uniquely gifted, the pioneer, the one who continued a family tradition.

HEAD GIRL

1914 Gladys Fraser	1915 Hilda Obott	1916 Ruby Hayes
1917 Agnes Osmond	1918 Lillian Styles	1919 Mary Callander
	1920 Mary Jewell	

One stimulated my interest in ECS' distant past. The OGA received a surprise legacy which enabled a student to undertake a Fine Arts course. Irene May Boggis, although a life member, had lost touch yet had harboured such pleasant memories. A live wire as school officer and student teacher, with a variety of prizes and examination certificates, she read a paper on Art and, as secretary of the GBS, wrote a learned article.

It was Marjorie Edith Payne who spent the longest time at ECS, from September 1914 to July 1924. With education and theology certificates, she realised that "I'm enjoying school now because I enjoyed it then".

Others who excelled at school included Sports champion Joyce Gentry (Hockey*, Swimming*) and Elsie May Smith, writer of a brisk narrative of the Peace Pageant in which she represented Elizabeth I. House and hockey captain, with seven Sports placings, Annie Tozer (Swimming*) won the General Knowledge prize and wrote a paper on the evolution of animals. Edith Margaret Woolgar contributed literary articles and most informative papers on the cause of a rainbow and on Jane Austen.

Others ventured further afield. Kathleen Foster broke with convention by marrying a year after leaving for the International Guild in Paris. Her paper on Chopin, "enhanced by pianoforte illustrations proved an instructive and pleasant evening"; the Society felt fortunate in having such a talented member. Edith Mary Levey married the brother of an OG who became a British Consul, and lived in many parts of Europe and the Near East. Librarian Rose Mary Chittenden married and emigrated to the USA, Gladys Olive Perry taught in Borneo. Agnes Mary (Nessa) Spencer, who kept the courts in good order, qualified as a dispenser, and, with her sister Isa Georgina, trained in Decorative Art, opened an Art shop. Nessa became a coffee farmer's wife in South America, but "deep down, our hearts are in England". Dorothy Hutchinson's schooldays were wartime ones; perhaps that gave her the taste for excitement. She, her husband and two daughters spent five tented years in the Australian outback, never seeing another human for months on end, forced home only by continuous drought.

Secretarial work increased in respectability; highly qualified girls, Edith Batson won a Scholarship (16 guineas) and Elsie Margaret Oliver an Exhibition (9 guineas) to St George's College, where both successfully prepared for the Civil Service, Edith gaining second place overall. Another first – her marriage to a refugee Belgian Lieutenant. The first twins, Gladys Jessie and Dorothy Lilian Wootton, arrived. Dorothy's netball report exudes enthusiasm and public spirit, with yet another appeal to prove worthy of Miss Bidwell, and even appreciation of the Crit. Book. A debater and reader of a paper on Wireless Telegraphy, she too entered the Civil Service.

Others undertook less usual trainings. Future hospital pharmacist Edith Margaret Ogilvie was thanked for marking out the ground throughout the season. Rose Emily Aird became a trained West End florist. Marjorie Chattey, Sports champion and County scholar, was school's first Inspector for school meals and catering. Actress Violet Wrenn contributed poems full of classical and biblical allusions, archaic words and a fey charm. After a polytechnic course, she acquired diplomas in English from London University and in Domestic Science and Canteen Cookery from *Good Housekeeping*, an achievement which remains unique. Gwendoline Martha Willmott followed her sisters to St George's College, but subsequently qualified in massage work, medical gymnastics and medical electricity at Guy's.

More went to university. Mary Jewell welcomed the diversions of Fire Drill, poked fun at attitudes to the weather, ably performed in the Peace Pageant and exhorted her House members to do their very best to help to build up a tradition in its first year. She won a £30 scholarship to Oxford to read History; school wished her all success and a jolly good time. After Quaker relief work in Germany, she became Head of a school in Kampala for daughters of African chieftains. An unrivalled pioneer.

Kathleen Jessie Gudgeon's first House report is virtually unique: no preaching. She succumbed in her second:"Let us carry on, and let us achieve wonders". Members did show great enterprise with a social, concert (17/- for charity), sports and a cycling club (formed, and disbanded, within a year), activities which partly excuse the House's bottom position.

Although boasting but one sporting success (1st in Egg-and-Spoon), future French graduate Margaret Gwen Francis sang at the Lit. Hist. and Deb.; for another student she was the ideal of what a Head Girl should be. She too admonished her House: "Unless we all pull together and do our bit, we can never make the most of it". When she died, the MLA offered the Francis trophy for French Verse Speaking.

Hilda Frances Obott's well-researched piece lamented the destruction of old Enfield. No-one was surprised when she won the Quain English Essay prize and graduated with 1st Class Honours, as did Dorothy Trotter who set a good example for her sister Cicely Mary (Hockey*, Swimming*), primarily an active person with no fewer than 13 placings in Sports events, and more as a visitor. She cherished *Poems of Today*, a present on her 11th birthday from Miss Bidwell. Both taught Geography, Cicely at Hull University. Evelyn Mary Spratley, junior and senior tennis champion, wrote a vigorous cliché-free hockey account. Her scholarship (£29) took her to Reading, but ill-health forced early retirement.

Marjorie Cozens Cooke was joint Sports champion as well as treasurer of le Cercle. Sister and House captain Kathleen Sylvia wrote *Night*, another skilfully written poem full of literary sentiments, and acted Widow Twankey in *Aladdin*, performed, perhaps inappropriately, at an Armistice Day celebration. Their paths diverged when Marjorie's scholarship took her to Training College. Kathleen won a teaching scholarship, plus a princely £3 book allowance, to Reading. She too was a first: – Doctorate in Philosophy, Student Assistantship in the department of Psychological Investigation. "One never knows how real, living and even jolly, religion can be till one comes into contact with the Student Christian Movement". In 1935, disaster struck. The magazine recorded her death in a black-bordered paragraph. "We remember her as a gentle and charming girl, always kind and unselfish. Her life leaves beautiful memories for those who knew her best".

A wider fame came to four. Hilda Constance Dean, school's second doctor, clearly enjoyed everything – friends, sports, lessons, drama. Beryl Leal Allen "had a leaning towards medicine, but my father, a man who assessed things from the practical point of view, suggested that as I had a very efficient and sympathetic pair of hands, dentistry might be a proper outlet for any talents I might possess". Her school career included 13 Sports placings and the captaincy of St Margaret's when it rose to top House. Her academic glory ranged from the best collection of dried flowers to the almost obligatory distinctions in French. Not even school's first dentist was allowed to be one-sided in approach.

1913's intake provided school's first professional musician in Mary Hutton Callander. As first House captain of St Ursula's, her report, albeit somewhat bossy, is not devoid of fun. She and her younger sister, Catherine Reid Lang (Katie, Sports champion for three successive years and House captain in her turn), had the impressive total of 38 Sports placings. Katie more than held her own, playing tennis for School, and, as netball and Sports captain, fumed against slackness and lack of enthusiasm. Mary arranged Latin songs for Prize Giving before going to the Royal Academy of Music for six years, becoming Sub-Professor. Augener published *Four Little Pictures*, the London Symphony Orchestra played her *Rhapsody* and other compositions have been broadcast. This did not go to her head. Sometime OGA netball secretary, she enlivened a Reunion with a brilliant performance on the piano.

Phyllis Margaret Pickard began auspiciously with an admirable performance in *Hiawatha*. First of the new members to swim a quarter-mile, she commanded all to attend the Baths in near-lyrical reports. "There was not a girl who regarded swimming as a duty that must be gone through with a smile; the smile came naturally". She struck new ground by doing brilliantly at the Froebel College, working at the Caldecott Community school and becoming senior lecturer in Psychology, member of a Government committee and of the National Association for Gifted Children, Head of graduate training at Maria Grey and author of *If you think your child is gifted*.

CHAPTER ELEVEN

Lest we forget

It is impossible now to feel the emotional appeal of the Armistice. Many have affirmed that it was the day they remembered best of their schooldays.

The magazine was published with much happier feelings, the near hysteria fresh in the editor's mind. "The excitement knew no bounds when the news of the signing came. We at once assembled in the Hall, where we gave vent to our feelings by three ringing cheers. After a short impressive address by Miss Broome, we sang the hymn *Praise the Lord*, followed by Kipling's *Recessional* and the National Anthem. Never had such hearty singing been heard in the school before. A party accompanied Miss Broome to the Thanksgiving service in the Parish Church. In the afternoon, a half holiday was granted".

"We were waiting for Latin, in one of the rooms overlooking Holly Walk, and when we heard the church bells ring, we all crowded by the windows. Miss X came in and was angry. What a strange reaction!" Another pupil thinks that "most of us went nearly mad with joy and excitement". A third, excited at the time, admitted later that none of them realised as their elders must have done the real implications of that day.

Celebrations followed. On July 3, 1919, School assembled in the Market Place to hear Colonel Bowles read out the Proclamation of Peace. As it poured with rain throughout the proceedings, the Colonel granted a half-holiday to all the schools which attended. ECS was well placed for such bonuses.

With EGS, girls presented a pageant of the town's history; Council bore the expense of hiring the chief costumes. On the eventful Saturday, the sun shone at intervals, but, the dresses being thick and heavy, no-one minded that it was not hot. The Angel of Peace, daughter of a fallen soldier, led the procession followed by elementary schoolchildren representing the Allies, then by ECS and EGS. Groups met at the Town Park gates, all making their way to a stage erected near the river.

Tableaux showed Cardinal Wolsey presenting the Papal Bull to Henry VIII at Hatfield House: Prince Edward, accompanied by his sister, Princess

Elizabeth, receiving the news of her accession to the throne, 1547: local resident Sir Walter Ralegh laying his cloak upon the puddle for Queen Elizabeth: the meeting of James I and the Tinker: the first Enfield Volunteers, 1798: May Day celebrations at Chase Side House, 1850-1860. A truly English occasion from first to last, for "just as we finished, it began to rain, and so we hurried back to school, pursued by the admiring comments of the onlookers". And how else to end this enjoyable afternoon but with a revivifying tea in the Hall, kindly provided by the Town Council?

During the holidays, on the fifth anniversary of the outbreak of war, the Thames Pageant commemorated the Navy's role. The Embankment and bridges were crowded; the more fortunate had places in stands. Two naval cutters, of the type used in the battle of Zeebrugge, led the procession of river police, the Royal Barge, in which sat the King and Queen, rowed by the Royal Watermen, the Lords of the Admiralty in their royal blue barge with its golden figurehead, several launches, one bearing models of the modern 18-inch gun and earlier weapons, a long line of boats carrying representatives of shipping companies and the association of wireless telegraphists, rowing boats manned by boys from training ships, with 70 lifeboats from the Mercantile Marine bringing up the rear. Many were black sailors, attired in white suits and small red caps. Indeed, a pageant of great historical interest.

Lest the euphoria be total, Miss Murphy sent an account of immediate post-war conditions in France: little street lighting, danger of power cuts because of the coal shortage, cobblestone pavements full of large, water-filled holes, houses dilapidated, prices astronomical, servants unobtainable, the parcel post system beyond description, telephones functioning but rarely ("one might wait hours and get no answer"). "Nobody bothers about anything and the result is chaos". Relieved that recent elections had proved a stunning defeat for the Bolsheviks, she ended, characteristically: "I think we in England are apt to forget what a large and important part of France has been devastated".

1919's Armistice Day celebrations, although less spontaneous, held more awareness of its significance – "a day to be remembered by all, from Cabinet ministers to schoolgirls". As 11am struck, all assembled in the Hall to hear the King's Proclamation. Maroons boomed out in the Town to herald the wonderful stillness of the Two Minutes' Silence. Then they sang with vigour *O England, my Country* and *England, Arise*. In London, every man stood bareheaded, all traffic stopped without the intervention of the calm dignified City policemen, every riverside flag was lowered to half mast, all dock work ceased until the maroons and church bells rang out. It was seen then as a great beginning as well as a great ending. "The girls of

Enfield County School realised, with millions throughout the British Empire, the individual responsibility of each one to make the future better than the past. In the evening by the fireside, members of the family compared notes and described their experiences".

Annual observance continued, the atmosphere in 1920 still emotional. "This simple way of honouring those who died for us has more in it than the flags and decorations. To be silent together, to think together, to pray together, to sing together – that is all: but like all simple, beautiful things, it is unforgettable". Ten girls represented School at the unveiling of Enfield's War Memorial in 1921, "to teach true patriotism and the spirit of service and self-sacrifice". It became traditional for Head Mistress to accompany Head Girl and Form Monitresses, each bearing a wreath, to the Memorial. On a weekday, the procession made its way along Holly Walk after the Silence; otherwise, tribute was paid on a Saturday, Sunday not being very convenient for school celebrations. This respect to the memory of the Beloved Dead continued for at least two decades, although by 1929 there was a single school wreath, the cost (between £1 and £2:2:0) being secured by collections.

Articles inspired by the occasion and submitted as late as 1932 seem to contradict the notion that war and armistice meant nothing to modern youth. Rita Ikin was two years old when the Armistice was signed, so that her deep emotions are amazing. She was stirred by the singing of those still alive, in homage to the dead. Then the gun sounded.

> Silence, deep silence, all England was silent
> Thinking and praying for those who were dead.
> Two minutes' silence and not a word spoken,
> Thoughts upon thoughts teemed in our head.
> Think how they fought for us, gave up their lives for us,
> Suffered so silently, triumphed so gloriously –
> Now they are dead.

She wondered at length what the present generation could do, concluding that sorrow was out of place because the dead were in glory and thinking of us.

> Yet God knows his own ones, the true ones who trust Him,
> They died thus rejoicing.
> 'We will die for our country
> Our all will we give,
> Remembering our dear ones, the true ones remaining,
> Far, far away in the land of our fathers.
> May God send them comfort, and help them and love them
> Though we cannot live'.

The Silence was over.

> And London, so silent, so still and so silent,
> Turns back to its labour.

PART THREE

THE TWENTIES

CHAPTER TWELVE

A Cloistered Seminary?

The Twenties are often thought to show the great divide between the haves (the Ritzy cocktail scene of the flappers and Charleston) and the have-nots (the down-and-outs). Although the relative stability of pre-war days never returned, Enfield suffered less than many areas. Such were the Head's ideals of service that girls were taught about social conditions, taken to see those less fortunate than themselves and encouraged to help constructively rather than by financial contributions. Girls could not avoid knowing of contemporary difficulties; many were actually enduring them. The criticism levelled at girls' schools staffed by unmarried women that pupils had minimal contact with the so-called real world was unfair.

If girls were aware of the facts of living, many were somewhat vague about the facts of life. Yet this decade saw the first woman MP, women over 21 gaining the vote, Marie Stopes holding birth control meetings. Limited contact with the boys was permitted. As well as the annual tennis fixture, both schools joined in a Carnival, culminating in a more or less comic cricket match. Even here, stereotypes prevailed: the girls managed to lose although the boys played left-handedly!

Meanwhile, Miss Broome admonished: "If you wish to talk to boys, you must do it in your own drawing-room and not in the street". Parents had to authorise, *in writing*, snowball fights with the boys in the field.

While girls spent, and still spend, more time out of school than in it, no-one was well informed. The BBC began radio broadcasting from 1922, the first talkies appeared only in 1927. No television, of course. There were few periodicals, clubs or meeting places other than those provided by School or Church.

Staff were badly hit. By the middle Twenties, salaries were 12% lower than in 1921 when Burnham pay scales were established. The new rates bewilder. One Mistress, receiving £250pa in 1918, dropped to £180, another to £240. One lost £60pa, four lost £20, another £72:10:0, yet one gained £40. Miss Florence's 1918 salary of £400 was reduced to £337:10:0. From their behaviour and activities, no-one could have suspected these severe blows.

Some often taught more than the 18 hours (27 lessons) which were regarded as the maximum.

Although more girls were born between 1921 and 1931, with Middlesex showing the highest rate of increase in population of any administrative county, getting into, and staying at, school were affected by national economic policies. For the first time, in 1923, numbers decreased slightly. The following year, a local authority could give up to 40% free places, increased to 50% by 1930.

The scholarship examination came accordingly into sharper focus. From mid-decade, 80 entrance scholarships covered fees and maintenance grants of £3, fathers' incomes being reviewed annually; four were honorary, A Vicar's scholarship was awarded in four years. Junior county awards (fees plus £8-£16) numbered 110 (six honorary), intermediate 32 (£20, one honorary), with six bursaries or maintenance grants (£12-£20), which ceased mid-decade, and two for intending teachers. Twenty-one girls were helped by training college grants of £20pa, plus £3 book allowance, for two or three years – a total of 269 receiving public help.

Although the Labour government increased money for those over 14, some had to seek supplements from Enfield Church School of Industry or from educational trusts. Books and uniform, not to mention such desirable extras as the magazine, caused strain to many families. Between 1927 and 1933, girls were allowed to bring sandwiches, only the 'better-off' having set lunches.

Recognising the physical results of financial hardship and war, the Government introduced Medical Inspections, to be held at least four times during a pupil's school life. Much disliked by girls as they were usually conducted with scant regard for contemporary modesty and not altogether approved by parents at both ends of the financial scale, they were wholeheartedly supported by Miss Broome. Prevailing pride, ignorance or penury gave her cause to lament that, although school already did much to promote girls' physical welfare, she received requests for exemption from Inspection, and found that advice given was not always immediately followed. By 1929, every mainland authority provided school clinics.

In 1928, she invited girls to spend a week at Dymchurch Holiday Camp, which she had long encouraged; this was essentially for girls whose parents could not afford a holiday. Glowing accounts and glowing faces indicated the tremendous success of this adventure which became a tradition; some 20 girls went each subsequent year.

They rose at 7:30 for breakfast at 8, some too excited to eat; dormitory inspection was at 9, then letters and orders for the day were distributed. From 9:15 until 12:15, there were walks, bathing or any specified duty until dinner at 12:30. From 1 o'clock until 4, walks again or an outing with Miss Broome. After tea, more of the same from 4:30 to 7:30, or games in the field. After supper (hot cocoa and cakes), the next hour was spent in the dormitory preparing beds before lights out at 9:30. A small prize was awarded at the end of the week for collecting pretty stones.

Throughout the war years, national and local money shortages had affected school. The Head's lamentations of limited accommodation grew tedious with almost annual repetition, yet she remained, unjustifiably, optimistic.

Inspectors supported her. As ECS was intended for 250 girls and was housing 410 by 1921, it required no little ingenuity to find room for them. Art, dining and cookery rooms became classrooms; some post-matriculation study and, later, all French conversation lessons took place in corridors and on landings, seated at rickety tables which regularly collapsed. This remained true for more than thirty years. They reckoned that the Head could look forward to an early extension of "the noble red edifice", which would render her arduous work a little lighter. Inadequacies thus officially recognised, plans were prepared for a whole new wing. Outside buildings had to be used. By 1925, one new classroom made life easier and a new cloakroom proved a boon and a blessing. By the end of the decade, E.R.B. was more than ready for the promised additions, which, in fact, she did not live to see.

Still, a new entrant of 1927 was struck by the building's impressive exterior, the field, including six or so gardens at the side to which individuals applied themselves, and the wooden gym-pavilion with its verandah at the far end near the present car entrance.

As big improvements were outside their control, everyone concentrated on smaller items. Mistresses brought back two pictures from Italy, girls statuettes and pictures from Paris.

"Mark! Girls of the County School! That piano of yours – no wonder you win Silver Cups – was won twice over by the enthusiasm and energy (not to say talent) of Staff and parents". Helpful too were a summer Garden Fête, enjoyed despite the usual rain, and a Staff Whist Drive run by F.M.F. A red letter day was a Staff concert. "With shame I confess that I was surprised how good the show was, and it certainly made us realise what poor stuff we ourselves are made of". Five years later, a second grand piano (resting-, indeed nesting-, place of many cats) was acquired, with a gramophone to keep it company. That meant a request for a record; consultation with Miss Woods was advised.

Self-help, from Form, House, Staff, always came to the rescue. Exhibitions, plays, fêtes (with such joys as frog races and skittles) contributed much-needed funds for stage properties, books, a lantern for the geography room, handicraft apparatus. A whimsical appeal was made for new stage curtains; the existing ones had, over nine years, served also as table-cloths and as mermaids' tails on Trafalgar Day; they were now transparent.

Although Governors provided ferns for the Hall, School was not very responsive in bringing flowers for formrooms. "Let us hope that girls will bring [them] habitually rather then in response to continuous requests".

Girls were cheered by the installation of a drinking fountain, deplored by their successors forty years later, which dispensed with mugs which might have been used for tadpole raising, and which proved a subject for conversation with shy visiting games' teams. This had a fellow in the cloakroom, but much wanted more: "We still await the day when we shall be able to introduce our visitors to a looking glass". A distinct gain were new chairs to be carried with care.

Sir Henry Bowles, missing Prize Giving as ill-health rendered necessary a short change of air, gave his most enduring and appreciated gift: an Honours Board on which the name of each Head Girl was entered in gold leaf.

In 1927, Miss Broome made a world tour, enjoying a summer on a bush farm in her homeland. On her return, at a reception of Governors, past and present Staff, Old Girls and Prefects, and enlivened by the Choir, Sir Henry presented an oak lectern for the Hall and a personal present to her in recognition of 21 years' service. Four senior Mistresses gave her "a large lump of coloured crystal on a long cord". On a similar occasion, EGS' Head had received silverware. One junior Mistress felt that it was to E.R.B's credit both that she accepted the pendant and disliked it.

From the Librarian came a two-fold appeal: for books (new and historical novels, general literature) and that every girl would make as much use as possible of them. She, realistically, believed in getting more books and finding room for them afterwards. Stock soon doubled. The swing of the pendulum now meant complaints of under-use. "There should be a larger membership: far too few realise the advantage that they have to hand. The reference library should be used more". Helpers drew praise for conscientious work. Coupled with a special appeal for English reference books went the idea that each leaver should present at least one book. There seems to have been no library grant before the Second War, so gifts were vital. By 1927, the French library was far famed as one of the largest in England. "The marvel is how it is housed in so few cupboards? The 'secret' is perhaps that half the books were always out – a matter for congratulation". Perish the unworthy suspicion that they may not all have been read. This same year saw the beginning of the oft-to-be-repeated plea for a proper library for books and for private study, a physical home with comfortable chairs and desks rather than shelves or cupboards in corridors, classrooms or even cloakrooms. "Would there were a possibility of seeing our desires materialised".

It comes as a shock that a long-felt want was a telephone. "We feel sure that small business matters could be transacted more quickly and with less inconvenience", although the writer was thinking less of administration than of arranging matches.

The magazine editor, naïve in the ways of the world, refused to be pessimistic, albeit remaining cautious. "For long years, editors have lamented over our lack of libraries, telephones and electric light. At last faint whispers are abroad of some of our dreams coming true in the near future – but let us not raise our hopes too high, in case ... We have waited so long and patiently in vain".

Matters were not helped when a hole in the roof allowed "a Niagara" to flood through.

Nearly a quarter of a century's patience was still needed.

The Spirit of Helpfulness

With little spare cash available, the Savings Association could hardly be said to be flourishing. Despite reminders of the simplicity of the system and the interest gained even on savings stamps, despite repeated appeals for increased membership, only a few individuals saved just over £200 over three years.

What were called, slightly patronisingly, Charities, brought School into contact, sometimes directly, with the hardships and sufferings of others. The influence of the Head and Miss Forrest is reflected in the choice of some recipients, but girls must have approved. Sure that the past four years had awakened higher ideals, E.R.B. hoped that their thoughtfulness would remain strong and that they would carry this spirit to fuller growth on leaving school.

Distress resulting from the fighting aroused generosity throughout the Twenties: French Red Cross £10, Russian Famine Relief £8, Polish Relief 5 guineas, Friends of Armenia 2 guineas: St Dunstan's for war-blinded soldiers 15 guineas, Edmonton Soldiers' and Sailors' Club and Earl Haigh Memorial Home, 2 guineas each, Edmonton Hospital for wounded soldiers £1 and ex-Services Welfare Society 10/6: Australian Ship Libraries 3 guineas, Navy League 10/6: Edith Cavell Homes of Rest for Nurses 3 guineas, Royal Soldiers' Daughters' Homes 1½ guineas (£1:11:6).

Amounts meticulously recorded, including the 2/- charge for each of ten cheque books and 10/10 for petty cash, mean little today, but the total collected and disbursed of over £350 is considerable, despite a marked drop during the decade. Whether because of reduced patriotic impulse, greater personal hardships or a fear of being shown up as mean, straightforward weekly collections became much disliked, raising in all £75:7:9. Collections on Trafalgar Day, £53:2:9, financed donations to the Mission for Deep Sea Fishermen and British and Foreign Sailors' Society £8:10:0 each, British Sailors' Society £9:2:0, and the Arethusa Training Ship £3:8:6.

Drill and dancing displays £102:17:6, big bazaars and modest formroom sales £63:1:1¼, carol singing £16:19:0, plays £11:2:6 and parties £3:13:0, all helped. Five donations totalled £2:5:0 and lost property fines boosted funds one year by 6/9. The Head felt diminishing support needed comment at three Prize Givings. "I hope that our girls will feel that their educational privileges are a preparation for service to others, and not merely advantageous to themselves".

Children respond to the needs of other children. Dr Barnardo's Homes still supplied an annual lecturer. The Young Helpers' League, with F.M.F. as treasurer, had individual collecting boxes which "would be more valuable if there were more members". The scheme lasted some sixteen years, fading out several times before ceasing finally in 1928. With them and a bazaar, £53:18:6¼ was sent. Also supported were the Shaftesbury Society £15:16:5, Save the Children Fund £15:10:0, National Refuges for Destitute and Homeless Children £5, a local girls' and infants' School £22:5:0 and Invalid Children's Aid Association 1 guinea. A House concert raised 17/- for the Starving Children's Fund. The names of several of these indicate the severity of need. Nearer home, a blind girl received £4:9:5, the Enfield Cripples' League/Mission/Union (its name varied) £27:13:0, and Halliwick, the local home for the handicapped, 16/- plus flags for its newly formed Guide Company. Girls proved efficient hostesses at several parties for these youngsters. On the last Saturday of one summer term, an OG brought a group of small children from a poor part of London to spend the day on the field. Happy faces and lusty cheers crowned their fun.

Other major recipients were the physically suffering, those more traditionally helped. The Cottage Hospital, renamed the War Memorial in 1922, received visits and gifts of £47:14:0, in addition to over £18 from the Carnival. Slight snobbery touched one visit of the Head Girl and VIB who took

Ten guinea purses
To give to the nurses,
Who were having a newly-built wing,

for the money, profit from home-made cakes, was accepted by Princess Helena Victoria. The National Hospital gained £8 and Enfield Infirmary £5: as silver paper was collected for the Royal Free, two Mistresses and six girls were invited to visit the hospital. Miss Florence took all VIA in one taxi to the North Middlesex Hospital.

Miscellaneous good causes included, until 1928, OAPs, with £51:5:0, the League of Mercy (supported annually) £10:11:6, Guides' Ambulance Fund £33:4:0, School's Thanksgiving 3 guineas, Our Day £1:3:6, and the League of Remembrance 10/-. A low priority in comparison with human needs, the RSPCA received only 1 guinea. One girl pondered a poster: Dogs make blind men see. "Were we meant to be kinder (ie. not blind) to dogs' feelings?" No-one would deduce that today.

Care for their environment was again shown one dinner-hour by a band of noble volunteers in short gym-tunics invading the churchyard with wire brushes. They brushed the tombs and railings, leaning over the tops of monuments to assail the weather-beaten faces of ancient effigies.

Awareness of the more specifically economic distresses of the decade is evinced by the continuing National Egg Collection, the Unemployed Christmas Fund, Winter Distress League £2:12:6, Flood Relief 1928 £3:10:0, and, in 1929, the Coalfields' Relief Fund 10 guineas.

One girl could affirm nearly 60 years later that "there is scarcely any of my present interests and activities – and these are many – which has not developed quite spontaneously from school's activities. Quite naturally, I have learnt to live up to the School motto".

We have survived a World War,

... but there is tension in the world.

Miss Broome wished to broaden their horizons: visits were made to Chase Farm Schools, Enfield Police Court, Birkbeck Laundry. "We owe much to our Governors who have given us the opportunity of seeing some of the social work of the neighbourhood". Hampstead Garden Suburb offered a glimpse of a different lifestyle. Civics lessons remained limited to post-matriculation classes and by woefully narrow terms of reference – "the work of women in the State, first in the home", for marriage was still what parents and most girls expected. Mrs Porter gave an entertaining address on Infant Welfare and also generously offered special prizes to three girls who narrowly missed becoming Sports champion.

References to public events are sporadic. In 1928, about two o'clock one afternoon, School was called out onto the field to see the R101. "We were just in time to see the airship surrounded by its bodyguard of aeroplanes drifting over the treetops". One form was disgruntled; the invasion interrupted their much-valued games' period. Alas, in the following year:

> From Cardington she sailed away;
> Across the Nile her pathway lay;
> 'Twas India she hoped to see,
> But little thought her fate 'twould be
> To fight against an eastward gale
> And never more her homeland hail.

A sense of established order prevailed. All leavers attended a Service ("a sad occasion") in 1926 in Southwark Cathedral, subsequently at St Pancras Church, to hear an impressive address. Poems frequently and unshyly call on God; one writer explained: "I felt that we could never praise the great God enough for all He has given us". Woods after rain brought one a step nearer to God; in the evening, God's work was done. Equally longlasting was the belief in fairies, the ubiquitous Great God Pan and talking animals.

> Each rabbit holds a twinkling light
> (Really a glowworm rolled up tight).

Empire Day celebrations continued traditionally except for one year, when, after the formalities, ECS and EGS went to the nearby Rialto cinema to see "pictures of life in our colonies, after which our Choir led the singing of patriotic songs. We were all filled with patriotic fervour". After 1929's inspiring service in the Parish Church, the March Past took place on EGS field, voted a great improvement on the dusty gravel playground with the overhanging branches of the walnut tree.

The Monarchy was part of that order. When Prize Giving fell on the same day as a Royal Funeral, postponement was immediately considered. "On the day when the nation is mourning the loss of the good Queen Mother Alexandra, our programme will be shorter and more subdued in tone". School joined in a memorial service in the Parish Church; with its solemnity were mingled thanks and praise for the example of noble womanhood set by the late Queen. "The memory of her life with its numberless deeds of thoughtful kindness will inspire us all as we strive to attain the Christian ideal".

School was not cancelled because of the 1926 General Strike as an OGA Reunion had been by an earlier coal strike. Those on a Geography expedition experienced great difficulty in buying tickets and finding the platform at London Bridge station, but, as a result, "I don't think anyone will ever forget what a scarp slope is".

Other excitements included viewing an eclipse of the sun at Interval through small pieces of smoked glass, a conflagration in the churchyard which provoked thoughts not, as it would today, of arson but of the Day of Judgment, and the first burglary. Cups were removed from the new trophy case in the Hall. Outrage turned to delight with the arrival of real flesh and blood detectives.

The weather always caused the same surprises, particularly when seven tennis matches were scratched in 1920; a poem asking for *Rain in Summer* in 1925 suggests a drought. One winter, butter, sugar, milk, the water in the bedroom jug, all froze. Even seven years after the day, "what memories we cherish of December 22 [1928] – memories of cold, grey rain, of streets covered with a sheet of glossy ice, of people sliding, falling, sitting suddenly with a bump. Never has it proved so difficult to get to school". Of course, there were always pea-souper fogs and windy days when loose chimney-pots and slates tumbled down.

Societies ("invaluable features of our school life"), all extra-curricular activities wax and wane with stupefying regularity. The enthusiasms of the young, perhaps especially of girls, seem inherently subject to change; the delight of one generation automatically meets the scorn of the next, and a school generation is between five and seven years. Certain clubs too were struggling to find their real motivation. Staff, the key factor, come and go; their successors' concerns lie elsewhere; if they do stay, their pursuits tend to be regarded as old hat. The novelty of Houses, and, more importantly, their involvement with competition, may have detracted from the quieter satisfaction of less frenetic interests. The elderly regret that the young do not join in corporate events; records suggest that, although they *joined*, they did not stick at things for long.

The small but excited membership of the Scientific Society, launched in 1927, ventured as far as Waltham Cross Gas Works. At Tottenham, they learned of the elaborate processes by which coal was used to make gas for domestic purposes with the best modern equipment. Sponsored by local MP Colonel Applin, a few went to the House of Commons when members were debating the Scottish Land Bill and the administration of the Lord Mayor's Fund for the Relief of Distress in the mining areas. They felt fortunate in hearing Mrs Dalton's maiden speech. This visit was particularly interesting in view of the then impending General Election. The GHS toured the *Daily Express* works where some 80,000 newspapers were printed, folded and pasted in one hour. The Guide had a stamp of their names made for each one. Two girls won 1st Class certificates in an essay competition of the Royal Colonial Institute. Staff spoke about different countries, Frances Mary Gates (Hockey*, later a lecturer) gave a lantern lecture on China, Fifths and Sixths heard a paper at the Philharmonic Hall, entitled *By car from England to India.*

On occasion, minds turned outwards to discuss, for example, the influence of environment on man. As well as debates on such parochial matters as Hobbleskirts or Crinolines, Should cats be allowed to run loose at night? or the unexpected topic of Hypnotism, one was held as early as 1920 on the nationalisation of industries, whilst in the following year, two members nearly came to blows over the Irish Question. Other contemporary issues included Sunday opening of cinemas and Co-education. Although each subject was thoroughly investigated with great animation by the faithful few, interest was less than with the earlier, more serious girls.

School hats were seen in various places in and around the Metropolis as girls explored not only their architectural, religious and artistic heritage, but how institutions flourished, for people worked every Saturday morning. "Although we live so near our great city, we know far too little about it". It was exciting when they lost half of the company at London Bridge. Fifty years on, Miss Rudkin saw the girls' conduct through rose-coloured spectacles. They were "wonderful to take around. We had nothing to worry about behaviour. In buses and tubes, unbidden, they sprang to their feet to offer people seats. I remember feeling very proud on the Embankment outside the Tower, when some rather scruffy pupils from another school said:'Oh, look at those girls. Don't they look nice?' – and so they did, green-print dresses, blazers, Panama hats".

However, few day-long expeditions were undertaken by modern standards, hence the apparently greater appreciation. London was at once inviting and repelling, both "crowded with people and the loneliest place on earth, where the tragedies of life are naked and unashamed. Here are the passions of men scorching and consuming, the muffled cry of hearts in bitter sorrow and the potent healing power of human love and sympathy". Style apart, have matters changed fundamentally since 1925? "You may pass a hundred beggars in the street without a thought other than they are a great nuisance, and then you may see one who will give you quite a different feeling, not the compassion which prompts you to take out your purse, but rather a feeling of responsibility for sordid, unhappy lives". References are frequent to tall smoking chimneys, squalid narrow streets, hurry, bustle and noise, although one girl did spend a happy summer holiday in the City. Paris gained in comparison: no factories, no smoke, no obtrusive slums: yet, on returning home, "our hearts leapt within us at the thought of our smoky London streets". Compared with the beggars and the poor folk who work from early till late, the fellow seen on the Great North Road, with his old tin can of rabbit stew and onions, his ragged shirt, buttonless overcoat, newspaper-patched boots and his trilby purloined from some scarecrow, seemed a happier fellow. One girl had a vision of London without slums, without poverty, without smoke or dirt and with silent transport, where people would be happy and healthy, and life none the less interesting because calmer and more natural.

The Lord Mayor's Show attracted crowds to see and hear the soldiers, with their guns ("murderous, awful machines") and the sailors followed by four old Edinburgh fisher-women. A few very peculiar motor cars, some of the first made, preceded a cart sponsored by the RSPCA. Scouts led a crowd of schoolboys, all arrayed in pink, vans of printing machines and, finally, all the dignitaries, "most of them old men with beards".

As always, Mistresses helped girls to increase their knowledge of their own country, their awareness of other lands. The thrill aroused by each trip is, to later generations, incredible. Public transport being limited, expensive and slow, even short distances posed problems. "St Albans lives in the mind as a visit to Green Pastures. It is a pity that we are not near enough to go oftener to see the Abbey and the country round". That Waltham Abbey should be new to most, although some students made the journey daily, is indicative of their circumscribed outlook.

Those going to Oxford for Recitation competitions travelled by open-top char-à-banc, which necessitated rugs and woolly scarves. The inhabitants of country villages turned out to cheer them along traffic-free roads. One girl dropped her hat overboard; a boy on a bicycle retrieved it and chased after them. The bicycle racks in the playground were, incidentally, over-subscribed.

An early autumn walk in Devon offered a glimpse of another world, for folk walked then. They went for rambles; indeed, those whose feet were sore after 13 miles were patronisingly pitied. A weekend in Sussex brought the customary delighted references to cows and chickens and wild flowers – primroses, bluebells, oxlips, daffodils, wood violets – growing in profusion in meadows and under hedges. On a second visit, one lazy day was spent in the woods, reading and pressing flowers. On a third, never a plant did they pass but some zealous person plucked a specimen, for the best collection won a prize. Forbidden to bathe one Whit, they paddled, resulting in sadly bedraggled petticoats and frocks. At the roadside, Miss Crombie once skilfully pumped out water for them to drink. Milkmaids, lambkins, the ploughman urging on his unwilling horse – all seemed miraculous. At Blackpool, many saw for the first time the sun set behind mountains.

Countryside trips had a spin-off. After one such, for the purpose of studying the geology of the district, during which girls worked hard, they lamented:"Why does time fly most quickly when we are the happiest?

With the deepest regret we realised the inevitable termination of our delightful holiday. Besides extending our knowledge, we learned a great deal about each other and became more broadminded in consequence. The knowledge of this fact was the consolation afforded us for the speedy conclusion of our visit" – after four days! What better justification for a school journey? Guide and Cadet camps, even travelling to away matches, gave the same excitement of discovery of self and others.

The Head praised individual Mistresses, always on the alert for fresh opportunities of widening girls' interests, who valiantly attempted to combat the insularity evinced in an article on Las Palmas. Twelve hours justified these judgments: "The people are rather lazy and therefore the town is dirty. All the little boys were smoking; one stole a cigarette out of Daddy's hand. The women are very pretty and wear mantillas". It is unclear how far visits, by introducing girls to ordinary people and by taking them to different religious services did succeed in dispelling misconceptions, for the most frequent comments suggest that they simply appreciated England all the more.

They could fairly boast that they were among the pioneers of school journeys. Miss Forrest flourished at the height of her powers; for foreign visits, never less than annual, strenuous and out of school time, she made all the arrangements personally; no travel agents for her. All difficulties were settled with masterly ease.

The first set the pattern. Wearing close-fitting caps for the dreaded Channel crossing, later arrayed in their morning suits of navy serge and bar-strap shoes, they visited the Louvre and le Palais de Justice on Day 1, the Louvre, St Germain l'Auxerrois, the Champs Elysées and Versailles on Day 2, la Madeleine or another church for Mass on Day 3, St Germain again, Notre Dame and up the 279 steps to the topmost gargoyle, la Comédie Française for a matinée, l'Opéra for an evening performance on Day 4, shops, le Panthéon, les Invalides, lemonade at the top of the Eiffel Tower ("in a curious conveyance, known in these parts as an 'ascenseur'") on Day 5, and, on the last day, the Louvre again, Cluny Museum and l'Odéon. A later record goes for the Louvre, Panthéon, Notre Dame, Sainte Chapelle, Palais de Justice, Conciergerie, Eiffel Tower, Arc de Triomphe, Invalides and Versailles – in one day and a half!

L'Hôtel Louvois came to expect their visits. In 1923, Rouen was added to the giddy week in the city. A jolly party, this one; with F.M.F's usual kindness, she gave them an exceedingly enjoyable time. Flowers were placed on the grave of the Unknown Warrior "as a token of our respect for the dead and sympathy with the French nation".

Cenotaph, 1919

Peace Pageant, 1919

Form Group, c1920

Camping, West Whittering

Left: *Uniform c1920, the Papworth twins*

Below:
Blackpool Choir 1922, Miss Woods, Miss Bidwell

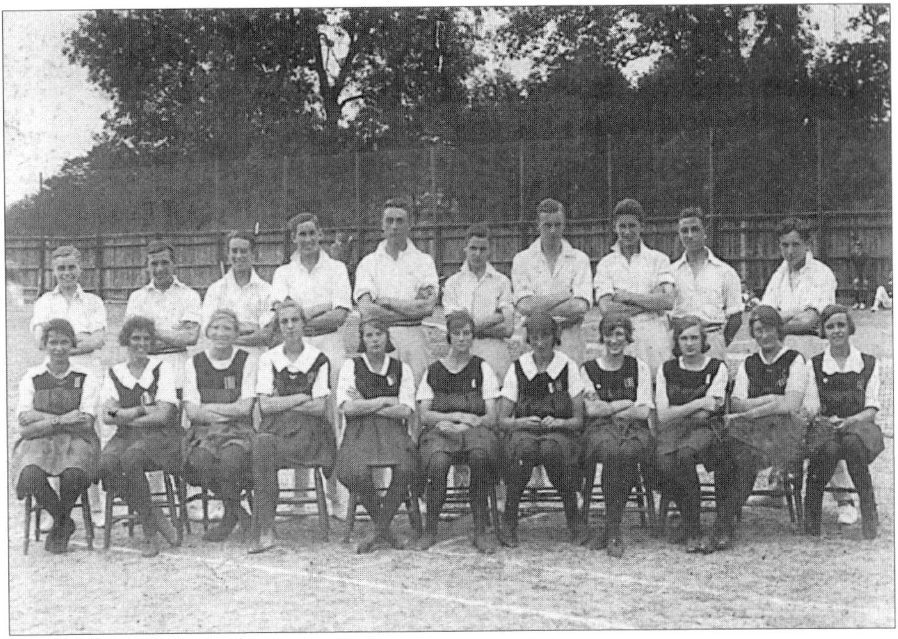

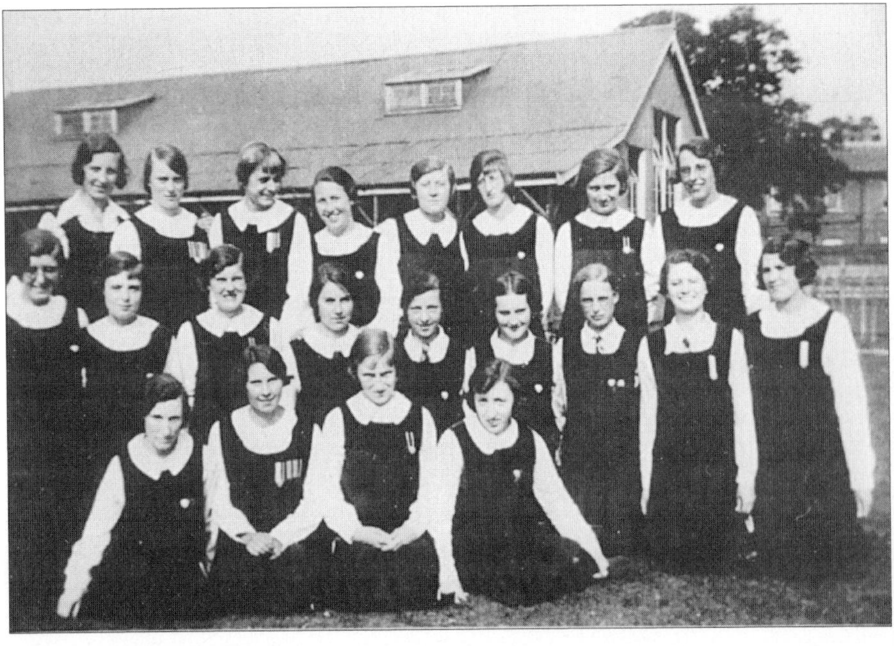

Empire Day

Facing page
Top: ECS Hockey, EGS Cricket
Bottom: Form Group

Frances Perry (courtesy Britain/Stockwave)

146

*Uniform,
1931*

*Greek Play
c1931*

Miss E.R. Broome, MA, Head Mistress

Travellers bought excellent silk kerchiefs and ornaments for the hair at very low prices. A group once visited a London school to tell of their delights. Magazine descriptions became cleverer, indeed cute.

"Yearly pilgrimage to ye ancient city of Lutetia, now yclept Paris in ye year of grace nineteen hundred and twentyfive". How many younger girls ploughed through that, or the lengthy, learned and well-sustained version written in the style of the old Testament Book of Chronicles, or the 48 lines of verse?

F.M.F. was rightly proud that over 100 girls had so far accompanied her. To overcome parental resistance to venturing too far into Europe, she itemised costs and justified the whole idea. Travel, porters, hotels, theatre tickets, excursions, transport in and around Paris, entrance fees, lunches and teas out, everything, in fact, except the child's own personal postage and shopping was included in the total which varied from £10 for eight days to £15:10:0 for a fortnight in Paris and Switzerland. Interestingly, she called the travellers children. She pleaded that with twelve girls, half-price tickets could be obtained, thus reducing the cost to £8. She felt certain that travel not only stimulated linguistic enthusiasm, but that also "the whole School is permeated with that understanding of a foreign nation which alone makes it possible that wars shall cease". The effect of the Great War on grown-ups was deep.

After Switzerland in 1926, 1927's Easter fortnight revealed another side to this astonishing lady as she shepherded her flock to dance at San Remo's Kursaal, or as she dressed as a Persian lady, complete with yashmak, for a midnight feast with dancing on the balcony to gramophone music. For some raised on egg and bacon, a continental breakfast came as an unwelcome surprise. They were impressed to see soldiers everywhere on the Italian frontier, and somewhat shocked by the drinking of cocktails and the wearing of obtrusive lipstick. They considered themselves untidy for being hatless in a fashionable restaurant. This complicated trip, with hotels in three countries, suffered a famous calamity when the Swiss tickets were handed in at Milan. F.M.F. had to go repeatedly to Venice station; "all the officials knew her quite well by now".

1929 took in Chartres and the Loire valley, 1930 Provence. Plans were announced for the first visit of the Thirties, to Normandy and Paris, by a party of ten to "ensure reduced railway facilities", an unfortunate phrase to indicate lower fares.

Maybe F.M.F's appeal for more participants resulted from competition. With Miss Hyslop, at Easter, 1924, Miss Crombie struck new ground, taking to Belgium six girls who had persuaded their parents to allow them to join the adventure. Clearly an adventure: seen off by family and friends, they went by train from Enfield Town to Liverpool Street, thence to Harwich for the sea crossing to Antwerp; they had to wait for the tide to carry them over a wreck. Twelve jolly days in Bruges were filled with excursions. Although "the cobbled streets cobbled our feet, the last day came all too soon for us, though not for our pockets. That does not mean that we were extravagant, but that we were very dutiful in writing home regularly", which reveals the contemporary postal service. The return crossing was to be "not a calm one. Taking this to heart, Miss Crombie advised us to get as much sleep as possible before we got to the North Sea. Soon some of us succumbed to the much-dreaded malady" on the unstabilised, therefore pitching and tossing, ship. "The Customs officials, when they say our white faces, opened and closed our cases for us". Nevertheless, they would very much like to go again, partly because Miss Crombie always allowed them to go off on little jaunts of their own, provided no fewer than three went adventuring. It worked.

A second visit, with the energetic cooperation of Miss Rudkin, was paid three years later. The old city of Bruges was much appreciated, not merely architecturally ("no fewer than seven churches"), but also the women in their black hooded cloaks, the clogs of the children, the carts drawn by dogs noisily rumbling over cobbled roads and the lace-makers sitting at their doorways. These young feminists declared that the women seemed decidedly the most hard worked. Good Friday offered a glimpse of intensely religious habits. Irène Van Trappen conducted the party round Ghent.

During a subsequent Rhineland fortnight, the best laid plans to visit half a dozen well-known towns were thwarted as misfortunes dogged their footsteps. Investigations into lost luggage forced a unexpected stop in Brussels, where one girl was laid low and had to be left behind in a comfortable, spotlessly clean *clinique*, kept by some charming nuns, watched over by an O.G. expatriate. The rest of the trip by train, boat and motor was a delight, apart from an awkward moment at Strasbourg when an official declared that collective passports were invalid. Two days of incredibly strenuous sightseeing in Paris left them tired and weary but happy.

Elderly ladies remain grateful to these Mistresses who seem to have derived professional and personal satisfaction from their involvement.

Still with remarkable enthusiasm

Like the whole country, School took time to settle down from the euphoria aroused by the end of hostilities. There was a feeling, short-lived maybe, that peace meant a return to the past, rather than, as after 1945, a determination never to go back.

Whereas 1919 saw a gradual restoration of normality, 1920 gives an impression of liberation, of new vitality. People were no longer living in wartime patriotic pride, sorrows and deprivations, no longer simply content to enjoy the relief that it was all over. There was an excitement in the present, owing something to the lifting of food restrictions, a hope for the future, apparent in work, play and social life, a sense that "we are beginning to create a tradition" anew.

This was symbolised by the revival of Miss Forrest's jolly Junior and Senior parties, "among the most enjoyable events of the whole year", when Mistresses were mobbed by the long-dressed party-goers. With the added excitement of prizes for fancy dress, then in vogue, and entertainingly organised by Prefects (doubling as waitresses), they culminated in 1930 with an indoor fête, with sideshows, competitions, hair-raising film scenario and Christmas presents to suit even the slenderest purse. In addition to the regular "petite soirée dansante où naturellement tout le monde a parlé français", *un bal masqué* was held in the Hall.

Teams combined in a summer party at which Staff were invited to engage in impromptu sports on the field or to dance in the Hall. Although thoroughly enjoyed, it had no successor. IIIA ran a Dance for Juniors and their friends. By making a charge for admission, this enterprising form was able to hand over £4 to School Fund. Fun, yes, but, as ever, with a serious purpose.

This sense of renewed life made itself felt even in a negative way. Trafalgar Day was celebrated in 1922 still with remarkable enthusiasm, especially in Lower and Middle school, whose inventive genius was productive of some extraordinarily original schemes of decoration. By 1925, "it continues a test of originality which our potential geniuses never fail to pass". A year later, a hint of desperation crept in; it was difficult to find good ideas as incidents in Nelson's life were felt to be limited. For schoolgirls, quite so. The writing was on the wall. They therefore departed from the usual set-up. "We invited friends to visit the school to see the work and to hear a short concert of sea shanties and sea poetry". The afternoon thus became an Open Day with entertainment, plus the inevitable collection. A pupil noted that Trafalgar Day had "ceased to be the wild sport we had heard about from our sisters".

It remained an obsession of the Head. She impressed upon all that it was "a token of our gratitude for all our naval and merchant seamen were doing for us in the Great War. Nelson's famous signal has always been prominent in the School's decorations for the day". Intriguing. To revive interest, 1931 turned the clock back with the re-establishment of a prize for the best decorated blackboard; lessons stopped for the afternoon's sea songs. The 1936 magazine reported that "this day becomes more popular each year, giving parents the unique opportunity of seeing their daughters at work", yet it was the last. It died with the arrival of the new Head.

The tradition which lasted over forty years and which, according to the Inspectors, provided a markedly successful contribution to active corporate life, was the House system. Sisters joined their elders, otherwise Staff and girls were allocated randomly. With four Mistresses and three Prefects, each of the five Houses sent five representatives to School Parliament, an idea ahead of its time and mentioned just this once. It was the descendent of the whole school in conclave to choose a motto, the ancestor of School Council. At its inaugural meeting, Saints' names and colours were decided; Catherine (Ca) dark purple, Cecilia (Ce) cerise, Margaret (M) saxe blue, Ursula (U) emerald green, Winifred (W) chocolate, later orange. Houses were to bring together the elder and younger girls, to encourage public spirit in work as well as in sports, to improve the general tone.

The Captains' notes reflect varying fortunes and interests as they tried to build loyalty, to create something unique with which its members, present and future, could identify. As with all innovations, enthusiasm ran high, yet, even in its first year, St Winifred's was "not as successful as we should be", but cheered up when able to donate £2:12:0, the profit from an operetta *Prince Constant*, to inaugurate a fund for stage curtains. St Catherine's concert pleasantly surprised all by the talent displayed. Most enjoyed a social and a jolly tea judging by the high spirits of those present and their reluctance to go home. Exhortations never ceased; for too many, keenness meant only the wearing of an identifying strip of coloured ribbon on the left breast and cheering lustily on sporting occasions. "Our failure has made us all determined to work harder than ever this year". "Come on, St Ursula's. We must not forget our School motto". "Unless we all pull together and do our bit ...".

Inter-House, replacing Inter-Form, competitions encouraged all games, swimming (with the first real Gala in 1921) and particularly Sports Day. Miss Broome offered a prize for the first Senior Inter-House team race. The effect on behaviour, with Conduct Marks (Cons) counting against the overall House totals, is less clear, although the system generated much administration for the officers. The magazine committee took the opportunity of gently suggesting that literary activity, in respect of House magazines or debating societies, would be worth consideration. Members decided otherwise, although St Cecilia's apparently produced an untraced number.

When published House reports ceased for several years, all was obviously not well. Each House had its practice day, but girls were rebuked for not turning up regularly. One netball report contained stronger criticism: "Captains would be exceedingly grateful if girls would come punctually without being sent for, and if they would provide suitable substitutes when they are unable to play themselves". Hockey players received the message: well-attended practices meant more exciting House matches. "This shows that School has realised that House hockey is not to be despised, for it is the nursery of full-grown First Eleven Warriors".

A further stimulus was provided by the Honours Shield to be won by the House gaining most points in each term's examination results. It was hoped that the House spirit would be as strong in competing for this shield as for the others. The mind boggles at the calculations necessary, the wide possibilities for error, the return to payment by results and the emphasis on competitive mark-grubbing.

We must wonder how far memories of House keenness are but nostalgic dreams.

An older institution underwent change. In mid-decade, a new method of selecting Prefects and School Captain (the sole use of this term: the Head preferred Dux, School favoured Head Girl) was introduced. "These important members of our community are now elected by vote of Miss Broome, Staff, Prefects of the previous year and members of the Sixth forms". Democracy was on its way. "We feel as if a Reform Bill has been passed, but we are still anxious to widen the franchise", although Fifths did not receive the vote until after the Second War. E.R.B. paid tribute to these twenty senior girls "whose good influence and helpfulness are among the happiest features of our school life". They checked late arrivals and departures, "with pen in hand and pencil too and teeth that chatter fast".

More importantly, each had close contact with the form to which she was assigned, vetting the girls, and standing at the end of the form's double line in Assembly. Ianthe Hoskins, having lamented this duty, concluded brightly,

> So let us with a joyful smile obey the golden rule,
> And with a cheer which all may hear,
> Shout Enfield County School.

In return, they received heroine-worship from their charges.

Another long-lasting way to generate the spirit of service was the introduction of School Colours, ECS' equivalent of the OBE, for Sense of Responsibility and Public Spirit, or SORPS. Recipients, usually from the highest prefectorial ranks, received a personal bronze badge.

The third tradition, also long-standing and with the same aims, was the creation of a company of Girl Guides, every term increasing its activities. Under Miss MacGregor's leadership, girls were trained for the various badges. Its first camp at St Leonards proved a delightful fortnight. Twenty-six girls formed three Patrols: Skylark, Poppy and Thistle. "As we are a School company, we are unable to attend Church Parades, but we go to the School Empire Day celebration and salute the flag as a company". When Miss MacGregor left, her place was ably taken for almost as long as school involvement lasted by Miss F.Sharp (Effie or F.S.), the F always included later to distinguish her from the second Head, Miss M.C. Sharp. Miss Broome expressed her pride in the company, sure that the influence of their ideals was most helpful and that every girl ought to have the opportunity of taking part in the great adventure of belonging to the girls' branch of the biggest ever youth movement. "Many of the girls who pass through a school such as ours are just those who will be best qualified to run companies of their own".

With the editor's hope that some literary member would write about the delights of camp life, the floodgates opened. 1924's camp with three other companies on the Kent coast was the first to be described, and at length: the mingled feelings of excitement and curiosity, the shrouded stillness of the countryside at six o'clock in the morning. Activities were listed and explained; réveillé, fire-lighting, table-laying in the marquee, fetching water for the morning toilet, preparing breakfast: hoisting of colours, hymn, prayer: tent and patrol inspection: bathing parade at 10:30 ("a time for much excitement"): grace before noon dinner ("a perfect triumph, [cooked] on an open wood fire and an oven constructed out of sheet iron and sods"): private visits into the town (provided they had the captain's permission and were accompanied by an officer), country dancing, excursion: tea, organised walks or games. An especially jolly song around the crackling camp fire, varied once by dancing to music on the farmer's gramophone, made evening perhaps the happiest time of the day. Finally, Taps, prayers, then to bed by the light of lanterns extinguished by 9:30pm. On a state visit to the next camp, armed with umbrella and galoshes, Miss Broome sampled the cookery, but, despite endorsing F.S' view that camping was the supreme test of character, declined to stay the night. At Stoke Poges, thirty-one relished filling up sheets with hay to make fragrant smelling beds, sewing up everybody's pyjamas and bumping the captain. The daily routine – tracking, which led them to the treasures of toffee, although 16 pieces remained undiscovered, brewing tea, bathing, hiking armed with butter, leaves, tea and a kettle – varied little, apart from a Court of Honour where camp welfare was debated in solemn conclave by officers and patrol leaders.

As numbers and activities increased, Guides were urged to pay in regularly in the hope of buying Colours. By 1926, the company, although not large, was becoming more efficient, winning cups in both musical festivals and district rallies. Meetings took place on the field and a successful camp held in Epping Forest despite first night lack of tents. We are informed of the precise method and snags of tent-pitching, and how the site was restored to its former beauty. One member soon gained her 1st Class Badge, and the company evidently had a jolly time near Dorking. An exciting journey in a lorry with badly stowed luggage, the pleasures of homemade candy, delicious homemade jam and marmalade sent by Miss Crombie, culminated in the camp adviser's praise of their dinner. Leaders were honoured to be invited as waitresses at the 1930 Jamboree.

Despite school's more sophisticated holidays, camp retained its popularity. Every year saw similar pleasures enjoyed by an increasing number: a bag of over-ripe tomatoes, pillows of dry straw mixed with thistles, the oven full of unwanted porridge at the time of camp inspection, heifers, an uncooperative water-pump: in short, a "delight in all the peculiar experiences of living, eating and sleeping out of houses".

The Guide company being almost full, about a dozen took the Guide, Ranger and Cadet promise in 1929. Cadets were 16-year old Rangers belonging to companies attached to schools and colleges, their purpose being to train for service in the Guide movement. They met between 7:30 and 9:30pm on Fridays. Until Miss Hodgson enrolled as her lieutenant in the Thirties, F.S. ran everything singlehanded. She appealed in glowing terms: "From the very beginning, a Guide is taught to put first things first", namely character development, worthy citizenship, useful hobbies, training in health and hygiene, and learning to live for others. For Miss Broome, all this was supplying a longfelt want. The first Cadet camp at West Wittering provided a fortnight packed to bursting point with pure enjoyment – taps, campfire, rest hour – and treacle pudding. Such interests lasted throughout the lives of more than a handful of girls.

CHAPTER THIRTEEN

We shall always remember their many kindnesses

The beginning of the decade saw an almost clean sweep of the Governing Body with ten members replaced; disappearances and re-appearances were frequent. Two died. County Councillor Spencer Hill "showed much kind interest in our activities, even after his term of office was over; we shall miss him, especially on Sports Days when he never failed to be present". Rev. Howel Brown's death proved a great loss. In spite of many calls on his time, he attended most public events, making "happy speeches showing his sympathy with us in our work and play". His generosity was life-long. Several entered ECS with Church scholarships which he inaugurated; others recognised their indebtedness to the good training they had received in neighbouring church schools which were his special care. One Mistress vividly recalled Father Abraham, with his wide, white beard reaching to his chest. A typical, if unkind, way of paying tribute was a Scripture essay competition. His successor, Rev. G.W. Daisley, became Vice-Chairman.

Commitment remained great. Individuals, in the time-honoured way, donated prizes for Improvement in Forms I and II, Neatness, Writing and Drawing (the Klara prize), whilst one lady encouraged Art, Drill, Home-Making and Darning. David Mason, Governor for seven years, later Vice-Chairman, is remembered by an annual VI History prize, awarded through the good offices of the Co-operative Society.

Cllr Goodwin, presiding at Junior Prize Giving in 1921, assured girls that they must consider themselves more important than usual in having a ceremony all to themselves. Mr Gibberd succeeded him, until, in 1925, Colonel Bowles resumed his rightful place. His fortunes rose as did those of ECS The following year, he is Colonel Sir Henry Ferryman Bowles, Bart, MA, DL, JP. The magazine waxed lyrical: "Heartiest congratulations on the honour which His Majesty the King was pleased to confer on him, that he is in name as in character 'a verray parfit gentil knight'. Sir Henry has done much for us in Parliament, on the Middlesex Education Committee and in innumerable local affairs, and has always taken a great interest in the School".

Black gowned figures sailing majestically down the corridors

This body of very able teachers kept excellent discipline, according to the Inspectors, retaining, despite reduced salaries, a corporate sense. One OG feels that they probably had the same feeling of pride in the school as the pupils had. They continued to give freely of their leisure. This was the era of 'pashes' or G.Ps (Grand Passions), of devotion to Mistresses – some attracting more adoration than others.

Inspectors again paid her handsome tribute. "If the school is in a thoroughly healthy condition, the credit of it belongs in large measure to the Head Mistress". When she had leave, Miss Forrest, in addition to everything else, acted as Junior First Assistant with Miss Baxter. During her later extended Grace term (two terms), Miss Florence officiated as acting Head, her success being noted by the ambiguous comment that it was due to her able control, supported by Staff and girls, that Miss Broome found conditions the same as when she left.

At 1919's Prize Giving, she noted the addition of "several new and valued members to the Staff of Mistresses to whose fine work the School and myself owe so much". The total of 19 included 10 graduates, the Physical Instructress and two visiting teachers for DSc and Art. Ten years later, there were 19 full-timers, with five Science graduates instead of two.

Two part-timers, Miss Fanny Blamey and Miss Olive Braidwood (who earned £165pa, £15 more than her predecessor) taught Secretarial subjects and acted as the Head's secretary.

When one year's results were disappointing, the Head explained that three senior specialists had been absent for ½ to 1½ terms: "no substitute, however good, could make up for this severe handicap to our pupils".

Yet there were 16 of them, seven in less than one year, three of them OGs (Misses Cooke, Biggs and Denham). All were experienced and qualified, two with 1st Class Honours degrees in Mathematics and Science; several had itchy feet, one having had at least nine posts in seven years. Their remuneration ranged from 7/6 a day to £190 a term. They stayed one week (one), two weeks (three), three (three), a month (two), half a term (one), a term (four) and two terms (two), which, if all added together, comes to less than four years.

In addition, eleven temporary appointments were made, again of well qualified and experienced women. Again, they disappeared after one week (one), two weeks (three), five (one), a month (two), half a term (two) and a term and a half (one). Miss Gladys Winifred Wormell bears a unique distinction; she taught General Elementary Science and Mathematics in Junior and Middle school for – one whole day: remuneration, 10/-.

"This craze for leaving among the Staff is causing the girls much anxiety and serious alarm". Indeed, these comings and goings do not support the view now conveyed by contemporary pupils of an unchanging staff. At least, temporary and supply teachers were available, as well-qualified women were unemployed. Yet 27 in a decade? Did they make any impact, short-term or more lasting?

Greater stability is conveyed by most of the remaining 15 appointments.

In the DSc department, Miss Jessica Dorothea Byett graduated from King's and, enterprisingly, had taken classes for Unemployed Juveniles. She offered Needlework, Cookery, Housework, Hygiene, Mothercraft and Housecraft, collected silver paper for Charity and helped with drama. Miss Olive Yeoman's skill in cooking as camp lieutenant was much appreciated. She must have enjoyed it for she returned after leaving school; "right glad we were to have her back".

Two Mathematicians and Scientists, Miss Clara Hornby helped with netball and drama, and Miss Lillie Marian Eyles (£230pa) enjoyed a year-long holiday. Miss Nesta Frances Soyer involved herself in all scientific activities.

The Art department had three short stayers. Although remaining but one year, Miss Mildred Grace Dodd made her mark, "art concealing art", in her acting, and receiving hearty thanks for making scenery which added greatly to success. Another willing helper with dramatics, Miss Kathleen Mabel Milnes held the secondary teacher's Drawing certificate. Miss Rolda Gladys Hutchinson, with a 1st Class Diploma in Teaching and the Theory of Teaching, the Board of Education's Art Class Teacher's and Advanced Design certificates, was appointed for two, then for four, days a week. She first received 17/6 a day, then £40 a term. These women studied for pleasure, certainly not for financial reward. Girls spent a lovely morning with her at the Royal Exchange and the National Gallery. "A tall thin lady given to such eccentricities as fur capes and three-quarter length overalls", Miss Hetty May Hicks taught Art and Handiwork throughout and middle school English for 17 years, taking up a six-months' travelling scholarship in 1931. She entered a choir in the Regent Street Polytechnic festival.

Modern Languages enjoyed stability and benefited from Assistantes Mlles Deswarte and le Quintrec, 1928-1930. Miss Margaret Campbell Wicks taught French throughout and German to VI, receiving the standard Burnham award plus London area allowance, a total of £250. From Llandaff, Bedford, the London Day Teachers' College and a year at the Sorbonne with various certificates in phonetics and French, the well-equipped Miss Kathleen Joy Gibbey whose Guide choir won a cup at the EMF, stayed only two years before leaving, much mourned, to "embark upon the sea of matrimony". When her replacement was appointed, it was hoped that she would do nothing so foolish for many years to come. Miss Jean Ramsden obliged by waiting nine years. She offered French plus middle school Latin, yet we find her teaching Spanish, with a Spanish assistant to help her. Involved with Guides, her main interest was drama; she helped the Juniors to present *The Pied Piper* at the 1935 Shakespearean celebration and did stimulating work for their next production, *Alice.*

Miss Gwendoline M.E. Jones stayed until her retirement. With a London Pass degree in French, Latin and Philosophy, she had twelve years' varied experience in Public and Grammar schools, girls', boys' and mixed. Appointed as assistant specialist to F.M.F. at the high salary of £398:15:0, she left an impression of somewhat colourless kindness. The other long-stayer, Miss Mary Barron, was the first, but not the last, to die in harness. She secured the elementary teacher's certificate while studying at the Northern Polytechnic for her BA. She added the London certificate (1st Class) in French phonetics and subsequently in French. She had come up the hard way, having taught in the tougher parts of London. She took over the languishing National Savings Association which owed her much. Energetic in helping Cadets with their badge preparations, she was remembered for her kindness, patience and interest in the girls' personal affairs. She was, "I think, the thinnest person I've ever known: she seemed positively hollow in the centre and this was accentuated by the cross-cut brown crepy dresses she wore. Her face was equally thin and boney with yellowish skin stretched over high cheeks and a large toothy mobile mouth. She prided herself on how much she moved her lips, both in English and French. 'Joli moulin à vent', we repeated over and over again, struggling with the elision. She would smooth back her close cropped hair, purse her lips, bend slightly in the middle". She taught the oldest group in each year, using only phonetics for the First form.

Although appointed several months before war ended, historian Miss Margaret Elizabeth Grace Johnston belongs to the Twenties for she had two terms' leave of absence without salary (£170 rising to £200) in 1919. She led visits to London and took part in the Staff play.

Two ladies ran the History department for 35 and 30 years respectively. By December, 1919, Miss G.V. Barker (Barkie) already played an important part in school life. Born locally, educated at co-educational Tottenham County and loyal to its Old Students' Association, she attended London Day Training and Bedford Colleges, gaining her Teacher's certificate. After supply posts, she offered English, English Language and Mathematics, with particular emphasis on junior work in her special subjects of History and Nature Study, at a starting salary of £160, with the dazzling prospect of nine annual increments of £10. She went to the British Museum in her first year; after the Second War, she repeated this expedition annually with First formers. Her strength and her weakness alike stemmed from the fact that she never changed, a loyal, helpful friend and colleague, concerned but unimaginative and conventional. Like so many contemporary spinsters, she had a string of elderly relatives of whom she took devoted care.

Miss Olive Durrant Rudkin (O.D.R.) graduated from her home University of Liverpool. With her diploma in Pedagogy (Bedford), MA (London) and her published thesis on the English Socialists of the late 18th and early 19th centuries (not, she confessed, a best seller), she was one of the most highly paid, £395 pa. She had spent five lively and exciting years in Cardiff, her Head rightly calling her a character. Miss Crombie's indefatigable supporter, she recalled with pleasure, at the age of 90, GHS expeditions and European travels. Her heavy teaching programme from year III (where Barkie left off) bore particular fruit in the Sixth; many read for History degrees.

"Guiding Stalwart Dies": the local paper thus referred to Miss Florence Sharp. For those who came under her influence, it is chiefly as a Guide that they remember her. This does not do justice to her zest and brilliance as a teacher of Classics. She pioneered the Direct Method. "Bonas statuas fecit, O Pygmalion", and the song *Flevit Lepus parvulus* are still talked of with bewildered pleasure. Results were unusually good, both for University entrance (for which it was then obligatory) and in external competitions. Inspectors once felt that, although the method was excellent, the chorus was of doubtful value as admitting individual and uncorrected errors. They underestimated F.S' knack of detecting weakness, whether in pupils or Staff. Any girl who did not attend in class was quickly cured by the brief command "Tu es magistra". Thus summoned to the front, the unfortunate girl was left to continue the lesson. Yet "of all who studied Latin here only very few have asked if they may drop it before the public examinations because they have loved and enjoyed it so much, in spite of its constructional and structural difficulties".

"She was both loved and hated. When she was our Form Mistress, she was generally adored. When she was ill, we sent flowers; forbidden to collect for a present at the end of the year, we denuded our gardens of flowers. The table and platform were piled high, and several journeys by a procession of porters were needed to squash them all into the back of her car. We loved her sense of humour – others hated her sarcasm. But the thing that most came over was a sense of fairness. Nothing was ever condoned, rules were to be kept, but she was never angry or upset. There was no evading work to be done". One colleague felt that she should have been a Colonel in the army. Another student felt that "she exuded authority to such an extent that it was only years after I left that I realised that for most of my school life, I had been taller than she was".

At the appointments committee, one unfortunate candidate was completely forgotten by both Governors and Head. When the poor soul put herself forward, it was to discover that Miss F. Sharp had already been offered the post and had accepted it. My reliable informant wondered wryly how the Governors dealt with that situation.

Miss Broome rightly thanked her Staff for "their aid in maintaining good tone and in the work of character training". Good tone – character training – typical educational aims of the Twenties.

Appointments

45 Miss Johnston	1918-1924	47 Miss Hutchinson	May 1919-1923
49 Miss Barker	1919-1954	51 Miss Fisher	Jan-July 1920
52 Miss Wicks	1920-1923	53 Miss Eyles	1920-Dec 1921
54 Miss Blamey	Dec 1920-Dec 1921	55 Miss Barron	Jan 1922-Mar 1944
56 Miss Braidwood	Jan 1922-Dec 1927	57 Miss Westaway	June-July 1923
58 Miss Bloor	Sept-Dec 1923	59 Miss Jones	1923-1946
60 Miss Dodd	1923-1924	61 Miss Norris	Jan-Mar 1924
62 Miss Boynton	Jan-Feb 1924	63 Miss Mitchell	Feb 1924
64 Miss Yeoman	Jan-Mar 1924	65 Miss Gilbert-Cooper	May-July 1924
66 Miss Milnes	1924-1927	67 Miss Rudkin	1924-1954
68 Miss F. Sharp	1924-1959	69 Miss Arnott	Jan-Feb 1925
70 Miss Gibbey	Oct 1925-Dec 1927	71 Miss Byett	Apr 1926-1930
72 Miss Soyer	1926-1930	73 Miss Biggs	1926-Apr 1927
74 Miss Craig	Oct 1926-Dec 1927	75 Miss Finlayson	Jan-Feb 1927
76 Miss Brackley	Jan-Feb 1927	77 Miss De Vinney	May-July 1927
78 Miss Evans	Sept-Oct 1927	79 Miss Hicks	1927-Apr 1944
80 Miss Smith	Nov-Dec 1927	81 Miss Wormell	Oct 1927
82 Miss Hornby	Jan 1928-1930	83 Miss Ramsden	Jan 1928-1937
84 Miss Irwin	Jan 1928	85 Miss Goodwin	Nov-Dec 1928
86 Miss Mead	Nov 1928-Mar 1929	87 Miss Brown	Jan-Feb 1929
88 Miss Skinner	Jan-Feb 1929	89 Miss Cooke	Feb 1929
90 Miss Wright	Feb 1929	91 Miss Wheatley	Apr-July 1929
92 Miss Denham	Jan-Mar 1930	93 Miss Angood	Jan-Mar 1930
	94 Miss Ridgeway Jan-Feb 1930		

CHAPTER FOURTEEN

How Smart We All Looked

The constant torment to future Staff and girls was still rarely mentioned. More conformist, many pupils were proud of belonging conspicuously to a grammar school, and especially to ECS. The wearing of uniform was respected and strictly enforced.

The tailor-made outfit changed little until Second War rationing. Girls still knelt on the Hall floor, although gymslips now had to be 1" above ground: still green, still longlasting, with three large pleats back and front, and the superior but not hardwearing dark green velvet yoke. Unless a daring mother could be persuaded to move the keepers to a more fashionable level, belts rested on the hips rather than encircled the waist. Long-sleeved white blouses, of flannelette or cotton according to season, had deep Peter Pan collars. Cardigans were forbidden: a white woolly Spencer, a Vedonis vest, a long Liberty bodice, worn underneath, provided insulation. Ties were now obligatory. Black knickers matched the obligatory long black stockings, alas easily laddered. Plimsolls were worn during the day. Girls fretted: would square-toed shoes be fashionable for long?

The green blazer, introduced in 1927, bore, on the left breast pocket, the Middlesex arms of three scimitars and the school motto. Uncomfortable for sitting, the garment wore badly. Cloakroom monitresses checked that they were properly buttoned before girls left the building. Whilst school hats were obligatory, because useful, on excursions in this country, they were not now expected on overnight stops nor on visits abroad. Where and how to place its vast disc? "On the back of the head? Looks foolish. Well forward? Too severe".

Summer frocks varying, the entire School assembled for the annual inspection of both them and hats. The Head had to approve. How humiliating to be branded publicly as lacking sartorial good taste! For the 1928 fête run by games' teams for Charity, which included a cricket match with a soft ball, girls were allowed to wear their best dresses. The tennis team, earlier resplendent in white tennis dresses and white lisle stockings or long socks covering the knees, now wore frocks in different styles. One was daringly sleeveless.

There was as yet no undressing for Gym. At the Drill competition, it was "a great relief to the artistic eye to see more or less one shade of green instead of twenty, as in the days before the school tailor came amongst us".

Current crazes included scarves peasant-fashion round the head, hiding all hair, worn with beltless dresses for camp, cloche hats and bar-strap shoes gracing a visit to Versailles.

These glories are only ephemeral

At Prize Giving, to which parents of prize winners were invited, Staff wore caps and gowns. All "four hundred maidens [looked] too seraphically good, cherubically smiling, angelically garbed", but buying the obligatory white dresses did hurt the pockets of the less well-to-do. OGs were immediately and charmingly addressed as Miss.

The Head stressed repeatedly that "my Staff and I fully realise the harmfulness of making success in examinations the sole aim of school instruction". Rather did they hope to give a useful and inspiring education to girls who had no very definite studious tastes, by fostering a love for Nature Study, the reading of good literature in English and in French, and Health, Strength and Public Spirit, so that all would be better able to use and enjoy God's gift of life, as well as to do their duty to their homes and their country.

Nevertheless, results were published for all to see, in both magazine and Speech Day programme, and often in the local press. They were worthy of pride, remaining well above the average for Middlesex. Variations occurred, naturally, when they were less good, "in spite of the fact or possibly because of the fact that at my suggestion our school hours were slightly lengthened while the number of subjects taken was not increased".

School's first State Scholarship was won by Joyce Rudland in 1930. Candidates in London University examinations from 300 schools competed for 21. She returned "as our accompanist so you will have an opportunity of appreciating her musical talent".

Recorded for the first time in 1921, 35 girls acquired Higher School Certificates (HSC). Miss Broome explained that the standard of the new examination was higher than that of Intermediate Arts or Science as Honours had to be taken in one subject, French, naturally. Six gained senior county scholarships, £25-£35pa, for Oxford or London colleges. English, History, Latin and Music accounted for the four Distinctions; six gained special credit in French O and one in German O.

149 matriculated and 180 more passed Senior or General School Certificate (GSC); one took Oxford Senior Locals, another the Senior Commercial certificate, so an excellent total of 331. The certificate "shows that the winner has satisfactorily completed her secondary school course and no girl should leave without it ". Sadly, too many did if they were already 16. With 95 special credits in French and German Orals, French led the list of written Distinctions with 39, History rose to 20, followed by English 10, Botany 6, Geography and Mathematics 5 each, Latin and Drawing 2 each. One passed in Greek. In 1930, three girls gained 11 Distinctions between them.

Other qualifications were increasingly sought. Of the RSA's numerous examinations, those in French were taken with apparent gusto: – Orals* 45, 272 Passes: Advanced (less popular) two 1st Class Hons., Orals 3*, 31 Passes. Seven sat Elementary Spanish over three years. L'Institut Français du Royaume-Uni (henceforth French Institute) awarded, from 1927, 13 certificates and 7 scholarships of 21 guineas. Secretarial courses waxed and waned, with, over eight years, RSA Elementary Typing 15 passes, Shorthand 16 (2*) at 60wpm, one at 80wpm, and Pitman's Elementary Shorthand (over five years) 39 Passes and, once, Theory 3, Typing 2.

Forms increased to 16, but prize numbers varied considerably, being awarded in merit order except for VIA (now meaning Upper Sixth), where they were for one or two subjects. A total of 538 were distributed thus: Year I 29: Year II 42: Year III 109: Year IV 144: Year V 100: VIB 70: VIA 44. Books were again given, each beautifully embossed with the school badge in gold. Girls had a choice within fixed price ranges.

Non-form prizes multiplied. French took the lion's share, the result of Miss Forrest's craftiness as much as of her teaching. In addition to 5 senior and 2 junior special prizes and 1 for special improvement, came Verse-Speaking, competitive in that certain marks had to be reached; 133 were distributed among four age groups. Then came the Domestic Arts: Homemaking and Housecraft, donated by individuals or the Parents' Union, 28: Needlework 12, ranging from 10/- to 2/6: Darning 2, and 8 certificates named after an early 19th century industrialist, James Watkin. Horrocks' material was always used. Twenty-eight won prizes for General Knowledge, 9 for Botanical collections, 5 for improvement in neatness and writing, 2 for Drawing and, in 1930, 11 "unhappy maidens [faced] 100 atrocities" in a spelling competition for 2 prizes. Some other subjects stood up for themselves: Geography 5, Mathematics 3, Art 2, German, Map-drawing and Singing. That for Scripture ceasing on the Vicar's death, 3 were donated anonymously; an essay was rewarded in 1929 and not again until 1957.

Girls were encouraged to enter outside competitions:– Essays for or on the Navy League, New Zealand and the Shakespeare Association. Two sisters won the first of many part- and full-time scholarships (fees and maintenance) to Hornsey College of Art.

"Whilst we rightly feel proud, we must remember that these glories mean hard work to win again next year, but our motto is 'Onward Ever'".

The pattern of Prize Giving remained unchanged, although proceedings opened at times varying between 6:30 and 8pm. After the introductory hymn, Head's report and prize distribution, the Guest of Honour addressed the audience, was thanked by the Deputy Head for so doing and songs and recitations preceded the National Anthem.

The audience was entertained with 14 items on average, although at the morning's final rehearsal, the Head had been known to cancel a much practised song. There was one dreadful occasion. She had warned the girls: "When I pause, clap". Unfortunately, when she announced that Lady Bowles could not be present because of the death of her sister, she paused! Girls performed French songs, recitations and dramatic extracts, a Latin song, *Adeste Fideles,* an Eleanor Farjeon scene, a mime of St George and the Dragon; they opened once with *Who would true valour see* and once closed with Walt Whitman's *Pioneers.* The words were printed in the programme, so that no-one could miss the message of battle and determination to face the future.

Quite properly, Miss Broome used such occasions for four purposes: an educational survey, a public report to parents and notabilities of achievements, as a platform from which she could ask MCC and parents for practical and moral support, and a pulpit from which she could repeat her aim of character building. Girls were to reinforce these messages by their demure demeanour, immaculate garments and their singing. She stressed the increasing need of qualifications in order to secure paid employment. Parents and girls would do well to make full enquiries before deciding on a career. Although school took no direct part in finding or even advising on posts, she rode her hobbyhorse of stressing the scope which existed overseas. "A girl with the spirit of adventure and not afraid of hard work might make a very happy career for herself in Canada or Australia".

Two Prize Givings in one year were unusual, but they boasted of this in 1920, 1919's having been postponed. Both were held in the Bycullah Atheneum (The Assembly Rooms), to which girls marched in a great straggling crocodile. This venue unavailable the following year, two took place on successive nights in the Hall, Juniors subsequently holding theirs in the afternoon, with the wife of the Chairman of Governors as presenter, although on one programme no name appears.

The Guest was expected to spur the girls on to further endeavours inside and outside ECS. All too frequently, speakers came from the narrow world of education, such as the Principals of East London and Bedford colleges, Dr John Adams "the distinguished educator", the eminent Ernest Barker, Ll.D, and Miss Barnes of MCC (the report then "ably" read by Miss Florence in the Head's absence). Miss Broome was defensively coy in front of Sir Benjamin Gott, Secretary of MEC when school opened, indeed since 1898. "I am glad that he fully understands school's life and work, otherwise I should have regretted more than I do that our Honours list is not as long as we hoped it would be". A hearty welcome was extended to Dr. Rendall, Ll.D, MA, late Head Master of Winchester College. "We hope he will be as pleased with his visit to us as we are, and then he will be very pleased indeed". Quite so. "Many girls will long remember his speech, particularly those working for examinations, who appreciated his sympathy when he spoke of Latin Grammar and Euclid". Professor Winifred Cullis, OBE, DSc., obliging at short notice for "someone who had died", gave an interesting and original address.

A few from the wider world were welcomed. Mrs Pember Reeves, writer on social problems, performed the ceremony with much grace. Her speech, interesting and sympathetic, drew three cheers. Miss Broome was intensely proud of Sir James Allen, KCB, High Commissioner for New Zealand, saying "I feel the truth of Kipling's words: 'What do they know of England, who only England know?'". On his second visit, he donated two prizes for an English essay. His daughter presented the awards; her request for a holiday was, as always, kindly granted. Dame Meriel Talbot, Intelligence Officer of the Society for the Overseas Settlement of British Women, was 1930's speaker. E.R.B. was nothing if not both consistent and persistent.

Sir Frank Spickernell, KBE, DSO, RN, was, in 1929, the catch of a lifetime, "the first time we have had a representative of the Royal Navy to address the school". He rose to the occasion with yet another interesting and original address. What a pity these rarities have not been preserved. His wife pleaded successfully for a holiday. "Great was the rejoicing".

The School is performing its functions admirably

In 1921, school had the advantage of frequent supervision and advice from Inspectors of both the Board of Education and of London University. No wonder Miss Broome was pleased to broadcast this, for they had stated that the school deserved the warmest support and judged that she might well feel proud. The 1923 Report, unlocated, had the usual helpful results. The earlier one combines with other evidence to give a picture of school life and of the subjects as then taught.

School had been, was, and generally continued to be, over-subscribed, to use the modern term: applications exceeded places. Assurance that it had not been necessary to reject anyone of good average ability is questionable, for, at least once, Miss Broome had been obliged to refuse girls ready to benefit from secondary education and to take only the best candidates. Promotions were, wisely, made only at the end of the summer term, only a few, for unspecified reasons, changing forms at Christmas. Each form had 26-32 pupils.

Miss Forrest wielded a large calling bell. In Assembly, seniors sat in front, juniors stood behind. Staff, robed, were on the platform. All awaited in silence the arrival of Miss Broome in gown and mortarboard. Silence is the well-remembered dominant feature. Prayers on Monday were followed by a breathless hush when the list of unfortunates given Conduct Marks in the previous week was read out. Those of the Red Ink kind (heinous, such as making a noise before a Mistress arrived) were recorded on the termly Reports. Minor Order Marks meant Staying In, to write lines. Whole forms were occasionally kept in either for this futile exercise or for extra tuition. Detention, never popular, was even less welcome then, more because of after-school activities than even for travelling problems.

Each day was divided into four morning and three afternoon lessons, each of 40 minutes, announced by the ringing of a handbell. The first began at 9:15; break was reduced from 15 to 10 minutes, "a pity"; the morning ended at 12:05; afternoon lessons lasted two hours from 1:40. Weekly classwork was, therefore, 23 hours 20 minutes, times varying slightly throughout the decade. Holidays totalled 13 weeks.

Now much increased, homework was considered reasonable in amount; girls were told to let their Mistresses know if it took more time than was specified . Between the 'top' and the 'lower' forms, a distinction was made. VIA (average age 17y 4m), preparing for HSC, received theoretically 12-15 hours, VIB and some in VC, preparing for GSC, 10h and 11h55 respectively. Work set in Year V varied between 12h and 7h25, in Year IV between 8½h and 6½ and in year III between 5h20 and 4h35; Forms I and II (each with 30 pupils) had 4h5 each.

Inspectors judged the curriculum well-balanced, all subjects receiving an appropriate amount of time, corporate life active and the new House system markedly successful. They reviewed each subject.

On enlightened and inspiring lines

Although not everyone would have agreed, "Scripture is particularly well attended to, being in the hands of the Head Mistress throughout the School: by this means, she is able to get in touch with each girl and by this happy method of drawing out their ideas and connecting religious teaching with their daily life, she is able to influence them indirectly in the best possible way. A thorough and inspiring study of the Bible is carried out". In one lesson with Upper IV on the Israelites' journey to Canaan, with maps, without any approach to preaching, real religious lessons were brought home. It was, incidentally, felt that the old unattractive Bibles, with their excessively small print, could well, if only gradually, be replaced by a shortened edition or by the Revised Version.

More oral work would involve less strain

English teaching has changed, for Grammar and Analysis were taught well on sound lines, Forms I and IVR being involved with "colour parsing". Form II was reading *Ulysses,* IIIA *Kidnapped,* IVA Lamb's *Chimney Sweeps* and VA Keats*' Ode to Autumn.* The more critical study in the upper forms was in excellent hands. Essays were written with care. A tendency to overdo the amount of writing meant that the teacher's work in corrections was apt to be out of all proportion to the effect produced. With some forms, too much indiscriminate answering meant insufficient attention to style.

Whereas Inspectors judged handwriting neat and legible without being uniform, the magazine editor wailed: "I have not once felt the thrill of pleasure from the beautiful handwriting of the author. Nothing could be more irritating to read than handwriting with a backward slope, which seems to reach a more dangerous angle with every page". A competition ("O ye gods and little fishes") was held, with prizes of fountain pens.

In view of the time devoted to it, reading aloud – fast, careless or even stumbling – was less good than it should have been. Poetry, however, memorised on a voluntary basis both as to choice and amount, was recited with feeling and intelligence. A hint that Houses should take over the Poetry competition was apparently ignored. Miss Baxter instituted Verse Speaking as a new method of teaching clear speech and self-expression. Miss Broome considered it a delightful help to the understanding of poetry. As everything soon became competitive, individuals and choirs entered at least four different festivals, winning first prizes with pleasing regularity. They were invited to give a public demonstration. Girls competed in all three age groups in Oxford when judges included future poet laureate John Masefield and Sir Gilbert Murray. Those with the highest marks were allowed to spend another day there with Miss Woods and Miss Bidwell. By 1930, Verse Speaking in both English and French at the EMF had won three Challenge cups, one Trophy, four first prizes and four certificates of merit.

For the Head, April 23, Shakespeare's birthday ("one of our most important anniversaries"), was, like Empire and Trafalgar Days, to be used to teach true patriotism and the spirit of service and self-sacrifice. Not an obvious reason for such commemoration.

Girls were, rightly, more concerned with the theatrical aspect. In 1919, three forms presented *The Tempest, Twelfth Night* and *Hamlet* to privileged spectators, receiving hearty applause for very enjoyable hours. Sixth and Second forms, having seen a professional performance, combined in *Midsummer Night's Dream*: "the little ones as fairies came up to all expectations and the lovers, in the opinion of many of us, excelled those at the [Royal] Court". Over £2 were collected for Save the Children Fund. Scenes were re-enacted at both Edmonton Infirmary and Chase Farm schools. The matriculation form was expected to produce its set play with minimal Staff support. *Macbeth* is joyfully remembered: "We thought that we were extraordinarily enterprising in borrowing for the feast a *papier maché* model of a chicken from the Gas Company's showrooms. The whole school came to the performance, in school time, of course. It was vastly entertaining – for the actors", all of whom were complimented, especially Lady Macbeth and the Porter. *Henry IV, Part 1,* was presented to an admiring audience of schoolfellows. "We congratulate Falstaff on the dignified manner in which he sustained his alarming proportions".

"Sensible of the honour of representing school at an historic ceremony", Miss Baxter attended the Foundation Stone Laying of the new theatre at Stratford-on-Avon, then still unspoiled. She kept girls informed by an economically vivid account of processions, robes, singing and personalities. "I wish you had been there, for it is not a superficial emotion, but a rendering of real homage to a great genius". She felt it appropriate that a woman architect shared in the glory of planning the theatre "in which to act his plays that you all know and act so well".

1927 was special as this memorial theatre appealed for financial assistance. A collection and money-raising festival in which all could, and did, participate was organised. F.M.F. created a competition, Mistresses arranged classes, selected poems and speeches, invited two judges and presented a trophy to the House gaining most points. House Captains acted as stage managers and producers. Many were astonished to find that girls could be so keen in a sphere outside sport.

Dramatic work was now fully established as part of school life rather than as public presentation with the spotlight on a few girls, and rather than visits to the theatre, of which few are recorded.

One OG praised the Staff's wonderful efforts, especially with male parts, Miss Woods having "the knack of the man". *Quality Street* also brought more library books. Another OG would have liked Barrie to enjoy Miss Bidwell in the title role of the delightful *Kiss for Cinderella*. At the Staff concert, Miss James sang in a little fluting voice *The Sweet of the Year*, Miss Brooks played the 'cello and Miss Baxter read *Tam O'Shanter*, "inaudible to many, incomprehensible to most".

The centenarian Miss Bidwell declared excellent *Caedmon*, which she wrote with, and produced for, Form II. It seems only decent to draw a veil over IIIA's fairy play in the magazine, *Why the Lark sings in the morning early*, with characters such as Fairies Anemone and Kingcup and Gnome Redcap.

Juniors formed a club which promised well, although soon plagued with the ever-recurring problems of poor attendance and the committed few. Producer-stage manager-dresser-prompter all in one, Biddy chose a dramatised version of *Bee, Princess of the Dwarfs*, which the children found very interesting; the dwarfs, unfortunately, found difficulty in speaking with their beards on. After initial stage fright, the play went well as "most of the actors threw themselves into their parts with animated vigour".

The younger ones finding the parts too long to learn, they contented themselves with reading *Midsummer Night's Dream* in 1926. After this fiasco, they tackled Biddy's dramatisation of the shorter *Bowl of Mist*. By 1928, apparent lack of interest allowed only the recitation of A.A. Milne's poems, yet the indomitable lady pressed on with *The Slippers of Cinderella*, to roars of laughter from the audience and panic behind the scenes.

Although VRemove showed spirit and talent in *She Stoops to Conquer*, pride of place went to playreadings and recitations. "We are always ready to welcome new members with or without dramatic talent".

Read first, *The Rivals* raised much-needed funds for stage properties and books. Rumour has it that Sir Anthony split his breeches and that Mrs Malaprop tried to mend the rent. "Here he comes", and the gentleman rushed on, "the needle still dangling on black thread from his seat".

Writing a play wrought havoc with their style. "Can we not inspire others to join our ranks, by our own enthusiasm and determination that our work shall go down to posterity as the outcome of the united efforts of the budding dramatists of ECS?" "School will long remember *The Tragedie of Sir Walter Raleigh*, surprising for its good style and historical feeling. Some of us, when we are old, and when the play is published – as we hope it will be – will point out little phrases and passages to our grandchildren." Sad to say, it has sunk without trace.

After enthusiastic study, *The Critic* materialised, despite the trampling underfoot of the ingeniously contrived Tilbury Port. Undaunted, they dramatised the Bardwell-Pickwick trial, thoroughly enjoyed by audience and performers alike. *Twelfth Night* proved problem-ridden, actresses succumbing to mumps, measles, chicken pox and other childish ailments.

Their choice of *Tilly of Bloomsbury* was judged unsuitable. *School for Scandal* was postponed because of a local outbreak of smallpox. All was finally well; profits permitted a donation to charities, payment of expenses and a comfortable balance for the purchase of properties.

Preceded by Miss F. Sharp's lecture, Euripides' *Alcestis* was performed by Upper III; Miss Woods produced with Miss Hodgson in charge of dances. Alas, the bathos of this artistic, not box-office, success: attendances were too small for the two performances, originally planned for outdoors but forced into the gymnasium by bad weather.

Bewailing decreasing interest, the Lit. and Deb. extended membership to VB. A Social enticed a few – temporarily. Girls again read papers on, or extracts from, *Abraham Lincoln* in a secluded corner of the field, Tagore and, again, R. L. Stevenson, but interest flagged. Not even a good attendance mustered for a House evening, so it quietly faded into the Dramatic Society.

This Very Illustrious Periodical

> Behold in this our own School Magazine
> The works of both the loyal and keen.

Generally two, once three, once five, joint editors worked with a committee of between six and twelve until 1927 when a single editor controlled a body made up for two years of prefects; the efficiency of a group of about twenty is doubtful. 1930 saw, more realistically, one editor – the masculine form was always used – and a committee of four.

"Many and varied are the trials of an editor, not the least being the fact that he has to ask the supporters of his magazine to contribute twice – as writers and buyers. We hope that those who have been public-spirited enough to do both, no less than those who have done but one of these necessary duties, will enjoy their own efforts in print as well as those of other notabilities". Their notes remain a mixture of chronicle (Staff arrivals and departures, regular or unique events, excitements all too often undated and with little indication as to importance), exhortation (to produce a School Song, to live up to the School motto), and matters pertaining to the periodical itself. Mostly coyly written, with lavish use of the editorial *we* and such adverbs as heartily, they exemplify their times.

The magazine, varying between 24 and 36 pages, was never conveniently compiled. The Honours list of results was normally preceded by details of School Fund, games, sports and OGs, although not always in that order. From 1927, names of Head Girl(s), Prefects, those gaining Colours were included. Original contributions and reports were jumbled together.

Purchasers were cajoled, especially when the price was doubled in 1921. One shilling was surely a fair amount for an annual production of impressive quality. The 2/- OGA subscription still bought a posted copy. At one Prize Giving, Miss Broome asserted that it was not a heavy addition to school expenditure and every girl ought to have a copy. Miss Baxter felt that the support it seemed to deserve was lacking. Girls were encouraged by photographs, tiny, black and white, blurred but doubtless evocative.

1928 saw the first advertisement. Disregarding official disapproval of poorly paid clerical jobs without prospects, the whole back page was filled by a Shorthand and Typewriting School whose full course of tuition cost £12:12:0 (Bookkeeping £3:3:0, books 11/- extra, plus Shorthand exercise books and typewriting paper); every student remained until she secured a suitable appointment, returning if she failed to retain her first job for twelve months. Even this advert. did not solve the cash-flow problem, although no more appeared until 1933. Great, however, was the satisfaction that one edition was travelling to South America, sixteen days by ship from Vigo, "following the route used by that hero of geographical exploration, Ferdinand Magellan".

Contributors too had to be wooed. Despite one year's excellent articles, "there's enough talent in the School to achieve finer things". A competition to encourage output failed; the editor, clutching at straws, felt that perhaps the fact that it was an innovation accounted for the small number of entries. Soon, only lack of space prevented the inclusion of more pieces, although a OG's long letter was printed. Those whose offerings were rejected were kindly and apologetically urged to try again. It is difficult to know how far a later editor was content: "Great is the satisfaction when the volume appears in its final garb. At last, one realises the marvels of the English tongue and rejoices to find a poem or essay with some interest. All too often, an editor has very little to choose from, and after the strenuous work of editing, is not assured of an appreciative public".

In short, a fairly typical magazine was produced with absolutely typical problems.

Apart from several who wrote anonymously, 150 girls saw their names printed after what they had written, of whom 65 were simply reporters. Most enjoyed a single success; it seems an occupation for a few such as Norah Kathleen Scopes and her younger sister Joan. Norah was remarkable less for her many and varied prizes (from Botany to Homemaking), and her EMF Verse Speaking solo, than for her writing. From a 14-year old came the imaginative prose of *The Wonderful Voodoo*; the 16-year old's *Under the Cherry Tree*, more complex in thought and structure, told of "The joys, the tears, the wondrous things /Hidden in old Japan". She vividly depicted the excitement of party travel and laughingly commemorated Guide camp disasters. Five vignettes of Provence, helped by a certain erudition, are more romantic and imaginative than the stereotyped diary-form articles.

Verse outnumbers prose by 4 to 3. The most obvious inspiration is literary, compositions from English lessons or homework being simply transferred – Edith Ford's *Tossing the Pancake* and Phyllis Lismer's *Roast Chicken*, after reading Charles Lamb. There are several sets of quotations, usually of philosophical or moral import, or applied to parochial matters. The debt is often stated: – Edna Harper's *Rabeyan, the West Wind* (Longfellow), Beatrice Cole's *Thanksgiving (Rupert Brooke)*:

> Thanks I here give
> For all the myriad beauties that will live
> Long after I am dead.

The South Downs mixes Kipling's verse with the girl's own prose.

Along with over-use of the second person singular and much invocation of the deity, writers sometimes included as many classical references (Pan especially), as many literary devices (apostrophe, pathetic fallacy) as possible. *A Meadow* is full of literary flowers, *The Oak Tree* is dominated by personification. For *A Nymph on the Death of her Faun*, "the trees sobbed and murmured as she passed them ... whispered to her, bowed their branches to her".

Interest in the darker side of life is evinced in *Shadows*, a complicated poem ("What is the wild witch Maeve?"). The tone is elegaic and religious in the skilful *Sursum Corda*, in which Dawn, Noon and Sunset are differing revelations of God.

The second source of inspiration is childhood. Their modern counterparts would surely be abashed by such public sentimentality and appeals to the fey. Fairies are everywhere. Brownies and Fairies hold a council meeting concerning mortals:

> This time the doors of a violet opened.

1922 saw the heights, or depths, of this with *The Fairy Dell*, excusable perhaps in a contemporary 13-year old:

> In the dell do the fairies live
> By the side of the silver stream;
> And once I saw them dancing there;
> Nurse said, 'twas only a dream.
> > But I know that the fairies dance
> > By the light of the moon each night,
> > They keep their glow-worms for their lamps,
> > To make the dusk wood light.
> And I have seen the Fairy Queen
> With her wings of a beautiful hue,
> I wish I could join in their nightly games
> And dance with the elves, don't you?

Two pages are spent in searching for a fairy's lost wings.

Not only fairies. "If you are good, then the Blue Bird, who is in the wood when a blue moon is shining, will throw you the most wonderful gift in the world, the gift of happiness". *A Tricksy Elf*, with the sweetest little face imaginable, was lying under a mushroom. Jack Frost's family includes Fog, Snow ("the fairy maiden"), Dew ("the pet of the family") and all the other elves who paint the sky and flowers.

The clichés of nurse and nursery continue, although it is unlikely that the writers had experienced this affluence. *The Wonderful Woods* follows young Bobby from the nursery on a magical flight to the King's Court on Christmas Eve. Childhood and motherhood are idealised: Baby Pearl has "two pretty blue eyes / Smiling at me".

More personal, more felicitously phrased, less obviously striving for effect, and therefore good fun are offerings, even by a 17-year old, on forsaken or rejected Teddy Bears, each with his own personality. *Nursery Rhymes (Slightly Muddled)* are modest in aim:

> Santa Claus is jolly and sweet
> His dear old face is kind and merry.

A lighter note was attempted in the Victorian-style morality tale of Lazy who sailed round the world *In Quest of the Land of Nothing-To-Do* – in vain.

Children were children then.

Other themes recur: the Sea ("Green heaving waste of waters wild"), Fire, the times of day (specially Evening and Night), the Seasons ("Come to me, I prithee, / Proud Autumn's golden leaf").

A few poems remain effective seventy years later, either because of the writer's competence or because a hackneyed theme is treated in a simple, genuinely child-like way. Eva Mann's *Song of the Faun* calls

> O Wind, you have taught me the joys of life,
> Have shown me hidden forests,
> And open moors, bird-haunted,
> The shadowy fields, where morning lies,
> The streams in whose music each night dies.

Marjorie Barwick evokes *The Wind* differently.

> The wind blew up in a frightful flurry,
> He came from the north where the snow lay thick;
> He said to the earth, 'I'm going to hurry
> And sweep from the trees their leaves very quick'.

Phyllis Hodgson's *Spring* pleases, after eighteen lines of conventional notions, by the bathos of her conclusion:

> All those joys the spring doth bring,
> Flowers and trees and everything.

A personal choice includes *Winter-Time* (Phyllis Hall), a simple 8-line poem, each alternate line being "Now 'tis winter-time", Violet Hopkins' *Clock*, "a callous, relentless friend", Olive Appleton's *December*.

> The Christmas roses, and brilliant noses
> That sniff, and snort and sneeze.
> At-ishoo.

and *Things I have Loved*, where Phyllis Edwin enjoys, together with rain and horse-chestnut candles,

> Cape gooseberries, and sand washed up by the tide.

My prize goes to *The Tramp*. Joan Scopes depicts his habits and appearance in unhackneyed words.

> The tramp smokes a reeking blend
> Of odd half-inches of cigarette ends.
>> Stowed away inside
>> His pockets wide
>> Are coppers, pencils, paper, string
>> Dog-eared cardpack, tin watch, ring.
>> Matches, ties, comb, spoon and map,
>> Mug, handkerchief and rabbit trap.
> At every step he well could feel
> The sharp hobnail and blistered heel.

Few prose writings grip; imaginative fiction is almost unknown. An OG, "pioneer in an unknown land", tried to "bottle a few drops of the rich and pulsating stream" – of college life in Reading. Virtually unique are *The Madonna of the Snows* (Norma Scopes), who tells how the little Infanta was saved from death by the Jester's unrewarded sacrifice, and Grandfather's stories of Good Queen Elizabeth and her cedar trees *In Old Enfield* (Rita Ikin).

Whatever the topics, emotions, skills, the magazine, while remaining a record, was fixed in its literary way.

We see changes in living as contemporary conditions are referred to or taken for granted: girls' slang, their in-words ("my chums"), their habits. Breakfasts were large and cooked, the midday meal was called dinner even if it were a picnic. On holiday, a compulsory afternoon rest still preceded tea, which was generally bread and butter, or, at home, bread toasted on the end of a toasting fork in front of the fire. Bed followed supper.

Many homes were, like school, lit by gas. A glowing fire was the focal point of the room; the chimney was warm. Aspidistras flourished in green art pots. Alarm clocks were manually operated. Washstands stood in many bedrooms; the water in the jugs in winter was, understandably, extremely cold, as Jack Frost turned it into an icy lump.

Fountain pens were an exciting invention; previously a nib was inserted into a holder and dipped into an inkwell fitted into the right hand side of the desk (so awkward for lefthanders), and filled by the caretaker from a large jug; it was then spattered across desk, books, hands and garments as the nib invariably crossed.

Looking forward to 1950, one girl foresaw an aeroplane fund, television ("a system by which the Head Mistress could see each form at work"), an automatic school bell (albeit broken so that it was back to a Prefect with a hand bell) and the need for another escalator.

The Nineties would require some changes. Hockey is unlikely to make the player "yet gayer". No longer can a girl in all innocence write about "my sleeping partner", – especially in Paris.

Very Promising

History needed pulling together and a modernisation of method, so that pupils did more of the work. Whilst approving that the syllabus dealt with movements and types of men rather than with facts and dates, and that form albums were encouraged, the Inspectors urged that a place be found for a course of broad European history.

Form I studied the age of Pericles; simple talks on Egypt, Assyria, Phoenicia could surely replace Greek and Roman history textbooks. IIIB were learning about the Normans, Upper IV Henry VIII's ships and VC elections in Queen Anne's time. IVB's lesson on the Reformation by an inexperienced teacher showed how ineffective it was to impart a stream of information to a class not overeager to receive it, without even the alleviations of a map or blackboard work. Civics classes were commended.

The well qualified main teacher of Geography had full command of her subject, proved by her care to give no more than a class could successfully assimilate. Everything was praised: – clear and accurate teaching, simple and painstaking imparting of elementary work to Form I, practice in drawing sketch maps, proper and regular revision of notebooks. Sympathy was expressed that the Mistress had to migrate from classroom to classroom so that no equipment could be used properly. Criticisms aimed at the Local Authority stressed the need for a black globe suspended from the ceiling, for pulleys to support wall maps so that the blackboard need not be obscured, and for a judiciously stocked museum.

The dominant society, meeting fortnightly on Friday afternoons, was the G.B.S., Miss Crombie and Miss Rudkin responsible. The emphasis was at first botanical. One Trafalgar Day, the group conducted experiments in the laboratory to the great interest of visitors. Miss Crombie gave an instructive demonstration of the art of lantern slide making, the Geography room being eventually complete with a lantern as there was no electricity throughout her time; it must have resembled What the Butler Saw. More significant was an outing to the National History Museum in Epping Forest. Papers were read on such topics as the Flower, Idols, Salt, Caves, Pyramids, ancient and modern modes of travel. Mistresses again described their holidays.

The change to GHS wrought a miracle. The Club became the means for many to get out and about. Their knowledge of local history and geography being vague, members undertook a long ramble via Waltham Cross through Epping. During the winter, they heard lectures on different countries. Most evenings being already appropriated, activities were limited to "occasional" Saturday excursions.

Occasional? Just the first year saw them at the Houses of Parliament, the National Portrait Gallery, the Tower, St Albans and inspecting the Cunard liner Ascania (they wanted to sail at once to New York as stowaways). A circular tour from Enfield to Woolwich, thence through the East End and over the bridges to the West End made them feel that they had really travelled; it was almost enough to make History lessons superfluous. "It is amazing how helpful and considerate the attendants, policemen, conductors and various public officials are to us wherever we go". Saturday mornings became so overcrowded that clubs were rationed.

Within two short years, the trips were not well supported despite their marvellous scope: Hampton Court, two more liners, London Docks (through the wine vaults and warehouses of teas and spices), Peak Frean's biscuit factory (where they received samples), the Mint (where they did not), Fleet Street, museums; and, in one afternoon, the Temple, St Paul's and the Guildhall. The octogenarian Miss Rudkin shuddered to remember her bygone energy.

Longer stays, much welcomed for truly educational work, became the done thing. On the first recorded, eleven girls, Miss Crombie and Miss Hyslop spent four short days at Redhill to study the local geology and the formation of the Weald. They learned much in this new and wonderful world, both scientifically and aesthetically, during their long walks; the countryside was a revelation.

1925 saw the same Staff with Sixth formers at Crowborough, invited by one-time Mistress, Miss Johnston. Everyone enjoyed the fun of a tight fit in a dilapidated charabanc, travel still causing both excitement and fear. Everyone went to church. No-one thought anything of walking 8, 10, 13 miles. Sitting in the stocks, an inquisitive goat, dancing the Highland Fling on a highly polished floor, spending all their money (one student returning home with ½d) – such were the ingredients of their topping time. They enjoyed the quiet intimacy of villages, beautiful flowers in fields, straw-filled palliasses; never a mention of traffic, although the noise in neighbouring bedrooms and the uncanny cries of screech owls banished sleep for *one* night.

Miss Byett joined the party to Seaford. Travelling through bluebell woods to the sea proved intensely thrilling. Forbidden to bathe, they too paddled, tramped, drank copious draughts of water, watched pony races, followed a flock of ewes and lambs and climbed 1,000 feet.

"A number of damsels, with minds geologically bent", spent one Whit at Dorking. A thoroughly enjoyable impromptu concert, more tramps through woods, services at the parish church, tea in a meadow, climbing up and down the slippery sides of a waterfall, country dances and community singing in the lovely countryside made them reluctant to return to brick buildings and books.

Over two years, books were presented for snapshots, account of a visit and plans for a continental tour.

Working together harmoniously

... in accordance with a well-constructed syllabus".

That "genius in tracing of thefts, [the] senior specialist, the remarkable excellence of whose work has been praised on previous occasions", F.M.F., was helped by four Mistresses, without exception of more than average ability. Fourteen forms were divided into nineteen divisions.

Yet the Inspectors dared to criticise. VIB should do their corrections. Pronunciation, whilst distinctly creditable, could have been more clearcut and precise. A few minutes of sound drill at the beginning of each lesson were recommended. Such lapses must have resulted from nerves, in view of the triumphs in examinations and at the EMF, the only festival to offer prizes for French Verse Speaking. Girls participated in Inter-School French, and, later, Greek and Spanish, competitions, "a delightful help to clear speech and the understanding of poetry". F.M.F. believed firmly in competition, especially as her pupils usually won. German, Spanish, Italian and Dutch joined French in the Modern Languages department. When Mlle Deswarte took weekly oral lessons with Sixth forms, ECS was the first Middlesex school to be granted this much appreciated privilege. At le Cercle,"tout le monde a été charmé d'entendre ses bonnes paroles".

The Sixth furthered the dramatic tradition with a public performance of *Les Précieuses Ridicules*. Prize Giving recitations included *le Songe d'Athalie*. Although numbers in le Cercle varied, F.M.F's encouragement continued unabated. To her, "nous devons tout le succès de nos réunions". High-spirited activities – the annual fancy dress party, theatre visits, lectures (one by Maurois), learning new songs – all inspired. More significantly, they underlined school's assumption that it was normal to write in French for the magazine, to speak French at meetings and to read "des compositions qu'elles avaient faites pour le Ministère de l'Instruction Publique". When, after nearly twenty-one years, the lady enjoyed a term in Italy, "rien d'important ne s'est passé", although everyone agreed that Willy the Mouse would not have dared to take up residence in the French room had she remained in Enfield. Missed but heartily welcomed back, she received a present from the OGA.

Good Work prizes were added to those already instituted for poetry recitation. Each girl, within her own form or division, aimed to achieve certain marks. This practice and the insistence on correct pronunciation were twice rewarded when school entered the MLA competitions and won the Middlesex Cup, more than 50 marks ahead (with 241 out of 300) of their nearest rivals, with three team and ten individual First Class certificates. The Dux scored full marks. Another year, they obtained all the first places in the different categories of those learning for fewer than two, three or five years, for which teams of five were entered. Schools came great distances to meet their regular, inevitable defeat. The record of prizes (at least eight) and certificates (at least fifty-seven) becomes, dare it be said, monotonous reading.

Miss Broome proudly reported that the work in French was one of the strongest features of the school. In 1926, F.M.F's *Anthology of French Poetry*, more popular than later books of formroom plays and of test papers, appeared to heartiest congratulations. Visitors from several continents came to study her methods. By 1930, she was a member of London University's Examination Council and a representative of the four Teachers' and Heads' Associations at an international conference.

Latin, begun in the fourth forms and taught to all in VA, VB and VI (but not to VC) was "fortunately assigned to the management of an exceedingly capable Mistress, whose methods of capturing enthusiasm were, judged by the lessons heard, modern, enterprising and very successful". Nothing but praise. Results continued to improve. The results in Greek, as with the newer Modern Languages, showed what could be done if the best use were made of very limited time.

The power of dealing satisfactorily with exercises

... on the propositions is not conspicuous".

The three male Inspectors concluded that most girls found geometrical reasoning one of their greatest difficulties. Lower forms could benefit from more mental arithmetic.

The four Mistresses who taught Mathematics had, notwithstanding, taken great care to coordinate the teaching, thus avoiding differences of method and overlapping of syllabus. Despite only four hours of instruction each week, attention was paid to acquiring habits of neatness and system in setting out work.

The whole of the Science teaching

... may reasonably be included under the heading of Botany".

Elementary instruction in Nature Study in Form I and Chemistry and Physics lessons in the middle school were correlated with the Botany syllabus and their main purpose was to serve Botanical requirements. Times *have* changed. "Judged by this standard, Chemistry and Physics, taught in groups of four, were properly arranged and suitably taught, although if considered as subjects *per se*, the standard was low". Botany secured interest and aroused enthusiasm. The well-designed and well-kept laboratory, with sufficient equipment and abundant material, was in constant use. This was several years before an escapade therein, when three culprits, caught by the Head, received Red Conduct Marks. The incident was denounced in Assembly, but, much to the general chagrin, not described.

OG Edith Gill lectured on Bees to a good audience, including eleven Mistresses, of the Scientific Society. One of the bees caused much amusement when it escaped. Two girls also read papers. A museum was begun with the gift of a beautiful mahogany showcase and a specimen of a wasps' nest. Two years later, however, very slow progress was reported.

Members visited the Science and Natural History museums annually, and attended a lecture on Invisible Light. The usual problem soon arose. With the difficulties of arranging lectures and expeditions so that they would not clash with other activities, they were unable to do as much as they would have liked. A summer expedition did reach the borders of Harpenden. At Jevington, with Miss James and Miss Soyer, seventeen girls delighted in a truly rural experience and Botanical orgy: references are frequent to cows, chickens – and the size of their own appetites. 1930 saw outings to Kew Gardens.

Interest clearly ebbing, membership was extended to the Thirds, informing them that "the aims of the Society are to further scientific knowledge, which is extremely important at the present day, and will become even more so in the future".

CHAPTER FIFTEEN

One of the more gratifying forms of work

Despite good accommodation, teaching in the Cookery room was seriously disturbed by talking and other noises connected with dinner preparation and washing-up.

Domestic Science received considerable criticism. Standards of neatness in notebooks should be higher, appearance of tables smarter and more businesslike. There was uncertainty of aim and too much wandering about. Immediate silence and cessation of movement were needed before any general instructions were given. Elementary mistakes were highlighted such as pastry mixed with hands instead of finger tips or knife. Directions, although clear and good, should never be offered in the middle of pastrymaking, speed being essential to lightness. Advice? Instructions given by one girl who has shown herself efficient in any detail might prove an incentive.

This treatment of a Mistress whom she supported totally and of a subject which she commended so frequently upset Miss Broome. "I should like to emphasise again the great importance of training all girls for home life. We do our best in the limited time at our disposal by carrying out a carefully planned course which every girl must follow. Our Mistress is very highly qualified, but we need the cooperation of parents to enable girls to get the necessary practice and to make them feel that there is nothing degrading in housework. I feel sure that many of our pupils could be entrusted to prepare a family dinner or to make a frock for a younger child, for what could be pleasanter than to make people comfortable and happy? I have been shocked to hear a mother say to me: 'Since my daughter has come to your school, *of course* I have not let her do any housework'. Such indulgence is quite unnecessary and I feel that it does harm".

She enlarged the syllabus with experimental Home Making, which included decoration, furnishing and maintenance of rooms, a practical application of Art forms; the first term's work was displayed to visitors. There was also a full course of Dressmaking, Cookery, Hygiene and Mother Craft. By specific request, some of the results were exhibited at the

Head Mistresses' Conference. Perhaps a visit to the 1926 Ideal Home Exhibition inspired.

This was a transitional period between Victorian and 'modern' approaches to the female rôle. A letter to *The Times* sixty years later pleaded for a return to Home Economics as a compulsory subject for all pupils, regardless of ability – or sex.

Fewer propose to take up clerical work

The approach to other subjects considered non-academic was somewhat patronising. Agreeing with the Head, the Inspectors found it satisfactory that the numbers of those who intended to teach were increasing and were reluctant to accept commercial studies as proper for girls in VA, VIB, and C. "There does nor appear to be any great demand for this kind of work". Figures scarcely support this assertion, although the average leaving age was rising as posts became harder to find. They did approve the stress rightly laid on a good general education first and that permission for the course was given only on the parents' written undertaking to keep their daughters at school until they had taken their GSC. Some OGs feel, with justification, that they were regarded as second-class citizens.

Great life and activity in both teachers and pupils

Perhaps Design "a little overweights the whole scheme for Art". There was too much practice in crude drawings out of the head, for figure drawing should be accurate by instruction as to correct proportions and immediate correction of bad mistakes. Admitting that girls loved the work, Inspectors felt that poor execution was permitted, along with cramped scribbling, hard lines and smudging for shading. In school, pictures containing small detail should be hung low enough for the average child, and might profitably be arranged according to subject matter or school of painting.

Many orders were received at two early displays showing developments of applied art in leatherwork, painting on wood and stencilling. 1928's exhibition of Art and Needlework, organised by the Misses Byett and Hicks, raised money for handicraft apparatus. Some girls did demur at putting their best frocks at risk in such jollities as cork-stabbing. Many visits to London's galleries and museums stimulated appreciation.

School's newest group, the Sketch Club, despite clashing with choir practice, achieved the commendable membership of 35. In winter, they drew from models, usually girls themselves, or, on one occasion, Miss Woods' cat. Prizes were awarded for the best sketches after a summer picnic. Drawing from life and sketching took place in every nook and cranny of the field and during a weekend at Cuffley. "Next year we mean to do great things", thanks to the untiring efforts of the founder, Miss Milnes, always ready to help. This initial euphoria soon gave way to the usual complaint: her work was worthy of more members. On her departure, the Club died.

Inspectors' Reports changed little over the years. School did build on strengths noticed and tried to reduce weaknesses.

Thursday afternoon is now sacred to us

One of school's greatest strengths seems to have received no inspectoral comment, yet the most significant change was the emergence on a par with French of Singing. That this excellence was the result of Miss Woods' tuition, energy and drive, there is no doubt. Her ability was recognised by girls, parents and Head, by outside musicians and adjudicators. To many who loved Music and Singing, the choir proved a never-failing source of interest and its weekly practices were eagerly anticipated. A appeal occasionally occurs. "If girls will come to choir meetings with the spirit of *giving* and not of getting, there will be no dissatisfaction. We only wish School as a whole would be more enthusiastic".

It would have taken more than this to daunt the lady whom Miss Broome commended as an enthusiastic musician. One mother enjoyed sitting behind the choir at Prize Giving the better to appreciate Miss Woods' facial contortions as she almost physically extracted the sounds. Maybe the change from Saturday morning practices increased participation as did a lecture by Geoffrey Shaw on Conducting, which included a novel demonstration with the senior choir.

Triumphs in competitive singing, unfair to omit, tedious to list, were in addition to performances at Speech Day (when, to take a year at random, nine songs were sung), at two Parents' Union concerts and once to a seemingly appreciative audience of the Enfield Literary Union. Regular practices for, and successes in, outside events provided the experience for the decade's highlights. In 1920, at the North London Musical Festival, the choir won the Silver Challenge Cup for choirs of equal voices, for which eight choirs competed. Miss Woods was well repaid for all her time and trouble. However, Tottenham High wrested the Cup the following year by two marks. Nevertheless, the Judge was so impressed by the beauty of ECS' singing that he gave them a silver medal. The newly formed junior choir was similarly rewarded. Neither group sank lower than second, juniors gaining 1st place with perfect charm to the delight of all who listened on at least six occasions and seniors on three. First class certificates were won by girls' duet and ladies' trio.

In 1926, the school choir, with four 1st prizes, triumphed over the other six entrants at the Elizabethan festival, but suffered defeat the following year at Westminster. The girls subsequently worked frenetically for the self-trained novice choir in the London Inter-Secondary Schools' competition, in which they won Honours certificates in three consecutive years. Martin Shaw, adjudicating, was so impressed that the senior group was honoured with an invitation to sing at the Cramer Concerts annually between 1927 and 1936, to much applause.

EMF provided great results. Seniors held the Targe or Shield, presented by Mr McEwen, without a break from 1921 until 1933 – not always a satisfactory victory, as, at least twice, there were no other entrants. Prizes (1st, 2nd, and, rarely, 3rd) were won for choirs, soprano and contralto voices, duets, trios, French songs, pianoforte, violin, and, from, 1927, choral and individual verse speaking.

The major triumph had come in 1922, so that it says much for Miss Woods' tenacity that impetus was maintained. Girls covered themselves with glory by obtaining 1st prize, which gave the Lancastrian Mistress particular satisfaction as the venue was Blackpool. A fête raised £50 towards the enterprise (also to purchase those much-needed stage curtains), so that School felt totally involved. The event remained indelibly marked on the minds of participants.

Up about 4am., they assembled in the Market Place before 6am. "Some of us had difficulty in recognising each other: we had been so voluminously enveloped in warm clothing by solicitous parents". They travelled in a high char-à-banc (a solid-tyred coach with inadequate springs) on a foggy October morning. The sun began to shine after Northampton where they ate a second much-needed breakfast. They thoroughly enjoyed the journey especially the part which lay through the picturesque Peak District. When Blackpool was reached at 11:30pm., cosy beds were never more welcome. By 8 o'clock next morning, they felt like giants refreshed. Sunday was spent quietly in view of the coming contest and the Winter Gardens saw a merry band of girls on Monday night, although all were inwardly ill at ease. "We donned our clean blouses, just as white and sparkling from our Mothers' hands as from the modern washer with its foaming detergents. We lovingly smoothed the well-pressed pleats of our tunics, gave a last hitch to our long black stockings and were ready for the opening bars of music under what seemed a blaze of light on a flower-decked stage. There was a hearty round of applause before we began". A hour or two later, a telegraph boy arrived at school bringing news of victory. Miss Woods and Miss Bidwell shared in the universal delight, not only at the result but at the glorious weekend adventure. They were accompanied by a very sober Head Mistress, lending her customary dignity to the expedition. Some parents had taken their daughters by the more expensive train, dubious of road hazards. Having already enjoyed press interviews and photographs, they sang most of the way home. A local Councillor greeted them: "You have put Enfield on the map".

Staff grumbled privately at the abstraction of girls for rehearsals. On this occasion, Miss Woods heaped coals of fire upon their heads by bringing back peppermint rock for them all. "Hardworking Staff, busy in the Staff Room, had just seriously misshapened their jaws with the delicacy, when the door few open and a young First former marched in without knocking. She was scared out of her wits when our Senior French Mistress rose, speechless, mouth rock-distorted, and ushered her out. I wonder what story went round the school?"

As a direct consequence of Blackpool, an OG choir was formed, which, with mothers of past and present pupils, became the nucleus of the Enfield Ladies' Madrigal Choir. Performing at the EMF from 1925, it was soon winning prizes at more than half a dozen festivals.

Miss Broome was thus able to report that the choir was becoming known in musical circles. Girls seized their cases and rushed home for Children's Hour, broadcast at 5:15pm. "Hello, children. The Enfield County School's Choir is going to sing for you". It is difficult to say who enjoyed the greater thrill, the youngsters in the studio or the listeners-in. The singers never forgot the excitement of sitting there silently, behind the scenes, with real, live BBC Uncles and Aunts. In 1930, they made a wireless record for the Corporation.

ECS was once requested to send representatives to join the massed choirs on the steps of St Paul's Cathedral during the Lord Mayor's Show. For this great honour, Miss Broome accompanied Miss Woods and choir on a cold, wintry day. She urged that each girl take a folded newspaper to use as a cushion should anyone feel faint. On the day, the only person who needed to sit on her newspaper was the Head herself.

In short, musically, "we blossom and blossom". After a decade productive of tradition, the choir continued to win laurels wherever it competed. Miss Woods must have prepared hundreds of songs of varied kinds, but it was felt that something was lacking which every school with a sound reputation should have. "We are still waiting for a genius to produce a School Song. Such a feat would ensure fame *in omne aestum*". The gap would, sad to relate, soon be filled.

How much is done for the physical welfare of the girls!

While Miss Forrest, then Miss Woods, put ECS on the cultural map, it was the excellently qualified Mistress in charge of PE, Miss Hodgson, who, despite, or perhaps because of, her strict and old-fashioned training methods, was best beloved. Girls felt a desperate urge to be a credit to Hoddie (later Hodge), who believed that physical work played a full part in promoting not only health and strength but also the much desired SORPS. Sixty years after leaving, an OG could write: "To her, we all owed a love of Fair Play and Gamesmanship" – this last not in the modern cynical sense.

She faced no easy task. Except for Forms I, IIA, IIB and IVB, no lesson was timetabled. The gymnasium, field and playground, none too big for a school of 400, were shared until 1925 with EGS. Half the lessons were still given in the Hall, to the distress of those teaching in classrooms which led from it. No Swimming Baths were near. Such problems proved a stimulus.

Although it was difficult to see how Hoddie could find time to do more, Remedial Drill was undertaken after the first Medical Inspection had criticised girls' poor posture when writing. Mr McEwen sponsored two Sports Day events – Curtseying and Good Carriage. "My brothers couldn't believe that anyone could enter for [the latter], walking gingerly, balancing a two pound jamjar on one's head". Quite. Another strange contest involved walking on Golden Syrup tins tied to the feet with string. Prizes rewarded posture as well as speed. The Head reported publicly that she often received congratulations on the fine carriage of the girls, which she rightly attributed to Miss Hodgson's invaluable training.

Junior and senior Inter-House shields and cups for the various physical activities proved markedly more stimulating than the Work shield. Most matches were hotly, indeed screamingly, contested. Each House elected captains and vice-captains for each speciality. Their exhortations to their flocks suggest an annual swing between enthusiasm and slackness. "Once more, the fates were unkind to us, and we finished up in a humble position. Yet are we downhearted? No!". "There is plenty of talent of every kind in the House, but unless we all pull together and do our bit, we can never make the best of it". Staff participation in coaching and writing in the Crit. books was fulsomely acknowledged.

When the legitimate grouse of shared facilities was removed, "the School Field and the Gym. are ours and ours alone! Oh! the joy and relief of it! We are hugely thankful that our beloved Hockey pitches are no longer profaned by the devastating football boots". Feelings a mere ten years later might have been different. Miss Broome, in more measured words, commented on mutual delight, "although of course we shared the ground very amicably while this was necessary".

With the exception of 1922 (even then the form showing the greatest keenness received a shield), Hoddie, with untiring perseverance, held her annual Drill Competition, with an external adjudicator. As in many contemporary schools, every girl participated, full of secret feelings of doing her best. Although the event was torture to some, editors enthused:"It is inspiring to see the School so neat and fresh. We positively shine with respectability, not a hair out of place". "Bravo, Sixth! You should always lead". Competitors were "proud to receive the high praise of the judge, not only for their own sakes, but because we feel we are a credit to Miss Hodgson". "The smart appearance and high level of excellence reflect great credit on the skill and patience of Miss Hodgson, who must be gratified by responsiveness and enthusiasm in her pupils".

Even the OG Gym club made excellent progress, being over-subscribed for several years. Members had, however, to be reminded that a spirit stove in the gymnasium was absolutely taboo.

Not content with competitions, Hoddie organised displays in alternate years. So successful was 1920's entertainment that a substantial balance funded the purchase of dresses to be worn on future occasions. Proceeds went subsequently to School Fund. In 1924, exercises and an exceptional variety of dancing held the attention of interested audiences for two successive evenings. Not surprisingly, to the disappointment of many, every ticket for the next event was sold long before the day when they again performed before the admiring and amazed eyes of their parents. The modern title of Gym Display appeared, although the items (dancing, team games, drill) remained similar. The reviewer remained narcissistic: "We again delighted our relatives and friends – and ourselves – by our physical skill and beauty". Armed with petrol and eucalyptus, they had waged war on obstinate spots on their drill tunics and prepared to do or die.

Colours, ribbons given out at a routine Assembly with due applause, inspired further endeavours. In the decade, hockey received 58, tennis 32 and swimming 57. From 1927, these last proved harder to acquire as the RLSS Bronze Medallion became a pre-requisite. Netball from 1922 won 43, sports and drill, irregularly recorded, 18 and 16 respectively over four seasons.

The returned field was bleak. "Let's plant trees and endow our successors with a sylvan shade". With great ceremony, House captains rammed home the earth, straightened their backs and sighed. Alas! Naughty boys were at work – over seventy years ago – and, next morning, no trees. Hoddie's perfectionism even asked the girls to pick out scores of dandelion heads, the Yellow Peril of the Field. Whatever its condition, annual Sports Days were held, usually on Saturdays, but once on Thursday and once on Wednesday.

With 1921's heatwave, everyone was thankful that the competition took place in the evening. The magazine no longer recorded events and winners, but the 33-43 races remained not dissimilar into the Fifties and included the usual oddities (Cartwheel Ball), plus those for OGs, parents and Mistresses (won more than once by Hoddie herself). The climax, with excitement at fever pitch, was the Inter-House team race, or, more simply, the Relay. The OGA once stumped up 10/- for consolation prizes. Chase Farm school band continued to enliven proceedings.

If any of us ever play for England

... we shall have Hoddie to thank".

Haphazard mid-course departures led to lamentations on the loss of team players in all games. Grumbles against the weather or, in 1929, the 'flu epidemic, must be discounted, as obviously opponents complained likewise. Much bad weather was reported, elderly ladies recall only sunny summers.

Hockey retained enormous popularity among the élite. Three collaborated on *Hockey Fever*

I must go down to the pitch again, to the rolling pitch and the
    sky,
And all I ask is a clean white ball and a stick to make it fly,
And the forward rush and the whistle shrill and the white
    sleeves flapping,
And the grim look on the ref's face and the two teams
    scrapping.

I must go down to the pitch again, for the thrill of a hard-fought
    game
Is a wild thrill and a living thrill that for ever is the same;
And all I ask is a winter morn with the hoar-frost lying,
And the quick pass and the wild rush of swift feet flying.

I must go down to the pitch again, for the rollicking winter sport
Has a lure of its own, a thrill of its own, a joy that can never be
    bought,
And all I ask is a cheering call from a laughing fellow-player,
And a breathless end to a well-fought game that makes one feel
    yet gayer.

A new small pitch proved a great help to juniors.

The main aim was the League Cup, retained 1920-1922, then lost. "Girls! How lonely the Singing Cup looks without its companion". Five years passed before success, mostly due to good combination rather than individual prowess. In 1929, it was shared with Finchley, who, with Latymer, too often proved school's undoing. Two teams played regularly; a third and a reserve started and ceased according to the enthusiasm or lack thereof in the middle school. Slackers received frequent rebukes. League results were not, perhaps intentionally, fully recorded, the magazine noting that, for example, all matches were won/lost except for one drawn; we can infer that teams won about half of the 150 played.

Fun events against EGS and the Mistresses were traditional. In 1927, for the first time on record, a Staff team sallied forth fully equipped as to members and impedimenta.

Although the first team once reached the second round of the Association's Cup, the proportion of wins for 1st, 2nd and junior netball in League and friendly matches was lower than that for hockey, yet the pleasure in "this delightful game that has come to stay" appears genuine. They were glad to have a court in the gym., especially in unsuitable weather; this helped to improve passing and dodging. All were advised to give it a try because of the chances presented for scheming and team spirit. Each House had its practice nights; deplored were irregular attendance, slackness and lack of stamina. The comfort of losers everywhere was invoked: "after all, the game's the thing". Miss Bidwell's patient, able and untiring coaching ceased in 1930; henceforth, a House Captain would help the new trainer. Maybe the enthusiasm thus generated would triumph over 'flu, leavers and sheer inertia.

1920 saw two tennis courts, one asphalt, one grass; the sole use of the field added only one more, that by the pavilion being no longer usable. Stop netting was soon provided. Competition for junior and senior cups was fierce; to Gertrude Parr (netball*, tennis*, indefatigable in Sports) belongs the unusual distinction of winning both in the same year. Six schools competed in the Schools' Championships. Although feeling that it was theirs by right, ECS failed to win until 1926. As many matches were lost as won, but all were thoroughly enjoyed, "which is, after all, the main point". Even the Staff won in 1930, albeit for the first time in nine years. "Juniors, do not be afraid to play, it will be hard at first, but with practice you will soon learn".

Help as ballboys, or scouts, was not always forthcoming, unsurprisingly, as services were required on Saturday mornings. It was vainly hoped that 1924 would show an improvement in many ways, that the courts would be surrounded by scouts, and the teams would send their balls with such devastating swiftness that their opponents would fail to return them. The game gave much pleasure to individuals playing in their own lazy fashion, especially between and after examinations. Indeed, "if all girls took as much interest in school matches as they do in their own games ...... "– the implication is clear.

Swimming was, as ever, the most deprived: the nearest Baths were at Edmonton, Wood Green or in the open at Barrowell Green, where Galas were held. Captains lamented this annually and monotonously as did the Head, for her girls lagged behind pupils from more fortunate districts. "We do hope something will be done soon to give Enfield the long-desired Baths". Pious hopes for a generous donor fell on deaf ears. Still, girls could watch club swimmers, so that those naturally inclined to remain feebly splashing at the edges might be inspired to nobler deeds.

Paradoxically, the sport continued to arouse more sustained enthusiasm than any other physical activity. The Club, with over 120 members, gave satisfaction to individuals of all ages who could continue to enjoy it at all times; it was associated with holidays; a team needed fewer members. Swimmers voluntarily gave up time after school on Tuesdays and Fridays. They obeyed their captain's command: "Needless to say, next season, every girl who can will visit the Baths regularly, so that she may compete in House races". Inter-Houses Galas were noisy affairs. 1925 saw an individual championship.

RLSS awards attracted many; 33 took Proficiency certificates only as they were under age, most, 103, gained the Bronze Medallion, which involved oral, land and water drill, 12 the Silver Medal and two the Award of Merit. Few failed. Participation in Galas, including a mixed team with the boys which came second, was regular and fervent, although only once did ECS come first of four schools; once, they were last because one of the team swam crookedly.

The attitude to success was typical: "these glories are only ephemeral, but our motto is Onward Ever".

CHAPTER SIXTEEN

Most of our pupils will have to take up some form of paid employment

That the majority needed work on leaving implies that some still did not. Home conditions never resumed the relative stability of pre-war days; by the time that many left, the market showed a considerable deterioration. It was paid work rather than a freely chosen career; this remained the prize for the minority.

Fifteen girls had strange, almost peripatetic backgrounds, two schools being quite common. One 16-year old came from Forty Hill Evening Continuation School, another via Newcastle-upon-Tyne and the Ursuline Convent, Ilford, a third from a South African High school. One wanderer had been to a Public Mixed Elementary in the Isle of Wight, the Transvaal Normal College and a Central School in Barnes before arriving at the ripe old age of 13; six months later, the family left the district, address unknown. Taught at home, the daughters of missionaries stayed a brief month. In a single year, one came from an orphanage, one was taught at home, one suffered from ill-health and one had been to three local institutions.

Over 700 had attended public, mainly local, elementary schools. Fluctuations in popularity intrigue: 8 from Chase Side in one year, 21 the next, total 78; 5 from Southbury Road, then 21, total 97 – variations which reflect only partly the changes in annual numbers accepted, from 64 to 112, averaging 84. Chesterfield contributed 97, St Andrew's Upper Grade 89, Bush Hill Park 86, Lavender Road 76: 20 local schools provided more than one pupil each, 7 only one. Others came from outer London and different parts of England, County Antrim and Holland.

Forty-three had already studied at secondary grammar or county schools locally or in the Home Counties, but mostly in over thirty different areas, from Birmingham, Bournemouth and Chester to Scarborough, Taunton and Worthing, not forgetting the Rhondda and Scotland. The world, it seems, came to Enfield.

A high proportion was still privately educated, although all but one of the Dame Schools faded after 1924. Of the 143, 25 came from further afield, from Bridge of Allen, Hampstead, Southampton, Miss Beale's at Margate – to name a few. There were so many local establishments that only four reached double figures: Miss Gardner at Woodstock sent annually from 1921, in all 16; Enfield Preparatory 14, Shirley Lodge 13 and Enfield Convent College 10; Palmers Green High 8, Miss Bassett, Miss Buckley and Winchmore Hill College 7 each, Roanoake, Elmcroft and Bycullah 6 each, Waltham Cross Convent and Wynward House 4 each, North Middlesex and Grange Park 2 each. Individuals had been at two commercial colleges, Edmonton Polytechnic Day School (Private), Hornsey Priory College, Miss Starrs', Miss Stevens' and Miss Temple's Private Classes and Miss Welsford's High School for Girls.

Some families had been profoundly affected by the death of father, brother or uncle. The 57 fathers who had been killed, had died or simply disappeared (2) had had a variety of jobs: on the land, in skilled occupations (eg. a Master lastmaker), trade and shops, civilian and service uniform, clerical and professional posts. A boxmaker and a foreman joiner died while their daughters were pupils. Three were abroad in the Civil Service and the Services. Two stepfathers were a motor mechanic and a steel hardener. A Master draper, a lithographic overseer and a police officer had retired. One belonged already to the black economy, a tramdriver who owned his private business. At least 69 mothers struggled on their own, although the phrase one-parent family was not yet current. Noticeably at the other end of the scale was a lady of independent means. Five girls had one male and two female guardians.

The normal fathers with over 150 different occupations? There is little discernible variation throughout the decade; the distinction between Master and OA still obtained. A rough division into white collar workers and those with trades, the majority, remains possible.

The biggest single group, 201, together with some 9 manufacturers (of gas apparatus to silk), is in some 25 different retail outlets, as sales' assistants and journeymen, buyers, directors, managers and partners: breadmakers, confectioners, pastrycooks 13, warehousemen 13, Master butchers 9, tailors and upholsterers 8, fishmongers 2, cleaner-dyer, draper, hairdresser. Small businesses accounted for 133 more: carpenters (one a saw doctor) 25, builders and general contractors 20, printers and publishers 20, decorators (one combining it with window-cleaning) 19, 14 in the drink trade, 13 in motoring and individuals such as advertising sign fixer, laundryman, locksmith, 2 furriers and 2 Lawn Tennis 'bat makers'.

There were 67 engineers in every possible specialisation, 52 factory hands and 9 labourers, including a road sweeper, of some 30 different types, plus 38 in RSAF from armourer's assistant to rifler. Other skilled men defy categorisation: brass finisher, embroiderer and designer, gold blocker, 2 marble cutters, mason, oilman (owner), 2 wire workers.

In Enfield's rural surroundings, 42 worked in farms, dairies, stables and nurseries, one being a rockwork and garden specialist.

Mostly in uniform were 34 in transport, all on the railways (even a doorman farrier) except for a tram conductor, 9 post office workers, 6 Gas, Light and Coal Company men, 4 policemen, 4 Water Board officials, 3 caretakers, 2 commissionaires, hospital porter, lift attendant, Master Mariner, Staff Sergeant RAOC and Royal Marine Light Infantryman.

Community workers include 3 chemical analysts, examiner of patents, rate-fixer, Relieving Officer. Other so-called white collar workers form more homogeneous groups: 92 clerks and secretaries, 16 Civil Servants at various levels in various spheres: 22 in education (Certified Class and Elementary schoolmasters to University lecturer): 22 accountants: 19 commercial travellers: 9 in Music (performers, tuners, instrument makers): 7 solicitors: 4 on the Stock Exchange: 4 in religion (Church Army officer, Clerk in Holy Orders, missionary, Primitive Methodist minister): individuals in architecture and draughtsmanship (surveying, showcard designing, ticket writing), dentistry, journalism and a library.

The leisure industry was making a slow start with a film company representative and a hotel superintendent.

These multifarious jobs constitute a cross-section of the population, thus giving a wide divergence in approach, way of life, social, cultural and financial standing, of which most girls must have been well aware. With but one shopkeeper jobless, fathers did not, at least initially, form part of the growing number of country-wide unemployed.

What did parents call their daughters? Not always by the most popular names nationally. Of those joining between September 1919 and June 1930, 84 were registered with a single name. Obvious surnames are again ignored. Of the 202 different names recorded, over 100 appear for the first time, some becoming more popular (Betty, Doreen, Yvonne), others remaining the choice of only a few (Adela, Augusta, Gwyneth, Lorna). A few belong only to the Twenties – Ernestine 4, Wilhelmina 3, Alfreda, Alberta, Noreen 2 each. Remaining unique are botanical (Pansy, Sultana), classical (Aglaia, Athena, Hypatia, Ianthe, Jessica, Octavia), seemingly old-fashioned (Beulah, Emmeline, Essie, Euphany, Theodora), more familiar (Bella, Olga) or just unusual (Anice, Eunita, Lina, Mena, Nesta, Patty, Reva). 71 did not reach double figures. Four increased noticeably in popularity: Lilian/Lily/Lillee/Lillian from 1 to 29, Madge 1 to 27, Joyce 2 to 21, Audrey 1 to 12. The top ten were Dorothy 40, Elizabeth 42, Joan 43, May 45, Doris and Kathleen 49, Winifred/Winnie 50, Marjorie/Margerie/Marjerie 55, Margaret 57, and, way ahead, Mary 88, plus 7 Mari and 1 Maria.

She should be given her full time here

Some 185 came in mid-year. Fathers' jobs presumably caused this wandering, which continued to make curriculum planning difficult, and both learning and teaching frustrating.

The term 'premature leaver', although not used, is appropriate for those who left in mid-year and/or before they reached the public examination form and who did not transfer to other schools. No fewer than 466 leavers come into this category, the highest number, 59, in 1927. From 1920 to 1928, 32 stayed one year or less, the record being held by one who remained but a brief fortnight. Five left in the summer holidays just before their 16th birthdays to get jobs. Economic problems were beginning to impinge.

These early withdrawals were repeatedly lamented. The course was planned to terminate at 18. Worthwhile employment would not be found by these unqualified girls. "A girl who does not excel in her studies is sometimes withdrawn for that reason. She may develop later, but even if she does not, she needs education all the more because she is slow to receive it. Incomplete education is not as good as a complete Elementary or Technical course". The Head hoped, more modestly and realistically, that all parents would influence their daughters to make the fullest use of their opportunities and would keep them at school until General School Certificate.

We know what all but 47 did on leaving. Only in mid-decade did unknowns reach double figures; there is little reason to assume that most of these swelled the growing ranks of the officially unemployed, some three million by 1930. Seventy-two are known to have married, one in Panama, several to schoolfriends' brothers; more undoubtedly did without informing school or OGA; 130 notified progeny, including two sets of twins; one had six sons and one daughter. At least 56 daughters and a granddaughter came to ECS in their turn, one teaching there after the Second War.

Seventy went to other institutions , including private convents here and in Europe, private and public boarding schools; three returned to elementary schools as unfit for secondary education, two were excluded for health reasons, which saved face; 41 left the neighbourhood and seven the country, going as far as New Zealand and South America. For one, there was no secondary school near; another's school place could not be transferred.

Like all similar establishments, ECS publicised the academic results of those who stayed the full time, always noting the class of degree and praising the 1st Class Honours, thus making clear where it thought real success lay, and lauded those who went in for teaching. News was relayed in Assembly, in magazines and at Prize Givings. These girls who reflected glory on the Staff were in the minority.

Annual numbers leaving for universities varied little; they totalled 43. Four went up to Oxford, four to Reading, the others to six London colleges, King's 11 and UC 10 the most popular. This concentration would surprise the next postwar generation. Thirteen Training Colleges, including two for DSc. and two for PE, received 40: St Katherine's, Tottenham, the nearest, took nine and Hockerill six. Not all taught or lectured, although 34 did locally. Of the 18 uncertificated, one became a florist and another was advised to change her profession.

Three attended the Royal Academy of Music, eight received private tuition, one girl's father having the suitable forenames of George Frederick Handel. One studied at the Ginner Mawrer School of Dancing, another became an assistant dancing mistress. The girl who began dramatic training was forced by ill-health to return home.

Two left for Hampstead Nursery College, seven, including a Norland, trained as nurses, one later working in India, three as physiotherapists, one as a masseuse. Entry into what are now called the caring professions was encouraged: "Hospitals want well-educated girls, and offer an interesting and useful career to those who have the necessary ideals of service to others, but attract few, in spite of their greatly improved conditions of service".

Other trainees included apprentices (eight milliners, two drapers, two in beauty culture and in dispensing, an upholsterer, a learner tea-room cake maker, three dressmakers, three designers and draughtswomen) and students: seven at Art colleges (one specialising in industrial design, another subsequently changing to chiropody), seven at local polytechnics, two at trade schools, one at Swanley Horticultural. After Regent Street Polytechnic, then a spell at home, one took a London University Diploma in English language and literature, a Good Housekeeping Diploma in domestic and canteen Cookery – and became secretary to the engineering manager of an insurance company!

Of those with immediate earnings, 18 worked in shops (three as cashiers, one running a home-made cake shop), 12 were hairdressers, four in domestic service, two each in factories, floristry and photography, as ECS laboratory assistant (such were called technicians comparatively recently), and library and dental assistants. One had a studio in Paris, another was a poultry farmer.

These account for fewer than half. Two groups remain. Seventy-three went in for some form of business, clerical, commercial or comptometer training, under half in private classes or schools, with fifteen at Pitman's, nine at St. George's, six at Clark's, four at the French Institute (two with scholarships of 21, later 24, guineas) and one at the London Chamber of Commerce.

Two hundred and forty-five went directly into clerical work, with a small but increasing proportion in banking and insurance, four already calling themselves secretaries rather than clerks. Miss Broome remained scathing about parents who sent their daughters into the overcrowded ranks of half-educated clerical workers. "I pity these girls if they have to live on their earnings in later life. I fear some regret their choice. I recently heard of a girl who left at the age of 16 to work from 9am to 6-30pm, as a clerk at 17/- per week out of which came 5/- fares to and from London. She would get £1 at the age of 18, but will be dismissed at that age, the policy of her employers being to economise by using cheap girl labour".

The Civil Service took 42. The Head urged parents who entered daughters for the Writers' Assistant examinations to be more selective and choose the Clerical Class intended for girls with a secondary education. "I feel they may realise their mistake too late". One worked in the Foreign Office, another in the LCC, several were post office telephone operators. One qualified later as a DSc. teacher.

Clerical training and work accounted, therefore, for nearly 300 girls.

And the remaining 222? They stayed at home. Some obviously got jobs later, sometimes much later, but 222 left in order to stay at home. The Head's loyalties were divided; although urging a wider vision, she had always maintained that, for all girls, a home was the best career. These amazing figures hold other surprises. Why were 52 specifically *required* for Home Duties, especially as two of their fathers had retired and one was unemployed? Ages ranged from 13 to 19, but 30 were over the contractual age of 16 and only six were under 15. A further 26 left through family circumstances or because earnings were required, yet 10 of these remained at home. Seven more stayed there because of the death of a parent, for one, of a widowed mother. Another had to take charge of younger children as her mother was seriously ill. A 15-year old left although family means were good and an older sister was earning, but mother required her companionship. Twenty left because of their own ill-health, including one "serious heart and nerves affection", which led to at least five early deaths at 12, 13 and 18 years of age; three more died before they reached 35. Girls were less healthy than their grandchildren would be. An influenza epidemic swept through school in 1929.

Governors exacted penalties in four cases, in one of which the father refused all information. One 14-year old had to help her parents, and parents wished that another should begin to earn. There must have been more to it than these recorded facts. In all, over 80 were removed for reasons which were probably outside their own wishes and which would not be tolerated later. In the Twenties, school was reluctant to tread on parental toes.

On a more cheerful note, three became respectively an ECS Governor, a Magistrate and a Mayor, one appeared in a television show and two received the MBE.

Head Girls

1922 Evelyn Leclair	1923 Florence West, Marjorie Payne
1924 Winifred Allen	1925 Edith Hopkins
1926 Helen Whitfield	1927 Kathleen Martin
1928 Margaret Cowing, Doris Partington	
1929 Kathleen Pangbourne	1930 Phyllis Edwin
	1931 Mary Gates

Additional School Colours,

... awarded for public spirit and service to the School

1923 E. Coverdale, D. King, E. Little, M. Tanner
1924 M. Arnold, B. Butler, B. Edwin, P. Warbey
1925 V. Mumford   1927 G. Gibbons, M. Watts
1930 E. Hance, J. Rudland   1931 O. Boshier

I had always been very happy at school

School was rightly proud of editors, prefects, House and Games captains, winners of scholarships, colours and a wide variety of prizes, who participated in clubs, wrote for the magazine, matriculated and enjoyed examination successes and often unusual careers. Three sets of sisters were among the twenty future graduates who won eight of the twenty-six School Colours in eight years. It is difficult now to see why more girls did not achieve this high honour.

Swimmers included Silver medallist Eileen Slater Price, future Coutts Bank secretary. Captain and champion Winifred Linley Allen advised: "If girls who swim would have a one-length race every time they went to the Baths, their speed would increase rapidly, and we should then have a better chance of gaining first place in the Gala". With literary and linguistic leanings, her travel accounts convey excitement. With an Oxford Modern

Languages degree, she trained to teach. No-one was better known to more generations than Barbara Butler; the OGA would have faltered without her quiet, dignified but determined secretaryship and her continued contact with school and with leavers. She became Secretary of the League of Nations Union (LNU), lecturer in Office Arts and Head of Commerce in a Further Education college.

With over 150 colours awarded, Sports addicts and reporters proliferated, many going on to Training Colleges. Mabel Winifred Watts (drill*, tennis*, netball*, Bronze) felt that netball was a delightful game that had come to stay. With EMF prizes for reading and singing, she wrote crisp notes on the choir which she trained and conducted at Prize Giving during Miss Woods' absence. Olive Laws won sports*, swimming Silver, and special drill prize: Marjorie Kathleen Pedrette scouted for tennis matches, participated in such events as Modes of Progression, Tennis-Balls-on-Rackets, Balloon-on-Plate: Freda Agnes Pratt with seven placings, tennis*, netball*, was a member of netball junior and first teams simultaneously: Phyllis Mary Warbey (swimming*, tennis*, netball*, captain of all three) stayed almost two terms, then returned a year later and remained seven years, wrote eight encouraging reports for different games as well as of the very jolly Belgian holiday: champions Muriel Annie Luxton achieved twelve placings, Nellie Rose Elizabeth Scholl (hockey*) won at the tender age of 13: Lily Constance Clarke won events alone (Egg-and-Spoon, Slow Bicycle) and with her sister, Bursar Rita Marjorie (3-Legged, Addition), both becoming tennis champions. Secretary of the Lit., Hist. and Deb., Lily won the first magazine competition.

Hockey experts Maud Ellen Arnold was the first to be selected by the County, while Margery Florence Haywood (tennis*), arriving aged 14, went straight into the first XI; after a spell of home duties, she trained as a physiotherapist.

All-rounders: Brenda Olive Woodfield, netball and swimming captain and one of the select band of Vicar's Scholars, added five prizes to her five colours. Surely Marjorie Richards was uniquely distinguished in that the tennis championship was postponed until September because of her illness! Twice champion, she was hockey captain and won two colours. Olive Eileen Boshier's sporting career (drill*, hockey*, sports*, swimming* with Teacher's and Instructor's certificates, tennis and swimming captain) did not suggest her premature death. No narrow specialist, she won a senior Technical Exhibition (£30 for three years, which took her to Chelsea PT college), prizes for Home Making, EMF vocal duet and GHS snapshot competition, and was a Cadet Star with Ranger All-Round Cords (Campcraft*).

Five were GHS officers. Winifred Mary Pulling wrote technically skilled verse and a shared account of a Paris visit which conveys honest pleasure. Kathleen Maude Pangbourne (hockey*, drill*) won prizes for Home Making, Classical and Modern Languages, qualified for the French Institute but chose to train as a masseuse at Guy's Hospital as did president of the dramatic club, Margaret Annie Cowing, encouraged unexpectedly by F.M.F. as she had all possible honours in French. Her involvement politically and with the work of Dr Steiner led her to become matron of a home for mentally defective children. Audrey Ellen Freeman (hockey*, Bronze) wrote *The Coming of the Night*, 45 lines of hypnotic blank verse, mixing academic and personal, before reading Classics. An active member of both French Circle and choir, Helen Louise Whitfield recalled for the Jubilee the competitive excitements of Empire and Trafalgar Days, but kept silent on contemporary escapades as "the present generation of schoolgirls needs no encouragement in the breaking of rules". With 100% in Middlesex French Verse-Speaking, she wrote the first published French poem, *A la Pâquerette*.

Others were primarily literary. Beatrice Annie Edwin (hockey*) set a hard example for sister Phyllis (drill*, campcraft*), who rose to the challenge with EMF, school and Middlesex Verse Speaking and Beethoven essay prizes and French Institute certificate (*assez bien*); later an Inspector, she served on Modern Languages committees and such public bodies as UNESCO. Marjorie Wrenn was one of the few Honorary Junior Scholars. Presumably her father's post as a chartered secretary and accountant precluded financial support. She wrote lively poems as in *The Seasons*:

> Old winter is a fussy fellow
> He walks on carpets white.

Before training for DSc.at Battersea Polytechnic, Gertrude Annie Payne claims attention for her evocative and personal poems: *Moonlight*: *Stream*: *An Old World Garden*. *Storm*, despite an invocation to mighty Thor, has force as she goes through the silent anticipation, the thunder and lightning to the radiant sunrise. Choir member Edith Gladys Coverdale received a Governor's prize for her essay on the League of Nations Union and nurtured the junior dramatic society.

Among future teachers was Kathleen Martin, who won a Shakespeare Association award, Mathematics and English prizes. Daisy Ethel Wright read Botanical and literary papers and graduated with a training college scholarship in History. A shining light in all sports except swimming, Florence Annie West became a Grammar School Head. With prizes for General Knowledge, Vera Bertha Mumford was the first to win a Dudin-

Brown scholarship (£50pa, French) to Westfield. Future lecturer Gwenneth Olive Gibbons reported on hockey, a scientific visit, the successful senior dramatic society, played tennis (despite collapsing in one match) and won EMF prizes.

Two linguists with French Institute certificates were Doris Adeline Dean, who became a French correspondent and Eileen Vera Chapman, Vicar's Scholar, who won a Modern Languages bursary of £20 to Oxford, augmented by a senior county scholarship of £80pa. Another distinguished in French, Ethel Doris Partington (netball*, drill*) worked for the unemployed, organised an East End girls' club's dramatic work, refereed netball matches at the Foundling Site and ran an Anglo-German holiday camp.

Two were particularly distinguished at school and after. It is impossible to mention all the examination successes, prizes and certificates (at least 36) gained by president of the dramatic society Joan Dabbs, who won a Drapers' scholarship (£60pa), also to Oxford. Her travel scholarship (a return ticket to Paris by the shortest sea route) was awarded by la Société des Professeurs de Grande Bretagne fondée à Londres sous la Présidence d'Honneur de Victor Hugo. No mere academic, she was House captain (Bronze and two colours), author of *Suggestions for Improving the School Hall*, qualified as an almoner, did social work and became studio manager of the BBC European Service.

A frequent and talented contributor to the magazine, co-author with Margaret Cowing of the choir history, Joyce Rudland was musically gifted, playing the piano for *Alcestis*, coming fifth in the *Daily Express* London area Pianoforte Playing competition, winning singing and verse speaking prizes and becoming an Associate of the Royal College of Music. With RSA successes in French and Italian and a scholarship to the French Institute, she, as expected, took a 1st class degree.

Joyce Eastwick was reported at home. On her death, however, an unusual career came to light. In the Foreign Office at the age of 20, she spent the Second War deciphering for the War Office. Her 23 years as a diplomat took her to Washington, North Africa, the Tehran conference, Paris and Morocco – after which she wrote children's books.

Bronze medallist Gwendoline Beatrice Kerlogue, youngest of three sisters, chose a clerical career and became school's first known Mayoress. Ethel Bertha Willmott won two colours and prizes primarily for singing. She is the first, maybe the only one, whose husband has been knighted.

Bursar and student teacher Winifred Violet Ellis changed direction to become superintendent physiotherapist at a local hospital. Sadie Marion Ingham, House captain with two colours, became school's first known company secretary. Following sister Dorothy, all-rounder Lillie Margery Papworth, with excellent prize and and scholarship records, left to learn the business of floristry. After a normal career and a time at home, Frieda Mabel Goodall took a 5-year millinery apprenticeship. In a shower, her first home-made hat of plaited crepe paper poured disaster on her face in the form of cerise dye. After wartime Fire Service, then free-lancing, she trained at the college of Aeronautical Engineering, enjoying work on Radar. All this despite loathing two subjects at school – Needlework and Mathematics. Her pictures were accepted at Enfield's Art Circle's 50th anniversary exhibition. She bequeathed £6,000 to help Enfield's older citizens.

Scholar Ida Mary Hope Robinson won £100 as the 10,000th visitor to the British Empire exhibition and its wonders. A nursery governess, then a nurse, she subsequently spent thirteen years, some of them grim, in a Methodist missionary hospital in China. Her account of six weeks' sea-journey conveys her excitement: "What untold experiences and pleasures were in store for me?" She later joined the staff of a Nigerian leprosy centre.

Which leaves two, both MBE, one of local, one of international, fame.

Winifred Emma Cowley, with distinctions in campcraft, her Cadet Star and Gold Cords, became acting Brown Owl, Guide captain, chairman of Enfield Ranger committee and secretary of Middlesex Rangers. OGA faithful, teacher, welfare officer, hospital trustee, founder member of the local Guide Dogs for the Blind, she has been an indefatigable organiser of sponsored events for good causes. She inaugurated the Mayor's Charity Walk of 27 miles. Joining Middlesex RLSS at the age of 14, executive member then president, with a bar to the Bader recognition badge, she has been an active inspector and adviser on swimming, especially for those handicapped mentally and physically. This voluntary work is all the more remarkable as she left ECS to stay at home under threat of blindness.

Frances Mary Everett (hockey*) is undoubtedly school's most celebrated OG, although not by that name, which was first in print for coming third in the 12-and-under Circular Jump. When a third former, she received as chance gift of tickets for Chelsea Flower Show. Such leave of absence troubled Miss Broome, who periodically regaled pupils with some of the frivolous reasons proffered by pupils. Why – a girl even asked for the day off to go to a Flower Show. Frances' early enthusiasm was encouraged by Miss James and Mr Edward Augustus Bowles, Vice-President of the Royal Horticultural Society, who recommended her to Swanley, then a gardening school for women. Practical work (carting manure) followed the diploma course and she joined Amos Perry's Hardy Plant Farm, where the water plant business was in its infancy and "I was fortunate in being able to work with this right from the start and eventually took charge of it". Marrying the owner's son, Frances Perry began the other careers which made her into a household name. Her first piece netted 15/- from *Country Life*. Direct, full of common sense, she subsequently wrote 19 books, the first on water gardening (1938) remaining a classic. She was the *Observer*'s specialist for 26 years.

Well known on radio and television, a Fellow of the Linnean Society and the only woman member of the Royal Commission on Allotments, she was the first woman outside the USA to receive the Sarah Frances Chapman medal, presented by the Garden Club of America for *Flowers of the World*, and probably the only OG invited to make a lecture tour in the States.

She became horticultural, then agricultural, adviser to Middlesex, Principal of Middlesex Horticultural College (1953-1967), receiving the MBE, the Royal Horticultural Society's Veitch Memorial Medal and its Victorian Medal of Honour. One of the first women exhibitors, she was the first woman member in over 160 years of its council and was later its president.

Sociable and supportive of the OGA, active vice-president of Enfield Preservation Society and president of the Floral Art club, her greatest service was saving Capel House and gardens from demolition, persuading Enfield Council to establish a college of horticulture in the 17th century manor and playing a large part in its development. It is hoped to convert an old stable block into a library in her honour. She is already immortalised with flowers named after her including an arabis, a white rose and a sweet pea.

Widowed in 1964, she later married another eminent gardener, Roy Hay. Her local memorial service was followed by a tree-planting ceremony in the Frances Perry garden at Capel Manor.

On a firm constitutional basis

Even former students, or as they preferred, then and now, Old Girls, were inspired to make a new beginning. By 1911, leavers from the Pupil-Teacher Centre could have formed an Association had they so wished. They visited school, wrote articles, gave presents to, and parties for, leaving Staff, and organised a social for those in Training Colleges. They kept in touch with each other, but there was no formally constituted body. The war focused their endeavours; apart from serving team teas, singing and acting, they enjoyed several interesting meetings of the literary society formed in 1917. Although the Head commented on the excellent programme of the dramatic and gym clubs, it was all hand-to-mouth. Would-be attenders, whether Staff, former or present pupils, simply gave their names to Miss Broome.

So, in 1920, all was reformed at a meeting of 80 potential members. With Head and Staff as Hon. Vice-Presidents, affairs would be managed by a president, treasurer and secretary. F.M.F. was an energetic committee member. They tinkered constantly with the constitution. Attempts to recruit girls as they left were not, and never have been, consistently successful.

At 1927's badly attended AGM, new proposals were carried to promote the interests of, and social intercourse between, OGs, at an annual cost of 2/6, or one guinea for life membership. The Head was now Hon. President; president and vice-president would be elected annually, treasurer and secretary for one year but eligible for three consecutive years, and a 12-strong committee for three years, one-third retiring each year. Catering and social committees were formed. Each Head Girl was an automatic member. The Report would be circulated to all and published in the magazine, although subsequently news only was included. Subscriptions no longer covered copies.

Appeals for new members were repeated as fortunes flourished then fell. One year, events were not sufficiently patronised: the next showed signs of real vigour and growth – or *vice versa.*

The dramatic club illustrates this clearly. With 20 members, "success is inevitable when talent and enthusiasm are combined". Not empty words, for 1922 saw two performances of *The School for Scandal.* Hiring 18 costumes and wigs with the services of a make-up man cost £13:5:0, plus 5/- for his fare. After other expenses such as floor polish 3/-, orchestra £3:3:0, printing £1:12:6, caretaker 10/-, hire of hall £1:7:6 and transport of extra chairs from and back to a local school 24/-, receipts from tickets sold to 53 OGs and 77 OBs gave a profit of £3:5:8. Miss Broome claimed that the Association was showing new energy, yet, a year later, it proved impossible to produce a play, as so many could not attend rehearsals. Dramatised versions of *David Copperfield* and other Dickens novels were not forthcoming.

After discussion as to whether Miss should precede names on programmes, scenes from *Cranford* were presented; 350 tickets (1/3 unreserved, 2/4 reserved) were printed at a cost of 11/6, furniture and costumes hired (£1:9:0 and £3:13:6 respectively) and 25 window bills prepared (6/6). Alas – a tram strike prevented a good attendance.

With the exception of a Wild West scenario in dumbshow, which required ability and ingenuity, performed to over 100 at the 1929 Reunion, dramatic shows lapsed until 1930, when the committee accepted with appreciation the proposal that a newly-formed society should mount an informal presentation of *The Canterbury Tales*. Miss Florence offered the use of school scenery and a small grant of £1. Rather more time was spent on discussing the varieties of sandwiches, cakes and sweets.

In 1923, the AGM was held in conjunction with Miss Broome's At Home at which she desired the pleasure of the company of Old Girls for coffee, music, dancing and a discussion of progress – a Royal Command. The next two Reunions were postponed indefinitely, only 28 tickets being sold. Despite a joint committee, even Reunions with EGSOBA were unsure of regular support. Yet in 1924, 60 had attended a successfully jolly and musical AGM.

The most regular meeting throughout the Twenties was a Dance to which prefects were invited; these were advertised in the now defunct local *Observer*. An early one had to be limited to allow 60 couples to dance comfortably. 1921's programme reads thus: waltz, 3 fox trots, the Lancers, valeta, 2 waltzes: supper: waltz, 3 one-steps, 2 waltzes, the Flying Boston, 3 waltzes. Entertainment included songs, pianoforte solo and a Sketch. *Sir Roger de Coverley* and *Auld Lang Syne* concluded the evening. Mrs Hill agreed to be responsible for supper on condition that OGs settled the bills and paid her separately. The lady told the committee five days before the dance that she could not undertake the same, so they were forced to find a firm. No small undertaking. Painters of Chase Side provided 50 fancies at 1d and 50 at 2d each, 60 tart and 60 sponge cases and loaves worth 5/7½. Milk and cream cost 11/4 (4½ a pint) and floor polish 2/3. The bulk of the food accounted for £1:13:5: 4lb sugar, 1½lb demerara, 2lb raspberry jam, 2 tins tongue, 2 jars each of ham and salmon-shrimp paste, 4 pineapple, 4 lemon and 4 raspberry jellies, 1 raspberry and 1 chocolate blancmange, 1 tin custard powder, ¼lb almonds, 18 lemons, 1 tin peaches, 1 tin apricot, 2 tins pineapple, 2 tins Nestlé coffee, 1 tin "Good Coffee". Food worth 3/- was sold after the event and 11d had to be found to replace a missing glass dish. Actually 81 were present: 15 girls (1/- each), 11 mistresses (who do not seem to have paid) and 55 OGs (2/- each). Even with an extra shillingsworth of sponge cake and 1/- for 8" trays, there was a profit.

In 1922, two were held with Old Grammarians. A ticket (single 3/6, double 6/-) included refreshments. In 1923, it cost 3 guineas to hire the Arcadians. Miss Brooome expressed satisfaction with the arrangements. The following year, the Felix Dance Band required £3:12:6, hire of Hall £1:1:0, with a double ticket costing 8/-. Joint dances were discontinued after trouble with overstaying the time limits.

It was next suggested that a social evening be held on the first Thursday of each month and a gramophone and records of dance music bought with the money in hand. Despite Miss Broome's kindness whereby the event was held in the Hall, so no gramophone purchase was necessary, numbers soon dwindled to vanishing point and socials were discontinued in under a year.

Individual secretaries were responsible for hockey and netball (both affiliated to the Middlesex OG League (5/- a year) and, later, tennis. Members benefited from renewed exclusive use of the field on Saturday afternoons. School lent hockey sticks, the Club provided balls; membership, which included a fixture card, cost 3/- a season. Teams twice carried off the Cup. Each paid for her tea and in tennis for her partner's. The keys, kept in Mrs Hill's charge on her pantry window ledge, were posted through her letterbox after play.

OGs were thwarted in respect of swimming; the open air baths were so well attended in the evenings that no special terms or times could be arranged. The gym club gave heartiest thanks to Miss Hodgson, who also donated tennis prizes. Much knitting was done when badminton, for which the old school tie was *de rigueur*, was added twice weekly at Enfield Court Riding school. As early as 1922, OGs were invited to join the Enfield Rifle club – emancipation, surely. Whist drives, 2/-, began at the president's house in 1926. A ping-pong table was installed in 1927.

An odd effort was made at the end of the decade to promote *esprit de corps*: how about an OG blazer, green naturally, with the school badge embroidered on the pocket? The secretary invited girls interested in Art to submit designs. The pattern of the badge is all that resulted.

Contact with school continued. OGs ran a stall at one bazaar. Some lamented the lack of a tangible connection; could an Honours list be the missing link? Present pupils would be stimulated by the success of their predecessors and school would have a record of which to be proud. It is unclear how this would have differed from information published in the magazine.

A general pattern was now established: Autumn AGM: winter Reunion on the first Saturday after term opened in January, provided the Hall be free; summer Reunion in July to which married members were encouraged to bring their children and which offered a tennis tournament, a treasure hunt and other competitions.

Those who doggedly supported the OGA in the Twenties and early Thirties remained its most faithful members.

To which all parents belong

Not only former students: new family association and responsibility emerged. Locally, few parents, especially mothers, had gone to Grammar schools. With pride tinged with fear, they had been mere spectators, coming in large numbers to public events, fathers competing in races, but that was the extent of participation expected or even allowed. Prize Givings were well patronised; parents grew bolder and requested a change of venue so that all who wanted to come could be accommodated.

School had early adopted an enlightened scheme of public relations, beginning with afternoon receptions and continuing with Trafalgar Day. In turn, parents gave practical support – School Fund, entertainment of Belgian refugees, patronage of bazaars, jam-making for the hospitals, providing cakes and china for Sports Day teas.

Greater involvement began with the Grand Piano Fund. Individuals had presented prizes, as for the 14-and-over Potato race. The Parents' Union was thanked for the generous gift of a House Challenge cup, a cup for the Sports champion and a brooch for the runner-up. These were followed by junior and senior tennis cups, a trophy to be competed for by six Middlesex schools and, later, a Home Making/ Housecraft prize. For Miss Broome, it "was delightful and stimulating to know that we have their good will and sympathy". Inspectors approved their serious purpose, and the varied evidence of their warm interest.

Miss Broome commented at six Prize Givings on parents' helpful meetings on careers, home training, ECS' methods of education, nursery nursing, Art. Girls enjoyed their lantern lecture on London. Parents, as a body, were now an accepted feature of school life. They could, therefore, be warily scolded when they failed to do their share, when the magazine did not have its deserved support.

Notes remain of the Head's challenge to the parents who were finding that they could count. Some of her words are still appropriate. After thanking them as individuals and particularly as members of the Union, she had one little complaint; on reflection, she had crossed out 'little'. "Some parents have too high an estimate of the powers of a teacher. However skilfully and faithfully her work is done, she cannot guarantee that all her pupils will pass a given examination. Whilst the pupils' own efforts and abilities are an important factor, results vary from year to year according to the proportion of girls who have the industry and mental gifts which ensure success. Parents may rest a assured that everything possible is done to educate their daughters on the right lines, but this will not result in every girl qualifying for admission into the University".

She outlined what *they* could do towards training mind and body, to enable girls to be better able to use and enjoy God's gift of life. "Parents may give us most valuable help by supervising their daughters' reading and leisure. Homes where the cinema, the daily paper and the lighter periodicals are the only possibilities of intellectual recreation are at a disadvantage compared with the girl who has learnt to share her parents' enjoyment of good literature and art. We cannot give her equality of opportunity". Her conclusion is delightfully patronising: "The success of some of our best pupils is due quite as much to home influence as to our own efforts. How very fully we appreciate this".

PART FOUR

MISS BROOME'S LAST YEARS

CHAPTER SEVENTEEN

We must hope the nations will accept our school motto

Midway through Miss Broome's last years as Head, ECS celebrated its Silver Jubilee. "It has been most interesting and delightful to watch the development of the school and I am fortunate in having with me four who were at its opening and who have rendered invaluable aid in many ways": Sir Henry, Miss Florence, Miss Forrest and "our faithful caretaker, Mrs Hill".

After commenting on some 5,000 Assemblies and some 2,000 pupils, the many marriages and, yet again, the sad fact that the most favoured and often the worst paid occupation was clerical work, she proudly recalled many successes in various professions, including five on the Mission field, three running their own private schools and the grand total of 52 Oxford and London graduates.

She recalled the Great War: "those of us who passed through those troublous times must hope most fervently that they will never come again, but that the nations will move Onward Ever to peace and happiness, not backwards to the horrors of another war. I am glad to remember that when in 1918 we assembled to give thanks to God for the Armistice, our VI form came to ask if we might sing Kipling's hymn *Lest We Forget.* This fine hymn expresses all that is best in our national aspirations and we thankfully realise the strength of Britain stands for peace". Nowadays, with its unfortunate references to lesser breeds without the law, it could be considered to be racist. The Head felt, however, that girls who entered upon the hoped-for peace would surely ever strive to do their duty to God and to their country.

Yet neither atmosphere nor outlook during her last seven years was rosy. The effects of the slump and increasing unemployment were visible in the girls' lives: stress caused by fees (the Means Test bearing harshly on some), cost of uniform, outings, sports equipment. For some, 1/- for the magazine represented twelve weeks' pocket money. The Savings Association was not flourishing, despite the efforts of the Mistress in charge and of the Head. Its fortunes, like those of the country, fluctuated considerably. She wrote a note to remind herself to emphasise the value of thrift, an unpopular virtue. By 1936, only 30 members remained; the total saved since 1927 was £455:5:6.

The unsurprisingly huge increase in premature leavers resulted in fewer entries for public examinations, fewer actresses and a lack of stability in games' teams. Only one entrant of 1928 stayed long enough to take HSC; in 1936, only four of the hockey teams remained for a second season. The Head warned yet again that sixteen was not the age of termination, but the minimum age at which a girl was normally allowed to leave, but was reduced to pleading that all should stay at least until the end of a school year. Job prospects were worrying. Miss Florence gave *Careers and Openings for Women* to the library to offer inducement to aim higher than clerical work.

Public concerns impinged. The Columbia Gramophone Company invited the choir to make a record. "Great was our disappointment when we heard that, owing to the present depression in trade, the making of all records by choirs had been deferred until a later date". Eileen Good turned such matters to school's advantage.

> Buy British is the slogan
> For everyone who shops,
> No matter if it's house-linen
> Or if it's mutton chops.
> We each must do our duty
> To help our Country through,
> Prosperity or failure
> Depends on what we do.
> It's difficult to write a verse
> I really must confess;
> But never mind, buy British goods
> For England's happiness.
> I hope each girl will do her best
> To keep this Golden Rule,
> And buy the British Magazine
> Of Enfield County School.

Yet the home picture is confused. Winnie Axford notes that

> The trade returns are up again,
> And things are on the boom ......
> There's talk of some reduction in
> The rates and taxes here.

During an excursion along the Thames, they saw something of the great commerce and industry, the pantries and storehouses on which the nation's prosperity depended.

Insularity persisted. The simplest details of foreign life ("No tea!") were still recounted as if features of another planet. Normality came as a shock. "In one memorable fortnight, we travelled more than 13,000 miles by boat, train and coach – not one limb broken and no-one lost herself irretrievably", which implies at least one near miss. Even a trip to the Isle of Wight provided excitement.

Fascism and Bolshevism seemed virtually synonymous; one pupil acknowledged that her interest in politics might sound unusual for a girl. Yet international problems were neither hidden from, nor ignored by, them.

Muriel Clark, the only girl in 1933 to win a scholarship to Perugia, told how Mussolini's secretary inspected the Fascists one August Saturday. Bills posted everywhere invited the Perugini, vibrating with enthusiasm, to take the opportunity of welcoming the illustrious representative of the Duce. The town swarmed with men in black shirts which did not add to their beauty. The inspiring speech was greeted with cheers and the cycle corps, unable to restrain their feelings, picked up their bicycles and shook them wildly in the air. To his credit, Mussolini himself was supervising the excavation of the Forum.

Spain came vividly into focus when Mlle Morénas, the French assistante, retold her experiences, hair-raising then, more commonplace today. She accounted it thrilling to have been kept a prisoner in the early days of the Spanish Revolution and brought back in a destroyer to Morocco, yet what happened was chilling. General Franco, chief of the Spanish Foreign Legion, had crossed the straits with his troops. Placards on train waggons, some bearing the hammer and sickle, referred to strikes: "To die or to vanquish". Bullets ripped through the compartment windows at night. Khaki-clad soldiers wearing red-tasselled caps ordered passengers to raise their hands. They spent five hours in the train in scorching sun without food or water, then three weeks at Córdoba, where they depended for water on the station fountain. Finally, a convoy of charabancs for foreigners was escorted to the port by lorries, two of armed soldiers and fifteen full of lead for making bullets.

Discussion of "the Saar plebiscite, Fascists riots, questions of the Far East was left to our dull contemporaries, the newspapers". Travellers could not, however, avoid awareness of conditions in Europe. 1931's visit to the Ardennes, under wartime German occupation, drew attention to the plight of cultivators in Rheims who could not sell their grapes because of over-production of wine. Unemployment in France rose less severely than in Germany, where, a later group heard, students, after studying until their late twenties to become teachers or doctors, were obliged to sell papers or sweep the streets, as there were practically no openings. The universities were crowded with people who continued studying because they could not find a job; in medical colleges, students worked on the stairs. Unemployment at home night be serious but in Germany it was infinitely worse with seven million jobless.

A subsequent visitor, escorted by an airman to a village ball, saw portraits of Herr Hitler and Nazi flags on all four walls. Another writer wondered what Mr Eden had been saying to Herr Ribbentrop. Yet border Customs men were formally polite, new roads were a marvel of engineering and "the warm-hearted German people welcomed us, and, before we left, drank a toast to friendship and happy relations between our two countries". Most perplexing.

The intrepid Miss Crombie spent a term in 1937 exploring the mysteries of the Far East, her return being greeted with pleasure. High, relatively barren granite hills reminded her of her native Scotland. She took a lively interest in modern Miss China, with permed hair and her long straight dress down to her feet and slit up to the knee, coolies, poor women doing hard physical labours, a typhoon, sampans, school-life, a Soya sauce factory, rice-planting. After she had enjoyed the crowded Chinese areas of Hong Kong, the Sino-Japanese War forced curtailment of her travels. Her story and a letter from Ida Robinson ("How good that she did not forget her school") told of bandits, brigands, disease, primitive superstition and cleanliness, although during Public Health Week, the healthier children received prizes: "it was great fun cleaning up the streets with brushes, brooms, spades, watering cans and Lysol". Yet Bands of Reds were less than ten miles away; inhabitants felt relatively safe, however, as the city gates were closed at night! The Chinese were unlikely to want Britain to give back Hong Kong, full of refugees from Shanghai, Canton and Macao, for they needed it as a funkhole under the Union Jack for all the generals who became fabulously wealthy.

The conclusion was naïve. England was the best country after all.

What is worthy of remark in the girls' England?

The trivial things taken for granted are now of historical interest: freezing linoleum on cold bedroom floors: blankets and eiderdowns on beds: collecting tram tickets: garden fires and Harvest Homes; queuing for the bathroom at holiday boarding houses: ammoniated tincture of quinine, the only remedy for colds: another outbreak of smallpox. There's nothing new at waiting at the doctor's in an atmosphere of deepest gloom, but

Once he's said you're O.K.,
You sigh and have a bill to pay.

Amusements? Mostly at the weekend, because "after tea, I have 6 sums, 4 preps and a comp. to write", while Father read *The Mail*. When gardening was unthinkable because of the weather and Uncle found the evenings rather dull, he, submerged by batteries, accumulators, valves and a cabinet, and with his leaflet *The Man's Dearest Hobby*, made a wireless set, a wonderful companion. It took several weeks and several fits of temper.

Canned music was beginning to displace home entertainment; whereas father whistled tunes learned in the trenches, mother sang old-fashioned refrains from her childhood, choirboy brother hymns, the girl sings "pop jazz" in the bath and camp (that is Guide camp) ditties. The cinema was becoming respectable; "a dozen years ago, who would have dreamt of taking a School to the cinema?" After a visit to the Exchange, "now when I telephone, I can picture the operator plugging in the connection".

Although the craze soon faded, a verse praised

this nimble magic thing,
That dances on a piece of string,
Nor even stops when bell doth ring.

Why, even the Head Yo-Yoed occasionally. In these "gay old days", what about a visit to the exhibition of children's books at South Kensington museum; "Good little Janes and Naughty Willies".

People walked more, carrying rucksacks on rambles. Bicycles remained the commonest daily transport. Third class train compartments, normally seating six each side, were often crowded, but "it is among ordinary people that amusing incidents are common".

"Intense excitement! Eager expectation! Hopeful anticipation! Anxiety, fear, dread!" – a first trip from Croydon in an aeroplane. One 4-engined giant weighing 14 tons carried thirty quite comfortably and a large quantity of luggage; tiny single-engined planes were flying about easily and naturally. "Aeroplanes can ascend and descend quite safely at times, yet our hearts were throbbing as though they would burst". The plane reached an altitude of between 1, and 2,000 feet, at 80mph – "What a speed!" Jean Batten and a seaplane on the Sound thrilled.

There was an almost automatic acceptance of religious observances; indeed, should the BBC Orchestra play on Sundays? On school holidays, there were often prayers and always a Sunday service, whatever the nearest church might be. Articles assumed the existence of God, several actually praised Him.

Royalty was distantly revered, Royal occasions enjoyed. The arrangements for a Royal Wedding might safely have been entrusted to the organising ability of Miss Hodgson. For the Royal Silver Jubilee, all other Enfield schools were turned loose in the park and presented with bags of buns. Not so ECS nor EGS, who traipsed to Winchmore Hill cinema. The celebrations "added brightness to our outlook, giving us ever-welcome extra holidays." The Head commented: "It is only those who have not tried teaching who think that we have too many holidays already". Five guineas were contributed to King George's Jubilee Trust Fund.

"The opening of the Spring Term was saddened for us all by the death of our well-beloved King George V, who will always be remembered for his devotion to the duties of his high office, which won for him the love and admiration of his subjects. School closed January 28, the day of the Royal Funeral, in token of our grief and our sympathy with the Royal Family".

The Abdication of Edward VIII received no official mention, although girls undoubtedly took sides. For George VI's Coronation, each pupil received a beautifully illustrated book and a week's holiday. The Hall was artistically decorated in the national colours. Juniors successfully produced a little play depicting the actual ceremonies. One lucky prefect had a seat for the procession, three favoured seniors attended a Youth meeting in the Albert Hall, the Empire youth service in Westminster Abbey and watched the State drive to Guildhall.

In 1933, the Underground reached Southgate, then Enfield West (now Oakwood), changing the character of the countryside. Not everyone applauded the frequent service of cheap trains, fearing the invasion of hordes of East End vandals.

Then, as now, there was always the weather: peasoup November fogs and floods brought colds, influenza and pneumonia.

Our work is enormously handicapped

National difficulties were conspicuously felt in the continuing, indeed increasing, inadequacies of the building. The rapidly rising population caused problems for Middlesex in maintaining, by 1937, fifty secondary schools with a total roll of over 22,000. The provision of cloakrooms was insufficient, the Hall, a thoroughfare, had to be used for class teaching.

ECS would have accepted happily the reduced design for new buildings (eg. ceilings of teaching rooms lowered by a foot), but had no option. Hopes were raised, hopes were dashed. At Prize Giving in the presence of the Lord Chancellor's sister, Miss Broome seized her annual opportunity: fitting everyone in was worse than the hardest crossword puzzle. The hoped-for extensions, which would have cost some £8,000, were postponed indefinitely. Girls still settled in the corridors and on landings, there perchance to work, perchance to bemoan National Economy, which cancelled the plans for the much needed and long promised new wing and library.

New gym equipment had to suffice: "we now mount roofwards on six new ropes and bruise ourselves upon two new saddles". In the Head's last year, two new gymhorses had been bought for "the benefit of those with vaulting ambitions", whilst "new shining yellow forms replace those worn out by the fairy feet of dainty (?) damsels". Suggestions for improvement were invited. The first notion was a revolving platform to vary the monotony of Assemblies, the second that armchairs and sofas should replace chairs and stools. Perspex glass should be put in windows, not as a primitive double glazing, but to make them proof against the excitable waving of arms and legs performed by people on the window-sills. Water in fire buckets should be frozen to prevent spillage, walls adorned with photographs of film stars. Zip fasteners on carpets would facilitate laying and removing. Six full-length looking glasses and a continuous spray of Yardley's Lavender from an arrangement in the ceiling would increase the pleasantness of life. The simplest would, of course, be a new Hall!

Clearly, the girls could offer no solutions.

Surprise was expressed that the Music room ceiling was still intact, for, despite redecoration in 1933, internal conditions were poor. The same old pictures hung on the walls, locker doors still swung open disclosing their intriguing contents to passers-by, table-desks still collapsed at inappropriate moments. Replacement of the kitchen curtain by a frail-looking asbestos partition was not considered advantageous.

Self-help came to a partial rescue of the library, housed "Outside the History Room Corridor". There, instead of behind the curtain, could be VI preparation periods in silence: could be, but whether there ever were, ever have been, such silences is questionable.

"Every new book is a joy to the Librarians' hearts". MCC provided books proportionately to the school population, but the contents were generally deemed old-fashioned. Miss Crombie lent twelve and presented others, as did three other Mistresses, six girls, three forms, the Public library (eg. *A Handbook of Commercial Geography, Twenty Years After*), and the Governors, who gave those indispensables, the *Encyclopaedia Britannica* and *The New Oxford Dictionary*. Not only books: in mid-decade, a blue feather duster and a new pair of steps, then a fine oak suite of furniture "worthy of the dignity and of the studiously inclined who do Prep. within its sacred precincts". Thanks to the devoted efforts of librarians and Sixth formers, the library was open daily from 4 to 4:15pm.

Excitement rose in 1935 because "next door to the balance room is resplendent with glass cases displaying sundry stones, butterflies and birds' eggs", in other words, a museum, which also housed stuffed birds and the grisly skeleton of a rabbit.

For girls, poorly-lit cloakrooms were the greatest source of dissatisfaction.

> In the school of Enfield County
> There's a place they call a cloakroom
> Called the lower downstairs cloakroom.
> There the thirds and fourths assemble
> Hoping there their clothes to hang up,
> Vainly hoping, for they never
> Even see a peg or a locker.
> Place of mystery, place of wonder,
> Where the shoes at midnight wander,
> Where the pairs all turn to triplets,
> For the left shoe with its right shoe
> Never are they seen together.
>
> But the hats aloof above this
> Watch with silent, deepening wonder
> Well they know each hurrying owner
> Never will her own hat discover,
> For the cleaners and the sweepers
> Always mix them up together
> In the school of Enfield County,
> In a place they call a cloakroom
> Called the lower downstairs cloakroom.
>
> (Two Losers)

An effective lament, resulting in a series of swaps. Staff took over this horror, First forms used the enlarged Staff cloakroom, small for 100 girls but well-lighted and the duty prefect could see everyone. The Middle school acquired the large cloakroom: "never again will the Prefect on Late Duty have to listen to grumbles and complaints of lost shoes". Foolish words.

By 1931, girls were startled at all hours of the day by tinklings from the Office. Someone had not, for the hundredth time, fallen over the School bell. It was the telephone: a telephone but still gaslight.

The inquisitive mouse, overhearing lessons as he pottered along the stone passages, frightened by Bunty in the Cookery room and terrified by the bell, provided a half-welcome diversion.

Outside? Near the gate were ten respectable gardens. On the rubbish dump behind the bike shed, haunted by a cat of unknown origin, girls held the funeral of a blown-down tree. Where later Sixth formers were allowed to do private study in the summer, trees were planted in the field, partly to screen the decaying Gym. The Gym might decay, but for the main building, only an earthquake could alter such a sound constitution.

The Head herself was unusually, indeed uniquely, silent on the building's shortcomings in her final Report. She felt, perhaps, defeated by the economic climate and relieved that they would henceforth be someone else's anxiety.

CHAPTER EIGHTEEN

Poor little new girls

The 214 different names recorded of the entrants in Miss Brooome's last six years show changes such as the first Shirley and Sheila; 97 had one name only, 20 received also surnames. Again, one or two – Davida, Laurie – suggest parental disappointment. Three – Adelaide, Mireille, Valentine – reappear only once.

There is a new leader, Joan, 73 of them, displacing Mary 70 and Margaret 68. Nearest rivals were Eileen and Joyce, increasing in popularity, with 40 each, Kathleen 35, Dorothy/Dorothea and May 30 each. Eighteen were the first, but not the last, of their names, but 13 remain unique; Abigail, Agatha, Allix, Ceirwen, Damaris, Dorcas, Druscilla, Finella, Margaretta, Milvena, Ninon, Theodosia – and Peace.

A few had had chequered schooling at three or more establishments; one had changed five times, returning thrice to the same one. One had received some education in the Rhineland, another at an Egyptian convent. Whereas 36 came from the London area and suburbs, the influx of 23 from Scotland, Wales and no fewer than 12 different counties is noticeable; 82, already uprooted from familiar surroundings, suffered the double misfortune of arriving during a school year.

With the virtual disappearance of Dame schools, fewer had been educated privately; Enfield Preparatory sent 11, Holy Family convent 9, other RC schools 7, Bycullah 7 and various nearby institutions 12. Elementary schools provided 90%; of the local ones, the most favoured were St Andrew's 54, Southbury Road 77, Lavender Road 79, Chase Side 88, Bush Hill Park 96 and Chesterfield 104.

First recommended by her Head teacher, a would-be entrant had to sit an entrance examination, marks for this and any other tests, such as Intelligence, being considered together with her school record. Apparently, just over one-third qualified and just under one-third went on to secondary education.

The standard annual fee of 15 guineas, which still included books, stationery, apparatus and the games' fee, was paid by relatively few – 70 in all. As the decade progressed, most received reductions to 12 guineas, and, through ten gradations, to £1:2:6 or total remission. The LCC paid one girl's fees. All could apply for remission, total or partial, or interest-free loans. A special free place might be awarded for one year. Junior awards, discontinued after 1937, and Intermediate grants (£3-£9) helped many; many more received maintenance grants, generally £1-£3 but for some up to £9, and one 10/- towards travel. At least 11 enjoyed free dinners 1934-1937. Overall in Middlesex, about 52% had free places in 1934 and 27% paid full fees, for Enfield almost 75% and 9·3%. There were clearly cases of poverty and hardship, some genteelly concealed.

From Stage Coach Driver (deceased) to Cinema Organist, relieving officer to tennis racket bender

Of the 629 girls who enrolled in Miss Broome's last years, OA fathers 99 and labourers 90 were more noticeably numerous than proprietors.

Differences, social and financial, are marked, some the result of the past, others forerunners. A compositor and a clerk were both unemployed. Another had two part-time jobs as manual instructor and staff carpenter. A lift attendant had lost his left arm in the War; another disabled soldier was an occasional nightwatchman. A painter and three nurserymen were invalids, one being subsequently divorced. A medical missionary was divorced by his wife who received no alimony. Three mothers were separated, one deserted by that Music Hall figure, a commercial traveller in corsets. Six fathers had retired.

At least two fathers, and one mother, died during their daughter's time at ECS, but the huge total of 41 had already died, including two regular soldiers. Three widows worked as cook, dressmaker and Ladies' Cloakroom Attendant. Five had remarried. Two stepfathers were a bookbinder and a railway guard. Five girls were looked after by two guardians (one a barrister), two uncles (one a farmer) and a 'Single Woman' (Father's late occupation unknown). The family unit was becoming less stable; girls had to cope with unhappy changes, as well as financial crisis. An extreme example: – father's business failed, he took a menial job from which he had to retire, the family let rooms to paying guests, the girl won a Junior scholarship and an Intermediate award, yet they could not make ends meet.

The largest number, 74, was connected with trade, mainly retail: 18 commercial travellers (a few already calling themselves sales representatives) tried to sell, among other things, buttons, health products and ladies' underwear; 75 more worked at all levels in every possible outlet – food and drink, clothing, household, luxury and leisure goods. Interesting now are an Oysterman (Lab.), a Mantle manufacturer and a Sign and Glass writer (Prop. retail).

Clerks, including a Sports Club secretary, numbered 69, civil servants (eg. chief foreign surveyor) 14. Education supported 12 and local government at least 15, as dustmen, controller of public lighting, superintendents of the fire brigade and ambulance services, librarians 2. Twelve were caretakers, janitors, porters, commissionaires, a Conservative club steward and the manager of a children's boating pool.

Work at RSAF, 26, and other factories, at least 50, absorbed many, ranging from bosses through charge or bench hands, warehousemen and storekeepers to the humblest artisans. Fourteen were general labourers, two navvies, a ganger, ashhopper, ebonite turner, goldblocker, rubber moulder, veneerer, wheelwright.

The Post Office employed 24, 14 were in various ranks of the police, five in the Services, one in the Merchant Navy. The scope for many varieties of engineers, 35, widened in electrical and wireless businesses. More were in transport: 20 on the railways, manual and clerical, mainly LNER: roads, directly and indirectly, took 68, from chauffeurs to cycle dealer and A.A. patrolman. Eleven were in printing and four in the Gas industry.

Landwork remained important for 34 owners and labourers, from pig-dealers and greyhound trainer to the Clerk of the Royal Agricultural Society.

House workers, some 35, varied from bricklayers to scaffolders and window cleaners.

In the professions were: two chartered accountants, a company secretary: two ministers of religion: architect, draughtsman, fine etcher, engravers: glassblower and scientific instrument maker: four musicians helped by six piano tuners, makers and checkers.

A helpful feature of our school life

The Thirties saw closer relations with the Parents' Union to which school owed much, especially financially. So many parents participated on Sports Day that two races had to be run. While Miss Broome everlastingly inveighed against premature leavers and clerical jobs, she similarly, but warmly, commended medical inspection and homework supervision.

In 1931, the Union had its first magazine report; it needed, as always, fresh organising blood. Besides the AGM, interesting lectures and enjoyable Whist drives, the committee and members held a Garden Fête from which they granted £20 to the Dymchurch holiday fund. All parents were urged to become *active* members. There was, and is, no subscription. Four years later, even social events were not well supported. There's nothing new.

Long and unwearied service

Considerable changes took place in the 15-strong Governing body. Sir Henry, the sole original, resigned as Chairman in 1935, to everyone's sincere regret. Vice-Chairman for ten years, H.A.D. Brown, Esq., assumed the office, his wife, of course, presenting Sports Day prizes. Only four others served throughout these last years, including Mrs Rothwell, now Vice-chairman, and Mr Collier who presented a Cup; its purpose is unrecorded and he was not present for its award because of bereavement. Members for shorter periods were (ten years) Mr Taylor, (seven years) Mr Mason and Mrs Davies , wife of the local MP, who twice officiated at Sports Days. Sir Henry, lady members and E.R.B. gave prizes for OGA Whist drives.

Relations between Governors and school remained close.

With unfailing support and encouragement

Although by their own wish, she mentioned no individual names, Miss Broome continued to pay tribute to her Staff. "They realise to the full that school studies are almost worse than useless if they are not accompanied by the formation of a fine character and the cultivation of good manners".

Further temporary reduction of 10% in their salaries in 1931 was not restored for four years. Women always received less than men: a graduate started at £264 (men, £276), and, with annual increments of £12 (£15), reached a maximum of £420 (£528). Non-graduates fared less well: £192 (£204) by £9 (£12) to £342 (£432). Even the subscription to the Association of Assistant Mistresses (AAM) had to be reduced from 2 to 1½ guineas. Graduate qualifications were the norm; those who taught non-university subjects were expected to hold a recognised diploma. Several appointees, although highly qualified and some with experience, were on a term's probation. Maybe this suited both parties; the Head could dismiss with little reason given, the Mistress could apply for another post without stigma. Many still had to supervise games, whatever their subject, ability, willingness or state of health. Three or four graduate student teachers were accepted most years for two of their three teaching practice terms.

Of the old stagers, Miss Forrest remained the dominant figure, continuing to organise le Cercle, holidays and Christmas parties. She helped the Chief Inspector elect to run a course on the correlation of Arts subjects in Sixth forms. The Vice-Principal of le Lycée Français commented that ECS figured annually at the head of the list, distinctly above all other schools in written and oral work.

Substitutes, visiting or simply unsettled Mistresses numbered ten, of whom six were scientists; despite staying a year or less, they involved themselves in activities. Miss Sempronia Alice Baker was remembered less for a ramble to Bayford (she lost the way) than for indoor fireworks skilfully manipulated.Another scientist received 25/- each working day for less than one month. Miss Lydia Grace Sewell, with a doctorate in literature from Peru, had had six posts in thirteen years, and taught Spanish, German, Junior English and Geography.

A few left more impression. Miss Eileen Margaret Farrell taught Mathematics to lower and middle , Science to lower and Botany to middle, schools, and helped with both scientific society and swimming, leaving " for a more important post". Miss Marian Whelan thrilled with a much appreciated demonstration of liquid air and escorted 40 girls to Enfield Cable Works, where, in school time, they enjoyed a splendid tea. Indeed, "what an excellent President the Scientific Society had – a bumper year of events. What fun!" Leaving after five terms to "embark on the sea of matrimony", she returned to give a talk on the things seen on the tea table.

Truly did the magazine comment that some Mistresses were as ships that pass in the night.

Fortunately, two Scientists remained longer. Miss Elsie Mary Bruce studied the flora in Tanganyika (Tanzania) for one term during her eight years' stay. Guide captain, she examined for Cadet badges and gave talks and bird imitations. Miss Julie Pheasant held lab. teas, donated books to the library and accompanied both rambles and a Paris party.

Netball soon improved with the energetic coaching of Miss Gladys Victoria (Jane) Bowen, a sharp-tongued character. She played in the Staff team, helped in the Scientific society, on holidays and at several Guide camps. Her Mathematics lessons were, inevitably, old-fashioned: "Merchants buying at X pence a pound and selling at £Y a ton, or express trains which overtook slow ones", yet girls felt safe working through the textbook to secure a sound GSC result.

Apart from one transient, the DSc. department enjoyed stability with Miss Hilda Gertrude Sturgeon, "the best organised teacher we ever had", who took Needlework for one day a week. "Each lesson, she began by teaching one basic step – how to run and fell a seam or how to cut bias binding – and issued us with a small piece of material on which to work a sample. While we began this in strict silence, she went round and marked last week's homework, finishing just as the bell went. Our task was to finish the sample, press it and stitch it into a Needlework book opposite our summary of the instructions ready for next week's lesson. Efficient – and deadly!"

Graduate Miss Pattie Jarvis taught Cookery, Needlework and Hygiene to Forms I-IV, so was a popular helper with preparation for Cadet badges. She enquired whether girls' mothers used butter, margarine or the "new white cooking fat". *Her* sewing lessons were "more colourful, creative and enjoyable, but not at all useful. She brought a breath of fresh air; addressing us as people was not a mannerism". She read unorthodox books to them, commented on current affairs such as Munich, encouraged discussion and later collected signatures in favour of a crèche to help working mothers – ahead of her time. She became an Inspector then joined the Flour Advisory Bureau.

Art had a 2-term substitute, Modern Languages a visiting linguist ("a real life señorita") and, the last appointed, Miss Margaret Conway who also coached netball. The school Secretary left in 1936 to be replaced by OG and one-time Guide Lieutenant Joyce Schollick.

These few years suggest an instability comparable to that of recent times. Only one Mistress stayed until retirement; 18 averaged less than four years each.

Miss Broome's last appointments

95 Bowen G.V.	1930-Dec 1946, 1947-1965		
96 Farrell E.M.	1930-1931	97 Jarvis P.B.	1930-Sept 1942
98 Lowe K.M.	Jan 1931-June 1931	99 Smith E.C.	Jan 1931
100 Southans E.W.	Feb 1931-Easter1931	101 Relf E.M.	1931-1932
102 Sarmiento E.	1931?	103 Stewart M.	1931-1932
104 Whelan M.	1931-Apr 1933	105 Bruce E.M.	1932-1940
106 Pheasant J.H.	May 1933-Easter 1946	107 Green F.	1934-1935
108 Baker S.A.	1934-1935	109 Eyre L.I.M.	1935
110 Sewell L.G.	1935-1936	111 Sturgeon H.G.	1936-1939
	112 Conway M. 1936-1		

Assistants:

French: Mlles. Broglio, Foulon, Morénas, Ollier, Pignochet, Serres

Spanish: Sta. Sarmiento

A 'Pre can only be in one place at the best

And those Senior mortals, the twenty or so Prefects? Two tell their stories.

All is not gold that glitters

The duties of a prefect are many and are fair,
But the best of such fine glories prove a nasty snare.
You nearly wrench your arm out with ringing loud the bell
And are always kept on tenterhooks to mark the minutes well.
And if by chance the bell should be a minute fast or slow
Of course that was the prefect's fault; it always is, you know.
Well, lesson bells are not as bad as having to go out
To tintinnabulate it in the field and round about,
To gather in the maidens when interval is done,
To watch them unconcernedly straggling one by one.

Of course, the school is very good, there never was a form
That did not have its own form 'pre' and strive to keep her warm.
However much you push and shove to keep them all in line,
And hit and nod and sh! and sigh and pine,
They always seem to talk and laugh or look the other way
As if it's nought to do with you whate'er they say.

I'll tell you now a glorious task known only to VIA,
And that's collecting registers – it really is O.K.
When you begin, it seems light work, just one or two, you know,
But when you've got but half of them you do not quite think so.
And then when lots are missing and the time is getting late,
And oh! your arm is aching and feels as though 'twould break,
You go up to the staff-room to find they are not there,
You miserably totter down – you've half a mind to swear.

Another glorious privilege I do not dare leave out
Is going on late duty (without a shade of doubt).
When usually you roll to school at five or ten to nine,
You have to be there early in weather foul or fine,
And then you have the glorious joy of standing by the door
To take the names of those who're late – you wish that they were more.

And so, dear little children, when you get into VIA,
Remember this, a tip from me, it is not all – "I say,
What a jolly time those prefects have!!!"

(Rita Ikin)

and

The Pre's lament (1934)

Who are they that come into the hall
For morning prayers come last of all,
And then in lines uneven fall?
    My Form.

Who are they when they go upstairs
Forget that they must walk in pairs
Until I catch them unawares?
    My Form.

Who are they when they're coming in
Always make a frightful din,
Till I must scold them for this sin?
    My Form.

Who are they now will ask me why
I look dejected, often sigh?
To them I'll give this brief reply,
    My Form.

(Josie Barker)

CHAPTER NINETEEN

Appearance is very near becoming immaculate

Uniform not merely blurred social distinctions, it helped to provide an identity, yet it was not wholly compulsory until 1936. A photograph in 1930 of the Study (VIA) shows only one in uniform; in contrast, all but one of VIB in 1937 wear regulation summer cotton frocks with white cuffs and Peter Pan collars. The school tailor or clothing lady still measured and took orders. The pupil, duly dressed, was then carefully inspected.

Badges, which included a strip of material for Colours and an unfortunately large P for Prefect, were sewn onto the velveteen top of the all-wool or special serge gymslip, which, 21" long, cost 4/11¾. Green and white ties crept in; they have now virtually disappeared.

The magazine reminded pupils that hats (coat and hat, 14/11) must be worn daily. The stiff sailors were replaced by panamas in summer. Even this mercifully lighter headwear became unpopular because it clipped the ears. In winter, girls dared to wear velours tilted on the back of the head and turned up all the way round. On one expedition, 400 hats set out but the wind ensured the return of but 399.

Still no-one changed for gym or games, although divided skirts for tennis matches were recommended in 1936 as a good pattern, smart and allowing more freedom.

Minor details altered as girls became more clothes-conscious, more emancipated. An early article, intended to be hilarious, indicates one revolt: belts were worn higher and higher.

In magazine advertisements, school knickers, all wool, with removable elastic to make washing easier, in green, navy, scarlet or fawn, 12", cost 1/11¾, other sizes at proportionate prices. A maid's corselette, 28"-34", was offered at 3/11¾, a short-sleeved vest at 2/6½, silk stockings at 2/- a pair, wool scarves 1/11¾, fur-backed gloves 5/-. "Kosi-clad for Little Folks" was neither explained nor priced. In more frivolous vein, a cashmere frock and knicker set, Eton collar, silk embroidery and ruched waist, was advertised at 6/11¾. A party dress of "art silk crepe, daintily ruched at shoulder and waist", Peter Pan collar and puffed sleeves, was a snip at 4/11¾. Animal nightdress sachets, "the most popular gift", cost 2/11¾.

The Greatest of Schooldays

Picture, if you will, 400 maidens clad in white array,
We all sing hymns in descant, and rousing school songs too,
While French and Spanish classes both show what they can do.
All this is most enjoyable, but what we most admire
Is the sweet melodious concert by our talented School Choir.
We see short witty plays and scenes from Molière
(Which are added to the programme to give a highbrow air).
We laugh – when others do – and applaud, for there's no doubt
That they're excellently acted, whatever they're about!

The School Report. We listen with pride and interest keen
(We never even dreamed before how clever we had been).
The Governors make speeches and more of them propose
Long votes of thanks, and after, the remaining few thank those.
Ah! now I had forgotten, and I haven't mentioned how
Before all this happens, quite a hundred damsels bow
To a lady, flower-fêted, who kindly gives to each,
In turn, a prize, and follows up with a most gracious speech,
And with becoming modesty thereafter will declare
That she always has admired the clever girls who gain
Such prizes, as while yet at school she used to seek in vain. ...

She's found out that, as a general rule,
The Great were never very good, or very bright at school.
This sentiment we (mostly) are ready to admire,
Although of other platitudes we very quickly tire,
Feeling rather fearful lest after all she may
Forget to ask the Governors for an extra holiday.
(She did, alas!)

(J. Scopes)

May we detect the birth of modern cynicism? The Lord Chancellor's sister was the wretchedly forgetful lady.

Speech day programmes were long: small wonder there was neither refreshment nor reception afterwards. There were rarely fewer than 15 items, in one, two or more of the five languages taught, countless part-songs, choral verse-speaking, even a mime with music. Everyone was expected to join in the opening and closing hymn: *Bright the Vision that delighted* (with descant), *Now Thank we all our God, Let us with a gladsome mind, Praise to Jehovah, the Mightiest King in the Highest,* the perennial *I Vow to Thee, My Country* – the sort they sang on Empire Day – and, of course, *God save the King* to close proceedings.

The vocal offering causing the greatest sensation was the School Hymn, given its première in 1932. "We are especially proud as it really is *our* hymn, written and composed by Miss Broome"; on the programme, Mrs. Crofts, wife of the former Master, is credited with the musical arrangement. What distressed the Music Mistress was that E.R.B. insisted on composing the music out of a mishmash of old hymn tunes, although some parents thought it wonderful to have a poet and a musician for a Head. The lady herself, "sadly aware of its present dirge-like effect", hoped to find happier music. This implies satisfaction with the words. Yet when her successor, relying on this remark, commissioned a new tune which was played at her first Speech day, E.R.B. was heartbroken.

> Onward Ever! Onward Ever!
> Strong to toil with brave endeavour,
> Till the task be done.
> To the joy of work well ended,
> By the hand of all commended.
> Onward Ever!

> Onward ever! Onward Ever!
> Fear and doubt shall stay us never,
> Till the goal be won.
> To the vision of our dreaming,
> To the hope before us ever gleaming,
> Onward Ever!

> Onward Ever! Onward Ever!
> Faith the darkest clouds will sever,
> O'er them shines the sun.
> To the glory of awaking,
> Where the dawn of Heaven is breaking,
> Onward Ever!

How much these words mattered to Miss Broome is clear from her annual request: "I now ask the girls to voice for me in the School Song the hopes and ideals which I desire for them now and for ever".

Tuesday, December 1, 1931, was the last time the school used the Assembly Rooms; they were burned down the following night. Future gatherings in the Hall meant both separate junior and senior events and inviting fewer guests. However, the unanimous verdict was that the advantages of having Prize Giving in school outweighed the disadvantages.

The speaker at 6:15pm, Wednesday, November 30, 1932, was Mrs. Wintringham, president of the National Council of Domestic Studies, which gave the Head the opportunity of revealing yet again her servantless upbringing and her delight in homecrafts. For Friday, November 16, 1933, the Danish National Anthem was learned in honour of Mme Genée Isett, former chairman of the Anglo-Danish Society. Miss Broome had paid an official visit to Danish schools.

Fittingly, Sir Henry ("who has discovered the secret of eternal youth") and Lady Bowles were the Guests of Honour at the Silver Jubilee Prize Giving at the odd time of 5pm, Thursday, November 12, 1934. "We are most happy to have him with us still and we hope to have this happiness on many future occasions. We gratefully remember his valiant help in the past and today he has added to these by undertaking what is always an arduous task" of speaking and distributing prizes. He subsequently performed a more arduous task, that of presenting a Jubilee Medal to each pupil. The magazine contained the unintentionally ambiguous comment: "Of the speeches, we will say little, for we know that they are well remembered by all who listened to them".

The next speaker, Miss Felvus, retired Head of Tottenham High, gave "a wise and graceful speech and got us a holiday".

The Head annually begged parents to let their daughters complete the course, warned that premature leavers secured only the same work as girls from elementary schools and repeated her hope that each girl would render true and faithful service to God and to those with whom her lot was cast.

Deceiving repetition of results under different headings is perhaps why 10% of the magazine was devoted to recording them. They do confirm that few, relatively, completed the 5-year course.

Over these years, 9 girls achieved Inter-Arts, one Inter-Science and 16 their HSC, with 10 special credits in French (O), 7 distinctions in French, 2 in Italian and one each in Geography and English. Individuals secured two State Scholarships, four going up to Oxford (three with scholarships), four to London (one Exhibition) and two to Chelsea and Homerton. Not quite the Higher Education figures of earlier years. Matriculation numbers (at least 101, 9 Honours) were often more than twice the national average. Almost all succeeded at the first attempt and in the minimum of years, French again dominating with over 100 distinctions and over 70 special oral credits. Three girls each had five distinctions in 1933. Another 103 passed GSC. Much sympathy was expressed for one matriculating girl prevented by illness from coming to receive her well-earned certificate.

RSA provided certificates: Spanish (Elementary 14, Oral 2, Intermediate and Advanced, 2nd class, one each), Italian (Elementary, one), French Oral 73 (16*), Advanced 2 (one 1st and one 2nd Class, both with Oral*) – a grand total of 94 passes. The few who entered for the Concours Spécial and Grand Concours achieved at least 13 prizes, 5 certificates, one medal and £5. The French Institute awarded 18 scholarships and 23 certificates, often with "Mention Très Bien".

Form prizes, in order of merit and not given lightly, varied in numbers, several forms going ignominiously unrewarded. Year I received 86, Year II 71, Year III 51, Years IV and V 68 each, and, for named subjects, VIB 38 and VIA 20. Prizes for Housecraft totalled 31 and for the annual French Poetry Recitation/Reading competition (two entrants from each form) 98. An outside firm donated three awards for improvement in handwriting. Many girls chose books on animals, birds or flowers.

Although Colours were distributed at the end of the appropriate term, Games and House shields and individual championship cups led up to School Colours. The Dux medal for each Head Girl brought the ceremony to a fitting close.

God giveth speech to all, song to a few

The choir pursued its ways of pleasantness, performing nobly under Miss Woods' incomparable tuition. As well as carol singing, it delighted the Parents' Union, and, in the Tudor Room, the local Shakespeare society. Even when three choirs competed against them at the EMF, School carried all before it, seniors and juniors coming first always, and the self-trained and novice choirs, double trios, French singers (groups and soloists) and individual entrants frequently. They won, at a conservative estimate, 51 silver cups, 7 targes, 5 pictures, 10 silver and 11 bronze medals, 79 1st, 9 3rd and 5 4th prizes and 161 certificates.

Let us not rest on our laurels

Traditions continued. Empire Day followed its customary pattern, culminating in saluting the flag before Sir Henry. "We realise that, with a few exceptions, women will vocally never become sergeant majors". Seemingly more popular, Trafalgar Day, with old and new sea-shanties, remained an Open Day, when parents, "fond or proud have the unique opportunity of seeing their daughters at work, and how angelic they looked".

Although it was past history to girls, Armistice Day remained the same: a short address in the Hall, the Silence, the wreath-laying ceremony, and a donation to Services Welfare Societies. "The fact that we received several articles inspired by the occasion seems to contradict the notion that war and armistice mean nothing to modern youth".

General events in school were few. Roy Newland's masterly dramatic version of *Macbeth* became an institution. When Engel Lund gave a folk song recital in several languages, "how we enjoyed his rendering of *La Cigale et la Fourmi*".

French Prayers enlivened *le quatorze juillet*, France's National Day. Another attempt to vary Assembly was less successful. Given the opportunity to choose a hymn, the Sixth assumed, correctly, that the Head would not check, and, wrongly, that she would be stunned on opening her hymnbook on the platform to find that it was in Welsh. "The girls must have given me the wrong number"; school had to sing either the preceding or the following hymn. *Onward Christian Soldiers* was one of her favourites; puzzled as to why only the first and last verses were ever sung, girls reached the astonishing conclusion that one verse mentioned hell and the other Christian brothers.

The whole school and subsequently a netball match were filmed by three cameramen on a cold November morning. No-one knew the reason and the results remain untraced.

It is undeniable that the theft of the tailor's money and a fête to replace it created welcome excitement.

Stamp collecting was introduced one year: "School will be renowned for its collection"; another short-lived enthusiasm, for this is the sole reference.

House reports remain a mixture of praise for achievement, exhortation to support and pleas to reduce the number of Conduct Marks. Potted biographies of the five Saints ("St Winifred is the patron saint of virgins") failed to inspire. Chronicles continued interchangeable: "the House was climbing the ladder of success ... Everyone must work together as a team ... What, no trophies? Woe is me! I cannot think of anything on which to congratulate the House ... United we stand, divided we fall ... We did not shine with our customary brilliance ... It is UP to you all".

Two stand out. "You (ie. Margarines) now hold the wheel of fortune in your hands. Steer the vessel to success". "Hail! St Ursulines! You have once more been faithful votaries of the learned Minerva. The Work Shield is ours for the 6th year – to us *labor voluptas est*".

A very attractive publication of its kind,

... which sounds like damning with faint praise.

The Head was forced throughout to support the magazine publicly and to urge its purchase. Individuals provided delightful posters, others copied out articles – and the editor wrung her hands. Readers were invited to sympathise with a rapidly ageing editor surrounded by a harassed committee. "The room resembles a large waste paper basket; articles on grubby scraps of paper, articles resplendent on gorgeous notepaper, articles of all sorts and sizes litter the window-sill, tables and desks, while the occupants are obliged to stand". Or girls were treated to heavy sarcasm. "It was undoubtedly with the kindest of intention of not distracting the already overworked VIA that the majority did not respond to the appeal to send in something". Brilliant contributions were deliberately withheld. Juniors did compensate for their elders' deficiencies, several pieces scintillating, apparently, with flashes of genius. The next problem was choosing what to publish.

Better was to come. "In this year of grace, 1934, we, the editors, present our 25th Anniversary Number. We keep our old price, and hope the numbers of our patrons will increase in proportion to our generosity". This silver-coloured 44-page issue was sold out.

There is again more original verse than prose. Homework surely inspired *Le Coquelicot* and *Amici et Inimici* (bird and cat), poems on homework, the first day at school, work based on set authors, parody, pastiche or misapplication of quotations. *What's in a Name*, a so-called narrative using Staff names, is parochial. More aim to instruct: *Travelling back through Time (Camelot), The Gay Old Days* (a village school sixty years ago), *Personification of the Past.*

Many remain childish with yet more fairies, little bunnies at play, King Winter with Jack Frost and Prince Hailstone. Most are on the familiar subjects of the natural world, the glories of the seasons, the weather, the stars, *A Contemplative Cat*. Too many clichés in subject choice, thought and expression make it impossible to select any offering as indicating future writing triumphs.

The pleasant custom of exchanging magazines with other schools continued, although none of those received remain.

Advertisements undoubtedly helped its survival. A long article on The Secretary and her Work – a Career for Educated Girls, included blurred photographs of blind-folded touch-typists and details of trainings from various ladies and colleges. Others hold an antiquarian charm: an offer to print a better, brighter Sports Day programme ("Cut this out and show it to your Head Mistress or Games Mistress"): the Paris Academy of Dressmaking and Millinery: Woodlands School of Domestic Science: Bluemell's Bicycle Accessories, Smith's Cycle Speedometer (19/6 complete) and the Apex Inflator Co. Ltd. (cycle pumps 1/6 or 2/-): Dunlop Blue Flash Tennis Rackets (from 42/-): Bassett's Liquorice Allsorts (3d a quarter loose): local businesses advertising jewellery, Christmas presents, laundry: faithful Grays, newsagents, "special attention given to phone orders for books of any description": the Froebel Educational Institute: London Radio College Ltd., which offered a fine career – "for any boy".

Charity begins at Home

An annual fête raised £20-£35 for Dymchurch; the financial circumstances of participants were common knowledge. This patronising and insensitive approach does not seem to have upset girls, at least not publicly. Each had to save all the year round; the 30 who went in 1931 pointed the way by collecting £19.

Keen anticipation gave way to hasty goodbyes and the loading of luggage as a shrill whistle announced the arrival of the train at Enfield Chase station. Once arrived, the first thing most did was to write home. Miss Broome concerned herself with literally everything, from buying ice-cream and supervising meals to taking evening prayers. A Parents' Union mother acted as her lieutenant.

The weather was always good, the amusements invariable. On one walk, they sang all the way home, so someone kindly threw them a penny. A barrel organ provided amusement; as there was no monkey, girls offered their services. They were lucky enough to find a haystack which provided a good background for photography. They enjoyed a fancy dress party, shell collecting, a concert and dancing. E.R.B. presented pocket money to winners of a laughing competition. Presents were bought for parents, the Head and any helpers. In the year of her retirement, 33 went to St Mary's Bay holiday camp, where she allowed them to paddle. Deep gratitude was regularly expressed to her for her organisation and good care.

What parts of the outside world were considered suitable charities and how was the cash raised? Special collections on Armistice Day and, as ever, at carol services, profits from events, from special ventures (such as a collection of 1,392 farthings) were added to the increasingly unpopular Form monies handed in on Mondays. The Armistice Day wreath dropped to 15/6, then to 10/6. Ex-Services Welfare received £10:19:6 and Miss Broome's favourite British Sailors' Society regularly benefited from Trafalgar Day, £21:18:0.

The sick and needy, always with us, were helped; over various years, Enfield Cripples' Mission £8:10:0, Save the Children £6:1:0, the League of Mercy four guineas. Other beneficiaries included Dr Barnardo's two guineas, South London Mission £2, a Middlesex blind girl and the local committee for the blind £1 each, and two London, and two local, hospitals £46:11:0.

Closely linked to the contemporary situation were the Enfield Emergency Unemployment Committee £22:5:0, the Winter Distress League

£7:1:0, the Central Fund for Tuberculous Persons £2, the Memorial Fund for the pioneer gynaecologist Mary Scharlieb £1:11:6, the Necessitous Middlesex Children's Fund £3 and St Bartholemew's Stocking Appeal 5/-.

Three donations recall specific troubles: Welsh miners received five guineas in 1931, Relief for the 1934 Indian earthquake three guineas and for the Gresford Colliery Disaster six guineas.

The most generous year was the first, with £32:7:6 distributed, whereas 1936 provided less than half that amount.

CHAPTER TWENTY

So many delightful opportunities

"Among our many activities, each girl should be able to find something to help her to occupy her leisure moments happily and profitably. The right use of leisure should be one of the results of satisfactory education". Still the Victorian approach: mere enjoyment is not enough.

It is the desire of the society to find a future Ellen Terry

Sincere appreciation was regularly expressed of the untiring efforts of Miss Baxter in producing plays, Miss Rudkin in back-stage work and, later, Miss Hyslop in ticket-selling.

From comparative oblivion, the junior dramatic club raised its drooping head in 1933. Members learned to use their voices properly and to speak clearly; in memorising portions of the classics , they hoped to acquire an intimate knowledge of the great dramatists. If not an Ellen Terry, perhaps a Sarah Bernhardt, or, by 1936, an Elizabeth Bergner? One critic wrote frankly: "Few girls are handicapped with ugly voices, few are ever silent, yet the number to whom it is a pleasure to listen is small". They recovered to give a version of *The Pied Piper,* subsequently of *Oliver's Island* and two playlets for Shakespeare's Day, *A Pleasant Holiday* and *The Swineherd.*

Choice at Prize Giving and the EMF continued varied. Scenes from French classical plays matched an ambitious English content: *The Rehearsal* which actors enjoyed as much as the audience, a scene from *Kenilworth,* dramatised by O.D.R. to commemorate the senior society's 21st birthday, a playlet in Chinese fashion, an excerpt from A.A. Milne's *The Four Friends. Alice through the looking glass* was later presented for the Parents' Union. Pride of place went to wide-ranging choral Verse Speaking – Lewis Carroll, Sir Henry Newbould *(Pulchritude),* Christina Rossetti (*From Goblin Market*). Verse choirs won three 1st prizes, two Honours and five certificates at Regent Street Polytechnic festivals.

Public performances were, by later standards, few and unadventurous. In *The Knight of the Burning Pestle*, one actress had a fit of giggles on stage. Does a 70-year old blush at the memory? Judged very successful, it raised

£9 for Charities, despite the fact that two members of the cast were changed at the last minute. A planned *Hamlet* was cancelled as "our one and only moody Dane was forced to withdraw owing to pressure of work". More members ("Do join!") were obviously needed.

One production, scheduled for the notorious month of February, was announced well in advance as "you have no idea how discouraging it is to play to a half-empty Hall". Although several older girls left during the Christmas term, *The Rivals* duly materialised. School was urged to become more involved, if not by acting, then by selling tickets and coming to support their friends.

One good year, the next less so. Seniors, modestly, acted scenes from *Pickwick Papers* and the modern one-act *Thirty Minutes in a Street*. Some problems were overcome by the capable handiwork of a member's brother. "Every member performed her part well, and individual praise would be invidious".

"You shy damsels with latent histrionic ability please attend our meetings". Perhaps they did, as 1935 was one of the most successful. Little time was wasted over the choice of a play. As tickets sold slowly, everyone felt discouraged, but, after a special appeal, *Quality Street* played to two full houses, and made enough profit to permit membership of the British Drama League.

The next year saw *Pride and Prejudice* – and three changes of President. As well as studying Dramatic Art and Mime, seniors presented *Dear Brutus*, scenery and props clearly causing great fun. Its success resulted from the endless hours spent by Miss Baxter coaching self-conscious schoolgirls in portraying the characters as Barrie had invented them.

In short,

in triumph at last
The curtains closed upon the happy cast.

Do not be deterred by youth or modesty

It is easy to feel that there's nothing new when the resuscitation of an old society is trumpeted as the birth of a new one. Such was the Sketch club in 1933 in which Miss Hicks showed unfailing interest.

Art was enjoyed by encouraging original work and by learning to appreciate the work of "mature artists". This led members to London's Galleries, Royal Academy Exhibitions and to Westminster Abbey, where they noted the architectural styles.

At first small, with very keen juniors, it held a pen-and-ink competition; entries were few, but of a high standard. Later came holiday competitions and displays, prize-winning posters for the plays, sketching outside, clay modelling, printing on material, weaving, murals, calendars, work in oils and, perhaps the favourite, lino cuts. The secretary humbly felt that "complete satisfaction must always evade us, when so much lies before us". All seems modern until you read of the very jolly weekly meetings to paint wooden boxes and letter racks.

We do our best, which is reward enough

"Young ladies, you are well advised to get your sports requisites at the Sports' Outfitters to the Enfield County School, the Middlesex Education Committee and Wood Green Education Committee". Briggs survives.

Although PT was enlarged by the new 1933 syllabus, reports changed little. Disappointment was still regularly expressed that spectators were few on Saturday mornings. Sir Henry offered "a beautiful and valuable Cup, a great treasure and a fine incentive to excellence in Physical work and games", for the House whose practices were best and most punctually attended. Neither he nor the writer envisaged the extra work which this unusual benefaction, his last, would cause. St Catherine's was the first winner with 96·8%.

Lest all be thought hearty, a poetic player waxed lyrical about dew, sunset, birds.

> The sacrament of beauty is revealed
> To all who will but see it in our field.

Hockey remained the premier sport, although practices were not attended with any show of enthusiasm, despite a film and lecture by the legendary Margery Pollard. In league and friendly matches, four teams, reduced latterly to two, experienced mixed fortunes as inexperienced young players replaced premature leavers. Individual play was not bad, but the power of combination was still lacking. *Jupiter Pluvius* was also mostly unkind. Details for one season were not, perhaps wisely, recorded; for the rest, W 42, L 48, D 13, 40 colours. One popular fixture was against the Staff, "clad in armour strange". Girls flocked to join in the blood-curdling roars at thrilling Internationals.

The Netball League ceasing to exist in 1932, only friendly matches were played. Staff bravely endured frozen feet and hands to referee. Whilst one year was the most depressing on record and players failed to learn from their mistakes, results could have been worse: W 113, L 54, D 9, 29 colours. Again, premature leaving was lamented. "We are not able to include a photograph of the team as several members left before it could be taken".

The tennis team won the Sir William Prescott cup in 1931. Subsequent teams were below standard on the new asphalt courts. House matches drew enthusiastic players but few onlookers. Eventually, there were insufficient entries for even the individual championships. It did not help when the courts in front of the pavilion were waterlogged. Despite Miss Hodgson's unfailing encouragement, figures are bad: W 46, L 48, yet 30 colours were granted.

These reports could well apply 10, 20 or more years later. There was one innovation. VIB, allowed to work outside, sometimes stopped for unofficial and greatly enjoyed games of rounders. The highlight was the match at the end of the summer term after farewell feasts.

The activity which had least in its favour was the most professional. Its popularity increased with the Open Air Baths, opened in 1932 and then the largest in the country (200' long), with accommodation for 2,000. Up to 120 swam, still on Friday evenings, although only 40 could receive tuition. Thanked were Miss F. Sharp and especially Hoddie, whose chirpy and reassuring presence at examinations resulted in 51 bronze medallions, two bars, one silver and nine Instructor's certificates of the RLSS and 26 colours.

Efforts to arrange lessons in school-time failed, except for two forms, who, from 1935, enjoyed swimming in Gym. lesson-time. Staff muttered about time and, on occasion, pupils, lost on the journey.

An invitation card was issued for the annual Sports held on a July Saturday at 5pm., unless the treachery of an English summer caused postponement. The crowd of onlookers included many OGs. Nobody was allowed to receive more than two 1st prizes and one 2nd. "Few of us aspired to more than one and those whom the new rule affected didn't mind. Although prizes are very nice, we can do without them". One year, however, in "King's weather", Dr Dunbar, the Guest of Honour, evidently considered the programme too short, for she called for another race and gave a beautiful racket to the winner. Twenty colours were recorded.

A mixed bag, therefore, but, as one reporter wrote: *"Nil desperandum"*.

Le français n'est pas mort dans notre école. Vive le français!

"Mlle Forrest mérite plus que des remercments". Le Cercle *was* F.M.F.

Her absence meant no reunion 1933-1934, but every other year saw the customary varied entertainments. The long list includes at least three plays of Molière, two of Racine, *Le Cid*, and a few more modern pieces, *L'Anglais tel qu'on le parle*, *Fin de Bail*, in which she herself acted, and *Le Voyage de M. Perrichon*. Scenes were performed on one glorious occasion to some 600 visitors. She relished all the *vieux jeux et vieilles chansons*, every *soirée dansante traditionelle*, each party when French only was spoken. She took members to the theatre, specially to see the touring Comédiens de Paris, to lectures and exhibitions, with excellent attendances even on Saturday afternoons. Each *dîner à la française* ended with a toast. She gave "un discours amusant et instructif sur Paris 1800-1900".

Roll up girls and join the Scientific.

Despite the high turnover of Staff presidents, tiny progress with the museum and ritual complaints of difficulties in arranging meetings, this was the heyday of the Scientific society. A hearty welcome was extended to Mistresses and girls, "the more the merrier".

Juniors virtually took over one year, lecturing on reptiles and decoloration of flowers, but concentrating on birds; several became expert at imitating their calls. Their elders read papers on the universe, enzymes, fire extinguishers, wood, crystals, sound. They held debates – "How schoolgirls love to argue" – one on vivisection. Visitors spoke on electrical sparks and on physics. Fifth and Sixth formers talked to Enfield Aquatic Society on life in ponds and streams.

Practical work provided excitement: piscatorial expeditions for some thrilling hours at Hilly Fields: Whitewebbs and Crews Hill yielded snails' eggs, leech, water beetle and boatmen for the new aquarium. They explored Perry's plant farm and Mr Bowles' wonderful garden. There was a jolly Christmas ramble to Cuffley, others to Hadley Wood, for "Enfield's surroundings are superb for country walks, you know". Epping Forest was the annual venue for a fungus foray and pond-dipping. At Kew Gardens, "how they enjoyed themselves and how quickly the time flew by".

With light hearts and heavy cases, six biologists accompanied Miss Bruce and Miss Pheasant to Stockbury, the journey involving six changes of train and bus. Everything delighted: bees, calves, chicks, donkey, goose, jugs of hot water, candle-light, even getting up at 4am. (albeit too late for the beginning of the dawn chorus), a 20-mile nature walk. They brought back birds' eggs for the museum's new glass cases.

None of these activities, however, held a candle to the fun of the annual Lab. Tea, the most favoured feature of which was the consumption of jelly with spatulas from evaporating basins. Tea was, of course, drunk from beakers, sandwiches eaten from troughs. Gastronomic delights were followed by amusements: treasure hunt, "progressive games", photographs of Staff when young (provoking much hilarity), fireworks, chemical conjuring. Hard as it is to imagine nowadays, an increasing number – 90 in 1935 – happily joined in this innocent caper.

The Society distinguished itself

"Arranged as only expert organisers like Miss Crombie and Miss Rudkin can manage", the GHS gave girls a glimpse of different worlds, although, even here, lack of support was occasionally lamented.

School was invited to make a map of the neighbourhood for the utilisation of land surveyors, as Miss Crombie's work was known beyond the classroom. Every available Saturday, armed with notebooks, maps and pencils, members surveyed the area and recorded accurately its uses; one heroic person transferred it by means of strange symbols and colourings to the 6" OS maps.

At the Science Museum, machines and models were likened to those then found on seaside piers but without their financial limitations. O.D.R. long remembered one visit to Covent Garden, watching "women in gayly coloured overalls, knee-deep in peapods. Good, obedient girls, they wandered about on their own and duly assembled at the time fixed for our departure. We lined up the long crocodile, staff in front, prefects in rear". Half got lost, but one prefect marched the late-comers to Liverpool Street and sent them home in charge of another.

Miss Brooks brought examples of native work and products to her lecture on Grenada. Miss Crombie showed beautiful slides of glaciers (after a jolly tea), talked on place names and Edinburgh, and encouraged the preparation and reading of papers by members, thus contributing directly to their awareness of the outside world. Films on the Rockies, Everest and the mystery of the Blue Light were shown in a local cinema. Fortunate Sixth formers were escorted to Dr Stamp's lecture on North America, "so interesting that we were all sorry when it ended and surprised to find how late it was".

As "Geography is a subject as wide as the world, History is as all-embracing as eternity, so the activities of the GHS are by no means limited, yet it is surprising how one may search for things of interest far and wide and quite overlook what is close at hand". Never did these two Mistresses make that mistake. "Onward Ever ploughed twenty brave damsels", studying river action, visiting Waltham Abbey, the local brickfields, Tottenham Nesta factory for mattresses and tram seats ("we had no idea that so much of the work was really manufactured home-made"), and always St Albans. Once again, they collected very generous samples of Peak Frean's biscuits.

London never palled: churches, museums, the City, Charterhouse, Whitehall on Armistice Day, the printing of *The Sun*, Bushey Park, Hampton Court by water to see "something of the fine uses to which wealth can be put".

Highlights? – a unique expedition, armed with OS maps, to Whipsnade, which, perhaps because "we did not spend all our time learning the topography of the zoo", was voted the happiest outing of 1934: and the regular exploration, which continued agreeably post-war, of London Docks, when the whole school (later Fifths only) sailed down the Thames in *The Royal Daffodil*. "We went in double file across the road at Tower Hill and held up the traffic to the joy of the girls and the anxiety of the Staff".

The society felt that it distinguished itself by the magnitude of its undertakings.

"The lively but well-behaved lambs of the First Form" still went to the British Museum, studying art, architecture, literature and theology at one fell swoop. Theatre visits were treasured rarities. Charabancs took 200 to see *Charles the King*, and Gielgud as Hamlet and as Richard of Bordeaux. The Open Air performances in Regent's Park were well patronised, although *Comus* and *The Comedy of Errors* suffered from heavy thunderstorms; *The Tempest* and *As You Like It* were uninterrupted. All but the Fifths went, with EGS, by tram, to the cinema for *A Midsummer Night's Dream*. Seniors saw *Victoria the Great*. As well as glorious Kew and the Oval, one coach party to the Crystal Palace enjoyed the Thames by night.

Full to bursting point with pure enjoyment

In the old Gym, 30-40 Guides in six patrols and 15-22 Cadets assembled; all over 16 were urged to join their jolly meetings. They collected awards assiduously: five Cadet stars, the Enfield District Challenge Cup for first class work, at least 12 distinctions in campcraft, a Camper's licence, Ranger All-round and Gold Cords, the picture in the Rangers' Ambulance competition. With various appointments as Pack and Company leaders, Tawny and Brown Owls, lieutenants and captains, the supreme accolade came when Miss F. Sharp was appointed Commissioner for East Enfield (1935-1941). All this delighted the Head: "When I began to train our first OG candidates, it was with the great hope that they might finally become officers and help in the movement wherever they went. It was a very real joy that my hope has in some measure been justified, through the very fine work of the Mistresses who relieved me of my great undertaking when I was still endeavouring to master the mysteries of flag-wagging. One OG has courageously started a company of her own – *floreat*!"

Exciting events included celebratory parades, two Brownie "Flying-Ups", a Coronation rally at Wembley where they sat just behind the Royal Box, the Leader's Investiture, a Ranger rally and conference. They represented Enfield at the 1937 Wembley Festival of Youth, where they performed a Maypole Dance, looking gay in summer uniforms, coloured aprons and ties worn as triangular scarves.

A meal of smokey sausage and bacon was cooked on the field. An Open Evening explained the joys of camping. The jolly weekend Coronation camp for all Enfield, with a magnificent firework display, was held at East Lodge.

Varying numbers went further afield. Journeys, long and complicated, began early in the morning. Stereotyped reports list pleasures, some traditional, some surprising: navy blue linen camp hats, erecting screens, laying cook's fire, mutton, suet rolypoly, "soup, soup, beautiful soup", picnics, lunch still followed by one hour of perfect rest and quietness, cocoa or, again, soup. "Scraping dixies is such a noisy, messy, happy job". They loved beach games, playing "hats and no hats", and fancy dress cricket. Too often, the heavens wept copiously or the weather clerk had a little weep. In fact, the Guides' supreme happiness was camping. They learned that many hands make light work and returned, like snails, unwillingly to school.

Well, our own country isn't too bad after all

The European trip, the first for the lucky few, became more important. Guide, philosopher and friend, Miss Forrest, whose jolly holidays remain the stuff of legend, took parties to Italy, Switzerland, Normandy, Brittany, a château near Pau (handy for an exciting excursion into Spain) and the "gay city of Paris, la Ville Lumière". The other adventurous ladies, Misses Crombie and Rudkin, continued to accompany girls to Belgium and Germany. They were astonished by their hospitable welcome in Austria and fascinated by the religious intensity of life.

The Channel crossing, often overnight, by the longest but cheapest Newhaven-Dieppe route was usually tempestuous. "Do not eat milk chocolate in front of pale-looking voyagers when a boat is behaving like half a dozen switchbacks rolled into one".

They giggled at linguistic problems, listened through earphones to dance music from London, took long, healthful walks, climbed, "chugged gayly up in the electric trains, feeling out of place in our 'Sunday' clothes, surrounded as we were by girls in sleeveless jumpers, breeches and Alpine boots". They were thrilled to see Swiss mountains, to meet Customs men on the train, to visit a French school. Suspicious of French food such as *vol au vent*, they found that the natives spoke a slightly different, somewhat faster, language: "we discovered that we still had much to learn if we wished to use the French language proficiently". They too still rested before or after lunch, still picked flowers, they played table tennis, they enthused over hot tea and buns. They accepted strange Italian ways: "As we were wearing cool short-sleeved frocks, we were told that our arms were not sufficiently covered, so we had to enter the cathedral in relays in the only coats available". They were as fascinated that the boatman who rowed them across Lake Como was an Italian as that their coachdriver was the son of the Royal Coachman to the Emperor Franz Joseph.

They learned recent history in discovering that every bit of glass had been removed from la Sainte Chapelle during the war. Geography came alive when they altered their watches to Central European time. Economics meant something when they discovered that the fall in money values was particularly exciting as they had never before handled anything less than a farthing. Politics became more vivid in the encouraging work of the League of Nations in Geneva.

CHAPTER TWENTY-ONE

A Regrettable Wasting of Opportunities

Of those who left before the new Head arrived, the immediate whereabouts of only 11 are unknown: 41 moved elsewhere, 13 changed to private or different local institutions, or, mostly at about 13 years of age, to Junior Technical Schools. These are not true premature leavers.

Personal health accounted for ten departures: returned to elementary school, not strong enough to continue to attend, "duly entered but never attended" as long illness preceded removal from the district. Despite an entrance scholarship and General Progress prize, another left after two years because of a bone disease of the leg. One, aged 14, left three months before dying of a double mastoid. Death had a different vocabulary: "We shall hold in loving remembrance" two 17-year olds, Kathleen Naylor who died after a long, painful illness, and Joan Rawson, "a girl of a lovable character and intellectual promise". One invalid and one deceased father, the ill-health of six mothers and the death of one caused premature departures; daughters had to look after families.

One child stayed a term before being withdrawn because of Father's "temporary belief that he was leaving the district"; he then sent her to an elementary school. Perhaps the fees were too much. Another, admittedly on probation, failed to make good over two terms. One became a shop assistant, partly because her earnings were required, although lack of progress had resulted from ear trouble. Two more parents, one a widow, withdrew their daughters, aged 12 and 14, for poor progress. A 17-year old was readmitted after a gap of several years, remained five terms and was then again at home. One returned to her elementary school, relinquishing her award after just one month.

Numbers rose and fell. In September, 1932, 418 were on roll, by the following summer, 372 remained. The shocking number of 253 left during a school year, peaking at 76 in 1934-1935. Many went as soon as their 16th birthday was reached or would be reached during the next holiday, but one child was removed at the age of 11, eight at 13, 64 at 14 and 65 at 15, with only two penalties enforced. More shocking is the return of N.F.C. (Necessitous Family Circumstances) and S.R. (Services Required) for 54 girls – 1935 again the infamous year – the agreement with the Governors being frequently excused or broken. The problem was compounded as these leavers, lacking qualifications, could take only the lowest paid jobs. The Thirties were making themselves felt.

The annual Leavers' Service (once at St Paul's), with the full panoply of a C of E service and Hymns Ancient and Modern, would have sounded hollow to many of these youngsters, told to reverence and speak the truth, choose their friends wisely and honour the traditions of their school.

The following figures add up to more than the number who left, as, for example, girls first at home took jobs. The general picture remains true.

Again, most, 225, went immediately into clerical work or training, in banks, insurance, railways, local government; at least three were dealing with comptometers or "calculating machines". Later, some became supervisors, child welfare officer, magistrate, mature students or joined the Forces. Civil Service took 66 more, one in the Foreign Office, one in the Metropolitan Police and one eventually science assistant at the Royal Naval Physiological laboratory. Thirteen were telephonists.

Again, the next largest number was immediately at home, 134, of whom one "had to leave", and only two were actively seeking work.

Trainees and apprentices pursued the same careers as earlier leavers, plus dancing 2, lampshade painting, embroidery, commercial art, housekeeping, Lyons (to be a manageress) and "homemade catering". Shops took 38, factories 16, hairdressing 9, domestic service 33, kennels 2.

Some fit into the grammar-school-leaver stereotype: assistants (4 library, 4 laboratory), 10 in various branches of nursing (including a future Deputy Mayoress), 2 dental receptionists.

Numbers going on to higher education decreased. Ten studied at the French Institute or Lycée (six with scholarships), three at Hornsey, three at Polytechnics and one each at the School of Retail Distribution and the North London Commercial School. Three became student teachers, one trained in Medical Massage at Guy's before setting up her own physiotherapy practice.

Seven Training Colleges, including PE and DSc., accepted 13. One became a junior school Head, another personal assistant to UNRRA (for refugees and relief) in the British Occupied Zone of Germany, a third taught in a training college. Seven took London degrees with one senior county scholarship and two exhibitions, whilst six, all with scholarships or bursaries, graduated from Oxford, one subsequently gaining an award to the Swiss Institut Préalpin ("Bravo, Kathleen!")

School was notified of 121 marriages, one, a future translator, to an Hungarian. Another accompanied her husband on a mission to the Chinese government. Of the 146 known children, 40 followed their mothers to ECS.

Although Dame Meriel Talbot had strongly urged girls to leave over-crowded England to seek opportunities in the colonies, only nine emigrated before the war – to Africa, North and South America, Australia, Denmark and Jamaica.

HEAD GIRL

1931 Mary Gates	1932 Joan Scopes	1933 Marjorie Clark
1934 Mary Parsons	1935 Eileen Saunders	1936 Edna Mansell

1937 Mary Nickolds

Additional School Colours

1934 M.E. Clark, J. Martin	1935 K. Cox, J. Howe
1936 D. Johnson	1937 M. Downes

MBE and OBE

We now have to list some and omit so many all-round achievers, who formed the backbone of the school and gave it its particular character.

Kathleen Winifred Connor, hockey captain, entrance, junior and French Institute scholarships: Ruby Elizabeth Boorer, country dancing, Home Making, drill*, Gladys Annie Cox, Kathleen Helena Dabbs who followed her sister to Oxford with a State scholarship, all won prizes for French reading and recitation in school and at the EMF, Kathleen teaching drama, then joining wartime censorship in Bermuda, then the WRNS: another French achiever, Marjorie Winifred Brewer, later a pillar of the Mothers' Union, whose son became York Minster's Master of Music: Mabel Audrey Perry, Science, Needlework, Cookery: Winifred Evelyn Sarah Townshend, swimming, writing, Guiding: swimming and House captain Mary Parsons with distinctions and colours: Lorna Beryl Claxton, drill*, sports*, tennis*, swimming* with silver medal, editor of the OGA Silver Jubilee magazine: French graduate, swimming and tennis captain Jean Martin and Dorothy Mary Kathleen Johnson, both House captains with five colours: Ianthe Helen Hoskins, with poems comic and emotional, 1st Class Honours degree, MA (Education), a future Training College Principal: frequently confused Marjorie Alice (Training College) and Muriel Ethel (Oxford) Clark, both academically gifted, their results bristling with distinctions, with an impressive number of prizes: Joan Scopes, three colours, active Guide, editor, GHS president, English graduate and teacher.

Well-known as the personification of Enfield Reference Library, House captain Olive Eileen Bunting specialised in such work at a time when vacancies were few.

Elsie Cracknell, with the highest marks in English and Geography, came first out of 1,273 entrants in the Civil Service Writing Assistants' (Female) examinations and reached the executive class. She was the first to gain her LL.B., completing it in three years instead of the five allotted, despite working during the day – not surprising for an entrance scholar with five distinctions in matriculation, netball*, prizes galore, writing and acting talents.

Which leaves the two with public awards. Writer, Principal and Director for over thirty years of Cordon Bleu Cookery, Muriel Grace Downes, MBE, trained at Regent Street Polytechnic. As well as the Coronation Lunch in Westminster School Hall, she has prepared a Reception for 400 at the British Museum and dinner parties at 10 and 11, Downing Street. Naturally, she had been House and hockey captain. She makes chocolate mousse according to the recipe learned at F.M.F's parties.

The OBE? – the actress Brenda Bruce, although at E.C.S. for only five terms, during which she was training as a dancer (which she gave up at 12). Chorus girl at 13, she was in repertory at the ripe old age of 14. She has graced a number of parts at the National Theatre and with the Royal Shakespeare Company in Britain and on world tours, given solo performances and was television actress of 1962.

A Tradition of Public Spirit and Self-government

The energetic leadership of Dr Lily Butler gave new life to the OGA. Her first report as Hon. Sec. in 1927 was, like all her others, brief and to the point . Praised for unlimited service, she resigned as chairman only weeks before her death sixty years later.

By 1930, for a subscription of 2/6 (later doubled for hockey players), there were three hockey and two netball teams, for which shorts and school tie were obligatory. Although an XI won the Shield three years in succession, results were usually poor; with floods and 'flu, they rarely managed a full team. On Wednesdays until 10pm, badminton flourished. "Romance is not lacking among the smiters of the shuttlecock". Tennis tournaments were still held at summer reunions.

Most popular were, as ever, Whist Drives and the Madrigal choir. Not content with community singing, it won the Challenge Cup for Ladies' choirs at Bromley for four successive years, first prize eleven years out of twelve at the EMF, eight cups at different metropolitan festivals, a cup and a shield at Stratford and top marks for madrigals at the North London festival.

Meetings were enlivened by an exhibition of arts and crafts, games, treasure hunts, a mime by the Cadets and supper. It would have been impossible to organise refreshments without the help of Mrs Hill and her daughter.

Acting flourished only in the first two years with two short radio plays, a French drama and scenes from *Alice in Wonderland*, the humour of which was duly appreciated. Almost 100 danced in the newly decorated Hall to the Ronald Bateman Dance Band, whose pianist wife was an OG. As not all those attending had paid their current subscription, a proposal was made, belatedly, that a book be signed so that records might be kept. One January fog and one July deluge affected attendance.

1933 saw the first dinner. For 2/6 a head, about fifty enjoyed themselves at Pinoli's restaurant in Wardour Street on the auspicious day of Friday, October 13. At the second, the three lady Governors were guests, each making an appropriate short speech. Henceforth a annual success, the meal preceded the Loyal Toast, a recitation and songs, F.M.F. once delivering a topical ditty. Miss Broome still held regular At Homes.

An interesting meeting was arranged between the first Dux, Ida Bullen, and the then Head Girl, Mary Parsons: "prehistoric recollections of the School were discussed over the teacups. We hope to follow worthily in their footsteps". Presentations continued to Staff of 21 years' standing – even to Miss Crombie's sister who was marrying. At a special Jubilee function, books were given to Miss Baxter, Revelation cases to Miss Hodgson, a folding tray to Miss Bidwell and a leather portfolio to Miss Crombie who had made the birthday cake. The last three also received book tokens. Twenty-five candles were blown out by the joint efforts of the Head and Mr Quilter.

Contact with school remained close. The Association noted the sentiments of loyalty and affection freely and happily expressed in tributes to the Old School.

CHAPTER TWENTY-TWO

The School is in a thoroughly healthy condition

What was Miss Broome's legacy? Reports by Inspectors for the University of London and School Examinations Council in 1931, and twice in 1936, give the official view of subjects where there were at least three examinees. The curriculum was judged normal, apart from the commendable enterprise, expensive of Staff, of having four Modern Languages.

Each year had two or three parallel forms. Parallel is misleading when A contained the best material, B the less good and C or Remove forms were made up of pupils with very little aptitude for secondary education. Ten forms had over 30 pupils, five reached 35. The effort, albeit unsuccessful, to keep girls until the age of 16 was commended; eight were in VIB, a sad remnant of four in VIA.

VA and VB, 25 students each, averaging 15 years 10 months, had 11¼ hours of preparation (homework) each week. The differentiation now becomes marked: IVA, 31 girls, had 8h40, IVB, 35, 8h20 and IVX, 10 only, 7h40: IIIA, B, C, 33, 32, 30, had 7h, 8h and 6h40 respectively. All three Second forms had 35 pupils, prep. being 4h, 4h15 and 3h40.

The day was divided into four morning lessons, each of 45 minutes, and three afternoon sessions each lasting 40 minutes. The first bell was hand rung at 8:55 before Assembly, although the school clock continued its irregularities. Another bell at 9:55 indicated a short 5-minute interval, Break coming later. The morning ended at 12:45pm, the afternoon at 4pm and out-of-school activities at 5pm.

Scripture, to be dignified by the name of Religious Instruction, was still taken by the Head, and still taught in the Hall. Constant interruptions and lack of equipment meant that Bible reading had to be "done in simultaneous chorus. Such conditions are particularly bad for producing the thoughtful mood desirable in this subject". The wide syllabus ranged from Genesis to Church History, from great Christians to the history of the Bible; the method of teaching, necessarily dogmatic in the circumstances, was extremely reverent. The old Bibles should be replaced.

The syllabus in English was comprehensive and well-arranged, the allocation of time judicious. Teaching was on the formal side, giving a thorough grounding in grammar, with précis work, composition and history of the language. Perhaps a little too much time was spent in the lower forms on elaborate niceties of grammar with the coloured chalk analysis scheme, and in unfruitful writing out of small corrections, and not enough on accurate paraphrase. Writing was universally neat and legible, if occasionally too small. "Do we press the 'classics' too much?" Oral work was good, if too often inaudible to the whole class. Essays should be fewer and shorter.

Internal examinations,, sometimes too hard, received general praise. However, "if there is a free choice of questions, the marks for each should be the same". All slips of grammar and spelling should be ignored, "facetiousness and fine writing" discredited, but rigid attention paid to style – good paragraphing, happy phrases and apt words.

The examiner agreed heartily that written appreciation of poetry in examination conditions was impossible; that it was compulsory caused him astonishment. Probably because it featured in GSC?

A magazine contribution knocked contemporary poetry.

> When we attempt to write
> This modern
> Poetry,
> We find it easy
> Just to put a word
> Here
> And there,
> Sans metre
> Anywhere.
> Our first attempt seems rather good,
> But anyhow
> We thought it would
> When we began
> It.
>
> (The Inspired Ones)

History was again strong, taught by an inspiring specialist (O.D.R.), whose manner was of one not imparting knowledge but working at a common problem with her equals. Good textbooks were sensibly used. The subject benefited from the sound English teaching, as examination scripts almost without exception were clearly arranged, paragraphed and concisely worded. It was difficult to praise sufficiently the industry of the large forms, in which failure was almost non-existent.

That almost all offered Geography at GSC reflected careful teaching of this living subject, treated mainly on humanistic lines. Enough time was allowed for a well-devised scheme, books were well chosen, great stress was laid on accurate sketch maps. Unhappily, all lessons were in one room without power ("an epidiascope would prove so valuable") and with no special facilities. The walls were adorned with illustrations, maps, diagrams and photographs, many taken by the Mistress herself. In HSC, "avoidance of the question on the Union of South Africa and that on maize was most marked".

French, taught throughout, enjoyed distinctly fair conditions with five periods (six for VIB, seven for VIA) and considerable reclassification of pupils. An exceptionally able Staff, headed by a teacher of unusual skill and enthusiasm, secured remarkably good results, especially in oral work. The unusual sound of voices issuing from behind the curtain on the top corridor with the Assistants was noted. The girls, accustomed to answering questions in French, expressed themselves nicely. Nothing was left undone that could interest them in French language and literature. Skilfully set examination papers were marked conscientiously. Even the most backward division of Year IV had creditable results, despite difficulties with pronouns. The only flaw observed was a tendency to paraphrase rather than translate.

A capable teacher taught German on sound lines to nine girls in VIA (only three for HSC), to VIB and to six beginners in IVA on two lessons a week; results were very creditable.

The 3-year course in Spanish, with four periods weekly, had 26 students in Year III, 16 in Year IV and 10 in VIB. With good pronunciation and results, the subject was especially helpful to those preparing for clerical work of good standard.

F.M.F. taught Italian to VIA beginners.

In Modern Languages, therefore, the work in all aspects was so satisfactory that no detailed comment was called for.

The highly qualified and enthusiastic Latin Mistress found thinning classes. Although 21 Fifth form candidates in one year achieved seven distinctions, Inspectors regretted that so few were left to pursue the subject in the Sixth, "where the real fruit begins". Five lessons and three homeworks were adequate, but, to improve matters, the subject was now begun in IIA.

Criticised were uninteresting manufactured Latin and the rather laborious translation of dull sentences; the ablative absolute should be appreciated, not as a trouble, but as a happy device. Grammar work was good, handwriting firm, "a healthy symptom". IIIA showed clarity of thought, being trained to think in Latin. Some still remember chanting: "Qua, Qua, canit ibi rana".

A sterling personality pervaded all Mathematics teaching, which was thoroughly sound even if not of a very high standard. There were no post-matriculation survivors. A more flexible approach to all three components would ensure that initiative was not checked. Compound interest proved a stumbling block; there was a long trail of weak scripts, book work was not mastered, trigonometry was ignored. "It was refreshing to find one girl note on her answer that it was obviously wrong".

Science accommodation still consisted of one large, well-planned and equipped laboratory, a smaller unsuitable one and a balance-cum-store room. One more lab., one more teacher, classes of 30+ being too large, more microscopes, more readable books and electric power were necessary. Years I-III spent four weekly periods on general elementary science, Year I still doing Nature Study in the summer. Biology, which now replaced the rather academic Botany as the sole GSC science, was begun in Year II. In order to inculcate scientific habits, the syllabus needed simplification so that fundamentals (weighing and measuring) and simple experiments (heat, barometric pressure) could be covered.

After GSC, a short course on light, magnetism and electricity would be profitable. There was no post-matriculation work; to tie up one highly qualified Mistress for two girls would be wasteful. What sounded anti-feminist then is now called rationalisation; they joined EGS which was well-equipped.

Physiology and hygiene in the Fourths were "wisely not studied for examinations, a factor that has perhaps assisted in arousing the keen interest evidently shown".

The close connection between Art and such subjects as History, literature, Needlework and house decoration, the good library and the encouragement to develop personal tastes were praised. Too many sketches covered the walls; few, frequently changed, were more attractive. Whilst imaginative illustrations were promising, pencil work often delicate, colour washes well arranged and all work careful with feeling for perspective and proportion, considerable weakness showed in design, too often appallingly crude or neatly executed but depressing. Marking was as fair as any decisions on art work could be. "More ability for drawing would have helped considerably" – a judgment reached long ago by teachers and pupils alike.

Domestic Science included Cookery, Needlework, laundrywork, hygiene, First Aid, interior decoration and care of invalids and babies. The capable, even-tempered and pleasant Mistress commended the subject by her real personal interest. The Head was especially proud of the Home Craft Model Room.

The PE Instructress had served long and successfully, giving due care to girls' physical health. Inspectors repeated that the gymnasium was unsatisfactory and inconveniently situated.

Girls attending evening classes were allowed to practise typing during the day on ancient black machines.

Music and Drama aroused much interest. Praised were the vigorous corporate life, the House system, visits, societies, the well-edited magazine, the flourishing OGA. and the helpful Parents' Union. Girls gave a pleasing impression of good manners and of good relations with the highly competent Staff, with some teachers of outstanding excellence. In short, Miss Broome "had reason to look back with pride on these years during which she has laid sound foundations and established good traditions".

At the previous Prize Giving, she had voiced similar sentiments. "We cannot but feel proud to belong to a school in which we get so many delightful opportunities, and whether we be Staff or Pupils, despite the distasteful drudgery that must come into the day's work, we like to think of all the beautiful things we enjoy together, and which we shall remember when our School days are over".

We shall remember her

After the unforgettable year of three Kings, 1937 brought to ECS the end of an era and a new beginning.

Miss Broome retired at the age of 65. She had made a quick recovery ("we hope it may be complete ") from an accident and clearly had no wish to go. Yet the excitement of post-war days had faded. Some of the more modern, better educated Staff were becoming impatient with her fixed ways. School was losing momentum in difficult times.

Expected tributes abounded. "At the helm, she had safely guided the vessel through troublesome waters". The magazine wished their beloved Head Mistress every joy and good health after a lifetime's work, the choir acknowledged her encouragement by attending concerts and camps, school gave her a diamond ring and the OGA a travelling rug, diamond brooch and bouquet. OGs recognised "how fortunate we were to have such a sincere, tactful and sympathetic Head Mistress. It must be a great pleasure to her to know that many of her girls have attained important and worthy positions".

After a year in South Africa, she attended one Sports Day and one Prize Giving, but never revisited ECS, although her successor recorded that she retained her lively interest in its activities. Only a week before her death, she asked for a plan of the new building so that she might picture school in surroundings so different from those with which she was familiar.

She died in her 85th year. Her obituary referred to the highest regard in which she was held by Governors, Education Committee and her many pupils. "A fine example of devotion to duty, she, with the aid of a loyal Staff, built the school from a small beginning to a high peak of scholastic excellence".

One other person retired with E.R.B. Mrs Hill, Keeper of the Tuckshop, left, "knowing that her service has been deeply appreciated by all".

PART FIVE

THE NEW HEAD

CHAPTER TWENTY-THREE

A warm and friendly welcome

Mary Constance (Mollie) Sharp (M.C.S.) was thirty-eight when she became school's second Head in September, 1937. She followed her good Oxford History degree with diplomas in theology and education. Having taught in three public schools, she was amused to hear ECS described as snobbish. She had twenty-five hectic years ahead of her before retirement, and actively enjoyed twenty-two more, never dwelling on the past, always interested in school's present and future.

Some found her deeply shy, but she was an enthusiastic, cheerful person, with a wicked sense of humour, sparkling eyes and gurgling laugh, intensely curious about people, sometimes embarrassingly so.

Sharing the worry of parents confused by worsening economic difficulties and growing tension in Europe, always concerned about individual problems – combining a career with marriage, awkward journeys to school, finding suitable posts – , she once told girls that she pitied "children from small families who lacked the freedom of large families, for no-one could possibly keep tabs on you the whole time", but confessed that she shrank at the memory of how she used to sit about reading, leaving her mother to do all the work.

By reading out the new form lists at her first Assembly, she made herself known to everyone. In her first magazine, she wrote diplomatically of her sense of privilege in coming to a school of high traditions and such a record of interest and enthusiasm in work and play, and hoped that all would work together first to maintain, then to enrich and develop, these traditions.

One new girl felt lucky that Miss Sharp was part of her change-over. As *her* year, the first that she saw through, "we felt a rapport, a freedom of access, and were incredulous when later she was referred to as Olympian, and not knowing the names of her VI form".

New girl Mary Penman wrote a sad ditty.

1937, The First Day

Poor little new girls,
First day at school,
Afraid to make a whisper,
In case they break a rule.
Black looks from the big girls
When in their way they get,
Cowering in a corner
When by a prefect met.
Poor little new girls!
The first day as a rule
Is really quite bewildering
In a brand new school.
So if you are a big girl,
Be very, very kind,
And take pity on the new girls,
They'll be grateful you will find.

"We took our 11plus at the school, and I was very impressed by everything, from the large sash windows of clear glass, just low enough to see out of, to the officious prefects, who, in spite of it being a Saturday, stood at the vantage points on every staircase calling out 'No talking on the stairs, please'. As if we would have dared! My parents were very pleased: my father sent my mother and me to the Off Licence to buy a celebratory bottle of beer. There were no promises and no rewards for me except the excitement of entering a new life. However small and simple in design that school seems now, it was quite disorientating ; a form prefect shepherded us from one lesson to another, lest we got lost in the sea of green and white surging along the stairs and the top corridor". Prefects loomed large in the new girls' first days.

Miss Sharp accompanied expeditions, taught First form History and RK up to Year IV ("a weekly pleasure, but much broken into by telephone calls"), and coached individuals for the Oxbridge general entrance paper, all with tremendous gusto yet with dignity. Her wide-ranging intellect and scholarly approach, her cultured background and her experience helped her to broaden girls' outlook and to set a standard for academic work.

When she cancelled afternoon Assembly, lessons lasted 6-8 minutes longer. Teachers welcomed non-interference in the teaching and conduct of a subject and admired her modern approach to curriculum and her skill in timetabling, which ensured that 'free' or marking periods were honoured. She provided the ideal daily lesson for French and Mathematics divisions. She allowed a school radio, rearranging lesson times to accommodate a particular programme. Staff's professional pride and confidence in her leadership grew.

One veteran Mistress considered that M.C.S. was lucky to inherit a united, loyal and intelligent Staff which included the brilliant Misses Forrest, Hodgson and Woods. This was not an unmixed blessing; latterly, Miss Florence and Miss Forrest had virtually run the school. Although the soul of discretion and loyalty, the former was upset at losing the supervision of examinations to Miss Rudkin, as, rightly, the Head wanted her Deputy to be available. Accustomed to free afternoons in order to attend London meetings, F.M.F. was a trickier proposition. Although all were now to enjoy a weekly CCP (Continuous Correcting Period, euphemism for a free afternoon) and were allowed to leave the premises except during examinations, the visit of a VIP or Official, and the first and last weeks of term, the particular perks which F.M.F. considered her right disappeared. Confronted by the lady's temper and tears, M.C.S. simply walked away and left her to it.

Pre-war new Staff numbered five: Miss Eileen Mary Bell (one term): OG Kathleen Martin and Miss Agnes Hilda Davidson (both 1937-1941): Miss Dorothy Fisher (1936-1941), shared with another school, who married and was allowed to continue during the War: with her Chelsea diploma, Miss Joyce Ethel Bass (1938-1944), assistant games' Mistress, who was a member of the Chartered Society of Massage and Medical Gymnastics.

Two departed. "We envy whoever has succeeded in depriving us of Miss Conway's services. It would be appropriate to close on this farewell note:

> Fare thee well,
> The elements be kind to thee, and make
> Thy spirits all of comfort".

The loss of Miss Florence seemed irreparable. The evening of Friday, June 23, saw assembled in the Hall, a considerable number of Mistresses and girls, some "ancient of days", connected with ECS for thirty-three years. After a delicious supper at flower-bedecked tables, solo and community singing preceded tributes to her inexhaustible patience, her gentle but quietly strong personality, her counsel and unremitting labours. She was presented with an oak dinner waggon, a handbag and three books.

There was another new arrival. Caretakers occupied, perhaps still occupy, a special place in schoolgirl affections. Each seems in a blissful land somewhere between pupils and Staff, a normal adult who will retrieve the tennis ball from the roof or see to an ailing bicycle. ECS was fortunate in Mrs Hill's successor, Mr. Whitehead (Charlie), who came on the same day as the new Head, to whom he was devoted. He just had time to make the interior a model of perfection, to cultivate gardens and to make the cottage, empty, desolate, its windows broken, into a home with his wife and son, who also became a schoolkeeper. Charlie's chase and capture of the thief whom he found asleep on the sofa in the Staff room became the stuff of legend.

Mr Scudder took over during the war. His good humour and philosophy helped much through days of air-raids and nights of fire-watching, and girls were sad to see him go. Called up in 1939, Charlie's war was frightful. After a silence of fifteen months, Mrs Whitehead received from the War Office in 1943 the intimation that he was officially missing. Everyone shared her hope that he was a Prisoner of War, and so it proved. On the day before Prize Giving in 1945, a cablegram announced that he was on his way home from captivity in Java. He finally reached Enfield the following year. One father returned from a similar experience a broken man; although the magazine reported Charlie as vigorous and cheerful after four years in prison camps, it was some time before he regained his natural ebullience.

This sturdy, independent character, forced to join the local Union, got into trouble when one of its officials, leaning over the fence, saw him cleaning the storm-splashed windows of Staff and Head's Room. In everything he did, he strove for perfection, which occasionally had its drawbacks, for he was upset when anything was damaged in use.

He had a kindred spirit in Groundsman Bartrop, who also organised an illicit trip on the roof.

Miss Sharp inherited a Governing Body on which there were already five women. The only new member, G.S. Rawlinson, Esq., FCA, CC, MBE, always took an active interest.

Miss Sharp's School Council was an important and lasting development in 1939. She presided, all Staff were present initially; most vocal were the old stagers, F.M.F., F.S., O.D.R. and Hoddie, although at least fourteen others spoke before the war. Girls participated through representatives of prefects, deputy prefects and forms. Resolutions were submitted after an official form meeting; voting was by ballot. Democracy was on its way, so fast, indeed, that M.C.S. decreed that no rule could be changed until one year had passed.

Uniform was frequently on the agenda. Correctly measured by the tailor, the seemingly everlasting tunic still had buttoning belts, fitting, officially, at the hip. A proposal to substitute House girdles failed. White blouses still had Peter Pan collars, cardigans were again rejected in favour of warmth-providing undergarments. For gym, girls now exercised in blouse and black knickers, for which white cotton linings were encouraged, black not being considered nice next to the skin.

Outdoor uniform was usually a dark blue gaberdine or reefer-coat, rarely a green one, with a black velour hat adorned with the school hat-band, and difficult to twist into more fashionable shapes. Some wore a close, ear-hugging serge affair, with a large badge on the front, more sensible for cycling or in wet weather. All attempts to make panamas optional with summer dresses (green cotton, with a check of white and black threads) or the disliked blazers, on the grounds of convenience, pleasantness or health were dismissed. "Hats protect hair". They remained obligatory for expeditions.

Dark green shoebags, named in white on the outside, should contain gym and house shoes, although few ever acquired the latter, so plimsolls were often worn all day, a practice acknowledged as bad for the feet. The bag should also contain an emergency pair of stockings, although girls thought this wasteful. Council approved a specified shade of fawn instead of the black so useful as penwipers.

Other essentials were overalls and caps for DSc., and green, long-sleeved overalls for lab. work. How to transport books, equipment, sandwiches was left to the individual.

Council discussions were traditional. School ties must be worn, Miss Hodgson an unexpected dissentient voice. Pleats should be allowed in summer frocks, Hoddie again disagreeing. The notion that socks be worn all the year round could not even find a seconder, whilst Miss Rudkin's proposal for a new gymslip was ruled out of order. Not permitted were shorts for gym or tennis (expensive and time-wasting), white or green woollen jerseys instead of blouses (Miss Bowen feeling that there would be inadequate washing). Agreed were green hair ribbons with summer frocks, subject to the amendment that colour, width and material be clearly limited.

Miss Sharp's first set of rules, more simply expressed, resembled those of Miss Broome.

Silent double file was allowed only *after* Assembly and break, otherwise it was single file virtually everywhere and at all times. Council later allowed talking when in double file, it being deemed wiser to have a few rules which must be kept. "The harassed and overworked Prefects have been freed from the painful duty of imposing silence upon the unwilling schoolgirls going up and down stairs". Running in the building was forbidden.

Unless she had permission to stay in or to visit a classroom, every girl had to go outside at break and lunchtime; no-one was to leave school without the agreement of the Duty Mistress; no girl could, even if her parent sanctioned it, eat in the town. The pre-War lunch 'hour', 12·15-2pm, gave ample time to go home. Staff lunch, cooked in the small room off the DSc. room, was served in the Office, two flights down. Miss Jarvis, regarded as *avant-garde,* introduced the Oslo meal and encouraged girls to take lunch in her room, but most preferred to eat in the Music room their sandwiches made from white tin loaves, enlivened with jamjars of jelly and triangles of cheese wrapped in silver paper. Feeling that she must educate in manners, and despite Staff protests, M.C.S. would not let girls eat their packed lunches in the grounds. Arrangements were complicated and overcrowded.

More general rules covered trivialities or the obvious: books to be covered with brown paper, personal belongings to be marked, jewellery still forbidden, money to be kept in the pocket (risky, surely?) or handed to the Form Mistress, loss of a locker key (replacement 1/4) to be reported, caretaker to be informed immediately of spilt ink.

Detention on Mondays from 4-4·30pm punished any sinner who, after a warning, broke any rule or failed to do her prep. properly. Anyone with three detentions in one term was reported to the Head. She still required a note on return after a week's absence. "A note to be written if homework not done is to be placed on the desk on the platform before Prayers and collected after from the Head and shown to the Mistress(es) concerned".

The personal involvement of the Head with day-to-day matters causes the biggest surprise today.

Council took care of matters not otherwise covered. Each girl should clear her own lunchtime litter into a basket provided at each table. Cyclists could use the back gate, provided they dismounted, first at the junction of the main road and Church Lane, and again at the gate, and that they did not ride in double file. Walkers entered also by this gate for an experimental period of seven days. As no-one was injured, both concessions became permanent. In the Hall, a locked Lost Property Box,"with a wide aperture for the reception of articles", was opened daily by a Prefect and marked things claimed. Anyone claiming an unmarked object after one week paid ½d fine.

M.C.S. tried small innovations. By screening off a small area at one end of the Hall, she introduced preparation times in school, thus lightening homework. A weekly hymn practice of twenty minutes after Assembly acquainted seniors with the new hymnbook. Effort, rather than success, was encouraged by a Good Work list for each form, read out after Assembly on the last day of term. And a school photograph: "Never before have we been lined up in the field, row upon row, awaiting the moving camera with fixed smiles upon our clean and shining faces".

She also wanted to keep senior girls in touch with the deteriorating political situation. They approved. "The September crisis roused the British Lion from untroubled slumber. Perhaps if we had not been made uncomfortably aware of the nearness of events in Europe, we should not now be looking forward to our lesson on Current Affairs each week, which, it has been rumoured, the Staff have expressed a desire to attend". Was this lesson the cause of a briefly renewed interest in Empire Day? Incidentally, references to 'Mistresses' virtually ceased.

Official meetings with EGS were encouraged. As well as the usual matches, Spelling Bees were popular. The local press "witnessed our defeat, announced by the raucous clanging of a gong" in the first, and "our ultimate triumph" in the return event. In debate, the boys staunchly defended their opinion that women's place was in the home; despite convincingly eloquent opposition, women were relegated to their pots and pans as of old.

Some early lessons and teachers are well remembered. Miss Woods gave a special flavour to junior work. They made their own bamboo pipes which they played in the EMF. With Biddy, they mimed Greek myths and practised choral set pieces:

> The tap at the top of our pipe
> Pours with perfect precision.
> And when you would stop
> Not a drip or a drop
> Appears to upset your decision.
> But some taps pursue
> Their plans without you
> And splutter and splash in derision!

Still worth trying. Less favourably recalled are writing two pages on How a Bunsen burner works or copying notes on How to clean a gas cooker.

Their general naïveté and unworldliness amuse now. Girls thought nothing on learning that James I was unpopular because he had 'favourites', and, even during the war, they studied Shakespeare's *Richard II* and Marlow's *Edward II* without the faintest idea of what was implied. Every day, the field was full of girls arm-in-arm or with arms around each other's waists; to have a 'crush' or 'pash' on an older girl or a teacher was almost obligatory.

Other highlights? Every junior could count on one visit to the British Museum. At a well-remembered First form Christmas party, Staff and Prefects lined the stairs from cloakroom to front door to sing Good Night as each girl left. Pre-war, these were events. Girls changed into what were called party dresses, long white socks and, preferably, patent leather shoes with a strap. Traditional games were played: Musical Chairs, Spin the Platter, There was a Jolly Miller. There was the exciting ordeal of partnering Prefects and Staff in veletas, polkas and waltzes. Of course, the evening closed with *Sir Roger de Coverley*.

Of the 197 who came between the new Head's arrival and the outbreak of war, only 21 appeared at unorthodox times. Whilst 26 transferred from schools within a 20-25 mile radius, 11 had been brought up in 19 different towns (one at a private boarding school), so these students too knew something of other parts of Britain.

Five had been given surnames at birth. In this small sample, the pattern of first names changed slightly. Margaret 22 now led the way from Mary and Joan 17 each and Joyce, Doreen and Elizabeth 16 each; only Betty 11 and June 10 reached double figures. New ones appeared which would become popular – Angela, Annette, Denise, Hilary, Jacqueline, Judith. Five remain unique: Elvina, Ginette, Golda, Gunnild, Meiron.

Previous schools were not always named. Eighteen were educated at other county or grammar, 13 at local private, one at Central, schools and one at home; 125 came from 13 local institutions, the top three being Lavender Road 20, Chase Side 22 and Chesterfield 24. These girls were the first to benefit from the new trolley buses, "silent, fast and no fumes".

There seem almost as many different jobs as fathers. One was unknown, one unemployed, one in India. Two (fruiterer, domestic store owner) had retired through ill-health. A cableman, too ill to work, died while his daughter was a pupil. Grandmother looked after one motherless girl, another had an uncle as guardian. One girl's parents had separated. Eleven fathers were dead, from bus conductor to Civil Servants, proprietor of a fancy goods shop to a Metropolitan Police Superintendent. The Master Coker's widow was a dressmaker. Three widows had remarried.

The land had lost its importance; there was but one gardener.

No-one is labelled OA, the omission doubtless reflecting the attitude of the new Head and society. Local firms and factories (although RSAF is named only once, clearly more worked there) supported the largest number, 38, mainly skilled hands such as 6 cabinet makers, 4 decorators, 3 works managers, 2 stampers, glass blower, gauge maker, machine-gun examiner, monumental mason, steel hardener, stropper, ventilator fitter. In contrast, five labourers, two cleaners were unskilled.

Thirty-two worked in trade, retail and wholesale – all the usual clerks, assistants, supervisors, proprietors, 4 commercial travellers, plus the less usual advertising specialist, costumier, French polisher, market porter and Multiple Shops Inspector.

Twelve, manual and clerical, were on the railways; on the roads, 12 were drivers and 2 conductors. Eight worked in the Post Office, 5 in electricity or gas and 7 were engineers.

Of the basically non-manuals, clerks and secretaries in a wider range of posts were the most numerous 25, followed by Civil Servants 8, bank officials 6, teachers 3, police constables 3, accountants 2. Unique were Fine Art Dealer and Picture Restorer, Professor of Languages in France (whose daughter had a guardian as mother was abroad too), turf commission agent and works chemist.

A different financial pattern was emerging as most fathers felt the pinch, fees rising and falling at the annual assessments. Immediately on entry, 110 received totally free places, 32 paid partial amounts (12 guineas a term down to £1:5:0) whereas 29 paid full fees. One had a junior and four had intermediate awards of £3-£7, 14 had maintenance grants. On admission, 16 gained outfit grants, four free dinners and six travelling expenses from 10/- to £1. During their schooltime, five more enjoyed partial, and 23 total, remission. Intermediate awards benefited 13, outfit grants six, mainly supplementary to free places. Two families refused those, one applied unsuccessfully as did another in respect of free meals.

Tentative plans

Miss Sharp and Mr Whitehead vividly remembered dirty walls, peeling paint, lack of hot water, for the school fabric had been neglected; how, indeed, could Mrs Hill have coped? Self-help, make-do-and-mend had effected slight improvements: *Cornfields in Provence* presided over every Assembly and gay posters made bright patches of colour in dark corridors. The Gym, the old tin-roofed wooden pavilion (the Pav), did have a new practice goal, a polished lino floor, wall bars, a horse, an adjustable beam, and, behind, a changing room, Staff shower and office. A revolution occurred in the Cookery room with the acquisition of modern stoves, a gas refrigerator and a drier. Despite the original prospectus, there were still no separate, specifically equipped laboratories for Physics or Chemistry.

"How much longer must we wait for electricity?" wondered the new Head. Well might she wonder. This lack was regularly deplored by those using "the black holes of Calcutta" (cloakrooms), in which the new mirror was quite useless in the struggling, fighting mass. Miss Broome had apparently refused electricity when EGS had it, on the grounds that all the gas fittings had just been overhauled. Miss Sharp's first undertaking was to have the stage footlights electrified; the stage curtains caught fire during the first year, but all was subsequently well.

The Library housed quite a collection of books, but they were difficult to locate. "Have you discovered that there are as interesting books near the window as those near the door, and that new books are added 2 or 3 times a year? Do not complain that you cannot find a book you like if you do not tell one of the librarians what you had hoped to find".

All these weaknesses were as nothing compared with the chronic lack of space. Every nook and cranny, every corridor was pressed into use. The sick-bed couch, already in an unsuitable position at the end of a passage, was used for French conversation groups, and one landing remained permanently timetabled as Room 3, Behind the Curtain.

No-one could accuse Miss Broome of having kept silent on the matter. Everyone wondered how this lively and determined young woman would fare. Whenever any VIP was expected, she deployed the Staff to teach in all the awkward holes and corners to draw attention to the crying need for new buildings. At her first Prize Giving, she repeated the tired phrases: overcrowding, many rooms unsuitable for the purposes for which they had to be used, the Hall an obvious example with unavoidable exclusion of parents. Having cleared the matter with Higher Authority, she continued; "However, on the urgent representation of the Governors, Middlesex Education Committee has lately given instructions for the preparation of plans for a large extension to and alteration of the existing building". She had had the fullest opportunity of making suggestions in respect of a new Hall, library, gym, laboratories, classrooms and cloakrooms.

Patience was needed during the necessary formalities and processes, all the more aggravating as the daily progress of the Grammar school's new building was obvious. The following year, she expressed her hope that by the next Speech Day, ECS's new structures would be on their way to completion. The design, approved at a cost of £46,000, envisaged the existing school as one side of a quadrangle. Munich and the armaments drive dampened expectations; nevertheless, work was scheduled to begin the following summer.

Workmen arrived with the first load of bricks on August 21, 1939. War broke out two weeks later. All was postponed "for the duration".

That same year, MCC, in commemoration of its Golden Jubilee, presented a book of facts, figures and history to all in their last year at county elementary and secondary schools, to afford an opportunity to study and to take a really live interest in it.

ECS wanted more than a book.

CHAPTER TWENTY-FOUR

Pleasure is our chief preoccupation

In the Sketch Club, in the spirit of enquiry and adventure, everyone was free to choose her own medium. Apart from making two expeditions, members met on Tuesdays to learn various crafts, or, in more orthodox fashion, to sketch.

School Council approved the creation (more accurately, the re-creation) of a debating society, to broaden the outlook on life. Miss F. Sharp dismissed this as a waste of time.

Choir members ventured through the snow to sing to the Governors, raising more than £5 for Charities. They were again asked to perform at a Cramer concert. As always, girls competed successfully in Edmonton and Enfield festivals, entering classes in the whole musical and French ranges, amassing 30 awards and 46 certificates. Their singing so delighted the Head's sister, Miss Evelyn Sharp, that she gave them several copies of her own *Nativity Mime*, which was acted by IIS and sung by the choir. They also sang her song *The Thrush* for EMF's 21st anniversary.

The Head and Staff were thanked for their interest, Miss Woods for her untiring efforts and Miss Kenworthy for the time she devoted to practices and her help with the double trios and duets.

Nous remercions Miss Forrest de tout notre coeur

With the new Head as *présidente d'honneur*, F.M.F. as permanent *présidente* and girls as *vice-présidentes, trésorière et secrétaire*, le Cercle flourished. In addition to "notre soirée dansante traditionnelle où nos invités d'honneur ont fait des discours très intéressants", they saw seven more plays; *Le Misanthrope*, "pas entièrement comprise, a été cependant agréée par tous". Theatre visits to see *Matre Pathelin* and 17th and 18th century classics were especially enjoyable as the King and Queen attended performances by la Comédie Française. A dramatic group, in which F.M.F. participated, entered the Oxford poetry competition. Adjudicating, Poet Laureate Robert Bridges commented: "not quite keeping to the rhythm, but a charming voice". Mlle Soussana was the first year's assistant.

The number of talks given by girls was exceptional and considered a great help to self-expression.

"Miss Sharp looks upon our efforts with approval; we should like to welcome her as a member, and hope that when she has the time, we shall see her at some of our meetings".

New interests of the Scientific Society included liquid air, Cheddar caves, electricity, Rowntree's chocolate factory, modelling plants in plaster of Paris. Records of birds' songs provided two pleasant evenings' entertainment. Girls ventured out into the woods on a winter fungus foray, and rambled in search of wild flowers. They saw Covent Garden in the dawn; they visited metropolitan museums and the Zoo; the Gas Works thrilled. Twenty-two underwent a three-hour lorry journey to the Downs to enjoy a lovely weekend on a farm: – animals, bats, birds, village cricket, church.

The GHS beat scientists in a Knowledge Bee by guessing more names of scientists than their opponents could of distinguished geographers and historians. However, the cause of science triumphed in the joint discussion: Which is the more beneficial to mankind, Science or Geography and History?

Tired, but with happy memories

Among happy GHS outings were the time-honoured London delights plus Old Street Nursery school and, through the Head's influence, the House of Lords and its precincts closed to the public. They heard a Commons debate on unemployment, enlivened by the ejection from the gallery of a disturber. Miss Crombie talked on her exciting adventures and showed photos and an OG's coloured film of life in Hong Kong.

A serious event took place in both years; a General Knowledge Quiz. Girls were asked to identify authors, literary characters, scientific pioneers, musicians, painters and famous people by their activities, to locate characters in their right books, towns or buildings in their countries and to explain abbreviations.

Never let it be said that the muse of drama sighs neglected

"We have always eagerly welcomed any opportunity to see a play, be it English, French, and even in our more ambitious moments German. We have produced sketches and mimes on our own account. Our production of French plays deserves to be noticed as a venture not often attempted by other schools".

In addition to demonstrating, by request, verse speaking at a teachers' conference, seniors presented their stupendous epic, *The Chinese Lantern*: gay costumes, incidental Eastern music, drumrolls, flickering light, all contributed. Miss Bidwell gave invaluable help in preparing *Jerusalem* for Speech Day. Staff received renewed thanks as did the Art classes responsible for scenery and programmes.

Fifth formers saw *Geneva*, Shaw's sardonic commentary on present-day politics, and *Henry V. Thank you, Mr Pepys* and the film *Victoria Regina* provoked the comment: "How much do we owe to those two great characters for increasing the power of Britain on both sea and land".

Full of excitement

Sea-weary travellers explored a real Belgian seaside town before a train took them, stiffened, to the Bernese Oberland. The delights included Lucerne's old houses, glaciers, stalactites, river erosion, changing English money into Swiss francs and seeing Miss Rudkin and Miss Crombie on toboggans.

Intrepid members of Staff took girls to Fécamp, Paris and Chambéry, and brought them back in their entirety, in spite of suffering a choppy sea crossing, ready to win further linguistic laurels. On this their first foreign holiday, they enjoyed standing in the Métro: eight hours on the railway ("not one dull moment"): the thrilling drives in the mountains: Rousseau's delightful cottage: beautiful wild flowers: the two "sliders" who didn't even ladder their stockings (no trousers, no tights then): lizards and a long snake. In Paris, they bade Miss Forrest goodbye; "thanks to her, we had enjoyed every minute".

The thrill of a first night in camp

Cadets were deposited at one of their four camp sites "all but swooning from the fumes and joltings of the lorry". They wanted, and expected, to have fun, so they did, even in "performing our ablutions under the trees", or building barricades against predatory deer. They cooked a special dinner when the Head visited them. Pleasures remained simple: daily bathing in the river: rest hours "dipping our toes in the water and sucking lollipops": hikes: paddling to get water from a natural spring in the rocks: camp fires with a nearby Scout troop. Not even the theft of Fanny, the camp bicycle, spoiled their delight.

All enjoyed a Christmas reunion in the Hall, and twice participated in a Stocking Trail, picking up and counting beans and playing many games.

Several became Cubmasters, Brown Owls, Lieutenants, Captains. The best way to thank Miss F. Sharp and Miss Hodgson "is by disseminating the knowledge we have gained in any sphere in which we may find ourselves".

If we had played and worked hard together

Ah, but St Winifred's did in 1937-1938, winning hockey, tennis and netball shields, the senior Relay *and* the Work Trophy. "So now who says work and play don't mix?" Top the following year were the Margarines, with hockey, sports and Bowles trophies. "We must not let that team spirit flag".

St Catherine's received moderate praise and comprehensive exhortation: "Do turn out regularly for games practices. Work counts too, you know". Alas, St Cecilia's, 1939: "This year we have done nothing. This must be very depressing to read, and it is just as bad to write. We mustn't let it happen again! The main thing for us to remember is that however feeble we look in comparison with others at present, next year is still ahead of us. We can all do something, and each of us best knows what". Virtues suggested were keenness, perseverance and punctuality.

Two years of woe for St Ursula's, with only the sports shield, made Phyllis Whitfield burst into verse.

> Here begins the tale of sorrow
> Of the mighty Ursuleans,
> Mighty once in days now byegone,
> Days of conflict and of triumph.
> Days of mastery and of conquering,
> Conquering all the other Houses.
> In the fight for Sports and Work Shield,
> Hockey, Netball, Tennis, Bowles Cup,
> All her efforts were but useless,
> And she strove in vain to grasp them
> As they sailed to other Houses.
> But be not downhearted, Brother,
> We will yet win back the glory,
> Glory of those prized possessions
> On away, O Ursuleans.

But the *universal* sense of commitment had gone for good.

This auspicious occasion

School Council defeated two motions: that captains of House and House games wear badges, and that prizes, not colours, be awarded for sports, so that girls not really clever might receive prizes.

On Sports Day, girls wore their House ribbons like military decorations. A record number of Governors attended the last pre-war one; the Head presided, Miss Hodgson and Miss Bass were the starters, three Mistresses acted as recorders and no fewer than 13 as judges, four supervised tea and 11 girls formed their own committee. All this organisation was essential for 50 events and 595 listed competitors (some entering several times) who included celebrated academic names and a future Mayor of Enfield. Everyone was expected to perform.

The 8-page printed programme shows a mixture of old and new, orthodox and bizarre. Eight pairs of juniors opened the proceedings with a Subtraction race, followed by 13 pairs of seniors in a Kangaroo race. Three age groups competed in Circular Jump, Obstacle, Potato. Unknown to today's athletes were the ever-popular Egg-and-Spoon, Snake, Three-legged, Slow Bicycle and, uniquely, Hop-Skip-and-Jump, Basket Balance, Nursemaids (?), Bunny Jump; for the athletic were 80 and 100 yards and senior High Jump. Races for visitors (4:25pm for U-10 and U-14), Mistresses (5pm), Old Girls (5:25), families (5:40) preceded the final Inter-House Relays.

An almost illegible programme of a Gym. Display shows a similarly wide range of exercises, dances, marching, agility work and Inter-House netball shooting. Five colours were awarded. An outside adjudicator judged the annual competitions.

A Country Dance party in E.G.S. Hall listed 14 dances, separated by supper. "Gay tunes tinkle across the consciousness of students engrossed in sterner things, and feet beat to the infectious rhythm".

The visiting coach, who had them all staring with admiration, doubtless helped the tennis pairs, who, although defeated by the usual rivals, won 44 out of 48 matches played and received seven colours. In 1939, the first VI won the North Middlesex Inter-Schools shield, last held thirteen years earlier. Staff and girl umpires were most warmly thanked.

Although still without a swimming pool, the sport continued to generate enthusiasm. A long crocodile hurried off daily: "to everyone comes the blessed hour when the coach stops outside the Baths and one whole period is snatched out of school time. We troop out with impeccable coiffures as one bell sounds and creep in again with dankly dripping ends as the second is heard forty minutes later. It is an added excitement to gaining the right to a green cap". All thank the new Head for this development.

Champion Sheila Weekes won the all-Middlesex finals of the Breast Stroke and ECS came fifth out of eleven competing schools in 1938 and second out of eight in 1939, the last season for some time. Many gained RLSS awards; 60 could swim ¼ mile. There were four Life-Saving classes. PE Staff presented a new trophy, won for the first of many times by St Ursula's.

1937-1938 began in style with a new, level netball court, and most of the previous year's team. "It is a pity that more girls do not watch as such support may even help to win a match". Staff coaching was appreciated; five won colours, four teams played 76 matches, W 52, L 22, D 2.

Having regularly lost hockey matches in 1937, they were so cheered at an International that the clever, hard-hitting Welsh defence could concede more goals than they had ever done that they won all the remaining contests apart from that "against our formidable opponents from the other side of the fence, whose football tactics baffled us completely". The speed and precision of play during two more visits to the Oval cast them into despair before arousing "feverous emulation", but the encouragement both of Staff and "the perpetually approving smile of our kilted mascot, the far-famed Jimmy Ethelbert" did not prevent depressing results: colours 7, matches W 23, D 1, L 39.

The Mag's i Cumin Out

Publication was henceforth postponed from December until July. "It is a far more satisfactory arrangement, when there are no parties to distract us, and the activities of three terms are ready to be recorded".

Hammonds (Opticians), Arthur H. Brown and Son (Turf Contractors, Florists and Garden Constructors), Dryad (Crafts), Winsor and Newton ("Scholastic Colours and Materials"), United Dairies, Enfield Highway Cooperative Society ("Entrance fee 6d for Pass Book and Book of Rules") – some advertisers still survive. Two rival concerns had connections through daughters: Ebbens "for three generations have sold Bread and Cakes: support Enfield Enterprise": and Freemans: "Try Freemans Jubilee Luxury Loaf and Vienna Rolls. Our roundsman passes your door. May we call?"

All school magazines are multi-purpose. Girls have the heady experience of seeing their names, writings or lino cuts in print for the first time. It provides a useful record of achievements which may stimulate similar or greater endeavours. Activities and expeditions are an agreeable reminder or a foretaste of future delights. A pleasure well worth the money turns out to be the writer's hobby of recipe-collecting, from such diverse sources as literature, different countries and her grandparents.

Grievances can be aired: "Where the advice 'Every man for himself' is carried out to the letter turns out to be Our Cloakroom at 4 o'clock". Neville Chamberlain's harsh world outside appears in *Prologue – to Peace*, Chaucerian in style, and, possibly, spelling.

It is, of course, a literary organ. Whereas *Four Hundred Princesses and the Ogre* is a prose "Fairy Tale with a Grain of Truth in it", most contributions are, yet again, in verse, most with stereoptyped titles indicating natural beauties and hazards. For *The Traveller*

> Your feet are weary – your heart is glad,
> You may be hungry – you are not sad.

Truly individual, Nancy Thompson's *Lament* eloquently expresses the feelings of many would-be poets.

> I am unhappy when I write in rhyme.
> My thoughts are eager, and they won't keep time
> To metre, when I try to make them drill
> Like soldiers, or dance in a quadrille.
> Or words
> They're birds,
> They fly unfettered in the groves of prose.
> But rhymes are cages, and the fresh life goes
> When bars of ruthless rhythm hem them round
> That burgeoning forth of colour and of sound,
> Rare,
> Fair,
> Aeneas' golden bough in a dark tree,
> After much striving may it come to me –
> But never – if that striving be for rhyme.
> My thoughts are prose thoughts, and they can't keep time.

The School Fund was closed

Special collections enabled donations to be made to national (Services Welfare £2), local (Memorial Hospital £5 and Infirmary £2) and particular causes (Cripples' Mission £2, Save the Children, Centre for the Blind, Ida Robinson in China £1 each).

When a cheque book, 2/-, had been bought, the balance of £4:1:8 was handed over to the Head. Weekly amounts proved insufficient – £11:12:11¼ in twelve months. £1 was put towards a wireless set, despite lack of both electricity and space; pictures, frames and vases were bought for £8:1:11.

A fête being considered too time-consuming, collections were now taken simply for specific needs. Traditional charities were not forgotten: Armistice Day Poppy Fund £2:12:4½ (no more wreaths), Hospital Day Fund £1:6:0, Alexandra Rose Day £1:3:7½, British Sailors' Society £1. Support was particularly generous for those connected with current political and economic distress: Czecho-Slovakian Refugees' Relief Fund £16: Winter Distress League £3: Germany Emergency Committee, International Peace Hospital, Milk for Spain £2 each. In all, £31:3:10.

No-one could foresee the amounts which would soon be forthcoming.

CHAPTER TWENTY-FIVE

The results may be considered satisfactory

Form prizes for Good Work (129), for Homecraft (5), for French recitation (16) continued to encourage the competitive spirit. La Société des Professeurs awarded one silver, one bronze, 16 book prizes, one certificate and *le prix Régnier* – to just seven candidates! Ninon Boyall received one of four Italian government scholarships to Perugia; after a 36-hour journey, her term proved a happy combination of study and amusement. With a scholarship to the French Institute and a 1st Class Honours degree from Oxford, she trained as a librarian in South Africa.

The reports of the examiners for GSC (English Language plus at least five subjects chosen from at least two different sections), yardstick for Grammar School 16-year olds, indicate both curriculum and standards. In Miss Broome's last year, 37 candidates gained 28 certificates, 11 matriculated. In 1938, 60 from three forms achieved 42 certificates and 20 matriculations; in the last peacetime entry, 36 secured 39 with 23 matriculating. Four certificate-winners added extra subjects. Total failures numbered 44.

No official review was provided for subjects with fewer than four candidates.

Comments are occasionally bewildering, sometimes amusing, often acerbic. HSC reports, creditable one year, highly satisfactory the next, were even more trenchant. After two years in the Sixth, the best candidates achieved Inter BA or BSc., prior, usually, to going on to University.

GSC English Language results were variable. 1937's essays were inclined to be short, thin in matter and often immature, but free from gross errors of style; the following year's were unusually good, showing original thought, well-arranged material and a clear, interesting and unaffected style. Commas needed attention as did set books. Too often the story was retold in a mixture of Biblical and modern schoolgirl idiom. Appreciation was preferred to analysis; girls were extremely vague about poetry. In short, whilst many wrote pleasant and fluent answers, these were seldom based closely on the texts.

One unfortunate HSC candidate displayed serious spelling weaknesses; essays were damned as limited in vocabulary, thought and imagination. It was, perhaps, some comfort to know that thought had been given to structure.

Clearly, there was considerable scope for the next Head of Department.

English and European History, although of a reasonable standard, showed too much note reproduction and inaccuracy; presentation left much to be desired.

Sketch maps in Geography were often extremely crude with far too many errors. The course seemed somewhat restricted in scope, yet questions covered four continents! Still "good on Scotland. Weak on N. Africa". By 1939, Geography had 60 candidates.

But GSC French! Written work was generally highly satisfactory, pronunciation often almost faultless, oral work extremely good and dictations exceptionally good. Yet, even here, syntax (weak), accents (carelessness or ignorance), idiomatic phrases (not always well handled), composition (lack of knowledge of the rules of grammar) and verbs (the most frightful source of trouble) received criticism.

Without being outstanding, HSC examinees had been so well grounded that they could make full use of their powers, "such as they were. One or two were in that subjective frame of mind which induces writing nonsense while hoping for the best". Even the weaker essays showed a delightful capacity for thought and maturity of outlook penetrating through the still difficult medium of half-mastered French". Verse translation left some with few resources. All read fluently with a good accent and talked without hesitation.

Despite creditable oral work, papers in German (31 over the three years) varied from excellent to decidedly weak with imperfect knowledge of the elementary rules of accidence and feeble comprehension of verb forms.

Spanish (32 candidates) was mainly creditable, although 1938's entrants spoke with ease but with a good deal of inaccuracy.

Latin GSC, with 45 candidates, achieved one distinction each year. Several showed merit; accidence was well known with one faultless paper; in scansion, one was completely correct, one an utter failure; *oratio obliquo* was well understood. Set books, however, showed a "want of common sense; quotations enhance the value of the answer, but if both accidence and syntax are at fault, they are useless". The prose (from *Robinson Crusoe*) gave a few bad blunders; "explanations added in brackets might well have been omitted".

Trigonometry was again left severely alone. Arithmetic was judged intelligent if inaccurate, although one candidate did give weight in gallons.

Algebra was variable and often incomplete, although six girls gained full marks for graph work. Geometry, sadly, produced few good scripts, as the syllabus had not been fully covered. Despite these strictures, work was generally clearly set out and showed intelligence, even when final success was not attained.

Biology was taken by 137 well prepared girls who had worked hard without using sufficient common sense. With weakness in respect of earthworms and frogs, curious thoughts about alcohol being absorbed in the stomach, and occasional unwise choice of mistletoe, all candidates were badly penalised by knowing practically nothing of the peaplant beyond that it was a peaplant. What a relief to read that all had a good general knowledge of the caterpillar and practically every candidate showed a sound knowledge of the bone. No-one then attempted the question on ecology.

Fifty-eight sat for Drawing, in which great variation is inevitable. Elegance of execution sometimes masked deficiencies. Drawings from nature, with few exceptions, did not sufficiently express the beautiful qualities of the plant, an iris. From life, results were unsatisfactory. Although some design ideas were excellent, there were hardly enough to go round. Perspective was too difficult for most. Candidates needed to have their attention drawn to the principles governing good composition. Yet the pass rate was high.

One State Scholarship was gained in 1938, which left 27 for the rest of the country.

All have combined to make me feel at home

At Miss Sharp's first Prize Giving, the Chairman of the Education Committee caused amusement with his stories and much delight with his promises – enlargement of the school and less homework. The new Head, incidentally, was accident-prone and totally unpractical. A member of Staff on these occasions had to act as her maid, armed with safety pins and the like! She thanked those Governors and parents who had called on her for their cooperation and friendliness and paid a characteristically warm tribute to her Staff, who had begrudged "neither time nor pains in explaining school matters, and who have borne with unwearying patience my endless questions", and thanked the pupils from Head Girl to newest entrant.

She used the occasion not merely to lament the state of the premises, but to proclaim her view of the purpose of education in general and of ECS. in particular. A school catering for all-round development and preparing for life and service to the community should provide a "content of knowledge, a body of belief, a standard of conduct and a sense of values", so that scholar or artist, professional woman or homemaker, could all face life with dignity, judgment and common sense.

She could sound like E.R.B. "Every girl should try to finish the school course planned as a continuous process of mental training". Distressed that girls left mid-term or mid-year, but conscious of financial stresses, she urged at least one year in the Sixth, because of its wider outlook, increasing responsibility and greater freedom which should result in the exercise of initiative and wise judgment. This became her annual crusade. After so much given by Government, County, Governors and Staff, "you should feel that you must not leave school until you are ready and fit to repay what has been so liberally given you".

Her second Speech Day was her own. The girls were no longer a sea of every conceivable tone and shade of white, for gymslips were the order of the day for which everyone was truly thankful. Canon Norman Sykes, Professor of History, gave a helpful and well-delivered address to which girls listened in a silence that showed well their interest and appreciation. The Head was pleased that distinguished people were willing to visit schools and hand on wisdom and counsel gained from their valuable experience. Proud of examination successes, expeditions, sports and entertainments, she too was happy to proclaim the various occupations and achievements of former students, and a record number of marriages.

She wished to bring home to all the troubled situation: "we are living in the shadow of world danger when we fear at best an international war and at worst the collapse of civilisation as we know it". Although the horror had been averted, no-one could feel certain that peace was permanently secured. The bewildering world of Fascist, Nazi or Communist ideas needed modern knowledge plus disciplined characters plus self-control.

Her peroration, bloated in cold print, would have been delivered with a firm, sincere optimism, which gave confidence in those troubled days. She thanked the Staff who "hand on to the new generation the best and finest that they know and are then proud to stand aside while the young set out to build Jerusalem in England's green and pleasant land".

Not all girls, however, were impressed with the system. Council debated a motion to abolish prizes and award certificates only. Miss Sharp told them that the money saved could not be spent in school. Deflated, the proposer then advocated that prize-winners should give their books to the library. The suggestion was firmly rejected.

A sudden change in living and thinking

The magazine printed a few articles from OGs. Phyllis Lismer described the training and possible posts in chiropody, her definition of which was distinctly off-putting: it "means the treatment of malformed nails and superficial excrescences occurring on the feet". M.M.S. detailed life at the National Society's DSc. training college, where "hardened British maidens" poked the eyes out of potatoes, made and washed clothes, stuffed chairs, managed the college flat, cooked,

> Peeling all the onions
> Filleting the fish –
> Finding out your bunions –
> Dropping down the dish.

Less discouraging was Kathleen Dabb's description of Oxford college life.

HEAD GIRLS

1937, 1938 Mary Nickolds   1939 Madeleine Boyall

Additional School Colours

1937 M. Downes   1939 E. Burton, S. Keay, N. Thompson

The large number of 203, which included two sets of twins, left in the remaining peace-time years, no fewer than 29 in Miss Sharp's first term, two even during September, 1937. One girl stayed a brief three months; 63 left at times other than July; two came in April, and departed, four years later, in April. Five, all under age, disappeared for undisclosed reasons. Far too many who had shown promise, with several prizes, colours and Bronzes between them, left from the Thirds and Fourths in 1939.

Most had free tuition, but that did not prevent 15 going for domestic or financial reasons. One mother was deserted, another a widow, two (plus one father) were invalids, and one had died. Three girls were ill and another died in her twenties from tubercular meningitis. Eleven remained at home, eight moved and, it was feared, finished their schooling, although aged between 12 and 14. Three fines were enforced. Five were evacuated in good time, three to Canada, one returning later, one remaining to teach the village children before becoming a dentist's secretary.

Whilst 33 have no recorded posts, school was subsequently informed of 58 marriages, 35 sons and 38 daughters, 9 of whom came on to ECS. Clerical work accounted for 98 in all: 45 in the Civil Service, 40 as clerks or secretaries, 13 in training. Other posts were held by 22: 6 telephonists, 3 shop assistants, 3 factory hands (one aged only 14), 2 hairdressing and beauty culture trainees, 2 in domestic service (despite junior awards): individuals were trainee buyer, pioneer engineering draughtswoman and assistants to a pastry cook, a dispenser, in Enfield Foot Clinic and a laboratory.

Three trained as nurses and three as nursery nurses, one becoming a midwife and another changing to training college. Further Education claimed the others. Despite five full and two half scholarships and three passes for the French Institute, only three took up these places. Enfield Business College, Hornsey (scholarship for original work) and Hertford College of Agriculture (for a scientific study of farming) each accepted one student, seven went to training colleges and eight to universities – to London colleges, the Royal College of Music and three to Oxford, with several awards between them.

An ill-documented feature is the changing of careers, mostly post-war; one read Sociology, three changed to teaching, one to voluntary adult education, two became librarians, one entered men's preserves as a Technical Officer at de Havillands. At least five emigrated.

Although these girls belonged mainly to Miss Broome's headship, their achievements added lustre to the new era. Virtually all were actresses and prefects, with matriculation, HSC and form prizes, French remaining the dominant subject.

Rosemary Alice Blaxhill gained a senior county award (£50) to read Classics at Westfield. Vera Phyllis Angel (drill*) acted also in English plays, helped with Sports Days and reported on Cadets. Mary Louise Nickolds (hockey*) and Sheila Annella Keay also won French Institute scholarships, Sheila being treasurer and Mary secretary of le Cercle, president of the GHS, editor of the magazine and winner of multifarious awards: junior grant from the Church School of Industry, four prizes from la Société des Professeurs, a Middlesex grant for a summer holiday in France, an Exhibition to Westfield and the Drapers' Company scholarship which took her to Oxford. Predominantly a writer, Sheila too helped at Sports Days. Nancy Joyce Thompson (hockey captain) spoke at Council, translated a French play, won Grand Concours and Sketch club prizes, State and County scholarships, graduating from Oxford before teaching. Another teacher and Sports Day helper, House captain Eileen Alice Burton read Science at London.

Winner of a prize for Improved Handwriting, Margaret Annie Flowers was a musician. Kathleen Alger, junior and twice senior tennis champion, won a Bronze and five colours. Many are grateful to Marjorie Brenda Read for her work for the Conservation Area Study group, her embroidered pictures and her gift of the Art prize.

The results of the ECS training,

namely the ingenuity and resourcefulness of Old Girls.

Winter reunions included an orchestra (with the aid of hockey sticks, tennis rackets,and a dustbin lid), a play, a monologue. The summer reunion was still devoted to tea and tennis.

At the London dinner, Miss Forrest, unanimously voted into the Chair, introduced their new president. The following year, 45 attended. In between the recitations and *Auld Lang Syne*, it was agreed to invite the Head Girl automatically and to reduce the subscription for leavers to 1/- for two years. Prefects were already privileged to enjoy the friendly atmosphere of an Old Girls' party. Miss Woods and Miss Hyslop received the customary presentations for 21 years' service.

Whist Drives died through lack of support. Badminton was still played regularly, shorts being obligatory; knitting and sewing were still done in the happy atmosphere. The netball team, re-formed and affiliated to the area league, won 13 of 15 matches and was promoted a division (W 9, D 1, L 1). They even beat school by 4 goals. The hockey XI was enthusiastically successful: "What better way of spending those first precious hours away from the office stool?" For games and especially for tennis ("a very jolly evening, for we are allowed to use all the school courts"), the appeal was, as ever, for more participants. It was, in fact, their peak.

PART SIX

THE SECOND WORLD WAR TO 1946

CHAPTER TWENTY-SIX

1939 will probably go down as the strangest in school's history

Tiring years of disappointment and improvisation had followed the collapse during the slump of 1931 of plans to extend the building, first mooted in 1923. At the first wartime Prize Giving in March, 1940, the Head commented wryly on circumstances so different from those anticipated on the last peacetime occasion. "I was in the middle of exciting and prolonged discussion with the architect and officials. Final plans, complete to the last electric light switch, were ready and the last obstacle had been surmounted. I alone, for some ten days only, had the joy of feeling that the long fight was at last successful". Now, hopes were again deferred, perhaps destroyed.

In 1945, at the first peacetime Prize Giving, after reminding her audience that school affairs, "although important to ourselves, seemed of small moment when set against the great world events of that year", Miss Sharp pointed out, certainly not for the last time, the disquieting, indeed serious, inadequacies in both specialist and ordinary rooms, with 584 on roll.

Between these two speeches? Permanent overcrowding which grew annually worse as the local population increased.

Enfield was just outside the evacuation area, but some pupils left for so-called safer districts, returning after, and for, varying lengths of time. Normal school was temporarily cancelled; Staff called personally on every girl on the registers. New First formers met in small groups in parents' houses; several teachers took classes in their own homes. Miss Woods had "French verbs chanted in her unaccustomed ears and the ignorant schooled within her walls". One exciting morning was spent in a vain search for suitable premises. Otherwise, girls went in for a few hours each week to hand in work and collect their next assignment. For some, this provided a welcome chance to think; for others, it meant unwelcome domestic chores. Never once did Staff find fault with anyone for slackness; the trouble lay in finding enough material to satisfy voracious appetites. "If for a time we rejoiced in seemingly truant afternoon excursions, it was not long before we began to wish for normal life again". Double periods, twice weekly, became the norm.

The girls assumed that it was considered dangerous to have too many congregated in one place; in fact, by Government Order, no school was allowed to open officially until adequate provision against air-raids had been provided. "Instead of seeing the walls of our new building rising, we watched the construction of shelters on the very site where we had hoped to see new classrooms, cloakrooms, hall and gym. Progress seemed maddeningly slow, and we longed to seize spades and help. The arrival of a grab cheered us considerably and we had difficulty in tearing ourselves away from watching its fascinating operations".

"Dubiously we watched the oily black waters drain away, until at last we could venture down the damp, dark corridors. Then came day after day of air-raid practices, when to the cheerful blast of Miss Hodgson's whistle" (from which she was rarely parted) "we escaped from the classroom to the lusty singing of *Roll out the Barrel*". Singsongs often took place when it was hopelessly dark for lessons. After one of the coldest snowy winters for years, the first of three consecutive unusually bitter ones, these shelters were ready in the spring of 1940. About the same time, 750 non-evacuees from Edmonton and Tottenham, whose buildings were closed, descended in never-ending streams upon Enfield for almost two months. ECS' numbers rose to 1,000 with 25 extra Staff. The building was made to expand in miraculous fashion, with girls packed in every corner, and "this by no means metaphorically speaking". Forty years on, Miss Sharp could still see her door opening, "and a sergeant major woman leading in eight schoolmarms and saying 'I'm Miss X of the High'". Professional relations remained reasonably harmonious, considering that they all wanted separate rooms in which to teach only their own girls. Just as many as could be accommodated in the shelters were allowed in at any one time. Every desk, every cloakroom peg was shared by three.

The French Assistante had been obliged to wear her bulky lifesaving belt the whole way across the Channel. Girls took up more space as each carried coat and gasmask. Miss Hodgson umpired hockey and tested gasmasks simultaneously, withdrawing two players at a time to the sideline while the game continued. Normally girls sat in a visiting van to have them checked. Gasmask cases became examples of what would soon be called one-upmanship – gold mock leather or brown suede being judged 'better' than the standard cardboard issue.

When the other schools departed, all revelled in the unaccustomed spaciousness, in not being obliged to suffer Music in the Hall or dogfish in the museum. Miss Sharp was pleased to return to normal timetable and full sessions, a state of affairs denied to many schools. EGS, who really needed all their space for their own members, kindly lent their new Hall, "its newness and magnificence the incarnation of all we had imagined and desired"; lunch there aroused both gratitude and jealousy.

Staff volunteers for night duty received training before firewatching became compulsory. The caretaker was bribed to deal more meagrely with the coke or alter the time of feeding the boiler, which suffered alarming intestinal rumblings, so that they could get some sleep. They had not enough gasmasks and only the largest oilskin suits as protection from the dreaded gas.

So far, "we are proud of the way in which we have carried on, despite the many difficulties which lay before us. We are determined to live up to our motto, Onward Ever".

The life of a country can depend on the way you behave

By July, 1940, a general sense of insecurity prevailed, as news became stale as situations changed. The first local fatality occurred during the summer holidays. Heavy autumn rains depressed.

Miss Crombie read from *Wind, Sand and Stars* of men who had to survive without water for three days – to loud groans. Many lessons and dinner-hours were spent in the shelters which were concrete tunnels sunk half in and half out of the ground, with one door facing school and the other the field. There was room for three classes in each as girls sat back to back, and close together to keep warm, on the double bench down the centre. The walls of one displayed paintings – officially. Inadequate candles provided the only lighting.

When there was a warning, there was a general rush to 'bag' the best seats by the door. "I have a memory of hearing Miss Flint read the first chapter of *Pride and Prejudice* between French songs on one side and Spanish on the other". Everything was thoroughly enjoyed.

Sirens often wailed by 6pm. Girls spent the nights in their Anderson retreat, together with family, pets, sleeping bags, meals and books, sleeping, brewing water for tea on spirit stoves, perhaps transferring to bed for an hour or so before coming to school. All were tired before they arrived. One girl was woken by the *On Parade* programme on the Forces station; mother entered the lounge, now her bedroom, to take down the blackout. After searching for gloves and hat, she and her friend walked to save the 2d busfare and to discuss the night's raid, hoping the warning would sound during the most hated lesson, but it seldom obliged. Another turned up, handed in her prep., and went about her business cheerfully although her home was in ruins. If the All Clear did not sound until after 6am, school did not begin until 10am. This relief occurred infrequently as Enfield's alerts were shorter than those in Ponders End and the industrial east side with its targets of Power Stations, Powder Mills, railways, reservoirs, gasworks. Enfield, Edmonton and Southgate heavily sandbagged their important buildings to withstand the 569 high explosives, 44 oil and 30 phosphorus bombs, over 5,000 incendiaries, and, later, long-range rockets and flying bombs; more than 20 people were killed, more than 20,000 injured and thousands of homes damaged.

Miss Sharp must have been exhausted; she took time and trouble to rearrange timetables, made necessary by the alterations in school hours, and to organise escort parties to ensure girls' safe passage home during air raids, as when one lasted beyond 6pm. One girl moaned: "Why do I live so far from school?" One teacher, returning home, had to shelter in the undertaker's storehouse.

In 1941, Hitler sent "his Huns to bomb the magnificent building in which we labour unceasingly". Three Staff were firewatching when a string of bombs fell across the field, demolished the Gym, the Tuck Shop (which all agreed was a Good Thing) and two of the shelters ("What happened to the hundreds of bulbs we planted on one side?"), blew out all the windows, brought down ceilings and demolished the wooden partitions separating classrooms. Miss Sharp cycled to view the damage at 3am. "School was quite safe and sound. No words could express my joy".

Miss Bass, on duty that dramatic night, awoke about 2 o'clock to realise that it was time to take over the watch. "At that moment, there was a roar of planes and very loud gunfire – followed by a lull – I decided to wait. Suddenly there was the roar of planes returning, extremely low; without any warning came the familiar whistle of bombs getting louder and louder, nearer and nearer, for what seemed many seconds, followed by terrific explosions. The unbelievable had happened. Things came shattering down from all directions and through the dust and soot I looked up to see the sky where the blackout curtain had been. I scrambled out of bed, over glass, to find the door jammed but a convenient hole was blasted in the panel at the side. My first thoughts were to retrieve my clothes, which I found by the light of a torch (still upright on the table), beneath the rubble, very dirty but still intact.

"Meanwhile Miss Pheasant had located Miss Davidson, somewhat bewildered but unhurt, in the Staff Room. An endless stream of people flocked into the building through all the entrances: policemen, wardens, soldiers and civilians proudly displaying warm pieces of bomb. Everyone was asking questions, the main concern being the sound of rushing water (later discovered to be a broken radiator) and the escape of gas. On my anxious enquiries as to the fate of my car, I was led over the endless pieces of glass, earth, wood and cement to where the mudguards were just visible, underneath the remains of a garage and broken boughs. As the raid was still in progress, we sat in the black miserable lobby, passing the time drinking tea from a milk bottle to rid our mouths of the persistent taste of dust, and extracting small pieces of glass from our clothing. At 4am, at the all-clear, we were sent away from the building to walk back to our lodgings. Nothing appeared more peaceful and normal than the rows of houses and the deserted streets, on Good Friday morning, after such a hectic night of firewatching. The glory of the day seemed to overcome the horrors of the dark hours".

Joyce Armsby adds graphic details: partitions lying on the dusty floors "had linen and cellophane squares nailed to them in what appeared to be a haphazard manner, leaving the Hall resembling a Moorish palace formed from the high arches of the classrooms. In the centre were piles of wood and glass, gym. apparatus and plenty of plaster. During the first week, entry to the Hall was strictly forbidden, so there was an unusual number of willing helpers to carry the dust-laden gym-horses, boxes and mats outside for gym. lessons. The bicycle sheds were bicycle sheds no longer". The Pav. "consists of heaps of doors and other wood; the brick foundations remind one vaguely of a Roman hypercaust. Wood from the Pavillion has reappeared as garage walls, but rosebushes planted on the opposite side of the stone steps are not what they were". Many desks had accumulated glass and wood chips. Vases, tins and boxes were irretrievably lost. Doors were replaced wrongly and many of the Mistresses' platforms developed a nerve-racking squeak. Some remaining windows could be opened by hauling on lengths of rope, but most were nailed up with hardboard, so that gas lights were on all day. Shelters were renewed in the shortest possible time. The sculpted heads from the Art room emerged from the debris surrounding Shelter Five. For weeks men worked.

Sixth formers were allowed to volunteer in pairs for firewatching with two Mistresses and so to sleep in school. They apparently received no formal training in fire-fighting, First Aid or survival techniques, but the evenings were much enjoyed by the girls, less so by the long-suffering adults. Discussions continued long into the night, once so engrossing that the kettle was left on the gas; it says much for the pressure that, after two hours, it was still only gently boiling. One girl found it almost impossible to visualise a life without these spells of duty. She remembered being invaded by Wardens who shone torches into sleepy eyes, demanding to know if they were alright. "School ought to be grateful to Staff and Sixth", some of whom have vivid memories of the hot water system in the Office which kept up a constant thumping, so that they were forced to pack up their beds and re-camp in the Staff Room. Vera Babington dedicated her Byronic poem to a firewatcher.

> She walks in trousers in the night
> Of endless shocks and search-lit skies.
> One curtain more, one blanket less,
> With curlers in each raven tress.

Air raid warnings continued. Girls studying GSC Chemistry obtained permission to transfer equipment to the Music room downstairs to investigate the properties of nitrogen uninterrupted. The concentrated nitric acid used, too corrosive for the drains, was poured, a few drops at a time, onto the field. To avoid wasting drinking water, rainwater was collected by caretaker and Staff, using shovels, saucepans, bowls and other vessels of assorted sizes, then used for cleaning.

Assembly was also held in the Music room until the Hall was repaired, the hymn sung as strongly as ever after a night made hideous by a 12-hour raid. Many now recognise a unique sense of community spirit.

Together with drawings of iron rations, firebuckets, bombs and stirrup pumps, Air raid Wardens and Home Guard insignia, magazine writings show how the war dominated life. Not all the contributors' names have survived. Doreen Stableton's *The Sheltering* (Song of the County School Girls) was written with yet more apologies to Kipling.

> As the form was working a sound was heard
>   Once, twice and again!
> And the girls looked round, and the girls looked round
> Disturbed at their work by the wailing sound,
> Each one guessing what had occurred,
>   Once, twice and again!
>
> As the form was working, the sound was heard
>   Once, twice and again!
> And a girl went out, and a girl went out
> To bring back word there was no doubt,
> And we reached for our coats, and were told not to shout,
> Once, twice and again!
>
> As the form stopped working, the whole school stirred
>   Once, twice and again!
> Feet on the staircase that clatter and crash,
> Voices that pass in a flash – a flash,
> Run, do run to it! Dash! O Dash!
>   Once, twice and again!

Satchel full of books, gasmask, outdoor coat and "any other articles needed to amuse myself. How can one hurry with all one's luggage?" pondered Anne Cleveland. They huddled together, both to keep warm and to try to see by the flickering light of a candle, frequently blown out by draughts. "Algebra gives me a headache in the shelters". Rain forced its way in; girls put their feet on the wall, shifting position every five minutes to avoid cramp. Water soon covered the floor, then dripped through the roof, so that by afternoon only one shelter was usable. Girls were allowed an occasional run outside to warm up. Legs cramped, back aching, eyes dazzled, "Oh, Mr Hitler! If only I could meet you!"

Mary Hill Cottingham's *Thoughts during an airraid* were more elevated.

> Mother nature carries on
> The same as we have got to do.
>
> Take a walk along a lane
> (Don't mind the airraids, or the rain).
>
> There's beauty still in Nature's dress
> And all her former loveliness.
>
> And all this beauty will endure
> Long after war has lost its lure.
>
> And dirt and dust and smoke will cease
> And all the world have perfect peace.

And what about the sinners?

The Shelterers

> Is there anybody there? said the Warden
> Knocking on the offender's door;
> And the guns broke the silence,
> And the offender broke the law;
> And some shrapnel fell on the roof top
> Above the Warden's head.
> And he smote upon the door again a second time;
> Is there anybody there? he said.
> But no-one descended to the Warden,
> No step was heard on the stair.
> ….. And he felt in his heart a great anger
> That no-one had answered that sound.
> And the light shone out in the darkness
> And the shrapnel was falling around.
> ….. "As I have come and no-one has answered,

I am going in", he said.
At this out came the shelterers
In dressing gowns arrayed.
This was by no means the first of their offences,
Therefore a fine was paid.
And the light was turned out quickly,
The light that had cost them dear –
But the Warden was listening intently
In the distance was heard the All Clear.

Patricia Brett conveys the atmosphere in *The Life Story of a Rumour*: gypsies in the wood; are they troops disguised? Germans? Grenadier Guards?

Miss Sharp felt that 1940-1941 had been Annus Mirabilis, the Year of Wonders; she hoped, vainly, that 1941-1942 would be Annus Felix.

Everyone had her own story. One family, complete with all the necessary passes, motored down to Bognor Regis, passing many sodden-looking soldiers in capes and gasmasks. "Thousands of spiders had been busily at work, weaving miles of gigantic webs that trailed and coiled all along the promenade", or, more prosaically, horribly spiked barbed-wire intended to make short work of any invader who tried to get past it. Having suffered only one or two small bombs, although enemy aircraft passed overhead most nights and the siren disturbed day and night, Bognor welcomed them as heroic survivors. Hotels, normally flourishing and important, looked neglected and dilapidated. Weeds grew unheeded, paint peeled off doors and window frames. It was agonising to see stretches of empty sand but to have to keep to the land. A piece was missing from the middle of the pier to prevent enemy landings; soldiers with gasmasks guarded its entrance. The girl was impressed by the weird hollow whistle of shells fired out to sea in target practice and by soldiers firing at a dummy of a man. The absence of signposts caused the family to lose their homeward way. Enfield's boisterous siren greeted their return.

There was a normality of sorts. They played netball if there was no gunfire. The War did not impinge on one newcomer. Irene Cater's joy at passing for ECS changed to nervousness on arrival, awe at the noise in the Hall, fear of being lost in the corridors. She soon discovered that Mistresses were perfectly pleasant human beings. She decided that this was one of the happiest years of her life.

1942 continued its somewhat miserable way. Council requested more frequent shelter drill and complained that gasmasks were being badly treated and not brought regularly. Almost immediately after, Government decreed that they should not be carried – not because the danger had ceased, but because rubber was in short supply. With a heating ban in force, all shivered in cardigans, coats, gloves and scarves in the winter cold. Dreariness was enlivened for some; the Sixth whiled away an alert lasting most of the afternoon by playing cards behind the shelters. On the All Clear, deciding that Miss Rudkin would not bother with twenty minutes of History, they continued their hilarious game of cheat. F.M.F. caught them. "If it had been bridge", she moaned, "but a game of chance!"

Shopping caused problems:

> Oh, is there anything to buy?
> Some hairpins? Only one.
> O well, the fresh air's done me good,
> Though shopping's not much fun.
>
> When goods are plentiful again,
> When storesmen hear my plaint,
> And say 'O yes, we've plenty, ma'am',
> My joy will make me faint.

Almost as important was the worry over coupons for new gym. slippers.

And the sirens continued:

> Come, dear children, let us away
> Down and away below.

Towed along in the air by a powerful-engined transport plane, gliders were a new development.

But with

> Bombers swooping from skies smoke grey
> Over lands though grim yet gay,

patriotism burned fiercely as First former Diana Stewart confirmed in

Army, Navy and Airforce

> Out in the Channel I watched a troopship,
> Steaming full-speed ahead.
> Men who keep war from Britain's shore –
> These men Britain has bred.
>
> Out in the Channel I watched a convoy,
> Steaming right into the gale;
> O'er waters rude, they fetch our food –
> From Britain these men hail.

> Out in the Channel I watched a Spitfire
> Flying with steady hum;
> Men who down Huns and dodge German guns –
> From Britain these men come.

1943 brought a long-lasting novelty. "Not even in wartime, when we try to put up with difficulties cheerfully can our old building be forced to hold the steadily increasing numbers". Five minutes' walk away, Enfield Court, 1690 with many mid-19th century additions, had housed lavish entertainment such as Hunt Balls when Enfield Chase stag hounds had lived in the grounds. EGS had bought "that magnificent Plaisaunce" to house their juniors. Surprisingly rapid repairs were made to roof and rooms ruined by incendiaries.

ECS' First forms were accommodated on the first floor of the three-story red brick building. A flight of tall steps led to small rooms, some with low, slanting ceilings. Formerly a stable (the rooms above, bedrooms for stablemen), the laboratory now held stuffed birds and an aquarium.

Immediate access to the shelters was by means of open ironwork fire escapes. Many recall the diminutive figure of Miss Barker in charge. She taught her last lesson, booted and spurred, ready to catch the bus home for lunch. Firedrill had to wait until she was suitably attired.

Sixth formers had an attic room to call their own. They spent a happy Saturday morning staining the floor with Darkaline; they pinned a notice on the door: "Abandon hope, all ye that enter here". Its occasional use as an alibi was accepted, the relief to overcrowding being considered worth that inconvenience.

In the bleak snowy winter of 1944, university entrance examinations took place in an unheated upper room; candidates wore every garment which they possessed. At one point, the caretaker poked his head in; a few moments later, he crashed in, stamped across the room with a shovelful of coals straight from the boiler which he threw into the grate. He had carried it three storeys up through a draughty building – probably as great a danger as German incendiaries.

By then, the low-ceilinged basement, full of pillars blocking Staff view of miscreants, had been rebuilt and arranged as an a additional canteen for both schools, although the arrival of cookers was delayed. For too long, girls showed their hands, palms and backs, to the long-suffering Duty Mistress.

The use of the Court meant the achievement of a cherished dream, modest by today's standards. The library could have its own minute room off the top corridor. In their holidays, Technical College students made fitted shelves, Don Gresswell, school's supplier, sent several hundred new and secondhand books, so that friends could choose one to give; the donor's name would be inscribed. The Head was proud of such efforts in the fifth year of war. New books numbered 130, the total 4,216. Even this small improvement could not last. The Sixth formroom opening off the Hall was inadequate; VIB had to be hived off into the tiny library.

Joyce Armsby's *Thoughts in the Library* were a cry from the heart.

> Some people never realise that books have proper places;
> That they are arranged alphabetically;
> Instead they come along and replenish all the spaces
> With Science, French and Fiction most illogically.
> They never seem to think it isn't quite convenient
> To call Greek and Italian 'History'.

> There are some other people who find it most oppressive
> To read a book in less than half a year;
> We cannot understand why their zeal is so excessive
> Unless they study more than would appear.
> There are some worse offenders yet, who commit dreadful crimes,
> Some borrow books and not sign their names,
> Or lend them to friends who lend them to friends – several times
> Who lose them 'somewhere on the way from games'.
> To arrange a school library is a most arduous task
> Involving much attention, time and care,
> And we are as surprised as you, should you come in and ask
> 'Is Keats here?' and find that it is there.

A dilapidated library book, thrown into a corner, read during meals, mended clumsily, marked with pencils or pens, its corners turned down, touched with dirty hands, or even suffering fish paper as a bookmark, appealed "to all readers that we have feelings too, and to treat us accordingly".

Home and school conditions continued to deteriorate as makeshift sleeping and working arrangements resulted from things that went bump in the night: doodlebugs, Purring Percies, pilotless planes, V1s and buzzbombs. It was back to lightning movement between school and shelters, to whole days in the gaily frescoed catacombs, to the trials of Maths, French and scientific formulae competing with newly-learned songs, back to lukewarm potatoes eaten picnic fashion.

When the V2 raids began in 1944, the Sixth enjoyed the doubtful privilege of sitting outside the seven shelters for lessons and dinners. If they had to dive for cover, they returned to a mass of half-eaten puddings with dishes of congealing custard dotted about on the grass. HSC examinations took place in a ground floor room with windows on three sides crisscrossed with brown paper. If EGS' bell had not pealed when the rocket cut out, Mr Scudder, posted at the door, blew his whistle. Girls "should lie on their faces with their hands over their ears", preferably under the desks and aim to keep their bodies off the ground. The Mistresses' problem was throwing themselves flat and keeping their dignity. Papers were scattered, ink blotted desk, floor and person. Fifth form candidates never forgot the Algebra paper in the middle of which they all went to ground while a flying bomb passed overhead; they returned a few minutes after the crash to cope with X and Y with trembling hands but resolute determination. All thirty passed!

Some girls were evacuated; the sturdy majority remained.

On D-Day in June, the Head invited the Sixth to hear the news on her radio; most of them were already listening – in a local shop!

The immediate post-war dreariness was expressed in Kathleen Shafford's version of *If*.

> If you can stand in queues,
> If you can cope with bills, coupons, rations,
> If you can bear to see the things you've queued for
> Be sold before you even reach the door,
> If you can fill each unforgiving minute
> With sixty seconds' worth of queuing done .....

Let's go to it

Girls dispensed with margins, drew extra lines at tops and bottoms of pages, even divided the spaces between lines. Exam questions were written on the blackboard and girls did their bit by writing the answers in pencil in tiny letters. Any wildly hit tennis ball was retrieved, a task made easier by the bomb damage to fences.

This was not enough. Fund-raising was of prime importance. The more parochially-minded constantly requested additions to the wireless fund, £2 in 1939. By mid-1946, this wireless *was* acquired; the next aim was an episcope and projector.

Weekly wartime contributions rose from £25:19:1¾ in the first year to £32:10:9½ in the second and £122 in the third. Appeals never ceased: "let individual strivings be intensified and multiplied". In five years, nearly £1,000 were donated. In 1943-1944, each girl averaged 1/- a term; all were urged to aim for 1/6, "not a great effort in view of the sacrifices our Forces are about to make".

In the autumn of 1939, a War Work committee was formed of form representatives, two Prefects, the Misses Bowen, Beall and F. Sharp and the Head, to consider ideas and coordinate efforts, to use the special powers and gifts of girls and Staff alike. "Every girl has felt she must do something to help her country".

The main source of income was the annual Sale, with its accompanying amusements, held on a December Saturday from 9:30am to 7:30pm. Competitions sometimes preceded the event: the best Christmas gift, toy, calendar: treasure hunt, dropping pennies into a pail of water, table tennis, hooking the neck of a bottle with a ring attached to a cord, knitting: guessing a doll's name, book titles, the Staff from baby photographs, the date of Miss Rhodes' etching, the weight of a cake or of Miss Hicks' picture of the Cambridge countryside.

As rationing bit more deeply, the Sale became ever more popular, the means used ever more ingenious. The first raised £75, the next £80, then £140, a sad drop to £72:12:8, but up by 1945 to £206.

Amid tremendous excitement, what fun and hard work they caused. The large and enthusiastic audience was summoned by a bell to entertainments, which, over the years, included carol singing, innumerable charming and amusing playlets, including Miss Rudkin's *Potted Plays*, which, although requiring little scenery, were performed under conditions of great difficulty in the Art room. The hilarity broke records when Hitler's moustache fell off. These five-minute dramas, acted with panache and makeshift props and costumes, were on such topical themes as a Girl Guide capturing a parachutist, the young lady who rejected both the suitor with under-the-counter chocolates and the spiv with his black market onions in favour of the good citizen who offered nothing but a seat at the communal fireside – all a welcome diversion from doodlebugs.

Other attractions were the Hornpipe, Grecian dances, Mazurka and Irish reel, choir concert, demonstration of pipe-playing, senior vaulting. A Science exhibition gave VI the chance to create an artificial sandstorm and to turn water into wine. There were displays of war souvenirs, of foreign and old English curios, of African weapons and an axe.

In Music room and Hall, stalls showed great ingenuity, some selling out immediately: toys (1943's centre of attraction), plants, bags, leatherwork, stationery, sweets and provisions (in the early years), books ("tremendously impressive"), flowers, Guide literature, white elephants, "all those things that are usually found at sales of this kind". One year enjoyed "Mdme Arabel's Cavern", while from the depths of the caretaker's workshop, moans and giggles issued throughout the afternoon – both phenomena unexplained. Miss Hicks painted silhouettes, Miss Bidwell and Miss Woods sold handcreams and lotions made from rose petals dried in their dilapidated greenhouse. One student vividly remembers what happened to one purchase of laburnum seedlings, 6d each. When an incendiary fell in the porch of a friend's house, her father grabbed the plant by the stem and smashed it, pot and all, on the flames. It saved the house. All was colourful, goodhumoured and exceedingly noisy. Staff were especially thanked for frenzied time spent setting up and clearing away stalls and for the harassing work of providing refreshments. This once took the then novel form of a "cafeteria, run on the serve yourself idea, with delicious cream cakes and a most welcome cup of tea".

A fête planned for 1941 was cancelled because of rationing. Two Dances, one with EGS, were highly successful. Trimming dusty laurel bushes and cleaning cars for Staff, a concert (£11:7:0) and at break sales of Lost Property (£1:11:9), of Christmas seals, cakes, garden produce, book marks and other homemade goods gave pleasure and profit.

Council decided the recipients, the committee and Miss Barron the actual amounts, not regularly recorded, after deductions for postage and cheque books. Old favourites were not forgotten: hospitals, local and metropolitan (£38) and the deprived (£60), cripples, blind, orphans and Waifs and Strays, lepers, animals, and, unexpectedly, the Musicians' Benevolent Fund.

Most money went, of course, to war needs. At home, these included Winter Distress League, appeals by London's Lord Mayor and by radio's Uncle Mac for Mobile X-Ray apparatus, Enfield Air raid Disaster and Ambulance Funds, the Red Cross (local, French and Greek): British Sailors' Society, Navy League, King George's Fund for Sailors, British Merchant Seamen's Department, Fighting French Forces (£2), Army, Navy and Forces' Comfort Funds (£7) and for Spitfires.

Wider needs were well to the fore. In 1939, £3 were sent for Polish Relief, £16 for 12 parcels and £5 for books and games for POWs in Germany. Later responses were made to Mrs Churchill's Aid to Russia Fund, Bengal Famine, Jugo Slav relief, UNRRA (refugees, £16:16:0), United Aid to China (£7) and Inter-Schools' Committee for Warsaw (£20).

Apart from collections for Princess Elizabeth Day (£6:7:9) and Poppy Day (£3:13:6), five nation-wide appeals succeeded one another. War Weapons Week netted £978:11:0. During Warship Week, Commander Campbell, "even more charming in the flesh than on the air and admired, if for nothing else, for his courage in disagreeing with the redoubtable Professor Joad" on the radio Brains Trust, addressed schools in a local cinema. He told the dramatic story of the battle of the River Plate, of young German boys in action for the first time, the gallant fighting of *HMS Exeter* and the sinking of the *Graf Spee*. Form I danced the Hornpipe yet again; the Head Girl and EGS' Head Boy shook hands with the famous visitor, whilst the Sixth had the dubious honour of sitting on the platform behind him. The target was £1,000 to equip a destroyer's sick-bay; £1,400 were raised.

Wings for Victory received overall £2,646:16:0, encouraged by Inter-House contests designed by Miss Flint, entertainment given in the Market Square, Miss Blair-Brown's special indicator and the local schools' competition in which three girls won prizes. During Air Force Week, each form aimed to pay for a specific piece of equipment or clothing, but the response was unusually poor. "Let us make the success of our united and now justly famous 'Special Efforts' even more stupendous", appealed Miss Barron, opening the Salute the Soldier Campaign; two won prizes in a dollmaking competition and VI won the poster design. The target was also £1,000, the result £2,598:7:0.

The hope was expressed that, after the war, home charities would need less and that more could be given to countries liberated, rather than to those occupied and depressed.

Money was also collected for National Savings, considered a direct war contribution, although Council worried, unnecessarily, lest this was to the detriment of war efforts and charities. Individuals saved for 6d and 2/6 stamps, sold in formrooms on Mondays and converted on Fridays in the Hall into 15/- certificates. Membership rose by 1940 to 200, with a monthly average of £30 saved per girl, and by 1943 included 84% of the school, totals having increased eleven-fold. Miss Beall exhorted all: "We are constantly reminded by the wireless, the papers and from many platforms that it is our duty to save for victory and that we ought not to be satisfied unless we are saving every penny we can". From £168:16:0 in 1941, the total rose to £1,844:5:0 in 1943 and remained over the £1,000 mark. When the war seemed to be entering its final phase, savers were reminded of the need for Victory savings as their contribution in the great struggle. In Victory Week itself, girls saved £1,342, nearly doubling their original target. Miss Bowen was thanked for working out averages, drawing up graphs, organising special drives: "she has become, in short, a Propaganda Agent". Leavers were urged to keep up the good habit.

Fund raising was not the sole war work. Youth Squads, disbanded in 1942 in favour of united effort, organised each form's activities. With competitions and raffles banned, money had to be earned. Most popular was knitting, mainly squares for blankets for hospitals, minesweepers, Forces, civil defence and badly bombed areas of London, ten forms(VC achieving three), eight undertook gardening, seven collected books, five silver paper, four magazines, three stamps, two newspapers, two general salvage (eg. jamjars), two farthings and two firewatched. Single forms collected waste paper, clothes, tinfoil and eggshells, made and delivered sandbags, gave out fire watching rotas, made bookmarks, lavender sachets and 'felt buttonholes', helped in a hospital, volunteered for blood transfusions and sent a parcel to a POW.

Near the doorways in the shelters and if Staff agreed, knitting was popular; wool, rationed for personal use, was supplied by the Comforts for the Troops organisation. Exhortations continued: "if sufficient supplies have not been built up, men may have to go cold". They relied increasingly on such voluntary work as relations lacked coupons. Miss Bowen spent time and trouble procuring the wool and packing up parcels before Miss Tomlinson took over. In a single year, girls knitted 12 pairs of seaboot stockings ("not nearly as formidable as they look"), 22 pullovers, 20 pairs of socks, 9 pairs of gloves and 6 balaclava helmets. By the end of 1943, 500 Comforts had been despatched. In one December week, 90 pairs of gloves were made and sent to Russia.

Volunteers were sought to darn socks for soldiers billeted locally. A later generation would doubtless wonder why they couldn't darn their own, but no such questions were asked in public in the Forties. Indeed, each volunteer had to bring a sample to qualify; although £10 was spent on wool and although the four military centres did have some socks mended, the project failed.

A far corner of the field, once waste ground where the groundsman dumped his grass cuttings, was divided into neat plots, each flourishing with rows of healthy vegetables; girls went several times a day to assist the progress of these precious crops; firewatchers gave valuable assistance by watering in the cool of the evening. "Do ask for a plot if you haven't one now"; not only was the work healthy and tremendously enjoyable, but also fine for the war effort by growing more food and making money for war charities: "so if the War is still on next year " (this was 1941), "and even perhaps if it isn't, please consider having one".

When the gates were opened after the bombs, a few girls came every morning to rake the seemingly endless stones to grow seeds – and that in the Easter holidays. Every spare moment was devoted to these allotments. Great was the rejoicing when a row of pale green lettuces appeared as reward for many weary hours spent with obdurate dandelions and plantains. A few enterprising souls grew marrows on top of the shelters, scrambling up and down to pollinate by hand. Eventually, potatoes, tomatoes and marrows were on sale. Dig for Victory was the slogan.

Other work was less backbreaking. Books for the troops were dumped in a shed; girls removed any suitable for school or libraries, but this merely nibbled at the edge of the huge mound. Collecting reworkable stuff was encouraged by a visit to the Salvage Works where waste was burned in large furnaces at very high temperatures to provide heat. In a large shed at Carterhatch Lane 'dust-busters', women sorted and boiled newspapers. Tins were compressed into less than a quarter of their volume. "Everyone who came will want to save more salvage in future". Recycling is not a recent notion.

Outside school, new ration books were 'marked out' one year. A Christmas fortnight at the Post Office provided useful pocket money for patriotic but impecunious seniors; they felt they were doing their bit and a good day's work for the first time. They emptied bundles tied with a special slip knot so that the string could be reused – "interesting while the novelty lasted". During the twenty minutes' morning break, shove-ha'penny, darts and tea were popular.

Sorters had to face an oral examination, correctly placing towns in areas eg. Crewe distribution, Home Road (Waltham Cross, Cheshunt); after passing their geography test, they collected mail emptied from bags onto a long table, put letters the right way up for the stamping machine, removing packets, which had to be hand-stamped, into coffin-like trolleys. Amused by letters addressed to Father Christmas or to Colonel Daddy, Middle East, girls bore a deep grudge against those who tastefully decorated correspondence with halfpenny stamps, such having to go through the machine several times; strongest fury was reserved for those who sent 'high' chicken. When work was slack, they threaded pieces of lead on to string to tie up mailbags. Such was the desire to deliver post that girls were chosen by lot. It was safe then to travel in the dark and clock in at 7:45am; each queued for registered packets, put letters in order and collected fares money. One was tickled by a householder's comment: "Do you know, they've got children doing it!"

Girls visited Rowley Lodge, Arkley, which housed the last refugees from an earlier conflict, the Spanish Civil War, whose parents were either killed or political refugees. Already entertained at ECS, these youngsters, especially the Basques, showed their rooms, paintings, games, gardens, dances. In financial difficulties because of so many appeals on behalf of more recent victims, all the boys who were old enough to work gave all their earnings, except one shilling, to the home and the older girls worked hard cooking and cleaning for everyone.

The commitment to such unfortunates survived the war. Council in 1945 successfully moved the adoption of a European town with contributions towards equipment for schools being rebuilt. Arnhem was withdrawn in favour of Warsaw (24 votes), a clear winner over Fécamp (Miss Forrest's connection), Oslo (8 each), Lyons and Malta (5 each).

After public examinations, cyclists were encouraged to go fruit-picking. One year, three or four declined in favour of Science lessons. They received a stern lecture – from a Classicist – on the proper sense of priorities and their refusal to sacrifice. The 1943 magazine extolled the virtues of a Forestry Camp, where "sensations not thoughts are at home": the scent of crisply burning wood and of fragrant earth, fires, singsongs, physical sweat, straw beds, bacon and strong tea, birds, morning thanksgiving and praise, saluting the colours, friendship between teachers, clerks, students, nurses and schoolgirls, British and foreign, all united by the same ideals, feeding pigs, chasing cows away, stroking horses, mud, water buckets, sketching, even one wrenched ankle, one arm in a sling.

The Suffolk Harvest Camp, arranged by Miss F. Sharp, held similar excitements. At 8am in the Market Place, press-gangs of fathers and brothers helped to load bicycles and luggage onto the lorry; they travelled singing and eating. Pleasures included apple-picking, stacking sheaves ("more interesting and less tiring than carting"), leading the loaded carts over the railway line to the stack, struggling to avoid the gateposts in fear of imminent trains. On their first venture, they waited three days before anyone wished to employ them. By 1943, farmers were queuing for the good services of 55 girls and 11 Staff. Non-Guiders faced problems with a leaking tent and collapsing trestles. Storms raged overnight even bringing a frog into one bed; hands and ankles were battle-scarred and skins itched from barley inside clothing. This was WORK: 10½ hours a day, 5/- a week.

Lady Whitehouse kindly allowed them to swim when they pleased, they took tea with Lady Gordon Findlayson, inspected churches and attended services, the Rector praising their sweet young voices, visited the American aerodrome, enjoyed the cinema, the local Youth Club Dance and the village fête and patronised the Tudor Tearoom," a charming little place where one does not serve oneself". No-one ironed their clothes and no-one cared. Permanently hungry, they ate supper in a big marquee with a hurricane lamp on each table. They consumed vast quantities of fruit, chocolate and sandwiches as well as cocoa and Syrup of Figs and got through bottles of Sloan's Liniment. They still wrote to their parents and rushed for post even three days after arrival. Facilities?

> Glorious things of thee are spoken,
> Bucket, bucket made of zinc!
> You whom I cannot wash plates in,
> How I wish I had a sink!

They were pleased to have new washplaces in 1944, with the privacy of four walls of hessian.

Seemingly indefatigable, Mistresses "work like heroes until late at night, tucking us in, bringing found hot drinks and influenza mixture and getting us up every morning, as cheerful and capable as ever to deal with problems like sick girls and wet fuel, clothes and food". They justified their privilege of sleeping in beds. Miss Neilson, in charge of all the rations and cooking, never gave them a dull meal.

Although too tired to be disturbed by gunfire, girls were fascinated by hedge-hopping fighters and 4-engined bombers. Trees swayed with the rush of air when 600 flew over the day after the war with Japan ended, August 14, 1945. The Rector, whose fox-terrier Judy was their mascot, hung an enormous Union Jack from the attic window, and all stood up and cheered. Amidst great excitement, they wished they were in Enfield to celebrate; several hours later, they realised that the war was really over, but it was too wonderful to take in, so they went on working. "We shall be very proud when our grandchildren ask us what we did on V-J Day". Despite "shoes muddy, dungarees and shirts creased, hair untidy and hands and face dirty", they participated in the Church Thanksgiving Service, although they lost their way irretrievably to the celebratory bonfire.

CHAPTER TWENTY-SEVEN

Can Europe be saved?

That is the question we must ask ourselves

The main source of news, bad as it generally was, remained the wireless, but Miss Sharp kept the seniors informed in her weekly Current Affairs period. She somehow managed "in spite of another retreat from Tobruk or a disastrous air raid to leave us feeling that to face the facts was a kind of moral victory in itself. She communicated a quality of vision and concern".

Discussion continued on serious topics of contemporary and future importance. The case for Federal Union was argued by Constance Coxall as early as 1940. Contrary to 1918's armed truce, peace needed thought to avoid incurable stupidity. She analysed the causes of the war, the crippling of the League of Nations by the USA, the inadequacy of government and labour plans ("an impartial, and even kindly, survey of the Socialist and Trade Union leaders does not lead one to believe that they would work salvation"), and advocated some loss of national sovereignty, machinery for economic cooperation, and money diverted from armaments to reconstruction. "It is an ironical comment on modern civilisation that it has taken a war to give us a chance of saving Europe".

Sheila Keay's article on the Vimy Ridge Memorial to the eager young men who had died far from home, set in a peaceful countryside, fruitful by the hard work of its peasants, showed the same horror of war. "The last thing we saw was symbolic – the silky wrinkled petals and spidery green leaves of a tiny Flanders poppy". Yet the same mess recurred with the second contingent of Canadian troops on January 1, 1940.

One of the greatest honours was the visit of Rebecca West; a post-war student, Thelma Hawkins, became her secretary. After tea with Sixth and Staff, she presented a copy of *Black Lamb and Grey Falcon*. "As women, we should not think that our lives are important only while we were young and pretty". Referring to Jewish dead and Balkan problems, she warned that this generation or the next might reach complete barbarism, and worried lest the State took over more and concluded that the present situation was too exciting and glorious to take lightly.

Another thrill of this exceptional year was Miss Sharp's participation in the *Living and Learning* series. When the BBC telephoned, she assumed a reference for a job applicant was required. The very nervous Head recounted the experience: "I came at once up against the security regulations instituted to prevent Fifth Columnists or unauthorised people breaking into the headquarters of British broadcasting", being stopped by police and two officials, then taken to the enquiry office enclosed within a stout wire grill before gaining a pass. A secretary took down on 55 foolscap sheets the three hours of informal discussion between Kent's Director of Education, Harrow's Head Master (Mr. Moore), the Director of Congregational Youth Work, a War Office Colonel and M.C.S., the statutory woman. All was reduced to 25 minutes of debate. They criticised the draft before rehearsing for a couple of hours; the producer rebuked them for being dull and unconvincing. A final rehearsal, timed with a stop watch, took place in intense heat in a small, windowless room; they had to sit so close together to be near the microphone that a notice in capital letters was raised: "You are making too much noise with your papers". Terrified of losing her place, Miss Sharp was later surprised to receive fanmail. "It was a strange experience to hear our Head Mistress' voice, mysteriously and subtly changed". Girls lamented: "Why can't we have more discussions like this instead of having to listen to dreary women moaning about White Christmases?"

Miss Sharp used every possible occasion to make girls, parents, Governors and the general public (for her remarks were usually quoted in the local press) think about ideas. "Ideas are just as real as machines and the peace will not be won securely in spite of all treaties, social security plans and Acts of Parliament unless we have thinking men and women who know how to handle ideas and discern spiritual values, how to understand languages and sift scientific evidence. The ability to arrive at independent conclusions is the only safeguard against the dictator or the mob, and it is for this that we are fighting today, not only for ourselves, but for the coming generations. When we look back at the ruin of our modern civilisations, can we doubt that the basic reason of the disaster that has overtaken our generation is that in our different degrees we have been stupid, greedy, lazy and selfish, forgetful of God and unmindful of our brother?"

As an historian, she pointed out that war always brings the replanning of education. 1815 brought the instruction of the Lower orders, the end of the Boer War the establishment of Secondary education, 1918 and 1944 new Education Acts. She felt that the State should organise the present system so that over-worked teachers, bad buildings, huge classes, organised competition between children at the age of 11, the false antithesis between different sorts of education were eliminated. She did not foresee the result of her hopes.

She aimed to fit girls for life, to enable them to take their place in the community as responsible people able to think coherently, to work vigorously and to judge rightly. Pessimistic when confronted with football pools, vulgar advertisements, poor films, litter, cheap novels, she was sure that more discriminating education could provide the opportunity, the energy and the will to put first things first. Girls hoped that they possessed the necessary straightness of vision and keenness of heart.

Democracy was stimulated by a School Election, run by Miss Rudkin, before the General Election, for which ECS enjoyed a day's holiday. Two VIB representatives for each party coped with heckling at meetings, gave their eight-minute election speeches and answered questions before the whole school assembled in the Hall.

All candidates claimed to solve the housing shortage and provide jobs for everyone and equality of education. The Communists also advocated the nationalisation of all land, transport, banks and health services, a minimum weekly wage of £4:10:0, raising the school leaving age to 16 and equal pay. Liberals required state control of railways, electricity and mines, equal pay and security for all (via Beveridge), free trade, ultimate self-government for the Dominions, the removal of all emergency powers which strike at the liberty of the subject or the freedom of the press, and Parliamentary reform to include payment of candidates' expenses so that young and poor alike could compete. Labour stood by the old maxim of government of, by and for the people now that the better educated masses could think for themselves, and better social services. Conservatives, the National Party, pro-Churchill and his team, would conclude the war with Japan, restore peace to Europe, and, at home, modernise farms and villages, stabilise agricultural markets and prices, stimulate employment by returning industry to private enterprise, whilst admitting that some controls on raw materials, rents, food and clothes were still needed.

School did not conform to the national trend: Conservatives triumphed, followed by Labour, Liberal and Communist.

Thoughtful and educated citizens will be needed after the War

Aware that young people would face a world more chaotic then ever before, the Head used 1940's Prize Giving to continue her crusade against premature leavers, for school life was all too short and competitive.

Wartime jobs, seemingly soft and easy, were temporary; only the well-qualified would be kept on in peacetime. Surely it was unpatriotic as well as foolish to break off a girl's education. Although broad daylight detracted somewhat from the customary thrill, and there was no entertainment, the afternoon was generally enjoyed.

It was 1942 before a full-scale Speech Day took place, and that was in EGS' beautiful Hall, kindly lent at some inconvenience to themselves. The arrangement continued for thirteen years. It was probably the first time that so many people connected with, and interested in, the school had assembled under one roof.

Sir John Catlow, Chairman of Middlesex Education Committee, spoke of the disappointment when war broke out, making a new building impossible; it was promised high peacetime priority. Tributes were paid to Sir Henry Bowles, to Staff, even to Miss Sharp's mother! "Helpful and amusing", Chuter Ede, Parliamentary Secretary to the Board of Education, asked girls to remember that the older generation had been through the same things at school, and that "wherever you go, you will be ambassadors of this school". He described the Head's report as the best he had heard. First formers presented button holes to platform guests, bouquets to Lady Catlow and Mrs Davies and a basket of roses to Miss Sharp.

The *Gazette* described the second one as even more enjoyable.

Miss Sharp was pleased that, when war news from many fronts was of overriding importance and papers restricted in size, education was judged headline and front page value. More openly patriotic, she felt that war should act as both tonic and inspiration. The girls had been privileged to grow up during Britain's finest hour. So that sacrifices should not be useless, they must "uphold the spirit of integrity and devotion which has united our country. Your part is to help in the re-building and re-creation of the world". Mr Moore (from *Listening and Learning*) spoke in lighter vein. Pleased that books as prizes ("an admirable thing") were restored thanks to the Governors, and urging girls to read Greek literature if only in translation, he compared education with measles: not serious complaints, albeit uncomfortable while they lasted, each leaving only a few small scars.

A barely legible programme for June 1944 shows that school sang *The Song for Peace* and the choir *The Shepherd* and *Cargoes;* the speaker was S.G. Rawlinson, Esq. Miss Sharp thanked the parents, who, "in spite of wartime difficulties and increasing home claims, realise that we are trying to keep up our standards and give their daughters the best possible start in life, and cooperate willingly with us in our efforts". She appreciated the combined efforts of County and Governors who repaired and altered

Enfield Court and thanked EGS for allowing First forms to be happily housed there.

1945 was a busman's holiday for Head Mistress Miss Strudwick, OBE, MA. The Head again used the occasion for propaganda. Present standards could not be maintained; there was simply nowhere for specialist teaching or to house books or scientific apparatus. Enfield was denying its girls opportunities available in similar Middlesex schools. Sixth forms, 62 strong, were the biggest ever. Sure that the glory of English education had always been its freedom from regimentation, she looked forward not only to the new Governing Body and the raising of the school-leaving age (ROSLA), but to close collaboration with colleagues in the new secondary schools. She could have had no idea of how close that collaboration would eventually be.

In 1946, Ernest Davies, MP, spoke, his wife presenting the prizes. First forms had to be excluded and not all parents invited, so the Head again stressed slumlike conditions: for example, three Sixth forms of 22, 38 and 10 had form rooms measuring 19'× 11', 17' × 10' and a curtained-off end of a corridor. Gaslight still forced early stoppages on dark afternoons. Yet this had been one of the most successful years on record.

We have not been able to produce the magazine in its usual form

1940 saw the last normal edition. The Editor expressed doubts: "The sun which, while we write, is beating down upon a peaceful Enfield, may shine upon a different scene by the time the magazine is printed". Primarily still a chronicle, there were but eight original contributions, four being touched by war.

On Mary Flanders' *Wise Isles*, gold and silver were despised as life was happy and not overshadowed by war and poverty; each received according to his need, all was in common ownership, women were economically independent. Pat Denton's *Path* to the sea led through the Normandy apple orchard to a tiny valley, the nearest thing to paradise on earth, and along it one foggy night, hastened a number of British troops making for the boats they never reached. More personal, Patricia Platt on *Keeping Diaries* tells of the shortlived will to record one's life. This wartime one on odd scraps of paper clipped together looked untidy but would certainly remind her of the paper shortage. Small brothers, no respecters of private property, appropriated it to draw aeroplanes or to make a war scrapbook. The unsigned *Tale of the Three Ivory Balls* is an Arabian Nights story dominated by war.

Evelyn Dennis' *Blizzard* is the only one to express childlike delight:

> I wake up in the morning
> To find a world that's white,
> Great icicles are hanging,
> Oh,what a lovely sight!

Advertisements generally suggested normality. New were half pages for Birkbeck Hygienic Laundry Ltd., Vincent Burgess and Son, Coal Merchants ("Order your usual quality fuel while it is still available"), Gladys Grigg ("Eugene Permanent Waving a Speciality"), R.C. Appleby (Qualified Optician), R.L. Triggs (Watchmaker, Jeweller and Silversmith) and Schoolwear Ltd. The Cooperative Society waxed eloquent: "To delay is dangerous. An emergency might arise when you would be glad of assistance. By becoming a member, *you save without effort*".

As the usual magazine would hinder the war effort, a single copy, hand-written on widelined paper 8"× 6½", appeared from 1940; it was pasted onto drawing paper 21"× 15", then put into an art file, unmanageable then, disintegrating now. This first edition, fully representative of school activities, was so popular and so much more economical that "we have even had a request that, after the war, magazines should be produced in this form as well as in a printed edition".

The second brought a major crisis. "We succeeded in losing all the official accounts, but House officials and Games captains valiantly produced new ones without demur". Editors, pleased to receive more poems, which still outnumbered prose offerings, tactlessly expressed surprise to find such talent, but remained disappointed that juniors made little effort and that the same names recurred. The Head noted in her foreword that she laughed at some contributions, took real and permanent interest in the more serious offerings and liked the tiny illustrations, drawings, water colours and paintings – of tennis, mathematical ideas, a bus queue, scenes in nature, a mother putting her child to bed. There was even music, for pipes and to poems.

1944's edition saw the light of day, despite flying bombs, evacuation and other attendant evils.

The war continued to inspire. On a visit to this ancient seat of learning in 4441, some interesting frescoes (on shelter walls) came to light; the strength and symmetry of the 20th century gymnasium were visible through the tangle of jasmine and roses.

In the Jewish refugee's first impressions, "people going about in large mackintoshes looking very strange and uncomfortable" were unimpressive; the trolleybus frightened in case the top fell off, the language was strange, the school arrangement displeasing. Courageously adopted by Miss Rudkin, Greta Glauber gained three distinctions in GSC. Unable to find openings after studying Dress Design, she took a secretarial course, worked in publishing and taught in a village school.

An unsigned poem concluded that future men would wish they had seen our war. *The Crystal*, living in a beaker in the lab., told his story.

> he's never had such moments in his history
> As when from bomb and workmen he escaped.
> A Scientific student from the Sixth Form
> Rescued him and kept him safely by.

Would any pre-war writer have commented that the little heads of the three park cygnets "popped out of the swan's back like soldiers looking out of their tents at the sound of reveillé"?

Could anyone rival the poem to Général de Gaulle?

> Vous fûtes le premier à lever l'étendard
> Des Français de la Croix de Lorraine.
> Symbole de la foi, de fierté souveraine
> Vous vous êtes offert pour prendre votre part
> A ce combat pour hâter la victoire
> Et qui rendra la France à son peuple français.

Cadet leader and House captain before graduating and working in university administration, Ena Vallé wrote a pleasant pastiche, *Extract from the Diary of Miss Mary Bennett*. In her continuation of *The Great Lover* (again Rupert Brooke), Doreen Stableton enjoys the murmur of large crowds, the sound of water gushing from a spout, the smell of newly-printed books, the shining backs of pigs, parcels tied with string.

Comedy emerges from set homework: *How the Lady Bird got her Spots* from the hot things which fell on her when her house was on fire: for Patricia Davolls, *The Hyena got its Laugh* from seeing its own image in the water. Margaret Cash cheered herself with *The Pleasures of being Ill*, when Sherlock Holmes, "a very sensible present and much nicer than Pythagoras", took precedence over French poems.

Nature provided the usual powerful stimulus: cawing rooks fly homeward to their rest, flowers are nature's jewels, the avaricious bees find their hidden storeroom, the red squirrel's eyes are "mischievous with glee / As he fingers the hazelnut lovingly".

Joan Hardwick writes with complete certainty.

God made the trees,
God made the flowers,
God made the birds,
And pleasant hours.
He made the sky,
He made the earth,
He made ourselves,
And gave us birth.

There are still pixies in the glen, tiny elphin fairy men to whose music the fairies dance. Anne Bowes' mongrel ruined several hats as he lay in front of the fire. *My Cat,*

He really is a little pal
I'm very fond of him,.
Although he is only just a cat,
I would not part with him.

Daphne Gardner's pet aversion turns out to be chickens who won't produce eggs, so end up as Christmas dinners.

Others touch on school life. *Homework* is the despair of pupils and the perpetual bane of teachers who surely expected it when they entered the profession. Why not try an experiment? Let children choose how much to do. "Quality of work, health of pupil, temper of teacher, all would improve".

Perhaps Margaret Theobald's simple *Roaming* is characteristic in several respects.

I'd like to live in America.
I'd like to live in Spain:
I'd like to roam far over the sea,
But I'd want to come home again.

More sophisticated is the reworking of some emotion or experience, or the purely imaginative piece: *The Enchanted Statue* who wanted to move, the hopelessness of things, the failure of humans, Betty Bentley's view of *Fear* – "no person should ever laugh at fear for fear it will one day come to them".

Sonnets galore were entered for the competition in 1946's edition which reprinted some of the handwritten wartime versions. Editors felt that the ideal magazine should be entirely produced by children, not merely as a record, but, more importantly, "a repository of the ideas and aspirations of budding authors in various stages of school life".

CHAPTER TWENTY-EIGHT

It seems almost incredible that School life was carried on at all

Rationing and the blackout affected many activities. Christmas parties being the first casualties, a request for parties of some kind, Form or House, appeared regularly on Council agenda; they resumed only in 1945.

Whist Drives and Dances were suggested as means of bringing together Staff, girls and parents, but the Hall was not blacked out in 1940. Miss F. Sharp opined that working parties would be far more suitable than social events of a purely pleasure-loving kind. Towards the end, daylight saving with double summer time allowed some events to give useful training in social manners. One early evening dance with EGS was interrupted by a doodlebug. Although an attempt to set up a joint VI society during 1944 for rambles was shortlived, a social club the following year enjoyed regular meetings which included a Brains Trust. A junior Chess club failed.

"I do not understand a word of German, but I could follow the play perfectly by the acting". The precaution was, however, taken of reading a summary before three productions: scenes from *Don Carlos, Wilhelm Tell* (after school hours to a large and enthusiastic audience) and *Maria Stuart,* preceded by a short humorous sketch. Apart from annual performances of French plays, few other occasions are recorded. Miss Morrell kindly judged the Poetry competition, choosing four poems to be spoken by girls selected by the English Mistresses as the best reciters in their forms. No-one suffered from stage fright, all were clearly audible, criticism was constructive and tension relieved by loud and prolonged applause. Two prizewinners received poetry books. Her own extensive recital ended with the sudden climax of *The Ice Cart*, which "effectively wakened any girl who might have allowed her thoughts to wander". Miss Malt later recited a beautiful selection of verse.

Miss Miller's trio's recital with explanations was of music on pipes and flutes; Miss Hamlin gave a lecture-recital to both schools, and, in a blacked-out Music room, Miss Davis two varied puppet shows depicting the Nativity, *Au Clair de la Lune,* negro spirituals, *Macbeth* and a fashionable lady in Westminster Abbey. The war having affected puppet manufacture, seven had to suffice.

Immediately after the war, events did not multiply greatly. Guests spoke on a wartime visit to Canada, *Hiawatha* (prior to a performance at the Albert Hall), the Industrial Revolution in relation to modern times, and the woollen industry.

It was enjoyed greatly by all who were able to go

Excursions in 1940 were conspicuous by their absence. A ramble, a musical outing were suggested. Would a matinée be on a convenient day? If not, how many could go in an evening? What about air raids? Would permission be given to go into a danger zone?

Many saw the films *Fantasia* and *Henry V*. Allowed out ten minutes before the end of a lesson for a cold lunch, forty excited girls in three parties, each with a Mistress, then set off on two buses for Enfield West Tube station, thence to Piccadilly, whence they marched in a crocodile to the Royal Haymarket Theatre, chocolates and programmes. After the National Anthem and the *Marseillaise*, they were enthralled by *The Beggar's Opera*. Considerable analysis of opera and performance concluded that Michael Redgrave was a most dashingly wicked hero who sang with a captivating air. They came away humming the tunes that London has heard since the 18th century, and, although tired, did not mind the terrible crush on the train, the atmosphere smokier and more stifling at every stop, or that some girls got on the wrong train *and* that it was raining.

Several trolleybus loads went to *see Twelfth Night* . They considered production extremely good, settings ingeniously contrived, costumes bright and colourful. Avice Landone's Viola was original even if she had to stand on the steps to be of a height with her twin. Maria was too old and the Duke gabbled, but he was handsome enough to cause heartthrobs.

At Golders Green, they enjoyed a thrilling climax to much action in *The Devil's Disciple*, Robert Donat being perfectly suited to the blustering, swashbuckling hero. Four relays travelled by bus and Tube, Miss Flint being stranded, so concerned was she in getting everyone out of the train, to the Open Air Theatre for *Lady Precious Stream*. Although girls had to stand all the way home in the rush hour, "I think the Mistresses ought to be thanked for arranging the expedition and for taking us". Robert Atkins' peculiar laugh became tiresome in *Henry IV*, Sir John Martin-Harvey was superb and Helen Cherry was "a versatile young actress who should prove herself worthy of the West End".

Another busy year saw them queuing for balcony seats for *Hamlet*. Helpman, albeit noble and tragic, was hampered by his small stature.

"There was certainly a great deal of difference between his acting before and after he was mad". Pamela Brown, unconvincing as mad, had a "curiously mature voice, hut she has not acted in many plays". Other judgments were more cruel. Basil Sydney (Claudius) could have been more villainous, Margaret Grahame (Gertrude) was unsatisfactory, the fight was comic, Laertes panted too loudly and everything was too dark. A later *Lear* fared better. Most had heard unimpressed criticism of Donald Wolfit, but the young critic was bowled over by him (*"hors de concours"*) and by Richard Goulden, very moving as the Fool. Others saw the Comédie Française production of *M. Perrichon* at Edmonton.

Wartime theatrical visits included some of the great performances of our time. One actress dominated. In *The Corn is Green*, Sybil Thorndike was the progressively-minded middle-aged schoolmistress and Evelyn Williams, the author, her pupil. In 1941, anxious beforehand lest rain postpone the Sports and so prevent them from going, they travelled to the New Theatre for Gilbert Murray's version of *Medea*. Despite the lack of intervals, time went too quickly. "I should say that Miss Thorndike is at her best in Greek plays", even making them sympathise with the unattractive Medea and throwing other actors into the shade. She received a burst of applause on her entrance and a final roar on her exit, when the First forms, accompanied by four Mistresses, were excited visitors to *Alice in Wonderland*. "When I recall this play, I am sure I have never enjoyed any comedy more" – the moving scenery, the glass table that changed its height, the lighting, giving the illusion of water, Roma Beaumont as Alice.

And there was Gielgud. In his presentation of *Macbeth*, praised were the scenery, William Walton's atmospheric music, Leon Quartermaine's Banquo, but not Gwen Frangcon-Davies' Lady Macbeth (unconvincing) nor Thea Holme's Lady Macduff. Yet all surpassed everyone's expectations and the general feeling was that, given the chance to see the play again, they would certainly go. Gielgud himself excelled in *Lear* ("one of London's most successful productions"), with simple scenery but also with Jack Hawkins, Fay Compton, Cathleen Nesbitt and Jessica Tandy. In the enjoyable *Importance of Being Ernest*, the supporting cast included Hawkins, Gwen Frangcon-Davies, Edith Evans and Peggy Ashcroft.

Post-war expeditions to London resumed gradually. Seniors visited Art and Craft, Constable and Greek exhibitions, heard lectures on British architecture and saw Shakespearean and Italian plays. Meetings of the Council for Education in World Citizenship (CEWC) were open to the Fifths.

Why are there examinations, and why, O why, are there results?

Each form I-IV was awarded prizes, or, in mid-war, Good Work Certificates (GWC), and, in one year, both, so that near misses could be rewarded – in all, over 280. VIB (Arts, Science, Commercial /Secretarial) gained nearly 50, VIA about 30, usually for named subjects. General Knowledge competitions gave one junior and two senior prizes.

The three Fifths received 80 or so GWCs and/or prizes on their results, again generally better (82%-87%) than the county average (79%). Failures were not recorded. At least 116 gained matriculation standard and 222 GSC; more than 80 took additional subjects, at least three matriculating thus. Commercial subjects were offered once; Shorthand and Display merited high praise, but Typing lacked the necessary accuracy.

Other examinations successfully taken included Nursing Prelims. and RSA Italian (1946, one Intermediate, two Advanced). Candidates continued to win a disproportionate number of awards in competitions set by la Société des Professeurs.

More stayed the full seven years to take HSC: 3 in 1940, 18 in 1946. Only four failures were noted out of 54 candidates in fifteen main and two subsidiary subjects (Scripture and Spanish); they gained distinctions in French 8, English 6, German, Botany, Zoology 2 each, Latin and Chemistry. Special credits in Modern Language Orals were the norm. VIB internal examinations were one year not invigilated; there was no cheating, but once a few comments were exchanged. Miss Forrest got to hear of this; result, "a monumental row".

The magazine printed what these girls thought of the emotional stress of examinations taken at the sunniest time of the year, when shouts or whistles from the field combined with rattling windows and open lockers to disturb. Whilst trying to be sympathetic, "no Mistress has appeared, or ever will appear, human during Exam. week", wrote Cubmaster Joyce Armsby. Trained as a teacher herself, she changed career to become a company secretary. An Assembly reading was gloomily prophetic about reaping the just rewards of one's labours.

Rita Wollen, a future homeopathic nurse, wrote a 5-stanza *Dirge*, with apologies to Tennyson.

> Half a mo', half a mo',
> Then ends Assembly.
> Into room five they trooped,
> Wobbly and trembly.

'Put all your books away!
This is the frightful day!'
Into the dread room five
After Assembly.
    'Forward the monitor!
Set the chronometer!'
IIIH watched petrified –
'Give out the paper!'
Their's not to make reply,
Their's not to reason why,
Their's just to do – or die,
Inside the dread room five
Each heads her paper.

Shirley Jarvis also wrote a parody.

I remember, I remember,
The room where I was taught
Avoir and être, owe and ought,
The noughts and crosses at the back
Safe from the eagle eye.
Alas no angle ever drawn
Was so obtuse as I.
    Oh, life could still be full of fun,
    But for fate's scurvy trick,
    The further off from First Form days,
    The nearer to Matric.

We are determined not to fall behind in the quality of our work

Miss Sharp was, rightly, hurt by the "current tendency to suggest that in our curriculum and lessons we are cut off from life. Girls are just as much in touch with reality when they are reading Shakespeare or making music or when practising Cookery or learning Arithmetic".

Several Board reports remain for most examination subjects. Remarks might suggest poor results; this was not so.

Some Religious Knowledge candidates showed a confused grasp of the subject, muddling one gospel with another. A Christian Way of Life club was proposed.

This year's praise for GSC English Language (précis, spelling, punctuation), becomes next year's criticism. Entrants were reproved for lack of attention to the rubric, the habit of attempting only half a question, using quotations without any indication of their relevance, even disobeying instructions. Their elders neglected aesthetic considerations, their answers on poetry being "limited by lack of flexibility in expression, partly due to lack of sympathy for the more imaginative side of literature" – a dangerously sweeping statement. Set authors changed little: Chaucer, Marlowe, Spenser, Wordsworth, Keats, Jane Austen and Shaw.

In February, 1940, a council member asked what steps had been taken towards the formation of a debating society. The answer was simple: none. By May, one meeting had taken place and a debate arranged with the boys. It seems then to have been suspended for the duration to resurface in 1946.

A well balanced performance, cleverly staged and sincerely acted

Blackout restrictions and part-time schooling destroyed 1939's plans. Dramatic efforts were reduced to Shakespeare Day and morning form shows, such as *Alcestis, X=O, Mme La Baronne.*

Miss Flint produced *Robin Hood* in 1942, Miss Hicks again providing scenery in next to no time. The youthful critic praised the lighting ("a very new invention"), the costumes (colourful and effective), the shooting (good), elocution and pronunciation (beyond criticism as every word could be heard). Even so, make-up was somewhat overdone, the appearance of the knights occasionally strained credulity and the atmosphere failed to convince when the bold, bad men sang in sweet soprano voices.

Despite problems, *The Tempest* was judged one of the best productions of recent years, although the outstanding actress was at times too lively even for Ariel. Small Second formers performed a little dance as wood nymphs. "The many hours of real hard work of the indefatigable producer were a delight to us, a credit to all concerned and a real tribute to Shakespeare's genius".

There were three performances as *St Joan* proved so popular. Apart from some harsh criticisms of individuals, " for the most part, we forgot that the players were girls, which is rather a hard thing to do, as a rule". The new dimming apparatus pleased everyone.

A Midsummer Night's Dream, 1944, gave the sensation of being in another world, especially as the prosaic school was transformed by the extension of the stage and by new curtains. Puck grew so much in the summer that she became Starveling! Praised too was the black and white production with its use of light, jewels and costumes of *Twelfth Night*.

First post-war productions were *Elizabeth and Essex*, which reached the customary high standard and *Two Gentlemen of Verona*, with scenery judged luxurious but realistic. The calamity of one actress falling ill on the day was overcome; almost all Thirds and Fourths contributed, with forty actors, three scene painters, twenty-one costume makers and ten stage hands.

A Poetry competition began after the war, a development of Keats' and Brontë afternoons when an appreciation of the writer's life and work preceded readings or play. "One girl had only a minor part, but she could have put it over much more forcibly". The critic took time to work out that there was something wrong in stage effects which produced pink almond blossoms against green sky. Another offering was "so polished and engrossing that it satisfied even the most critical mind. Neither play nor reading reached perfection, but neither was far from that point".

Rejoining the British Drama League and borrowing copies made possible the important Staff-Sixth play-reading group, which flourished for sixteen unbroken years. Miss Flint ably managed the stage directions and led the casting committee of the Head, Miss Rudkin and VI representatives. Everyone prepared her part so that all went smoothly. An interval for refreshment helped its avowed educational purpose of furthering understanding between Staff and Sixth, "essential for combined operations". Many Staff enjoyed these afternoons. Miss Sharp read Caesar in *Caesar and Cleopatra, Hamlet* was given to the Firsts before they saw the play, *The Apple Cart* was shared with EGS, boys and Masters being invited to *Viceroy Sarah.* The choice was wide: *Outward Bound,* Galsworthy's *Little Man, The Good Companions* and several one-acters so that they could finish before the blackout. *1066 and All That*, reserved for the private amusement of members, presented a formidable task for the committee.

Taking over from careful Miss Baxter, Miss Flint, with skill, energy and imagination, raised dramatic work to great heights. Comparable with Miss Forrest, she had the same dominating bounce and apparent blindness to certain subtleties, whilst being extremely sensitive to others. She certainly possessed the mysterious gift of being able to recognise and nourish latent talent, whilst being disliked by those who did not fall under her spell. One girl felt that "we existed only in so far as we imbibed her enthusiasm for Keats, Shakespeare, Drama and Marion Richardson handwriting".

Activities were not unduly restricted by war conditions

Fifth form historians covered the Chartists, Italian and Greek Revolts, Castlereagh and Canning, Peel, Napoleon and Bismarck; a detailed list of errors in both European and English papers was shamingly given.

Some geographers provided evidence of much guesswork, as well as an extraordinary ignorance of the British Isles. In one dreadful year in HSC, in no case did the sketch map or the comment show any real appreciation of the distinctive landforms of the area.

The GHS was kept alive not only by the indefatigable Misses Rudkin and Crombie (and, later, Miss Barker), but by the Head's involvement. She discussed historical judgments to help members to understand what was happening in their world and talked interestingly on alpine mountaineering, outstanding 12th century people, St Francis and medieval scholars. A Czech pupil told of her homeland, Miss Phipps Jones described teaching in West Africa, the secretary of the Historical Association gave an instructive account of the great prison work of John Howard. Girls read Linklater's *Corner Stones*, brought historical and geographical items for discussion, saw historical films and talked on Bunyan and Stratford-on-Avon.

Despite fewer excursions and reduced field work, members did get around. They rambled from Cuffley to Northaw, using OS maps, lunching in the fields, returning home in time for tea. A conducted tour of Waltham Abbey preceded a picnic in Epping Forest where a climbable tree provided a diversion. They found depressing the shattered altar of St Paul's, but were cheered by, first, lemonade and sticky buns in the Embankment Gardens, then the temporary loss of two Staff in Westminster Abbey. A small but enthusiastic party paid a four-hour visit to the City, having viewed it from St Paul's Gallery, which proved comforting as London was not as full of ruins as they had expected. They saw Russell Thorndike and Herbert Lomas in Drinkwater's *Abraham Lincoln*.

An interesting and profitable experiment was an exhibition and lecture on China, proceeds going to the Chinese Red Cross. At the Royal Academy, a Greek display pleased them with embroidery, national costumes and statues of, for example, Princess Marina. All the juniors enjoyed a Jugo Slav exhibition.

As the geographical aspect lessened, the historical divided into junior and senior sections. More significantly for the future, they began to go out not as a specialist society, but as form or year groups. The Thirds inspected the local Tudor Room, all that remains of Henry VIII's palace, and a hundred travelled by coach to the Tower. Fourths were in the City on 1945's Election Day.

The Board's comments were helpful

In French, Miss Forrest's classes shone by their customary command of written and oral vocabulary. In HSC, Language was uncommonly good one year, the better essays a pleasure to read. Well-prepared set authors included the 17th century greats, Beaumarchais and Anatole France.

Even the linguistically able found German grammar somewhat difficult. In Literature, much was mature, well-ordered and attractive – but stereotyped.

Spanish one year produced a moderately favourable impression, as most candidates had some grasp of the essentials, although another year showed ignorance of ordinary conversational idioms.

Latin set books were less well handled than the grammar. Sixth form candidates were commended, although Roman geography was once considered weak. In Roman history, not much knowledge was revealed; indeed, statements were often inaccurate.

A lack of generality in the work

Girls still encountered trouble in dealing with compound interest, stocks and shares. One girl tried trigonometry, "apparently in error". Attempts to do Arithmetical working mentally resulted in disaster. "Whilst statements were too often made at random and instructions disobeyed", Algebra, on the whole, received praise. A possible reason for the lack of success in riders "was the entire ignoring of data".

Join us! It is open to all forms

General Science was taken one year. Chemistry gained qualified praise, Biology showed much evidence of sound teaching.

After the temporary inactivity of the dreary months of the early blackout period, the Scientific society's energies went into enjoyable and instructive Saturday and holiday rambles – Whitewebbs, Crews Hill ("a few funghi and mosses"), Bayford (fairy rings, " the rare and beautiful bog-bean, orchid and yellow iris"), the River Ash at Ware ("patches of dainty red poppies"), Cuffley ("animal prints in the snow"), the Stort valley. Members left at 7:30am to see the picturesque Beane valley with spring bluebells, wild garlic and marsh marigolds, part of the river covered with a mass of snow-white flowers, the dainty water crowfoot, and the mosaic of cultivated fields.

1941-1942 was the most successful in the society's history. Restrictions limited indoor meetings (a talk on fossils found in coal), but each wood and hedgerow, pond and stream provided fresh objects of wonder and beauty: catkins, blue dragonflies, blood-sucking water scorpions found during pond-dippings with "fishing nets we had made ourselves and jars with string handles", when wellingtons were sucked off by mud and one hat mysteriously disappeared. They saw the ice-filled furrows of the Roman Road near Hoddesdon, Dick Turpin's Cave (mineral water and ice-cream), deer, autumn toadstools and a 3-foot long snake in Epping Forest. Not only did the Head join one ramble, but she talked on her unique experiences of bird-watching, with recorded bird songs.

In chemical experiments popular at various Sales, plant-like growths emerged from crystals in a water-glass; they produced a snowstorm, an explosion in a treacle tin, water fountains, miniature volcanoes, invisible handwriting – and a Chamber of Horrors with bones and skulls.

Post-war scientists too became more adventurous. Seconds adopted a monkey when they visited the zoo. VIB attended a Chemical exhibition. Increasing scientific awareness appeared in talks given by Sixth formers on evolution, heredity, disease, DDT, followed by questions and discussions; these were enlightening and amusing, making everyone realise how great the realms of science were. Handsome tribute was paid to Miss Bruce and the aptly named Miss Pheasant (who wrote on *Careers in Science*) and Miss Finch. Brenda Knudson felt that they had inspired girls to love and believe in the study of science". They prepared the way for the specialisation to come.

Alas, girls are not taught how to wear them

... lamented one writer, comparing their party dresses with those of yesterday. Nevertheless, Needlework, despite uncertain mending and insecure fastenings, and Housewifery were generally better than Cookery, which attracted caustic comments. Food in pans was allowed to burn, rissoles were unknown, sauce-making was most uncertain, and the choice of breakfast meals for a war worker displayed great lack of variation. The dishing-up, however, was attractive and improvements were effected.

They should sketch at home and in their spare time

In Art, Fifths offered plant drawing ("good on the whole, but a little tired looking"), design ("flair but not always fitness for purpose"), object drawing (faults of perspective), pictorial design, life, posters, embroidery designs, pictorial composition, lettering and water colours.

The revived Sketch club broadened into an Arts society. Members discussed each other's work, which must have been daunting. Pencil drawings and green abstracts were created for the home-produced magazine. Many were simply artistic: a flower, a windy day, the butcher, the circus, the road mender (slightly bizarre, anatomically); others related to contributions; comparatively few reflected the war: greeting a soldier, ration books. Graffiti existed even then; on one drawing of a depressed boy sitting at a table, someone has written clearly: "What a nana!".

Mr Sanderson, artist and teacher, lectured on the evolution of Modern Art. Members spent a day sketching in Hadley Woods. Visits continued to the Tate to see what good painting really was, to St Martin's School of Art for an exhibition of free adolescent work, to Heal's to inspect house interiors, handprinted fabrics, glassware, pottery, furnishings and modern paintings, to lunchtime ballet and to Sadlers Wells, with Fonteyn and Helpman ("a flight to fairyland with the perfect beauty of the music, the poses and the colour effects"), and to Charing Cross Road booksellers. At the Leicester Galleries, they were amazed by Epstein's *Jacob and the Angel* and his bronzes and by Proctor's Impressionist paintings. The National Gallery displayed Rembrandt's portrait of *An Old Lady* acquired for the nation, war pictures and an exhibition recording the changing face of Britain by artists whose normal livelihood had been altered by contemporary conditions. Girls visited the Future London Display, awed to see Mrs Churchill.

Appreciation was expressed to Miss Sanderson and particularly to Miss Hicks who planned the outings.

When the war ended, enjoyable Saturday mornings were spent with Miss Rhodes at the Wallace Collection and the Courtauld Institute.

What about it, Choir?

Girls were disappointed when the Cramer concert was cancelled. Despite the blackout, regular practices continued until air raids put a stop to them. In 1939, a repeat performance was given of the *Nativity Mime*, but, alas, "carol singing outside seems to be a thing of the past, and those of us who remember the happy gatherings of muffled-up singers, trooping forth in the snow, equipped with lanterns and torches, look forward to the time when the Governors will once more hear ECS voices singing *Good King Wenceslaus*". Parents were invited to carol services, based on the Festival of Nine Lessons and Carols. Should an air raid prevent the service, they hoped to hold it at the same time the following day.

On Shakespeare's Day, choir and Sixth sang a 3-part song taken from *A Midsummer Night's Dream*. It was frustrating to be unsure whether raids would permit concerts at the end of terms or at functions such as the Empire Youth service at the cinema, where they were invited to lead the singing, receiving many compliments, "including one from the minister personally", or at Speech Day, when they performed tirelessly, giving their finest efforts. In 1946, a concert and gramophone recital helped the church hall funds.

Apart from their own singing in the shelters, girls enjoyed recitals in school by Maurice Jacobsen and Miss Fiona Addie. They heard an orchestral concert at Westminster Central Hall and enjoyed an opera. When hopes were expressed for a School song to replace *Jerusalem*, suggestions were made for a competition, for an approach to literary and musical celebrities, for adaptation of a hymn, even for a revival of *Onward Ever*. There the matter rested – and rests still. It was agreed to sing Amen after the Prayer as well as the hymn, but for unspecified musical reasons, Amen after the Prayer only was opposed

The suggested formation of an orchestra met with little response: "it is doubtful whether there is sufficient talent in school". In 1945, a club to arrange concerts and lectures was proposed; the Head explained that, with the new Education Act, no fees were paid, therefore there was no games fund, which had hitherto paid the fees of musicians, lecturers and the like. A voluntary levy of 6d or 1/- for members, non-members to pay for admission? Carried unanimously – and never referred to again.

Only one or two entered for Music at GSC.

The highlight continued to be the successful and well-attended EMF, one of the few festivals still carrying on, the sole concession to wartime being that it became non-competitive. The one day to which it was reduced went by far too quickly for many girls. At the first, Dr Herbert Howells congratulated them on singing *June the Piper* and *Wind from the West*. The humour and helpful advice of adjudicators was much appreciated, although Dr Geoffrey Shaw threw the choir by asking who had composed the song which they had just sung. Different years saw additions: rhythmic movement, a 6-part round, an undescribed experimental class. Criticism remained exceptionally favourable. Prizes were reinstated after the war, ECS gaining twelve in addition to many certificates.

Although "more regular and punctual attendance at practices would express our appreciation in a more concrete form", verbal tribute was always paid to Miss Bidwell and especially Miss Woods for her "patience, unflagging interest and sympathetic guidance".

Her retirement caused great fears, but Miss Thomas upheld worthily the choral tradition so well established.

Miss M.C. Sharp, MA, Head Mistress

The Staff, 1938

Hockey, Miss Hodgson

War Damage, April 1941 (courtesy Enfield Gazette)

Staff, 1947 l to r

Back row *Misses Bowen, Collins, Mrs Dean, Misses Anderson, Campbell, Mrs Parker, Misses Neilson, Cox*
Second row *Miss Maude, Mrs Hart, Misses Kirkby-Johnson, Browning, Heller, Mrs Harper, Misses Russell, Walles*
Seated on chairs *Misses Tomlinson, Marion, Morley; F. Sharp, M.C. Sharp, Hodgson, Rudkin, Barker, Flint*
Seated on ground *Misses Ellis, Thomas, Flowers (Porcheret), Robinson (Hill), Wright (secretary), Crook (Tavener)*

Miss Benjamin

Miss Hodgson

Miss Marion

Mrs Taylor (secretary)
and Mr Whitehead (caretaker)

Geography Field Class, N. Wales, 1948, Misses Ellis, Neilson

Fruit picking, Histon, 1949

Scripture Union, c1948

First form, 1947, off to the British Museum

CHAPTER TWENTY-NINE

Because the general discipline was firm,

our small transgressions were sufficient to satisfy us

As an "attempt to express in practical form the lessons of democracy which should be learnt by all citizens", the Head encouraged Council to look at every aspect of school life, even if hitherto considered the prerogative of Staff. Resolutions, filed in the library, were translated into action by the committee. Form periods were made available to discuss both agenda and decisions taken.

Parochial concerns were aired. Washbasins should be left in a clean state and new mirrors acquired for the cloakrooms. Enquiries into the acquisition of a hymnboard should be initiated. Staff agreed to weekly assignments of homework, but only for seniors and only in certain subjects. Council rejected what would be welcomed a decade or so later, namely one 'free' night each week, as well as preparation periods in school ("girls don't know how to use them"), and more voluntary prep. during lunchtime.

To inculcate good habits, some suggested Good Behaviour Marks, Bad for the opposite, which would count for, or against, Houses in their bid for the Work Shield – not a new idea. Many opposed this mercenary point of view. At the beginning of a lesson or prep., if no Mistress or Prefect arrived, the Form Monitress of forms I-IV should tell the form to work in silence and then report to the Staff room. Fifths were expected to work on their own, although both Miss F. Sharp and Miss Bowen felt that they lacked the necessary sense of responsibility. Rules were generally less rigorously enforced, Staff being too busy and too tired. Some viewed this leniency as the forerunner of a rapid decline.

"No-one below the VI form may leave the premises at lunchtimes or during the school day" was interpreted literally by some Sixthformers who silently invoked it to justify errands of gastronomic self-help before cream buns and chocolate cake were rationed. If they met the Head in Holly Walk, "an innocent Good Morning as we passed guaranteed a safe passage". M.C.S. would certainly have known, or guessed, and been amused by, and sympathetic to, their trip.

341

Wartime Sixths were, in fact, the pioneers of modern freedoms; there was, after all, no rule saying that they should *not* climb in from the cokeheap through the Music room windows, play leapfrog over trestle tables, do prep. in the churchyard where they could ignore the airraid warning, remove their prefectorial hats to spend the afternoon at the cinema watching *The Lamp Still Burns* about wartime nursing. After such an escapade, they returned for after-school activities! Another group held an undiscovered poker session in their study drinking cider brought in by one aged 18plus. They ran a complicated sweepstake as they read *Hamlet*, drawing names of girls against those of characters in succeeding scenes; 1d stake, winner takes all, or a share of, 9d. These self-same girls were pillars of rectitude as Prefects.

Council in 1940 wished for an extension of the right to vote for Prefects. The principle was agreed as supporting democracy rather than popularity. Miss Forrest was the sole dissentient to the suggestion that they be allowed to give punishments and detentions with the approval of a Senior Prefect. The Report book gave them sufficient authority. By 1946, they were taking a daily, yes daily, Prefects' detention, so that punishment could speedily reflect the crime.

Their identification with their forms and their forms with them continued intense, occasionally unhealthily so. Form Monitresses frequently modelled themselves on their Prefects. Council's undemocratic motion that Form Mistresses should select these lowlier officials because the girls voted for their personal friends was referred back, and decently buried.

We can all do something and each of us best knows what

In no other aspect of school life do clichés abound as they do in House reports. For those who win, for those who lose, there is congratulation, exhortation, rebuke, a frequent whiff of desperation. "We came 4th this year in the Sports, which is at least an improvement on last year's 5th. ... Keenness and enthusiasm count and will reap rewards in the end. ... Juniors must remember that the Juniors of today are the Seniors of tomorrow. ... It is not the winning that counts, but the keenness in turning out to practices regularly and having the true House spirit"; SORPS again. "Take a pencil and paper to write this out and pin it on your wall. *Please turn out to every practice!* ... The more effort you put into it, the more you will reap in the end".

One Captain gave specific admonishment. "Next term make up your mind that YOUR House is going to win the Bowles Cup" by four simple rules.

1. Find out your House day for hockey and netball.
2. Always look on the House noticeboard to see if your name is there, the day *before* the House games practice.
3. Always turn out *promptly* to House practices.
4. If you simply cannot come out, tell the games captain and provide a substitute.

"Winning the Cup requires neither brain nor brawn, but only enthusiasm and a little memory".

St Catherine's took the hockey cup four times, sharing tennis honours with St Ursula's which maintained a virtual monopoly of both netball and swimming and won the reinstituted post-war Sports Trophy. St Winifred's twice gained the Work Shield, Margarines enjoyed the odd win.

But St Cecilia's! What tales of woe! 1940: "Where are the shields and the Bowles Cup we were going to win? Go to it next year!" 1941: "One of the worst years. Things are serious. Consistently last". 1943: "No shields! A very depressing record. I advise you to forget the past two or three years and keep your eye on the future. If you aren't good at games, you can help us to win the Work Shield" – clearly second best.

Although the original fervour never returned despite individual enthusiasts, the shouting at House Relays never diminished in volume.

Council confirmed that Houses should be the means of instituting other activities, but this ideal remained unrealised. Winifred's enjoyed innumerable cakes, blancmanges and games at their party. Community singing and a play on the saint, written and produced by Miss Flint, made the Captain feel that they "should be well on the way to being, as our brothers would say, 'Cock House'". Cecilians also welcomed First forms at on November 22, day of their patron saint. Ursuleans formed a large Savings group, the amounts being added to school totals in aid of the country.

Perhaps Houses were too big and should be split in two? Should there be competitive play performances, with judges? By 1944, nothing definite had been decided and Houses remained simply a focus for games and sports.

Meanwhile, *"Work and Play for your House always. All depends on You.* See if we can't make this House the House to which every newcomer will be proud to belong".

Gymslips seem to last for ever"'

A 1937 new girl was still wearing her original when she was a Fifth former; then, the edges of the box pleats were worn through and the yoke, originally of fluffy dark green velvet, had attained the threadbare dull yellowish tinge which was the mark of a senior. Inside the yoke was a pocket to which a purse on a chain could be attached, so that the front sagged drearily. Buttons fastened on the shoulder. Council's motion that gymslips which had become too small should be made into skirts was firmly quashed. Still the same blouses, although the more daring girls, or more enterprising mothers, enjoyed shirt styles which better suited a tie.

Council's request for pegs in classrooms, as girls had to keep with them at all times their outdoor coats because of air raids, was rejected as not ideal. "One of the worst garments ever designed – bulky and awkward to wear in the winter, but sticky over a summer dress, quickly losing its soft new nap to reveal a coarse dull underweave wherever it had rubbed on desks and walls", the blazer yet continued. The black velours hat still resisted all efforts at twisting, pulling or even cutting into more fashionable shapes – boater, 'po' or porkpie. First Years wore theirs with a piece of grubby, knotted, chewed elastic under the chin, whilst older girls attempted to anchor theirs with hatpins. An early resolution that berets should replace this ill-fitting, old-fashioned headgear was defeated as impossible to arrange in wartime. This was probably because there were four to five dozen hats still in stock. The war did bring one great blessing: supplies of panamas ceased. Although the Head really wanted a fawn hat suitable for all occasions, girls had already voted unanimously that hats be optional in summer.

The other essential, not formally prescribed, was luggage; satchels were falling into disfavour, music cases were the in-thing, however unsuitable in size and shape, especially for seniors.

The stern, pre-war attitude was slightly, grudgingly, relaxed; as rationing took effect, everyone began to have different priorities. Gymslips lost their velvet trim. "Anxious that no black die should enter any wounds we might sustain from battles on the hockey pitch, and to bless us (in some respect at any rate) with the fashions of 1940", lisle stockings were permitted, as were, at long last, green cardigans. Nevertheless, Vedonis vests and liberty bodices worn with navy knickers continued.

With their silver badge of office and hatband in silver/white with two narrow dark green bands, Prefects were allowed to wear dark green dresses, made of the itchy gymslip material and condemned as unhygienic by a later generation, with tussore collars and cuffs. The usual summer dress material was replaced by check gingham. Council requested some safeguard that skirts would be of suitable width and length for games.

Ankle socks, similar in colour to stockings, were suggested for gym; colour matching with wartime dyes and general preference for white ruled them out. Shoes provided never-ending problems. Shoebags were recognised as unsuitable for muddy shoes and inadequate for wellingtons – but "don't you know there's a War on?"

Council conservatively condemned obvious cosmetics (rouge, lipstick, eyebrow pencil). Hair styles were in the melting pot – short, longish, long – although disapproval was expressed of such extravagance as long hair hanging down over the collar and hair which "is impossible to wear a hat with". They agonised: should there be a limit on the height above the forehead? compulsory tying back if shoulder length? The Sixth opposed, again on grounds of hygiene, the proposal that white hair ribbons as well as dark green or black be worn with dresses; they would dirty too quickly!

A day before VE Day 1945, "a fitting time for Staff and girls who had shared wartime difficulties", a panoramic photograph (5/-, at least 75 must be sold) was taken, although winter uniform was decreed. Virtually no seniors and only a few juniors wore ties with their mostly buttoned-up blouses. Many sleeves reached the elbows as if long-sleeved ones had suffered surgery.

Any real change was deemed impractical until rationing was relaxed.

The Scramble and Crush of the Dinner-Hour

Food rationing emphasised the importance of school dinners.

Government policy was to make a cooked meal available cheaply for all. Numbers taking advantage of this increased satisfactorily: 30 (1934), 130 (1939) 200 (1940) and by 1940 320 stayed regularly.

Specimen menus for two weeks in September 1941 survive.

Monday   Irish stew, root vegetables, boiled rice and jam

Tuesday   Cold beef, green salad, baked potatoes, syrup tart, custard

Wednesday Vegetable stew, runner beans, potatoes, baked sponge pudding, jam

Thursday   Shepherd's pie, greens, potatoes, plum or apple pie, custard

Friday   Hors d'œuvres (lettuce, cucumber, watercress), cheese, tinned meat or sardine, rolls and butter, trifle

Week two showed little fundamental difference.

Monday   Hot pot, haricot beans, potatoes, steamed pudding

Tuesday   Corned beef, tomatoes, potatoes, ground rice pudding or jam tart, custard

Wednesday Cold roast lamb, green salad, potatoes, apple tart and custard or ground rice pudding

Thursday	Pressed beef, carrots, runner beans, potatoes, batter pudding and jam or treacle tart and custard
Friday	Hors d'œuvres, gooseberry tart and custard or chocolate trifle

The food cost, on average, 5½d. Just over 12% had free dinners, under ·5% paid 4d, almost 84% paid 6d and roughly 3·5% the top price of 9d; 3,238 meals in all were served. They deteriorated as rationing bit; memories of an Oxo cube with salad and unpalatable British Restaurant type of fare remain. Staff ate at a separate table and had coffee afterwards. The Sixth, daring to complain at such discrimination, heard that Mistresses paid extra for the privilege, although the burden of dinner accounts and understanding the catering regulations would have justified it.

Girls still trooped over to EGS Hall. Cards of five tickets were bought on Mondays, one being torn off daily, signed on the back and posted in a box outside the Staff room. If the count revealed a discrepancy, names were read out to girls seated in the Hall to see who had not posted her ticket. The simpler, more effective way of collecting tickets on entry was soon adopted.

At Council, dinner was the topic most frequently raised. A clear majority passed the extraordinary motion that school should start earlier so that the dinnerhour might be lengthened to permit both lunching at home and resuming House games. They asked for special places; Miss Barron, with incomprehensible logic, suggested that better behaviour would be a more fitting remedy; it was decided that girls should arrange themselves in the queue in the order in which they wished to sit. It was later agreed that, in suitable summer weather, those bringing lunch should leave earlier so as to be out of doors, the elder ones being responsible for maintaining a tidy field. Miss Rudkin warmly agreed, adding that plenty of fresh air was essential in wartime. Eating on the field was again firmly refused, Miss F. Sharp expressing doubts as to whether daily picnics in the grounds constituted a suitable feature of school life.

Dinnertime air raids were the worst, "for we all love our dinners in peace, and it was most annoying to be in the act of putting a piece of roast potato in one's mouth and then to have to pick up one's knife, fork and spoon and take cover". If a raid began before mealtime, steaming dinners were pushed over from EGS on trolleys to the shelters by Staff and Sixth who also issued beakers of milk, free after the war, at Break. It was difficult to manipulate plates without a table. Occasionally, the Sixth sat outside the shelters. "I remember the whistle blowing when we were all on our pudding course. We took cover immediately and briefly and emerged to the incongruous sight of little groups of puddings scattered on the grass. It was much harder to identify one's own than we had imagined". If the raid began during dinnertime, lower school girls dived under the tables, one being surprised to find herself nose to nose with Miss Rudkin.

One delightful memory remains. Staff brought the Sixth tea during 1944's examinations, It was "soothing to have nice warm beakers and teachers saying 'Sugar? Is that enough?'".

Games were all the more enjoyable as there were so few

At first, it was difficult to organise any sporting activity since at no time did all Forms meet together. Practices had to cease well before dark to allow cyclists to get home before blackout time. Cutting the grass presented problems when petrol was rationed; lines were marked by volunteers when the groundsman was called up. Possible matches were fewer as many schools had been evacuated.

Thanks were offered by Captains to cooks and refreshment committees. In 1946, cordial for winter matches cost £1:5:0, fares 5/11 and Sports Day teas 7/6.

Reports for both winter games are virtually interchangeable. Hockey, still *the* game, still inspired verse; with renewed apologies to Wordsworth, Joyce Armsby evoked

The Solitary Centre

Behold her foremost in the field
Yon solitary County lass,
Running and hitting by herself;
Shoot now, or quickly pass!
    No centre forward ever passed
    A stronger ball from off her stick ...

eventually, she, weirdly, scored a goal to win the day.

Results of the two or three teams are incomplete: W 45, L 20, D 6, scratched 6 (1946), Colours 23. Girls lost to the boys, drew once with the Staff, but lost 5-1 to combined Mistresses and Masters. "Fortunately, no German airman has dared to drop a bomb on our pitch", although one came unhealthily close in 1942. "The ATS played us in thick mud and battledress with disgraceful results", for which no excuses were offered. Peace brought not only a good spirit and increasing success on Wednesdays and Saturdays, but also second place in the North Middlesex tournament.

"An account of a wartime netball season does not make the interesting reading we should like". Netball was tolerated. Only the Knock-Out inter-form tournament aroused enthusiasm. The traditional Staff match, still the favourite, had a rival, that against EGS. "If only school turned out in half the number to inter-school matches as they did to that match, I am sure we could be urged to better play and the school could not fail to benefit by watching". Maybe continuing during a warning, if there was no gunfire, helped the three, four or even five teams to some 17 Colours and to their massive wartime wins: eg., 1941-1942, W 26, L 12. The first post-war season was less glorious: P 25, W 12, L 12, D 1.

Be sprightly for you fall among friends

The half-mile trek in all weathers to not always enjoyed gym lessons in the Presbyterian Church Hall gave another legal excuse for unavailability; one future Head Mistress skipped it from day 1, thus not being registered. With Miss Hodgson, "an orderly lesson ended with the command 'with a step forward, dismiss', at which we took a step forward, clapped our hands and dispersed". In the summer of 1945, a two-day Gym Display "miraculously overcame the difficulties under which physical training laboured since the destruction of the gym.". In the first peacetime year, Remedial Drill was reintroduced.

Little more than a pleasant pastime

ECS kept the Inter-Schools Tennis Shield throughout the war, competition ceasing after 1940. After the air raids, courts could be booked between 4 and 6pm, but prestige came slowly. Three teams played in white blouses and skirts: P 42, L 12, 7 Colours. Junior and senior championships continued. EGS won regularly, the closest score being 51 games to 48, the Staff occasionally. Seniors sometimes umpired with Staff, one of whom taught them many tactics, including net play. More matches were arranged post-war as other schools returned, but the weather forced many cancellations.

"If you keep trying and practising, you will win through in the end". The game of rounders, comparatively new, was greeted with great initial enthusiasm but less skill. Two junior teams increased to four: W 30, L 24, D 7. Seniors were castigated in their first season for bad fielding. Council accepted Colours in principle, but only two were awarded.

Many learned to swim, thus gaining House points

Life Saving classes, RLSS Bronzes (at least 40), Bars thereto (a dozen or so), 1st Class Instructor's certificates (about 14) and one Award of Merit – swimming was a popular individual sport. They were pleasantly surprised to learn that the baths could be used during school hours again in 1941. The ever-lengthening list of names on the Hall noticeboard showed that many more were learning to swim and dive.

Annual Galas were a popular morning out of school, although, by 1945, points collected during the term meant that the winning House (usually Ursula's) was already known. Senior inter-form Relay (in nightdresses "to much amusement"), half-width wading race for First form non-swimmers, the judge (Mrs Angus), who gave an exhibition of swimming and diving – it was all great fun. In the winter of 1946, activities expanded to include Life-Saving Land Drill; the standard soon rose dramatically.

> A Day to be remembered
> Is the Sports Day of our School,
> When we in our excitement
> Perchance might break a rule.
>> The thrills and disappointments
>> In every kind of race,
>> Are soon to be detected
>> On every scholar's face.
> And then amid the praises
> Of parents and of friends,
> The victors take their trophies,
> And thus the glad day ends.

Sports Day once had to be postponed to Tuesday morning because of the cold and rain. A Governor or local worthy presented pictures to winning forms, cups to champions and savings stamps to winning OGs and visitors, including fathers. Proudly wearing her House colour, each girl loudly cheered any member of the same House. The 1942 Mistresses' race (Miss Collingwood an easy winner, followed by Miss F. Sharp and Miss Bowen) proved popular.

One July Friday, 1944,"a small number of parents and visitors braved the darts of the enemy"; indeed, two alerts interrupted the afternoon, juniors being despatched to the shelters. As some girls were evacuated and races were not completed until the following Monday, there were no official championships. This was doubly frustrating as books had been displayed in the hope that some would be donated to the library.

In 1945, on another Tuesday, the sun shone all afternoon; parents crowded in. This was the first most could remember when there was no fear of raiders or flying bombs. The Sack and Cloakroom races were pronounced amusing, the Mistresses' event (which included such odd tests as knitting) was won by Miss Bowen, followed by Miss F. Sharp and Mrs

Westwood – in all, "one of the most successful the school has ever known". 1946 reverted to type – interrupted by storms.

Minor sports? The table tennis club, begun in 1939 with two tables proved immensely popular; by 1940, however, it was unofficially suspended for the duration; that same year, Council voted its revival. Nothing more is heard of it until 1946, when Fifths played thrice weekly.

Post-war saw, at 5:30pm, two years of country dancing for the middle school, culminating in a summer party in EGS Hall.

Of the nine Mistresses thanked, two were singled out repeatedly; Miss Bass, "for making it possible for us to uphold the English reputation for sport even during a war", and, of course, Miss Hodgson, despite absence with rheumatism for nearly two terms. She wrote:"How much I have missed you all. Compulsory holidays can become very wearying". Finding it strange to envy others turning out of bed at 7:15am, she was forced to be in bed or baked in an electric tunnel or steamed in a vapour bath. Urging girls to appreciate having the use of all their limbs, she threatened to be "an even greater dragon warning you off sitting on the grass. Real campers never sit on damp grass". She was pleased that Mrs Brown ("a silver lining to the cloud") enjoyed her time at ECS, "proof that you have 'come up to scratch', and done your best for her". She received from heroine-worshipping pupils many messages, letters and gifts.

Considering the many difficulties that have cropped up

Guides and Cadets worked closely together, Miss F. Sharp and Miss Hodgson being supported by Lieutenant Beall (who later formed her own company), Captain Murrant, Miss Bowen (lessons on First Aid), Lieutenant and Quarter Master Neilson ("excellent suppers") and Miss Davidson.

Meetings were restricted and weekend camps cancelled. Signalling and camp making took place on the field, outdoor work being considered proper Guiding. Members recall a camp fire lit with only one match (a test in the rain),"cooking some of our precious rations, helping to make a field kitchen and learning how to erect tents, only to pull them down again without having slept in them. We all give a helping hand with the clearing up". Day, and later, weekend camps became the annual highlight, when they enjoyed sandwiches and a rest hour before tracking, then cooked teas over their fires.

They dug a potato patch on the hockey pitch, which fully repaid them for their time and labour. They participated in all war efforts, helped the WVS to deliver letters, cleaned Staff cars and bicycles, ran a jumble sale

(£7:4:0 to their ambulance fund), held a drill competition with other companies; "there was great rivalry when we sang *Our Chief Guide* as to which company was the best". Junior recruits were some of the few who were distressed to find that the gym had gone, and that their patrol boxes were in a muddle, only a lid being left of one. Guides, with renewed energy, began two new patrols, one called, embarrassingly, the Blue Tits.

Noteworthy events included a Memorial Service in the Parish Church for Lord Baden Powell and a concert for his fund at which they read a play, deemed competent if uninspired. A demonstration of an emergency field kitchen caused great excitement when a thin spiral of smoke issued from the chimney. They loved Christmas parties on their own and with the Sea Rangers, the usual services at St George's Day Parade and for Empire Youth in the Town Park (with a March Past to the Market Place), hikes (tea at Miss F. Sharp's house), cycle rides (compass and mapreading) and running their own Bring and Buy sale. Two volunteered for relief work in Europe, one represented Middlesex on Youth Sunday in Westminster Abbey, others participated in the Wings for Victory parade. They felt privileged to spend Whit at an international camp.

Training continued for competitions and badges (Child and Sick Nursing, Cooking, Toymaking, Knitting) and teaching new recruits their tenderfoot. Cadets exchanged Guide hats for bright blue berets and school hats for white ones. Discarding emblems and badges, they were invested with new blue and white enamel trefoils. They scrubbed and cleaned a room in Enfield Court for meetings.

Although numbers increased, the end of the war saw no real change; there were simply more meetings, more camps and campfires, more cocoa and cakes, more training (Lifeline Throwing, Flag Hoisting), more parties when everyone brought food or each patrol provided a game. They delighted in a fun fair, a treasure hunt, Visitors' Day, and in 1946 ten excited girls spent 2½ weeks in the French Alps ("scanty food") with three Staff. The following year, they appreciated the food but judged the weather doubtful.

The war had seen the best of Guide and Cadet endeavours.

"I am proud of these activities, the record of a London school in wartime", proclaimed the Head.

CHAPTER THIRTY

The measure of a school is the quality of people who work in it and are turned out by it.

At Speech Day 1946, Miss Sharp paid tribute. "In certain fields of national life during these often difficult and frustrating post-war days, it has been remarked that the volume of work and output is limited and declining and that greater efforts are needed, I can confidently claim that this does not apply to us, for ever-growing numbers, shortages of books and other tools of learning, alarming and exhausting conditions of overcrowding only act as a challenge to the Staff, and, as a result of their unflagging labours, *our* exports are healthier in body, wealthier in knowledge and wiser in outlook than ever".

In addition to their normal teaching and participation in school life, the war had brought extra obligations: checking on home problems, holding lessons in their own houses, fire-watching, selling savings stamps, dealing with dinner accounts, issuing rationed rubber shoes, preaching fuel economy, showing resourcefulness after air raids. Although unaware of it, they were the first to fulfil the ever-increasing functions of social workers. Health was affected, Miss Rudkin being seriously ill in 1940; "we trust that the period of convalescence will strengthen her". The secretary's work too was becoming more complicated; there were three during the war, the Misses Schollick, Auger and Franklyn.

The turnover, worst in 1946, was great, sometimes welcomed, sometimes provoking tears. Temporary, visiting and substitute teachers were plentiful; some preferred non-permanent posts, some were alone as husbands were called up, others had failed to secure regular jobs. "The only time we were badly behaved was when we had a student whom we unkindly christened The Flop. The poor girl was unprepossessing, tall, gangling, with a bun and thick glasses, and so nervous that she took the lesson while perpetually popping her hanky in and out of her pink directoire knicker-leg".

Between 1940 and 1946, thirty-five Staff left, twenty-two for other posts, not always in education, for at least two did specific war work.

Of the new appointments, eighteen left during the war. Eleven came – and went – staying from 2½ weeks to 2½ terms. Miss Gwendoline Trice Martin (six previous schools in four years) made an impression during her one term by participating in Council, theatre expeditions and harvest camp. Miss Beatrice Flora Cunradi was more extraordinary: educated in England, graduating in Illinois, she taught in Argentina before spending twenty-seven years as secretary/ translator/researcher in North and South America, moving on after five terms at ECS.

Other leavers, generally after two or three years, must have seemed fixtures by comparison. Six married ("all the young ones going" wailed the girls): the Misses Thompson (Music), Paternoster (PE), Lindsay (PE, member of the Play-Reading group), Noble (Science) and Bruce. The last had given unfailing support in netball and taken instructive and varied outings on Saturday mornings. Miss Joyce Murrant not only remained six years but made history by staying on as Mrs Westwood. Teaching German, she is affectionately remembered for her energy, interest, help and ingenuity.

Miss Davidson and Miss Fisher departed after four and six years respectively; Miss Jarvis, after twelve years, was especially blessed for her parting present: "two really large mirrors to replace the old ones with their curiously dappled reflections". Miss Beall became a Head, Miss Hicks a lecturer, Miss Bass joined the Swedish Institute as a physiotherapist. Both Miss Sanderson and Miss Finch were experienced, the former a visiting Art Mistress, the latter a biologist. Miss Kathleen Martin had been a pupil. Miss Pheasant, thirteen years, did a stint at a Training College before renewing her connection with ECS as an Institute of Education tutor. Miss Bowen's relationship was more complicated; she returned after two terms to stay until she retired in 1965.

The old order changed with six major retirements. After twenty-three years Miss Jones and after thirty Miss Hyslop both departed, although the latter was only 55. Long identified with dramatic work, Miss Baxter's theatre parties, deep personal interest and keen sense of humour were thought to have earned her a rest; she later married. Miss Crombie, after teaching during two wars, and still only 53, had, despite difficulties inconceivable today, created a sound tradition of Geography teaching, and opened the eyes of many to the outside world. Girls were agreeably surprised when she married a year later.

The major change of 1944 was the departure of the two great friends. Miss Woods, appointed in the middle of the first war, left near the end of the second. She made the choir, arranged songs and solved make-up problems for plays, cheered them in the shelters with *Lilli Bulero* and *Old*

King Cole, leaving "us happy but very thirsty". In short, she established school music. "Every generation of new girls passed through her hands and has owed to her the firm foundations of good work and discipline laid in that important first year' – tribute to the diminutive Miss Bidwell. Together, they created the EMF.

Both ladies visited the Mediterranean to photograph and paint. Their sherry parties and fundraising continued for school causes. In the early Fifties, they arranged London visits, even "toiling up the steps to Big Ben, accompanied by a talkative bevy of young girls" on Anglo-French holiday courses.

Miss Barron, aged 57, died in harness after twenty-two years at ECS, and remembered particularly for systematically slogging through F.M.F's text books.

A deep sadness was the sudden death in 1940 of Miss Florence, aged 61. A broken arm had hindered her search for war work on retirement, but after Dunkirk, she was soon looking after refugees from the Low Countries, which must have reminded her of the past. "There is no generation of girls that does not remember her with affection and gratitude". Actions speak louder than words. A memorial fund provided a perpetual reminder of thirty years of unselfish care and thought for the girls' best interests. Despite wartime problems, subscriptions, ranging from 1/- to £20, soon totalled £788:4:9, £300 being invested in 2½% Defence Bonds. This made possible grants towards training or professional qualifications, or for those who experienced hardship in mid-course or who changed courses; often a guinea made all the difference. It also endowed an annual prize for a Sixthformer with good results at HSC/AL Mathematics; there was never a dearth of suitable recipients. Much used in its early days, the well-managed fund stood, by 1952, at nearly £1,000 and had helped 123 girls with a total of £900.

The magazine editor commented that girls were so used to frequent changes that they could not realise the thrill experienced in earlier days on the arrival of a new member of Staff.

What of the stayers? Two shared a flat, somewhat to their own wonderment, as they were so dissimilar – but they did laugh at the same things. Vigour personified as she sped round the Old Building, the life and soul of fire-watching, Miss Mollie Kathleen (Kate) Flint (1940-1950) introduced a new femininity, being the first to appear in wingswept glasses and the new Dior look when everyone else wore skimpy, knee-length, rationed Utility suits; she and her sisters operated their own lending fashion library; no-one could compete with her slender elegance. Perhaps she was the last to evoke a GP, a 'pash', a 'crush'. She turned the magazine into a literary organ and gave plays a professional polish rarely seen in school drama. Whereas she could not boil an egg with even a modicum of success, her flatmate, Miss Mildred Edith Tomlinson (1940-1970) was neatly and precisely practical as befitted an Oxford 1st Class Honours Chemistry graduate. Her influence on all scientists was tremendous.

These two symbolise the new wave which took over in the Forties and Fifties.

Eight Governors, including "our much loved chairman" Desborough Brown, Mrs Davies and Mr Mason served throughout the war; another spent a year on war service. They once charmed the girls by granting a half holiday in honour of "an excellent and record-breaking year at the conclusion of a greatly disturbed school course"; it was added to the summer half-term.

With the death of Mrs Rothwell, Governor for nineteen years, school lost a staunch and loyal friend. The first chairman, Sir Henry Bowles, died in 1944. ECS was probably as much his creation as it was that of the first Head, perhaps more. "He was always so keenly alive to all we were doing, never too busy to help in any difficulty, full of keen sympathy with us in our ever-present problem of inadequate accommodation. Many OGs have cause to remember his generosity and continued interest. Only a few days before his death, he was still busy devising new ways to help us".

We do look forward

1,1008 joined ECS during the war and up to December 1946. No fewer than 442, almost 44%, had their entire secondary education in wartime or immediately post-war, when conditions were as bad, occasionally worse. Returning evacuees cause problems as previous schools and fathers' jobs were not always mentioned at interviews, were sometimes repeated or different information supplied. Several stayed one month, two a fortnight, one just over a week; 126 arrived at times other than September.

Evacuees, nine girls with at least three previous schools, one with four, three European refugees, two English girls returning from Holland – all must have been confused. Old favourites kept their lead: Chase Side 90, George Spicer and Lavender Road 78 each, Chesterfield 71, St Andrew's 50. Increasing numbers came from Raglan 35 and Suffolks 30. Others kept their low position. Ten schools contributed for the first time: for example, Merryhills 26, Cranbourne 20, Ladbooke 19, Oakwood 13 – in short, 704 girls from 28 establishments.

Private fee-paying institutions, mainly local, some unnamed, sent 67, Enfield Preparatory 16 the only one to reach double figures, with 12 from convent schools; 40 came from secondary schools in more vulnerable areas – Tottenham and Edmonton 10 each, Hornsey 6, Dalston 3 and 11 from other parts of London. 106 had been in 82 different places in the United Kingdom, from Edinburgh to Southend, not to mention Canada, India, New Zealand and the USA.

Limited areas? Similar backgrounds?

Three girls called Margaret Rose and three Marina bear witness to interest in the Royal Family; 31 had a surname, few had but one forename; indeed, some 281 different names, some just spelling variants, are recorded. Some have a masculine air: Alberta, Arnoldine, Frederica, Roberta, Thomasine. Margaret 98 and Mary 90 continued to be most popular, others in the top ten being Jean 80, Joan 74, Patricia 59, Ann/ Anne/Annie 53, Elizabeth 42, Joyce 40, Eileen 38 and Audrey 35. Newly favoured were Barbara 30, Shirley 29, Evelyn and Betty 27, Maureen 21 and Valerie 17; 86 had names unique to them, such as Alwyn, Babette, Cisca, Ethaline, Ethne, Hatty, Hedda, Jilda, Kerstine, Lorle, Magali, Petronella, Sigrid, Tegwin, Thali, Zella.

Financial details are copious and complicated. Most needed more money, especially when father was called up. Not untypical was one girl paying termly full fees of five guineas, then £1:5:0, who then gained free tuition, grants for maintenance, travel and uniform, free dinners and an Intermediate award. Many families paid or received different amounts each year. Until fees ceased, 372, almost 37%, had free tuition for most, usually all, of their school lives; 147 only, for at least part of their time, paid in full; partial payments were due for 188, most £1:5:0, fewer £2:5:0. Two other authorities contributed for four pupils.

Maintenance grants, reassessed annually, varied even more. One father, refused one year, received £14 the next. Accuracy is impossible, but 221 enjoyed an average of just under £5. After 1945, grants decreased to 32 but averaged almost £8; 31 won Intermediate awards, £1-£13, averaging £4.

Uniform grants, mostly £2-£3, went to 61, two receiving £10. Those 76 travelling from the outskirts were helped by carefully judged travel money of nine different amounts from 10/- to £2:6:0. The final help was free dinners, felt to be humiliating by the 19 recipients, their poverty being obvious when the others were paying. One girl's financial and other problems caused her to move temporarily to stay with her fiancé's mother. What would Miss Broome have thought? One mother who had been helped unofficially wrote delightfully: "I do appreciate it very much and as soon as the girls are off hand, I hope to be able to repay in full once again. Thank you".

The domestic scene was obviously less settled. There are no details of 49 fathers; 26, of whom one was unemployed, 2 in the Navy and one a Japanese POW, were already dead or died before their daughters had left ECS. Two widows remarried, eight girls had stepfathers, six were orphans. Three divorces and one separation were noted; 25 girls were in their mothers' care, some because father had been called up. Only four women admitted jobs – cleaner, housekeeper, school canteen and domestic workers; maybe social prejudices affected replies, or some worked only after their daughters became pupils. Two fathers had retired, another, war-blinded, retrained as a physiotherapist. One student lived with mother and uncle, another was sent to stay with her aunt. Two refugees had guardians, one a parson.

Over 200 fathers were white-collar workers. Clerical work, 87, covered the usual wide fields and varying levels to include a Trade Union general secretary and a registrar. Civil Servants numbered 24, managers and directors 20, accountants 18, journalists 8, local government officers 7, stockbrokers 4, architects, commercial artists and ministers of religion 2 each, plus 31 in education, with still the distinction between schoolmasters (Grammar) and teachers (other ranks).

Retail trade provided a living for 146. Proportionately more numerous were 46 commercial travellers, 31 were owners, managers and the like. A narrower range of goods was sold: clothing and tailoring 23 (including fur and leather), catering 14, grocery 11, meat 7, hairdressing 5 (one master barber), drink 4, newspapers and tobacco 3, jewellery 2, furniture 2, fish 1.

The pre-war pattern changed slightly as manual and transport workers shared third place. Many skilled men remained, such as wire drawers, cordite worker, aluminium polisher, jute goods supervisor, turbine greaser, but fewer labourers and factory hands. In printing, 19 performed all manner of jobs from compositors to packer. On the roads, 62 fathers worked as conductors, chauffeurs, drivers and mechanics of all possible types of vehicle from cabs to cranes; the railways employed 22 clerks and 22 skilled men. Four, more unusually, were with ships: dock checker, ocean cable operator, ship surveyor and general worker.

More were in construction work as builders (one doubling as a funeral director), inspectors, merchants, decorators, plumbers, foremen and charge hands. The large total of 38 worked specifically with wood.

Engineering, at several grades, continued to support more in wide spheres, from bakelite to ventilation, pattern making to radio, cinema and television. Ten electricians were busy men.

Some fathers may have been counted twice depending on when the war claimed them; 41 were directly involved in the RAF, the Army, the Navy or the RNVR (marine wireless operator), in Civil Defence, or in munitions, 11 in RSAF; also mostly in uniform were 16 connected with the Post Office, 14 with the police and 6 with the fire service.

A higher proportion was in health work, as chemists of different types 7, makers of medical aids 8, plus nurses, an optician and 2 dentists. In bottom place, now of minor importance, was the land, with 4 in nurseries, 3 in gardens, 3 on farms, and a mixed bag: cemetery supervisor, head cowhand, dairyman, groundsman, riding instructor, seedsman and smallholder.

Unusual? Fewer: auctioneer's assistant, coin meter collector, musical director, district representative and the first Member of Parliament.

What greater mixture could any sociologist dream?

People will judge you by what you are and what you do

VIA leavers were again fêted after the war. In 1945, they took part in a service in St Paul's Cathedral. The following year's event in the Central Hall, Westminster, was less impressive, but at least everyone could hear. Hats were, of course, obligatory.

Discussions began with a IV parents' meeting in 1945, but there was still no official careers guidance; the assumption was still that a girl knew what she wanted to do or she would take a clerical post and no-one had the right to interfere. They saw an ATS film show. OG Hilda Tucker enlightened magazine readers with the minutest detail on the nursery school and lamented the lack of trained helpers to guide the mental and physical growth of young children.

In mid-war, a request for a reference for nursing training asked: "Is Miss X intelligent, lady-like, amenable to discipline? Is she likely to treat her patients with kindness and consideration?"

A bank, post-war, wrote about a 16-year old: "I shall esteem it a favour if you will inform me in confidence what is your opinion of her character, and, whether, so far as is known to you, she bears an unblemished personal reputation". Even more surprising is the conclusion: "Thanking you in anticipation of your reply which I shall be pleased to receive by return of post". Colleges asked if candidates came from "a Good Home" with "a Good Cultural Background".

"This record represents what one school out of thousands is doing in this country". Some 442 left up to the end of 1946, 128 at odd times; 168 had known both Heads and 197 had joined in the last two years of peace. At least 30 were evacuated (one, strangely, to Dover), half returning after relatively short stays; several emigrated. There were misfits: six returned to their old schools, five moved to others, one to the convent, one left through family circumstances, another broke the agreement; one retired with nerves, one died, one was killed; a fourth died later aged only 36.

The jobs of almost half are unrecorded. Only three seem to have joined up. Two worked on the land, one went into a nursery garden, one studied dairying at Studley college and another horticulture at Swanley. Two worked in factories (one on a slicing machine), eight in shops (two sisters running their own, two hairdressers), five were telephonists. Five became librarians, four were trainees (as a tracer, with a comptometer, two in a drawing office), three worked in laboratories. The caring professions took at least 26: chemist's receptionist, trainee hospital almoner, masseuse, two at the London School of Speech Therapy, two dispensers, three physiotherapists (who found it difficult to get training), three apprentice pharmacists and at least 13 nurses.

Stimulated by rising numbers in VIB Commercial, 60 were attracted to clerical work, in factories, industry, local government, Odham's Press. At least 16 joined the Civil Service, in, for example, the Ministry of Supply and the Air Ministry. Ten followed secretarial training, four at Pitman's; Tottenham Technical college and various Polytechnics accepted 12. One studied Economics, Business and Commerce.

Multiple applications had to be made to colleges and many received heart-breaking rejections. At least nine went in for DSc, one attending a Dress Designing school, another studying Canteen Management. In addition to those following Music (two at Trinity College, one with a scholarship), Froebel and Dramatic studies, one trained as an architect. Three colleges took eight for PE. At least 30 went in for teaching at 11 different establishments. Wartime saw 8, and 1946 18, scholarships (full, part-time, evenings) to Hornsey and 15 to the French Institute, although, again, not all were taken up.

About 40, every school's pride and joy, went up to universities. Competition was fierce, both for places (especially when servicemen and women began to return) and for State scholarships. At least 8 college scholarships ("the blue riband of achievement") and nine exhibitions were won to Oxbridge, London and provincial universities. In 1945, three winners were invited to a reception at Middlesex Guildhall. Miss Sharp was proud too that five played in their university teams in their first year.

HEAD GIRLS

1939 Madeleine Boyall	1940 Patricia Denton
1941 Mary Flanders, Winifred Rayner	1942 Jeanne Tucker
1943 Beryl Eaton	1944 Olive Stephens
1945 Audrey Lane	1946 Barbara Williams

Additional School Colours

1942 M. Lahee, Margaret Stone	1943 M. Allen
1944 Mary Stone	1945 B. Stone
1946 G. Murfitt	

Some achieved local, national, indeed international fame; so many won so many prizes – form, linguistic, scientific – and gained so many examination successes, four distinctions being not uncommon, that choice becomes increasingly difficult.

Madeleine Ginette Boyall (1st place), Eleanor Patricia Denton (3rd), returning evacuee Jeanne Patricia Tucker (the examiners considering her diction perfect) and Patricia Marjorie Brett all gained scholarships to the French Institute, and with Winifred Patricia Rayner and Audrey Lane (hockey*, actress and school's Conservative candidate), Honours in le Grand Concours and Concours Spécial. House Captain Madeleine secured matriculation, RSA, HSC and a Middlesex award to spend two months in Italy, and, as a teacher, ran French verse-speaking competitions as did editor Winifred, a future Head, who won a senior County award of £70 to Bedford. Both acted as did Pat (Brett) who won an Exhibition to King's and entered the Civil Service. Audrey chronicled the Cadets' activities and, as if four subjects in HSC were insufficient, began Greek before studying Psychology. Writer and secretary of the French club, Pat (Denton, tennis*, hockey* captain, swimming*), with EMF prizes and a State scholarship to Oxford, became a Sergeant in the Intelligence Corps, teacher, examiner and journalist. Jeanne described scientific rambles, and, after her ATS service, also read French at Oxford and became a personnel officer.

Another editor and active member of le Cercle and choir, Christine Mary Flanders became ECS' first Child Psychotherapist. After graduating, Olive Bertha Stephens (hockey*, swimming*, 1st class Instructor) taught, then worked with her husband in British Guiana. Swimming champion and another 1st class instructor, future teacher Mary Elizabeth Stone wrote on the scientific society as did Margaret Stone, who represented Middlesex Cadets and became a Guide Commissioner. She was a House captain with swimming* Bronze and Bar as was Cadet Margaret Helen Lahee, who participated successfully in gardening, the EMF, le Grand Concours and achieved vacancies at one London and two Oxford colleges.

Two more were House captains. Sussex physicist Violet Holland gained most of the possible Sports awards:– Colours for drill, tennis, netball and swimming, captaining the last two – and was 1st Class swimming instructor and twice champion. Muriel Helen Allen, tennis and swimming captain and actress (in *Robin Hood*, "her acting was up to her usual high standard"), read at French Prayers. When National Service initially delayed her university entrance, she taught locally before taking up her £20 exhibition to Royal Holloway. A grant from an educational trust helped her to take an Oxford education diploma. She, her husband and family became known by their appearance on Robert Robinson's television show.

Ruthless pruning still leaves a goodly number of successes. First, writers. Doreen Evelyn Stableton won the *Oxford Book of English Verse* in a magazine competition. Editor, Greek beginner, winner of a French Institute scholarship, choir member, and, later, Oxford graduate, Mary Hill Cottingham also contributed drawings and dramatic criticism.

Actresses, often in French and German as well. Pamela Langley wrote, won Grand Concours and Wings for Victory competition prizes. Although considered too French mannered for Warwick in *St Joan*, Hilda May Sharpe, dramatic critic herself, received praise for many performances. She became a Head and Mayor. Joyce Wright won a Botany exhibition to Westfield, giving up research when she and her husband became farmers. Cadet Lieutenant and scene-shifter, Betty Margaret Young (hockey*) won prizes at the EMF and for French recitation, and saw printed not only articles *(Knitting, The Post Office)* but also her pen drawings. She joined the WRNS. Betty Edith Stone, another Greek beginner, EMF prizewinner, writer, critic and editor, won a scholarship to Exeter and exhibitions to RHC and Girton, where she continued to act, "really immersed in her part" as she had been at school. She and Stella Arnold had both been school's Labour candidates. Stella (rounders* captain) acted "with immense wit and vigour" before graduating from London. Another writer and French certificate winner, Faith Warburton studied Italian at Bedford.

Two took up religious work, Barbara Frances Russell with the Society of Friends. After winning silver and gold medals at London Academy of Dramatic Art, she became an Associate of the London College of Music, teaching elocution and speech training. After composing, and winning prizes for, Music and with a scholarship to Trinity college, Joyce Kathleen Westall went as a missionary to Nigeria.

Harvest camper, magazine contributor, "a sturdy and dominant figure", Malvolio, Bottom ("the perfect clown"), St Joan and Caliban, Brenda Saunders (rounders*) gave up her exhibition at RHC to act with the Young Vic in *Knight of the Burning Pestle*, the Old Vic school and Salisbury Arts theatre. She became a Pastoral Head and Head of Drama in a comprehensive school. Acting was coming of age, a possible and respectable career.

Other scholars. Cadet patrol leader, Marion Helena Ebben (hockey* captain, junior tennis champion and later captain) acted and achieved a Cambridge place, State and Biology scholarships to Westfield before doing laboratory research work. Betty Ada Rampton (tennis*, hockey*), with a silver medal from la Société des Professeurs, relinquished her French Institute place in favour of a Drapers' scholarship and a trust award to go to RHC. Two won Florence prizes. House captain Kathleen Mary Evans (swimming*, hockey*, tennis* champion for two years) gained her BSc at King's College of Household and Social Science. Scene-shifter Audrey Todd (swimming*, Bronze, captain of hockey* and rounders) gained an Oxford Exhibition, State and college scholarships to Girton and a Fellowship to Princeton, USA, which led to the post of principal research officer with the British Gelatine and Glue Research Association.

Wider fame has come to six. Everyone in Enfield has heard of Phyllis Oborn MBE, who, from laboratory worker, rose to be General Manager and Director of Thorn EMI Subsidiary and President of the Enfield District Manufacturers' Association. The third woman Mayor, she sponsored The Helping Hand and Enfield in Bloom. ECS knows her as OGA speaker, long-time chairman of Governors and staunch supporter of all activities.

Clelia Madeleine Riccardi travelled much after her linguistic prize-winning schooldays. Graduating from Southampton, she learned Russian stenotyping at evening institute, becoming not only Modern Languages tutor to Donald Peers but an interpreter, with a record of 35 international events in five years, from the Liberia Rubber Group to the Geneva conference on the peaceful uses of atomic energy.

Many nationwide have cause to thank Vera Babington. Member of the Poetry Reading society, Cadet, Guide Lieutenant, she became school's first speech therapist. She and her husband invented an artificial larynx for those who have lost their vocal chords.

Two more career firsts. One of the last pre-war admissions, Laone Mary Hammond had illustrious examination results (HSC with 4*, including Italian learned in two years), a French Institute scholarship, and, only six months after GSC, a bursary to Oxford, gaining a prize there. Finding few choices for Arts graduates, she joined the Swiss Bank Corporation, dealing particularly with the estates of expatriates. As a result of three years' part-time study, she became a barrister, the only woman to gain distinction in the first Bar examination, and a legal advisor in the Ministry of Health. Sonia Gertrude Porte illustrates the contemporary problem, for she applied to no fewer than six universities: this with an excellent school record of form and linguistic prizes. A Modern Languages graduate, she took a Social Welfare course at LSE, sponsored by the Home Office, before becoming a probation officer.

Brenda Mary Knudson is the second to be immortalised. Captain of House, hockey and tennis, junior and senior champion, Deputy Head Girl (DHG), actress, she won a State scholarship to University College, then a Goldschmid scholarship (£40) for the outstanding performance of the year by any girl from a Middlesex secondary school. Achieving her 1st Class Honours degree in two years, she became Demonstrator.

More scholarships such as St Dunstan's Exhibition for Women in Science were gained by this Senior Research Scientific Officer and lecturer at an international congress. After working, with her algologist husband, in the Sudan for the Forestry Department, she discovered, at Windermere with the Freshwater Biological Association, an hitherto unknown species of underwater plant life, known for all time as Tabellaria Quadrisepta Knudson. Rare fame indeed.

More notified school of their private life than of their jobs: 287 marriages (several more than once), 150 sons (plus four adopted), 153 daughters (two adopted, at least twenty following their mothers to ECS) plus three of unspecified sex.

The era of working wives and mothers, of greater flexibility in changing jobs, began. A clerk studied at a polytechnic, a telephonist went to Bath Academy of Art, a fashion model to the Civil Service. At least forty emigrated and worked all over the world. Margaret Alice Sigrid Buncey wrote on auto- and motorcycle- racing; in California, she became a university counsellor in the treatment of alcoholism. Work took others to Germany (Allied Control Commission), Peru (Medical Unit), India (a one-time shop assistant trained as a nurse there) and Italy (British Consulate). Choice widened: BBC, Enfield Grand Opera Company, secretary in the economic section of the United Nations, orthoptist, psychiatric social worker, industrial nurse, aircraft pilot.

A survey of their activities is both impressive and gratifying

Although the Arts Club lasted a while, the OGA was a war casualty. Individuals involved themselves in various school events and continued to use the tennis courts, but other sports clubs ended, never to be revived.

The Head referred to careers at Prize Giving: two were the only girls in the French section of the United Nations; one was breeding mosquitoes and other pests in an attempt to stamp out disease in Africa and India. She viewed Income Tax officers with amused admiration, finding it awe-inspiring that some OGs actually understood PAYE (pay as you earn) in all its ramifications. Some helped the war effort in the WVS, Red Cross, Civil Defence, Land Army, Reuter's and Intelligence work.

Thinking continued meanwhile. Should a subscription be reintroduced? If so, when? As thousands were now eligible, should group secretaries look after years or groups of years? This idea should have been pursued, as year groups now frequently organise their own gatherings. Twenty-five who joined ECS in 1945 met again when most were 21 to enjoy dinner and the theatre; the 1938 and 1943 intake held their own Golden Reunions.

Dr Lily Butler invited all OGs and children to the first post-war 'do' on Saturday, July 7, 1945. Margarine, sugar, milk and preserves presented problems; if the numbers of under-ten-year-olds coming were known, it was possible to receive an allocation of these comestibles.

Tea was at 5pm. Tea, bread, Swiss rolls, sponge, miscellaneous items, milk cost 15/-, kitchen staff, 3/-, 195 biscuits from school cookery classes at 1d each, 16/3, printing, 12/6, postage, £2, *Gazette* advert., 5/-, caretaker, 10/-, book tokens, £1:1:0. To balance this, 132 members paid their 2/- subs. In the autumn, besides discussions on forming a choral society, 77 attended the first post-war London dinner.

Presents to long-serving Mistresses continued, but the pre-war fervour had gone.

Officier d'Académie, Guide, Philosopher and Friend

The end of the war marked the end of an era almost less than the retirement of the last of the Old Guard, Miss Forrest, known to some 150 Staff and 3,717 pupils. She represented a ladylike age of hats, gloves and class distinctions, for she was a snob, socially and academically. It was impossible to visualise school without her.

Examining Boards, critical of some aspects, never failed to pay tribute to the conversational fluency of her candidates. Yet lessons were unpredictable. It might be a poem to be learnt with the help of a picture drawn in coloured chalks, plays to be read, a dissertation on some pre-war activities, an introduction to the complexities of ending a letter in French. Her temper was legendary; a row could erupt over the agony of her beloved France, war conditions, leg trouble, new Staff. Wrath would overflow from classroom to corridor, where victims, sent out perhaps for smirking or not knowing a verb, would be harangued until they wept. She too would weep, but with vexation at girls' stupidity or because they were specialising in Science, and could threaten not to teach for a week.

Clashes were not, unfortunately, confined to girls. She and the Head were poles apart. Before Assembly, girls waiting in silence, Staff seated on the platform, all could hear raised voices coming from the Head's Room. Finally, the door would be flung open and F.M.F., "red in the face and tearful, her halo of white hair escaping from its pins, would sweep out of the double doors at the end of the Hall, leaving Miss Sharp to carry on as if all was well". On better days, she hovered in the lobby to join in the hymns in a gruff monotone. As she attended the local Presbyterian church, her abstentions were not on religious grounds.

On July 14, she kept alive the spirit of France as she had done in the Great War. Not only was *Notre Père qui es aux cieux* solemnly recited by all, but the special hymn which she composed, and to which she added *une strophe nouvelle*, was sung to the tune of *Londonderry Air*. Incomplete versions in her handwriting are all that have survived of this "très beau cantique qui exprimait tout ce que nous sentions".

> O Seigneur Dieu, en ces jours de détresse,
> Nous te prions pour tous les malheureux,
> Les vieilles gens, en leur grande tristesse,
> Et les enfants au destin malheureux.

Two incomplete stanzas dealt with the wartime situation.

> O Seigneur Dieu, soutiens de ton courage
> Tous ceux qui sont en pays occupé.
> Que leur prière au milieu du carnage
> S'adresse à toi qui seul peut les aider.
> Celui qui sert, qui se met au service
> De son pays, dans sa simplicité:
> Nous te prions, pour que ce long supplice
> Suscite en nous la solidarité.

She ended in fine style.

> O Seigneur Dieu, dans ta grâce infinie
> En nos grands maux, ne nous délaisse pas!
> Que nous fassions, au cours de notre vie,
> Toujours le bien aux autres ici-bas!
> Bien loin de nous le péché et la haine;
> Que tout dépit soit toujours repoussé!
> Nous te prions, pour que malgré la peine,
> L'avenir bientôt nous ramène la paix.

Speakers from the Free French Forces and escapers from France were welcomed. Fifths were stirred by "le privilège d'assister à la commémoration à l'Albert Hall de la célèbre proclamation de Général de Gaulle en 1940: 'La France a perdu une bataille, la France n'a pas perdu la guerre'".

The French choir sang French and English songs at a 1945 reception to French Asssistants; F.M.F. loved music and used songs in her textbooks and her teaching, but she herself was incapable of singing in tune.

She ably arranged classes when war broke out; her administrative skill made her positively enjoy wrestling with forms and returns. Yet few knew of another side to her nature: she paid for the education of two orphan sisters.

In the Sixth, practically all the 17th century plays were carefully studied, together with ' approved' modern writers. She refused, however, to teach the Romantic poets; once, she averred, girls, as a result of these gentlemen, had asked her to take them to Hadley Wood to look at a pond by moonlight! She disapproved of two-way dictionaries; French Larousse should suffice. In 1939 alone, three went up to Oxford to read Modern Languages, two with scholarships, one gaining a First; there were university entrants each subsequent year. Her candidates were well-known at the Society of French Teachers, twelve awards being won in the first year of the war, then medals, certificates and prizes for the four best candidates in prose composition. Not a year passed without scholarships and entrances to the French Institute, and many successes in RSA Orals.

Her girls were less inhibited linguistically than most. Many magazines contained articles, even poems. They are incredibly good for the age of the contributors. *Les Saisons*, written in alexandrines and full of Nature, does end with unfortunate bathos:

> La neige au manteau blanc qui recouvre la terre
> Nous amène l'hiver et la fin de la guerre.

She remained the very active president of le Cercle. Although *la soirée dansante* was abandoned as in the Great War and gone were the lavish evening affairs, she produced five or six plays annually, performed of necessity in the afternoons and on Saturdays, with excellent attendances; proceeds went to School Fund. For *Les Femmes Savantes,* tea was served during the interval. *Andromaque* received such acclaim that it was repeated at an educational conference.

One year alone saw two plays by the Thirds, *Tableau de l'Histoire de France* by the Fourths, *Le Bourgeois Gentilhomme, La Fleur de l'Âge* and *Act V of Bérénice*. She, and the girls, considered this "une des méthodes les plus intéressantes et les plus efficaces d'apprendre une langue vivante". Sadly, standards declined: one girl played her part in *Le Cid* with the text concealed in her voluminous cloak from which she prompted in sibilant and mid-European whispers. Later girls remember F.M.F's tears as they romped through to a final tableau of Marianne declaring that France would live again, and, later still, when she rang down the curtain in mid-performance.

Visits were made to the French Institute to see more professional performances. Actors brought *Le Malade Imaginaire*, Pamela Stirling took tea with the Sixth after producing scenes from Molière. Out-of-school activities resulted from her tireless efforts to reinforce l'Entente Cordiale: an exhibition of French paintings, "un discours très intéressant" by a Commander of the Free French Forces on French colonies and their wartime rôle, talks by Professor Saurat on fighting French and by Capitaine Neurohr (not merely interesting but amusing) on Brittany and aspects of modern France.

Although F.M.F. seemed lively and reintroduced exchange visits quickly after the war ended, her last days at ECS were saddened by her distress at being succeeded, although it was some comfort to need *three* successors. Two were *in situ*: Miss F. Sharp became Deputy Head, Miss Marion Head of Department. She was heartbroken at having to interview whoever would take over her classes. I had never heard of her when I thus met her. Having unwittingly ventured an opinion which clashed with a cherished view, I was taken into a conveniently empty classroom, my face was slapped and I received a dazzling impromptu lesson. Feeling that all was lost, I dared to argue, albeit somewhat tentatively. I gathered subsequently that she thought I'd 'do'. Her Fifth set frightened me by their oral fluency, their ability even to argue in French and by their grammatical range, yet tuition over the previous few terms had been mainly by remote control.

Her retirement was marked by a full programme in which 26 girls took part. An Address was followed by songs (Spanish, Italian, German) by seniors. A lengthy *Hommage à l'Auteur* took the form of scenes between new and old pupils and readings from 13 of her 40 or more books, which were used also in the Dominions and the USA. Not all would seem suited to such treatment: *C'est un Secret, Form Plays, Contes et Récits, Par Retour du Courrier, Apprenons le Français 1,2,3, French Poetry, Junior French Poetry,* perhaps; but *Test Papers, Graded Test Papers, Comprehension Tests* and *Exercices de Lectures Expliquées*? The Head gave her *Allocution*:"It is difficult, if not impossible, to chronicle adequately all that the school owes to her". She had ensured that ECS remained on the national and European map for both the teaching and the learning of Modern Languages.

Miss Sharp paid public tribute at Prize Giving. "For 37 years, Miss Forrest has made ECS her life. She spent her brilliant gifts and unflagging zeal on the countless number of girls who have passed through the school. A recital of her achievements, were it to be comprehensive, would fill the whole of my report". She noted the interest and thrill of using the books she wrote, the unrivalled knowledge of trainings, careers and places of Higher Education, the amazing memory which never forgot a face, a personal history or even a birthday, her 37 school journeys. "Despite her many interests, we always felt the School and the girls came first".

To wish her godspeed, Old Girls flocked to an evening in her honour in the New Year, when they recalled the inspiration of her enthusiasm. The Head Girl's introduction preceded more songs in different languages and a sketch, *Nous avons tous le même auteur*, to prove that her books were exciting. Dr Butler praised her human understanding, sense of humour and broad outlook on life. The delighted lady received a wallet containing a cheque.

She continued to provide information about, write to, and stay with, many former pupils. She was especially proud of one working at French Government Headquarters and of another in the French Secret Service. When the OGA was at a low point, she compiled a new register. Her kerchief party raised £6:15:0 for its Jubilee Fund. Gregarious and a compulsive joiner, she was advocating, even in 1960, a Staff association; it might have got off the ground if she had been able to run it. By 1962, she was permanently in a Nursing Home, thus missing the OGA Dinner for the first time.

Her funeral brought tributes from OGs all over the globe, literally from China to South America. "As a junior, I was scared of her, but as a senior and especially after a week in Paris with her in 1923, she was a friend". "Now that she has gone to her heavenly mansion, there must be many who are grateful for having known her".

CHAPTER THIRTY-ONE

We are hoping to return to the unknown conditions of school in peace

Yet in 1946, the Head reported that pre-war conditions were sadly slow in returning. Of course, they never did; school remained gas-lit and virtually laboratory-less and the building was soon in complete chaos. Whilst girls felt satisfied in having had a small part in the great happenings of the world, they had hoped for form parties, flourishing societies, expeditions, after-school activities without blackout.

After two days' holiday, they paused for Thanksgiving. The programme for the Service for Victory in Europe, May 10, 1945, was printed after the occasion, so that every girl had a copy. Reading from Isaiah XI, prayer, *These things shall be*, reading from Micah IV were followed by the oft-repeated anthem *England, Arise, the long, long night is o'er*. Miss Sharp's address preceded prayer, *O beautiful my Country*, extracts from Pericles' Funeral Oration, *What heroes has thou bred*, two poems (Binyon's *The Living Cause* and Owen Seaman's *Midnight and Morning*) and *Jerusalem*. The service concluded with parts of a speech by Abraham Lincoln and the National Anthem, still *God save the King*.

One prayer was comprehensive. "Let us give thanks for the victory and for the mercies vouchsafed to the efforts of our nation, commonwealth and allies; for our confidence in the righteousness of our cause; for the deliverance of the early, dark years; for the unremitting watch and ward of our Navies; for the wonderful skill and unwearying valour of the Air Forces, for the great and magnificent victories of our armies and the armies of our allies; for the magnificent courage of men, women and children who have disregarded danger and discomfort; for those who have endured pain and loss and refused to yield; for those who have laboured to provide us with food and the tools of war and have not faltered; for the ready sacrifices of the whole people; for all these and other blessings from God's hand, let us give thanks".

Miss Sharp spoke of the excitements: flags and banners, safety of father or brother, world freed from terror, end of siren and coupons, hopes for return of supplies and packed shop windows – but warned of the needs of the liberated and the problems of peace-making with the Germans. She urged that, although the English are an inarticulate race, this was an occasion for patriotism, to be unashamedly proud. "See to it that you continue proud of your country and worthy of it, so that they shall say of us that it was still our finest hour after the war was over". She turned to the reasons for fighting the war. While it was to save democracy from conquest and to help an ally against tyranny, we had three aims: Democracy, where the people's will is expressed, justice openly administered, criticism free, opposition allowed, opportunities for all, which demands clear thought and right judgment: Liberty, not licence, not static but requiring eternal vigilance: and Peace, which must be made creatively, worked for energetically and built out of the materials of life, so that "in the days that lie ahead, you are all peace-makers".

Thanksgiving Week early in the autumn culminated in a Youth rally in the cinema. Girls represented Enfield at the later Albert Hall celebrations.

Miss Sharp took the opportunity at Prize Giving to comment on the new Butler Education Act, on which high hopes were set. "It is a fine thing that during the greatest war in history, this nation should place on the statute book an act embodying its determination to provide secondary education for every child over 11 instead of confining this privilege to a small minority. If Waterloo were won on the playing fields of Eton, the Battle of Britain was made possible by the secondary school". The Act's provisions included compulsory religious education, transfer at 13+ and 15+ between the different types of school (difficult for organisation, curriculum, parent and pupil) and free places without an entrance examination, in the hope that existing injustices could be removed.

She was rightly disturbed by the need for more teachers, buildings and equipment, and by the administrative machinery of government reports and statistical returns which seemed to suggest that education was a matter of forms correctly completed and lists properly tabulated. For her, together with reasonable discipline and good conduct, scholarship and independent work – intellectual, aesthetic, spiritual, physical – this was what mattered.

She spelled out what she envisaged for ECS. "Each school has its own unique character and tradition and is not just like any other school. Ours will in future be known as a grammar school and while we shall gladly welcome the chance of working in close cooperation and amity with the technical and secondary modern schools, we also look forward to keeping our own special outlook and standards". Despite the popular implication that a combination of applied science, cheap publications and continual broadcasting was going to make it simple for everyone to be healthy, wealthy and wise, she put her faith in Aristotle's aim of a right judgment and a delight in fine characters and noble actions.

PART SEVEN

AFTER THE WAR

JANUARY, 1947

The story changes, for ECS now became part of my life. First impressions altered but little during the life of the County School.

Two or three Mistresses were of my vintage; some belonged to the era of my own schoolteachers. All but two were unmarried; there were no men. They divided into two not always harmonious groups: those who retained pre-war attitudes and those who were orientated towards the present and the future. The teaching was far superior to any I had known, with staggeringly good results. Girls were enthusiastic and welcoming, well-groomed and well-mannered. They too seemed old-fashioned in their attitude to school activities and their willingness to learn.

But the building! Five of us shared one small table in the Staff room, and the flickering gaslight, worked by a rusting chain, was not immediately above it. In formrooms, desks were old-fashioned, floorboards squeaked and the platform blocks giving access to the Mistress' desk and to *most* of the blackboard were terrifyingly rickety. Some Sixth form lessons were still in corridors.

Yet it was a flourishing and lively place. I stayed over 33 years.

CHAPTER THIRTY-TWO

I'd like my school to be just like the school in story books

We'd all have private studies and a tuckshop full of sweets,
    A swimming pool with diving boards and chutes;
A "gym" where we could execute the most enthralling feats,
    And six-course dinners followed up by fruits.
A huge school Hall with tip-up seats and softly shaded lights,
    A stage on which I'd dance or act or mime;
And every time the good girls fall in any awkward plights,
    The bad girls always get found out in time.
We'd have adventures every day and lots of laughter there,
    A school like this would suit me to a T;
Of course, I'd do a bit of work when I'd have the time to spare,
    And that is how I'd like my school to be. (G. Bax)

"Enfield County school refuses to be beaten by the conditions in which it lives, and looks forward to the future with zest. In spite of post-war problems, housing shortages, lack of labour, and the consequent necessity for patience, our hopes are fixed more strongly than ever on our 25-year old dream of new buildings – a Hall that will hold us all, a real gymnasium, a proper Library, Sixth form and other classrooms, more laboratories, a stage worthy of our plays, a craftroom, an adequate kitchen, electricity, hot water, cloakrooms with light and ventilation, storerooms instead of corridors lined with cupboards – the list is unending. Patience is wearing thin".

Head and Staff struggled to cope with 600 girls in this building made for 250. Miss Sharp railed tirelessly against the slumlike conditions. A tiny room intended as a store- or prep-room had 15-20 VI trying to do microscope or dissecting work in space more suitable for three or maybe four. "On dark days we are compelled to stop proper work early in the afternoon since the gaslight in many rooms is so poor that it is impossible to read satisfactorily or see the board clearly". Ironically, electric light was in the huts but not in the main building which showered plaster and unglued ceiling tiles on classes.

All continued to perform a perpetual steeplechase between the Church Halls – Presbyterian (too small for large forms and, fuel-less, soon unusable) and St Andrew's – the committee room of the Education Office, the junior school and the Grammar school itself. This last faced the awkward choice of either injuring the advanced work of its own boys or denying the loan of laboratory space altogether to ECS chemists and physicists.

For 37 terms, school had the workmen in.

Although the cry of "Don't you know there's a war on?" could no longer justify every shortcoming, peacetime conditions remained absent. 1946, 1947, 1948 – the building was in absolute chaos.

In compensation, Council voted £4:16:0 for rosebushes, £10 for bulbs, 14/- for Woolworth's seeds and £2:10:0 for plants. The front was beautified by a new fishpond which Mr Whitehead made on his return. Shelters were replaced by prefabricated huts, which 'temporary' structures remain in use to this day. The pride of their owners who could switch on electric light and read with ease, each was adorned with pictures (£12:11:0), a notice board and curtains (£7:16:5½). Despite the noise and dirt of coke deliveries outside, the Fifth Year tenants enjoyed their separateness.

Making-good war damage followed.

Jan. 7: workmen remove windows

Jan. 8: IIB, IIBr excluded am, IIC pm

Jan. 9: IIIT, IIIE excluded am, IIIB pm

Jan. 30 to Mar.9: "owing to the excessively low temperature in all rooms on the North side, first lesson cancelled, school began 9:30".

The window of VIA's room was removed, the aperture blacked out, gaslight on permanently. Draughts were so fierce that, even with a coal fire, their room was too cold for lessons which were transferred to the committee room. The temperature in VIB's room, albeit only 17'× 10' and housing over 20, fell to 35°F because of an ill-fitting temporary window.

All this in 1947, the worst winter in living memory, with its attendant burst pipes and illnesses.

Miss Sharp's record book, begun in the first year of 'peace', constitutes a detailed study of building operations during terms and holidays: daily confusion, shortages of materials, timber still being kiln-dried, need for permits, make-do-and-mend, demarcation lines, innumerable site conferences, tired or inexperienced labour force, countless varying official and quasi-official bodies and forms, changes of mind and procedures, modernity's struggle against different vested interests, securing permission from the War Damage Commission, which, unsurprisingly, came late in the day. All activities, to say nothing of teaching, had to go on round, or in the middle of, this upheaval.

Giving a cheery rendering of the top hit of the moment, knocker-downers rather than builders swarmed all over. Slowly and painfully, most rooms taking 5-7 days each but several, including the Art and Staff rooms being out of action every single day for a whole month, electricity was installed. "Behind our backs came a noise which can only be described as a herd of wild elephants crashing through the undergrowth" – actually the new heating system. "Judging by the heap of twisted, rusty metal excavated from our cellars, it is a wonder that we have had a warm school all these years".

"Other workmen, having heard that there was space for a few more piles of equipment, set up their claims". Decorators came to make good (or cover up) war damage; they hid the scars with cream, peach, eau-de-nil or turquoise; the Old Hall lost its institutional dirty brown varnish.

With no corner safe from workmen, the Head, years later, reminded girls that "we really must stop grumbling when painters dare to stay a month".

Members of the Education Department held periodical inspections of both damage and progress. All windows had been removed for copying in the workshop, Music and DSc classes had to be housed elsewhere. Then every window was altered so that each could be opened. Staircases were out of action. Fortunately, the top corridor ceiling was pulled down and replaced during a half-term, but scaffolding was ubiquitous. The library was unusable for one week, a laboratory for three. Three new labs were created out of three formrooms. Then, after two hectic terms, word came that all but seven ceilings were unsafe and must be replaced.

Eventually, forms had again to be excluded for a morning, afternoon or whole day. 1949 was one entire year of chronic disruption at a time when girls and Mistresses alike might have hoped for normality. Returning after four days, three forms found the canteen closed for a fortnight; the roof leaked so had to be refelted. By January 10, six rooms and the Hall were out of use; whole forms, including girls preparing for public examinations, were regularly sent home. Work in the laboratories fell behind – because the plumber was ill! In spite of this, the Head sent off a requisition for an additional £100 worth of scientific apparatus. In fact, February 9 was the first day on which all pupils could be present. Two days were added to half-term. As late as March, a downpour was recorded for two days in the top corridor, and there was no heating ("a major leak as radiators on top floors are empty"); when the Office arranged to deliver 30 oil stoves, all was well again. Teaching resembled a scene from a Marx Brothers film, as pipes, followed by a triumphantly grinning carpenter, emerged into a lesson from wall, ceiling or window. Clothes were thick with dust and dirt, although Staff were still somewhat protected by gowns.

Outside, roadways had to be drained and remade, existing bicycle stalls (made by the caretaker) roofed and a new cycle shed made. One parent complained that his daughter's footwear was being ruined by all this.

Some notes amuse – at this distance of time. The Clerk of Works was unhappy about the distemper in the corridor and Art room and thought that they should be repainted when the whole building was done. The newly installed windows had to be removed in order to hoist through new benches for the labs. The following day, M.C.S. explained that the girls couldn't use these bench tops and it was arranged that the size should be increased by 15"-18". One new lab could be used, but the fume cupboards had to be inserted later – when the blackboards arrived!

During the summer holidays, ceilings and lavatories were at last completed and gas fittings removed, but September saw the decorators return, so whole areas were again, or still, out of use. On no day in the term did school have the use of every room. In September, 1950, the Firsts were excluded because of decoration of Enfield Court.

January 1949 had seen plans for the new gymnasium, complicated because the field had to include, besides games pitches and hard tennis courts, a new dining unit. Twenty-two months later, Middlesex officials came to discuss these. 1951 was distinguished only by the purchase of new garden seats, £22:10:0 for five. By then, the Head felt that if the Middlesex Authority were really going to do something for ECS the next year, that would inevitably mean another national crisis. A magazine article envisaged the 21st century: 24 were struggling in the Algebra room, which had the same teacher's desk, pale green walls, white ceiling, panelled partitions, but no mistress, only a robot: there was no gymnasium yet, but there were lessons in aviation and visits to the planets by rocket. Still, September 22, 1952, did see the first lesson in the new Gym (cost £100,000), although permanent apparatus was still awaited. "The novelty of having somewhere to work without continual worry about noise or perpetual care about banging into other people is still with us". A weekly evening class in the following year gave an opportunity to many OGs deprived of apparatus work during their gymnasium-less schooldays.

One oddity: the Head was advised that she should record that the lease to the Eastern Electricity Board for the substation in the corner by the Gym, was completed on 24 June for a period of 42 years from 25 March, 1954.

"The long awaited extension to the school should be under way by next Easter", 1953. Everything was agreed – except the starting date. Miss

Sharp, wisely, refused to get excited. The New Building (NB), still so called, consisting of Hall, lecture room, canteen, administrative block with library above, and then two storeys of class and specialist rooms, was at last begun. It rose steadily on the then hockey pitch during Coronation year to supplement the Old Building (OB), erected in the reign of the Queen's great-grandfather; M.C.S. commented that the premises had been inadequate in the Royal grandfather's time.

"The process of building is seldom beautiful and never quiet". In January, 1954, discussions were held about wall schemes. In July, County representatives came to consider the consequent changes and redecoration in the OB. "Chaos is come again". The concrete mixer throbbed and churned noisily every day for two years.

Yet in September, 1954, the new block of 12 classrooms was in use. Girls had to be careful with satchels and avoid inadvertent kicking until the paint dried in 2-3 months. During the holidays, the former Art room, library and Room 1 (now the Advanced Biology lab), were taken over for conversion. Rooms off the Old Hall were put out of use. As this was to become laboratories, the last Assembly took place therein on October 18; for the rest of term, Prayers were held sometimes in formrooms, sometimes in the shell of the new library. One girl had never realised how valuable and unifying Assembly was until they had to do without it. The senior cloakroom became a storeroom. After half-term, the New Staff Room (NSR), Office and Head's room were in use; it was, however, another fortnight before the telephone was available.

The new field by the Gym was sown; then began the work of transforming the dock, thistles and tin-can-infested nightmare into a hockey pitch.

Did all this put paid to the usual Prize Giving airing of grievances? Indeed not, because of workmen, steam rollers, pneumatic drills, dust and disorder, equipment not delivered or else despatched long before the rooms were ready, library books in piles in a small classroom. At least there was no Sixth form coaching in corridors or on the Hall platform as there had been for over twenty years. There were even startling moments when for a period a classroom was actually empty. Still, "bricks and mortar, concrete and glass don't of themselves make a school". Throughout, school never closed, although the Head later felt that it might have been wiser to have bowed a little to the storm.

In February, 1955, the First forms moved in bitter cold from the Court to classrooms on the ground floor in the OB, which ended EGS' 15-year long patience and tolerance of daily invasion.

The canteen was the last section to be completed. All could then sit in the Hall, with more civilised and sociable family service instead of the former queuing and overcrowding of the cafeteria system.

On October 26, Visitors' Day,"we have entered on our inheritance and are amply and fitly housed". It was the greatest thrill to have "our noble and airy Hall", for Prayers, the time to feel a united and corporate body, meant much to the Head. She listed "our splendid and gracious library, our full complement of Biology, Chemistry and Physics laboratories, our magnificent Art and spacious Cookery rooms, our specialist provision for Geography, Music, Needlework and Secretarial training, our hard tennis courts and our own canteen". It is salutary to recall this delight, although criticism was, and still is, levelled against the so-called Covered Way (roof only, no sides) between the two buildings, which acts as a wind tunnel; crossing it can result in a soaking. Visitors and new girls can lose their way in this confused and varied collection of structures.

Twelve months later, OG Frances Perry advised on the planting out of the grounds. Measurements were taken over a year later for curtains for the lecture room, which can enlarge the Hall or be separated from it. Internal rearrangements occurred subsequently, but except for an Art storeroom, the County School had no further additions.

The last signs of the builders' tenancy were removed; the surrounding hedges and copses provided secluded places of assignation with EGS boys. It had seemed hardly possible to visualise the day when the concrete mixer would stop, when the piles of cement, brick and sand would disappear, when dirt would no longer be carried on shoes to every corner. By 1957, the only mention on Speech Day was an expression of hope to maintain the shining and unusually well-kept condition of buildings and grounds.

Problems did remain. Hut classrooms continued to be heated in an antediluvian and wasteful way, although some inhabitants happily fried eggs on the radiators. Once " we were all crowding round the window before afternoon registration, wondering why water was pouring out of a pipe by the library. Our Form Mistress rebuked us saying hadn't we seen water before, but it was hot water – something had gone wrong with the central heating. The fire bells were rung as the empty radiators could have blown up. No-one took much notice: the bell was confused with a lesson bell and there surely wouldn't be a fire practice when snow was on the ground".

An extra form could now be admitted, important because the post-war bulge was nearing secondary level. In five short years, the Hall became too small for all girls to sit during Prayers, there were not enough chairs, VI3 was housed in the museum and lessons again took place Behind the

Curtain. A representative from the Architect's department did come to consider plans for an extension. There were eight forms in the Sixth and Seventh Years, and, by 1962, 75 pupils more than the new designs had foreseen. When numbers reached 827, ECS was, for the first time, larger than EGS.

The Head wrote an anxious official letter just before she retired. "During Assembly, a nasty accident was, I'm thankful to say, averted by a most lucky chance. One of the glass covers to the electric light in the Hall ceiling crashed to the ground and miraculously fell just between two girls. I dread to think what would have happened if it had hit a girl's head. These circular covers are held by three springs and it appears that one of these had weakened. I am wondering if springs ought to be four". She would also like to see as soon as possible four extra classrooms and the second Gym approved by the Ministry in their original plans, there now being 167 Sixth formers.

1962 brought power cuts, ice and snow; yet more rooms were repainted. Beautifications, often suggested by Council, continued: yet another cloakroom mirror £1:7:8: vases for the library £1:6:6, 9/-, 10/- and £3:17:11: hairtidies for cloak- and wash-rooms £1:14:0: insulation board 16/-: fingerplates for classrooms 15/4: blackout materials £3:4:7: Sick Bay curtains £4:13:6. Outside the Staff room,a rosebed was presented by leaving Sixth students. Pictures (£18:7:0) remained popular, with framing £3:6:3 and renovation £1:9:5. Dishcloths and dustpans were agreed, but Hall mats were rejected as dangerous in an emergency.

Bigger items included timber and fitting for noticeboards £3:2:10: an electric polisher for the new Hall floor £50+ and, less than a month later, repairs to same £1:11:3 and additions £6:4:5: filing cabinet £12:6:11: renovation of loud speakers £10:17:6: an amplifier £61:5:11.

Although M.C.S. remembered when laboratories, practical rooms, storerooms and new Gym seemed unbelievably spacious, she grumbled that a new coat of paint did not make a new building, but characteristically cheered herself that "we kept our sense of humour – most of the time".

A fair conclusion is that "School is a History of School Building since the Education Act of 1902".

Not a factory but a living community

Miss Sharp urged her Prize Giving audience to "think more steadily and unselfishly, gracefully and lovingly, not only of the actual brick and concrete buildings, but also of the spirit and tradition of the school, able now to flourish and to grow to fuller stature". She asked juniors to reflect:

"Why am I at school? Why here? What for? Knowledge about the world and the learning about ideas and concepts which you are acquiring daily" would help to make school a good and happy place."Your powers are all being trained – learning to think things out for yourself, to choose between right and wrong, between the accurate and the careless, between good and bad taste, to work without advertisement and fuss, to understand and appreciate other personalities, to see, hear, feel, do and make things, using the abilities and talents with which you are equipped".

She explained to the older girls that the Sixth form enabled young people to develop their minds, form critical judgments, become adult in the use of their intellect and emotions, aware that it is not enough to rely just on hard work and memory and not even on good teaching. With the Crowther Report,"exciting, stimulating and beautifully phrased" on 15-18 year-olds, she felt that a good Sixth showed close links with university, specialisation or study in depth, independent work, intellectual discipline and social responsibility.

In short, "read, listen, look and hear, try, play, experiment. Choose life".

Aware of the divisive nature of the public debate, she admitted the weakness of the grammar school system in catering for the top dozen or so with the other eighty destined for vaguely secretarial work. As early as 1947, she discussed publicly the comprehensive school "which we are given to understand is the shape of things to come", but judged it unfortunate that its protagonists appeared to belittle what was being done in secondary schools. Merely a different form of organisation or the introduction of new methods would not produce a race of supermen. Many attacks on grammar schools exasperated and depressed. She rejected exam-ridden, snobbish curriculum, old-fashioned methods and customs, illiberal specialists, wishing to be neither in the old rut nor submerged by the new. Her school aimed for "Culture, that is Godliness and Good Learning". She encouraged the streams to mix – in games, subject divisions, annual parties, equal representation on school bodies – but the great academic divide remained even within a school with limited intake.

And the day-to-day? OGs complain of rules. Admittedly, Miss Sharp's draft in 1951 covered the same old concerns; punctuality, marking of property, single and double file, running, silence, money. Any note explaining homework not done was to be left no longer on the platform but outside her room. Food was to be eaten only in Break, out of doors (fine), Hall (wet). Ink spillage had now to be reported to a member of Staff. Breaches of rules could lead to a weekly detention; a card recording this had to be signed by a parent and handed to the Mistress in charge. Those detained for serious offences should not collect their slips from the platform after Assembly, as that meant playing to the gallery, but should have to stand in the Hall – a baffling distinction.

There was a weekly 'free' night, which meant that no homework was set, although any missed for whatever reason would then be made up. In 1950, there was one ("wonderful", to Staff) Silence Day.

Parents were involved by invitation not only to major events but also to Year evenings, which were occasions for general talks on careers for seniors, on subject choices available to Thirds, on rules and uniform to the new intake, or for individual consultations with form or teaching Staff.

School life? "We have to beseech people not to come too early in the morning and have to ring a bell to make them go home in the afternoon". Milk was left in crates at the end of the OB corridor; "it was sometimes still frozen by playtime". Ice-cream was later popular at Break, bringing in a useful profit. Bright spirits enjoyed climbing over the coalheaps on to the roof when the caretaker left ladders around. For Monday Assembly, each form in turn chose the hymn and a passage which was read by the Form Prefect.

HEAD GIRLS

1947 Evelyn Woolnough	1948 Jean Nightingale
1949 Patricia Butt, Christa Stubbs	1950 Mary Archdale
1951 Joan Dickinson	1952 Joyce Wilkinson, Ruth Tucker
1953 Suzanne Carter, Gillian Cardy	1954 Maureen Harvey
1955 Margaret Putnam	1956 Margaret Putnam, Patricia Quick
1957 Patricia Quick, Susan Page	1958 Beryl Parsons, Ann Hatch
1959 Janice Butler	1960 Brenda Sledge, Tessa Ormandy
	1961 Frances Freedman

Additional School Colours

1948 S. Wood	1949 M. Mackenzie, P. Widlake
1950 A. Cammack	1951 J. Hall, S. Hinder
1952 S. Eastman, B. Liddiard	1953 J. Freeman
1954 G. Goreham, P. Wilson	
1955 D. Barsham, J. Binnington, D. Grieves, J. Rand	
1956 J. Howling, J. Steer, J. Welch	
1957 G. Belchier, R. Whiting	1958 J. Evison
1959 M. Farrant	1961 P. Knight, A. Matthews
	1962 J. Lock, V. Turner

Fifteen years saw twenty Head Girls, as seven first choices left after two terms in VI3; six DHGs succeeded to the office. Most, together with twenty-six Prefects, received School Colours, the supreme and hotly discussed accolade.

In 1946-1947 only, ten Deputy Prefects were chosen on a trial basis. When school numbers increased, some forty were nominated from first year VI (VIB, or, as it sometimes called itself, *Sextus Nobilissimus*) and Fifths to act as Subs, half in autumn, half in spring. If they proved themselves, a summer election gave full status. Staff were again divided: more should have the opportunity of exerting authority as against the view that to increase the number would cheapen the office.

Prefects' uniform changed little, although the short sleeves of the Forties gave way to long. Ties were generally worn as were tunics until the mid-Fifties, although a few preferred their dress. Socks were accepted footwear until 1960. Hair was now short to medium length. Common to all was still the huge P sewn on to the left bosom. Flashes for blazer or coat cost 3/- and hatbands 6/- and 11/-.

Prefects once held their own dance. Staff invited them to tea two summers. The privilege most enjoyed was the June Staff-Prefects Lunch, inaugurated in 1949 and slightly subsidised by School Fund. Chatter was agreeably free, despite initial awe at both the occasion and the Head's Grace.

> Benedic, domine, nobis et donis tuis
> Mensae, caelestis participes nos facias
> Rex aeternae gloriae.

They felt that ECS was a good place to be.

The good teaching made academic work relatively easy

Loving her work, Miss Sharp was careful to praise publicly her Staff "in the most responsible, the least advertised, the worst paid and the most richly rewarded profession in the world". Aware that "they keep from me and solve many problems that I hear of only after the event", she extolled her happy working community for its enthusiastic, unselfish interest, team work, enlivening spirit and sense of humour. An OGA speaker agreed: "In your hands and those of your predecessors, ECS has flourished. In your hands, we leave its future and we have a supreme confidence in that future".

Girls and parents were encouraged to consider the role of teachers. "Do we expect the Staff to push all the necessary learning into our heads and rules to be made for everything so that we need not take thought? The best teacher in the world can accomplish nothing unless the pupil cooperates and comes to meet the teaching". Television already made too many viewers expect the Staff to do the work.

All new features were not totally beneficial. Married Staff left to have babies. By 1959, sixteen were married; by 1961, eleven were part-timers. The frightening shortage, in Science and Mathematics especially, extended to other subjects, so that, nationally, it was nearly disastrous. As most highly qualified Mistresses did stay, ECS was never in the position that teachers needed five OLs and were welcome if they were not actually on a life support machine, yet M.C.S., rightly, felt anxiety for the future supply of specialist teachers now that so many more fields were open to women.

Meals, milk returns, registers had always been part of the job, but now there were more lists (season-ticket holders, families receiving income support). More significantly, they were becoming involved in the social and emotional problems of girls and their families. Illness, not unexpectedly, took its toll: the strain of war and contemporary shortages was catching up. Colds were the main problem, thirteen in one term, sixteen in 1957 when the absence list reached epidemic proportions. Annually recurring influenza came second. Indisposition was now rarely given as a reason: tonsillitis, ulcerated throats, nervous strain, pneumonia, bronchitis, laryngitis and debility might well be occupational hazards, but Staff had their share of serious and minor operations, acute dyspepsia, anaemia, gastric 'flu; one sprained an ankle, measles defeated one, chicken pox another. After 1961's half-term, school ended at 2:40pm, because of Staff absences and the resulting exhaustion of the sturdy.

There were other reasons: religious (Jewish, Catholic), professional (conferences, lectures, county hockey, examinations, interviews), public (jury service), personal (illness of child or husband, death in the family, trip to the USA, wedding, investiture of an aunt for services to the Red Cross, establishing the necessary residence for marriage).

At Staff meetings on the eve of the autumn term, form and personal timetables were distributed. A weekly session before Assembly dealt with everyday minutiae. A July supper was the occasion for presentations to leaving colleagues; in 1951, six and two guineas were thus spent, which gives an idea of the value of money, as does the same year's Staff insurance premium, £1:9:0. One menu lists cold ham and salad, rolls and butter, fruit sponge flan, savouries and coffee. One year's milk for Staff teas cost £1:11:3.

An entertainment in 1948 consisted of a recital by Miss Thomas ("she sang most charmingly") and two plays produced by Miss Flint: *Tudor Thorns*, a serious drama, and *Wayside War*, a comic play on the Civil War. Lack of time, illness and the winter weather excused any shortcomings, although they won general praise. The old social pleasures, however, died; there were no more.

Miss Stella Wright, whose personality and work were much appreciated, was chief secretary 1946-1951. Miss Hadfield took over for three years with Mrs Wheal who remained throughout this period. In 1961, Mrs Taylor, who had already been Miss Sharp's secretary, returned to stay until she retired in 1984, having worked with three Heads. Friend and guide to new and longstanding teachers as well as to pupils, Marjorie knew, better than anyone else, the school, its business, its oddities, its present and former students and whom to contact when any difficulty arose. These ladies were involved in daily life, on school holidays or with Scripture Union. In the Office, there was never a dull moment.

In addition to Head and Deputy, there was now the Third Mistress, who organised Assembly, the notices, invigilation, the day-to-day substitution for absentees and the like. Regarded as helpful to promotion prospects, this tiring and unenviable job was, after the retirement of Miss Hodgson, held for one year only.

Many departments had long-staying members, some remaining after school became comprehensive. Most were afflicted with transients, especially in the shortage subjects or during illnesses. In 1949-1950 alone, there were seven temporaries, two supplies and three visiting. One lady survived eleven days; one had had eight posts in twelve years, another nine in twenty-four with at least two periods of not working at all.

The King has been graciously pleased

to approve that Mr Whitehead, our Caretaker, be mentioned in recognition of gallantry and distinguished service whilst a POW in Japanese hands and has awarded him the Bronze Oak Leaf Emblem". A marvellous sight he was in his best uniform on formal occasions.

It is "a perpetual wonder how our much loved school-keeper finds time to keep our buildings and grounds so clean, shining and beautiful". The dirt from the building site made this a heartbreaking daily task in termtime and holidays alike. A 1951 order survives: – 56lb wax polish, 1 gross toilet soap £2:10:5, ½cwt hard yellow soap, ½doz balls of ¼lb string, 10 gallons of paraffin £1:10:0. Inkwells needed Ink Scholars Washable Blue, 6 jars, 7/6 each, inkwell filler 5/6. One gross relief nibs cost 8/-. A paintbrush cupboard £24:19:3 plus paint £2:10:0 gave him the means of repairing wear and tear in the Old Hall. Remembering the April Fool introduction of permanganate of potash in the water tank, he still talked thirty years later of the thousands and thousands of tons of coke which he shovelled into the greedy furnaces, which, on his retirement, were torn out and replaced by gas-fired ones for Mr White, his successor! When Staff gave him a farewell dinner in 1971, his table was decorated in Arsenal colours in acknowledgment of the many times the school bell went missing for Saturday afternoon matches.

"However untidy the site may look, it has, nevertheless, been one of the joys of the year that, when time allowed, it was always possible to stroll behind the hut classrooms and there enjoy a magnificent display. I shall never forget the way he utilised some of the turf and earth being displaced in the building operations to create, in an extraordinarily short time, a new garden of grass and flowerbeds". Some fifteen years after the bombing, the Authority finally extended and improved his house.

Charlie's main concern outside the line of duty was for deprived children. He and his wife ran their parties impeccably. Every single guest one year wrote to thank him. As Father Christmas, he gave each a present from school's Christmas tree, provided games (helped by First formers), film shows, a conjuror, food ("salads, plates piled high with sandwiches and cakes"). Students, past and present, helped to raise funds. An Old Tyme Dancing gold medallist, he later ran dances, which he loved, to help pay for the presents. A good time was had by all.

CHAPTER THIRTY-THREE

A rich variety, expressive of many sides of life

is to be found in school activities today

Girls were more aware of the world outside than their mothers and aunts had been. Living near London encouraged involvement in Royal events. Princess Elizabeth's Wedding Day meant an enjoyable holiday. Then the magazine referred to the sorrow and sympathy with the Royal family which was felt on the death of George VI; school collected over £25 for the Lord Mayor's Fund in his memory. The funeral provided another day's holiday.

IVL, on a visit to the Houses of Parliament, had the unique experience of hearing the Proclamation at Charing Cross of Queen Elizabeth the Second's accession. Listening to the radio, school looked back to Tudor times and forward with bright anticipation; this new Elizabethan age held out exciting possibilities for women. In Assembly, choir sang *The Hymn for a Queen.*

Coronation day was, of course, a holiday as it had been in 1911. Thirty-eight girls were woken at 4:30am, ate their bacon and eggs at 5am and, rucksacks full of food, cycled to school where Miss Marion and Miss Benjamin checked their uniform. The Union Jack, bunting and flags of all nations were everywhere. Two girls carried a board bearing the name of the school, the rest trooped behind in double file to their allotted places near the BBC's television unit. They saw the Lord Mayor's Coach and Escort, the Heads of foreign states in open landaus (the star being Queen Salote of Tonga), the Prime Minister with Sir Winston and Lady Churchill, the Peers and the Royal family. A thousand guardsmen heralded the climax: the Royal Horse Artillery, the Yeoman of the Guard, the Queen's Barge Master and Watermen, the Royal Horse Guards' Band, and the Sovereign's Escort of the Household Cavalry preceded the golden fairytale coach drawn by eight greys. "We shouted ourselves hoarse. She seemed to give those intimate smiles that were meant for each one of us". Last came the Royal household officers and equerries. All left a lasting impression of the pomp and pageantry of historical England.

"Up with the pageantry! Up with the Coronation! And up with the lark on the morning before!" Nine Sixthformers went independently, spending a happy if sleepless night on the pavement, with kitbags, ground-sheets, blankets, blazers, thick and somewhat ancient skirts, sweaters of all shapes and socks of all hues, glucose tablets, face flannels, cushions, apples (instead of tooth brushes), bread and chocolate. A policeman shouted Wakey-Wakey at 4am. News of the conquest of Everest filtered through. During the scramble for best places, "friendships, which during the night had seemed eternal, reached the last stages of icy enmity, but the friendliness of the school party as a whole was never shattered. Unashamedly crying, a wave of sincere and profound emotion" swept through them. The Abbey service was relayed to a silent and reverent crowd. All this was reported in the shockingly titled *Les Fleurs du Mall.*

School's Coronation Fair in the new Gym (gates open 2:45pm, fair 3-6pm 9d, under 15 4d, under 5 free) was opened by Miss Weavers, County Education Officer. There were stalls and exhibitions throughout the building: competitions for knitting, needlework, photography, gifts, cakes and flowers: pony rides: displays of gym and dancing, historical models, pottery throwing and clay modelling: teas: bran tub and sideshows. OGs sold sweets (£8:16:0). Despite the fact that most participants were soaked to the skin, £124:10:1 was raised. Everyone trooped to the cinema to see both Coronation and Everest films.

Princess Margaret's wedding provided another holiday, Empire Day a half-day until 1961 when Commonwealth Day replaced it. Nine girls heard the Duke of Edinburgh lecture at the Royal Festival Hall.

It again became difficult to find time and space for societies, for expeditions were many. Several visits were paid to the House of Commons. There was the great trek by rail to the South Bank Exhibition of the Festival of Britain. "Everything was so wonderfully designed even to chairs and letterboxes", from the Lion and Unicorn Pavilion and the Skylon (frail and small from the opposite side of the river, solid and strong close to), to the Pavilion of Health, from the Dome of Discovery ("from a wonderful working model of the solar system, we learnt more in five minutes than from all the textbooks") to the County Exhibition, Pit Tunnel, Homes and Gardens, New Schools and Ronald Searle's drawings. "Our 600 was merely a small cluster in that crowd. Oh how my feet ache, but it was worth it".

Firsts and Seconds made the customary 22-mile trip round the borough to give them a view of the varied terrain. School involved itself in local life. Visits were paid in at least six different years to the Magistrates' Courts and Middlesex Quarter Sessions. IVAlpha, in the front row of the public gallery, heard cases of breaking and entering, stealing, driving offences, assault on the Police (£5) and cruelty to a goat (£5, 3 guineas costs). Girls attended meetings of the Urban District (later the Borough) Council and took part in an Inter-schools Civics Quiz.

The Civic Reception and Dinner were twice held in the Hall, Patricia Davison singing at one. Parties toured Forty Hall for a Local Government exhibition, Council awarding essay prizes. Schoolchildren presented the Insignia of Office on the Borough's Inauguration, the Mayoress' Badge and the Deputy Mayor's Robe and Hat; Head Girl Margaret Putnam made the Speech. Girls visited the Mayor's Parlour on several occasions. School enjoyed holidays for the election of the first Mayor and Aldermen, for the Civic Luncheon which followed the first council meeting in 1945 at which Miss Sharp seconded the Toast, as both took place in the Hall, and for Charter Day celebrations. Five carriages in procession took dignitaries to the Market Place, where the church bells rang a Quarter Peal of Grandsire Triples, and soldiers formed a Guard of Honour. The ceremony, service (with the hymn *Before Jehovah's Awful Throne*) and reception were held in the Rialto cinema.

Town links were close: Town Clerk, Borough Treasurer, Chief and Deputy Education Officers were all fathers of pupils. Despite regular appeals by the Head, individual Governors were elected only in 1958 after a gap of over thirteen years. They toured school and soon became valued counsellors.

Yet one student regretted later "that we seemed so cut off from the community, from contact with boys, from opportunities to help local people in need, and from the world as a whole. We were very protected in a middle-class, well-educated female domain". How would she have felt in pre-war days? True, they were cut off from boys during the day, but most had contact through families, churches, social and sports organisations; Sixth formers continued to enjoy a mixed social club. They certainly involved themselves with the local needy. Individuals celebrated United Nations Day, others went on Aldermaston Marches. Schools were taking more interest in, and were increasingly affected by, the world outside, just as society was taking more interest in education.

Magazine writers reminded girls of contemporary events. One article recalled that "les Allemands ont détruit les ponts pendant la guerre. Les Français ont camouflagé [*sic*] les cochons, quand les Allemands sont venus". A Mistress described the Alamein battlefield.

There were even clerihews on topics such as General Mobutu and the United Nations, Ogden Nash and Tony Benn's rejection of his inherited title.

Members of the Sixth attended a conference on growth and change in the Commonwealth. Visitors to lessons (the Japanese Minister of Education, Professors, Heads and teachers from at least sixteen countries in the five continents) were closely questioned.

Fifths participated in a conference on the work of Government, Fourths and Fifths heard a lecture on coal and how to use it (1947). Fourths joined public meetings on USA, with Brains Trust, on Spain, Nigeria and Nansen. It is true that dissemination of information was largely to seniors, indeed mostly to the Sixth, who had newspapers in their study and heard papers on Austria, China, Ghana and the Caribbean (from slavery to federation). A father, J.B. Hynd MP, talked on Russia, a former Embassy official on Yugoslavia. The VI Inter-Schools discussion group reviewed the Colour Bar. The police came in – by invitation – to give Safety First talks, demonstrations and films. Sgt. Blanchard told the VI of the work of the Force.

In Assemblies and at Prize Givings, Miss Sharp referred to such problems as post-war atomic energy, "one of the greatest discoveries of all time, yet all are in fear of the use we may make of it".

Twenty senior girls spent three happy summer holidays fruit-picking. This provided an opportunity to discover each other, other girls, the Staff mainstays (Misses Cox, Ellis, Tomlinson and especially Morley) and the world outside. They slept in 8-bed dormitories in junior school classrooms. As they were careful with plums for one week, they received the great privilege of picking pears, under strict orders to eat none, then apples and damsons. One year, 22 tons of apples were picked, graded and sorted in two days. Working harder than most had before experienced, they gained a smug satisfaction from rising with the sun and earning money by the sweat of their brows, enjoyed midnight feasts and a holiday WITH pay, but appreciated less an all-pervading odour of boiling jam. 1950's plum crop failure cancelled their fun.

In 1947, "it cannot be said that it is peace: it can be said that it is post-war". Strikes, rail and bus, and power cuts hit hard. Later, girls had to hitch to school and a parents' meeting was postponed; there were fewer on the platform for Prize Giving. They suffered like everyone else from shortages; bread was rationed in 1946, potatoes in 1947. "I hate to drink tea in a café short of sugar". Abolition was gradual, sweets coming off ration in 1951 (when tea rose to over 10/- a pound), butter and meat in 1954, and, less significant for most then, petrol in 1958. The economic situation forced cuts in education as in other spheres.

By 1954,   The shop on the corner sells cakes and sweets

Chocolate mice and sugar sticks.

A penny for one and sixpence for six,

as well as chocolate éclairs, pink lollipops, green candy bars, cornets, ice-lollies, fizzy drinks, humbugs – alas

> we often go past
> For the money we have just will not last.

Other difficulties mentioned included shortage of housing, and first, second and third class treatment in hospitals, although the National Health Service provided many with spectacles. National Savings were encouraged to help the economy of both saver and country. Amounts increased most years, totalling over £11,290.

In a non-smoking compartment of a tube train were Shirl and Doreen, "real working class girls who generally travel in pairs", another in black velvet jeans, organdie sweater and dufflecoat, hair severely scraped back to form a saucy horse's tail, gilt hoops from her ears, plus schoolgirls who had been to the Old Vic and admired the acting, whereas others had heartthrobs such as Gregory Peck and Dirk Bogarde, plus old ladies discussing trial and hanging, and one knitting. The last trams were phased out in 1952. Conductresses with ticket machines caused excitement when you could jump on the bus when it stopped at the lights. Cars became increasingly important, although it was not until 1962 that a road safety film was considered necessary. Jean Dozell's *Song of the Car* is surprisingly modern.

> The car-park keeper scratched his head,
> Gazed all around and slowly said,
> "They all got in, without a doubt,
> But how on earth will they get out?"

An old car belonging to Sarah Bonfield's great-grandfather was found in the Fifties; "she had a fine old chassis and a good engine for a car of that age". After a picnic, the starting handle raised a splutter. A large American asked to buy it, for £200 for a veteran car exhibition. Of course, all Americans were fat and smoked large cigars in their cars.

Clothes rationing ended in 1949, when there were "flannelette pieces in my ragbag and the cat chewed mother's best hat's ostrich feathers", but magazine references to appearances are less frequent than might be expected. Daddy wore an Aertex shirt by 1954. For Heather Stephens, *Things I Hate Doing* included the perennials of getting up and going to bed, "of watching the 310 bus go whizzing by, of hearing my auntie ask 'What have you learnt today?'", but also "I hate to comb the tangles from my awful knotty hair".

There was a new phenomenon: *The Beatnik* (with apologies to Chaucer).

A man there was with hair full long and straight,
He loped along with an unseemly gait,
He had not washed, I guessed, for many a week.
A jumper he did wear that reached his knees;
It dirty was and frayed around the sleeves.
The trousers that he wore were rather tight,
With sandals on his feet, his toes in sight.

(Meryl Smith)

We can follow the changing amusements. At *The Fair* in 1949,

Try the roundabout and coconut shies
Penny a go on a chair-a-plane,
Tuppence a sugar-mouse, threepence a ball,
A pipe for father, a vase for mother,
A doll for sister, a hoop for brother,
The circus starts in fifteen minutes,
Performing bears and chirping linnets,
Clowns on stilts and elephants dancing,
Seals in tanks and horses prancing.

(Elizabeth Tyler)

A few years later, *The Hunt,*

The wild vibrating clarion calls, the sound
That quickens heart and pulse of all who hear

stimulated Dinah Barsham to ask

This gallant fox, does he enjoy the fun?

Soon there was *Brumas at the Zoo*, only *he* was looking at *them.*

What are these things that are looking at me?
They haven't fur
Or padded paws,
Beady brown eyes
Or ten white claws.
White, rounded ears
Or little black nose,
Or many pink toes.
Am I really so amusing to see?

I think they are children who are looking at me,
With pale pink skin
And each two feet.
With strange-coloured eyes

> And claws so neat,
> Soft flabby ears,
> A peculiar nose,
> What, not a tail?
> And I can't see their toes?
> I think they are much more amusing than me!

(Ann Taylor)

The Sixth attended a symposium on the BBC. The Head appealed publicly that girls should not spend seven days a week glued to the television. Father mended the apparatus; *Panorama* with Richard Dimbleby clashed with *Amateur Boxing*. Mother preferred VHF radio. As for commercials? Could they be true? Perhaps they were really an entertainment for the tots? During a Test Match, "people stay up all night listening. Reports are broadcast in every shop, factory and pub; every self-respecting newspaper places atomic bomb explosions second to cricket on the front page". 1960 records rock music and such new words and phrases as with it, beat, square, don't you dig, teenagers, teddy boys, hire purchase. "A specimen of modern youth" wore a black leather jacket.

When all is said and done, it's the weather which affects everyone most. 1947's freak winter gave the coldest February in 300 years with its attendant fuel crisis, and the wettest March in at least 100 years with some of the worst floods on record in the South – followed by a blazing summer. In 1948, school was sent home early on three days because of fog; again in 1950 and 1952, "the last great pea-souper, thick yellow smog, blanketed London for four days", killing many. A theatre performance was cancelled, buses gave up, a lorryload of cattle took seven hours to travel from Pudding Lane to Earls Court. The great North Sea storm of 1953 with the worst floods for more than 200 years affected ECS less than the snow during Mock examinations. In 1954, for more than a term both hockey pitches were practically under water, and one girl lost both home and clothes in Canvey Island floods.

Even the school photograph was washed out in 1959.

CHAPTER THIRTY-FOUR

Some parents find it difficult to afford all the items

There is no more emotive subject than uniform. Heads were so exercised by the matter that Miss Sharp, at the Authority'a request, asked her colleagues to complete a questionnaire.

Variations in costs were enormous: blouses 12/11-23/-, tunics 32/- to 70/-, blazers 25/- to 120/-, dresses 4/3-35/9, ties 4/6-6/6, knickers 3/11-5/6. One school specified a coat, 98/- to £5:16:0; most, optional, were quoted at 74/- to 96/5.

Some Heads wondered whether any item was legally compulsory; others insisted on total uniform, including a real panama 25/8, hats 12/- to 18/11, hatband 5/6, tunic girdles 3/3 and indoor shoes 12/11, declaring that parents considered the outfit a good buy. Most allowed greater diversity, making little obligatory and permitting different stockists. One Head had been forced to this latitude "in one of our national crises, when the government seized the whole supply of green serge for export, just when 64 new girls should have been buying their tunics". Another insisted only on the beret, 6/10, another the purse belt 6/8, whereas a third allowed a 'Sloppy Joe' tie. At one school, mothers bought the frocks for themselves. Several arranged the sale of secondhand items, as did M.C.S. Although parents might not have been ashamed to buy or sell clothes in reasonable condition, their daughters' feelings were possibly different.

And ECS? For several years, the school tailor still came to measure new entrants and those who had outgrown their kit. The completed form required seven different measurements. A leaflet specified basic items; green serge tunic, warm and hardwearing, compulsory for all functions, although too long for games, of two qualities (50/3 and 52/9 for 30"): green skirt and Moygashel shorts for seniors (from 44/9), knickers, black again or navy if black unavailable, stockings, black and/or socks (from 3/11), black felt hat or beret (5/11 to 6/11), badge (1/9), Science and DSc overalls (15/6-28/9), shoebag with name worked large on the outside, blouses, long- or short-sleeved, neck suitable for a tie (4/6), cotton (11/6-56/3, down to 6/10 by 1952), poplin (18/9 to 25/6), flannel (unpriced). Woollen jumpers were not allowed under tunics. Suspenders, not garters, should be worn. Optional garments were blazers (47/6-56/3), pocket badge (5/6), cardigan (22/6-33/11), later, T-shirt for gym, plimsolls (8/9), dark green or navy overcoat, green gaberdine mack, with detachable hood (£5:19:6-£8:3:0). As a compromise, transparent or uniform mackintosh hoods were permitted, but, because of the problems of identifying and counting on expeditions and to uphold the dignity of the carol service, berets would be worn for these occasions.

Progress was on its slow way.

Still with a stock of berets, School Wear Ltd., upset to learn that parents were discontented with both fit and quality, felt that they had been unfairly treated, but generously offered to take over again should a new supplier prove inadequate. Tenders were invited.

Prices, samples and other schools' experiences were exhaustively compared. Letters to D.H. Evans outlined stringent conditions. Could they guarantee a more adequate turn-up on the hems of tunics? at least two qualities for every item? really prompt delivery? One County Councillor, staunch supporter of the Cooperative Society, objected. Parents were not compelled to shop at D.H. Evans, although Miss Sharp admitted that, in practice, public opinion and school's attitude did amount to compulsion. Some parents bought green tunics elsewhere, many made blouses, skirts, cotton frocks; a few, with tailoring experience, made everything. The only thing needed then would be the beret badge and the blazer pocket badge, both specially woven.

Notes were available for those wishing to make dresses. Green and white candy-striped material, 4/11 a yard, was available locally at Pearsons. One suggested pattern was Butterick 7741. "The dress is a shirtwaist style, the belt, collar and sleevebands should be of the same material. The belt may be stiffened and made with a buckle. No white collars or coloured belts are to be worn". Stripes were not universally popular; how about checks?

Matters did not proceed altogether smoothly. Blazers were a different colour from the rest of the uniform; worn with the beret, both looked equally bad. Cardigans were too bright a green for the tunic. "You hoped to be able to make blazers of two quality weights. I gather that you can supply only one range. Are you able to arrange a supply of really crease-resisting shorts?" The firm bought all School Wear's stock and promised price lists; because of increased costs, tunics would be 8/- above that quoted. Problems resolved, D.H. Evans remained ECS' stockist. A small discount was credited to school. OGs remember looking forward to visiting Oxford Street, although representatives did come to school.

Council hoped, vainly at this time, for a nearer stockist. Rejecting a weekly inspection and a later motion that girls could wear their own clothes, members discussed individual items *ad nauseam*. Shirt blouses with tuckable tails, not elastic, were preferred. Dislike of ties was frequently expressed; distinctive ones were approved for teams, rejected for Houses. The Head of Art saw no aesthetic reason against a coloured version, but the danger was, apparently, that girls might wear coloured socks as well! The netball team had already taken the law into its own hands in this regard. Cardigans, to be purchased from one stockist, should be of one shade of green and, if knitted, of a regular pattern.

After three years of discussion and several rejections on the grounds of cost and practicability (crushed in shoebags, blouses come adrift), dark green pleated shorts for games, agreed: coloured girdles (2 yards, 3/-) for House matches, agreed: green and white scarves, agreed: if knitted, they should conform to one pattern. A special braid (3d a yard) could be put on blazers.

The most controversial areas were the feet and head. White socks were approved for summer, fawn (later, dark green) for winter; in 1954, nylons suitable for skirts should, because of expense and unsuitability for games, be optional, although, oddly, it was "obvious that it was not desirable that juniors should wear nylons". Black or brown shoes, but not white canvas in summer, were agreed. 1960 saw the problem of Italian styles, with long pointed toes and stiletto heels – the committee must decide. Gym shoes must be marked externally with the owner's name and initials; a tape might be attached to the tongue. After eight years of disapproval, white hair ribbons were allowed by 1960, provided they were kept clean, but no coloured hair slides.

A 1956 panoramic photograph shows 35 Staff, two secretaries, two groundsmen, Mr Whitehead in uniform and about 610 girls, all in long-sleeved blouses, yoked (not velvet) tunics, most with ties, socks, belts, Sixth in skirts – and with short hair. Four wear cardigans, several granny sandals, most a piggy bag round them, and very few have glasses.

In the immediate post-war years, those in dire straits were helped by outfit grants. Occasionally, money was lent and repaid weekly at 2/6 or 5/-.

If uniform was hardly distinguished, then White Girdles were. Held initially by any suitable person from the Seconds upwards and renewable by Staff vote, they were instituted in 1947 to reward good deportment and appearance. Inevitably, this became confused with courtesy and good manners. They were accepted neither readily nor regularly by Council, which suggested their abolition as girls were being polite for the wrong motives. This was generally agreed to be better than being rude.

Junior White Girdles, refused in 1952, were accepted, with one dissentient voice, two years later. Up to 10 should be granted then automatically lost at the end of the Third Year. Until Sixth numbers increased, senior girdles were correspondingly reduced from 30 to 25. Council members were still debating hard in 1959. Abolish, because impossible to know all girls? No. For deportment only? 28 in favour. A form award for appearance? 17. Each form to receive two? Maybe. For one term only? 6. Suspend the award indefinitely? Unsure.

An unsatisfactory state of affairs.

Meetings can be held whenever there is sufficient business

The composition and function of Council were argued about almost as fiercely as the agenda, which ranged from trivia to fundamentals. A list of all suggestions was posted and comments invited. Each form elected one representative; her deputy accompanied her but enjoyed neither speaking nor voting rights. Juniors did not always have a vote. The power of Staff (10), Prefects (10) and Sixth (16) to outvote the rest was questioned: 12 representatives for 500 and 36 for 100? Should not the whole school act as Council?

The Executive had one representative from each senior form, plus several Staff. The Chairman retained the casting vote, but any resolution must have an unspecified majority, as the Executive could not be expected to implement a scarcely popular decision.

Dinnertime remained a frequent topic. Passes signed by parents giving permission to go into Enfield were again rejected, Staff later agreeing, without discussion, that Sixth non-Prefects could go without permission. That this privilege be extended to III-IV because of shopping problems if they had to take or collect siblings was refused, M.C.S. stressing her legal responsibility and the potential damage to school's reputation if large numbers flooded the Town at a busy time. Dinner-hour prep. in the library, from which any talker would be debarred for the rest of term, should remain for seniors only, as juniors "had very little work to do as yet and didn't realise what hard work was", and would need supervision.

Requests for variations in timing had to be refused while meals were taken in EGS Hall. As a concession, each table of eight would be allowed out when all had finished – on fine days and with safeguards. Wireless programmes *(Eye Witness, Film Time, Cricket)* could be heard in one designated room and dance records were permitted in another. Such concerns diminished when dinner was served in the New Hall and Music room. First lunch remained primarily for seniors, who wanted to reserve places, whilst juniors attended various practices, although they could queue in the hope of spare seats.

Mrs Carpenter succeeded Miss Price as cook. While foods were rationed, an HMI and the District Organiser tried to solve the resulting problems.

Form matters: no girl should be Form Monitress twice in the same school year. She, but not her deputy, would wear a badge, although some argued that there were already too many badges. Despite F.S's fear of expense, the Head Girl and senior games captains and, later, Senior Prefects, should have distinctive emblems. There should be a fortnightly form period.

Assembly caused concern. The singing of *Amen* should be lowered or changed. For reasons of comfort and cleanliness, something was needed to sit on during the proceedings; its impracticability was recognised but resented. Separate junior and senior services were refused; school must remain one corporate body. Girls speaking should not now stand at the side of the Hall where they could be confused with Prefects and the point of the punishment lost. Several years later, detention replaced standing up.

Special occasions were considered. Where should 1957's carol service be held? Whereas the Old Hall had lacked dignity, the New Hall could accommodate all denominations. Could Roman Catholics, like Year I, have a separate service? A large majority voted for the Parish Church, noting the need for a rehearsal with the organ. School Christmas cards should be printed, but without the crest as that would cost £5 for registration with the College of Heraldry. Junior and senior Speech Days, so that more parents could attend, were not initially agreed. An annual Harvest Festival to collect food for the needy (voting 22-22) would bring organisational difficulties.

Although public examinations would be affected, they again proposed that school should run from 8:30am to 3:30pm, but for different reasons. It would relieve congestion on the buses, allow freer evenings, would benefit concentration and family life and, in summer, be cooler. Changed times did come – eventually. The warning bell at 8:55am should be rung on the field in summer. The whole travel pass system needed revision. Could not pressure be put on the Ministry of Transport to provide a school bus from Potters Bar?

And a mixed bag. Police should be informed of missing articles of value. Termly fire drill should be held. A school flag was, sensibly, rejected.

There are still a number of easily satisfied, passive pedestrians

House spirit was, on occasion, flourishing, especially with annual Christmas parties. Captains exhorted members to make a titanic effort in every respect. Over fifty Captains, democratically elected, some serving two or even three years, worked hard. In truth, devotion to House appealed less and less, certainly to seniors.

Council voted overwhelmingly, 93-22, to resume the pre-war custom of regarding Good and Bad Work Marks as points for and against. Each detention should cause the loss of one point. Members failed to agree that one extra Good Work Mark, and therefore point, should result when a certain number of Marks had been achieved. Badges (1/6 or cheap 2d metal) should replace coloured ribbons, which would be retained on gym knickers. Perhaps House Staff should wear the badge?

When, little foreseeing the work created for all concerned, VIB in 1956 presented a House Challenge Cup to include – everything, Council suggested a points system: work (scholarships, college places, exam results, Good Work lists, prizes, certificates, magazine entries, competitions), behaviour (White Girdles, School Colours, attendance, detentions) and Athletics (teams, Colours, records, awards).

Encouragement, lamentation, flattery, blind optimism – all are common to all House Captains' boringly repetitive reports. "Things are indeed looking up and it's up to you to see that they go on doing so", Ca, after a disastrous year. "No success except what is due to individual effort and that is not what really matters", M. First formers received praise for "constant effort. Let us hope that their enthusiasm will increase and help to keep up the House spirit", Ca. "Still a spark of House spirit, which I hope they will fan into a flame", M. "Good luck, anyway, and keep trying", Ce. "It would be more to your credit to work hard and behave well and cut down the vast numbers of bad work marks and detentions that you receive", M. "Everyone must put her whole heart into the matter at hand. Keep trying and the elusive shields will soon be yours", W.

Still, "you have been a pleasant crowd to manage, and I've enjoyed coming into contact with you", Ca.

A few outings might be thought highbrow: *The Marriage of Figaro, The Way of the World*, the Nutcracker Suite and the Royal Ballet in which Brenda Taylor, an old Catherine, danced. Leaving ECS at 14 for the Royal Ballet School, she, within two years, had performed, with Helpman and Fonteyn, for President Auriol of France, and later came second out of 953 in a television competition to design a Festival of Britain poster. Ice shows were popular; at least seven parties included *Aladdin*, most favoured and enjoyed, despite deep snow, bitter wind and a long wait for a tram, and the "beautifully coloured" *Holiday on Ice* and *Champagne on Ice*; "an amusing sight to behold were 62 girls (not in uniform) tucking into ice-creams!" *Simple Spymen* pleased several groups. Coaches for comfort and convenience were generally considered worth the cost.

"No Passengers Please". St Catherine's Captains had to put a cheerful face on regular under-achievement, praising such meagre successes as an OG winning the OGs' race, the lowest number of detentions twice ("Well done!", but not a lasting state of affairs), the highest number of Good Work Marks (once), eleven wins in hockey, netball and tennis (although, one year, "I think the less said the better, although I'm sure the team tried hard"), three individual swimming successes ("The House is devoid of really outstanding swimmers"), and, for the first time in fourteen years, the Sports Shield in 1956. Once, the team had shamingly dropped the baton.

The writing was on the wall, in spite of a few non-point-worthy activities such as a visit to Kennington Oval for the women's cricket match, arranging flowers and a record recital (3/- from refreshments for School Fund). One party enjoyed an amusing and entertaining reading of Ian Hay's *Little Ladyship* and a charade, "a fitting close to a year with the friendly atmosphere and mutual enjoyment so necessary for the generation of a really electric, vital House spirit".

Why cannot the House come top more often? St Cecilia's also notched eleven wins; these included a nerve-rackingly fast senior netball final, and rounders when the team was "chosen somewhat hurriedly". Poor support for Sports events meant double-edged encouragement: "even if you are no sportswoman, you can still enter for the egg-and-spoon or the obstacle and sack race, none of which requires much intelligence or skill". Unable to arrive on time, they were bottom in swimming.

The usual annual fluctuations meant: top Good *and* Bad Work Marks, flowers very good, detentions "on the average, fairly good". Either "we can feel quite proud" or "it is impossible not to be depressed by such a formidable list of disappointing results". Comprehensively, "work and behaviour are still our weakest points"; miscreants should try to curb their high spirits until break or after school.

The saint's day party was, one year, very successful and should be tried again. It was, but "could have been more successful if more of you had come".

"Happily our hopes have been fulfilled; members are keener and the majority have turned out to all sports in all weathers". However, St Margaret's went into the doldrums in the early Fifties. Proud of stalwarts with Colours and White Girdles, "there are many more people we cannot be proud of – those who don't even know when their games' practices are, and make no effort to come to meetings, who never come out to watch matches. The unfortunate Captains could be seen exhausting themselves in trying to drag you out".

Results were not too grim; Sports Shield after 16 years (although no entrants *one* year), thirteen wins, plus, the highlight of 1962, the swimming shield (after 25 years) *and* the House Cup. No wonder the party was hilarious.

Most congratulations were given to the Margarines who collected toys and books at Christmas. It took three of them to carry these greatly appreciated parcels to Great Ormond Street.

"We must not rest on our laurels". St Ursula's was more successful: 25 wins and one shared (one netball final exhausting even the onlookers), three times most Good Work Marks and four times the Challenge Cup. In 1959, Captain and Deputy presented a cup to Susan Pegrum and in 1961 to Pat Pollard, both having contributed most towards success. When an exciting hockey final was lost, Ursulines were properly reminded that the excitement of the game was as important as victory.

What everyone remembers is the Ursuline domination of swimming for 15 years. More than once, the trophy was won before the actual Gala; the winning margins were huge, from 93 to 294. Once, they amassed more points *before* the day than the runners-up achieved *finally*. 1958's loss was stunning; they lost again in 1959, admittedly by only half a point. By 1961, the Gala was written off with shame as experience for the few juniors who took part; it was undoubtedly the first time that the House came fifth. Was that why behaviour went from bad to worse?

"Good luck for next year and keep trying. The House spirit is still spreading".

"There is still an unfortunate tendency to leave everything to someone else". St Winifred's had most Good Work marks several terms and won seven games finals. 1947's Sports Day brought noticeable improvement; instead of being last, they reached 4th place. Once, they came first – for half of the afternoon; a third year, however, was shameful. The junior rounders team, ambiguously, "fought hard to lose two matches". Seniors seemed fatefully resigned. There was an appalling rise in the number of detentions.

Small consolations: flowers arranged most artistically: the Challenge Cup achieved once: "the intelligence of the House seemed to improve steadily". All-rounder Barbara Millard received the individual trophy.

CHAPTER THIRTY-FIVE

The younger generation is just as good as we were

Entrants continued to refute the assumption of narrowness of experience and vision by coming from over 250 contributory schools and from at least 20 different kinds, public, state and private. Apart from finance, the 1944 Education Act made little difference.

Over 65 moved from across the London area, from Tottenham to the City, from 51 schools. The astonishing number of 110 from 96 schools came from all over the UK, bringing with them different customs and speech patterns. One poor child had already been to four secondary establishments, the last in Nairobi. Others from abroad included at least six whose fathers had served in the Forces in Germany, one from the Royal Military College in South India, one from Madras College, two each from Australia, Canada and South Africa and one from Singapore. So some 200 girls from 160 schools brought new life to Enfield.

Most transferred in the normal way as a result of the dreaded 11+, from at least 85 schools. The main contributors were the ever-popular George Spicer 176, Lavender 150, Chase Side and Chesterfield 119 each and the relative newcomer Merryhills 109. Brimsdown 37, Worcesters 25 and Eversley 12 were new to ECS; in fact, 22 were first-time contributors. Thirty-three more sent 132 between them over the whole period, one from St Martha's Convent surviving but half a term before returning. The 58 from Palmers Green High went mainly into the Sixth.

Family backgrounds show similar diversity. At least 24 girls had stepfathers, three had stepmothers. Two fathers had retired, two were unemployed (one with a company director wife) and one was in prison. At least twelve mothers coped singlehanded; their husbands were serving abroad, had left them or separation had been mutually agreed. During their daughters' schooltime, 19 fathers and three mothers died, three fathers became invalids, seven were on their own, two remarried and six more parents separated. Eleven girls were looked after by guardians – aunts, grandmothers, foster mother, an unidentified Miss – or were in an institution.

More mothers worked, some as single parents, some from financial necessity, but often in the newer spirit of freedom and equality engendered by working during the war. Auditors, comptometer operator, draughtswoman and clerks of all kinds accounted for at least 81. The educational sphere was obviously convenient for about 83 ancillary and teaching staff, even one Education Officer. The caring professions, from doctor to home helps and hospital cleaners, offered a wide range to 45 as did factories 21. Others, such as two milliners and six dressmakers, worked from home. At a rough estimate, some 275 had gainful post-war employment, divided almost equally between full- and part-timers. The former included driving instructress, Salvation Army worker, four shop assistants, and the latter, florists and three barmaids. One became an ECS Governor, another had been a professional singer. Still more said Housewife rather than 'at home' or ' I don't work', as their predecessors used to say.

The list of fathers' jobs is far from complete; it can be divided, unfairly and arbitrarily, into generally non-manual, generally manual, and completely mixed. Clerical workers are most numerous, nearly 200, covering all possible areas including Civil Service 38, banks 31, accountancy 29, insurance 17, shipping – even the Royal Mint. Retail and wholesale trade absorbed over 100, in all capacities and in most outlets. Directors and managers of companies, including the Hippodrome, numbered 52.

Education and local government accounted for over 60, with 21 schoolmasters, 9 Heads (one with OBE for National Savings) 2 lecturers and a professor of Medical Science, a swimming instructor, the organiser of the school coach system, a county councillor and the Town Clerk. Various professions employed 15 draughtsmen, 5 solicitors, architects, engravers, a legal executive, translator and the Director of the Institute of Economic Affairs, 38 in all.

Over 170 manual workers were in factories, 10 at RSAF, with an ever-increasing variety of trades: – supervisors 26, electricians 20, computers etc. 12, with individuals as thread grinder, plastics designer, capstan setter, plater, measure cutter, strander, timer – to name but 7 out of 59 stated trades. The biggest single group was of 83 engineers. Transport supported 55: railwaymen 19, drivers of all manner of vehicles, a ship's furnisher; 43 were in building construction or maintenance. The land absorbed only 21 in all, with 8 farmers (one in Cyprus), managers, gardeners, nurserymen, a chicken manager, crop sprayer, farrier and stud groom.

With mixed skills were some 50 in general welfare: chemists, doctors, dentists and their assistants, optician, in hospitals or with human or animal institutions and 5 clergy. Leisure industries were supporting more, 28 in all, in the media, catering and hotels, a designer of dress patterns, bookie, commercial artist and actor.

The Services accounted for 20, the police 8, with a CID Sergeant, and one fireman; 19 worked for the GPO, one in the Royal Household. A few refuse, as always, to be categorised: bargee, checker of Bills of Quantity, credit controller, dye caster, meter tester's assistant, mutuality collector, progress estimator, Saw Doctor and a Tory agent.

What had these parents named their daughters? Some 350 different names are recorded, with considerable variation in spelling; 226 had one name only, one had two, 57 had three.

Names unrepeated in ECS' story numbered 45, ranging from Amena and Antonetta to Vita and Viva, with at least five of Celtic origin and only five or six noticeably foreign. Occurring uniquely in this post-war period were also Ione/Iona; Sheena/Shuna; Brigid/Bridget/Birgitta; Amanda, Cherry, Elunid, and Jasmin (with 2 representatives) and Gloria (5). Several occurred for the first time but not for the last; Karin/Karen, Kay, Marcia, Nola, Paulette, Sharon: Melanie 2, Beverley 6, Marilyn 10, Penelope and Sally 11, Sandra 21: 15 bore names more popular in days gone by, such as Ada, Audrey, Betty, Edith, Ellen, Florrie, Lily, Mabel, Nellie, Violet. Others achieved sudden popularity (Sandra 11), most featuring nationally, such as Sheila 40, Maureen and Pamela 42, Linda/Lynda 44, Barbara 45, Carol(e), Jillian/Gillian and Jen(n)ifer 48. ECS' top ten were Jean 67, Elizabeth and Valery/Valéry 69, Christine/Christina/Christeen 71, Susan 78, Janet/ Janette/ Jean(n)ette 81, Mary 86, Patricia 103, Margaret 127 and, runaway favourite, Ann(e)/Annie/Anne-Marie 187.

Let thy speech be short, comprehending much in few words

Whereas one OG remembers, as highlights of Prize Giving, Staff gowns and the dresses of returning leavers, the Head worried that much of her annual review was, inevitably, constant and traditional. Nevertheless, the triumphs, successes and failures are new to each generation and her cheerful reports sounded fresh.

It took place in EGS Hall for several years. Soon the New Building provided insufficient space. By 1958, Miss Sharp considered it sensible to have separate junior and senior events to accommodate many visitors and parents as well as the girls, including the new First Forms. Even though the Hall and Music room were crowded, there was soon not enough room to invite everyone who wished to come. When numbers increased to 700+, the new girls had to stay at home.

"Girls will be girls but they were 'boys' when a mouse ran across the Hall. They laughed! They are probably laughing still, for they are taught to love laughter as much as learning".

Expenditure included: refreshments from the Dutch Cake shop £10, transport of speaker £2:10:0, removal of piano £3:10:0, cards and invitations £11:5:0, alterations to the Honours Board £2:5:0, all in 1949: 59 books, £36: 12:6, 17/- for stamping them, 1951: Books £43:7:6, 1953; flowers £6, 1958.

Apart from Mr Pascal, Director of Education (later called Chief Education Officer) and a good friend of ECS, the Chairman of Enfield Education Committee usually presided.

The order of proceedings varied not at all. The evening opened with such well-known songs as *Glad Hearts Adventuring*, *Worship*, and *Creation Hymn*. Between the Chairman's remarks and the Head's report, before the Speaker and after the presentations, choir and/or small choir, often unaccompanied, sang, over the years, some fifty different items, showing catholicity of taste and representing more than twenty composers, classical, romantic and modern. Each ceremony usually contained a moving, melodic song and a comic one: – *Sweet Kitty Clover*, *Watching the Wheat*, *The Angelus*, *Orpheus with his Lute* (on three occasions), *The Owl and the Pussy Cat*. One year's highlight was Miss Benjamin's setting of four nursery rhymes, records being sold to girls and sent to the BBC, where nine nervous singers had an audition. Three cheers for the Speaker, Head and Guests were called for by the Head Girl, her Deputy and a Senior Prefect. The evening ended, always, with *Jerusalem* and the National Anthem.

Whilst the Fifths received 37 certificates over six years and 147 prizes, other Years collected annual prizes and Good Work Certificates for near misses. This clearly revealed which form was the 'brightest', especially when one received no such awards. The First Year (four forms from 1955) gained 107 prizes and 131 certificates, Year II (four from 1956) 128 and 119, Year III (four from 1957) 116 and 134, and Year IV, 113 and 109. First Year Sixth divided thus: two Arts forms (from 1959) with 59 and 42, two Science forms (from 1961) 52 and 42, Commercial (known more attractively as Secretarial) 27 and 25, and in 1947 only, Pre-Nursing, one prize. VIA Science gained 87 and 3, VIA Arts 73 prizes only. Special awards included the time-honoured prizes for Religious Knowledge, Mathematics, History and French, plus one for Classics when Miss F. Sharp retired.

1951 brought the funeral oration over Higher and School certificates, metamorphosed into General Certificate of Education (GCE) at Advanced

Level (AL), Alternate and Ordinary Levels (OL). Entry for desired subjects replaced the old system of a fixed number chosen from different sections. The new standard was higher, so girls and parents were warned not to aim for too many. The Fifths' *Operetta* told of girls invading the Ministry of Education, threatening to strike if GSC continued. After murdering this demon, the Monster "malevolently called from the vasty deep a creature more frightful, GCE". Suspending judgment –"it was not a loafer's paradise, nor has all the strain been removed"– Miss Sharp remained unrepentantly opposed to the regulation that candidates must be 16 by September 1. "The actual birthday has nothing to do with mental development or fitness for examinations". Later, discretion was allowed to Heads and distinctions were restored to AL.

Despite a disquieting increase in leavers aged 15, 16 and 17, with the consequent loss to the individual, the family and the community, more were realising the value of advanced courses. In HSC, 61 in the Arts forms passed 177 main and 36 subsidiary subjects with at least 31* (two girls gaining four) and 53 Goods. Scientists, 33 in number, passed 89 main and 25 subsidiaries, with 129 Goods. The Head was not disappointed when she looked forward to results just as satisfactory and triumphant at AL, which demanded independent reading, a scholarly and imaginative approach, meticulous, detailed study of texts and precise, patient, scrupulously accurate laboratory work. The two groups gradually blurred, some Scientists taking Art, some Arts students Biology. Numbers rose nationally and at ECS: Arts 204, Science 155. Passes in main subjects, from Art to Zoology, totalled 853, with, later, 47*; 90 or so who failed AL grades were granted OL passes.

Entry to universities in this 20th century of specialisation was still by examinations which dominated 8-10 winter weeks and caused problems of staffing and accommodation. Successful candidates twice attended Guildhall receptions. Until 1959, girls had won 44 Open Scholarships and Exhibitions, 34 State Scholarships and more than 180 places to at least 17 different universities – 80 to London, 13 more to London colleges which later became independent universities, and others to establishments all over the British Isles. One went on to Kent over twenty years later. "This splendid record is one of which we are all very proud". County grants were generous. The end of men's call-up in 1961 put pressure on places, especially in Science and Mathematics, and added to overcrowding, confusion with eight different GCE examining boards, over-specialisation, cramming and the inevitable raising of university demands.

Miss Sharp was delighted too with the 500 or so going on to other, often over-full, places of Further and Higher (FE, HE) education and training for

Horticulture, Physical Training, DSc, Secretarial skills: Art, Music, Drama, Ballet, speech and other therapies: libraries, laboratories, nursing, teaching. The range had become wide.

In the three Fifths up to 1950, 286 passed, 165 matriculated, which included all the 'top' form in that year, when four sat in December to defeat the age ban; 94 passed additional subjects, which gave two more Matrics. OL calculations are complicated by individual subject entry and recording remains ill-defined. Up to 1959, 2 girls passed in 9 subjects, 147 in 7, 91 in 6, 58 in 5, 128 in 1 or 2: 3,147 subjects overall, an average of more than 5. From 1960, coinciding with the increase to four forms and concern at the damaging importance attaching to numbers, figures were listed thus: with more than 7 passes 132, 4-6 passes 127, 3 passes 48.

1948 was "the most successful year in work and play since I became Head Mistress", with the largest number of School Certificates (80) in school's history. Ten years later, "academic results are the best I can remember"; some Fifths did brilliantly, but there was a higher proportion of failures: "a combination of laziness, too frequent television and going out most nights with the boy friend. Bad results are mostly deserved, the aftermath of indolence". The Head gave examinations general approval in a highly competitive world as they tested intelligence, memory, industry, common sense, self control, all virtues needed by society and the individual. To avoid being swamped by them, the experiment was tried of one annual exam-time for the rest of the school. This proved insufficient, especially as parents' holidays frequently interrupted the summer term.

It was well-known that Miss Sharp attracted interesting speakers. One startled her, and her audience, by wondering whether she wore a pigtail when she was a girl. (She did.) Another arrived about 9pm on a night of dense fog. Having walked in front of the hired car, he had stopped frequently between Central London and Enfield to give himself strength.

Charles Morris, Head "of the magnificent school that is so great a source of pride to the City of Birmingham" was the first in 1947; Kenneth Lindsay was MP for the Combined Universities, a one-time President of the Oxford Union and Parliamentary Secretary to the Board of Education. One family friend, the Very Reverend W.R. Matthews, Dean of St Paul's, outlined the qualities of the well-educated: the power to concentrate, "a capacity which modern methods of education do not always encourage sufficiently": a sense of proportion which gives the ability to grasp essentials: the power of expression which increases the power of thought: imagination, the sign of a probing mind: the critical faculty, judgment and discernment, plus a real sense of life's purpose, namely the enrichment of one's own life and that of others – a tall order! Another, Canon Marcus Knight, Chancellor of St Paul's, celebrated the first full Speech Day in the New Hall.

Professor Sisson was Senior Fellow at the Shakespearean Institute and Emeritus Fellow of English Literature at UC, then the most popular London college for ECS. A distinguished public servant and an expert on international finance described Sir Wilfred Eady, Principal of the Workman's College, Camden Town. Mr.I.J. Pitman MP, spoke "at this grave moment in national and international affairs", Suez, 1956.

Among eminent women were several Head Mistresses and two Principals of St Hilda's College, Oxford, where girls regularly studied, Miss J. de L. Mann and her successor Miss Kathleen Major – no sinecure, for the latter handed out 59 prizes, 8 cups, 2 medals and 3 shields. Miss Catnach had just returned from a world tour.

Three were perhaps the most outstanding. The then editor of *The New Statesman*, Miss Janet Adam Smith, was a "speaker of high distinction, daughter of a famous theologian, author, critic of poetry and noted mountain climber". Dame Dorothy Brock attracted many VIPs. The one who gave M.C.S. the greatest personal pleasure was her 'clever' sister, the first woman Permanent Secretary, Dame (later a Life Peer) Evelyn Sharp. Her theme was "Take what you want – and pay for it". Her mother and members of the family sat on the platform.

For seniors, the event brought assessment and remembering. For juniors, it was one "of challenge and of looking forward. You must start to work now to get good results in the Sixth". Speakers were mainly present or former Heads.

The Head congratulated parents on their sacrifices, at the same time appealing for cooperation on homework, set on about 165 evenings in the year! For her, Prize Giving remained the most important day of the year, when she could publicly sum up achievement and stand back to gain fresh inspiration.

A real milestone,

an exhilarating kaleidoscope, a tree bringing forth good fruit, grown from a sapling planted on 1909".

The OGA asked every member to make the Golden Jubilee year "memorable by attending Reunions and bringing back with you every Old Girl you know. Some have lost touch for so long that they will need persuasion. They are afraid of being lonely in a crowd but surely this is impossible if the crowd is big enough". A hard core remained devoted, some holding office for fifty years. Some 1,600, roughly 40% of past pupils, were traced. Many remained close friends, others had kept in touch with long-serving Staff, many parents still lived locally.

The first task was to raise money. In six months, they amassed £35:14:0, in twelve £136:0:9, but there was over-spending of over £52. Interest from investments, donations and the odd sherry party were welcome, a Bottle Bring and Buy sale raised £18:18:6, and coffee mornings were the order of the day. Most appreciated was the last one with Miss Bidwell and Miss Woods at their flat with its fascinating view of the Thames. Notices of these events were distributed, via Miss Campbell, by girls to save postage. Each form was invited to consider a gift to school. Profits from the Concert Music for Your delight helped. Everyone was praised for unobtrusive organisation and teamwork.

The Great Day, Friday, September 18, opened with a mid-morning Service of Thanksgiving; girls in immaculate uniform trooped along Holly Walk to the Parish Church. A printed Order of Service listed the hymns: *Praise to the Lord, He who would valiant be, Holy Spirit, truth divine* and the patriotic *Land of our birth, we pledge to thee*. Prayers were said for all in positions of responsibility, for members of the Staff, "that they may show understanding, enthusiasm and imagination", for all former members, founders and governors, and, at much greater length, for present pupils and for the future. Miss Sharp and the Chairman of Governors read from Ecclesiasticus and Romans. Canon Knight preached, the choir sang *With a Voice of Singing* and closed the service with the traditional *God be in my head.*

Lunch was hastily gobbled for school was open from 2pm until 8pm: a long day. Programmes in hand, visitors "received an almost overwhelming picture of the amount of work which has been accomplished and which was progressing – even before their eyes, as Staff wished to show, as far as such a thing is possible, the wide variety of work done and opportunities available".

Displays were mounted in no fewer than 24 of the possible 27 classrooms: work in Biology, Careers, Classics, Modern Languages, Scripture and Secretarial subjects. Art and Craft gave impressive demonstrations of pottery, fabric printing, tile making and oil painting. A two-hour Analytical Chemistry practical lesson took place in one laboratory.

A home-made folder explained that History consisted of project work, for example, after an expedition, and classwork in exercise books: Ancient History (Firsts), The Middle Ages (Seconds), Tudors and Stuarts (Thirds), 18th-20th centuries, English and European (Fourths, Fifths), the AL syllabus and two courses of Current Affairs. The outstandingly interesting Mathematics display showed that the subject could be understood and enjoyed by even the unmathematical. Geography presented carefully executed models and maps of expeditions and of the growth of both Enfield and ECS.

Two rooms were filled with photographs and magazines, "productive of a flood of reminiscence and hearty laughter". The library illustrated how it was run. It was hoped that parents would select a Jubilee gift from a display of books mounted by Don Gresswell.

Such was the press and throng that tickets had to be obtained beforehand for the indoor shows. The Dress Parade in the Hall aroused admiration for the practical clothes made and modelled by girls, while Room 1 housed a Spanish play, singing and dancing. There were two energetic displays in the gymnasium, where a packed audience watched "vigorous skilful vaulting and imaginative dancing" by pupils from all parts of the school, the favourite being a Third form dance based on Pandora's box.

At 3pm, Cadets on the field broke Colours and pitched tents. Excellent teas were served by the DSc department.

Proceedings came to a triumphal close with a tickets-only Music and Verse Speaking (English, Greek, Latin) concert, containing sixteen items composed during these fifty years. They ranged from Hungarian folk songs to an Irish lullaby, from an *Invocation to Science* to *The Ships of Arcady*. Whereas the candid magazine critic considered some reciting ragged, no-one faulted the excellent performance that was always expected of the choir. As well as various Prize Giving favourites, the programme included *A Song for Music*, composed for the occasion by Dr Eric Thimann.

The Head remembered afterwards "a sea of friendly faces and laughing crowds all over the school grounds, all activities most imaginatively and decoratively planned, showing school's rich variety of intellectual, practical and artistic possibilities".

This exhausting day came before the OGs' big day. At their previous reunion ("children welcome"), they had presented a portable radio, an embroidered tablecloth and a cheque to F.S.

Assembling from noon, 122, including one from Holland and mainly from the first 25 years and still addressed as Miss X, ate an informal but hilarious lunch. Present pupils washed up. Enthusiasm was high even if the temperature outside had dropped. Nearly 500 attended the service at the Parish Church. Eve Barsham (1947-1954) played the organ. They too sang *Praise to the Lord* and some Psalms, as well as *Blest are the pure in heart, Jerusalem* and *Now thank we all our God*. Passages from Job and Ephesians were read by Barbara Butler (1917-1924) and Susan Page (1957's Head Girl). Prayers of thanksgiving and blessing, conducted by the Curate, preceded a thought-provoking address by the Lord Bishop of Willesden. The collection contributed £17:0:5 to the Church Restoration Fund.

"As always beautifully prepared by our generous helpers", tea, inevitably, followed, graced by clergy and Governors. An inscribed teak table (£28:19:0) was presented for the entrance hall. On its first official appearance, it was piled high with books and certificates for Prize Giving and has been in daily use since.

Council, having refused to contemplate paying £300 to one artist, commissioned Muriel Archer, a member of Enfield Art Circle, to paint the first Head's portrait, which was then unveiled. "Those of us who were at school in the 1930s will say that it is Miss Broome as we knew her". It was partly funded by a sale, raffles (£4:6:6), coffee mornings, cocktail and tea parties, but they were still considerably short of the sum required, £75:5:0.

Several from the original Form I attended, some "enjoying the leisure of a well-deserved retirement", others boasting of their grandchildren. At least one retired Mistress was shaken to think that she had taught these truly Old Girls. Old Staff warmly welcomed were Miss Hunter, the only original, the octogenarian Miss Baxter from Scotland, Miss Bidwell then a mere 78 years old, Miss Woods and Miss Hyslop. There was disappointment that Miss Forrest, who had inevitably taken a leading part in the preparations, had fallen and injured a leg that very morning – "l'homme propose et Dieu dispose". A car service was organised, so she received more than 150 visitors over the weekend. The OGs "drifted home, tired, hoarse, deafened but very, very happy", and the Head could look back on two almost deliriously full days.

The OGA held a Jubilee Bridge Drive (2/6) in aid of Mr Whitehead's children's party and a Jubilee Dance (3/-). This proved an anticlimax: attendance was disappointing and only £23:17:0 was handed on.

At the annual Dinner (12/6) in the Hall, Frances Perry proposed the toast to School, coupled with the names of the Head and Miss Forrest, who, as the first Mistress appointed directly to ECS, proposed the health of the Association. Representatives of each decade wallowed in reminiscences greeted with laughter and a few moist eyes. Jubilee year ended only in the following spring with the play *Doctor in the House.*

What remained? Apart from many renewed friendships, the OGA received an influx of new members, so that the target of 250 Life Members was shortly reached. School felt, for a time, a new cohesion, a slightly bewildered, because unexpected, pride in belonging to the past. Reading and hearing of so many different careers was an undoubted eye-opener and encouragement. Even the magazine received a record 227 entries, "an increase in quantity matched by an improvement in quality".

Besides hopes that the next fifty years would be as prosperous and progressive, tangible reminders exist. In addition to the table, portrait and a decorated sundial above the main entrance, school's collection endowed the Hall and Music room with a permanent microphone system and modern record player. The library was in better shape: 200 new books received the commemorative label, the donors' names being listed in the magazine. The Governors presented another set of the *Encyclopaedia Britannica* and special prizes to the year's two Head Girls.

Still treasured, the OG magazine, 96 pages, 5/-, subsidised by coffee mornings and teas, included many memories and stimulated more. Providing a Who's Who list, "individual accounts of professions and jobs, and letters from all over the world – amazing when school's short life is compared with the centuries of boys' education – was a difficult undertaking for scattered amateurs". After many vicissitudes, such as sharply rising costs, strike, illness, lost copy, it appeared many months behind schedule.

Miss Forrest – who else? – summarised school at this time, as "a large and happy community of nearly 800 girls, with a carefully chosen Staff, who may well be proud of the work they are doing and whose initiative and self-sacrifice have done so much to ensure that the high ideals in work, play and behaviour should still be respected as certainly as has been the case hitherto".

"What pride to look back – what great hopes for the future!"

CHAPTER THIRTY-SIX

Some girls and some parents think that lessons are like a dose of medicine

poured into one and passively received instead of being an adventure which won't have a happy outcome unless all the people concerned in the enterprise take an equal and cooperative part".

Miss Sharp rightly claimed an unusually wide choice of subjects: 8 basic (RK, English, History, Geography, Mathematics, Art, DSc, Music): 5 Sciences: 6 Languages (one girl studying French, German, Latin and Spanish began Russian externally). She accepted the difficulties of timetabling for 21 regular GSC and 16 HSC subjects, 9 for the one-year VI course of General Education – plus PE. She introduced Sixth form Social Science which could be combined with General Science, Commercial or Pre-nursing studies, with one whole day for DSc, Hygiene, Civics and Local Government.

To strengthen our understanding

of spiritual truths and of the vital applications they have to our lives", the Head took enormous trouble with Assemblies. She was amused when a tame jackdaw invaded and no-one batted an eyelid. She supported those interested in religious matters, encouraged concern with the less privileged and fostered responsible involvement in activities.

Few took religious subjects in external examinations, but gradually academic respectability was acquired. From 1952, 28 achieved AL (one*) in Religious Knowledge. Perhaps because of tragedies in her own life, Miss Dorothy Alice Campbell (1945-1970) demonstrated what could be done in practical terms to help others and strenuously promoted understanding of widely different forms of worship, although unable to fulfil her own desire to become a Minister. An inveterate traveller, she showed slides of visits to Israel and Oberammergau and talked about the Church in the USA.

Several Staff were involved. Miss Maud Kathleen Penrose Thurston (1960-1969) joined as a specialist.

A fortnightly religious discussion group initiated prepared meetings on eternal themes: Evil, Prayer, Heaven and Hell, "religion in the broadest sense. *Please come.* The greater variety of opinions, the more stimulating the discussions". This soon merged into the world-wide Scripture Union, which, from the original 36 members, went from strength to strength. Although enthusiasm was not consistently maintained, an average of 70 attended Monday lunchtime meetings. Seniors ran a junior group which much enjoyed singing. Badges symbolising commitment to daily Bible reading became popular. On offer were Bibles, £1:7:6 with zip fasteners, 11/- without, and *Songs of Praise,* 1/10 (later, 2/6). In 1962, the Gideon Society presented New Testaments to First formers. However, Bible studies (St James' Epistle, the Ten Commandments) were "always indifferently received, but different methods were tried so that all could take part".

A weekly prayer meeting before school proved a source of support and strength to the faithful few. One year, St Andrew's was open for prayers before examinations, "a great help in our attitude to exams and their results".

Wide-ranging discussions touched on the philosophical (Equality of all men, morals without religion, the end of the world, the bomb, Spiritualism, the Holy Spirit, infant baptism and adult immersion), the educational (Christianity and Arts or Sciences, the New English Bible, Religion's place in History) and the practical (giving up sweets for Lent, contemporary Social Services strangling Christianity, careers in church work, denominations); "there was even a discussion when we endeavoured to apply our faith to such topics as clothes, careers and marriage".

Some topics were introduced by Miss Campbell or members, but most by outsiders: Ministers, a Sister and Mother Superior, representatives of religious bodies, who dealt with such themes as the Colour Bar and taking God on holiday with you. Guests described their lives in far-off countries, OGs Ida Robinson on China, Joan Restall on Nigeria. One priest brought an interesting tape-recording of his visit to the Holy Land, another talked on church music. Best remembered were two well-known women. Rev. Elsie Chamberlain told of her work in the religious broadcasting department of the BBC. Over 120 students and Staff felt privileged to hear Gladys Aylward talk on her work among the Chinese people. This stimulated a termly missionary meeting to arouse interest in the work of Christ in foreign fields.

They joined with other Christian Unions, rambled during summer holidays, listened to gramophone records, read medieval and miracle plays, enjoyed a junior performance of a "simple but attractive" Nativity play, Brains Trusts, Testimonies and a Quiz. Rain drowned a Sausage Sizzle, so instead they played a glorious game of Sardines. Films and filmstrips were popular, especially when shown jointly with EGS: God and the Atom, *Pilgrim's Progress*, to name but two.

Girls participated in an Inter-Schools camp, a Leaders' conference, the Keswick Convention and Student Christian Movement meetings, in Rallies and Squashes connected with the North London Fellowship of Christian Unions in the Billy Graham crusade. In 1954, the Greater London Crusade at Harringay claimed their attention, several counselling or singing in the choir. Approximately 50 members went in special coaches to the climax at Wembley Stadium. A weekly mission to Enfield held services for ECS, EGS and the public.

The Group "has reflected the Spirit of the whole Church in its emphasis on unity. We pray that you all may have God's richest blessing".

Three continued religious studies. Anthea Cousins was the first to read Theology (Sheffield). Brenda Green studied at the London Bible College. As singing always seemed so much more important and pleasant than work, Ailsa Morrison worked in a library until old enough for a full grant for Music College. With her ordained husband, she adopted a badly treated Jamaican girl. Later, in Canada, she felt the call, studied by correspondence, graduated and was the first woman to be ordained priest by the Anglican Church there ("Meet my mother, the father"), unique so far for ECS. Others worked for the C of E Children's Society, the Institute of Almoners and the National College of Social Services.

The whole school took part in the carol service, usually in the Parish Church and once attended by the Mayor. The pattern changed little; six or so hymns, six or so readings, although the annual number varied between 9 and 25. Each of the first four Years contributed until the choir took over in 1960 with carols new, English, French, Danish, German and, once, Polish.

Religious items in the magazine, many prize-winning, were almost exclusively connected with Christmas, as in Margaret Maxwell's *Carol*.

> Red glows the coat that Saint Joseph wears
> As he leans on his grey ash staff and stares
> At the Holy Babe, who, rosy in sleep,
> Lies curled in the manger so brown and deep.

or *The Stable*, by Diana Coltman, where, with the Magi, the Shepherds and the Angels bright, were

> The poor, unnoticed humble things
> That praised Him that holy night.

Margaret Putnam's entry concerned *A Strange Visitor,* a rich king of Ethiopia, who asked the innkeeper's wife, Martha, if he could spend the night in the stable to commemorate the Crucifixion of God's son born there thirty-three years earlier. He forgot to pay his bill, but Martha used the advertising to become rich. Less cynical, more traditional was Suzanne Carter's *Christmas Poem.*

> A low from the stable awakened the child.
> It opened its eyes at the mother so mild.
>> She turned to her baby and cover'd him o'er
>> To save him from draughts coming in from the door.
> The rugs, hung as screens on the porchway so bare,
> Admitted the shepherds who entered with care.
>> They gazed with wonder at Jesus so dear
>> For they were surprised at finding him here.
> They knelt at the foot of the manger with joy
> And showed a wee lamb to the newly born boy.
>> At last they were gone and the family slept
>> Then Gabriel came and watch over them kept.

Other verse described a glimpse of heaven in *Bird Song*, the peace of *Evening Requiem*, "the worthy tribute to our Lord" in Mary Cock's *Ruined Abbey*, while Beryl Egan wrote in prose of the pleasure given by Church singing to *The Tramp.*

Their Christianity was practical too. In close touch with the Shaftesbury Society, girls attended their annual London Festival, where purses were received one year by the Queen Mother with "a delightfully sincere smile", and another year by Countess Mountbatten. They knitted squares, often competitively, which Miss Campbell sewed up into 97 blankets. By 1962, fewer were made: "As the pattern of poverty is less acute in England, we are hoping to make babies' garments for refugees".

Many willing helpers ran Christmas parties for deprived local children and those cared for by House Parents. 1955 saw the first annual one for handicapped youngsters from Vale Road School, each paired with an ECS girl. They were ferried in their wheelchairs or carried from the field gate. Tea was followed by games – Pass the Parcel, Hide and Seek, treasure hunt, Pin the Tail on the Donkey – and singing. Soon they organised summer fun as well. Short concerts included tap dancing, mimed nursery rhymes, scenes from *Alice in Wonderland*. Guests loved a delicious party cake with Humpty Dumpty sitting on top, rides on a real live pony, feeding the ducks between the showers, building sandcastles and receiving sweets, a balloon and a posy of flowers. ECS had never seen children enjoy themselves as much and were thrilled to receive individual letters of delight, often with amusing drawings. Exhausted helpers had thoroughly enjoyed it all.

All were consulted on the choice of Charities. Miss King, Miss Bowen and Mrs Parker in turn coped with the administration. Main beneficiaries were the sick, the afflicted (blind and their dogs, cripples, lepers), children (sometimes through UNICEF and League of Pity) and animals (World Wild Life Fund £30, PDSA and RSPCA). Normal weekly collections, still, theoretically, divided between good works and amenities, brought in £2,366:15:4, ranging from £42:6:2 in 1952 to £306:8:10 ten years later. Christmastime collections raised £1,100.

Seals were sold to help Spastics £8:17:10, for Queen Elizabeth Hospital for Children £30:10:9 and for the prevention of TB £8:16:0, and Christmas cards for the Pestalozzi Children's Village £1:8:4. Two girls traded their own flowers and plants to send £7 to the Sunshine Homes for Blind Babies. IVL carol singers donated £1:6:0 to the British Empire Cancer Campaign, for which 65,000 used, untorn postage stamps were saved over four years. In addition to £3 for the Merchant Navy Comforts Fund, the 27 members of the Young Trawlers' Union, begun in 1960 with Miss Coster's encouragement, collected milkbottle tops, silver paper, magazines and money which totalled £66, "an active and successful year".

Disasters and those in need, whether at home or abroad, met, as always, with a ready response. A parcel of clothing (postage £3:4:7) went to post-war Germany in response to an OG's account of conditions: thousands cold and hungry, living in cellars and shelters, their energy absorbed by a grim struggle to keep alive, houses, families and savings lost, TB rampant, spiralling costs on the Black Market (coffee and tea £5 a pound, butter £10), prisons and remand homes full, people unable to go out because they lacked clothing, hospitals overcrowded, the official ration, long since unobtainable, for a baby – one nappy. Germans were cheered that their former enemies helped them. When floods devastated Devon, the East Coast and Holland, over £104 was collected; one OG lost her home and was married in hastily bought and borrowed clothes.

Also benefiting were Relief Funds for the Orkneys £11:15:3, the Chilean Earthquake £14:16:0, the Congo £60, United Nations Aid to China £3, Inter-Schools Committee for Warsaw £14 plus £69 for stationery, mathematical instruments and radio for a Polish school (although this fund closed "for economic and political reasons"), Save Europe Now £12, pocket money for Belgian children staying with local families £13, Refugees (First form collection) £11:13:0 and the Penhalonga Inter-Racial school in S. Rhodesia.

Annual support for Princess Elizabeth's Day raised nearly £100. English funds helped included the Lord Mayor's Thanksgiving £25+, the

Portsmouth Affray £41:5:0, George VI Memorial £26, Margaret Macmillan Memorial £5 and Westminster Abbey Repair £1.

Charities Weeks netted over £1,800 by the usual means of sales and displays of all sorts, plus funfair, marionette shows, Coronation Fête films, profits from Staff teas, exchange of Victorian relics, viola recital, raffle for Cook's cake, Mr Whitehead's Dance, surplus from the cripples' party and donations; the biggest boost came from ice-cream £202.

1960 was the highlight. "School is to be especially congratulated on its splendid work on behalf of World Refugee Year, both in individual form efforts and on joint occasions. Much ingenuity and imaginative planning were shown, especially in the quick and non-time wasting ideas evolved to fit into the busy working days".

* indicates also carol singing

IA*	£6:18: 0	Bran tub, Bob-a-Job
IB	£5: 5: 0	Raffles
IC	£35: 1: 6	Penny Race, Book Sale, Trading with 1/-
ID*	£5: 9: 4½	Pig Collecting Box
IIA	£3: 1: 6	Cookery competition, Pennies in Bucket
II Alpha	£2: 8:11	Scenes from *Midsummer Night's Dream*, X-Word puzzles
IIB	£10:11:10	Sale of sweets, biscuits, coin collection
IIβ	£11:19:11	3d bit guessing, treasure hunt
IIIA*	£18:15: 0	Sweet raffle, talent competition
III Alpha*	£10:11:10	Photographic competition
IIIB	£12	World Refugee Day
IIIβ	£11: 4: 6	Sale of boat race favours, Jive session
IVA*	£11: 2: 2	Slides of around the World in 25 minutes, Raffle
IV Alpha*	£11: 0: 8	Sweet making competition
IVB*	£6: 0: 0½	Sale of biscuits, coffee
IVβ*	£23:12:11½	Record Hop
VA	£35	Barbecue
V Alpha	£8: 1: 7	Beetle Drive
VB	£3: 6: 9	Sale of necklaces and earrings
Vβ*	£8: 8: 8	Raffle of Easter Eggs
VISec	£18: 3: 8	Christmas card raffle, sale of used gramophone records
VIB Sc	£16:18: 0	Christmas Hamper Raffle, baby sitting

VIA Arts   £3: 2: 6   Donations
VIA Sc   £21   Film show
Cadets   5/3   Sale of cakes
Staff Playreading   £17:11:6
School UNICEF film show   £16

Adèle Griffiths, later a student at Aberystwyth, ran a Garden Party (5 guineas), "with great skill for an 11-year old".

The grand total was over £480.

One former pupil touched school's heart. Christine Perrott contracted polio while at ECS. Girls provided small items and apparatus for turning the pages of a book (£17:10:0). After being in an iron lung for two years, she wrote:

> Thankyou for the lovely flowers.
> Thankyou for the cooling showers,
> Thankyou for the tall tree,
> Thankyou, God, for making me.
>> Thankyou for the dark, dark night,
>> Thankyou for the morning light,
>> Thankyou for Thy kindly love,
>> Thankyou, God, in Heaven above.

She was a Foot and Mouth painter, able to move only her face for six years and deserved the Endurance Medal of the Girls' Life Brigade. Her success in passing English Literature OL in 1957 "was really the proudest record of the year". She requested, when dying, that her life support machine and painting equipment go to a London hospital.

So feminine, so cultivated, so alive

Head of the all-graduate English department, Miss Flint is not forgotten by any contemporary teachers or pupils. Many had cause to be grateful to her for arousing their interest in dramatic work and several for their careers in the theatre. "Not everyone could take her perfectionism in drama, in VI Literature or in lower school essay-writing, but those who revelled in it were richly rewarded".

In the worst winter of the century, "she spread laughter which is a manifestation of a sense of proportion and often of courage too, for it remained with her even when she knew she was dying". The OGs presented handsome books to the library of which she was once in charge, in memory of one "so able professionally to communicate her love of our English Language, whether spoken, written or acted".

Meticulous, tireless and supportive of every aspect, with not a day's absence from 1943 to 1972, Miss Doris Cox was just as active. Wryly comic, Miss Winifred Walles (1944-1952) participated in drama as wardrobe mistress, in playreading, magazine and library and talked on Colorado to Historians and Geographers. With wide teaching experience, Miss Kathleen Millen (1952-1969) brought the library into the modern age.

Three, one OG Annette Wynne, remained one year only; two year stayers, numbering six, included Miss Joan Dickinson (Mrs Doig, drama), Mrs Elaine Dunford (drama, later a Head), Miss Jean Macgregor (also Scripture) and Miss Gillian Bliss. Now better known as Jill Paton Walsh and renowned for her novels and her prize-winning children's books, she is a Fellow of the Royal Society of Literature. Two stayed longer: Miss Margaret Bird (Mrs Cuthbert, 1959-1962) and Miss Jennifer Harding (1961-1964).

For Miss Flint's first Open Afternoon, the Old Hall represented an Elizabethan theatre, with a huge apron stage. Girls sat on floor, chairs and windowsills, so that all could see VIA performing Shakespearean extracts on women, friendship, marriage, Romans, magic. The quality of the acting seemed unaffected by the fact that sometimes there was barely more than a foot between characters and audience. On another occasion, "in spite of the attraction of the summer weather, in two or three minutes after the curtain rose, we were all deep in the story of the Brontës".

The Mobile Theatre's small van brought their properties and six members, including Brenda Saunders, to perform Chekhov's *The Bear*, *The Bishop's Candlesticks* and the hilarious *Proposal*. "The afternoon was over all too quickly".

Girls went out more often. Three coaches took them to Stratford. They ambled round Shottery before seeing their set play, *Julius Caesar*. Critical of production and, again, Gwen Frangcon-Davies ("she wandered about"), divided in opinion of Gielgud as Cassius (unanimous, however, that he spoke the verse beautifully), they approved Harry Andrews' Brutus and felt that Andrew Cruickshank (Caesar) did what he could. A later group attended the Oxford Experimental Theatre's production, and, despite travel sickness, agreed that this modernised version made them think. Anthony Quayle (Mark Anthony) was the idol of the audience.

VIB appreciated *The Taming of the Shrew*, with Wolfit the perfect Petruchio and Rosalind Iden "fiery red-haired and uproariously funny throughout". Although judging the play undeserving of detailed study, "we all agreed that we had spent a thoroughly enjoyable afternoon". *Hamlet* and Olivier's *Richard III* were enjoyed at different London theatres, as were both Redgrave and Wolfit as Macbeth.

New Building: note the 'covered way'

Laboratory demonstration, Miss Maude

Mathematics lesson, Miss Flowers

Art lesson, Mrs Hargrave

Middlesex Schools Junior and Senior Swimming Champions, 1951

431

Hockey team, 1952-1953, Misses Crook, Macfarlane

Netball Shooting

Gym

Keep Fit

Prize Giving, c 1951

Prefects, Misses F. and M.C. Sharp, 1952-1953

Fourth Year group, 1956

A morning in the National Gallery wandering from one exciting painting to another preceded the enjoyable and informative *Young Elizabeth*. Choice widened: *A Man for all Seasons*, *The Miser*, a Shaw anthology, *St Joan*, *Murder in the Cathedral*, *Samson Agonistes* (St Martin's-in-the-Fields), *Comus* (Windsor), the Wakefield Cycle of Mystery Plays (the Mermaid) and the Hogarth Puppet Show. They investigated Canterbury before seeing medieval and miracle plays, with beautiful singing by a concealed choir. Later students heard a talk in the Planetarium on Chaucer's Astrology, saw films of *The Flight of the Little Heron* and *Great Expectations*; both juniors and seniors heard lectures on acting, stage fights and make-up.

A pleasant and interesting weekly half-hour

Listening, reading and arranging programmes required planning and manoeuvring in the sharing of books. The élitist Staff and Sixth Verse Reading Society flourished for nine years; "although all individuals are welcome, the Group is found to be more compact and more pliant when fewer people attend. We all enjoy the exchanging of pleasure which the reading of our own particular poems to each other gives".

Each participant, bewilderingly, read a different part in *The Family Reunion* in weekly instalments. They found *The Lady's not for Burning* amusing and exhilarating. They explored a variety of writers from Milton and Keats to Dylan Thomas and Virginia Woolf; Christopher Fry's *Venus Observed* was a great success, C. Day Lewis' *Italian Visit* was only partly understood. Staff prepared a record programme of Shakespearean sonnets.

Usually, themes, not predominantly cheerful, were chosen: sound, dreams, the war, the lunatic, the lover and the poet, murder. The Group grew larger; they wondered if it had anything to do with the apparently irresistible fascination which death seemed to exert over obviously healthy and blooming members.

At the first meeting of 1958, they read from the less well-known Shakespearean plays. Alas, lack of Sixth form support brought activities to an end after only five sessions. A VI English Poetry Reading Group is next mentioned – that is all. A pity, as "after a busy day of school work, half an hour of listening to old favourites and making new discoveries is both relaxing and stimulating".

Competitive Verse Speaking in the different categories of the EMF was encouraged and always successful. 1947's total was nine prizes and twenty-six certificates.

Well and vigorously read

"It says much for the clever and witty interpretations that the cast gave of this amusing play [*Captain Carvalho*] that the audience was at times reduced to tears". The magazine sometimes criticised these termly delights of the Staff and VI Playreading Group, but was generally ecstatic. "It is hard to know whether cast or audience have derived the greater pleasure". In the summer, Fifths were invited – and charged for the privilege, proceeds to School Fund.

The thirty or so plays chosen were mainly modern: *Outward Bound* ("more unusual"), *Quiet Weekend* ("a most endearing couple of middle-aged schoolboys conspiratorially proud of their midnight fishing spree"), *A Question of Fact* ("well attended, topical appeal, cast doubled, all read intelligently"), *Ring Round the Moon.* Miss Flint, at her last meeting, dominated as Queen Elizabeth in *Will Shakespeare.* "We are most grateful to her for reading stage directions at all our meetings".

At least ten Arts Staff were publicly commended for their readings, convincing, engaging, amusing, spirited, effective, amazingly true to life, endearing, immaculate. Some fifty girls received similar praise, sensitive, moving, charming, humorous, masculine.

The Group was an example of happy fraternisation between the different Sixths and between them and the Staff. I enjoyed it greatly.

The ideal choice to attract people of all ages and tastes

Plot, characters, interpretation, production, all received detailed and constructive analysis in the magazine, usually by an OG who had acted earlier. Mr Whitehead, often with his son Ralph, constructed, and occasionally painted, scenery designed by the Art Staff, and managed the lighting effects as well as clearing up after rehearsals and performances. "How little could have been accomplished without him!"

A chest, £7:18:6, housed stage curtains, which, in 1950, cost £9:12:0 for cleaning. Various young teachers acted as business managers. One year's accounts read thus:

Samuel French Licence Fee	£13:13:0	Programmes	£4:11:0
Chas. Fox Hire of Costumes	£40:16:9	Sale of tickets	£5:15:6

Artricia photographs 4/6

In all productions, the main parts were doubled, so that over 60 girls might be involved. Thus Friday's performance differed markedly from that on Saturday afternoon. This, sound educationally, caused problems of costuming and rehearsal.

Juniors had their own productions, useful for talent-spotting. 1947's *Nativity Play* made a loss of nearly £10; 1950's was highly praised. "We never tire of it, new and original and old old". For *The Golden Apple*, they made their own costumes. Form and magazine prizewinner and swimmer Jeanne Duval ("charming") was the youngest in the BBC Repertory Company's performance of *Mad about the Boy*. Brenda Taylor and Ruth Nixon (gym*) both walked and stood beautifully as Helen. Ruth, swimming for school and county, gained the Award of Merit before reading Economics at LSE.

Midsummer Night's Dream, "the most charming of his plays and perhaps the most perfect, one exquisite whole", occupied 17 actresses, 4 fairies, 3 attendants, 14 costume helpers and 13 stagehands. Credit was given to Myra Lawrence's quiet queenly confidence and Joan Gardner's unusually pleasant and sympathetic treatment of Demetrius. Ann Taylor played Helena "enchantingly with a surprisingly mature appreciation of the humour of the character". The mechanicals presented "every possible ounce of humour in every possible way", notably Shirley Hann's skilled character study of Quince, whilst Wendy Hadwin won all hearts as Puck.

Miss Cox was producer, lighting director, stage manager and wardrobe mistress of *The Ivory Door*, which left nothing to be desired; Eve Barsham played her own music. *Beauty and the Beast* was wisely chosen since its delicate fairy tale atmosphere demands a young cast. Junior Sketch Club members made the simple, easily movable scenery and an enthusiastic and capable back-stage team greatly enjoyed providing noises off. Unfortunately, not all remembered their words, not all were audible, one was too sweet, another too calm, but Mary Cock's masculinity, " an authoritative and fine performance", deserved praise. Anthea Matanle gave "a most intelligent rendering of feline grace". *The Imperial Nightingale* received a mixed review: one actress found it difficult to keep in her part continually, another's voice had a tendency to squeak or to be lost altogether; not all sustained the essential dreaminess – but the lighting was effective and the use of scenery restrained.

The junior dramatic society, re-formed in 1960, was run by Sixth to include group work, mimes, speeches, a make-up demonstration, playreading and a competition.

Choosing a play presents problems for seniors in an all-girls school.

The extra seating space and roominess of the stage of EGS Hall made possible the more elaborate props and scenery for *The Immortal Lady*. Congratulated was Senior Prefect and magazine committee member Isobel Henderson, who won EMF prizes and a Scholarship to RADA before going into repertory and becoming a West End understudy. Future Oxford graduate Doreen Clarke (tennis*) displayed the necessary "glorious impetuosity and excitable artificiality". The aptly named Joan Cordelia Wollen also contributed to the magazine and won prizes. I found it hard to believe that the actresses were schoolgirls.

For *The Merchant of Venice*, greeted with the customary thrill of anticipation, Miss Thomas played on an exact copy of the Elizabethan virginals, kindly lent by the Dolmetsch family; Enfield Technical College lent lighting equipment. Prizewinners Diane Wells' Shylock "purred" and White Girdle holder, Senior Prefect, House Captain Mollie Mackenzie (gym*) gave a study of a sad man as Antonio. She won scholarships to two universities and became an SRN.

"A drama founded on human truths, on men and their feelings and thoughts and their relations with God, the beauty of the rainbow seen mistily, but steadily throughout", *Noah*. For a later production, "it was delightful to be able once again to buy materials, design and make most of the costumes". Praised were two White Girdle holders. Senior Prefect Doreen Russell, after Training College, passed the Executive Civil Service examination with the highest marks of any woman. Prizewinner, magazine contributor in English and German, choir member, Margaret (Peggy) Butt as Noah "never forgot the trembling voice and hands and the slow careful movement characteristic of old age". A "mature and sincere Bassanio",she won scholarships to Oxford, acted with the university dramatic society, touring in Paris and Berlin before becoming a speech therapist and counsellor, later a psychotherapist and writer.

For Miss Cox' first senior production, "dignified and magnificent", *Viceroy Sarah*, Miss Benjamin played charming incidental music; the scenery was rich, the costumes correctly elaborate. *Much Ado* aroused fears that memories of Gielgud might be too strong. Again two prizewinners were singled out. Nanette Webb (gym*, junior tennis champion) designed the scenery and acted with controlled hatred and bitter resentment. She was rewarded for recording Enfield in her skilful pen and ink drawing of Maidens Bridge, and read English at Oxford. Ruth Bennett (rounders*) was a member of the chess club and trained as a secretary; "as the simple and sincere Friar, she did full justice to Shakespeare's poetry".

The audience was transported into the medieval world of *Richard of Bordeaux*. Old hands acted memorably. Lorna Stone, another future speech therapist, gave the dignified charm of Queen Anne. Suzanne Carter's Lancaster was "an outstanding performance, mature, intelligent and sensitive"; prizewinner and House Captain, she won State and Classics scholarships to Reading.

"The cast made the most of the material they had and created memorable characters where there could have been mere cardboard figures. The play was made successful by the acting and the production" – so much for *Mary Queen of Scots*. As a challenge in the New Hall and with girls from all years, *Romeo and Juliet* was an ambitious choice. Whereas extra space was welcomed, the apron was useless because of lighting deficiencies, backcloths were fixed and wing space for changing limited. Still, when compared with the platform of the Old Hall, it *was* a stage. Newcomers Sheila Whatmore played the Nurse with an intelligence and instinct remarkable for her age and Kathleen Noall, an arrogant Tybalt, demonstrated good sword play. By the sheer force of her acting, Dorothy Grieves' Juliet was in a class by itself. House Captain, Cadet, DHG and Grand Concours prizewinner, she read English at RHC.

However unsuitable a choice, the strange and difficult *Winter's Tale* with "unpleasant theme, broken-back construction, elliptic language" was a set book. Some fine actresses were criticised for immobility and self-conscious gestures, but the cast was congratulated on doing as well as it did. Brenda Sledge, "enchanting in a fine performance of great beauty", read English at Exeter.

Caesar and Cleopatra gave ample scope for exciting effects with scenery ingeniously and effectively atmospheric. Mary Swainson's voice, movement, gestures were all convincingly male. Senior Prefect, debater, defender of Jazz, magazine contributor, Language prizewinner, she became President of the Union at Westfield.

Despite the problems of a mannered play, Miss Cox in *The Rivals* "led us into a world of comedy, wit and grace in which we were enchanted". Many received high praise yet one actress disregarded detail, another was too stately and failed to use her hands properly, a third was afraid to use her costume. Her thirteenth venture did nothing to mar her record of successes. A mixture of uproarious comedy and aesthetic charm, the perennial *Midsummer Night's Dream* did lack a little royal dignity as the rustics leant too heavily on slapstick. The bewitching fairy interludes owed much to delightful costumes and to Mrs Hargrave's unusual and enchanting background. In *St Joan*, "the entire lighting, the painstaking research into heraldry, the evocative scenery, visually pleasing and dramatically functional, the capable scene-shifters" all added up to a most attractive evening.

Of the many others who acted, Yvonne Walker, who enjoyed a fascinating range of posts and travel in Europe and Japan, and Helen Brockman, who worked for Granada Drama department, both studied at the French Institute. DHG Shirley Eastman ("poised and mature") won form, Greek Verse Speaking and magazine prizes before reading English, with a State Scholarship, at Oxford, became teacher, social worker and JP. Winner of form and History prizes, Margaret Putnam, subsequently a senior probation officer, gained an Exhibition to RHC after giving "the immaculate performance that has come to be expected of her" as Dogberry, Friar Lawrence and Shaw's Caesar.

"We are grateful to them for the pleasure they gave us; we remember too all those whose hard work behind the scenes did so much to make the plays a success".

More leavers studied speech therapy: Senior Prefect Sheila Arman, Lynette Beaven (Psychology Honours) at the London Hospital School, Philippa Doubleday at the West End Hospital, Elizabeth Stone and Betty Bentley, for whom many roles, especially that of Sir Toby Belch, were doubtless good preparation. Jocelyn Millis, French competition winner, trained at Drama School.

Prefects and prizewinners, 25 in all, read English, although one changed to Theology. They included music-lover Marylin Massil (Hull), Gillian Headland (Reading, with State and Open Scholarships), soloist Marilyn Finch, Anne Hallam-Jones (State Scholar, King's). After working, Irene Jones read English and American Literature at Kent in 1983. Library helper and State Scholar Jean King went up to Cambridge. Christine Dyke, Pat Allison and Gillian Shepherd (Queen's Guide, play reviewer, State Scholar) all won Oxford places.

Perhaps more tongues will work in the debates than in lessons

By 1954, the Debating Club was open to all except Year I, partly because of an increasing awareness of the world outside. Its fortunes fluctuated, but it kept going, supported by Miss Millen and Miss Kirkby-Johnson, both keenly interested in public speaking. Committee members were always receptive of new subjects.

The first debates tended to be lighthearted. The motion that personality was of more importance than brains was lost. The House, with Mrs Dunford as guest speaker, felt, not for the first time, that the Sciences were of more value to mankind that the Arts. It did not regret that the English climate was not under government control; "in spite of the dreadful summer, we did not want to control the English weather although the debate was held during a storm". If George Stephenson and Christopher Columbus were trapped in a burning building, this House would prefer to save George Stephenson: sadly, no record remains of the decision.

An unexpectedly large proportion of self-confident juniors soon attended. Obviously, that this House is of the opinion that the sexes are not equal was lost, seemingly on the basis of the superiority of Mata Hari as a spy, Joan of Arc as a soldier and the USSR women who drive steamrollers. The abolition of capital punishment was defeated as was the more topical proposition that television was the curse of the age; this debate produced much laughter. They narrowly approved of gambling and easily defeated the notion that Girl Guide and Boy Scout movements did not meet the demands of modern youth. A lively discussion surprisingly did not deplore the use of animals for scientific or medical research. They agreed to have more equality between white and coloured peoples. Many abstained at a well-attended meeting which agreed that it was better to be amoral than immoral. On the abolition of the monarchy, six abstained, six were for and forty against.

Motions drawn out of a hat produced witty and impromptu three-minute speeches: The United Nations is a useless body: Young children should be allowed to believe in Father Christmas: Rock 'n' Roll is a harmless pastime (an enthusiastic debate).

Over 90 attended, perhaps because it was with the boys against Edmonton Latymer, to disagree that euthanasia was the main cause of evil. ECS defeated EGS with their interesting presentation when preferring the past to the present. Two contests were held with Minchenden. That intermarriage is the only way to better international relations was defeated by twenty-six to six, with six abstentions. A woman's place is in the house was changed after sustained and heated argument to allow the insertion of 'married', but, as pre-war, it was still lost, by thirty-three to three, three abstaining.

But, as with most clubs, "enthusiasm with several, apathy as a whole".

The Centre and Hub of all our Work

Books, still the cheapest of commodities, were acquired by various means: – a sale, a special collection, a requisition allowance with 12½% discount (£61:5:0) bought 106, donations from leavers (687 altogether), money from the OGA (£200), an exhibition displaying one hundred books essential in every home. "We thank the Borough Librarian for his generosity in lending so many books [244] for which we have made special request".

"Our lovely and gracious library", with shelf space for 10,000 volumes, brought real delight in 1955. It is chastening to see how quickly the thrill faded. In two short years, it had ceased to be the wonderful place it was, its books and amenities taken for granted.

By then open from 8:30am until at least 4:30pm, it boasted some 6,800 books, 140 piano music sheets and 22 Ordnance Survey maps, although fiction remained poorly represented. Council agreed that new purchases should be made for the junior section, the stock being childish and in bad condition. As well as *The Spectator*, *The Times* was approved for its usefulness for geography, history and current affairs and for the literary value of its leading articles.

The Library's Grand Display was prominent in Jubilee year and brought in not only Arts and Science books (412 plus 100 more from Enfield Library) but also a useful and attractive folio stand for atlases and such-like.

Ten official librarians were sought. Each candidate had to state reasons in writing, submit two book reviews and mend one volume before undergoing short written and practical tests. So many suitable applicants resulted in twelve appointments. Learning the manifold and often dull routine duties, girls from the Seconds gave up willingly time and energy to keep things running smoothly and were thanked for their invaluable and unobtrusive assistance. A committee consisted of two Staff, two girls from VIA, sixteen from VIB and, for one year only, two from each of the Fifth forms.

Now a tidier, more regulated place, the bays were full almost to capacity when all the books were in for checking. By 1962, three new bookcases were requested. The Head on her retirement presented a set of the *Cambridge History of Literature*, four dictionaries (two Latin, two Greek) and a picture. Two new tables complete with bookrests and pen grooves stood in the bay reserved for VI, who also had a round table at the top of the stairs. F.M.F's *Britannica* in green leather, her last contribution to ECS, was housed in glass-fronted bookcases ; it was rare to have *two* up-to-date sets. Mr Whitehead cleaned and resurfaced the tables.

A more sophisticated system of registration became imperative to reduce losses and the heinous crime of deliberate withdrawal of books without signing for them. Books were systematically reclassified; repairing, recovering and devising protective coverings occurred weekly. Borrowers were urged to return books promptly and to replace them correctly as a tradition of respect for rules had to be established. The library remained open during checking to produce more sense of responsibility and fewer losses. A new procedure, successful but entailing more work for the librarians, was adopted for reserving popular works.

Miss Sharp advocated reading not skimming, admittedly an old-fashioned concept. An article *Why Read?* by Sylvia Ridgley, who won an English scholarship to Exeter, told how a small child wants a story, whereas an older one may read a book as a work of art. "We need to study literature with all our imagination and intelligence. Apart from fun, it helps us to see the inter-relationship of everything in life and to use our own powers of creation and sharpening of sensitivities. Literature is all-embracing and so gives happiness". Miss Millen organised a Readers' Club, some 45 strong, which met fortnightly to discuss such topics as mystery and detection, fun and humour, other people's lives and biographies, to read extracts and to participate in Quizzes – buns and orangeade 3d.

Delegates attended Ministry of Education and Librarianship courses, a literary Brains' Trust and book exhibition. Members of the School Library Association visited ECS.

Eighteen girls are known to have become librarians. Two French medallists were Sheila Wood, House and tennis* captain, Senior Prefect and prizewinner, who changed after secretarial work and Beryl Blunt who trained at Birkbeck after graduating. Margaret Marra and Elizabeth Shearman both worked in Children's departments, Pat Gibson in the Police College, Ann Hemming in the Nature Conservancy, Margaret Turner (gym*, junior tennis champion, Cadet, Senior Prefect) for EUDC. Esther Polkinghorn became assistant librarian at Birkbeck. Others studied at Southgate, Islington, Holborn and Enfield.

"We grow apace and continue to be busy and well used".

What a pleasure it is to have again the School Magazine in print

Its 64-84 pages appeared once more in December; the price rose from 1/6 to 2/-. Despite good sales, the deficit averaged £22:10:0, paid for out of School Fund or the private account. Copies were still sent to schools with which contact was close.

The pattern, incredibly, did not change. Miss Sharp's remarks remained joyous: "I am proud to write this foreword to a magazine which, in its accounts of great occasions, House triumphs and failures, games records and school expeditions, represents in some measure the varied activities that enrich our life in school".

Staff notes, headed *Valete* and *Salvete*, included tributes to retiring members and notes of any marriages or births. Lists of school officers preceded the calendar, full Prize Giving programme and reports of every activity in and out of school, plus details of monies collected, disbursed and saved, and of the library – it is obvious how at least half of most magazines was filled. As space allowed, a poem or drawing or a spread of photographs was squeezed in. The last nine or so pages were devoted to the OGA; occasionally, an OG wrote of her exotic doings.

In between were the original contributions. Even the chaos of building operations failed to affect creative output. Several, inconsiderately, wrote in French or German; "many of us will have to persuade our friends to translate for us". The indefatigable committee members coped with collecting items, planning layout and correcting proofs.

In 1947, "a splendid and happy year", Miss Flint and the committee found judging the annual competition unusually difficult as so many had entered for more than one category. Juniors had to continue from either "By the moon we sport and play" or "I stood tiptoe upon a little hill", the latter presenting the greater difficulty. Individual entries were discussed, mostly in kindly terms. Over the years, 52 prizes (senior 26, middle 9, junior 17) were won, 15 more efforts were highly commended and 17 commended. A manuscript of worthy but unrewarded items was often placed in the library.

Comments reveal not simply changing fashions, but the surge and ebb of ability, an up followed by a down. When space proved inadequate, it was deemed fortunate that many rejected contributions were below standard, quality failing to match quantity; some were unsuitable for inclusion – a tantalising remark. One year, a huge total of 195 produced a shortlist of nearly 100 essays and poems, the next 140 offerings of a low standard. One year 227 delighted the committee, the next competitors were scolded for a lack of self-criticism which gave the judges hours of fruitless work. For Miss Sharp's last year, the standard so improved that the committee's task was pleasurable and more difficult. There was one dramatic offering but, as usual, verse predominates in all but three editions.

Relatively few contributions can be called naïve, certainly not pejoratively: collecting pebbles from holidays: winter evenings ("How lovely they are /Letting our thoughts travel far"). Christine Dyke tells a fairy tale, so if such "are beneath your dignity, you need not read it". *Street Scene* tells of ragman, old clothes, blankets, sweep, milkman, carthorse and games. One girl records the smell of the city after a summer storm mixed with the aroma of fried onions for tea, one of the most delightful things she knew. *Eric in Lilliput* was a game: "You promised I could kill you first". For Jill Belcher playing hopscotch, "her hot plimsolled feet squeaked spasmodically as she darted from square to square". Gillian Frith's pavement artist's drawings were washed away by the rain and his only shilling fell down a drain.

Ronila Heybourne, with three large hampers, three large bags, numerous packages, caravan, horse and frying pan, concludes: "Take our advice and stick to British Transport – nationalised or not". Elizabeth Norbury disliked being outside:

Horrid cold wind	And January rains
How gay and bright	Are the firelight flames.
Dear Scrumptious Puss,	Make room on the chair,
I'll return to my book	And the happiness there.

Most evocative are Gillian Shepherd's *Childhood Memories* – winter bathtime, clammy steam, soothing paraffin stove smell, flannel nightgown, icy lino, hot water bottle and battered Teddy.

A gentle approach to the comic was encouraged. Cautionary tales appear over twelve years. As for Joyce Wilkinson's *Sonia Brown*,

> Unluckily she bit the end
> From which the pen-nib did extend.
> This pen-nib as she bit with force
> Prevented further rhymed discourse,

whereas Audrey Jarvis' *Mable Daw* put her fingers too close to the fire,
> The flames licked her up and she has passed on.

In *The Ballad of Welwyn Town*, Jocelyn Taylor told of Helen Fair, she of the long peroxide hair, who had ridden pillion on Mike's motor byke which plunged into the river:

> Alas for him, he could not swim,
> And neither could the motor byke.
> The moral here, all parents dear,
> Let not your daughter Helen
> Drive with her Mike, on a motor byke
> Down a greasy road in Welwyn.

Inanimate objects, contemporary society, moving house, the door which refuses to be painted, father's inefficiency, new shoes ("I simply love those little squeaks/ I hope they'll last for weeks and weeks"), Maureen Riordean's sorrowful soap ("Rubbed on a scrubbing brush, prickly hard scrubbing brush/ Only to keep the linoleum clean"), Helen Ford's optimist ("I bought myself a small recorder/ They'd none in stock: I had to order") – all raise a smile.

Animals amuse too. An elephant never forgets because "he has nothing at all to remember". Adèle Griffiths' octopus laments:

> Good gracious me! What would you do
> With eight long legs instead of two?

Nature in all its forms remains the main stimulus. Valerie Cottle writes simply:

> The first star glitters in the sky,
>   The little birds have gone to sleep,
> The tawny owl goes hooting by.
>   The foxes from their lairs do creep.
> The moon is shining brightly down,
>   The tawny owl has caught its prey,
> The rabbit in its coat of brown
>   Comes from his hole and starts to play.

Alive and growing things attracted: chrysanthemums, "Great shaggy flowers in colours bold": Sylvia Ridgley's prize-winning verse on the spirit of a peony: Sandra Payne's owl whose "hooded lids but ill disguise/ The wisdom in those enormous eyes".

The wind for Brenda Brotherton is

> Whistling and bustling and blowing and blustering
> Sweeping and flattening the rippling green grass.

The weather, the times of day, the seasons were popular subjects. Phyllis Fisher's foggy London caused trouble to vicars, the paper boy, the doctor, two newly-arrived Jamaicans, but the policeman, stolid and dependable, brought sanity back into an otherwise estranged world.

The sea, perhaps unexpectedly, is invoked several times, whether it be its cruelty, its attraction or the sadness of the seagulls.

When "thin cobweb mists enshroud the trees", autumn again wins easily. Ann Oliver thinks about its leaves.

> Gold, brown, yellow, red,
> Lovely hues from tan to green,
> Trees their pretty foliage shed.
> Soon upon the ground, quite dead,
> Small dry piles of leaves are seen.
> Such a short life their's has been.

Many writers were serious. Helen Brockman's character is moved "by this age of invention and discovery, of three dimensional films, television and the conquering of space, of the atom bomb and the space ship" to wish for real freedom for her children. The passing of time and death haunt. Shakespeare inspired at least eight, to reconstruct his times or characters, to add a new scene, to pay tribute:

> He took the tangled, twisted skein of life
> And wove it into a living whole.
> Mankind grew great, made mighty by his might.

Sir Walter Scott rubs shoulders with King Arthur and Hector; Pan is "beautiful – half man, half beast, but a god".

Magic, witches, ghosts, fears: perhaps Beryl Ward should have the last word: there was but one girl alive – so the world ended.

Some of these different elements are seen in Dora Birch's sonnet, *Life and I*.

> Kind life and I have roamed for many years,
> Like lovers arm in arm along the path
> Of endless time. We've shared our joys and tears,
> Our hopes and fears. He taught me how to laugh,
> And sing and play; he shared my sorrow too.
> I learned that hopes like Icarus soar high,
> But soon they quickly crash down from the blue.
> That dreams are castles built up in the sky,
> But when they fade, new dreams like stars shall rise,
> A birth to compensate a loss so sad.
> We kept and shared our secrets, joys and sighs,
> And all the things that made the other glad.
> But sometime I shall draw in my last breath,
> And break my troth with him, and join with death.

No wonder that the Head felt that opening the magazine was always one of the excitements of the year.

CHAPTER THIRTY-SEVEN

Many generations can never be too grateful

"History is not dull. That idea is quite outdated and it is a good idea to move with the times".

"Second year work was much enlivened by re-enacting the battle of Hastings with rulers and chalk, which was far more fun than first year History. Lessons had been spent staring at the bulging dimples above the stocking tops of a teacher who was compelled by the classroom fixtures to sit precariously on a podium and compelled by the chronological syllabus to describe in minutest detail the stomach-churning technicalities of Egyptian mummification!" Girls in another Second Year found the lessons so dull that a strike was initiated: "budding militancy was shortlived after 40 minutes' silence watching our teacher leisurely reading *The Telegraph*".

"I was astonished when I was told that the order for *Tudors and Stuarts* had lapsed; I am sure you must be mistaken as you have repeatedly assured me that the order would not lapse and that the books would be forwarded to me as soon as they were printed. We have kept on ringing you up". This note to the bookseller brings Miss Rudkin immediately to mind. She retired in 1954 after 30 years at ECS. Once coaching swimming and hockey, she contributed much to school organisation and life and to the OGA. She remembered sitting on the floor of the Head's room searching for the appropriate envelope of examination papers; glancing up, she saw Mr Whitehead at the top of a high ladder glaring down with the utmost suspicion. Over addicted to puns, she was often witty and always kindhearted, once comforting those reduced to wrecks by an excited Miss Forrest.

O.D.R. enjoyed a surprisingly harmonious professional relationship with Miss Barker, who, after 35 years, retired in the same year. She introduced over 3,000 First formers to the subject. "New girls are encouraged by being told that they would be taught by one who initiated their mothers into the study of history". I wonder. A loyal supporter of St Margaret's, she had accompanied countless expeditions, and attended OGA meetings as long as she could, seeming to shrink year by year. At her funeral, OGs learnt what had been a closely guarded secret: G.M. stood for Gladys Mary.

Barkie turned back the pages with howlers collected from examination papers. Elizabeth had been broken off by the Pope, and disposed of. After the Armada, when Elizabeth visited Drake's ship, she knighted him and he is now called Sir Walter Raleigh. A son was born to James II which was called the last straw.

Both received armchairs as retirement presents. "We hope that they will have pleasant memories to take with them. We can be sure that if they visit a museum and see a ghastly mummified figure in a glass case, they will be reminded of the present members " of the Historical Society.

The pattern continued much the same, but the pace quickened with the new Head of Department, Mrs Nita Martin (1954-1972), who exemplified the new trend of returning to teach after having children. "History came alive by her infectious enthusiasm". She encouraged freedom of thought and discussion on contemporary issues while clamouring for more opportunities to dig for the past. Young graduates, however short their stay, were all involved; Miss Mary Steele-Perkins (1954-1956) who became secretary to the UK committee for UNICEF, Mrs Shirley Levenberg (1956-1957, playreadings), Miss Margaret Healey (1957-1959), Mrs Jean O'Reilly and Miss Valerie Chancellor (both 1959-1961) and, in charge of Savings, Miss Dorothy Pyett (1961-1968) and Mrs Judith McConnell (1961-1965).

In 1947, only one took HSC; by 1962, 10 took AL, with good results. All future undergraduates won many form prizes, most were Senior Prefects: Grace Goreham, Margaret Grove, debater Dawn Tyler (hockey*), "one of the most experienced and mature actresses, an education to the younger ones" to Exeter, writer Merle Philo, Ann Hatch, choir member, debater and actress, "completely giving herself to her rôle", to London, and Sandra Marshall to Swansea, later living in Australia.

Three won State scholarships: Jean Ebben (hockey*) went to Southampton on an Open Scholarship, later teaching in Nairobi, DHG Ruth Whiting, library helper, debater and actress, who always showed "urbane polish", with Greek Verse Speaking prizes, to Oxford. Singer and House Captain, organiser of the Scripture Union, magazine contributor in French, participator in the Inter-Schools Classical Club, Joyce Wilkinson achieved high distinction in all examinations with full marks in History, won the Clothworkers' Scholarshop to Somerville, became President of the Junior Common room and, MA, B.Ltt, was research assistant on a medieval project, Head of the Institute of Historical, and member of the Inter-Varsity Fellowship of Christian, Unions.

Some studied Economics or Economic History with EGS. Four read Social Sciences including swimmer Josephine Hedger at Edinburgh.

In 1947, representatives joined 3,000 young people at the prestigious 4-day Westminster Conference on World Citizenship to listen to papers on the United Nations, Science and World Affairs, Trade Unions, Education for What? ("enlightening and thought-provoking"), and especially to hear Sir Stafford Cripps (obliged to leave early for a Cabinet meeting) on Reconstruction at Home ("sound and heartening common sense"), J.B. Priestley on Russia, America and Ourselves ("typically himself, even to the familiar accent") and Harold Nicholson who reviewed the Paris Peace Conference giving vivid imitations of the various representatives. All received a barrage of questions.

Two attended the 6,000 strong World Forum of Youth at the Albert Hall, sponsored by the *Daily Mail*, whose editor, Frank Owen, opened it. With delegates from Europe and America, it proved a real example of world citizenship. Three eminent men helped to make the afternoon memorable. The Duke of Edinburgh, "with naval brevity and sincerity", admitted that Utopia was unobtainable, "but if we know the sort of world we want, we can all work for it". Mr Attlee preached freedom, tolerance and a sense of continuity. Aiming to guide the Commonwealth to self-government, Mr Eden urged delegates to travel and to correspond.

Sixth formers enjoyed later conferences on the USA and on Parliamentary institutions, several debates in the Commons and a Saturday seminar on Tudor England, and discussed the teaching of History in schools.

Miss Sharp again set the standard by talking on subjects as diverse as local government, Pope Innocent III and St Catherine of Siena ("enlightening"), while her Wander in Rome made them want to visit that city. A representative from the Royal College of Arms explained heraldry, the county archivist described his work. The Historical Association (1959, tea 1/-, refreshments for lecturer 1/-) sent members to speak on, for example, famous women, Machiavelli, the Dissolution of the Monasteries, life in Nelson's time, the Industrial Revolution and Patterns in History ("explaining the National Debt"). They listened to C.V. Wedgwood on the English Civil War, Denis Brogan on Lincoln and Hugh Ross Williamson on What is History?

When there was a General Election, school, true to tradition, held its own, with the Sixth form candidates (praised for their courage) and all concerned thoroughly enjoying themselves with meetings, posters and sandwich men. The Communist skated lightly over contemporary problems at home and disarmament, generously promising 400,000 houses a year and £15million for new hospitals. Labour "chewed over the old and musty bones of contention", and offered a utopian state of leisure with pleasure. The Liberal wanted a Western bomb to end the Cold War, Scotland and Wales to have their own parliaments and promised £150million for roads and safety measures. The Conservative "did not try to win our support with fire and enthusiasm and tricks of oratory", but used heckling to advantage. Gladstone would have been horrified at the exchange of views that took place during the 'secret' ballot. The Conservatives won a resounding victory.

All Years went out and about to local institutions and delighted in the usual popular places. Hatfield House revealed a nearby piece of historical beauty of which they had been unaware. Also less familiar were Hampton Court, Lancaster House, Charterhouse and Windsor; they saw Colonial and Soviet exhibitions and the Royal Tournament. Fifths were shown round County Hall and heard a case involving stolen goods, the accused being found guilty, to everyone's disappointment.

Visual aids – slides, models, films, filmstrips – on all manner of historical events were used increasingly: Hadrian's Wall, an 18th century Election, the life of an apprentice, Palestine 2,000 years ago, Criminal Justice, cathedrals, Monarchy, Battle of Worcester, Cecil Rhodes. A notably large audience found the *Beginnings of History* extremely interesting; *Servant of the People* was revealing the experiences of a recently elected MP – when the bulb blew.

Displays were mounted of anything which might be considered historical. Firsts held a costume evening, juniors enjoyed a picnic. Each sent in a question and answer for Quizzes, chaired by a Sixth former. Form representatives described an historical happening or place or impersonated an historical figure. They voted for the person who had most helped the progress of civilisation: winner, Lord Shaftesbury.

In 1956, a specialist magazine, edited by future mathematician Pat Dannahy, was widely distributed. Interest in, and a sense of, history were reflected in the orthodox magazine: an ugly incident in 1916 Russia, the problems of an Irish émigré in Canada. Margaret Putnam wrote of *The Subject of Good King George*, an anti-Jacobite who yet helped a Jacobite to escape. Actress and House Captain Kitty Robers (hockey*) wished November 5, Guy Fawkes, gunpowder, treason and plot, to continue for ever.

They enjoyed comparisons. Anthea Matanle wrote *The Diary of Elizabeth Cummings (1606)*, when a friend saw in the fire a picture of what she thought the world would look like in the 20th century. As it was uncomplimentary, "all of us were glad to be back home again, out of the dreadful din and bustle". Helen Brockman in *The Family Album* described, first, a typical Victorian family, Papa's frockcoat fitting to perfection,

Mama and her little brood, the aspidistra, the age of the steam engine and the pennyfarthing; next, 1906 with an unmistakable Edwardian air; 1925 on Blackpool promenade, flappers, short skirts, no waists, flat chests; 1942, the WVS, airraids, bombed houses; 1953, holidays in the South of France. The young man wished a world set free from petty tyranny, with free speech and freedom of action; he hoped he could be proud to have lived today.

Legend played its part. Shirley Eastman wrote of the knight who rode off to war singing of his lady left behind to fade away. Senior Prefect Patricia Sharp, when a Second former, composed a scene between Joan of Arc and the Dauphin, which derived as much from Shaw as from History lessons.

In short, a wonderful time was had by all.

She marched them up to the top of the hill and she marched them down again

This was Miss Margaret Ellis (1945-1950), but could have applied to any of the all-graduate Geography Staff. This future Head took students on many day- and week-long excursions, played the piano on numerous occasions, was one of the few able to tame the contemporary apparatus, ran games practices and umpired. Her successor, Miss Kathleen (Kate) Coster (1951-1963) conveyed her seemingly inexhaustible knowledge of the district on annual expeditions to the North; not all Sixth girls were accustomed to 15-mile tramps. Others joined in the trips, notably Miss Bowen, Miss Neilson ("such an efficient MO"), the Languages Assistants – and Rex, who was unfortunately inclined to chase sheep. The dog belonged to one of the characters of the Staff room, fun-loving Steve, part-timer Mrs Wooldridge, a sturdy tennis player, who also talked about America; she retired in 1963. Mrs Marie Luxon (1958-1977) worked part-time in this period,coming into her own as a senior Year Head in comprehensive days, when she showed infinite patience, great kindness and motherly interest.

Girls taking AL Geography came from both Arts and Science forms, rising from two to ten by 1962, some 60 in all, nine or so obtaining subsidiary or OL grades. Increasing numbers went up to universities. Two won magazine prizes. Cadet, Senior Prefect, member of the Playreading Group, Barbara Fossey, who read Greek for interest, set the example in 1948 with an Open Scholarship to Girton. Jacqueline Welch, a "thoughtful and sensitive actress" and House Captain, went, after Oxford, to the USA on a Fulbright scholarship and, with a Ph.D. and as departmental head at Guelph, was seconded to advise on rural development. London took five:

Audrey Bailey (folk dancer and rower) went on to laboratory work, Jill Buchanan (junior Middlesex hockey reserve), Helen Bush (Town and Country Planning assistant, then New Zealand research officer on grass), Alison Tattersall (House Captain) and Inga Dunwoody, Ministry of Housing and Local Government, then ECS laboratories.

Leicester, Liverpool, Reading and Sheffield took, among others, Margaret Bass (Bronze and Bar, Cadet), Janet Bull (House Captain, later teaching in Belgium), Pauline Everall (RSPCA, Nature Club), Marion Littlechild (French Institute scholarship winner), Pamela Maunder (High Jumper), Brenda Strangleman (chess player, linguistic secretary). Valerie Bright joined the Civil Service as a cartographical draughtswoman.

Coloured slides of many different countries were explained, exhibitions mounted and films shown of volcanoes, the horsemen of the Pampas and the working of the Meteorological Office. They attended a lecture on the new Oxford Atlas; the cost of Ordnance Survey maps, housed in a map chest (£5:15:6), rose from 2/- to 4/6, less discount. The sound projector improved after long-needed repairs, £5 bought a cap for the film projector, filmstrips were 15/6, blackout material, curtain roller and fittings £3:4:7. Everyone appreciated the modern specialist provision in the New Building.

Staff talked of their journeys: – Miss Roberts on her year at a Madrid tutorial college, Miss Woods on Corsica, Miss Julia Kelly (visiting for two terms) on Australia, Miss Bowen and Miss Forrest on Norway. Pat Butt and Meriel Dasley told them about Madrid ("instructional and interesting") and Vienna respectively. Different forms heard about life in the Antarctic, deep sea fishing, Barbados. At the Royal Geographical Society, the first High Commissioner described a Nigeria independent for just three weeks.

School participated in a local survey. In addition to all the usual trips, different forms visited Dunstable, the Imperial Institute for a Sixth form conference, and the Commonwealth Institute.

One of the most enjoyable days for Staff and girls alike was the Fourths' annual expedition to the Port of London. After catching the train, sometimes as early as 7:30am, to Liverpool Street, they walked or took the tube to Tower Pier; later groups travelled by coach. Sharing the *Crested Eagle* or the *Viscountess* with other schools, they listened to an informative commentary and marvelled at warehouses filled with goods for export, the harbour master's launch, the Royal Naval College, Greenwich Observatory and over thirty large cargo ships. Nearly four hours, but over too soon. Tired but greatly enlightened, they thanked the Staff for making the journey so interesting. Final accolade: "It was well worth the money".

For the Sixth, work on field trips came as a shock, and dormitories provided a new experience for many. "Eleven rather doubtful schoolgirls, pioneers in post-war partying, for the purpose of geological, geographical and physical fieldwork" spent Easter 1947 in baronial mansion turned Youth Hostel. They suffered their first disillusion in the train, when a diagram of the route and notes on the structure of the country were distributed. Miss Ellis further alarmed them with a geological hammer, compass and thermometer. Once, with 1" and 2½" maps, they had to find routes in very hot weather.

North Wales was chosen for three years. Sixteen spent all day in the train to Bangor before taking a bus to Capel Curig, where two weather-beaten cyclists joined them. Much work was connected with glacial features in the upland areas, without diminishing their appreciation of the beautiful countryside. They enjoyed botanical scavenging as much as souvenir-hunting; it was fascinating to climb in brilliant sunshine and eat lunch in the snow. In addition to a somewhat amateurish ascent of Mont Siabod (2,888'), they were impressed by the grandeur of the mountains, the slate quarries ("largest in the world"; the guide showed all the processes), the woollen mill (which reminded them of Dickens) and the Fairy Glen. One group spent a fortune on TCP, another suffered blisters.

Thereafter, Keswick, three hundred miles away, was popular. Some swam before breakfast, others disliked washing in cold water. They too climbed, enjoyed spectacular views, "resplendent and glowing" scenery, visited Kendal's snuff factory and Penrith's four markets, pencil and notebook in hand, finding the locals helpful; they walked barefoot across Great Langdale Beck and covered a considerable area of Cumberland although they took several days to get used to being surrounded by mountains. One year, it rained almost daily; London rainwear was not designed to withstand the Lake District's brand of precipitation. Once they had to do an 85-mile tour in a minibus as the weather was so poor; too bad that one suffered from travel sickness. One year's bog became the next's frozen tarn.

They studied types of farming, forestry, volcanic rocks, the work of ice in the past and of running water in the present. They loved the sheep and dairy farms with hospitable and obliging farmers and admired hand-shearing. One old farmhouse had just got electric light. "We are very grateful for such an exciting though strenuous week".

The regular base for smaller numbers was Juniper Hall in Surrey. They used maps for more detailed geographical survey, especially of chalk areas. When they examined river terraces, these maps became too soggy to handle. Fun and jokes compensated for blisters and bites. They walked over hills and downs ("the clouds descended"), followed a transect line, took a coach trip across the Weald and inspected heathland and an historic camp.

"We unanimously agreed that this was the way to learn Geography".

CHAPTER THIRTY-EIGHT

The standard was extremely high and the competition very severe

"A passion for imparting the proper discipline and manners expected in an ordered society"; Miss Louise Irina Mélanie (Lisette) Marion (1944-1961), thus commended, had not found it easy to work in the same department as, to arrange a farewell for, and take over from, Miss Forrest. Highly qualified and experienced, she rushed around on her bicycle, "threatening to kill us if we didn't get out of her way". Many generations enjoyed her introduction to the French language and their initiation into the subtleties and profundities of French literature. OGs recall her vivacity, enthusiasm, tremendous capacity for hard work – and her excellent cooking – and gave her a travelling clock on her retirement. "If anyone ever gave more to the profession of teaching, I have yet to find her". She was discretion personified in her deep friendship with the Head.

Arriving as Miss Cherry, I became Mrs Hart after one term and succeeded Miss Marion ("The Boss") as Head of Department, having been hitherto mostly concerned with teaching and examinations. Miss Dora Bishop (1946-1948) returned as Mrs Scott (1967-1983). Miss Iris Sparkes (1951-1965) organised *Les Francophiles* with EGS' Mr Smith, and, although terrifying the shy and the wrong-doer, gave many the urge towards linguistic accomplishment. Junior graduate Staff included Miss Irene Anderson (1948-1951, then teaching in Kenya), Miss Heather Phillips (1959-1963, Mrs Crowter, daughter of an OG), Miss Judith Walker (1961-1962), returning as Mrs Kelsey (1964) and two who stayed but a year, Miss Fiona Eadie and Miss Jean Harrison who arranged a German Day. Assistants again took Fifth and Sixth conversation lessons.

Languages continued to dominate HSC entries; in 1947, all eight girls studying Arts subjects entered for French, three gaining Goods; altogether 17 passed, with but one failure. AL had 83 passes, reaching 15 in 1961. Over 15 years, Sixth formers won nine medals, twenty special prizes (reading, literature, poetry, translation at sight), five Oral prizes and forty certificates in Le Grand Concours and two medals, twelve prizes and seven certificates over five years in the slightly different Concours Spécial.

In 1952's Verse Speaking, with 894 entrants from 113 schools (each allowed a maximum of 12), 8 reached the finals to win, appropriately, the Francis Memorial trophy, with 527½ points to the next school's 410. A representative of the French Ambassador brought a reproduction of an Utrillo picture.

ECS also won the Twentyman Trophy; 865 competed. Charmian Walker came 1st in the U-16, and Eve Barsham in the 16+, groups. Two others gained third prizes. Ten years later, they were happy to win again despite fewer candidates. They lost the following year, although winning 1st and 2nd prizes. In 1956, Senior Prefect Hazel Alton came top nationwide. With a State Scholarship, she read French and Italian at Cambridge, spent three months in Sicily looking after children and won a £70 prize for a month in Florence. Janet Gamblin took 2nd prize, played both piano and violin, and went on, with State and Gamble Scholarships, to Reading. Not surprisingly, ECS received the Silver Cup presented by the French government for the eight best gaining the highest aggregate of marks. When maximum points were 700, school achieved 670 to earn *le Prix Spécial offert par la Maison Boucheron*. Margaret Lievesley, 6th with 615, secured the Air France prize; after Reading, she taught. Mary Stearns, 12th with 601, won that donated by *le Conseil Supérieur des Français à l'Etranger* before studying at the French Institute and becoming secretary to a lawyer.

Junior and senior F.M.F. prizes were first awarded for specific achievements. Medallist Andrée Sommerard won hers for Oral results. Actress and Senior Prefect,she played the piano in a family quartet. From QMC, she made a special study of teaching the mentally retarded. Elizabeth O'Toole (examination distinctions, Grand Concours awards, scholarships to two universities) took French, Italian, German and Latin in HSC. Junior winners, mostly with other prizes, included French medallist, German Verse Speaking prizewinner and State Scholar Julia Broadbent, singer, actress and DHG Frances Freedman, Mavis Fernee (TC), Senior Prefect and choir member Pat Thomas (Exeter) and Maureen Wicks (scholarship to the French Institute).

Later successful language students, mostly with F.M.F. prizes, included, alphabetically, Diane Ascroft (leader of Christian Union, later training as a pilot), her sister Eileen (Spanish specialist, who taught English in Madrid), Susan Page (actress, House Captain, later returning to teach), Mary Wilkinson (one of the three best scholarships to the French Institute) and Jennifer Williams (Senior Prefect, "robust" actress).

For pleasure, girls and Staff produced a Modern Languages entertainment in 1952. The Sixth and Francophiles enjoyed play readings: *Knock*, entertaining despite the deafening noise from the builders in the

Hall and *Le Petit Café Bernhard*, an animated performance. Other evenings included interesting *Souvenirs de Vacances*, a film on wartime resistance, a Brains Trust; "we helped to wash up after tea in EGS". An International Linguists' Conference took place in school. Girls attended an MLA meeting, heard lectures at the French Institute, and, several times, saw classical plays such as *Le Cid*, once produced by Michel St Denis, *Le Misanthrope* in modern dress and *Andromaque*, "la première tragédie que nous ayons vue. Oreste était un peu vieux", as well as works by later and modern writers. Sheila Wood reviewed two productions – in French. They were lucky to see all too rare performances by la Comédie Française.

What brought most personal satisfaction and a new awareness of different cultures and behaviour, as well as linguistic benefits, were visits to France. "Après avoir traversé la Manche, je posai pied sur la terre française et je me dis: 'Maintenant, je suis à l'étranger'". Even the smells were different. Vimy Ridge and the black mining districts overshadowed by slag heaps shocked Shirley Eastman. "France seemed a curious mixture of slowness approaching inertia and noise approaching hysteria, an intoxication as potent as its clear amber wine. Adieu, charmant pays de France".

Twenty-three girls benefited from summer schools at Grenoble, surprised to find themselves in a dormitory, larger than EGS Hall, of over 100 beds. The six nationalities represented spoke French and English on alternate days. *Antigone* and *St Joan* were read aloud. Visits, folklore, dancing, singing, *jeux dramatiques* and *concours* added to the fun.

Another group stayed in the Paris Foyer des Lycéennes, which led to lasting friendships. Apart from excursions, reporters mentioned the *concierge*, knobs for opening doors, the funny lift, modern furniture, a thousand little gadgets and knicknacks of whose uses they were ignorant, showers, superb food, two hours for meals, fish with rich cream in a rosette on top, mushroom sauces, celery with vinegar, pounds of tomatoes stuffed or served with oil.

Others were guests of families for an enjoyable intensive holiday course at Toulon, AL tuition alternating with expeditions. Sheila Curtis (French Institute *Prix d'Excellence*) spent a working holiday looking after French children in *une colonie de vacances.* Charmian Walker and her mother went camping in Corsica. Invited to share a family *kermesse*, they discovered that the baby was also called Charmian; the Corsicans believed the coincidence was a good omen.

Girls were encouraged to exchange visits with their penfriends and to relate their stories for the magazine. Maureen King found the Lyonnais hospitable: "Standing along the embankment of the Rhône are dark-tanned men and women with large baskets of melons and peaches. We could buy a kilo of peaches, which is, approximately, 2lb. for 25 francs, which in English money is 1/-". Fourth former Pat Lievesley extolled family meals (*soupe avec miettes de pain*, fish on Fridays, different cheeses, *tartines* for tea). In Paris, however, "la circulation dans les rues est terrible. Tout le monde klaxonne et tous les gendarmes sifflent sur leurs sifflets". *Plus ça change ...* Gillian Cardy noted that mother worked very hard, but approved of the Eiffel Tower, the champagne served at a teaparty and half a pound of butter slapped on a joint of meat.

The French Institute's highly competitive courses gave the training required for high-flying and managerial careers, indeed for a weird and wonderful variety of private secretarial posts: to the chief engineer of Leibig's Extract of Meat Co. Ltd., to a Danish Import Company in Canada, to a senior director of Nestlé. Twenty-four, many winners of prizes and White Girdles, were successful entrants: Jane Batt (netball*, tennis*) came 8th, Jennifer Rees 25th, both gaining scholarships. Linda Cook worked on a Fleet Street magazine: Margaret Stephenson became a translator with the Institute of Linguists: Janet Wragg (tennis*, hockey*), Senior Prefect and House Captain, obtained *le Prix d'Excellence* and taught French shorthand at the Institute itself: Barbara Turpin (hockey*, gym*), an 'original' Head of House, an energetic Cadet ("she would make a good cubmaster") took a Polytechnic diploma in Commerce and Languages.

Kindness and hospitality wherever we went

Miss Kathleen Russell (1945-1975, part-time to 1978) was in charge of two departments: stationery, which she ruled with such a rod of iron that even M.C.S. had difficulty in prising out a pencil, and German. She encouraged those with primarily linguistic interests; her French classes acquired impeccable pronunciation. Her work was recognised by Uruguay's Minister of Education who visited school, and, later, by eight foreign students. When she spent a year in Germany, ECS received Dr Liselotte Fauler in exchange. The first ever Assistant, Fraulein Muller Karper, ran a Christmas evening.

Over forty took German in the Sixth during this time. The two most successful were Senior Prefects and multiple language-prizewinners. Meriel Dasley, with the Gamble Scholarship to Bedford, taught at a school for the Blind, gained a University Tutorial fellowship at King's to study High German dialects, and became, amongst other things, lecturer and Dean at Goldsmith's and editorial adviser to her publishers. Mary Cock was accepted by Cambridge but took up her Exhibition at Oxford, achieving a double First in Prelims:, a First in Schools and her D.Phil. As an

Official Fellow at Newnham, she was a Foundation Fellow of the new Robinson College.

Girls sang carols at a school German afternoon and twice at the City Literary Institute's party. Their own Christmas festivities involved plays, poems and songs. Lectures and films were frequent, a number at the Rudolph Steiner Hall: on Goethe's poems, the contemporary scene, Germans in England (by an evangelical pastor), the life of Schiller ("the sound and action were not synchronised"). Sixths joined in a German Day at Woodford, saw *Wilhelm Tell* at Sadlers Wells and *Faust*, once performed by the Vienna University dramatic society.

Students competed in the Inter-Schools Verse Speaking, winning the Twentyman Trophy in 1953 with the highest aggregate of marks of the 84 schools entering 336 candidates, the prize being a modern still life. The cup was retained for two more years, Anne Hatch winning a First Prize.

A German girl, Antje Otzen, spent a pre-university year with VL. "My teachers' and classmates' understanding, friendliness and good will made this time a wonderful experience for me, being so far away from home". She returned to accompany 'her' form and Staff to the Lake District. Two girls spent three memorable weeks with a family; this included Easter with the local Girl Guides going down the Rhine and visiting the Grammar School. OGs worked in the Control Commission and on relief work in Germany; one was personal assistant to the Director of UNRRA.

La vida española es muy animada

Supported by Assistants, the Spanish department was run by Miss Christine Roberts (1943-1957). She read with relish such rôles as Polonius, Androcles and Sir Peter Teazle in the Playreading group, played comic parts in the Staff entertainment, talked to the History societies, took a party to Spain where she spent a year herself and wrote a textbook. She gave prestige and popularity to the subject.

Her successor, Miss Heather Spence (1957-1972, Mrs Leigh) carried on her good work, running a fortnightly club with experimental classes in Spanish dancing, handicapped only by the fact that castenets and Spanish music were scarce.

Over a period of nine years, 14 took the subject at HSC/AL. Girls entered three Hispanic Council examinations. Notable candidates were Patricia Butt and Una Leonard. With a scholarship, Pat travelled in 1948 by air to Madrid, where "la gente se mostraba muy simpatica conmigo, sobretodo, lo que es extrañar, la gente de baja clase". Sandra Simmonds had the same happy experience during her month's stay. White Girdle holder Pat gained Inter-Collegiate, State and Skinners' Company scholarships in Spanish and German to King's and the Jubilee Scholarship of £100 to Oxford. Una, French medallist, sang, wrote prizewinning prose and verse, took Matric. early, won countless linguistic prizes in and out of school – eg. for the highest marks of any girl from the Association of Teachers of Spanish and in the Inter-Schools recitation competition – State Scholarship and Exhibitions in French and Spanish at both Oxford and Cambridge. After working in the Ministry of Labour, she took a Divinity degree and became the sole woman lecturer in Biblical Theology, Church History and New Testament Greek at a Protestant Evangelical College in Catholic Barcelona. Her *Echange avec une jeune fille française* gives a clear picture of family life and behaviour in Tours; she urges others to follow her example.

Linguistic holidays were organised. 1951's preconception that Spain was a land of serenades and bullfights was hard hit by the noise, weather, markets, narrow streets and hedgeless unevenly shaped fields. An educational visit to San Sebastián was offered in 1953 for £22:5:0. A party made the 50-hour journey to Madrid. Marian Littlechild told how they soon became firm friends with Spanish students. They were struck by carvings on business buildings, gay café tables, shoe-shine boys, children and old people begging, the old grey donkey, strolling, talking, Segovia and face to face with Prince Juan Carlos. Easter week was exciting, a bullfight providing "the most uncomfortable, tense and nerve-racking hour and a half in our lives but one which we would not have missed on any account".

1948's Spanish afternoon presented songs light and gay, and well-acted scenes from *Don Quijote.* A larger audience including other schools later enjoyed songs and three short plays, "conspicuous rather for teamwork than for outstanding individual performances, as each part was equally important. Obviously everyone had gone to some trouble to get everything ready. Attractive programmes were distributed by girls in Spanish dress. The Hall was decorated with Spanish posters".

At the Spanish Institute, they saw various plays. In one year's Inter-School recitation competition, 30 schools sent 108 candidates; ECS had eight finalists. In other years, Eileen Carter won 1st prize, then the U-16 prize presented by Spanish teachers; highly commended Carolyn Allen reached the semi-final, later reading Spanish at QMC.

Altogether, 32 linguists studied at London, Exeter, Nottingham, Reading and Southampton universities: actress Gillian Bax: Carol Burrows French Institute scholarship winner: Marion Dale, pianist, classical verse speaker: Senior Prefect Carol Godfrey: Sheila Hynd, Exhibitioner, State

Scholar, teacher, organiser of School Travel Service, future Governor: Margaret Maxwell, singer, Cadet, returning as Mrs Hillson to teach: Scholar Sonia Morgan: Christine Murdie, Christian Union: Tessa Ormandy, House Captain, swimming champion, Exhibitioner: Barbara Williams, medallist.

Such a hilarious, exciting and unforgettable holiday

Jacqueline Welch described the Alps, chalets, flowers and churches of Switzerland; pillion-passenger Julie Neale travelled 2,000 miles through France, Switzerland ("problems of roadmending"), Italy (banks shut, lived on £3 a day for three days), Austria and Germany; Katherine Noall in Palma felt that "time is of no consequence to this hot-blooded Latin race. Spanish vocabulary is inexhaustible". The driver was protected by saints, waving his hands skywards and singing local songs. Gillian Shepherd stayed two months in Florence with a family discovered by an advertisement.

"We must have looked rather glam. as someone asked if we were a party from a finishing school.... Our arrival at Ostend was greeted with great jubilation on the part of the natives.... The Swiss officials, on seeing that we were schoolgirls, assumed that we had nothing to declare and ignored us.... At Dover, we were greeted by the customary enthusiastic efficiency of British Railways" – comments taken at random from accounts of the many post-war holidays.

Holland in 1951 provided nylons in abundance, meat and butter in plenty and most delicious real whipped cream cakes. Prices were considered high: 2lb loaf 1/-, margarine 1/10 lb., meat 3/6 to 6/-, and butter, a luxury, 4/8 lb. Only coffee was still rationed.

Mrs Leigh will be remembered by so many, over 200 in this period alone, for Easter, summer and Christmas holidays for which she was responsible, frequently with her husband. A postcard, signed by all participants, was always sent to the Head. Parents were invited to see slides.

Switzerland – "the funicular was a rather frightening experience but one which we took quite calmly", snow on Christmas Eve, glaciers, shopping, delicious packed lunches and 5-course dinners, voluntary, vigorous and exciting walks, excursions – "we made use of every moment of time – early to bed, early to rise" and, of course, skiing. Daily they improved their initial rather wobbly proficiency. One year, all achieved one-star badges after lessons with an infinitely patient instructor.

Toledo, Avila – gold and silver ware, poverty: Madrid – excursions, pelota: Costa Brava – swimming, sunbathing, dancing, the frightening experience of Spanish roads.

465

The work of the Leighs, sometimes accompanied by Assistants or by Mrs Wheal, in acting as responsible parents was much appreciated. They were thanked for their constant good humour in the face of all sorts of minor emergencies, as when " French railway officials went on strike and Mr Leigh found the linen cupboard and we made up our own couchettes".

Such was the Modern Languages Department. I was proud to belong to it.

The enjoyment of Latin

This was the title of Rev. C.J. Ellingham's entertaining discourse. Girls were fascinated to hear that many boys enjoyed learning the declensions of irregular and peculiar Latin names and collected irregular verbs in the same spirit as they collected conkers. On another occasion, he guided them to a deeper understanding of Virgil's significance.

Appreciation of Aristophanes' *The Frogs* was helped by Dr Sheppard's lecture which "infected the audience with his own enthusiasm". Other speakers covered the worship of the Lares and Penates, Greek tragedy, Ancient Science, the metres of Horace ("a scholarly talk"), Plato, a day in the life of a Roman wit. Mr Moore gave an inspiring address on Greek philosophy and the Socratic revolution, and the Rev. Elmsley's talk, well illustrated by Greek, Latin and English verse, appealed especially to those who enjoy poetry. At the British Museum, Sixths heard about the Elgin Marbles, recently moved to more spacious quarters. Pupils from nine schools came to see slides on Roman London. Three Greek students heard Professor Chadwick on Linnear B. Others felt honoured to attend a talk on Greek Life by Gilbert Murray, "one of the greatest classical scholars of our time"; two attended his Memorial Service in Westminster Abbey.

Greek remained a minority subject, seven gaining AL (one*) and three subsidiaries or OLs, but Greek literature and culture were still considered part of an educated person's experience, so fifty seniors visited the Greek Exhibition in Chelsea.

The main emphasis was on drama. Girls enjoyed topical allusions to such as Churchill and Tessie O'Shea in a version of *The Birds*. Seniors saw *Electra* ("very moving despite linguistic difficulties"), university productions of *Medea* and *Prometheus*, the gay and colourful *Helen in Egypt* at St Albans, and *The Clouds* ("somewhat vulgar satire") at the outdoor amphitheatre at Bradfield College. They were deeply affected by the presentation of both Œdipus tragedies by the Attic players. Some sixty girls had the unforgettable experience of *Agamemnon* acted by an all-male cast. The revised pronunciation of the original Greek made it easier. The excellent chorus included two who were strangers to Greek, which was incredible because they chanted, moved and sang completely in unison. Even girls similarly bereft were greatly impressed.

A coach took seniors along snow-covered roads to Cambridge for an undergraduate performance, again with marvellous singing and dancing, of *The Bacchae*, which everyone managed to follow. This came before the breathtaking sight of Evensong at King's College Chapel.

Interest was further stimulated by reading and verse speaking competitions, organised by the Inter-Schools Classical Association with entry limited to two seniors and two juniors for Latin and two for Greek. At ECS' first attempt in 1951, five reached the finals, gaining one Greek prize. This set the pattern. The following year, school won one of the only two prizes given to girls, while in 1955, of the eleven female finalists, five were from ECS. In 1962, the Greek Chorus achieved third place, the result of "Miss Elder's coaching, especially her painstaking and undoubtedly heartbreaking efforts in infusing suitable feelings into our insensitive souls". Over the years, 44 reached the finals, winning several times. As boys dominated the entries, there was especial jubilation when Nanette Webb, at third, was the highest placed girl.

Tribute was rightly paid to Miss F. Sharp, who retired in 1959, at a farewell dinner of grapefruit and melon cocktail, mixed salad with grapefruit, nuts and raisins, angel fool, white wine, cheese, biscuits and coffee.

"First and foremost, we think of the love of the Classics with which she has inspired so many girls; not only those who went to the university to read the subject, or those who tasted the all too rare joy of studying Greek, or who competed so successfully in competitions, but also those who, more humbly, learnt Latin with her for four years and forgot that it was a difficult subject in the genuine pleasure of speaking and reading the language and of understanding something of the greatness of the Roman people. Cicero, to whose wisdom she introduced many girls, used a now famous phrase which epitomises what she gave to the school – Summum Bonum, the highest good". Thirds later attended one of her demonstration lessons at the Institute of Education.

Deputy Head in the difficult post-war period of building problems, her zest and involvement in every aspect of school life were legendary; "her walk reflects her purposeful, energetic nature". Praised for her splendid maintenance of traditions and standards and firm but kindly discipline, she could seem hard, at least outwardly. Yet to many, she was, although strict, "lovable in a genial, friendly way". To one student, she exuded authority to such a degree that it was only many years later that it dawned on her how diminutive she was.

She was awarded the Medal of Merit in 1961 for outstanding service to the Guide movement. The companies did not long survive her retirement as Captain the following year. She found it difficult to come to terms with a different generation with a different approach to life and leisure, and was inclined to be dismissive of younger people who did not want to wear uniforms or to do their good work in groups. She refused to use Christian names and indeed titles, only surnames for Staff; a teacher should resign on marriage and illness should be conquered. "Perhaps she should have been a man, gone in the Army and become a Colonel!"

Few can have suspected the tragedies in her life. Her mother dropped dead when F.S. was in her teens, her only brother died of cancer, she and her sister arrived on holiday in Switzerland to be summoned back to a dying father.She was on holiday when her housekeeper died. Her sister, with whom she shared a house, also died.

Of her devotion to ECS, there can be no doubt; so great was it that she felt Staff ought to have resigned rather than allow it to become a Comprehensive school. She attended Prize Givings, committee and general meetings of the OGA, as Vice-President and subsequently Life President until the year before she died; there were never enough activities for her.

After her departure, the department of graduates was led by Mrs Lilian (May) Parker (1947-1965), once second in the Mistresses' race, who had a great sense of fun in the Staff room, but rarely let it appear in lessons. She coached girls for competitions, took outings and encouraged participation in the Classical Association. Miss Jane Elder won a European competition with her translation of Seneca's *Thyestes*, which was accepted by BBC radio. In 1982, she mounted an exhibition of stained glass and enamels at Forty Hall. Mrs Margaret Denbeigh (1951-1967) did personnel and welfare work after teaching both Classics and English. Two others helped for one year and one for two terms.

That not taking Latin caused social and intellectual division is still felt by some OGs, as only 25-30 annually began the study in the 'top' Second form. Some 80 took HSC/AL, gaining 9 distinctions, and, in the early years, 15 Goods and 7 Subsidiary Levels.

Ten, all Prefects or Senior Prefects, form and various subject prizewinners, five being State Scholars, went to university, five to Reading, four to London and one to Cambridge: Margaret Morley, Rosemary Taylor: House Captains Denise Warwick, Suzanne Carter ("outstanding, mature, intelligent, sensitive" as Richard of Bordeaux, White Girdle and Open Scholarship), Gillian Cardy (hockey*, actress, record number of House points, later a teacher of backward children), Margaret Farrant

(DHG, gym*, hockey*): Ruth Davies who gained a First before teaching: music-lover Juliet Boyd (Girton): Beryl Parsons (debater, showed "polished acting technique" as Mrs Malaprop, Exhibitioner, later MA, PhD and part-time lecturer at the University of California): Patricia Wheeler (gym*, hockey*, White Girdle, Christian Union organiser) who won the Millicent Fawcett Scholarship to Bedford and gained professional qualifications to become assistant librarian at Birkbeck.

A noteworthy record.

CHAPTER THIRTY-NINE

We think it's by far the best way of doing work

It was once assumed that Nature Study/Botany/Biology was the favourite science of girls. The subject certainly flourished at ECS, usually in tandem with Zoology. An OG prize was instituted in 1953. In 1947, a Surrey trout farm was paid 3/7½, the Regent Street Pet Shop £2:5:6, whilst fish cost 1/2. Three years later, preserved frogs (9 male, 9 female) cost £1:4:0 (postage 2/6), and freshly killed rabbits 9/6 each, plus a packet of seeds 4d. £1:11:0 secured the sharpening and setting of 13 razors and a new handle and 25/8 Utility overalls for the second lab. assistant in 1951.

Although less spectacular, less obvious to the outsider, Physics and particularly Chemistry increasingly attracted students, 16 already in 1956. Five years later, 28 girls were in VIA Science to 24 in VIA Arts. They felt themselves a cohesive group, held dances and presented *South Sea Fantasia* with the University Quartet: Admission 2/6: "Leave Your Spears in the Umbrella Rack".

Many expressed deep gratitude to the forward-looking graduate Staff whose numbers increased as syllabuses caught up with the modern world, although not until 1955 was there the full complement of laboratories. A pillar of strength to girls and Staff alike, Miss Tomlinson contributed immeasurably to school's interest and success in Chemistry by her "quiet but unquenchable devotion to her subject".

Despite suffering from a spinal operation which affected four terms, Miss Elizabeth Browning (1946-1952) led expeditions, activated a Nature Club, won the Mistresses' race twice and made Biology a popular and firmly based subject and bore cheerfully the difficulties of the cramped conditions. Miss Jessie Maude (1946-1955), thanked for her particularly successful work, was the first Mistress in charge of careers; the second, Miss Ena Kirkby-Johnson (1948-1967), was best known to the Staff as AAM secretary and first president of the North London branch. Mrs Jean Thompson (1948-1969) took many Biologists on field work. Mrs Margery Borshell (1959-1969) was a lively Zoologist. Five stayed for four years each: Miss Vera Heller (1947-1951): Miss Betty Walker (Mrs Breward, (1951-1955) who sent her first impressions of Cairo – "cockroaches 2" long scuttling across the kitchen floor and ants appearing miraculously from nowhere": Miss Elizabeth Johnson (1955-1959), involved in Cadet camps and National Savings: Mrs Susan Purvis, who looked after School Fund and Mrs Elaine Ashmore (both 1961-1965).

Three exemplified the new trend of coming later to teaching: Miss Sylvia Huggins (1960-1961), with industrial and Civil Service experience, Miss Meryl Fowkes (1960-1962), an assistant industrial chemist and Mrs Suzanne Hall (1961-1964) after six years' research. Three stayed for two years each: Miss Ann Dickinson (1958-1960), Miss Margaret Campbell (1959-1961) and Mrs Mary Appleby (1961-1963). ECS was fortunate to find three to do substitute work when needed.

A weekly Naturalist, subsequently Nature, Club encouraged interest with Treasure and Scavenger Hunts, a dog show judged by an OG vet., bird-watching, identification of fungi and talks on budgerigars and hamsters (by girl owners) and on mice. IVDS mounted a display of floral decorations, IIL included pressed flowers in their arrangements. Middlesex staged an Exhibition at which invited AL Biologists gave an impressive demonstration of the processes used in the experimental investigation of the functions of living plants.

By 1955, through the Club, 140 juniors were members of the RSPCA, with 103 new recruits the following September; many became Animal Defenders; all contributed generously to Animal Flag Day. One pets' competition included guinea-pigs, kittens, fish, tortoises and a terrapin, most well looked after; three OGs presented seven prizes of 5/- book tokens. Two tortoises, kept on waste ground outside VIA study caused amused interest; mice were cared for in the new Biology prep. room. Members told how to examine life in a fish pool, films were regularly shown and an OG recounted her trip to Skokkolm Island.

Regular visits were paid to the grounds of Forty Hall, Botany Bay, Rothamsted Experimental Station, Epping Forest (with fishing rods, collecting jars and foods to a somewhat smelly pond near the roadside), Chase Farm Path. Lab. and the Co-op Dairy. In popular Whitewebbs Park, they collected and identified toadstools one damp foggy November Saturday. They surveyed clay soil vegetation, or brought back insects, centipedes and spiders for classification. They once cycled there, having "smothered our exposed parts, which were in some cases quite extensive, with insect repellant and sun-tan oil".

Specialists enjoyed Kenwood, Whitbread's Brewery, Zoo, Science Museum and the Elizabethan garden at the Ideal Home Exhibition. They checked soil at Ivinghoe Beacon in windy rain and studied animal camouflage and movement at Whipsnade. Over 100 visited Kew Gardens;

when the lesser celandine was found in Potters Bar, plants were sent, at Kew's request, for research. Pond-dipping was carried out in the New River, Trent Park and at Enfield Court, netting dragonfly, nymphae, water boatmen, pond skaters and a phantom mite. They kept two locusts for a fortnight.

A Problem Day sent girls in pairs to find 26 species of plants and insects for exhibition in the lab. by 4pm. In 1953, VI Biologists discovered a rare weed, native of Central Asia, growing in the school garden. When they heard a cuckoo in February, they wrote to *The Evening News* and *The Times.*

Longer lasting expeditions were regularly made to Juniper Hall ("no juniper trees in sight"), an old building linked with French émigrés, smugglers and Fanny Burney; they enjoyed the fun of getting there, excellent meals (despite "cookhouse fatigue)", a dormitory and well-equipped lab., although one unfortunate dislocated her shoulder. Barefoot, they watched the sun rise at 4:30am. By long walks up and down chalk quarries, they learned to keep their centre of gravity low. One party, soaked to the skin, lost its way but found the flower of the rare cut-leaved germander. Another group, working in slimy brown bog to their thighs, counted badger holes. They found a mole. They tramped ("blisters and bites") and wrote piles of notes in the evenings. They sought beetles and bugs, glowworms, lice and spiders; they pressed specimens, spent an interesting evening making leaf prints using a mixture of soot from a candle flame and machine oil; they counted 956 musk orchids; they learnt the techniques of insect grubbing and the use of beating trays, kite and butterfly nets, killing bottles and other apparatus; they made line transects and quadrants to identify all plants in a particular area, finding nearly 100 different species; in pouring rain, they discovered a wild orchid which they left undisturbed. Church, swimming and slides (a pet badger, a fox cub) further enlivened the proceedings.

Physicists visited the National Physical Laboratory, heard a Royal lecture and a talk at Thorns Electrical Industries and inspected the gasworks, Ediswan, the Power Station and the Telephone Exchange. Sixths found the 1957 Atom Exhibition memorable; nearly 300 seniors gave thunderous applause as they watched silhouettes of the London skyline, night falling, the heavenly signs, a year's journey round the sun, all at the Planetarium.

Botany/Biology at HSC/AL had over 80 candidates, Zoology about 100 and Chemistry 100, of whom only two failed. Fewer, some 45, took Physics.

Ever-increasing numbers studied further. Contrary to popular belief, most scientists, as well as winning form and Florence prizes, were active in school life and sports, as Prefects, Patrol Leaders and House Captains. In all, at least 65 went on to 15 different universities, with 13 to London colleges and 9 to Oxford. Mavis Glibbery was the sole 1st Class MSc in Corrosion Science and Engineering from the City of London Polytechnic. One pioneer took Mechanical Engineering at Enfield Technical College, another a 5-year apprenticeship at Enfield Cable Works.

Ruby Hynes and Ann King read Natural Sciences, Heather Liddiard (Sea Ranger, scenery painter, hockey*, tennis*) Physiology before achieving a diploma in Guidance, Counselling and Teaching. Five pursued General Sciences including Anne Rogers (later a secretary), Vera Nixon (swimming Award of Merit) and "fearless horserider" Gwen Wager. Two physicists were Jennifer Evison (DHG, swimming* champion, reserve senior Middlesex hockey) and Wendy Gordon, who, after Oxford, gained her London doctorate.

Among the 14 Chemists were Eileen Eggington (netball*, swimming* champion, Award of Merit), Wendy Nial (hockey*), Pat Quick (tennis*, netball*, who worked in the Sultanate of Oman), Brenda Kennedy (State Scholar), with four to Oxford: Margaret Hey (gym*, future restorer of Old Masters in the National Gallery), June Linnell (gym*, rounders captain, later manager of a Citizens' Advice Bureau), Jill Rand (DHG, netball* captain) and Gloria Spurge who had sat OL early because of the absurd age rules and who became an HMI.

Nine concentrating on Zoology included sisters Anne and Elizabeth Robbins, senior Sports champion June Binnington, Charmian Walker (an outstanding Queen of Scots), Susan Froggett("works the school projector") and Anne Bennett (State Scholar, praised for her highly amusing rôles), the first woman to get a First at Leicester and who also went on to do research.

Microbiology claimed three: Helen McAleer, Patrol Leader Shuna Wallace and Wendy Riddle (swimming* captain, Instructor's certificate, Life Saver with nine medals, rounders*).

Jean Maudesley (hockey*, tennis*), Janet Freeman (Drapers' Company Scholarship), sisters Janet (Senior Prefect, gym*, netball*, rounders* captain, Pfeiffer Scholarship and a First in Botany and Zoology, teaching in New Zealand) and Alison Cormack (DHG, State Scholar, Exhibitioner), Cynthia Ridgeway (Exhibitioner, gym*,1st Class swimming instructor) and Pat Lievesley (95% in practical AL Chemistry, another State Scholar and Exhibitioner) were among the ten taking Botany/Biology.

Ten medical students were Helen Henderson (Edinburgh), Sheila Cameron (King's), Angela Fowler who ran the Christian Union (Sheffield), Heather Collins and Margaret Simmons (State Scholar, netball*, gym*, college prizes) at the Royal Free. Marjorie Williams, member of the County Association of Change-Ringers, was the only woman to get a First BA at

Trinity College, Dublin, before qualifying. Oxford claimed notable successes: Gillian Spenceley, Adrienne Barnett who became a Philosophy Tutor, and, perhaps the most distinguished of these highly intelligent scientists, swimming champion Julie Neale. Taking her OLs in Switzerland to beat the age bar, she acquired a bronze for skiing; State Scholar, she was one of two women to win a Studentship at Göttingen; she became the first woman on the staff of the Oxford Professor of Surgery and the youngest member of the Royal College of Physicians. She returned to judge a pet show, a change from participating in allergy conferences in Spain and Turkey; she became a Registrar in Dermatology and senior MO first with the Medical Research Council and then in Australia.

ECS was proud too of its dentists: Royal Dental School, Jean Bromley and Pat Knight (DHG, hockey* captain): Guy's, Susan Thickett: UC, Judy Wicks and Barbara Williams, last heard of studying Maori in New Zealand. Two others became dental auxiliaries and two dental receptionists.

Two trained at the Royal Veterinary College: State Scholar Janet Gibbons who acted ("deep vibrant voice, fine zest and sly wit") and Wendy Hammond (gym*, hockey*) whose Alsatian won nine awards, including three Firsts.

In 1961, a Mobile Nursing Unit paid day-long visits, for nursing still attracted many, despite off-putting college prospectuses. One stipulated that a student nurse be single or a widow aged between 18 and 30. After acceptable character and academic references, she would receive £40-£55 in her first year plus "board, residence, the use of and laundering of full indoor Uniform and personal laundry within reason". She would have 28 days' leave, one day off each week, 2½ hours free daily (four on Saturday) and three free nights in fourteen when she did her three months of annual night duty.

Thirty-seven took preliminary examinations between 1948 and 1958. At least 70, including many holders of White Girdles and School Colours, trained as nurses, only one having to give up through her own ill-health. At least 26 hospitals trained them, 50 at London and local establishments, five at Children's, and one at Homoeopathic, hospitals. Choice is unfair, but how to omit Laura Appleby (Christian Union, hockey* captain), Eileen Atkins (gym*, hockey*, tennis* captain), Rosemary Carpenter (WRAC Officer in Germany), Pauline Centa (Psychology prize, future Mental Nurse), Brenda Sharman (Baptist Missionary Society in the Congo) and Sheila Gibbons, both midwives, Janet Moscrop (working in an orphanage after training in a Mission hospital) and Dora Oakman (Chase Farm Gold Medallist of her year)? Sheila Allison, at the ripe age of 28, gained a County award to read for a German degree. One became a missionary nurse, another an Area Children's Officer, a third an X-Ray Assistant.

Three trained as radiographers, three as occupational therapists; 36 worked in laboratories (pathology, research, pharmaceutical, brewing, chemical, hospital), Pat Howes later changing to nursing, and Eileen Peatchey becoming an official guide to Plymouth. From the Hospital Board's Blood Supply Depot, Jean Spriggs taught and examined Dance in Portugal and Mexico. Jasmine Steer (DHG, House and hockey* captain, actress) qualified at the School of Orthoptics.

Jean Sowter farmed in Rhodesia, two studied at Swanley Horticultural College and seven at Wye, including Margery Andrews (later a secretary) and Mary and Winnie Thomas (DHG, prize for practical work, later demonstrator and lecturer).

A grand total of over 210 known to be connected, directly or less closely, with the Sciences.

With this upsurge went increased interest in Mathematics, stimulated by the prize in Miss Florence's name and by the all-graduate Staff led by Miss Morley, with the longest serving Miss Bowen. "You'd have to go a long way to find someone as friendly or as cheerful" as Miss Iris Collins (1946-1970, part-time 1970-1973), whose claim to fame lies less in the fact that she came second in a Mistresses' race, or that she had been in the WRNS, but more in her teaching, especially of the Sixths, and for her control of National Savings. Miss Jane Flowers (Mrs Porcheret, 1947-1954) was business manager of plays. After eight schools in twelve years, Mrs Elsie Matthews (1955-1959) did her last stint among the lower forms. Two OGs returned: Miss Hayes (1954-1963) and Miss Boshier, appointed 1960, who had spent seven years as a Housekeeper-Matron. Dogged by ill-health, she died after three years. A reading desk for the platform, designed by Mrs Hargrave and made by a local craftsman, commemorated her "quiet unselfishness, dignity and serenity, great integrity and fortitude". The younger Mrs Joan Goad (1957-1968) was joined by two others for two year stints, Miss Marta Cwynarski (1958-1960) and Miss Kathleen Tibbs (1961-1963).

Over fifty took Pure Mathematics in HSC/AL and about thirty-five Applied. Ten, most of them Prefects and all Florence and form prizewinners, read the subject at Durham, Leicester, London or Oxford; amongst them were Margaret Adams (32 Good Work Marks in *one* term), Patrol Leader Dora Birch (gym*, the first ECS Mathematician to go to Somerville), Exhibitioner Nancy Carter who had had to take Physics at EGS, State Scholar Patricia Scott (winner of Classical Verse Speaking competitions, tennis*, singer, actress ("a very amusing Flute"), Margaret Waite (netball*, gym*) and Senior Prefect Joan Wilkinson.

All these girls hardly support the view that such subjects are for the boys.

A gift which will be a source of pride and pleasure

The Secretarial Sixth presented an electric gramophone from the proceeds of its dance. Responsible for Lost Property, girls demonstrated business acumen by making a profit one year of 14/6½. Expenses included a stopwatch £4:10:0, "Gestetner: urgent Obliterene 2/3", examination fees £10:2:0, typewriter ribbons 2/3 each. In 1951, Pitman's were reluctantly compelled to increase the price of *Office Training* to 3d a copy. The cost of printing rose by 14% and of paper by 500%.

The lowliest of the Sixth forms, VIB Commercial gained five form prizes and three Good Work Certificates, and, as VIB Secretarial, 22 prizes and 23 certificates. 1952's new title coincided with its rise in esteem, virtually created by French graduate Mrs Amy Dean, its Head for twenty years (1948-1968) and helped by Mrs Lorna Dehnel (1963-1976). Many girls took at least one AL, usually a Modern Language or English. The New Building provided a specialist room. RSA and Pitman's added status, 35 achieving in Shorthand 60wpm, 72 80wpm and 6 100wpm: – Sarah Bonfield, Sonia Brown, Pat Edwards, Barbara Mitchell, Jane Murphy (EMF winner) and Pauline Howson, prizewinning Verse Speaker and "a most endearing" actress whose spirit never flagged. Nan Pollitt won a Pitman's prize. In Typing, 41 succeeded at 1st Grade and 79 (including two Firsts) at 2nd level. In 1954's GCE , 8 passed Commercial subjects and a further 7 Part I Accounts in 1957.

They too visited Gas and Electricity showrooms frequently, twice the Magistrates' Court and once the Spry Kitchen. They were more obviously excited by a Jacqmar Fashion Show, a lecture in good grooming and a trip to Greenwich, although the Business Efficiency Exhibition at Olympia and the Secretarial Exhibition at Hornsey were more strictly relevant.

At least 104 from Fifths and Sixths followed Commercial and Secretarial courses, more becoming secretaries later in their working lives, and at least another 216 learned on the job. They studied at seven different Technical and Polytechnical colleges, at several London establishments, one with a scholarship to St Godric's, one even in Perugia. Others trained after graduating.

Many secured interesting posts: with the manager of a film company (whilst training as a singer), advertising agencies, BBC (Joyce Bourne as secretary to the Head of External Broadcasts, Beryl Mills responsible for

700 broadcasts in 18 different languages), American Embassy (choir member, magazine contributor Ruth Tucker, gym*), Design and Research Centre, computing, British Council, New Scotland Yard, British Chamber of Commerce in Lausanne (as Director, Jacqueline Roberts, Vice-President of the Anglo-Swiss Club, enjoyed the title of Mme la Consule) B and B farmhouse holidays (magazine prize-winner Toni Cutler) and to the Artistic Director at Stratford Theatre, Ontario.

Sixty worked in banks, from the Bank of England and Coutts to Chase Manhattan and the Bank of British West Africa. Finding them impersonal, one turned to medicine, another to teaching. Civil Service Executive took 19, one with the Crown Agents for the Colonies and Singapore.

Over 60 joined firms or industries, such as building, cable and electric, Shell, ICI, Unilever; 40 are known to have opted for insurance, Trust and Finance Companies, 23 were in transport by air, sea and land, as well as in petroleum companies, travel agencies and the RAC. Kay Watkins subsequently beat 199 others to secure a post with the World Health Organisation. Fifteen went into local government and the GPO, and 13 to newspapers, one becoming secretary to the Sports Editor of the *Sunday Dispatch*. Jean Peck, from *The Listener*, went on to Audience Research whilst teaching in a local dancing school and ended up in Poona!

CHAPTER FORTY

The display in the Art room was particularly impressive

In no department are teachers more fundamentally important than in Art, and ECS enjoyed notably gifted artists, always ready with advice and encouragement. Miss Elizabeth Campbell (1946-1975) is known to most as Mrs Hargrave, and to later students as Mrs Westman. In addition to supervising the imaginative Christmas decorations and cards, judging the RSPCA flower competition, taking part in a television programme and the Playreading group, dressing First formers for a Gym and Dancing Display, her main work, apart from teaching of course, was for plays, providing many lovely visual moments. For *Beauty and the Beast*, she also made the props and the animal faces.

Fellow of the Royal Society of Painters and Etchers, "a rare and coveted honour", and the Society of Graphic Art, Gold Medallist at the 1970 Paris Salon and the Italian Academy, Associate of la Société des Artistes Français, Hon. Member with Diploma and Silver Medal of the Tomaso Campanella Academy, a Padua Award winner – few can boast of being taught by someone as gifted and as internationally eminent as Miss Marian Rhodes (1944-1947, a break for her own creative work, 1955 until retirement 1967). Her etchings, exhibited at the Royal Academy and bought for the nation, were freely given as presents. She retained Yorkshire accent and forthrightness, yet remained shy. Endlessly tactful, she was praised for her scholarship and great spirit of service to the community.

Another talented artist, Miss Sylvia Leeming, with a National Diploma of Design, (Mrs Deakins 1947-1955) was wardrobe mistress. Mrs Adams was OG returner Shirley Jarvis, Mrs Janet Margrie stayed six years (1957-1963), Miss Marie Jankovska two (1961-1963) and two others managed one year each.

School Fund provided rubber mats for the Craft room tables (£16:11:6) and a towel. The 1947 kiln (£110) was replaced four years later. Interest stimulated by Mr Margrie's talk, there was a long waiting list to use the potter's wheel (1952), a source of constant amusement. How "fascinating it is to watch the clay stretch and take shape under your fingers, even though

479

it occasionally takes the wrong shape". 1955's magnificent new accommodation caused enormous excitement.

Art, an academic and a fun subject, was taken by both Arts and Science students. For ten, it was their sole AL entry. At least 58 gained HSC/AL, some with distinction. Many went on to Hornsey; at least 142 from Thirds upwards obtained awards to attend Saturday morning sessions; one took evening classes. Forty-one pursued full-time study, ten with scholarships. One was accepted by the Constance Spry Flower School, three by Bath Academy and two by St Albans School.

Margaret King acted ("she screamed most realistically"), wrote and designed school's Christmas card and won the OGA prize for Art and a scholarship to St Martin's School. Celia Reynolds and Daphne Dall received prizes for lino- and wood-cuts of plays and games. Over four years, Enfield Arts Club gave awards to Dorothy Osbourne and Christine Paul (both Training Colleges), Gillian Harrison (French Institute, Palais des Nations) and Margaret Stobo who went on to a Fine Arts course at Reading. One student worked in the Design and Research Centre, another trained as a draughtswoman.

Visits were numerous: to the King's Pictures, the Pinto collection of Wooden Bygones, the Design Centre and the London Galleries – "a morning of enjoyment which passed quickly away as we wandered from one entrancing painting to another". Whenever there were special exhibitions, ECS girls were there: Tate, Royal Academy, Trent Park: Arts and Crafts, Peruvian Art (plus lecture), Impressionists and Moderns, Primitives, Portuguese, Flemish and British paintings. They heard the 1947 RIBA Christmas lectures on Architecture. At Great Bardfield, the Sixth recorded that the crafts and designs showed that the artists lived harmoniously together in the village.

The Sketch Club experienced such popularity that it closed its lists one year and thereafter split into smaller groups. A time for enthusiasts to anticipate with pleasure, it offered scope for many crafts – handloom weaving, such "useful home effects" as wastepaper baskets and scarves, for which a secondhand loom was acquired, making "contemporary" lampshades, and, of course, sketching, out of doors when weather permitted. Several paintings and specimens of pottery work were exhibited at Forty Hall. Each year, as they filed into Assembly, girls gasped with delight at the stunning Christmas decorations.

The beauty and musicality of the choir's singing

Many learned to play the piano with local teachers, notably Miss Eileen Sullivan, and ECS was exceptionally fortunate in its Music Staff. Council's proposal of a musical appreciation club was rejected: "the subject is dealt with in the curriculum". Music was, indeed , all around them. *A Glimpse of life on the planet of St Cecilia*, home of dead composers, told magazine readers of Schubert adding to his unfinished symphony and gave news of many others.

Miss Dilys Thomas was yet another notable contributor to musical success. In one single year, she was thanked for Carol Service, Prize Giving, EMF, Empire Youth Sunday and for weekly practices. Especially appreciated were her thoroughness, energy and "love of music which she has passed on to us". Every girl took part in her farewell concert, "a fine conclusion to all her good work": 15 solo items received loud and prolonged applause.

"Singing a favourite song with perfect artistry and restraint" – so said the Head at her retirement concert, which, characteristically, included solos (piano, clarinet, harp, voice), duets (piano), choir items – and Miss Benjamin (1950-1980, then part-time to 1986), the next departmental Head. Her cabaret items at private Staff functions delighted all. Envied for her ease and fluency in so many styles, Hetty composed and played effective incidental music for Dress Parades, encouraged entry for public examinations and stimulated appreciation by opera and ballet visits. Her own carol was published.

From 1950, Miss Mary Hosken, a regular visitor, trained mainly junior choirs, giving up much time to prepare many for the EMF. Mrs Isobel Mitchell (1952-1962, 1965-1989?, Mrs Stevens) impressed not only by her qualifications (ALCM, LCTL, LRAM, L.Mus, TCh, FTCL) and her elegance, but by her devoted work for junior and EMF choirs.

A recital by Miss Ruth Early inaugurated the new gramophone, bought when the Education Committee provided the grand piano towards which school had saved £60. Interest increased in the record played before Assembly. The Audix amplifier cost £61:5:11, a cabinet £16:14:4, records 17/3 and needles 3/11½ and 2/2. One concert's expenditure included tuning the piano £1:5:0 and blackout £4:7:1, another had a deficit of £1:15:0. Specialist provision in the New Building made a great difference.

How to select from the never-ending list of events which seniors and, especially, juniors enjoyed in London Halls and, between 1947 and 1957, over 40 in local cinemas, including one given by the London Philharmonic? Recitals: piano, woodwind (Archie Camden's Group), percussion instruments, viola and harpsichord, singing; Antony Hopkins' lecture on Brahms; concerts: Barbirolli's Elgar, County Youth Orchestra, Guildhall School of Music and Drama, the New English Orchestra when Leonard Rafter showed on several occasions what the different instruments were and could do. Particularly popular were the Robert Meyer concerts on Saturday mornings ("always instructive and inspiring") and the Ernest Read children's concerts.

Many heard *Judas Maccabeus*. Once prepared by Dr Jacques' illustrated talk, and once singing arias in school, different groups enthused over *The Messiah*, proud that three members of Staff sang in the London Philharmonic choir. Twice they appreciated *The Immortal Hour* at the People's Palace. Opera, after a slow start, became popular, from *Let's make an opera* to *The Magic Flute*, which "gay and charming opera was enjoyed, even by the less musically minded among us". Over 90 from middle school saw *Hansel and Gretel*; seniors liked *Figaro*; Sixths found *The Mastersingers* a wonderful experience. Over two years, at least 15 parties went to Sadlers Wells and Covent Garden, juniors thrilled by *The Sleeping Beauty*.

Appreciative of all the time and care taken by Miss Benjamin, so many wished to join the choir that, after strict auditions, junior and senior groups were formed. They loved recording at HMV *The Blue Bird*, *Music when soft voices die*, and, a Festival entry, *The Centaurs*, as well as singing to the local Derby and Joan club. Their memorable singing entailed much hard practice, for none of the teachers was easily satisfied. Fortunately, girls relished this almost as much as the important and successful occasions to which they led. One Christmas concert helped the Florence Memorial Fund. Six times the choir led and sang the anthem at the local Empire Youth Services. School's end-of-year service for dedication and renewed inspiration was twice held in St Andrew's.

Enfield String Players performed in school. Concerts for different instruments such as piccolo, accordeon and horn, often arranged by girls, were sometimes repeated for parents and visitors. In 1954, the first half was given by Festival prizewinners and the choir; the second was devoted to the *Stabat Mater*. *The Walrus and the Carpenter* began the delightful tradition of the comic item performed *con brio*.

As well as composing, accompanying and performing solos and duets with Miss Benjamin and for the OG, Eve Barsham took ALs in Music and Modern Languages before going up to Oxford. The first woman to gain a First in Music, she subsequently won a scholarship for three years' research for her doctorate. She played the harpsichord in the intervals of a London professional production of *The Provoked Wife* and contributed to the Cambridge Opera handbook on Gluck's *Orfeo*. A Festival Hall concert in 1955 was special to ECS as Eve's younger sister played the 'cello. State Scholar, junior and senior Sports champion, Dinah specialised at the Royal Academy of Music in conducting and choral training, lectured at Homerton and became a senior lecturer for the Open University. Her school Madrigal choir gave a recital. At the Jubilee concert, Tessa Ormandy's solo was rapturously received; an encore was "demanded and given, a moving and beautiful occasion". She won the Royal Academy Gold Medal. Mary Elvidge, soloist and leader of the Christian Union, who went on to the Guildhall School, arranged another concert the same year.

A Recorder group which won Festival prizes was run by Margaret Clark, who also trained at the Guildhall. Harringay Music Festival is mentioned only once, but that in Enfield continued to generate much enthusiasm. Many prizes and certificates were won in all age groups and in nine different categories, above all for choirs: junior, senior, small, U-17s, U-18s, Dinah's. By 1957, they were unchallenged. The prizewinners' concert in 1962, the Festival's 44th year, was held in the Hall to honour Miss Sharp.

Magazine readers were told that

The modern child wants jazz and swing,

And not the songs you used to sing.

The Jazz Club, with great help from Staff, flourished from 1957, with attendances of up to 80 to hear records of traditional and modern Jazz, Skiffle and Rock 'n' Roll.

Many appreciated music, for it was never the privilege of an élite. Eight more did become professional musicians: Jennifer Lilleystone, a well-known local teacher, trained the English Opera group: Jean Elmer (Royal Academy): Lorna Green (White Girdle, Royal College): Heather Stephens (London College): Megan Yorath (Trinity College): Angela Webb, who won an Enfield Arts Club prize (Oxford): and two more to the Guildhall School, reciter Sarah Tarring and Rita Dyke, soloist and actress, who won an Exhibition for Singing and defeated 2,000 entrants at the all-British Teenager Song Contest before doing cabaret (Vince and Rita Starr).

"How much is due to Miss Benjamin and Miss Hosken! It is their patience and hard work alone which are responsible for our achievements".

Beautifully neat and so carefully made

Once a Cinderella subject, but encouraged by both Heads, the Domestic Arts/Sciences developed enormously, even during rationing, in range of interest and importance. The new Cookery room and specialist provision for Needlework proved a great spur.

In a department notorious for the coming and going of marriageable young ladies, ECS fared better, needing a supply for only one term. Miss Jean Neilson (1943-1951), experienced and popular, helped with make-up for Spanish plays and is remembered for time and trouble taken with meals, which kept up a high standard, for camps, expeditions and Staff celebrations. She raised the esteem in which girls held the subject before she left for a Colonial teaching post.

Staff trained at either the National School of Cookery or Berridge House. Miss Margaret Robinson (1948-1955, Mrs Hill) acted as business manager for plays as did Miss Jean Roberts (1951-1962, Mrs Reddyhough), who made costumes for plays as did Mrs Jean Clapham (1959-1983) at this time. Also involved were OG Ann King (1958-1963, Mrs Mepham), Miss Barbara Wilson (1955-1958) and Mrs Margaret Patterson (1957-1959).

Odd facts: in 1950, six Morphy Richards irons were bought for 33/6, an iron stand for 14/6 and an ironing board for 42/2. Onions were 4d a pound in 1951, darning feet 8/3 each. Repairs to sewing machines varied between 1/1 and 9/-.

1948's expedition to the Mothercraft Centre cost 3/4½. The Ideal Home Exhibition was regularly patronised. Girls went to film shows and demonstrations at both Gas and Electricity showrooms, to Dickens and Jones store, the Embroiderers' Exhibition, the Courtauld Institute and the Catering Display at Olympia.

In 1953, VIB visted Stiebel House, feeling silly in their school uniforms in the richly decorated showroom with its luxurious grey Persian carpet. Seated on beautiful leather upholstered chairs, they admired a Countess' dresses for the Coronation service and for Ascot, Ava Gardner's dinner gown, "a marsh-mallow pink evening affair with 200 yards of tulle, and Adèle's hats which we longed to try on". They remembered that OG milliner Pamela Colwell began her career with Adèle. They were impressed by OG model Ann Gardner, who, after secretarial college, won the *Daily Telegraph* Ideal Model competition (1,000 entrants).

Vogue organised a Mannequin Parade in 1956, using what the Head called six suitably shaped middle school and senior girls as models. School enjoyed morning, parents evening, shows. Fashionable clothes for teenagers included smart town coats, attractive tailored suits and casual wear for the weekend. Hats caused controversy among the more conservative-minded, whereas accessories were universally appreciated. Help with make-up and care of clothes was received with hearty applause. Representatives of Yardley's also emphasised good grooming, urging seniors to enjoy fresh air, relaxation, early nights, a daily bath, perfectly clean undies and a well-balanced diet, to wear a smart suit, a neat white blouse, matching accessories and to do their daily dozen. Never more than two colours should be worn together, black to be avoided, grey and navy especially commended. Well-applied, carefully chosen make-up (rouge, eye shadow, mascara) "is not usually necessary for young people, but can be used as a 'prettifier' for parties"; better they held their faces under cold running water! Hands should be manicured once a week, hair brushed regularly and arranged in a 'suitable' style, and feet made comfortable in sensible shoes.

In 1954, Mrs Hill and Mrs Reddyhough were responsible for school's first Dress Parade. Firsts wore well-made dirndle skirts, most costing less than 15/-: Seconds, skirts and beach outfits: Thirds modelled "attractive sundresses, a school dress made with exceptional perfection for a 14-year old and smart and neatly made pyjamas": Fourths showed "a pair of jolly-looking shorts in blue striped linen", plus a red blouse. Sixths demonstrated "enchanting dresses suitable for any afternoon party, the outstanding one being blue with a very full skirt, a large square neck, an unusual overlapping collar and small sleeves".

For the fourth annual Parade, Firsts wore variegated aprons and matching caps. Seconds were more ambitious, their blouses and skirts being practical yet retaining their attractiveness. The middle school experimented: summer frocks, well-tailored sportswear, a Confirmation dress and 'saucy' nightwear, despite the models' reluctance to carry the generously provided Teddy Bears. Seniors, full of original ideas, provided a selection worthy of any couturier in adaptable evening-to-beach garments. The finale was a ballet-length cocktail dress of black taffeta designed by Jacques Heim. Twelve guineas had been advanced for the event; ticket sales brought in £10. 1959 saw the Butterick Dress Parade (Plain Ingleweave 4/11 up to Nylon Chiffon at 12/- a yard).

Barbara Husbands and Ann Merry won the OGA prize. Girls studied at seventeen or more different institutions, with more than twenty full-timers and seven part-timers following dress design courses at Hornsey. Ann Greening and Shirley Minchinton trained at St Martin's School of Art and Barrett Street Technical respectively. Beryl Shimmins became a dressmaker's apprentice. Cookery claimed Celia Baldwin (demonstrator), Margaret Shelley (training subsequently at the College of Occupational Therapy), Ann Lilley (Hotel Catering) and Eileen Fear (swimming Bronze and Bar), who, with Nottingham's Diploma of Institutional Management, won the Craftsmanship prize and became a caterer with the CEGB. More interested in management were Gillian Druce (Restaurateur in Blackpool), Queen's Guide Jean Nightingale (school matron) and her sister Dawn (in charge of a large firm's catering, then running a Guest House).

Other trainees were Valerie Dyke (Interior Decoration), DHG and House Captain Janet Lock (hockey*, tennis* champion, rounders* captain), Margaret Shimwell (Housecraft), Judith Burden with a prize for flower arrangement (College of Distributive Trades), Annette Mascall and Janet Noden (Home Economics) and Margaret Elmer who graduated from King's College of Household and Social Science.

The team spirit is more important than individual success

Council agreed that all matches should be announced the preceding day, that no-one below IV should nominate captains (one dissentient voice), and no-one below III should vote. Referred back were the nature and design of Colours: if detachable, might they be dangerous? or get lost? could anyone object to a 'better' colour? That the names of those good at games should be read out with the Good Work List at end-of-term Assemblies was not approved, nor was the motion that teams other than First teams should wear different coloured socks for matches. Juniors and seniors competed for House shields (engraving 7/6) in netball, hockey, rounders, swimming and sports (engraving 4/6), for form cups in netball and for individual trophies in tennis.

Heartiest thanks were always given to all Refreshment Committees, ball boys ("who worked conscientiously and well"), coaches, umpires and Staff. "We hope that the friendly relationship between Staff and Teams will remain". Expenditure on team photographs (1953, £9) was mainly recoverable; a set was given to the library in 1951 (£1:11:0). The games fund needed a subsidy that year of £2:1:1. Maybe more had been spent on food than two years earlier: "Rations £1:10:3. Tea for visitors, 2/11". Perhaps fares had cost more: Southgate 3/4, Latymer 9/2, Tottenham 14/6½.

Medication was needed for players and non-players alike. Council rejected the idea of pictures for the Sick Room, although they might have "the soothing effect of a tank of goldfish", but accepted a mirror. 1952's purchases were: – Hot water bottles 5/6 each, safety pins 7 for 4d, tweezers 2/6, clinical thermometer 4/1, Dettol 5/-, Veganin 20 for 3/3, Witch Hazel 2/3, ½" adhesive plaster 6/9, 6"×2" bandages 3/9, peppermint essence 2/4½ – and curtains for the sickbed window £1:14:11½. Sanitary towels were always in debt.

Medical and dental inspections were still loathed, even lessons being preferred to lengthy waits in the corridor and undignified proddings on a half-dressed body. They became more sophisticated: TB jelly patches, Mass X-Rays, BCG tests. The audiometrician tested the hearing of 12- and 13-year olds. Whilst colds were endemic, general health remained reasonably good.

Three lusty cheers

Long discussions on Sports Day concerned, firstly, the date. The summer term being too crowded would it not be better earlier when it would be cooler and avoid exam time? Secondly, the problem of fitting in the heats: Saturdays? Several seniors worked then. Weekdays? Finally, they reached the crux of the matter: 1952's enthusiasm for the existing type was low. For a Garden Party plus Sale, the vote was 21-22. The idea of separate junior and senior days was unanimously rejected, mainly because of over-complicated organisation. The only clear agreement was that everyone who survived the heats should receive points.

The day continued much the same, often dominated by the weather. 1947, evening; "half an hour before, the rain was streaming down and five minutes after hurrying home, the heavens opened". 1951: "the record smashed most decisively was that of the weather. For once, we performed in overwhelming heat instead of the customary cloudy dullness. Staff bore heroically the sun's glare. Enjoy it we certainly did". Many visitors seemed happy too, "perhaps savouring the comical tumbles caused by the slippery grass". 1953: cancelled, because the new foundations were being laid. 1959, 1960: it rained all day, so events were held the following morning, with consequently fewer visitors.

In the first half of this period, events averaged 36 with races for parents (who once ran faster than their daughters), visitors (one toddler remained on the starting line), OGs and Mistresses, who caused many a laugh or amused interest when they ran to the tape in Prefects' hats tied on with White Girdles, the winners being Miss F. Sharp and Mrs Wooldridge. Prefects devised a fanciful object race: "the sporting victims had to perform such tasks as scrubbing desks, threading very fine needles and skipping with blown balloons held in their mouths". Once, the efficient organisation was marred slightly by the photographer who, aiming to take interesting pictures, lay down in the middle of the course where he was in danger of being trampled on.

The cyclostyled programmes still listed events reminiscent of the Thirties: egg-and-spoon, leapfrog. More modern were throwing the rounders ball (record, 67 yards), and High Jump (middle school 4' 11", junior 4'9"). Serious Athletics proved difficult until the circular track in 1954 allowed the 220 yards flat. Perhaps the AAA film and Geoff. Dyson's lecture encouraged the new and keenly supported Athletics Club.

It is impossible now to recapture the importance of Houses for all physical activities. One year, a broken wrist "cast a temporary gloom over the proceedings, but the animal spirits of our five Houses were not to be daunted and the cheering soon reached its habitual ear-splitting pitch". Screams still encouraged Inter-Form contestants, but pandemonium broke out during Inter-House Relays, especially when three junior teams were disqualified and three senior teams dropped the baton. That year, the final points read: Ca 75, M 122, W 145, Ce 148 and U (often successful) 152. No fewer than 20 girls received the junior cup. Middle school championships began in 1952. Senior winners included Doreen Braybrook (rounders*, gym*, netball*) and Jean Scutcher (once junior, twice middle, twice senior).

A frantic rush followed to make a ring round the recorders' table for the announcement of the results, the Head Girl's mother presenting the awards. Flowers were given to the PE Staff.

Come on Seniors. Do not let the Juniors show you up

As early as 1948, Council discussed whether the weekly trek to the Baths, particularly dire in pouring rain, was a waste of time, and whether non-swimmers could do prep. This same motion was defeated again seven years later, Miss Hodgson insisting that girls could learn by watching and help by counting lengths. More to the point, no-one was left behind to be responsible for them.

To the smallish band of enthusiasts and particularly Ursulines, the 18 or so events constituted the highlight of the year. In the same breath, swimmers praised the customary gaiety (perhaps when the senior Inter-Form race was swum in nightdresses) and bewailed a lack of enthusiasm. With large numbers of competitors and good teamwork, early reports show the greatest keenness. "Every girl was keen to get marks for her House". In good weather, 70 swam a quarter-mile and a noticeable improvement in diving was commended (1947). Five years later, support given by most seniors left much to be desired; some races even had to be cancelled. Although points were awarded for standards attained during the year, a plea for more participants to make the Gala more interesting was soon published. Regular winter practices at Edmonton Indoor Baths were poorly attended until the juniors took them over. Yet, twelve months on, "swimming, both juniors and seniors, has shown a vast improvement. Well done!"

In the Middlesex Gala, seniors took or shared first place three times and remained second or third before sinking to sixth by 1959; juniors were always in the top three, winning, in 1949, the Broomfield Park Cup for Girls' Relay. Captain Brenda Stuchbury's swimming was judged an outstanding credit to the school. They lost first place by a single point in the North Middlesex Gala that same year; in 1950, they came first in every race, winning by 24 points.

Three swam in the county trials, one was reserve for an all-England Gala. House Captain Elizabeth Moore (RLSS Gold and Award of Merit, three times junior and once senior champion) represented Enfield and reached the Middlesex Junior Backstroke final. Girls participated in local events, coming second in Enfield's Coronation Cup.

At least 24 Colours were awarded. Champions, often more than once, included captain Myrna Brown (netball*), once tying with her sister Maureen who swam for Herts and Middlesex, and who, with Mary Kerr (gym*), was chosen to enter the National Championships, captain Christine Gathergood (netball*) and House Captain Susan Middleton.

Life Saving classes were popular. School did well in the H.D. Anthony Shield competition for schools without the use of indoor baths but failed to retain it. "Buck up you lifesavers!" Juniors responded, seniors did not. RLSS awards were avidly collected, however, – at least 26 Intermediate, 122 Bronze, 75 with additional Bars; five won the Unigrip certificate in 1962, 19 the 1st Class Instructor's certificate. Over five years, the Award of Merit, usually won by post-school swimmers, was achieved by 15.

Many scratched through inclement weather

The spring of 1947 was unique with every single match cancelled; over half were lost in 1952 when the hockey pitch was ruined. "We played in thick fog, severe frost, rain and driving snow", just one game being abandoned in a blizzard. When pitches were under water in 1955, practices were held indoors with a beanbag; despite skipping to keep in training, this was so dispiriting that many lost interest; only once did the first team manage a full turn-out.

Odd items of expenditure have survived: hockey socks (1959) £1:10:1: three pairs of hockey knickers repaired "as necessary", 8/-, 10/- and 12/-: pads £4:0:5: laces 3/-: stockings from the Scotch Wool Shop and Hosiery Stores, £4:16:0. Something was obviously wrong, as "I am returning only ten of the eleven hockey sticks you sent us. This is because the local Physical Training Organiser has taken the eleventh, and it is now in the hands of the Chief Physical Training Officer for the County".

Magazine reports still discourage the statistician: "pleasantly surprised at good results", a team was unbeaten, or one match was scratched and all the rest were won. First, second, IV and U-15 teams played regularly against Dr Barnardo's, 14 local schools, others in neighbouring boroughs, about 21 in all, secondary modern and grammar. Few exist today. They played the OGs, and, in a match "hilarious and unorthodox", beat the Staff 5-2. Arts Staff and girls played their Science counterparts. A

Shakespearean quotation was discovered for each member of the team which beat EGS in 1949: "He that escapes me without some broken limb shall acquit himself well. ... How hast thou lost thy breath? By running fast". "Now we must never let the boys beat us again". Alas, they always did. Some 60 Colours were received, in two years by all First team players. The overall results? Scratched 41, P 365, W 277, D 31, L 57. In one season, the First XI scored 127 goals, conceding only 39.

Affiliated to the Middlesex Women's Hockey Association, teams competed in the Inter-Schools Tournaments. First in the Northern area, seniors reached the final six times, winning in 1962. The U-15 won the 1960 local tournament and achieved the County finals twice. Girls watched a training film and international events at Wembley and proudly cheered Miss Ellis playing for the South against the West.

At the end of 1953, "our field was a mass of bricks and mortar as new buildings began to take shape. We were therefore pleased to find at the beginning of the season that the new fullsized pitch was ready for use", so the First team lost in the first round! The era ended well, however, with "team spirit high. Everyone willingly attended practices".

A special feature was the acquisition, in place of gymslips, of shorts for the 1st and 2nd netball teams, "which considerably improved their appearance". Soon new courts were also welcomed.

It snowed on the day of the Inter-Schools matches in that dreadful spring of 1947. Five teams (1st, 2nd, U-15, U-14, U-13) played as regularly as possible, P 780, L 109 (regularly to Queen Elizabeth's, Barnet), D 22+. Fortunes were mixed against EGS: W 7 (once with the help of the new rules), L 33. The boys asked "if one of the matches could be basketball, and, although we decided against this, it was doubtful which game we were playing". To school's delight, Staff won in 1953 by 14 goals to 12. Two years later, girls, playing in unaccustomed positions, won, to general disappointment and again in 1958, "although the Staff were given every encouragement".

All teams entered the Inter-County tournament, the U-13 and U-14 each winning once. Three times runner-up, the first VII succeeded in 1952, participated in the County Festival of Britain and won the 1960 North County Rally. The stars were the U-15 who played in the Battersea Pleasure Gardens in aid of the Playing Fields' Association and won the County Rally twice, coming second once. Many watched international matches at Harringay.

Do not forget those practices in the dinner-hour

By 1952, the Captain was deploring the increasing difficulty of finding opponents for senior rounders, U-15, U-13 and Third form teams being the the only ones regularly involved. Fortunately, juniors showed great enthusiasm, although the U-13s lacked match practice and coordination of field work. Standards fell; only seven Colours were granted. Of the 428 matches scheduled, 56 were scratched (23 apparently because of 1958's bus strike): W 242, D 25, L 105.

During Form and House tournaments, shrieks of anguish could be heard some distance away. The VI lost to the OGA at one reunion. Twice against the Staff, girls pointedly changed positions or functioned left-handedly – and lost both times. The Staff were patronisingly congratulated.

Council hoped for cricket, but lack of space and time prevented it as a summer sport.

Tennis, needing only two girls, was most popular; clubs exist outside school, there were indoor tournaments and the annual thrill of a Wimbledon visit. Staff enjoyed tennis duty until 5pm rather less. Council's proposals that courts should be used out of schooltime was rejected as bad for the grass and requiring more Staff supervision. The lack of hard courts was particularly noticeable, despite the encouragement of the Lawn Tennis Association coaches. In 1954, however, came the almost unbelievable luxury of seven hard courts. Tennis balls cost 28/- a dozen, rackets 63/- and 73/- (repairs 8/9), two nets £5:3:6 and shorts 20/-. 1951's sale of rackets raised nearly £100.

Battles were many, exciting and hard fought. Regular losers to EGS and to Staff, girls just managed a winning margin over the OGA. ECS and EGS combined against joint Staff and lost, 48 games to 51. For 1st, 2nd and later III teams, 37 matches were scratched and six abandoned during play; in only two summers were no matches cancelled. Out of more than 160 played, at least 110 were won and 39 lost. Thirty-two Colours were received. A recurrent problem was that most First team players left each year. Although one girl made the Herts junior team, school was unsuccessful in the Aberdare Cup.

"How gratifying it was to see such large numbers of entries for all the tournaments". Winners included: – juniors, Jennifer Flack (twice), Jennifer Ford (netball*, gym*), Josie Swallow (netball*), Sally Thornton (rounders captain), Hazel Underwood (hockey*): seniors, Pat Wilson (OGA games prize), House Captain Jennifer Hall, Senior Prefect Brenda Liddiard (hockey*, an actress of "noble dignity") and Myra Lawrence (singles and doubles, gym*, hockey*). Nanette Lucas (gym*, later a farmer's wife) reached the semifinal of junior Wimbledon and won the *Evening News* tennis singles.

Where do youngsters find all their energy?

Country Dancing for mainly middle school was greatly indebted to Miss Ellis. The privilege of holding it in the large EGS Hall made 1947's Christmas party ("lovely supper") most enjoyable. The Staff too learned the comparatively few dances which they did not already know. The OGs held a Square Dance party. A subscription (4/8) was paid to the English Folk Dance Society.

Dancing and Gym combined in displays of agilities, team races, Inter-House goal shooting and Country, Russian and Dutch dances. Three hundred attended in the small space of the Hall on two January nights, 1948, raising £57 for the Florence Memorial fund and school Charities. Firsts enjoyed dances, Seconds demonstrated balance exercises, Thirds vaulted on the long horse and played indoor games, Fourths and Fifths performed free-standing exercises and the High Jump (4'8") and Sixths did figure marching and vaulting. The Folk Dancers, for whom Miss Kenworthy played the piano, impressed everyone by their grace and lightness.

1951's display needed two day-long rehearsals. After a programme design competition the following year, "a bustle of anticipation pervaded the scene". For once, girls welcomed a rainy day in order to remain in the Hall at lunchtime to perfect dances and increase speed in games. "Juniors gazed through windows at agile seniors leaping in awe-inspiring attitudes over the horse". On the great day, everything was wonderful; even skipping had its share of applause and praise.

"The most exciting event of the new reign to us has been the opening of the new gym". A giant crane hoisted all the roof girders on in about eight hours. "We still impatiently await the new apparatus without which the building is not a true gym, but the novelty of having somewhere to work without continual worry about noise or perpetual care about banging into other people is still with us". The first display therein (tickets, 2/-, 1/6, 1/-) took place in 1956, with two performances of twelve items. The showers were markedly less popular.

A Gym Club was formed; at least 85 Colours were gained.

Unflagging energy and enthusiasm

Self-styled Granny of the Staff, Miss Hodgson spent thirty-seven years (1914-1951) at ECS, which included both wars when her whistle was much in evidence. She was thanked for umpiring, coaching, her interest in all games and for presenting a Cup for Inter-Form netball competition. She was MO at Cadet camps until 1962, when she could still teach campers something about Deck Tennis.

A good organiser, she was in her element on Sports Days and at Gym Displays. Many recall her deep voice, her ringing laugh and weather-beaten face, her "happy presence, invaluable wisdom and common sense" as well as her "box-pleated gymslip and blazer as if petrified from an earlier age". The Head praised her serenity and the wise advice of guide, philosopher and friend. She enjoyed a happy family life and a strong Christian faith, but never let her Catholicism intrude.

At the OGA reunion on her retirement, when she was presented with a gold watch and cheque, she took the salute from hastily sorted out matrons and mums at an impromptu march past. Representatives of each age group since 1914 spoke her praises – "lovely in a genial way", not a compliment applicable to many of her contemporaries, nor, indeed, successors. A burlesque gym display was mounted in the school uniform of the Great War. A celebratory iced cake was baked.

The collection (£165) taken at her Memorial Service funded an award in her name.

PE departments expect the quickest turnover of young teachers, but ECS was again fortunate. Miss Gwen Crook (1948-1957, Mrs Tavener) was always willing to help teams, giving valuable advice and umpiring tirelessly. Cadets missed her enjoyable Country Dance parties. She went to teach in New Zealand. As well as being involved in all sports, Miss Barbara Bush (1946-1948) acted in Staff plays. Girls were sad when she left on her marriage to Miss Bishop's brother.

Miss Pat Newby (1957-1962, Mrs Horrex), former House Captain and senior Sports champion, winner of three Colours in one year, greatly encouraged all players and admirably trained the fairy dancers for *Midsummer Night's Dream*. Miss Jill Hudson (1957-1960, Mrs Mapson) took part in Scripture Union and became the new Cadet Captain. "Our good results in rounders reflect her hard work. She leaves us with our regrets and good wishes". Mrs Mary O'Shea (part-time 1958-1965) was thanked for coaching swimming, Miss Pam Macfarlane (1951-1954) helped with Cadets and spoke in a debate on Jazz, Miss Gillian Gardner-Hopkins (1960-1962) scored three rounders for the Staff. Mrs Filer, grandmother of an OG, played the piano for gym and dancing. School was shocked when Miss Sheila Webb died suddenly in 1964.

Sixteen girls, several with ALs, trained as physiotherapists; they included House and games captains, at least 13 with games Colours and two with School Colours: Margaret Moore (netball*, Hodgson prize) and Grace Murfitt (DHG, Cadet). Twenty (including 19 captains of games and four of Houses) with more than 50 Colours between them, went on to PE/ PT colleges; among them were tennis champions Mary Halliday (thrice Sports champion), Pam Brodie (junior county hockey) and Dorothy Renwick: swimmers Jean Gilson (fastest girl swimmer in Middlesex, 1949), Maureen O'Brien (Bronze, DSc prize), Senior Prefect and Cadet Barbara Johnson (HSC, 1st Class Instructor's certificate and Award of Merit): White Girdle holders Joan Dickinson (running team), Christa Stubbs: junior county hockey player Jeannette Atkins: delegate World Forum of Youth Laetitia Freeman: actresses Eileen Pulford, Mollie Smith: senior sports champion and DHG Pat Widlake: Irene Tingley, later a missionary nurse and teacher: Rosina Williams, who "has an excellent throw for a girl".

For four years in the quiet of the DSc room , enthusiastic Chess players mainly Third formers, held a weekly meeting to learn the rudiments, the Head providing sets. Mr Adams (Enfield Chess Club) helped Mrs Porcheret who was responsible for its success. A junior American-style championship was won by Frances Heath (Training College).

"I hope that we shall continue to strive".

Apple fritters! Indigestible but none the less exciting

A party of over 70, with delicious cakes and jellies, celebrated the 21st birthday and the good old days of the 12th Enfield Cadet Company, perhaps the most continuously active of all school's post-war groups. They wrestled with long-forgotten knots, sang lustily round an imaginary campfire and looked at films of old camps. With their unfailing presence and friendly advice, the moving spirits, Miss F. Sharp and Miss Hodgson, cut a cake decorated with a campsite complete with tents, fire-burning and flag-flying. "There is no greater movement in the world than Guides and the aim of every Cadet to train for greater service in the movement is one of the finest". Apart from one year of comparative apathy, most years experienced an increase in members and excitement.

A local overnight hike prepared for investiture: in 1959, all VIB. Helpers included PE, five other Staff and more than one OG. Some OGs formed their own Trefoil Guild which met monthly.

At weekly meetings, Cadets played all games from Sardines, the most popular, to deck quoits and rounders. Once, disguised, they had to get a message secretly across Enfield without being challenged. They were challenged – by "a real policeman". In District Sports, they once won the Rayner Trophy. Country Dancing was popular at parties, on Thinking Day and to raise money for the County Camp Site Fund. Several Christmases, they ate tea by candlelight. Sales, Visitors' Day, District Displays, Birthday Teas at the first meeting of the year – these were special. In one concert, they represented two Dutch pictures in tableau form.

On the field, as all had done before them, they learned fire-making ("no easy task in drizzling rain"), loved brewing tea or steaming cocoa, and delighted in the aroma of fried bacon. Cooking sausages in wet brown paper proved most unsuccessful, whereas eggs inside potatoes were very good and melted chocolate in split banana tasted delicious. Two sinners once forgot their frying pan. A County Camp Fire in the grounds of Ally Pally in Coronation year was addressed by Lady Baden Powell; two carried flaming torches to light the huge, ready-laid fire.

Good Works involved collecting toys and fruit, filling children's Christmas stockings. They appreciated serious discussions, an Inspector's visit, camp conferences on training and child psychology, five lectures from the district advisor on campcraft (including the use of axe and saw) and talks on work in post-war Germany and on children's characteristics. During training to run a Brownie Pack, "all delighted in being Sprites, Elves and Little People for one day in the year".

In the all-England Cadet Rallies, they enjoyed 1951's Pageant, 1952's March Past and Service in Westminster Central Hall, 1968's Lunch at the Commonwealth Institute, followed by conference and Brains Trust. That same year, they won a trophy at the Jubilee Scout and Guide Handicraft Exhibition. They acted as Colour Party for services at St Martins-in-the-Fields and at St George's Day parades.

Five were selected for 1957's Windsor World Camp to celebrate the birth of Baden Powell, attended by 2,000 from the UK and 2,000 from 68 countries, addressed by the Chief Scout and visited by the Queen and her aunt Mary, the then Princess Royal. They joined in dances in national costumes, excursions and watched fireworks and the stirring closing ceremony along with 23,995 other Guides. Two joined F.S. at the Middlesex Jubilee International Camp of 1960. Sylvia Hinder became Assistant Headquarters Commissioner of the Cub Scout movement in Great Britain.

"The yearly camp is Guiding in the deepest sense of the word. It is there that all knowledge is put into practice and the gaps are filled up". A small group spent 2½ weeks in the Alpes Maritimes, where they helped during a mountain fire, ate scanty food and doubted the purity of the water supply. Stranded in Paris on their return, they stayed with French Guides.

The first two regular post-war camps were at High Leigh, when, of course, it poured with rain. The subsequent venue was often Theydon Bois, a charming village in the heart of Epping Forest, for a weekend "of conscientious objection to school work". Notwithstanding one riotous occasion (undetailed), camp was near the noise of traffic yet peaceful.

They camped twice in Wales and four times in Cornwall, once when the farm cat gave birth to eight kittens. Eight girls, plus rucksacks, spent six hours in the train before travelling sixteen miles on the top of a lorry; they felt "curiously regarded, probably on account of our blue-bloused and navy-skirted uniformity". They entertained the vicar to supper and a policeman dropped in on their campfire. They pumped water and waxed ecstatic over the radiant sun and the fallow deer. In Dorset, "no life is quite as good – even when it rains, we have fun". They tucked in to a wonderful tea at Lady Armitage's house.

1952 was special in Northern Ireland, what with tea in the members' dining room at Stormont, and, despite jellyfish, wasps and rain, lunches of dates, apples, tomatoes, mashed pilchards and sliced meats. On a brief visit to Eire, where foods were unrationed, they drooled ("What bliss!") over raisins, currants, cream, tinned fruits and salmon, all in plentiful supply, and cameras, films and watches all much cheaper.

Cooking mishaps did not spoil Jersey's Battle of Flowers, the bracing walks and the full day excursion to Guernsey. Night travelling to Dunoon was a new experience for most. Perthshire provided grouse, wild deer, a coach tour of the Trossachs and two flooded tents. After two local venues which resembled a commando course in the rain, they held their last camp with F.S. at their wonderful Cornish site.

Despite her appeal to all thoughtful members of the Sixth form, however busy they might be, to join for the good fellowship and consciousness of the needs of others and to pursue the Christian ideals in accordance with the true spirit of Guiding, 1961 saw only fortnightly meetings. Members learned that a well-established school activity required unflagging enthusiasm to maintain continued support and interest. The company broke up in 1962, as no leader was forthcoming. The hope that, at some future date, the long tradition would be resumed remained unrealised.

A 5-stanza parody of the radio show *Much Binding in the Marsh* immortalised camp's in-jokes.

Through much camping with F. Sharp,
We have never any time to be just lazy.
Through much camping with F. Sharp,
Recollections of rest hour are very hazy.
She always finds us lots and lots of things we have to do
From mending broken dixies to concocting Irish stew,
To get her from the kitchen is more than we can do.
  Such fun camping with F. Sharp!

Through much camping with F. Sharp,
We're improving from her early morning natters.
Through much camping with F. Sharp,
Poor Eggie's skirt is gorse-bushed into tatters.
On Thursday we go home again after our fortnight's fun,
And we will remember it thro' many years to come,
And how we enjoyed it, oh! yes, all and everyone!
  We love camping with F. Sharp.

CHAPTER FORTY-ONE

Is she of unblemished reputation?

Prospective employers still asked the Head to "kindly furnish us with your views as to her respectability". Some girls, students in the early Fifties, feel that insufficient and inadequate guidance was given in choice of external examination subjects, that school was geared to Higher Education, anything less being not quite the thing, even that the pressure to go up to university resulted in feelings of inferiority in those who did not. Whilst it was a marvel that so many did rise above various problems to follow further education of any kind, university candidates were certainly cossetted, their splendid record lauded at every Prize Giving.

"A memorable occasion for many of us", the annual Service for leavers, whatever their future, continued, most frequently in St Paul's Cathedral, with a traditional pattern of hymns, readings, Acts of Thanksgiving, Penitence and Dedication, and an Address. One year, it was attended by the Dean of St Paul's, the Bishops of Willesden and Stepney, the Moderator of Church Training Colleges, Harrow's Head Master and some 3,000 leavers. Miss Sharp read a lesson; school's 70-strong choir twice sang *God be in my Head*. Hats were still obligatory.

The Women's Education and Head Mistresses' Employment Committees sponsored lectures on nursing, working with children, local government and the Colonies. Progress towards a wider range of topics with new opportunities, and to more personal advice, was slow. Miss Barnes talked to groups and interviewed individuals. Gradually, meetings were held with IV, V and VI, and, later, III. A careers file was begun in 1952. At annual year meetings, parents could discuss their daughters' futures and progress, or lack thereof, with all who taught them. Middlesex' Chief Employment Officer, Miss Wanstell, organised visits of her staff to talk to individuals over 2-3 days.

Material support increased. The Thomas Wall Trust in 1949 invited applications for grants or loans from those in real need. M.C.S. reflected on the girls' good fortune in living in Middlesex, generous with its grants and assisting every year an increasing variety of training. School contributed, the Florence Memorial Fund offered small amounts. An OG later repaid hers, saying that it had enabled her to rest and do college work in the vacation instead of having to take a job. Many applied until State and County provisions expanded. In all, 129 grants were made of £1-£20 at a cost of £900.

By 1958, the Head noted an amazing revolution, although she wondered whether present girls were as enthusiastic in respect of careers, degrees and qualifications as their predecessors. Upset by impatience to take up an easy and lucrative career, she urged them to take advantage of the unique and unrepeatable chances available in their late teens and early twenties, for it was now possible to return to full- or part-time work later on. Marie Curie was her example of combining a wonderful professional life of hard work and service with marriage and a family.

She encouraged a broader outlook by telling parents and girls at Prize Giving what their immediate predecessors were achieving. One year, she cited a prize for Practical Horticulture and the craftsmanship prize for the best technical student at the National Training College for DSc, although she hardly expected a repeat of one triumph – wife of the financial adviser to the Chinese government.

Over the years, 150-160 failed to last the course. Fifty or so left the district, three going as far as Australia, one to New Zealand and one returning to South Africa. Ten transferred to schools nearer their homes or more suitable in ability range or for vocational training. Six passed the entrance examination for Wycombe Abbey. About twenty took jobs – window-cleaner, telephonist, shop assistants, clerks, hairdresser – three, surprisingly, informing school of their marriages. In the early Sixties, unemployment among the under-twenties was below 2%.

A few left against official advice or broke their agreement. One left "with our concurrence", another through "utter laziness". Some had to leave: – hypochondria, travel sickness, parents separated, mother unemployed and father an OAP. One felt that she must help financially when father abandoned mother and five children. For at least three, grants proved inadequate. One had been a temporary admission while mother was in hospital. In sadly difficult circumstances, the doctor advised that, in order to avoid a complete breakdown, another should take life more quietly. One had six months' convalescence from broncho-pneumonia at an open-air school, one lost a year through rheumatic fever, a third was in and out of the Royal Orthopaedic, two repeated a year because of ill-health, one became pregnant and a twelve-year old, Shirley Richardson, died of pneumonia.

Post-war years saw a staggering increase in numbers, 189 or so with a range of at least 18 subjects, going up to universities or university colleges, for such as Exeter and Leicester had not yet attained independent status. There was " as long a queue for places of Further Education as there ever was for a bus or at the fishmonger's!" Candidates took two, three or even four different entrance examinations, one girl, successful ultimately, applying to no fewer than twelve universities. Some faced a difficult choice when a 'lesser' establishment offered a scholarship or exhibition and Oxbridge merely a place. So much depended on the results of HSC/AL and State Scholarship papers. Staff remember October, November and February as perpetual invigilation until 5pm, followed by a trek to the Post Office to send the scripts by registered post. Only three failed to complete their courses. Five more went up later. Girls studied at no fewer than 33 institutions, 66 at constituent units of London (RHC now the favourite with 15). Some 18 went abroad, with VSO or OXFAM. Three continued research, ten became lecturers and one joined the WRAC. More exotic were a student of Anthropology on an island in the Indian Ocean and an adviser on American rural development. Six joined the Civil Service here and in Australia.

197, including PE and DSc specialists, went to at least 48 different Teacher Training colleges; most were House and Sports captains and champions, choir members, actresses, artists. At least 20 had three HSC/ALs, nine gained White Girdles and many held high school office. Sending 16 in 1957, the largest number in any single year, ECS made a modest contribution towards reducing the shortage of teachers. The most popular colleges were Balls Park 12, Goldsmiths and Homerton 9 each. Most taught but 15 changed direction totally.

Other leavers show considerable variety. Twenty worked in shops (including Ciro pearls, one as a trainee buyer), six in medical and welfare work (one later joining the British Embassy in Japan), three telephonists. Other individuals? auctioneer, on the Intelligence Coordination Staff, in New Scotland Yard, Middlesex County Cricket Club, National Advertising Benevolent Society, Evening Adult Education Institute, sorter of industrial diamonds, Goray trainee, Victor Stiebel model, Deputy Warden Cambridge International Centre, breeding and showing Welsh ponies. Less usual then, several spent a year abroad on exchanges, others worked abroad, others settled in the USA 17, Australia 9, New Zealand 8 and in Singapore, Europe and Africa. Two notified their 'betrothals', 515 their marriages and 515 their offspring; at least 10 daughters joined ECS. One died in childbirth, five adopted children and two are known to have married twice.

In all, school recorded what about 1,100 did on leaving.

We have all set forth from the seat of learning in Holly Walk

... convinced that we would conquer the world

The Florence Memorial Fund soon reached £1,600, but fund-raising wisely continued: – Bring and Buy Sale £6:6:6, Bridge Drives £11, a dinner £2:0:6, Frances Perry's sherry parties giving nearly £50 altogether, annual amounts from £5 to £50 being added from general funds. In 1957, a Scripture (later RK) prize was created in Miss Broome's name, which was in addition to the OGA prize of up to 30/- funded in 1952, which was to be awarded, at Staff discretion, to a girl who succeeded in some field not covered by any other award – DSc, Biology, captaincy of games teams. Money was provided in 1951 for Modern Languages and for travel grants in Miss Forrest's name "to cheer her in her very poor state of health".

Loyally supported by the Head, the OGA committee, with Evelyn Dupère as secretary, reconvened, feeling the need to rally round and start up again. "The scope depends entirely on the enthusiasm of its members, and there is no reason why we should not have a society worthy of the old school". Sports clubs never did re-establish themselves; just four replied when badminton was mooted, a netball VII could not be formed, a rounders team lost depressingly to the Sixth. In 1953, approving the new gymnasium, a weekly gym class was patronised exclusively by those deprived of the opportunity to do apparatus work during their gymnasium-less schooldays.

Closer links were forged with school. A Whist Drive brought in £10 to pay for printed information and application form for each leaver, as Miss Sharp warned that if any association is to progress, it must have the younger element. Mary Williams (Mrs Turnbull) gave a regular talk. The Association once organised a leavers' meeting and donated a brooch for the Head Girl – 25 ordered £34:7:6, plus 80 pence for engraving.

The committee became more representative with group secretaries chosen each to represent five years. Two staff members, for long F.S. and Miss Rudkin, were co-opted. Vice-presidents began with Miss Hodgson in 1952 and Elsie Luck (Mrs Gibbons) in 1956.

Life membership rose from 15/- to £1:1:0, 15/- of which was to be invested, then to £1:10:0, the lower amount still allowed for immediate leavers. By 1962, there were 300 lifers. By 1959, 248 annual subscribers paid 2/6 for two years, then, as there was only 2/4 in the bank, 5/-. This overlooked £14:2:0 in the Post Office and some healthy investments. One magazine printed a shaming list of defaulters. Everyone attending a reunion was asked to contribute 6d.

In the summer, OGs and their children (once 120 in brilliant weather) enjoyed the customary sideshows, competitions, tea, tombola, conversation, races (and not only for the children), tennis tournament, rounders, donkey rides and, uniquely, a Punch and Judy Show. An average of 80 attended the AGM and winter reunion, "for games, dancing and the laughter of reminiscence", plus monologues, shadow plays, laughter-raising sketches, musical items, ingenious competitions, square dancing called by Pat Newby, a short play performed by the Metro players, *Auld Lang Syne* and supper, once a Bring a Basket meal. The tireless helpers and generous providers of cakes were thanked. The first time in the New Building, members, marvelling at all they saw, were received in the library and entertained in the Lecture room as the Hall was unfinished. They celebrated Forty Years On. A few socials and dances were held with the Old Boys Association. Bridge Drives, suspended during building operations, were a constant source of both pleasure and funds, participants paying 1/- for cakes and sausage rolls. In 1961, "never have we had such well supported Drives, nor, incidentally, such good profits", which over the years amounted to £56:6:11.

Seventy-five attended the first post-war dinner at Stagg and Russell's restaurant. The following year, nearly 200 dined at Beale's in two rooms, because catering regulations then forbade more than 100 persons in one . At the next occasion in the Hall, Mr Pascal, a familiar figure, was present to hear Eileen Hance sing and Mary Jewell tell of her involvement with Quaker Relief in Germany. Subsequent venues were Miss Forrest's "delightful" Sesame Club (three times), EGS, the Comedy restaurant, and, from 1955, school's new Lecture room.

Two and a quarter magazine pages were devoted to 1952's dinner, tickets 10/6, which no longer covered the cost. "Perhaps the smaller number present is attributable to the general shortage of money". Guest of Honour was Ethel Willmott. Staff were urged to consider that "those ink-stained fingers upraised to attract your attention may well belong to a future Minister of Education. There are those from amongst us of whom the school can feel justly proud. We made our way out into the cold damp night, our hearts warmed by the knowledge that we are each a part of such a flourishing Association". Guest speakers included Kathleen Gibberd, Frances Perry, Mary Flanders, Elsie Smith (on her travels in China), Frieda Goodall, Laone Hammond, Edith Fraser and Doctors Brenda Knudson and Lily Butler: different ages, different expertise.

Presentations were still made to long-serving Staff when they left. A special cheque was given to the Head to replace items lost in a fire in her home. To help school Charities, the Association produced three one-act plays: *One Hour Alone* (Victoria), *Check to the Queen* (Elizabeth I) and *Cats of Egypt* (Cleopatra), with the two professionals, Isobel Henderson and one-time Guest of Honour, Brenda Saunders, known to most through television. "It was difficult to believe that there were only seven performers. The whole entertainment was an outstanding success". The intake of 1945 enjoyed *The Reluctant Debutante* before dining together to celebrate their 21st birthdays.

In 1962, OGs bought 150 copies of the magazine which kept them in touch with friends. The numbers of those choosing to leave Great Britain or emigrating with their husbands, in search of congenial well-paid work grew steadily. Some returned when opportunities proved disappointing, others married foreign nationals.

Intellectual integrity and personal charm

Although it was clear that the Head was, not surprisingly, weary, it was with deepening dismay that all heard of her retirement.

As her departure coincided with her Silver Jubilee as Head, 200 OGs presented Miss Sharp with a refrigerator, a cheque, 25 red roses, a cake adorned with the school crest and a tablecloth embroidered with 270 names and the crest. Staff enjoyed a farewell dinner at West Lodge. The Head Mistresses' Conference took place at ECS in her honour; all were inclined to boast about this, but it was an exceedingly hard-working weekend for Staff.

Never known to raise her voice or lose her temper, the words of her dignified Assemblies were, sadly, not always audible at the back of the New Hall. Prize Givings were made delightful by her comprehensive, beautifully phrased, often witty, review of the year. Her magazine forewords, in which she commented on parochial matters, encouraged a sense of corporate pride. She partnered Mrs Wooldridge in the Staff tennis team to beat all three school couples. At Staff and Sixth playreading , she proved excellent as the Professor in *The Linden Tree*.

Girls appreciated her wide-ranging talks, given particularly, although not exclusively, to the Historical Society: Renaissance Art ("extremely interesting and illustrated by several reproductions of the pictures about which she was speaking"), Abraham Lincoln, Wandering Scholars, Switzerland's history. "No narrow academic, she showed that academic work was always rewarding and could be intellectual fun. She assumed that everyone would give of her best as she herself always did". She judged displays and exhibitions, encouraged the Scripture Union and enjoyed the Shaftesbury Society parties.

She encouraged participation before it became fashionable.

Battling unceasingly to get new buildings for her ever-growing school, she made it into a community. Although feeling submerged by administration – "how many eat dinners, drink milk, how much is spent on science apparatus, whether consumable or non-consumable, how many broken chairs" – she spent hours juggling with the timetable, as people were what mattered. All were conscious of her personal interest in girls' choice of subjects and future ambitions. When she came in 1937, ECS was lit by gas, there were no classes in Physics or Chemistry, there were 21 mainly permanent Staff. On her retirement, there were 50, all graduates except six, and 11 part-timers.

That she was at the height of her powers in the Fifties was increasingly recognised locally and nationally. A vigorous participant in Enfield and Middlesex Consultative Committees, a Governor of several schools and of St Katherine's Training College, an executive member of the august Oxford Society and long-time president of the North London branch of the Historical Association, she represented secondary teachers on MEC for eight years and Head Mistresses on the salary-negotiating Burnham Committee for twelve – ample reason for her invitation to a Buckingham Palace Garden Party. The Middlesex Agreed Syllabus of RE was her work. These bodies benefited from the tact, persuasiveness and sense of humour with which she reconciled differences of opinion.

Each year brought some distinctive outside event: presenting prizes at other Speech Days, being a guest at a luncheon to meet the then Minister of Education, taking the chair at a conference on world citizenship.

Tributes were many. Inspectors were always impressed. Staff benefited from her respect for their professional judgment and the freedom she gave them; most felt that they must try to live up to her expectations. An OG extolled the kindness, helpfulness, understanding and dignity of "a very human person"; seniors valued "the excitement of encountering the keen scholarly mind and the tolerant objective approach". Even sinners appreciated her sympathetic probing to find and remove the cause of the offence.

She could seem an awe-inspiring and remote figure to the juniors, one whose power is unquestioned and who is regarded with great respect. Respect remained; affection crept in. A Thirdformer, Lesley Rayner, summarised M.C.S's achievement: "It is her influence, at times unseen and unrealised by us girls, that has earned ECS such a good reputation for being more than a mere set of classrooms". Many agreed with Eve Barsham: "At all times, her calmness and wisdom were much in evidence, and gravity when the occasion demanded. We owe so much to her leadership during our schooldays". Gillian Staines quoted from *Proverbs*: "She openeth her mouth with wisdom and in her tongue is the law of kindness. She looketh to the ways of her household and eateth not the bread of idleness".

In retirement, never dwelling on the past, never interfering, always interested in school's present and future, she enjoyed Prize Givings and gave a talk on her visit to North Africa's ancient sites. She remained in close touch with the OGA and with individual members.

Death came peacefully in 1984.

PART EIGHT

THE NEW HEAD

CHAPTER FORTY-TWO

'I cannot do it'never accomplished anything,'I will try' has wrought wonders. Mistakes made when trying mean more wisdom for the future.

School's last Head, Miss Iris Hogg, a Mathematician, had helped with dramatic productions and played hockey, tennis and badminton for her college, where she had been Women's President of the Union, and hockey for London University, although her abiding passion was cricket.

Speech Day, soon after her arrival, was her first test. She paid warm tribute to Miss Sharp, who combined "excellent qualities of heart and mind, true scholarship, dignity and graciousness, vision with a sense of reality, and a warm sense of fun", and thanked her for the inspiration of knowing a Head Mistress who seemed not to understand the meaning of self. Unable to be a part of ECS for very long without being fully conscious of the fine tradition, she promised to carry on all that was worthwhile in that tradition.

Having said "may the girls here tonight learn how to disagree without being disagreeable", she, characteristically, commented the following year that statements made by Head Mistresses often create quite a shower of dust, when phrases are quoted out of context, for her remark had been headlined locally, "Don't be disagreeable, says Head Mistress". She changed the 3Rs to the 3Ls: "Look, listen and perhaps learn", and differentiated between false freedom ("to do what I like") and true freedom ("to do what I ought"). It was imperative to strive for something beyond reach, though not unrealistically far away. Aiming for skilfulness rather than a particular skill, she hoped to train girls to face life happily and courageously, to distinguish the important from the trivial, to grapple with ideas and have respect for truth, honesty and pride in a job well done.

In short, "we offer the girls equal opportunity, so that they may grow intellectually, spiritually and culturally; the only limit we recognise is their own individual capacity. Each individual has to discover her own particular bent within *our* attempt to give freedom and discipline to everyone".

"Membership of a community entails the heavy responsibility of conforming to a certain extent", therefore, rules. All must have a purpose, although most always seem unnecessary to pupils, and, indeed, to ex-pupils – "an excessive amount of petty regulations which really didn't have any bearing on life outside; perhaps good preparation for the pettiness of commerce and society". Another recalls that there seemed to be little disobedience and great discipline which "could be fierce, rigorous and unpredictably applied by the 'old school' Staff. If there was too much noise in one classroom during a lesson, you had to sit with your hands on your head". I.K.H. would have been horrified if she had known this.

Her first regulations stressed punctuality. All late comers or early leavers had to sign the list, no girl below VI could go out without a permission slip signed by a member of Staff, a letter was still essential to explain absence, to cover work not done or to explain any non-uniform clothes. Some rules did not change from 1909 to 1966. Forbidden jewellery included small rings in pierced ears, not yet the fashion. Council decided that rings should not be on fingers but on a neck chain. A religious jewel was sanctioned, if inconspicuous, make-up was unsuitable in 1962, allowed in 1964, if discreet; this dispensation did not extend to coloured nail varnish. Running or talking at specified times and in specified places remained forbidden; single or double file at various times could not be maintained. I.K.H. merely stated that school books should be covered; E.R.B. had specified the kind of covering.

Other rules repeated Miss Sharp's decisions. No-one would be responsible for any unmarked property lost on the premises; money should be given to a Mistress for safe keeping, kept in a pursebelt or in a zip-fastened pocket or, during PE, placed in the boxes provided. One girl forgetfully left her busfare (3d) in her blazer pocket. During a search after several thefts had been reported, this was discovered and the culprit banned from a cinema visit. Nor must any money be collected without the Head's permission.

Some bore her own stamp, most after lengthy discussion in Council. There were to be no visits to the Medical room and no eating when in uniform in the street or on public transport. Girls choosing to stay in during the dinner hour must read quietly in formroom or library: greater freedom here. Forbidden were writing on blackboards and notice boards and taking ink into the library (the caretaker's job) and, later, bottles of any kind. Desks must not be joined in pairs. Girls must assemble in allotted places on the hard courts in silence for Fire Drill. Telephone messages were acceptable only in emergency. Non-urgent dental appointments should be out of schooltime. Council fought against the limitation of one rough note book per term: "Signature of Staff in old and new book should curb wastage".

Detention remained *the* punishment. Parents were still asked to sign the explanatory card.

Some even had a sense of humour

"We girls were alert to the divisions of 'Old School' and 'New School' amongst the teaching Staff, the physical separation of Staff rooms" (OSR and NSR) "provided visible proof in our eyes. The best of the 'Old School' were widely respected for their shrewdness in human relations plus bottomless funds of knowledge on the most obscure subjects", although one OG feels that very few came to terms with a pupil as a person. Perhaps she had been one of IIA, caught can-canning on desk tops and made to stand for twenty minutes outside the OSR – "in silence, watching the ceremonial staff teapot being carried hither and thither".

The Head regularly applauded her Staff, referring to marking, preparation, courses of further study, parents' meetings, all after 'hours'. "Teaching is not instruction but giving of themselves". OGs agree. "The range of extra-curricular 'growth' available was enormous, due largely to the love, time and efforts of the Staff who must frequently have felt it a thankless task. ... The quality of the Staff I personally came into contact with, even allowing for the rose-tinted spectacles of time, far exceeded the normal expectation. ... It is said that if you have been well taught, you should be a good teacher yourself. I can only hope there is some truth in that for the sake of the students I now work with. ... School widened my horizons in a way that only those who have experienced a caring educational environment can understand". Another praised their encouragement of self-confidence, individuality, human values and interest in learning and understanding.

The magazine reported that "we count ourselves fortunate indeed that already Miss Hogg has won the respect and liking of Staff and girls alike". She herself was very conscious of, and grateful for, the support of Staff and senior girls.

Staffing became less stable; the average number was 52, of whom a quarter worked part-time; 44 arrived before 1967, eight of whom stayed a year or less; there were three OGs, one had two daughters in school, one was on a year's exchange (the first male since 1919); twenty stayed into the new era. Of those already *in situ*, 27 left before comprehensivisation, including nine part-timers. As Deputy Head ("someone who is everywhere, seemingly indefatigable"), Miss Cox withdrew in 1963, Miss Morley retired in 1966, when I took over (surviving until 1980) in the trying year before ECS 'went' comprehensive.

Administrative and ancillary personnel changed little: Mrs Friars (who spent twelve years on school's finances), Mrs Wheal, Mrs Taylor (secretary) and Mrs Taylor (cook); Charlie King (who after fifteen years at Holly Walk went to Rosemary Avenue), groundsman Tom Pettifer (a familiar local figure), Mr Whitehead, of course, and a rapidly dwindling band of cleaners. A young caretaking assistant apparently appealed so much to some Fifths that "ink was purposely spilt on the floor and the young man called in to clear up the mess, causing us to collapse in giggles. We were forbidden to talk to him at playtimes; he disappeared one day, reputedly given the sack".

Their good will is a real asset

The Head was early aware of the happy leadership and readiness to help when needed of the Prefects. One junior was shaken by the insufferable superiority of this élite. Head and Deputy were photographed with them in their uniform of white blouse, green and white striped tie, prefectoral badge and dark skirt, several wearing ribbons denoting games Colours. Hair is generally short; few wear glasses. Head Girl and Deputy were usually supported by 7-10 Senior Prefects and 16 Prefects. Between 32 and 50 were Sub-Prefects, 9-22 being promoted.

The Sixth once ran an Oxford-Cambridge Penny race, three selling favours. They enjoyed Dances, especially with EGS, who were invited to well-attended lectures on such topics as Tibet and television drama. Staff gave them farewell teas, later coffee parties.

In a decade of naïve optimism, of "an expansion of consciousness", the transition to the Sixth became ever more difficult. One OG, who enjoyed VI, found the idea of a discussion somewhat daunting after five years of submission. I.K.H. appreciated the problem: "Girls will be women, growing up between two worlds, having to adjust to ideas of independence in a world of conflicting desires, interests, standards and beliefs".

Despite being an all-female institution, "the atmosphere was generally friendly but firm".

The stability of a good home

... and a peaceful atmosphere in school are essential for healthy growth of both mind and body.

Yet much conspired to unsettle this generation: icy fog and blizzards forced early closures, smog postponed the school dance, once cancelled because of gate-crashers: visits of HMIs: Reports on Education: changes in the structure of the Borough and of the Governing Body: transport strikes: Beatlemania: Cuban crises: assassination of President Kennedy.

The Head publicly acknowledged "this uncertainty about purpose and the all too frequent changes in social climate which lead the young to so much moral confusion. The problems are of a kind and order of seriousness which has never confronted a similar age group before".

Many magazines reflect this unease. A surprising number hark back to the wars which they never experienced. Mary Hawkins tells how the Professor, once a German prisoner, eventually loses his bitterness and could wish his captors well: "he saw clearly and with certainty that true justice will be done in its own time, for all men are brothers and no society can overcome the intrinsic laws of nature and creation". Fourthformer Sheila Fairbairn writes of a very young man who became a very old prisoner in Japanese hands, his only pet a bug in his rice which he trod on: "God, let me die". Meryl Smith recalled the pact of no fighting on Christmas Day, when "the game of soldiers would be interrupted. Silence was strange and somehow wrong. It allowed them to think and ask questions that would not be answered", instead of being bound to kill and maim in return for honour, glory, shellshock and foot rot.

The future troubled. Hilary Finch worried lest the button be pressed because of man's hatred for man. "Will it happen again?" After reading Music and English at Exeter, she is now a freelance writer on Music. Carol Sykes dreamed of all the people caught in the blinding flash of an atomic war:

> I saw the letters on the tomb.
> They didn't ban the bomb.

A social problem, perhaps after visits by West African students, touched Adèle Griffiths; a young girl, full of *joie de vivre*, applies for a room in London, and has to face the fact that she is coloured. Jocelyn Taylor in *Obituary* for a living poet writes of race riots in Alabama.

The Green issue struck Susan Birkett:

> Old tin cans, bubble gum wrappers, broken bottles,
> Stunted trees, broken fences, petrol cans,
> A waste area of all that's ugly and brutal and utterly
>   abominable.
> ... It goes on being defiled, continues to be contaminated,
> And nobody cares!

Secondformer and future Art student Barbara Aldridge writes *On Being Plagued by Others' Transistor Radios:*

> Beatles, Clark and Rolling Stones ...
> Tuneless, twanging, moaning voice ...
> Must I listen to them too?

Catherine Carlson scourges the TV addict:

> Before the television came,
> John's activeness had brought him fame,
> But with the fiendish goggle box,
> Inertia crept from crown to socks.

Jacinth Brand sums up the extreme despair in *My Generation.*

> Plastic homes with paper people,
> Church with instant concrete steeple,
> Dollar down, you can have a 'plane;
> Just smash it up, come back again.
> Instant coffee; no need to work –
> Waste all the time; try hard to shirk.
> No need for money – goods on tick.
> The telly's got a built-in kick.
> Just for fun, try to kill a man.
> Judgment's in an aerosol can.
> No love, no hate, can't live, can't die.
> Go to church, we could always try.
> Always old, never ever new;
> You must find something else to do.
> Sit and eat dehydrated cheese.
> Run your eyes over naked trees.
> Sit here and wish your life away
> And hope there'll be no other day.
> Hell's no threat; they've just dug it out.
> Tell me, just what is life about?

The increased size of the school prevents social contact

"Girls leave barely knowing their contemporaries, let alone those a year or two above or below". In 1963, 11 new girls were of the second generation. There were usually 120 newcomers to Year I and 22-28 to Year VI; 771 joined ECS during its last Grammar School period, giving an average roll of 800.

Although details of a girl's background were, increasingly, written on her personal file which remains confidential, the family unit was obviously less and less stable: at least thirteen divorces, two stepfathers, two stepmothers, six separations, nine deaths (four fathers, five mothers), two children adopted, one fostered, one in care, one mother permanently in hospital. One mother and several fathers were not to be contacted or had simply disappeared.

A few fathers were unemployed or had retired, three more had dual jobs – taxidriver/baker, postman/ lab. technician, driving examiner/hospital worker. Known occupations remain varied: 88 had manual jobs and/or worked in factories, one even owning one; others were labourers, mechanics, charge hands, foremen, managers, inspectors, skilled men. Engineers and electricians numbered 37, 36 were in retail trade (three proprietors), 35 in building and furnishing, 33 in transport, 28 were clerks/ secretaries, 25 in various professions (education, radio and films, medicine, surveying), 20 wore uniform (including one prison officer), 6 were Civil Servants, whilst individuals were caretaker, gypsy, golf club supervisor with his wife, Grenadier Guards bandsman, nurseryman (just one on the land, so different from years ago) and 'paviour'.

Similarly, not all contributory schools are recorded: 26 came from abroad (two sisters from Mauritius, others from the Antipodes, Barbados, British Guiana and Germany), four from Scotland, two from Wales and one from Belfast, with 18 from different English establishments from Peterborough to Portsmouth, Bedford to Billericay, 19 from what was known as the Greater London area, four from convents, one from boarding, and one from Army, schools. The customary 40 or so local institutions continued to send the majority, main contributors being Merryhills 17, Grange Park 16 and Lavender 11, with 18 sending each just one girl. Palmers Green 40, various convents 30 and Oakwood Secondary Modern 10 provided most of the 75 or so who went into the Sixth.

In fact, the usual variety.

For 478 one name only is listed, for 243 one plus an initial, 24 have two full names and 13 one name and two initials. There were three sets of twins. 73 boasted names unique to this short period, although only 29 are new to school: Alana, Anys, Armelle: Bernadette, Billie, Bonita: Clio, Colleen: Gaynor, Glenda, Glynne: Jacinth: Lexy, Liane, Libuse: Maxine, Michele, Miranda: Nanita, Narriman, Nicola: Rashmina, Rosetta: Shona, Simone: Teri, Tina: Zarah, Zoe. The favourites were Ann/Anne and Elizabeth, both 23, Gillian/Jillian/Gilian 25, Linda/Lynda/Lindy 28, Patricia 29, Margaret 30, Christine/ Cristina/ Christiane 36.

Susan Love, ID, commented on the phenomenon of the new outright winner with 65.

When I came to Enfield County,
I was most surprised to see
The largest batch of Susans
There'd ever been for me.
    There were several in One A,
    And five of us in D;
    It must have been a favourite name
    In nineteen-fifty-three.
When teachers ask a question,
Saying "Susan, answer, do!"
You look at all the others,
And hope it isn't you.
    But if the question's easy,
    Then you all reply at once,
    And even if the answer's wrong,
    You're not the only dunce.
But when you come to write it down
It isn't so much fun;
You have to give your surname;
Then you're the only one.

Forty barrowloads of boiler fuel have to be removed

... from the main fuel store in the Old Building. It is not easy to find labour willing to do this". Could a store, therefore, be arranged at the corner of the OB.?

Such problems were aired at termly Governors' meetings. ECS was grouped with Chace Secondary Boys and Secondary Girls, with whom ties were to become so much closer. Whilst presenting fewer maintenance problems, the New Building housed 750-850 girls by day and was filled to overflowing on four evenings each week with 1,000 or so evening students. The Hall was constantly used by outsiders: for concerts, drama festivals, badminton contests and by Townswomen's Guilds, Allotments and Gardens Association, Scouts, Enfield Brotherhood and Sisterhood. Special difficulties arose with Saturday evening dances, as adequate supervision of both participants and intruders proved impossible. Governors were concerned at reported infringement of regulations prohibiting smoking.

In 1962, the allowance for the upkeep of the building, minor improvements and repairs was £3,410. Complete redecoration was scheduled for the following year, externals costing £2,000. Clocks for eight rooms were deferred for over a year. His request for a new uniform being rejected, Mr Whitehead still had to make do with his original, although he did get a lighting point for a toolshed (£20).

The OB remained difficult. Room 1 and the two Cookery rooms, promised redecoration when the NB was constructed, were still untouched; the work proceeded, in 1966, one room at a time. The linoleum in two rooms was still the original. A faulty flue meant that if the wind were in the wrong direction, smoke was blown into the Old Staffroom. One of the large oak tables therein had woodworm. When the radiators broke down, "we used to jump up and down on the spot, reciting our 14 times table". Electricity cuts were unhelpful.

In 1963, gratitude was expressed for the installation of a bell outside the OB. To the delight of their inhabitants, it too was inaudible in the Huts, which was the point of the exercise. The Fifths always had these prefabricated, but permanent, structures, which saved inconvenience at examination times. Mirrors were provided for their cloakrooms. Heating posed problems, one Courtier stove in a corner proving useless. New name boards arrived for the Holly Walk entrance and by the caretaker's house. By 1966, the new Music room was built onto the end of the Gym, to be replaced in 1994. Rats enjoyed the derelict bicycle sheds; one was dismantled to provide extra parking space. Governors were asked to order drinking fountains for the outside walls. Repaired were chain link fencing £90, close boarded fencing £60, walls and railings £400, the asphalt roof over the DSc room (which needed electric clocks) £350.

In 1966, a fire in one cloakroom damaged girls' property. Less importantly, soap tablets (3d each) were still used, although three times as expensive as liquid soap in dispensers. Their pungency in the dingy rooms is not forgotten.

"The peeling NB showered crumbling plaster and unglued ceiling tiles and rejoiced in the most ghastly rainbow walls and ceilings rumoured to be painted with ends of lines no-one but a local authority would buy. Summer days were spent in a sauna when unlucky enough to have a lesson on the sunny side; jammed venetian blinds thoughtfully provided in some rooms could not repair the basic design fault". More were requested for the NSR, the Office and the Head's room (which was carpeted £40). Windows were "set almost in the ceiling, every sash-cord jammed".

Various improvements and equipment were approved: boarded floors in three rooms £400, entrance hall mats, step-ladder for the Stationery room, eight roller-type blackboards, one portable, and lockers with doors; the old wooden dining tables were replaced with Formica. Bought for the New Hall were a public address system (Council later urging full amplification) and photographic apparatus; brass rubbings were renewed on gold foil by Sixth and Art Staff. Permission was sought to move the Head's telephone.

Supervised after hours and presided over in style by Miss Millen, the new library, "meticulously administered, was an absolute haven for swots". In 1962, the capitation was 4/-, but 8/- for those aged 15+. The old tables were cleaned and reinforced, two new ones with bookrests and pen grooves arrived. Three new bookcases £30 and bookshelves £50 were needed, as, despite ever increasing losses, new books flowed in.

Sixthformers enjoyed special privileges: "there are many books that young adults would like to read and sometimes ought to read if they are going on to universities or colleges, and some such books cannot be on library shelves open to young children". These young adults borrowed and returned on their own, with no losses in the first year. A collection of 'special' books was housed experimentally in a small glass-fronted cupboard. Mrs Denbeigh generously gave 35 volumes, 200 more came through Mr Freakes at the Education Office and 49 from the late Professor Wooldridge. A week-long Penguin book exhibition attracted attention.

The changing room in the gym was chaotic at the change of lessons when three forms left as three arrived. Perhaps a pre-fab could serve for "surreptitious comparisons of pubescent development and anxious concern over when my mother will think I'm big enough for a bra". The showers hadn't worked in living memory. When, later, they did, girls perversely tried to avoid them.

Before 1945, the county paid, termly in advance, for apparatus and equipment. Subsequently, these were purchased from capitation allowance; at this time, the Governors were responsible. The PE department asked for one small trampoline, or trampet, two forms or benches for balancing exercises and two rubber mats 6'× 4'. Two hockey goals and nets cost £60, six tennis nets £35 and six umpire's chairs £120.

An emergency was formally reported in 1963. The connection between the main tank and jockey tank became obstructed, probably due to extraordinary weather. This might have caused an explosion in the boiler house with possible grave effects. The building was evacuated, the Fire Brigade summoned; engineers overhauled the system. The Head requested some form of alarm attached to the safety valves, a fire alarm in the OB: ("The NB alarm automatically calls the fire brigade, which might not always be appropriate") and measures against parked cars which obstructed access.

Regular tribute was paid to the caretakers for keeping school warm and clean, for the hundred and one little jobs they performed, especially when they kept one sweep of the brush ahead of the girls clearing a path through the snow in Miss Hogg's first winter.

We are most anxious to keep up the standards of appearance

In 1963, parents completed a questionnaire on uniform, and, specifically, its purchase; 229 were completely satisfied with D.H.Evans, 178 did not wish to change the supplier, whilst 163 more, although happy with the service, still regretted the journey to London. Telephoned orders were dealt with promptly, service was quick and efficient, delivery excellent. 151 were dissatisfied, criticising the accounts department, badly fitting garments, delays, lack of stock and insufficient visits to school. 345 supported the idea of a second supplier locally. Discussions were prolonged. D.H.Evans promised to come eight times in the following two terms to take measurements and orders, bringing with them a small 'travelling shop'.

In school's own store, small articles of new uniform were available as well as second-hand uniform in good condition at reasonable prices. Outgrown items were welcomed, especially shorts, skirts and gaberdines. In 1966, anything unsold was sent to OXFAM.

Parents received a uniform list and suggestions for dyeing or secondhand purchase if costs were prohibitive. All garments cost more. Basic requirements hardly changed: green pinafore tunic (58/11 – 73/6) or green skirt for seniors (flared 50/9 – 58/6, Terylene 80/6 – 92/6): any dark green or black belt, not of elastic, not more than 2½" wide: white blouse, short or long sleeves (cotton 17/9 – 22/6, poplin 23/6 – 29/9): black knickers (soon to be known as briefs, from 6/3). The cotton summer dress was unchanged. Socks could now be white, fawn, grey, dark green, or, later, black, from 2/11, although in the severest winter, they didn't keep the wind out. A shoebag, once essential, now became a good idea to hold shoes, black, brown or dark green, "with low or flat heels, of a practical shape and reasonably waterproof". Boots were deemed unsuitable for wear inside the building.

Optional items included: dark green cardigan or pullover (26/9 – 37/6) or handknitted: blazer (63/6 – 81/6): bottle green or navy overcoat or raincoat with detachable hood (£6:17:6 – £8:15:9) or, later, a white or off-white full-length poplin mack. Notes, signed by the Head, were sent home on occasion: "As your daughter has probably told you, we have been looking at school coats and we are sorry to find that her coat does not comply with the school pattern".

Trousers were still, of course, unthinkable for girls and Staff.

Games required a white, cellular teeshirt (16/6 – 18/6), plimsolls (9/11 – 12/3) and shorts (25/- 38/-). Council considered that the wearing of such garments indoors in winter should not be enforced and also complained against doing PE barefoot in the Gym: splinters, verrucas, dirt. A green overall (28/11 – 35/6) was still needed for Science and a white apron for Third Year Cookery.

In short, "high fashion trends are not suitable as part of a school uniform which is designed for continuous daily use. Any extreme of design in any garment is usually unsuitable".

Uniform was regularly reviewed. No longer black, berets (badges 2/3) were accepted for expeditions but much disliked, girls feeling degraded and ridiculous because of social custom and the complication of modern hair styles. Failed proposals included headscarves, a new style blouse and the abolition of ties. The whole school voted more than 3 to 1 against the introduction of a school badge or brooch.

1965 brought a transformation. Because many parents felt the present skirt was inadequate for cold weather, a referendum was held on the possibility of changing to tweed. School was overwhelmingly in favour. A green mixture Harris tweed skirt, made to measure, from D.H. Evans would cost about £4. Material was on sale at school for about 27/6 a yard. Especially woven in the Hebrides, it was expected to be hard wearing and good value for money.

In addition, an inexpensive green duffle coat, about £5 and hitherto frowned upon, was also made exclusively by the store. Cardigans and pullovers, twin sets in the Sixth, would be of a lighter ash green. Sally's Wool Shop stocked the wool. Stockings would henceforth be fawn or brown only, and socks fawn, brown or white, as green and black ones would be unsuitable with the new jumpers and skirts.

A transition time for wearing out 'old' uniform was naturally accepted. D.H. Evans' representative now visited fortnightly on Wednesdays, and the cooperation of parents was sought, with the result that the account for one six-monthly period was £2,739, which gave a discount to school of £68:96.

HEAD GIRLS

1962 Harriett Lott	1963 Susan Martin
1964 Lindsay Tattersall	1965 Juliet Thompson

1966 Sheila Cadge

Additional School Colours

1965 J. Barry, L. Rayner, W. Wragg   1966 S. Clarke, J. Spurgeon

CHAPTER FORTY-THREE

We had to practise for weeks ahead

Prize Givings, junior and senior, remained the highlights of the year, officially, socially, musically, sartorially and academically. Head and Staff wore academic gowns; the Hall was packed; the select few – Mayor, Education Committee members, Governors and platform guests – were 'received' afterwards with coffee. Inevitably, there was repetition in Reports and speeches, but the event retained general, if not unanimous, approval. Programmes expanded as numbers of girls and openings increased.

Juniors heard a range of gentlemen including the Chairman of Edmonton Petty Sessions and the Head of a Bechuanaland college. In 1967, Miss Sharp spoke at the last of its kind. Seniors were honoured by John Freeman broadcaster, Edmund Blishen author, Ven. Martin Sullivan Archdeacon of London, and by such eminent women as Dr Margaret Adams OBE, Dame Kitty Anderson, and, in 1967, Professor Margot Jeffreys, "when we are celebrating the old in the midst of the new after a triumphantly successful last year". The usual hand-hurting task confronted them.

Queuing up outside the Gym
before confronting the question papers

Over the five years, 144 sat 386 AL Arts subjects, 123 took 333 Science subjects. Distinctions were gained in two years. Arts prizes totalled 44, Sciences 33. OL grades were recorded irregularly, but it is clear that 269 passed in six or more subjects, 217 in four or five. Staff had been involved in local and regional board panels prior to the introduction in 1966 of the Certificate of Secondary Education (CSE), intended for 'the next 40%'. All 25 candidates passed in Arithmetic, all 25 in Mathematics, and all 18 in French, with 12, 2 and 11 respectively achieving Grade 1, regarded as equivalent to an OL Pass. Examination girls did not receive Good Work Certificates; 120 Fifthformers received prizes.

The first Year Sixth, 57 when Miss Hogg arrived, grew to 190 by 1966: 107 Arts, 62 Science, 21 Secretarial. These last girls, encouraged by visits, took RSA Typing (50 passes), Shorthand (45, including four at 100wpm, 2 at 90, 25 at 80), and, in 1966, Accounts (14). They won 12 prizes and 15 certificates, VIB Science 16 and 17, and the larger VIB Arts 24 and 26.

The awards over the period were Year I, 53P, 80C: Year II, 55 and 76: Year III, 46 and 81: Year IV 56 and 87. Specialist prizes were Forrest junior 10 and senior 12, OGA 7, Broome and Florence 6 each, David Mason 5, Classics 4, H.M's for English 3, Webb for Science 2, Physics 1. This gives the staggering total of 382 Good Work certificates, 515 prizes and, at least, 33,300 external examination subject certificates.

A number of seniors had Saturday jobs. A local firm sent this enlightened note: "Before we make any arrangements, we like to enquire that the applicant would have your support, since we realise how important it is for young people to have leisure or even time for study at weekends. We appreciate, of course, that should examinations occur in the future, it might be wiser to give up the post temporarily or permanently".

Youth Employment Officers talked to parents of senior girls and spent days interviewing their daughters.

158 leavers from the Sixth went to universities and 270 more to FE of all kinds. For those who came during these years and left in Comprehensive days, the figures are 134 and 230, giving a grand total of 292 and 500. Facing stiff competition, several secured places at different establishments on varying conditions. In 1965-1966, all would-be students attained minimum necessary conditions. Only two did not survive their course. Pressure was certainly exerted on intelligent girls whose backgrounds never suggested such ambitions. Miss Hogg felt it "a source of sadness that a school's reputation should be based purely on academic successes. The lives of the young are unhappily dominated by the need to surmount one educational hurdle after another".

London was the obvious choice for the majority, 29 at 15 different colleges. Special wide-ranging discussion classes were enjoyed by those taking entrance papers for Oxbridge, 9 achieving Oxford entrance (St Hilda's 6) and 4 at Cambridge. In double figures were Bristol 15,

Birmingham 13 and Reading, which held Open Days, 11; 27 other English, Welsh and Scottish universities accepted ECS girls.

Ten went on to Colleges of Advanced Technology (CATS). Despite the extension of the course to three years from 1962, 167, of whom 20 were PE specialists, studied at no fewer than 53 English and Welsh Teacher Training Colleges, or Colleges of Education as they were now designated. Balls Park accepted 12, 14 took individuals.

Trainings now show greater variety. At least 55 followed Secretarial courses, mainly in London, including Holborn 11; another 69 went to Technical Colleges which often had a secretarial basis, such as Southgate 39 and Tottenham 20. Ten trained at Turnford, three at the College for Comptometer Operators, two each at Glasgow Central College of Commerce and London College of Fashion, and one at the School for the Deaf.

Their posts varied too: banks 47 (Bank of England 10), insurance and building societies 36, Local and Central Government and Civil Service (including the Treasury) 28, general business 28, Public Utilities 11, Welfare 7 (one with the Distressed Gentlefolks' Association): accountancy, advertising, broadcasting: the Design Centre, Fire Research Station, libraries, newspapers. Non-secretarial work offered increasing choice: cartography, chemical research, display work, factories, singing, nursery schools, riding, telephone operating, travelling abroad, the Services. Shops took 13 at all levels; tennis champion, House Captain, magazine artist Wendy Wragg began as a trainee with John Lewis, working on the shop floor then in personnel.

What happened to 99 on leaving is unknown, although some had been secretarily trained; 51 moved or left for domestic reasons, one staying a week, another 18 days; 7 or so changed to local schools, one was withdrawn by parents, another went to a residential institution, 3 to boarding schools. In all, 27 emigrated: Australia 11, Canada 4, South Africa 3, Cyprus, Germany and Italy 2 each, Aden, Ireland and Portugal. School knew of 85 marriages, 4 divorces and 64 offspring.

Leavers still attended the annual London Service.

We thank all our Music teachers

In the EMF, juniors gained first prize in 1963; seniors obtained high marks in two classes, but could not feel the same sense of achievement as no other schools competed. Henceforth, girls competed individually.

Musical activity was intense. Two annual Prize Givings imposed a double burden. "You had to learn the words of *Jerusalem*. otherwise you were doomed to failure". Small choirs usually sang part-songs unaccompanied: *Pipe, Shepherds, Pipe, My Fisher Lad.* Choice was wide. Juniors practised ten songs, for example, *Where'er You Walk, Nymphs and Shepherds, In Derry Vale.* Seniors learned 15, including *Cronos the Charioteer, I wandered lonely as a Cloud, O can ye sew cushions?* A comic item usually stole the show – *Dr Faustus, Little Polly Flinders, The Deaf Old Woman.*

Carol Services, again junior and senior, followed a regular pattern. A member from each year read the different stages of the Christmas story, different forms and groups sang in English and French – *In Nightly Stillness, Nous allons à Bethléhem, Here is Joy for every age, Voici Noël* – and a member of Staff closed the afternoon with prayer. School sang many delightful carols, conventional (*The Holly and the Ivy*) and less usual (*Good Morrow, Masters All*), as well as time-honoured hymns.

In 1965, for the first time, everybody went to Christ Church, Chase Side; a donation and a letter of thanks were sent to the police for help in crossing roads.

The summer concert included vocal, clarinet, harp and violin solos. Two new clarinets were acquired; it was proposed that a 'cello be bought with money borrowed from School Fund. Miss Hosken and a German Assistant sang, and, of course, Miss Benjamin played the piano – "this instrument became overheated as it was in the Lecture room used as a dining annexe". Seniors formed a Guitar group which played at Assembly. Junior and middle school choirs performed the Jazz cantata *Daniel.*

GCE classes heard Leonard Bernstein lecture at the Albert Hall where IV and V listened to the Vienna Boys' Choir. Different groups enjoyed a Brahms' *Requiem* (Festival Hall), the Camden Players, Campoli, opera and ballet – *The Bartered Bride, Dido and Aeneas* (St Pancras Town Hall), *The Masked Ball, Cinderella.*

Those who pursued their pleasure in music were Barbara Hartston (Guildhall School), Fay Freeman, weekend riding instructor, member of debating and Historical societies (Durham) and Elizabeth Hetherington, member of the Enfield Youth Orchestra (London College of Music).

Additional part-time teachers were Mrs Annette Gates, Mrs Judith Kelner, who, with *Adventures in Music*, began a series of musical appreciation concerts for children. No-one can overestimate what individuals and ECS owe to Miss Benjamin.

We are conscious of our debt to the Art department

Prince, princess, ugly sisters, mice, pumpkin, horse, carriage, fairy godmother, witch, the clock at 12 – all in *Cinderella* at Christmas appeared larger than life in paper sculpture, suspended from the ceiling. *The Sleeping*

Beauty, St George and the Dragon, Alice in Wonderland received similar treatment. Figures and animals were based on Botticelli's *Mystic Nativity,* green devils being created from hundreds of painted egg cones. The winning theme of a form competition was *The Magic Roundabout.* Parents were invited to evening displays; voluntary donations yielded £15 for the WVS and six more eggs in each OAP parcel. School's Christmas card once featured two designs from *Alice.* The Art department virtually took over the layout of the magazine, with designs for pages and drawings to complement contributions.

Sixths once held an exhibition of their sculpture, pottery, jewellery, pictures and fabrics. IVB heard a lecture on Glass. The successful competition for Saturday morning places at Hornsey continued, 15 winning scholarships in one year alone.

Mrs Hargrave remained the moving spirit, Miss Rhodes' name appeared in *Who's Who.* New part-timers were Mrs Margaret de la Salle (1963-1966), Mrs Sheila Black (1967-1972, who exhibited ceramics) and Mrs Daphne Harvey (1963-1978).

Fourteen chose Art at eight different colleges as far apart as Cambridge and Plymouth, with three at Hornsey. Elizabeth Grint (Holborn), won the consolation prize from Enfield Chamber of Commerce for a new badge design. Senior Prefect and House Captain Susan Aldridge is not untypical of these trainees: with choral and orchestral accomplishments, she, in 1973, gained Honours in Graphics at Middlesex Polytechnic.

A longing for the comprehension of life and true knowledge of God

Trying to explain the colour of baked beans and God to her small brother who asked who made the first god, "there is only one god, I announced. I thought about this statement and was slightly surprised to find that I believed it. It seemed a most illogical thing for a 1966 teenager to believe, judging by all the things one reads about 1966 teenagers". Thus Mary Dixon's prizewinning magazine entry.

Several pieces show concern with the eternal verities which were increasingly questioned. Catherine Carlson longed to

> Bridge the gap that yawns between ourselves
> And oneness with God.

Angela Harris asked *How Far is it to Bethlehem?*

> In this Modern Age, it's but
> A brief jet trip away,

but decided that the pilgrimage lasts a whole lifetime.

With support increasing, junior and senior Scripture Unions flourished. Mary Leonard could feel in 1962 that the Union was really representative of the senior school. Membership cards were issued to about 40, although it remained 'open house'. A team system was inaugurated which encouraged regular attendance.

Staff, clergy, OGs, missionaries and visitors talked about personal experiences, different denominations and church unity, the Dead Sea Scrolls ("absorbing"), smuggling Bibles into Spain; Terry Dene, ex-pop singer, "gave his testimony". At a leavers' meeting, four recent leavers spoke of the way in which Christians were received in offices, universities and factories.

Discussions were wide-ranging: textual (the ten commandments), doctrinal (The Devil), political (Christianity and Politics), conceptual (prayer, honesty, temptation) and practical (How to run a Church Youth Club, the Christian's attitude to pop music, the Colour Bar, the use of Sundays). A series of meetings pondered the Armour of God. Girls joined EGS to consider Christianity in the emergent countries. Some took part in an SCM conference. Bible studies, always popular, grew more lively "through using the Candle, Question and Arrow method".

The Fifth form Challengers sang Gospel songs to a packed audience; twentieth century hymn tunes, compiled and taped by Sandra Channon, were well received. Members occasionally took Assembly, the rejuvenation of which exercised successive Councils. The sung hymn, mostly ignored, was discontinued. Girls sat, form members took over from the Form Prefect on Mondays, the orchestra played on Fridays.

Members discovered a synagogue and Coventry Cathedral; the Inter-Schools Christian Fellowship organised a ramble. They visited old folk and were impressed by the friendly atmosphere of a Barnardo's Home.

House Captain Helen Smart read Theology at Sheffield and Nola Parsons studied at the London Bible College. Two went abroad after training colleges; for Sylvia Coombs, two years with VSO in Sierra Leone preceded ten years in the Solomon Islands. Helen Ford worked in a Bangladeshi hospital.

Staff remained unchanged.

Compassion is one of the greatest gifts of Youth

In those days of Mods and Rockers, gang fights, vice and violence, Miss Hogg commented publicly on the deep natural concern within many young people. One Sixth form collected £600 for various charities. Grateful for their own schooling, they specified that some of the money should enable a girl in an undeveloped country to obtain an education. Julia from

Scene shifting, "The Immortal Lady"

"Much Ado"

Milk at break

School uniform, Miss M.C. Sharp, M. Mackenzie, P. Butt

Miss I.K. Hogg, BSc, Head Mistress

Bechuanaland appreciated their generosity. Girls continued to send squares to the Shaftesbury Society and to refugees, for whom they knitted babies' garments; apples sold at Break helped to fund these one year. Cadets collected for a generator to supply night-time electricity at an African hospital. Occasional lectures (Nepal, the National Young Life Campaign) stimulated interest.

Although "desks and chairs do need smoothing", some girls wanted less spent on amenities. Of 1962-1963's collections (£264:19:4), £202:6:0 went to good causes; generally, 80% helped the less fortunate. They voted, sensibly, to be told where their money was to go, even though that sometimes meant diminished support.

Previously specified targets benefited most. Mr Whitehead's Christmas parties continued to thrive. Dances, to which boys were invited, helped to provide £60 for OXFAM, £150 for the Pestalozzi Home. A jumble sale and parents' social financed a party for old people for two years; Rotarians ferried them to school, where each guest enjoyed entertainment, a present and flowers. One OAP received £15. One VIA collected clothes for an East End parish. Princess Elizabeth Day raised over £26, Freedom from Hunger £50:12:6. In sympathy with Miss Hogg on her father 's death, £8:6:8 was sent to St Christopher's Home.

For Miss Campbell's annual summer party for severely disabled children, there was no shortage of willing parents to transport the 24 youngsters; V and Mrs Swift provided an appetising tea, V Alpha organised games (Pinning the Trunk on an Elephant), III brought toys and others their pets. Each child received a small present and a posy. Sixth formers attended their school's Open Day. Linda Gilroy in her wheelchair followed some lessons, hoping for a Training College place for the physically handicapped.

The biggest single effort came in 1966, when 144 men, women and children in the small mining village of Aberfan were killed under an avalanche of wet coal waste. Donations of more than £1,750,000 came from more than 40 countries. Girls requested a collection and sent £103.

"We hope that greater effort will be made in the future". National Savings averaged £840 annually; enthusiasm was greater among the seniors and in the first years of the period, but attitudes towards saving money were changing.

This is a dangerous, highly infectious organism

The common pest which Leslie Burton was describing "is that peculiar specimen, the Latin teacher. It gives warning of its presence by rattling off declensions at a rate alarming to hear. If this danger signal is heard, it is advisable to disappear immediately. It has a dangerous habit of firing off awkward questions in a manner of a machine gun, always at the most unexpected time, especially if you happen to be engrossed in a netball match which is being played under the window. If the disease takes, which it usually does, the budding linguist will be hic-haec-hoccing happily along with the rest. Sometimes, it is fatal, in which case the unfortunate victim develops into yet another Latin teacher, to descend upon an unsuspecting world".

Miss F. Sharp returned part-time, and, with the Thirds, gave another demonstration of the Direct Method. Mrs Parker retired, receiving from the OGA a coffee set and tributes to her "happy and witty personality". Mrs Crisp took over the department. Miss Elder and Mrs Denbeigh remained.

In the Classical Association's competitions, girls regularly reached the finals in Greek and Latin Verse Speaking, winning several prizes. An 8-strong Greek Chorus came third and two won the Dialogue. Joyce Clarke compared ancient and modern Rome to the detriment of the latter, although "the idea that everything is temporary, as life itself is, imparts a certain gaiety to the people". Girls travelled to Cambridge for *Œdipus Rex* and *Œdipus Tyrannus* or to Bradfield, this time for Euripedes' *Hippolytus*. A group saw a film based on *Electra* in modern Greek with a Greek cast.

Four pursued Classics. Ann Hoose took a job, winning, six years later, a scholarship to Oxford, and, ten years later, studied Chinese. Two Senior Prefects: Winifred Upson also went up to Oxford after achieving form, English and Classics prizes and AL Greek in one year before becoming a Speech and Language therapist: Carol Masters, Dramatic Club organiser, French and Classical Verse Speaking winner, gained a scholarship to, and a First at, Bedford before running County Guiding training and teaching English to foreigners. House Captain and choir member Diane Clarke graduated from Reading.

Life in Paris never really stops

The Eiffel Tower delighted Stephanie Ebbels: "we were in a world of our own dominating Paris". Individual holidays gave considerable impetus to Modern Languages learning. Susan Gardner's *Promenade Nocturne* shows a range of both vocabulary and grammatical structures. Some were paying guests for up to eight weeks. Two girls, after 29 hours of travelling, spent Holy Week at a college in Valladolid, three stayed in Pontevedra, "rewarding in spite of the arduous journey". Exchange visits were arranged for Galicia; girls were interviewed on Spanish radio. Jacqueline

Hales wrote entertainingly of bricks dropped during three weeks with a family.

"Miss Hogg drove down to Folkestone to wish us *bon voyage*". With Mr and Mrs Leigh, school holidays, fully subscribed, really took off, eight per year becoming the norm. Slides were shown at subsequent social evenings with parents.

Most loved was Switzerland. "When midnight struck, we toasted everyone in apple juice – wonderful and unforgettable". Murren became the favourite venue, the Hôtel Touriste being totally reserved for them. Igloo building contests, excursions, walks, learning to ski, skate and toboggan, crossing icefields, breathtaking chairlifts – never a dull moment.

Italy: coach tours included at least eleven towns from Lugano to Rome, Pompeii to Pisa and Florence, with a friendly, helpful driver, who initiated them into the art of eating spaghetti. Cruising from Venice through the Corinth Canal, seeing the Parthenon illuminated and national dancing, on to Rhodes and Sounion, proved an unusual and enjoyable holiday.

Austria, once with far from successful skiing, once with walks and excursions, gave pleasure, as did Yugoslavia. Another party stayed in Grasse, exploring, bathing, being driven by a wild driver and returning bronzed or burnt, full of memories and laden with gifts. Appalling weather meant a somewhat disappointing visit to Denmark and Sweden; undaunted, they planned a trip to Finland and Russia. A few joined adults for America and Canada.

Whilst many of the facilities on the boat left much to be desired, "one of the many experiences in the true sense of the word", was to Tenerife, where they stayed in a high-class hotel and went up a volcano.

German pupils saw films of *Wilhelm Tell*, *Tor under Tod* and *Wir Wunderkinden*, and performances by students from the Max Reinhardt Drama School, and continued their annual Christmas parties. In 1966, out of 33 schools with some 300 entries, ECS came fourth in Verse Speaking , with Patricia Abbott (Bristol), Patricia Davison and Linda Williams as finalists.

Spanish students ran their own club; eight reached the finals of the All-England Speech contest, gaining third and fourth prizes, and in the Drama section came second with *La Zapatera Prodigiosa*, which they had seen at King's College. Linda Wallace (City of Westminster College, translator for Unilever) won first place and Memorial prize in 1964's Speaking competition and wrote two short, somewhat depressing, poems, *San Esperanza* and *Transito.*

In Year IV, an average of 15 began German and 20 Spanish, with about half continuing to AL. During any one year, over 700 were learning French;

113-137 took OL, 30-40 AL, other Sixthformers continuing the subject with no examination in mind.

French record and film recitals featured Classical and Romantic writers. Girls were fortunate to see plays: *Le Barbier de Séville* (at Notre-Dame de France), *Tartuffe* by La Comédie Française, *L'Alouette, Le Cid* and *Phèdre* at the French Institute.

Miss Russell and Mrs Leigh remained. The French department saw changes. Miss Sparkes left to become a Deputy, subsequently a Head, returning to speak to the OGA. OG Susan Page (Mrs Pettifer, 1962-1967) came back later, as did both Mrs Kelsey and Mrs Gething. Mrs Frances Hills (1966-1986) worked part-time, Miss Phillips (1959-1963) married and moved. Miss Daphne Giles (1965-1972) became Head of Department.

Girls attended a conference on careers in languages; many combined French with secretarial subjects. The French Institute offered, by examination, 120 places to 450 candidates: Josephine Stiff came 60th and Marion Moore (later bilingual secretary to Economic and Industrial Counsellors) 25th. From Holborn, Linda Eastwood went into the Foreign Office, House Captain Janice Heskell joined the commercial branch of the Spanish Embassy in Mexico before working in a news agency. Secretary, translator, interpreter, Barbara Winks, Associate of the Institute of Linguists, gained a diploma in Theology to become a secretary to a pastor in Germany and to the United Bible Societies, and Margaret Alexander was accepted for French Special at Training College.

Among the 19 university students of Modern Languages (one with English, another with Speech and Drama) were: Oxford, Elizabeth Hume (AL Latin in one term, four distinctions) and Ann Hedge, who both taught: London, Jacqueline Barry (rounders*, netball*), Pamela North (Spanish and Portuguese), Margaret Purry (librarian and research), Carin Schwarzloh (accordeonist), Patricia Thompson (junior and senior tennis champion): Bristol, Michèle Galat (French and Philosophy) and future Head Lesley Williams (gym*, Broome and Art prizes): Southampton, Jennifer Lane (teaching): Newcastle, Catherine O'Neill (German and Danish): Reading, artist Margaret Stevens (German and Dutch), Lesley Tanner (Botswana, then teaching): Bradford Institute of Technology, Dawne Brown (French and Spanish translator/interpreter for an engineering firm).

Field trips embarked on with enthusiasm

The Sixth "heavily laden hikers" remembered wonderful expeditions, together with a variety of souvenirs ranging from Geological specimens to old sheep's bones which were not welcomed warmly at home, torrential rain, Youth Hostel bed bugs, jam sandwiches, coach breakdowns, drawing field sketches and making notes; they lost their shoes in bogs, they trekked through forest mists; some found the pace at Ambleside too fast, but a younger member of Staff notably brought up the rear. Others spent working holidays on various courses, attended a conference, heard a lecture, with the Physicists, on meteorology. Seniors went to Greenwich, Thirds delighted in the Docks, Seconds the Commonwealth Institute, Firsts their customary tour of Enfield.

The only unusual expenditure recorded was £30 for " one globe suspension".

Apart from showing one film to the juniors, the 26 members of the Young Trawlers' Union contributed £7 and sent stamps and silver paper to HQ, although not enough magazines were salvaged. Miss Pyett's invaluable help was appreciated.

Miss Coster received best wishes for her new work as a Head. Her equally hardworking successor, Miss Jane Mancus (1963-1971) was particularly noted for a cabaret act with Miss Benjamin! Mrs Wooldridge and Mrs Luxon remained.

Six read Geography, including Queen's Guide Jean Barclay and Angela Popham who subsequently gained MA in Social Geography at Sussex. With a degree in Town Planning, Mary Woodroffe became Senior Assistant to East Herts District Council.

After being shown round, we thanked the guide

The History department continued the time-honoured expeditions. Seniors delighted in Windsor and, once, in a coach drive to Westminster Pier for a riverboat trip. By the Cutty Sark, they wondered how long it would be possible to offer nails from the ship as souvenirs. Seconds visited the Tower annually, once being startled, whilst eating their lunch on Tower Green, by a 42-gun salute for the King and Queen of Greece. Ten who did well in examinations toured the Royal Mint, which they found noisy; they had to hand in cameras but were allowed to hold coins. Six won prizes for work based on expeditionary work. The British Museum was, of course, known to every Firstformer, as was Verulamium, where, one year, exhausted by the lecture, hypocaust, Roman Wall, theatre, excavations and making notes for their projects, "in the middle of our programme, we ate our packed lunches".

Trips further afield gave great pleasure: to Cambridge: a peaceful and uneventful journey to Oxford on a typically English spring morning of low cloud and heavy drizzle. Shooed rather than shown round Blenheim Palace, they then spent a pleasant hour wandering through the grounds.

Visitors covered many topics: the work of an archivist and of an MP, Local Government and Education (Alderman Mackenzie), Prime Minister and President (Hansard Society), the Reformation, the Norman Conquest, the History of Science (Historical Association), Parliamentary procedures (Shirley Williams) which some saw for themselves, current economic policy (an MP). Individuals joined conferences on the Renaissance, World Hunger (one of CEWC's annuals), the problems of the newly independent countries and the work of VSO (Royal Commonwealth Society). Three thousand Sixthformers, including eleven from ECS, heard two MPs, discussed in groups, reported back and enjoyed a concert and dance (with the Twist). Proceedings were followed at Council debates and Magistrates' Court. Girls participated in an Inter-Schools Civics Quiz.

Two extra holidays were appreciated: July 5, 1965 for Magna Carta Day, and in 1966 for the Election, after holding, of course, their own version.

Most activities were arranged by the ever-inventive Head of department, Mrs Martin. Replaced by Mr Hupert, Miss Pyett spent one year in Virginia; she was Business Manager for one play. Miss Eileen Swaffield (1965-1967) sang at a Carol Service.

Fifteen followed traditional History courses, all deserving mention as House Captains, Prefects and award winners. Senior Latin and Historical Association prizewinner, Marilyn Gallyer (swimming*, tennis*) was an active Young Conservative: Carol Crowe, a "polished, regal actress", formed a junior dramatic group, won French prizes and was accepted into the Civil Service Administrative Class. Three won David Mason prizes: Averil Jones (gym*, Forrest and senior verse prizes) from Oxford joined the John Lewis partnership: Susan Gardner (Golden Jubilee prize and "a convincing male actress") told with maximum action and speech and minimal description, of early American days in *The Tattered Banner* and became the first Simmonds Student before going up to University College: DHG Joyce Clarke, with a First from Bristol, did Social work with the Commonwealth Service Group. Helen Howl read Ancient History and Archaeology.

After an active school life, three read Law: Pamela Carter, Stephanie Fitt and Gillian Gardner (OGA and Best Plant Collection prizes) who went into Social Administration, then to Social Science.

As scope widened, 25 took sociological subjects – Political Economy, Statistics, Comparative and General Studies – with interesting careers both at school and after university. Nine studied Economics in 1965, still with EGS. Mary Leonard (choir, Cadet) went from LSE to casework in the East End, Susan Lisney (David Mason) to VSO, Susan Quick to Saudi Arabia and Susan Phillips (House Captain, choir, Tawny Owl) to teach, as did

Susan Clapham. Actress Carol Fisk read Sociology then Psychology, qualified as a shorthand typist and worked her way from the BBC typing pool to be assistant to Melvyn Bragg and Martin Bell in the USA, before becoming TVam US correspondent – and a light aircraft pilot.

I came expecting to see schoolgirls acting, but I saw Shakespeare

Miss Hogg commented thus on *Hamlet*; the magazine agreed, whilst feeling that it seemed a curious choice for girls. This, Miss Cox's fifteenth, was her most ambitious.

Rehearsals always began after summer examinations. The sombre but versatile set, the rich costumes, the at times inspired lighting all contributed to a visually exciting performance. Not everyone received unstinted praise. Claudius was somewhat ill at ease, Gertrude had a tendency to drop her voice, Laertes offered great sincerity but also some inaudibility, Horatio's voice was too light and one Polonius was a bit too comic.

Both Hamlets avoided the trap of copying famous actors; Margaret Keeling was "warmer and sympathetic", Alexandra Romanes more militant in her thoughtful and individual interpretation. She doubled as Ophelia with Juliet Thompson, "delicate and far away". As well as the Head's prize for English, Alexandra was a finalist in junior Latin verse speaking and went, as did Margaret after university, to the Rose Bruford School of Speech and Drama, subsequently gaining a six months' contract in open competition. Her 126-line magazine poem told how St Simeon Stylites reached patience and self-knowledge. Later publications were short stories (read by Bernard Cribbens on radio) and five children's novels; she toured with her one-woman show, *This Creeping Worm*, and ran Maypole Dancing at the annual Sidmouth Folk Festival. Juliet (tennis*) trained at Holborn, but, sadly, died young.

In 1965, Miss Flint allowed the girls to perform her *Merely Players*, an ingeniously linked series of scenes which offered varied acting roles and opportunities for crowd work. Forty-three performed on a small stage with a many-levelled set, designed, as always, by Mrs Hargrave and erected, as always, by Mr Whitehead. Girls participated in prompting, stage managing, make-up, catering, musical and wardrobe work. "The whole school had that feeling of unity which comes from experienced skilful production allied to devoted effort from everyone concerned, seen and unseen".

Euripides' *Iphigenia in Aulis* was Miss Elder's choice; boys helped with lighting and set. Singer, clarinettist, cast of nine main, at least thirty minor, actresses, all were naturally delighted when, according to *The Times Educational Supplement*, the audience broke into spontaneous applause.

Grammar School Staff made history by inviting ECS girls to take part in *Measure for Measure*. Dürrenmatt's *The Visit* was a joint production in which nine girls acted, seven were townsfolk, four helped with wardrobe, two with make-up and one prompted. As talented actresses would be deprived of their parts, school felt unable to reciprocate.

Dramatic interest was further stimulated by seeing Shakespeare's plays at Stratford, *She Stoops to Conquer* by Enfield Youth Theatre and by films.

The Upper VI helped juniors with several performances – *It Happened that Night, The Princess and the Swineherd* ("a charming fairy tale"), *The Sleeping Beauty* and *Snow White*. They also enjoyed demonstrations of fencing, stage make-up (Mrs Hargrave) and of puppets and marionettes (Miss Morley). One year, they performed their own plays, judged by Mrs Effendovicz, subsequently entertaining school, their parents and OAPs.

Jocelyn Taylor studied Drama and Theatre Arts at Birmingham. With magazine, Spanish verse speaking and Forrest prizes, Jacqueline Ménage trained the junior dramatic society before going to the Royal Academy. The Central School of Speech and Drama accepted Lynette Chappell. Essentially comic actresses, Madeleine Gayler went from secretarial college to university in New South Wales, and Jeanette Alexander, Senior Prefect, netball and House Captain to Training College.

The Staff and VI Verse Reading Club read *Caesar and Cleopatra* and *The Lady's not for Burning*; the Playreading Group joined with EGS for *Under Milk Wood* and *Venus Observed*. The Debating Society was popular, especially when opened to Fourths. That society rests on class distinction was won; all others were lost: coeducation *was* undesirable, religion *was* the opium of the people, advertising, though economically justifiable, *was* in all other ways undesirable, and, against EGS, the emancipation of women had *not* been carried far enough.

Mrs Joan Effendovicz (1963-1967), Miss Margaret (Molly) Platt (1964-1967) and part-timer Mrs Janet Twine (1963-1972) joined Miss Cox's busy team.

Twenty-two read English, occasionally with another subject. Almost all had been involved with plays, language competitions, choir, magazine writing and production. Maureen Marchant, school champion, swam for Enfield, Angela Pink was Tawny Owl, DHG Gillian Staines led the Christian Union.

Careers were varied. Helen Fairbairn took up evangelical work, Sally Sellick (1st prize Greek Dialogue, Oxford) a Fellowship in Canada before teaching. Kathryn Derounian lectured in Arkansas on American literature and published books and articles, Gillian Maskens worked in BBC News and Information departments and as a library assistant, Alison Trehern joined the WRAC. Four went up with awards: Exhibitioners Elizabeth Talbot (London) and Catherine Coulson (Cambridge), and scholars to Birmingham DHG Susan Clarke and Diane Pearson, author of *Alcibiades to the Assembly, 415 BC*, who became an UCCA librarian.

Recording achievements of a small but happy community

The old 2/6 green-covered magazine appeared for just one more year. Reports filled 42 of its 72 pages, the OGA eight, two were blank, two featured photographs, which left little room for original contributions. Competitions (verse three, prose, humorous prose and verse one each) were judged by the committee of 3-4 English Staff and 5-7 girls.

Sad was Second former Penelope Gardner's *Lament*:

> Sobs the wind.
> Tears of rain
> Stream down the pane.
> Mourn the trees,
> Bowed to the ground
> The very air
> Weeps with despair.

Many, however, were light-hearted. In memories of childhood, Margaret Purry recalled the pride of her life, her ballet dress, and Adèle Griffiths the Christmas tree, which had never seemed the same since she and it were the same height. Jocelyn Taylor's Peke was a "much-praised and most precocious pet", Susan Aldridge's Yankibonk was a beautiful beast. Mary Dixon's verse *To A Slug* ("Black and slimy one") was strangely beautiful; appropriately, she trained at the Royal Veterinary College.

Jennifer Williams hated noise,

> The chug of the train that won't let me sleep;
> The screech of the brakes from that man's horrid jeep.

Early disillusioned, Diana Hill was selling 'flags' for charity – the children buy, then nick the tin.

Two prize-winners were Jane Byworth who parodied Masefield:

> I must go down to Southend-on-Sea, to the muddy beach and the rain,
> And all I need is a day off school and the fare to travel by train,

for Bingo, well-fried and greasy chips, and Jacqueline Hales who recounted the food and habits of Cockney Mrs Higginbottom: "It is to be hoped that her soul went to heaven, as she was always so particular about knowing the right sort of people".

After one magazine-less year, the new format showed on the cover Enfield's composite heraldic beast of medieval origin, in a different colour each year. More expensive and needing subsidising, it was not universally popular; a Council motion to revert to the old type was, however, defeated, girls being asked to consider how to meet the deficit. In the next edition, several stockists, colleges and firms seeking staff took full- or half-page advertisements. The Sixth watched its professional printing. Inviting constructive criticism and praising the hard work involved, the Head supported the venture, warning that, with any break from tradition, some are sad at the passing of what has always been and others greet the new with too eager acceptance of change for change's sake. As end papers and literally over, above, below and round all items were drawings, linocuts and patterns, sometimes taking a full page, often heightening or illustrating story or poem, sometimes making the text difficult to read.

Complimentary copies were still sent to other schools.

Poems show rhythmic experiments, Susan Birkett writing about a star in the shape of one. Many reveal a feeling for language and beauty, some call on childhood (Susan Chapman's freedom to squelch in the mud of a summer pool); others are affected by the transitoriness of life. Maureen Marchant reflects on the destruction of youthful happiness, Michèle Galat muses that man is dust:

He knew too much, forgot too much.

Adults were again made aware of the adolescent obsession with the vileness of war and natural disasters, of humanity's cruelty. Susan Porter found man trapped in horror because of the folly of human nature wanting to do what is forbidden, Monica Collingham reviewed the lunacy of war, concluding that man is sent backwards by progress. Ann Cammack contrasts

> The Peaceful world of clouds with Guns,
> And a World
> Of ceaseless, bitter strife,
> Peace
> And the hope
> Of everlasting life.

After reading English, she went with VSO to Thailand.

Happily, there are many comic entries, from the sheer fun of Stephanie Fitt's *Alliterative Allegory* ("Don't ask a Butterfly to drink and drive") to the First former Christine Goddard's story of *The Book* that was never opened because of the excitement, dreams, lunch of a train journey. Mary Porteous digs at interviews, Third Programme style, and Glenda Warren's *The Mask* concerns the hypocritical canvassing of a would-be MP.

Animals, especially alley and stray cats, provide the usual fertile source of inspiration. Meryl Smith portrays the meeting of two lovers in the wild exhilaration of feline revelry. June Blackburn writes of *His Majesty the Cat*:

The smiles of the Mona Lisa sends the art world quite ecstatic
But the look in the eyes of a thoughtful cat is far more enigmatic.

Cynicism is not infrequent. Jacinth Brand compares creatures such as tigress and snake which do and seem as humans do and seem:

You laugh at the peacock, who, with chest out, struts vainly,
Just as you do, seeking a mate.
So you return to the safety of your mirror
Which reflects only appearance.

Narrative is rare. Frances Smith describes the chaos behind the scenes at the Globe at the first performance of *Macbeth*. Susan Pluciennik writes a macabre story on a train.

School itself stimulated little, although Penelope Gardner reflects on *The Last Bus*, identified years later on the 7th level at N9 "as a sacrificial vehicle. We assume that victims were collected from small wayside shrines and transported to a temple where mass slaughter took place. Incense seems to have been burned in the upper compartment. Samples of the sticks have been discovered on the floor. Victims were well fed *en route*, as notices prominently displayed advised them to request the right fare".

First former Rosemary Goldfrap considers ghosts who haunt ECS:

They write upon the blackboards
You can hear the squeak of chalk!
Can you hear a mistress
Saying 'Girls, you must not talk!'.

All are personal, often astonishingly mature and inventive. Future Art student Judith Brown's *The Lotus Eater* is written in capital letters within her own design.

My ship has gone.
Now I forget from whence
I came.
No memory;
No such want.
I am only – happy.

Algebra is a form of low cunning

The Mathematics and Science departments were not in the limelight to the same extent as those of the Arts, but scope and numbers continued to increase. Sixth formers attended a course on Computer Science; from Southgate, Ann Vivian joined Lloyds Computers, Patricia Haggerty studied at the College for Computer Operators, Penelope Collier at Hatfield Polytechnic before working with Elliott Automatic, Linda Hampshire and House captain Leisa Munday at Northampton CAT for Applied Mathematics.

At six different universities, six, with form and Florence prizes, read Mathematics: Hazel Bowerman (with Philosophy), actress Dianne Crowder (Cambridge), Janet Gwynn (House Captain, rounders*, with Economics), Gillian Hyland, Juliet Harrison and Beverley Rowan.

Thanked for making that most incomprehensible of subjects have some meaning and reality, and remembered not only for her painstaking teaching and for her acerbic tongue in the Staff room, but for her thoughtful care of the Charities and Amenities funds for at least twelve years, Miss Bowen had the unique distinction of working with all three Heads. She received a watch and cheque from the OGA. Miss Morley (1944-1966), "a great teacher with a real spirit of service", who had led many expeditions, received book tokens. Both retired to her quiet cottage in North Wales, where she did wonders for the Women's Institute and exercised her dogs.

Miss Collins was joined by Mrs Allene Scrimshaw (1966-1976), Mrs Phyllis Baruch (1966-1985), Mrs Anne Cooper (1964-1967, 1970-1983), who broke a tradition of seven centuries by becoming a churchwarden at St Andrew's, having previously been the only woman on its finance committee, part-timer Mrs Susan Oldham (1964-1968) and three who stayed but one year each.

The Sciences acquired new striplighting and a viewer microscope, £45 each. Girls visited the Science Museum, Planetarium, Royal Mint and Dagenham and Enfield factories. Physicists attended lectures at the Royal Institution. VIA's Club heard talks on astronomy, genetics, Darwinism, legends and mythology. The Second Year's attempt to form a Pets' Club, however, faded through lack of interest.

New Staff included full-timers Mrs Jill McCarthy (1965-1979), OG Miss Kennedy (1964-1967) and part-timers Mrs Faith Reid (1965-1980) and Mr Webb who retired from EGS.

Over twenty universities and colleges gained over 40 students. There were seven chemists: Jane Byworth (London and Herts) returned as laboratory assistant: Judith Carr went to Birkbeck after working: Diane Beckford emigrated to California: prizewinners Jennifer Steel (Oxford) and Mary Mirams (Exeter) gained First Class Honours. Physicists included Valéry Borshell and Ann Deketelaere (Oxford), Susan Neville (Duke of Edinburgh's Gold Award), Angela Tippett (represented Enfield in athletics) and Jacqueline Boardman (Imperial College, thence to Australia). Susan Pegrum (hockey*, athletics*, Sports champion), Janet Putman (Chelsea CAT, Captain RAMC, research in chemical pathology, M Phil) and Maureen Allen (first at Birmingham, D Phil) all studied Zoology.

Among the six pharmacists and six medics were magazine prizewinner and actress Pamela Darroch, Jennifer Caddy (all possible Sports honours and achievements), Sarah Rouse (from Barts to the Mile End hospital) DHG Lesley Rayner (Girton, Goldsmidt Scholarship for three years' clinical work at University College hospital) and Ann Buxton (Bristol, prize for the most promising student of her year and the only woman to qualify with Honours).

Greater variety was possible. Wendy Knowles studied Microbiology, House Captain Susan Penn (General Science) became a nurse, Helen Oldaker got a First in Agricultural Economics. House Captain Stephanie Ebbels qualified in Horticulture (Wye) and Dorothy Renshaw in Electrical Engineering (Northampton CAT). From Bacteriological Studies (Battersea), Catherine Patrick joined a Forensic Chemistry laboratory and Jennifer Attwood the Civil Service. Dawn Adams applied for Administration in the UK Atomic Energy Authority, Barbara Meyer became a Junior Technical Officer, Radio Biological Research Unit.

A new sphere became popular: fourteen studied Psychology, Rosalind Adams (first year prize) with Statistics. Of the nine physiotherapists, Glynda Evans (London and Guy's) took her M Sc in Human Relationships. Eleven worked in laboratories at various levels, including the forensic department at Scotland Yard. At eighteen different hospitals, twenty-two followed nursing, three Radiography and two Occupational Therapy.

This year has brought few outstanding successes

The verdict fitted most Houses. Juniors and individual seniors remained enthusiastic, but more were increasingly disenchanted. Abolition was again debated. Houses often combined for separate junior and senior outings. Most popular were *The Sound of Music* (seven parties), followed by *El Cid*, *Pickwick* and *Aladdin* (five each) and *Half a Sixpence* and the film *West Side Story* (five). Other groups saw at least eight other productions, including two on ice; one set preferred a ramble.

Having found difficulty in conscripting players for the hockey team, St Catherine's did not win the Challenge Cup. "Perhaps with harder work, more exam passes, fewer detentions, better luck and more effort, each one of you can contribute towards winning the cup. As the symbol of St Catherine is a wheel, I hope that it will start turning and bring you success. Remember – Up, St Catherine's!"

"More selfcontrol is needed. Will each individual give of her best? The seniors could take example from the younger members. Some few girls let St Cecilia's down time and time again".

"These people could best use their energy in contributing to House activities". The behaviour of junior Margarines left much to be desired, several names appearing regularly on the detention list. In the final year, they won the Challenge Cup convincingly with 2,216 points, 682 above the bottom House.

"Successful". Thus, succinctly, St Ursula's, which encouraged by awarding an individual cup. The House won over 40% of the trophies on offer.

"Work and Conduct only average". Poor St Winifred's could congratulate itself only on beginning Miss Hogg's Headship in possession of the Cup. By 1967, it was fifth.

> Can anybody play? asked the Captain
> Banging on the classroom door.
> And her stick, in the general exit,
> Smote a dozen girls or more.

Albeit hitting herself with her own stick as she tried to drum up support, Ann Cammack's *Hockey Captain* won the prize for humorous verse.

Despite pages still devoted to games, names of captains and team members, rewards and scores, the change in atmosphere is marked, although Council did request that team photographs be on public display. Whilst "all mucked in to take teams of games or dancing lessons" when Mrs Burnay broke her leg skiing, whilst the Staff were all "mugged" up in tracksuits, not always were enough players found for teams or offices, although the juniors could, almost always, be relied on for enthusiasm. The weather was permanently against them, twenty-two hockey matches being cancelled in one season alone, yet it had to be below freezing before lessons were abandoned in favour of gym.

Staff who left were Miss Margaret Macdonald, member of the English netball VII (1962-1966), Mrs Sally Burnay (1962-1965) who returned after having a baby, Miss Daphne Crow (1966-1967) to train to teach in less privileged countries. Staying into comprehensive days were Mrs Sally

Downes (1965-1968), Miss Gillian Scott (Mrs Thynne, 1965-1976) and Mrs Pearl Burrell (1965-1979), the Keep-Fit specialist, "whose enthusiasts were nurtured". "How grateful we are for the encouragement that all have given, especially during the bad weather, when their indoor practices kept up our fitness and enthusiasm".

The ten who went on to PE Colleges were games captains, had 17 ALs and 16 Colours between them, seven were House Captains, six Prefects, one DHG and one Head Girl. Carolyn Freakes won an EMF Gold Medal for recitation, Celia Winch and Hazel Arbery were both Athletics champions who represented Enfield.

Hockey ran the usual four teams, form and House contests and matches (despite cancellations, P 194, W 121, D 32). One term, the first XI proudly scored 144 goals to one against. Best of all, they drew with EGS. They played in junior and senior county tournaments, six gaining county places and at least 16 receiving Colours.

Twelve won netball Colours. Although in the first season, ten matches were scratched, 1,000 goals were scored. Five teams played altogether 336 matches, W 279, D 13, L 44 (including to EGS). St Ursula's was top House most frequently. The 1st and U-15 VIIs gained the Enfield Schools tournament, the first was runner-up in the county rally, as were the U-15 and U-14 teams which won once.

The usual tennis singles, doubles and House matches took place; four or five teams played over 60 matches, W 47, L 14, D 1, but failed to advance beyond the second round of the Aberdare Cup. The annual visit to Wimbledon continued.

Five rounders teams – 1st, 2nd, U-15 ("lacks concentration"), U-14 and U-13 ("enthusiasm is rewarded") – were, apart from form and House events, reduced to the two youngest by 1967. Only four Colours were awarded. Of the 108 external matches, only 69 were won and five drawn.

Much more popular were Sports, soon to be known as Athletics. 1965's cyclostyled programme lists 32 events with current records: junior, middle and senior 100 yards (12 seconds) and 150 yards (18·4): Long Jump (16' 5½"): Throwing the rounders ball (201'), middle and senior Javelin (70' 6½"), Discus (74' 7"), 80 yards Hurdles (11·9 secs.) and 220 yards open (29·5, later reduced by four seconds). The highlights came in the last nine events: form relays (V, 55·5 secs.) and Inter-House relays (55·8). The Head Girl's mother still presented the trophies. Three individual championships were on offer, but "since the number of events for which each person could enter was restricted, it was not easy to find enough athletic seniors".

In 1965, three teams competed in the Enfield Schools Meeting, A and U-15 coming first, B second, in the 4×100 yards relay (54·3); all three teams recorded the fastest times and six girls were chosen to represent the town. Two years later, ECS was second overall, the juniors coming first. Four represented Enfield and one ran in the relay at the all-England meeting.

Enthusiasm throughout the school spurred the swimming teams to success. In the Gala, each House entered a set team; competitors had to choose two events (breast or back stroke, butterfly, free style, diving) plus U-13 medley and relays. The Swimming Association's new test for personal survival was warmly welcomed. Girls continued to win RLSS badges and the Award of Merit.

Matches against other schools were of minor importance. Three teams entered Enfield Schools' Gala for the first time in 1965; juniors won , the others came second. In the North Middlesex Gala, individuals did well, seniors winning the medley team race. The U-16 relay team was champion of Middlesex and Herts. Six represented Enfield in the Greater London Gala. In 1967, after coming second in the Schools' Championship in Cardiff, the team triumphed in the national finals at Leeds. Swimming was becoming increasingly an individual rather than a corporate activity; there was finally just a First form Gala, encouraged somewhat by seeing films.

The Importance of Simplicity

Apart from providing meals, refreshments and general help for special occasions, conducting expeditions and organising talks on health, the DSc department sought to bring girls up-to-date. Full-day Fashion Schools at D.H. Evans store for privileged Sixthformers were designed to "smooth our paths in choosing our first career-girl wardrobe". "A demonstration of the right and wrong methods of putting on a bra and girdle made many ears tingle". Indeed! *Vogue's* editor "pointed out some fashion howlers at which at least some of us looked guilty". A Yardley representative made up Susan Martin (City of London Secretarial College). "A magnificent lunch was not the least of the day's attractions". When free to roam the store, girls found that the money drained out of their purses. Thirds to Sixths also enjoyed a Simplicity Fashion Show in school. "Teachers observed the move from a self-conscious, gawky 11-year-old in white socks to a rather less self-conscious, gawky 19-year-old in a miniskirt anxious to establish her own lifestyle".

The lively department was headed by OG Mrs Mavis Swift (1962-1982) and joined by Mrs Ann Craig (1966-1970), Mrs Janet Vear (1963-1966), replaced by Mrs Joan McKenna (1966-1969).

Lynn Gladden, chosen by her form to be a representative on McCall's Teenage Fashion Board, and Pat Pollard, who became a private designer and dressmaker, studied at the London College of Fashion, Jacqueline Syrett Hotel Management (Hendon) and Stephanie Hayes Reception (Southgate). June Croll (Comparative Studies Essex) subsequently applied to the College of Fashion and Clothing Technology. Queen's Guide Harriett Lott, first recipient of the HG's personal silver brooch, won the only First Class Honours in her Diploma course (Battersea) in Hotel and Catering Management, then a Trust House's first year prize and Morgan Scholarship before working at the Strand Palace Hotel.

School meals compare more than favourably with much of home cooking

Dinnertime continued a major concern. Still only the Sixth enjoyed the privilege of going out. Why, the others, aimless and unsupervised wanderers, might even return late for school dinner! School's reputation was at stake, especially in the milkbars. IV-V could do prep, juniors had to request personal permission. Food must never be eaten in formrooms. That homework should be decreased when a form had a lunchtime lesson was considered a matter for negotiation with the Staff concerned. Girls could make acceptable arrangements for meetings.

Sandwiches, not to be eaten at separate tables, could be brought for religious or medical reasons. Water was allowed twice and forbidden twice; there were complaints of dirty water, a non-functioning tap, the draughtiness of going outside; an urn should be bought. A menu was judged necessary. Systems were tried and abandoned: hatch service: each table clearing first course before getting seconds: cafeteria self-service. Finally, they were to arrive in eights to sit at set tables. Such were the complications that volunteers generously offered to help new girls when they first encountered the ritual.

At break, ice-cream was sold one year, this time at a loss; the experiment went unrepeated, despite appeals. The sale of soft drinks was considered impractical.

The Association continues while there are those to go on

The OGA withdrew from the Federation of Old Grammarian Associations, thus saving 10/6 pa. Enthusiasm achieved 348 Life Members. From 1964, a separate organisation grew up, YOGA, Young Old Girls' Association, with an initially encouraging response of about 125. To judge by the noise made by over 80, their coffee evening was a great success.

Miss Hogg was welcomed as President at a sherry party. Janet Lock became press secretary. Mrs Turnbull retired as secretary after fifteen years, receiving a luggage set and bouquet before becoming treasurer. Miss Barbara Butler took over until 1983 with Mrs Ada Barsham and Mrs Welch as social and bridge secretaries. Life Presidents were elected for meritorious service to the Association, Miss M.C. Sharp being one such. The immediate past Head Girl or her nominee joined the committee. If a member failed to attend without adequate reason, another could be elected in her place. Titles of Miss and Mrs were strictly kept. Magazines would have to be paid for; 179 had been requested in 1964, only 85 two years later.

Contact with school remained close, not simply because 20 or more had joined the Staff. Even when tables had cost £14:2:2, ten Bridge Drives showed a profit of £42:9:8, part of which helped the Orphans' parties. Money was collected on Miss Forrest's death for yet more prizes and travel grants in memory of a staunch supporter. Other prize funds were still supported.

Dinners, at which the Head Girl proposed the toast, were less successful financially, one yielding 4/9 profit. As well as outside speakers, Jacqueline Welch told of her work in the USA, Phyllis Edwin talked interestingly on Abyssinia. Frances Perry not only continued her fund-boosting sherry parties but gave a commentary with slides on African animals and flowers. Fifty-four years separated the oldest and youngest attenders.

Summer reunions were too early for college students. The winter buffet supper was, weather permitting, more successful: attractive décor, magnificent food, songs and, once, an excellent reading from *Twelfth Night.*

1967's Prize Giving, with broadcaster Franklin Englemann as Guest, was a celebration of the triumphantly successful academic last year of the County School. Seniors over the next three years had had most of their education in the 'old' school, many remaining loyal to it. From 1968 to 1971, no fewer than 127 gained places at no fewer than 45 institutions. These girls fell between two stools. Head Girls and some winners of School Colours must be their representatives.

Such were Diane Burke (English), Pamela Carter (Law), Jacqueline Hales (Spanish and Drama), Diane Hamilton (French), Sarah Kippax (Hodgson prize, Botany), Jill Turner (Biochemistry, Oxford), Ann Burling (prizes for French *and* Science), Mary Garnham (Training College), Lynn Dabek (Local Government), Sandra Shadbolt (member of the Greek Chorus, trainee buyer Harrods).

They set an incredibly high standard of commitment and achievement for the 'new' school.

PART NINE

THE END

CHAPTER FORTY-FOUR

Once upon a time, there were two schools and they lived happily ever after

Miss Hogg, at the first Prize Giving of the new school in November, 1967, thus paid tribute to "the good will and cooperation of all our colleagues at Chace".

This was a gross over-simplification. She had been more forthright in the last magazine. "It would be quite wrong to assume that most of us at ECS do not deplore the end of a multiplicity of types of schools, a system which has proved its worth in providing the education most suited to all the different aptitudes of the boys and girls in the area. Inevitably, a minority must bow to the theories of the majority. We hope that neither children nor Staff will be expected to do the impossible, either physically or mentally, which would inevitably be the case if the plan is rushed through before suitable buildings are available". These "suitable buildings" were still unavailable twenty-five years later.

The nation had been bombarded by Reports on Education: Albermarle, Beloe, Denning, Robbins, Early Leavers, Student Grants, Day Release for the U-18s, Education between 15 and 18 (Crowther), and 13-16 below-average pupils (Newsome).

Discussions, locally and nationally, continued on the largely theoretical aspects of grammar and secondary modern versus comprehensive. Are standards in the 3-Rs failing? What is the role of IQ tests? of examinations? Do more passes at OL and AL mean better, or simply more? Is competition harmful or good? Is there a need for experiments? Should the proven virtues of the grammar school be sacrificed on the altar of egalitarianism? Should the intelligent suffer for the masses? We are not born equal and school ought to prepare for a life in which some will succeed, some will fail, and some will simply rub along. Should education be used not primarily to acquire learning, but to implement social change? Is transfer at 11+ unfair, as some 80% 'fail', which leads to psychological problems? Transfer at 13+ – is it too late? Why should we take *their* dropouts and lose *our* best candidates? Transfer at 15+ into the Sixth? This last had long been practised by the independent sector. Should selection by ability be replaced by catchment areas or by location of the parental home, which would mean selection by wealth or poverty? What might be the special problems of split sites? Fundamentally, why should a real community which took years to create be destroyed by a stroke of a pen?

Jargon proliferated: modules, playway, structuring, child-centering, blackboard jungle, balanced intake, self-learning, projects ("This is my project and I hate it"), mixed ability/streaming/setting, equality of opportunity/egalitarianism. "Never have we been subjected to so many obscure theories and misguided controversies, nor have so many people been so emotionally involved at all levels".

On March 1, 1966, Enfield Education Committee recommended the reorganisation of secondary education along comprehensive lines and in all-through schools from 11-18 wherever practicable. Parents were promised that detailed planning, to be submitted by July 12, would follow this policy decision. It was recognised that most schools would be split-site. Beginning in September 1967, the change would be completed over five years.

Seven Grammar and twenty-three Secondary Moderns were to form fifteen Comprehensives. A 'plan' was drafted based on square feet of 'teaching area' per pupil, without regard for specialist provision. Many of the 750 teachers had voted against comprehensivisation, some writing to the Authority and to the Press. Although "we shall give our support to the new system since the welfare of the children and their good education have always been our concern", they felt obliged to record their sadness that what had served the community so effectively for so long was to be swept away. All were addressed in April by the Chief Education Officer. Half the scheme was referred back for reshuffling and resubmission. The *Times Educational Supplement* printed a nice quotation: "I hear that many schools are becoming comprehensible, but I would rather ours stayed as it is".

Suddenly, the tempo quickened. Enfield County (Grammar), Holly Walk (HW) was to amalgamate with Chace Girls (Secondary Modern), Rosemary Avenue (RA), in a highly charged emotional atmosphere, in which truth and untruth became sadly confused.

This is a happy school

Formed in 1949 with Miss Phyllis Moore as Head, this Secondary Modern took girls mainly from Lavender Road and Chase Side schools. They were well taught, with a cheerfully old-fashioned emphasis on the 3-Rs. A corporate feeling might have been more speedily achieved had the school received a name. A few suggestions and several months later, the

Education Committee came up with Chace, the original spelling of the Royal hunting ground. Miss Eastaugh designed the badge which incorporated a Stag and the Tudor Rose. Uniform helped: maroon, later grey, tunic or skirt, white blouse or jumper, maroon or grey cardigan and tie, pink and white check summer dress. Whilst there was no regulation footwear, so-called fashionable styles in shoes, as in hair, were discouraged. Jewellery and make-up were forbidden.

The initial intake of 200 was joined by 110 annually, growing to a maximum of around 700. Parents gradually came to feel great loyalty; their Association raised funds to provide items such as projector, screen and record player for the French department.

The RA building soon proved inadequate, despite huts in the grounds. Miss Moore retired before she could enjoy the new building which she returned to open in 1962. Although formrooms were designed, alas, for 30 only, facilities for specialist subjects were good, the spacious stage encouraged dramatic work, although the Hall was open to the corridor which served as cloakroom and changing room. A modern kitchen provided lunches served at tables for eight.

Miss Moore accepted total responsibility, a necessary involvement as many girls felt that they were failures and were regarded as such. Her threefold aim was to build up their morale, to give freedom from competitive examinations and to establish parity of esteem with Grammar Schools; these last two were sometimes in conflict.

Staff were encouraged to develop syllabuses for new subjects such as Science, Biology and French. "Very Parisian in high heels and with beehive hair-do", Assistants took small groups for conversation. Mathematics, with adding machines, replaced Arithmetic, Drill gave way to Athletics and Gymnastics. Commercial subjects proved useful; soon Pitman's examinations were taken. Homework was set.

Despite disapproval by Inspectors, learning by rote was encouraged (French verbs, poetry, arithmetical tables), Years were divided into A, B and C forms; the less able received practical instruction.

When parents and employers began to demand objective proof of ability and achievement, ten local Secondary Heads evolved an Enfield system, marked internally but supervised externally; certificates were issued. Girls who wished took RSA examinations in French, a 13+ test for Tottenham Technical College and GCE.

Sports were played within forms and Houses and against other schools. A few lunchtime clubs flourished. Charities were not supported on a regular basis, pocket money being generally far from lavish, but a Christmas party with presents took place for the Sunshine Homes.

Form Monitresses, Prefects, Head Girl, Houses, visits and visitors functioned much as at ECS; simple rules emerged after discussions with Staff and girls. The choir sang at Assemblies and concerts, recorders played.

The need for expeditions was possibly greater than at ECS; mainly on Saturdays, Staff, on a rota basis, escorted them to London to enjoy galleries, museums, parks, churches, the Zoo, to St Albans and to enjoy ballet, plays and concerts. Most enterprising were Outward Bound courses and holidays in Western Europe, preceded by study of the region. For a memorable Swiss sojourn, 42 girls, 6 Staff and 4 parents paid £25 each – which included excursions. Girls were escorted to stay with French penfriends, French girls stayed in Enfield. Prizes were awarded for photographs and diaries.

Youth Employment Officers and representatives of particular careers came to school; jobless leavers were virtually unknown. Many secured clerical and secretarial posts in local banks and businesses; hairdressing, floristry, factories and stables took others. One became a waitress, another a trainee beautician – for dogs. Fifteen-year-olds wanting further education went to local colleges, thence to Teacher Training or Art establishments. One took a law degree. Others were assistants until they were old enough to begin nursing.

At their last Prize Giving in 1966, girls sang French, Welsh and English songs and spoke verse. Sixteen forms I-IV received one prize each, Year V two and three for the Sixth; 19 subjects gained 47 prizes, with two special ones from the Head and the Parents' Association and two for the best academic results: 10 OL or equivalents and 2 CSE, 3OL and 10 RSA. Valerie Johnson was the first Enfield girl to win a Gold Medal in the Duke of Edinburgh's Award scheme.

Miss Moore proudly encouraged her "cooperative and enthusiastic" teachers. Most who joined the new school retired or left in the Seventies: Miss Connie Harris (Geography, games), Mrs Mary Spry (History, English), Mrs Margaret Moore (PE), Miss Connie Powell (Senior Mistress, remaining at RA) and Mrs Gertrude Taylor (English). Miss Jean Eastaugh (Art) and Mrs Janet Phillips (French) contributed greatly towards the eventual integration of the two Staffs.

We shall have the stormy passages as well as the calm

"Pulling together, we shall ride them out". Some girls were excited, most frightened. Naturally, most teachers were unhappy at this 'challenge', and mutually suspicious. Some were too sensitive, others too insensitive. Staff anxiety about jobs and parental fears for their daughters' futures mounted.

That the transition was no more agonising than it was owed much to Miss Hogg's generosity of spirit, bubbling sense of fun and helping hand. True to her principle that persons matter more than things, subjects and systems, she aimed to keep the temperature low and to begin new traditions while trying to preserve the best of the old ways.

The statutory notice, pinned on the door on January 19, 1967, brought the change home to everyone. The Ministry of Education had to approve the closure of an existing school, the opening of a new one, or, as here, "the enlargement of an existing school to such a degree that it amounts in practice to a new one". Objections had to be lodged within two months. Some parents sought a Writ. The Judge found the Council in breach of law but declined to give an injunction because "complete chaos would ensue".

In the icy snow, the posts of Heads and Deputies were advertised. Miss Yvonne Edwards, Head of Chace, was offered the Headship of Albany Mixed Comprehensive. Miss Hogg was reappointed in February. By March, there were over 100 applicants for Deputies, with two days of interviewing. My own re-appointment was strange; the extra responsibilities clearly presented by the new establishment, almost doubled in numbers and on two sites, forced me to relinquish the departmental headship. My salary was, therefore, technically reduced, although it was actually safeguarded.

Choosing a name was a minor difficulty, although verification took a long time. Suggestions included North Enfield, Abernethy, Uvedale, Macleod and Clarendon, but these did not encompass both. Enfield Chace School preserved the County's initials, ECS, and the name of Chace Girls. This meant changing public notice boards and altering two sets of stationery. Years later, school became Enfield County again; in 1999, the new name of The Enfield School for Girls is proposed.

Summer terms are always hectic: normal examination chores (CSE, OL, AL, RSA, Pitman's), games and sports, reports, promotions and demotions, junior and middle school Prize Giving, career interviews and references, not to mention the odd extra of a Sixth Form survey for a research student. This one beat all records.

First came the confirmation of the number of teachers allowed, giving two extra to cover time lost in commuting between the two sites and more to plan new courses. Staff from both schools were offered contracts and many were upgraded. Retirements and departures meant 13 new appointments for September.

Enormous and time-consuming efforts tried to solve problems and create a happier atmosphere of cooperation – meetings, meetings and yet more meetings. After a successful one with parents of the new First Year, the attempt was made to interview all the new pupils; 204 were seen, 6 disappeared into thin air. Parents of the Third Year in both schools were invited, Chace girls came up to HW for an afternoon to be shown around and given refreshments by County's Year III whom they would be joining. Sadly, one OG feels that during the changeover years, the barriers between the former grammar and secondary modern girls were rarely breached. Staffs met, as a whole, in departments, Years, administration, the new species of pastoral, and socially. Sometimes, these gatherings simply developed mistrust.

The first major question was how girls should be allocated between two sites. The Authority, rightly, asked for a minimum of pupil movement. Division of the school being obviously, however regrettably, unavoidable, all suggestions were opposed by some. Even the words 'upper' and 'lower' were criticised, 'lower' being thought derogatory; there were even objections to going 'down' the road to RA. In this no-win situation, it was decided to use RA as a base for Years I-III, with 35 lessons and HW for IV-VI, with 40, perhaps differently timed. Other headaches – courses embarked on to be safeguarded, no-one familiar with all aspects, strange classes, unknown buildings, sheer numbers of Staff and girls, different habits and customs, and , above all, the logistics of sites separated by a mile – the list of imponderables grew longer.

Without counting time for checking, copying and revision, Head and Deputy worked seven hours a day for 14 working days to produce the first timetable outline in 1967. As we became more experienced, so problems multiplied and we took longer, as when three unfilled spaces occupied a whole day. Hours of alteration followed when Staff left at Christmas and again at Easter. A computer in those early days needed to know so much before it could begin that pencil, rubber and mental sweat were more effective, as experts who visited in 1970 admitted. Even the Head had to teach 18 periods.

Other issues were mulled over. As the Head could not be in two Halls at once, the Head Girl and her Deputy took an occasional Assembly at RA and were involved with some of its functions. Prefects were retained at HW; they commuted sometimes to help out. A junior prefectoral system emerged, but both Third and Sixth Years lost out, the younger ones becoming nobodies again on their translation to Year IV, the older ones having less chance to test their powers of leadership. Juniors in general missed the example of more grown-up behaviour and more scholarly attitudes. A trivial but unforeseen consequence was the increased number of badges required.

It was generally felt that uniform "wears well, looks smart, is an excellent equaliser and avoids a lot of family argument first thing in the morning". A new style would help to create a new identity, yet the old garments had to be worn out. 1967 coincided with the mini; County tweed did not lend itself to rolls of thick material round waists in order to shorten skirts. For ten years or so, there were compromises, changes, simplifications: skirt (maroon, grey, tweed, new kilts), blouse (long or short sleeves), tie (maroon, green, none), twin sets for the Sixth and a college-type scarf. The matter still cropped up at virtually every Council meeting, rebelling against uniform being as traditional as uniform itself. Seniors still rejected a school brooch. By 1970, Sixths were out of uniform, although jeans became their own version. Rules became more tentative: "We prefer" a dark green gaberdine or duffle coat.

A printed note reminded all that watches should be named because of their removal for PE. Despite this, there was always a stock of unclaimed, unnamed watches in perfect working order. Purses remained a similar problem, as thefts, not unknown in either school, did multiply.

Houses received their death blow. Council was divided into two parts; the junior one flourished, the senior was sickly. Clubs fared similarly, the vitality, if not necessarily the sticking power, being largely with the 11-13 year olds.

The buildings both posed problems and forced solutions which had repercussions on Staff and girls alike. Each school had had reasonable facilities for the pupils hitherto involved, although both suffered from the post-war over-use of glass, with blinds constantly out of order.

Holly Walk's New Staff Room was pathetically small for increased numbers. In 1969-1970's estimates was included a cedarwood extension (£1,000) rather than a permanent block (£5,000). The Sixth forms, increased in numbers and social maturity, asked for a home for coffee, washing-up – in fact, a Common Room. They asked in 1969, 1970, 1971 and 1973. Parents gave £50 for furnishing and the Games Fund £140 to provide a sink. The Hall needed sound-proofing from the adjacent kitchen. Over-use by outside bodies meant that curtains and chairs needed renewing – but that, in 1974, would have cost £1,410. Boarding strips in the ceiling fell off; the caretaker was instructed to nail them. With the proliferation of examinations, improved lighting was needed in the Gym, at an estimated cost (1969) of £300. Showers and drying accommodation had to be re-sited. Bulk refuse containers improved waste disposal arrangements.

Rosemary Avenue had more Art, DSc and Secretarial rooms and equipment. In 1970, an extra Needlework room was approved for HW, and when the school leaving age was raised, a DSc room for Basic Catering.

Conversely, RA had insufficient and inadequate Science laboratories and at first modestly requested the rearrangement of benches so that practical work would be easier, then more ambitiously demanded new labs. Subsequently, HW needed a fourth.

Also required were more cloakrooms, remedial units as trial and error dictated, offices for Year Heads and, later , for Heads of departments. A washbasin installed in the Senior Mistress' room transformed it into a new Medical room (at a cost of £89:93 from the Games Fund), the existing one to be used for Staff marking and for Year Heads' interviews. Repairs and repainting dragged on. The heating boilers needed renewing, major roof works were urgent. When the Ministry reduced the allocation for minor works, projects were severely restricted.

On roll were 1,223 with an initial First form entry of 210 which later increased to 279, almost twice as many as there were in ECS at its foundation. The total peaked at 1,403. Many schools tended to become 'neighbourhood' schools, so that the mix advocated by the proponents of the comprehensive principle could not materialise. This happened either when specific Primaries were designated 'feeders' to specific Secondaries, or when too many wanted to go to a particular school which became 'over-subscribed', the victim of its own success. The criterion of accessibility was then invoked; ECS lost many of its ablest intake from the eastern end of the borough, girls who had hitherto gained so much academically and socially. The worst effects, however, were minimised by strong parental desire that their daughters should attend a single-sex establishment. Computer selection was rejected.

The number of feeder schools increased, with even greater variation in standards. The 11+ examination, whatever its faults, had had the broad result of ensuring comparable attainments in at least English and Arithmetic. The need arose to have some idea of both knowledge gained and potential ability. Visits to contributing schools and discussion with their Staffs were helpful, but as 50 or more such institutions became involved, no real comparisons were possible. ECS, therefore, devised its own tests, taken , initially, in the first week, subsequently deferred to half-term.

The new establishment had to be further sub-divided, so that each girl had an immediate point of reference beyond the Form Mistress who might be teaching in the other building. Houses could not be the new unit which had to be lateral not vertical. Each Year had its own Pastoral Head, a mini-headmistress. Sometimes friction arose between Form Mistress and Year Head, particularly when a pupil tried to play one off against the other. The system, however, soon became accepted as a necessity. At first, the Year

Head stayed put; this was frustrating for she had managed to know over 200 girls, perhaps teaching a quarter or a third, when they moved on. Soon, Year Heads moved on too. Their work became more varied and more demanding: Thirds needed subject guidance, Fifths examinations and career advice. Familiarity could, on occasion, breed contempt. The Sixth Year Head remained *in situ.*

As practical lessons were best completed in familiar surroundings with known teachers, DSc and Art students from Chace Third Year (therefore in Year IV at HW) spent one or two whole days at RA. Obviously, some RA girls had to take their places at HW. Two First forms came for the day. No-one could have her own desk, although they could use the others' cloakroom pegs. This was nightmarish for the younger ones, who felt that they did not belong, who had to carry heavy loads of books, who could not easily hand in homework in the correct building, who had difficulties with dinner money (4/- on Mondays at RA, 1/- on Tuesdays at HW), different customs and the journey. Older ones had similar trials. No-one could participate in games, clubs or choirs on the day(s) of their exile; indeed, some seniors simply disappeared *en route.* Activities took on a different look, with juniors separated from seniors.

The greater range of ability suggested that those less able should be in smaller teaching units, which meant that those considered brighter were in groups of 35, 36, even 38. As rooms were intended for a maximum of 30, desks had to be pushed together, a recipe for chatter. For some Staff, such divisions were unsatisfactory, almost perpetuating what they considered the evils of the old system. In mixed ability classes, the less able should learn from the more able, who, in turn, help them. This worked for some, but not all, subjects and made enormously greater demands on teachers. With teaching geared to the slowest, some classes became fragmented, doing different projects with increased noise and decreased concentration, leading to less stimulus for the able and more despair for the weaker ones. Setting for French and Mathematics continued. Names had to be devised to blur the distinction between 'top' and 'bottom' groups, although no-one was really fooled.

Increased numbers caused more problems in narrow corridors with cloakroom pegs, in toilet accommodation and at mealtimes. Halls were unusable before, during and after lunchtime. This resulted in tricky timetable adjustments for Music and Singing, PE and Dance, a major headache on wet days. Girls then had to stay in formrooms, which caused greater noise and a different approach to afternoon school. As fewer Staff involved themselves in lunchtime supervision, the dinner ladies had more responsibility, and, as each building has many exits, local residents and shopkeepers were soon complaining.

Even identification became a problem. Individual record cards, much maligned, were essential for the protection of pupils, to do them justice in disputes, at parents' meetings, for Reports (now ordered by the 20,000) and references. Personal photographs were taken on a girl's arrival and at least once more. Sold to the girls, these, with a returned discount from the firm involved, provided a handsome sum for School Funds.

The two-ex schools, separated by a mile of busy road with two difficult crossings, presented all the difficulties of dispersal. The first was the physical one of travelling. Staff could not teach the period before a journey and it was not always feasible to avoid a double journey in one day. Those wishing to teach the whole age range had to commute for several junior/ senior classes in succession or even have their whole allocation with a single form in one or two sessions. Commuting brought a parking problem to both sites, requests for more spaces being made annually. Enfield, generous in reimbursement, regularly updated the amounts according to the vehicle's cubic capacity. Verifying logbook, driving licence, insurance policy and claim forms, working out amounts accordingly, then distributing the cheques, later added to salary, was a time-consuming chore. Some car owners were not insured for passengers on 'business' journeys or did not wish to be tied by them. Non-drivers had to be provided with a taxi service, which, in the first term, cost Enfield 6/- for a single, and 7/- for a double, trip. There were some 160 weekly journeys, 108 during lessons, 52 at lunchtime. Each traveller was urged to look in the travel basket to collect messages etc. for the other building. Commuting contributed greatly to Staff weariness and to lessening of discipline as a class waited with varying degrees of patience or exuberance whilst a car was held up by traffic or an accident, because the driver was absent or the taxi was late or failed to arrive. Absent Staff had to remember from their sick beds to notify each building not only of forms and work but of their day's transport commitments.

There were serious educational consequences. Some teachers stayed in their respective buildings, for proper reasons, so saw colleagues only at meetings. Others passed each other on the road. Part-timers, increasing to over 30, with all the attendant complications, came in on different days. This all resulted in a lack of identification with the school as a whole. It also hindered, even prevented, follow-up of learning or behaviour problems; a teacher could not stop to explain or exhort when the taxi was waiting.

The dissemination of information or instruction, the seeking of opinion or advice meant a weekly Staff meeting in each building, the construction of procedural or information files (one for each building) which had to be kept up-to-date, plus brochures on specific issues and for parents. A 'black' telephone between both Offices considerably eased matters. Eventually, more advanced switchboards allowed a direct link.

The struggle to unify practices was constant. Rewards and punishments had to be rethought. Some Staff felt that the former should be primarily for achievement (measurable, if not always fair), others for effort (not measurable and sometimes too subjectively judged). Transfer was impossible for a girl whose naughtiness was a reflection of her academic or social inadequacy. For trivial offences, the time-honoured detention (when not rendered impossible by commuting), exclusion from events and deprivation of privileges remained the usual solutions. A 'sin-bin' was tried. Being 'on report', that is collecting a written comment from each teacher after each lesson, helped some backsliders. For more heinous sins – defiance, truancy, misbehaviour in the town, bullying, swearing at Staff, lying, smoking, the odd affray, graffiti, obscene 'phone calls, theft, vandalism, all on a small but disturbing scale – exclusion for a limited period, during which parents were consulted, was initially more commonly used than suspension, with, rightly, the hassle of procedures with parents, Governors and Education Authorities. One girl's emotional, social, family and financial problems could take up most of a day.

Other difficulties arose with time. The Sixth forms, the Grammar's pride and joy, almost justified the old system for many teachers. Even a small Grammar school often had a relatively large Sixth because of an academically homogeneous intake, parental pressure and because success breeds success. The system was geared to continuing education. Now, the intake, no longer limited to the top 20%, comprised the whole ability range (apart from the verifiably educationally subnormal), and all girls were distributed throughout the borough. Considerable bitterness arose because Latymer creamed off many likely Sixthformers, resulting in fewer 'traditional' seniors. Calculations suggested that a roll of about 1,500 would provide Sixth forms of about 120. Even then, classes in some subjects might be too small to be effective, useful or even possible. Numbers kept up while the Grammar stream made its way through. Subsequently, marked changes occurred, both in numbers staying on and in courses – repeats, vocational, secretarial, mixed, general – that were in addition to orthodox ALs.

A major trouble was winning over the middle school, Thirds and Fourths, who had no wish either to join a new school or to be joined by outsiders. One unforeseen bonus was that the 'top' form of the Secondary Modern made enormous progress. These 20-30 girls who had just missed selection for the County seized the opportunity of a higher assumption of success, of obliterating the stigma of failure; they frequently outstripped those who had been just on the right side of the success/failure borderline. The less able, on the other hand, felt overwhelmed and insecure in the new establishment, especially those who had to move to a different building, where Staff for the most part did not understand their needs. One became embarrassingly incontinent during Assemblies. Teachers who were themselves Grammar school products had to learn to cope by trial and error. Expectations for the children differed which gave rise to conflict.

Justifiable bitterness remained. Grammar school teachers felt that their particular expertise was not being fully used. The 26 Chace Staff had more to lose, especially those who had been in charge of subjects and now found that they had to pay second fiddle to those with more academic qualifications or experience.

The question of the young leaver had to be faced. An Enquiry in 1968 established that most parents of children likely to leave at 15 thought that schools had improved in physical, curricular, out-of-classroom and general terms, and that pupils seemed happier. Worries were lack of discipline, of basic study, spelling and speaking. Whilst they felt that their less able offspring would gain little by further schooling, some being neither interested nor capable, others mature enough for outside work, the general opinion seemed to be that 15 was too young for a life-affecting decision and that they should stay on to acquire various certificates. This highlighted the need to inform honestly and adequately parents and the general public.

The Report led to the question of raising the school leaving age (ROSLA) in 1971. The advantages of greater maturity, of more learning time for making better citizens for better jobs proved often less noticeable than the problems posed by rebellious youngsters, accommodation not geared to their needs, the lack of space everywhere, financial considerations, and, above all, the lack of good, qualified and committed teachers. Roughly half judged, rightly, that ROSLA would present major headaches and readjustments, whilst one-half were actively against the whole concept.

When ROSLA was implemented, consequently with no more Fourths leaving, all sorts of approaches were bewilderingly suggested: curriculum development, day release, apprenticeships, special schools for the more/less able (a return to square one?), vocational training, community work, work experience, careers courses, team teaching, continuous assessment, mixed ability groups.

ECS approached this pragmatically, without recourse to theories put forward by non-practising teachers and by others who had never taught. Consistent with its history, school aimed to continue as far as practicable with a normal schedule and integrate the girls into normal school life. All who could pursued OL and/or CSE syllabuses. More trained remedial Staff for small numbers and more teaching Staff to ease the burden on Pastoral Heads were needed, as was more money for extra accommodation. ECS would consider issuing its own certificate to show what had been available, what attempted and what accomplished. Basic subjects must be English – reading, writing, speaking, as for an ever-increasing number, English was a second language – Arithmetic and Home Economics, with the emphasis on 'real-life' situations.

A pilot project, Me and My Environment, sought to encourage these teenagers to see themselves in relation to their families, to their immediate neighbours (persons, houses, amenities), to Enfield (geographically and historically) and to the wider world outside. The books, kits and equipment were estimated at £210.

Not startlingly innovative, but with practical validity.

1968 opened inauspiciously; the Head was called for Jury Service and snow closed the buildings! Nationwide student demand for more consultation and self-government suggested that they had found their teachers incompetent and ignorant, indeed superfluous. The movement spread into schools to the extent of requesting changes in the subjects taught: social studies/sociology, economics, politics, classical studies, car maintenance rather than Latin, Greek, a second foreign language and Music.

Society was changing rapidly and fundamentally, so that schools were expected to take on the disciplinary function hitherto associated with parents. All too often, the support of family and society was not forthcoming. When schools inevitably failed in this new role, they received all the odium. As all this coincided with a period of great shortages of Staff, suitable and otherwise, a number of appointments were made at ECS which proved less than ideal, leading to trouble in the classrooms, cliques in the Staff rooms, deteriorating morale and increased militancy. The mix of full- and part-timers, married and single, older and younger, mothers and probationers, women and men had, as in any other society, its pleasures and its tensions.

When school was fully comprehensive, the Head felt constrained to say publicly that ROSLA had much to answer for, as "those who have, emotionally and physically, outgrown school are now, to their way of thinking, 'imprisoned' for another year".

Surely we cannot let the Association die

Anxiety for ECS' future was frequently expressed, although the Head stressed that she was "endeavouring to preserve the spirit of the School of which we are all so proud". The Old Girls' Association sent a formal expression of sympathy to Miss Hogg and the Staff.

Three problems now faced the OGA. Could it continue as a body? What would be its relationship to the new Comprehensive school? What would be its finances?

The answer to the first question was fudged until the arrival of Miss Hogg's successor in 1975. Never having known the County school, Miss Pagan could hardly be president of its OGA. Discussions dragged on until the constitution was adapted for the ECSOGA, which fitted both constituents. When school's magazine ceased in 1968, an annual news sheet was circulated, and despite difficulties of duplication and dispatch, still is. It is hard to get new blood on the committee, which has several times been reappointed *en bloc*. Marjorie Read, the Butlers' cheerful successor, talked to summer leavers. Helen Dordevic took over on Marjorie's death.

Money remained of great importance. The subscription rose to £1; renewals of annual membership are few. Life subscription increased to £3:50. By 1977, there were 381 lifers and 500 members altogether. By 1970, monies were substantial: in cash £273:16:4: for Miss Broome £35 in Defence Stock: for Miss Forrest, £234:0:9: for Miss Florence £1,073:16:4. After the last Bridge Drive in 1968, which raised £47:4:5, cards and tables, much mended by Mr Whitehead, were sold to the Parents' Association. Cash came from coffee mornings, toy stalls at fêtes £20, white elephant stalls £18, a Bring and Buy lunch £25:4:3, a Baby Boutique and donations. Raffles virtually subsidised the spring meetings.

Twenty guineas obtained legal advice and the services of an accountant to make the funds more flexible. A new committee saw all transformed into a charitable society, with a single memorial fund which, by 1984, stood at £4,000, the interest only being usable. This still funded the Head Girl's brooch and commemorative prizes. Books were offered to the library. Grants and bursaries (£40) helped leavers or those involved with research and retraining for which no official funds existed. One year, Sixthformers who did not receive a prize were given £1 each towards the cost of books needed for further study.

Presentations continued to long-serving, retiring Staff, including Mr Whitehead, and to retiring Association officers. Flowers were sent for Miss Barker's and Miss M.C. Sharp's 80th birthdays, Miss Rudkin's 90th and Miss Bidwell's 100th.

Official meetings are now reduced to the spring AGM and the autumn lunch. Miss Hogg was guest on her retirement; she had asked only for the portrait for school, but donations provided personal gifts of a coffee percolator and a heated cabinet. Miss Pagan and past and present Staff have spoken, Dr McMullan on the Sahara trip which had been helped with £500, and Miss Bidwell, the first time more wanted to come than could be accommodated. Other speakers have included Drs Dinah Barsham, Mary Cock and Susan Love, Mrs Clements on Guatemala and Phyllis Pickard just back from a Mensa conference in San Francisco.

These events are, however, tinged with melancholy, for most pre-1967 members find it difficult, sometimes impossible, to come to terms with the loss of 'their' school. Unofficial reunions have increased, organised by various intakes (eg. 1909, 1947, 1956, this last boasting a specially commissioned cake decorated with ECS Onward Ever) and leavers (1968's attended by some 90 from all over the country). Comprehensive Years are now doing the same.

EPILOGUE

"Enfield Chace is an all girls' County Comprehensive School, with a total of over 1,300 pupils. The Upper School is situated in the centre of Enfield Town and is adjacent to Enfield Grammar School, an all boys' Comprehensive School, the Market Place and St Andrew's Church. It has easy access to the centre of London and the Hertfordshire countryside. Because Enfield Chace is the only all girls' County Secondary School in Enfield, pupils come from many Primary schools across the borough in accordance with the policy of free parental choice".

Opened in 1967, the school is now [1982] well established.

In the past, the new was tried from a base of stability. This cannot be true any longer. An older generation said *Onward Ever*; that confidence seems to have departed for ever. The hope must be that Miss Hogg was not too wide of the mark when she trusted that the school community "would continue to treasure the simple virtues of patience, reticence, courage, modesty, good judgment and wide sympathy".

SOURCES

SCHOOL MAGAZINES, read with caution, as misprints and wrong dates occur as frequently as in newspapers. Problems arose when initials only were used, when several girls, related or not, had the same surname, even the same initials, as when seven Paynes came from two families in thirteen years, or when a nickname was used.

REGISTERS. Seven bulky, stiff-bound books remain."The name of each pupil should be entered on a separate line in the index below, in a consecutive series. The number opposite the name in the index must coincide with that inserted in the top right hand corner of the page allotted in the Register". But no secretary. So scrupulous were the compilers that duplication is not unknown; better register a girl twice than not at all.

Partly overlapping, hundreds of single sheets, with holes punched in, gathered dust for sixty years; each is divided into innumerable small panels in which to chart a pupil's dated progress. Although legally compulsory, most bear no information whatever. They remain a mixture of fascinating details and unfilled gaps.

STAFF RECORD BOOKS, legally compulsory for over thirty years.

MISCELLANEOUS PRINTED INFORMATION, such as programmes, minutes, reports for various events, articles in local papers and reference books.

MY DIARIES, for facts and dates only.

INDIVIDUAL REMINISCENCES. Memory, especially as one gets older, cannot be fully trusted; all spoken testimony has had written corroboration.

Although publicising my investigations and trying to deal objectively with sometimes conflicting information, I apologise to any former student, teacher, parent or Governor who feels that this account is inaccurate, inadequate or biassed.

SUMMARIES

1. Forenames

Over the sixty-three years, 470 different names are recorded, more, if variant spellings (Lil(l)ian/ Lil(l)y/ Lillya/Lilley/Lilias) are added. Of course, these do not constitute a valid statistical sample. Fashion (Margaret Rose), literature (Cordelia, Wendy), entertainment (Amanda), religion (Naomi), nationality (Golda, Tegwen, Gwyn(e)th/Gwynne, Irénée), tradition (Ethaline), commemoration of a place or loved one (Hypatia), desire to be different (Dorinda), even a veiled wish that a daughter had been a son (Arnoldine, Frederica, Alfreda, Erica) all seem to have affected parental choice. Some girls were born in Victoria's reign (Agatha, Euphany), others (Suzannah, Maureen, Jill/Jillian/Gillian) in her great-great-granddaughter's.

Three hundred and sixty girls bore names unique to themselves in their period, but totally unique are 161, the largest number occurring after the Second War and ranging from Abigail to Zoe. Forty-seven names occur twice (Alberta to Zena); thirty-eight score three times (Adelaide to Toni) and thirty-four four times (Ailsa/Aylsa to Una).

Names space out now: fifty-one recur between five and ten times, thirty-five more between eleven and twenty, eighty between twenty-one and ninety, and nineteen between 101 and 161.

Some appear, however briefly, in the national top ten of the period(s): Evelyn (to 1914), May (Great War), Ethel (Twenties), Doreen, Eileen, June (Thirties), Janet, Linda, Valerie (after the Second War).

ECS's own top ten were:

10	Kathleen/Cathleen/Kathryn	173
9	Dorothy/Dorothea/Dora	177
8	Jean	193
7	Joan	214
6	Marjorie/Margery	215
5	Patricia	224
4	Elizabeth	236
3	Ann(e)/ Annie/Anna	291

and well ahead
2 Margaret   357
1 Mary/Marie/Maria   481
I have the full list if anyone is interested.

2 Good Works

¼d = one farthing, quarter of a penny, 1d   ½d = Half or ha'penny
1/- = one shilling = 12d (or 5p)   20/- = 240d, £1
1 guinea = £1:1:0   half a guinea = 10/6 (52½p)

Before the Great War, a labourer earned, on average, 7d an hour, a male teacher £147:10:0 pa, a doctor £265 pa. In 1909, butter cost 1/2 a pound, sugar 3d. Women's pay was, invariably, lower.

Fund-raising methods were ingenious and varied: displays, exhibitions, drama, concerts, dances: sales, the most obvious, whether run by an individual, a form, school or the OGA, of work, lost property, jumble, home-made produce, ice-cream, seals, art, needle- and craft-work: sponsored events: competitions: films, teas, marionette shows: collecting farthings, silver paper; and, eternally, knitting. Too often, an organisation received simply a donation, but actual amounts have frequently been recorded, figures which mean little nowadays, but which, in fact, represent great generosity from girls and parents who were not affluent.

Students were always moved by the plight of others provided they *knew* where their money was sent and were kept informed by the recipients. Regular Monday morning collections, divided between amenities and charities, were unpopular because impersonal.

Some charities were supported throughout the years – the disadvantaged young and old, the sick. Others were of their period, as, for example, the result of the distress of the Thirties' slump, or of single disasters, such as an earthquake.

Both wars offered great and wide scope both during hostilities and in the aftermath. Parcels of knitted blankets, socks, gloves (90 pairs) and darning wool were sent to soldiers and sailors. Prisoners of War were helped with cash and comforts. The Middlesex Regiment received £36:15:9, the YMCA Hut in 1914 £2:12:6 and the War Supply Depot £85:12:6. During and immediately after the Great War, local needs were answered: Edmonton News and Tea Room for Soldiers' Wives £7:16:0: Edmonton Soldiers' and Sailors' Club 3 guineas: egg collections for the needy (4 dozen for three weeks, plus £22:4:2): Enfield families in distress.

Those wounded were remembered in their various, mainly local, hospitals: Elm House VAD, Roseneath Voluntary £10:7:0, Grovelands £5,

Edmonton's Wounded Soldiers £1, although their concert was run at a loss, Bush Hill Park Military (more eggs, plus £54:7:2), Star and Garter Home £3:11:4. Girls subsequently contributed to Earl Haig Memorial Home 2 guineas, Ex-Services Welfare Society £11:10:0, the League of Remembrance 10/-, Royal Soldiers' Daughters' Home £1:11:6 and St Dunstan's (for those blinded) £29:7:0. School's Thanksgiving in 1918 raised 3 guineas. Collections for Armistice Day wreaths raised about £30, and for Alexandra Rose Day 31:3:7½.

Naval concerns were helped by Trafalgar Day proceeds, the Navy League receiving a single donation of 10/6. Allies were remembered: Belgian refugees by hospitality and £6:12:0½, French £10, Poles 5 guineas, Russian Famine Relief £8 and the Friends of Armenia 2 guineas.

Although the known total is £338, clearly much more was distributed.

Causes sponsored during the Second War were, generally, more closely linked to winning the war first and distributing relief later. National efforts were supported: Salute the Soldier, War Weapons Week £978:11:0, Spitfire Fund, Wings for Victory £2,646:16:0, Warship Week, Civil Defence, Airforce Week £2,598:7:0, Fighting French Forces, King George's Fund for Sailors £6:15:6¾, British Sailors' Society £32, Destroyers' Sick Bay £1,4000 – very large totals indeed.

Ambulance funds proliferated: Guides' (£7:4:0), Friends', Secondary schools'. Refugees were not forgotten in kind or cash: World Refugee Year £480, pocket money £13, Czech £26, Polish £3, Basques, Yugoslavs, UNRRA 16 guineas, general £11:13:0. Uncle Mac's appeal for X-Ray mobile apparatus was helped, money and clothes supplied for civil defence workers and those in minesweepers; OXFAM benefited from the sale of secondhand uniform and dances £60, Armistice Day Poppy Fund netted £11:19:4½. With high hopes, £12 was sent to Save Europe Now, and £50 raised for the Lord Mayor's Thanksgiving Fund.

Specific foreign appeals were warmly taken up from the Twenties: Earthquakes in India 3 guineas and in Chile, Congo Relief £60, China (Red Cross, United Nations, OG, International Peace) over £12:6:0, Germany Emergency Committee, Inter-School Committee for Warsaw £103, Bengal famine, African generator, Rhodesia Inter-Racial school £11, Hungary, Milk for Spain, National Young Life Campaign, UNICEF, and Freedom from Hunger £50:12:6.

National appeals did not fall upon deaf ears: Lord Mayor's Fund for miners, Welsh miners, Aberfan disaster, Gresford Colliery Relief – not less than £115 – Flood Relief £107:10:0, Portsmouth Affray £41:5:0, Orkney and General Relief 10 guineas. Westminster Abbey Repair Fund fared less well with £1. Memorial Funds were involved: King George's Jubilee Trust 5 guineas, Margaret Macmillan £5 and Dame Mary Scharlieb 5 guineas. Local needs before the Second War included Winter Distress League in the Thirties £15:6:0, Unemployment Christmas Fund 1919 £2, Emergency Unemployment Committee £22:5:0 as late as 1940, Poor Relief Fund £3.

In peacetime, girls concentrated on the disadvantaged and the sick, giving money, paying visits, joining in camps, especially Dymchurch, acting plays and , above all, helping with much appreciated parties run by Mr Whitehead and later Miss Campbell. In the early days, funds were needed to alleviate misery: National Refuge for the Destitute and Homeless Children £5, Clothes for poor children £20, the South London Mission £2, the Foundling Site, Starving Children's Fund 17/-, Fresh Air Fund, Invalid Children's Aid £1:10:0, Necessitous Middlesex Children's Fund 17/-. While always continuing to help the deprived, the waifs and strays, the attitude became more constructive and more personal: Handicapped Vale Road School, Helping Hand, National Children's Homes, Dr Barnardo's £80:2:0¼, Shaftesbury Society £27:11:0, Save the Children £27, St Christopher's Home £8:6:8 and the Pestalozzi Children's Village £2:13:4. They sponsored Julia's education in Bechuanaland.

The League of Mercy was helped annually throughout the Twenties £9:19:6, and, later, the League of Pity. Halliwick Girls' Cripples Home received small amounts as well as a doll's house, Spastics £8:17:10, lepers, TB £10:16:0, Cripples' League and Mission £40:5:0 and the blind – various agencies, including Guide Dogs, Sunshine Homes for Blind Babies, Westminster, Central London Ophthalmic (£1:10:0), and London Hospitals for the blind and an individual blind girl.

The old were adopted: £192:18:8 altogether plus an OG legacy of £6,000. Since the Second War, they received parcels, but were also visited and given parties, a more practical approach.

General 'do-goodery' was practised by the Guides, especially in the Twenties. Before then, Our Day raised £776, School Self-Denial Fund £2:8:6. Princess Elizabeth Day was supported annually, latterly raising £130. Later, St James' Girls Infants school benefited by £2:5:0 as did the Musicians' Union Benevolent Fund.

Those who work at sea were remembered almost wholly in Miss Broome's time: Merchant Navy £69, Arethusa Training Ship £8:8:6, Australian Hospital Ships' libraries 3 guineas, Sailors' Day one guinea, Mission to Deep Sea Fishermen £22:5:0, British and Foreign Sailors' Society £10, and British Merchant Seamen's Department.

Finally, the sick and those who care for them: in the Twenties the Edith Cavell Homes of Rest 3 guineas. At least £300 was distributed to national and local hospitals: the National £16:4:0, Queen Elizabeth's £30:10:9, Royal

Cancer, Royal Free, International Police, Great Ormond Street (mainly toys), Hospital Day Fund £1:6:0. The four Enfield ones were: Auxiliary 5 guineas, Infirmary £25+, Cottage £69:6:10 plus at least 250lb of jam, and the War Memorial £128:17:0.

These are amazing totals, at least £12,000, and undeniably much more, particularly if the differing values of the pound could be assessed. The impetus to help, whether with money, or, more rewardingly, with time and effort, never died, either in war or in peace. Many former students continue this support.

3. Intake

Girls came from every kind of school – primary, junior, evening continuation, Polytechnic, day, preparatory, Dame, Grammar, high, central, elementary, secondary modern, Jewish, Catholic, convent, C of E, Quaker, single sex, mixed, state, public, private, open-air, farm, commercial, technical, Army, orphanage, Orphan asylum – or, for 27 in the early years, from no school at all, having been educated privately at home, usually with governesses, although one was 'travelling' and another suffered ill-health.

Although numbers fell periodically during the Twenties, Thirties and late Fifties, they regularly outstripped accommodation, necessitating at times the use, inconvenient but welcomed, of other venues. The building, designed for 250, charmed the original 24 Pupil-Teachers who were joined by ever-growing numbers, so that their bliss was short-lived. The first Mistresses, however, were pleased, as the increase not only brought in more Staff, but improved their salaries. The annual intake was about 100, mostly of 10-11 year olds, although there was always a steady influx into the Sixth usually from fee-paying establishments which could not offer pre-university examination work. The average age of pre-1914 entrants was actually 12½. More came than left, so that in school by 1914 were 253, in 1919 358 and by 1921 410.

Vigorous protests were continually made about the inadequacy of the Old Building, for even when numbers dropped during the slump, there were still 302 students. In the first months of the Second War, this figure shot up to 1,000, as schools in more vulnerable areas were evacuated. By 1947, 827 were on roll. With the post-war bulge, one more form was created to enjoy briefly the space and amenities of the New Building, although its construction and the repairs of War Damage caused more chaos than the War itself had done. Justified complaints continued.

Numbers quoted are the minimum, as early registration was imperfect, with no professional secretarial help, but also because a girl may have been to two, three, even four, or, in one case, five, different previous institutions. The contributory schools of over half the entrants 1962-1967 remain on confidential cards. The general picture remains true.

A striking feature is the number who arrived at the wrong time, whether at the beginning of the spring or summer terms or during term-time: pre-1914, 138: during the War, 142: in the Twenties, 185: in the Thirties, 104, with an overall total of nearly 700, approximately 13·2%.

Some girls came from other parts of the country, as fathers' jobs dictated. No fewer than 110 towns are mentioned as sending some 143 pupils, in addition to 125 from 51 different schools in the Greater London area. Thirty more had been in 16 named areas of Scotland, Wales, Northern and Southern Ireland, plus one from the Isle of Wight. A further 47 transferred from countries in the five continents; this does not include European refugees.

350 girls, therefore, approximately 6·7%, had had their education seriously disrupted: difficult for them and for Staff. They brought different customs, ideas and speech patterns.

Most, of course, came from local elementary schools, some 71 establishments sending 4,358 pupils. The annual percentage varied between 70% and 90%. Some sent girls virtually every year, others spasmodically; some no longer exist, a few are post-1945 creations. Thirty-one sent fewer than ten pupils, 30 sent fewer than 100 each. The main contributors were:

Chesterfield *	542	Chase Side	454
Lavender **	433	George Spicer **	375
St Andrew's	368	Bush Hill Park *	331
Southbury Road**	275	Merryhills	152 (after 1946)

(*contributed throughout ** none before 1914)

Secondary fee-paying schools contributed more Sixthformers than 11-year olds. Palmers Green tops the list with 78. Five more had been in boarding schools. In all, 183 juniors came from 32 establishments. Only four reached double figures: Potters Bar High 12, Edmonton Latymer and Harlow 11 each, Winchmore 10.

Nineteen Dame schools, mostly local, faded after 1924; some simply disappeared, others renamed themselves High schools. Over 100 girls were taught well enough to pass the Entrance examinations. The names evoke a long-gone era: Miss Gardner, Woodstock 22, Miss Chambers, Shirley Lodge 19, Elm Croft 16, Roanoake 11, Miss Buckley 7, Bycullah 6, Wynwood House 4, Miss Lee-Jones, Ingleby High 2. Others sent one each: Miss Jones, Cecil Road, Miss Beale, Margate, Lynwood, Miss Starr's, Steven's and Temple's Private Classes, Miss Welsford's High School for Girls.

More than twice as many, 217, again often to the Sixth, had been fee-payers at 13 known convents and Catholic schools, but more unspecified) Holy Family tops the list with 65, followed by St Angela's Wood Green and Enfield 63, Enfield 25. Six more came from similar establishments in England (Ursuline, Ilford) and abroad (Durban, Dominican Louvain, Egypt).

A further 159 transferred from 25 private fee-paying schools, more were unnamed. Only two reached double figures: Enfield Preparatory 48 and Bycullah 41. Most were local, others were outside the borough ; one had been at the Friends' School Saffron Walden, another at the Old Palace, Mayfield.

We can say, with some confidence. that 82%+ came from traditional elementary schools and 12·5% had paid fees.

As 399 institutions were named, criticism of a narrow intake to a socially limited ECS is manifestly unjust.

4. Leavers

It is impossible to give accurate figures for jobs for at least the first forty years. By 1914, already 201 were unknown, with 139 more during the Great War, over 100 between the wars and 234 in World War II. Names and numbers in magazines do not always tally with those in Prize Giving programmes. Some found work several years after leaving, others changed jobs almost as soon as they had left, others notified changes, sometimes several, much later; a few worked in more than one sphere.

Virtually throughout school's life, for it is not a recent phenomenon, Heads, Staff and Inspectors lamented premature leaving and exhorted parents to allow, or compel, their daughters to complete their secondary education. Miss Sharp called it both foolish and unpatriotic during the Second War. Whenever economic conditions worsened and the school leaving age rose, so did the numbers.

In the early years, what might be called a negative attitude to the future of girls did not help. Just as they arrived at odd times, so too did they leave at odd times. Between 1909 and 1914, 87 failed to survive until the summer and 42 left before their 14th birthdays. Only 23 departed similarly during the Great War, but in the Twenties, no fewer than 405 failed to complete the school year. Most were trapped; they needed paid work; the market remained limited. Penalties were noted in only seven cases throughout.

Lamentations continued. Throughout the Thirties, when money was tight, more than 300 disappeared. It is unfair to include all who left in the autumn term of 1939, as over 50 were evacuated, of whom 17 returned. It was upsetting that, although an increasing number did stay on into the Sixth, some 250 failed to stay the course after the war.

In all, a known total of 1,358.

To be fair, some did go to other schools, including their previous ones or those nearer to their homes. Some 50 families moved from the UK. One girl was excluded, two left for the educational reason of poor progress. All these account for about 300. At least 55 moved but found no school either near or appropriate.

Health played a part in this shifting picture. Sixty left, at least nominally, for reasons of their own ill-health, especially before 1930. Some 18 died, at least 6 more dying within a few years, again particularly in the Twenties.

Sadly, Necessitous Family Circumstances and Services Required hurt too many girls, again especially during the Twenties, when 52 were withdrawn specifically for home duties. Even when family finances were poor, too many of them, well over 150, remained at home, to help mothers or fathers, to take charge of younger children. In the Sixties, there were more modern problems of unemployment, inadequate grants and family break-up; one girl was tried for theft.

All this affected not only the individuals and their families, but such school concerns as games teams, House activities and the prefectoral system.

Little choice of career was available when ECS opened. It was expected that girls would stay at home, go in for clerical or Domestic Science work, or, preferably, teach. They were urged not to get bogged down in an insufficiently rewarded clerical post held in low esteem, to think of taking advantage of opportunities in the Colonies – and to read. That was the extent of the careers advice offered. The odd helpful book was donated to the library.

After the Second War, changes in working practices, with greater diversity and flexibility, especially for married women, affected and sometimes overwhelmed girls. School gradually woke up to their needs. The first evening talks to parents mainly concerned choice of subjects. By the time of the Golden Jubilee, there was more helpful publicity of what former students had achieved; various clubs debated possibilities and a Mistress was put in charge.

Slowly, lectures on specific spheres gave way to counselling, a careers file was begun, parents were invited to Year meetings, girls were interviewed individually, financial help was investigated. In the last phase of ECS, discussion and advice became a recognised part of the curriculum, with the help of Youth Employment Officers. A room with a small library was designated for the work.

As with the intake, all figures given are approximate.

In the early days, one or two left the UK to go wherever their husbands' work took them. As travel improved after the Second War, an ever-increasing number worked abroad, some on one year exchanges, others with voluntary and relief organisations, as a break before or after university, with a temporary job or as an émigrée with a career. Two hundred and twenty-three girls were involved in over 50 countries from Brazil to China; most were in the USA (50), Europe (42), Australia (30) and Africa (28).

The Services were not popular, only eleven signing on in both wars or finding them an escape in the Twenties and Thirties; a few did temporary war work. Others in uniform included the police, an Air Hostess, a Thompson Holiday girl and an Assistant Cub Scout Commissioner.

The law also attracted few if we exclude one tried on deception charges and another for theft; six more were involved in the legal system.

Religion called to a few more. Four graduated in Theology, others studied it in Training Colleges. Two became nuns, one a priest, several with religious organisations or individuals. There were no fewer than 12 missionaries.

Writing mainly took the form of journalism (12), publishing and their own work (10+), which ranged from research to historical novels, children's and cookery books. Librarians trained at six different colleges. One did research, the remaining 25-30 worked in local or specialised libraries.

Some 25 were directly involved with stage work, others were, and are, in radio and television in front of and behind the cameras. Several, wisely, have a fall-back career, in, for example speech therapy. Twenty-five musicians studied at ten different colleges, all involved professionally as performers and/or teachers.

An ever-increasing number, up to 142 in the Fifties, achieved part-time Art scholarships to Hornsey; over 60 studied full-time, one eventually having her own studio in Paris. Others were apprentices and trainees in a wide range of applied art.

In the early days, the land was of vital importance to girls and their families; dependence on it much decreased. Farming, here and abroad, floristry (over 50), horticulture and, later, more scientific agriculture were popular, in all 90, most learning by experience, but a handful studying at specialist colleges.

Fewer than stereotyping would suggest were involved with animals; riding was mainly for pleasure. Workers ranged from kennelmaid and poodle clipper via attendant at Battersea Children's Zoo to breeding Welsh ponies – and mosquitoes. Four became vets, one judging dog shows.

Miss Broome would have approved of the 150 who trained for different branches of Domestic Science. Apart from teaching and lecturing, inspecting and demonstrating, cooks had their own shops or cooked for hotels, private and public bodies. Needlework was more popular in her time than subsequently, when dress design, modelling, personnel work and buying were more attractive propositions.

She would have been less pleased with those who found practical work yet those using their hands belong mainly to her period. Few of the 35 hairdressers, Beauty Culture trainees and a only a couple of the 50 factory workers were at ECS after the Second War. Although two of them had junior awards, the 6 in domestic service also knew her as Head. The 71 shop assistants came from all generations; they became more sophisticated over the years, from the humble Lyon's Teashop waitress to the owner of her own business. One post-1945 girl served a 5-year apprenticeship at Enfield Cable Works; another in the Sixties was a window cleaner. Greatly varied courses in engineering of all kinds were latterly followed at universities and polytechnics; there was even an engineering draughtswoman and an engineering manager of an insurance company.

Well over 200 in all.

Most leavers fit into three remaining groups. First, the once despised clerical, which increased in respectability and scope as girls gained higher qualifications, became known as secretaries and personal assistants enjoying more challenging work. Some later transferred, often to teaching; some graduates acquired secretarial certificates. School's own department rose in stature. Over 1,000 fit into this category. They trained at 43 named establishments; perhaps the élite was the French Institute, although many of the 115 scholarships and exhibitions awarded were not taken up as candidates subsequently received university places. Many achieved high-powered posts in foreign and international bodies. Non-linguists had an enviable choice: to work for powerful and interesting individuals and organisations, in local, central and colonial government.

A far cry from the pen-pushers of the early years.

Remember that ECS grew out of a Further Education establishment and provided the sole way for girls to realise their potential. That there was pressure, or, at least, that pressure was felt to exist, to go on to Further and Higher Education was frequently expressed, especially by those who neither aspired to it nor achieved it.

Teaching was the main, indeed the only, goal of the early bright students, although as many as 60 remained uncertificated. Five hundred are known to have studied at Training Colleges or Colleges of Education when the 3-year course was introduced in 1962. No type of educational establishment was without the presence of an ECS girl; many became Heads, lecturers, inspectors and governors.

Physical Education attracted 120, most of whom taught; 30 preferred Physiotherapy, mainly in the Forties and Fifties. During and after the Second War, applicants exceeded places; at the same time, this period saw many more successful candidates, stalwarts representing school, borough and county in orthodox games and sports.

Girls reached university sometimes against parental wishes and always against fierce competition, which often led to cramming. School broadcast its successes which reached their peak in the Sixties. The new Colleges of Advanced Technology accepted students. Scholarships and exhibitions, State and College, made all the difference, financially to families and in prestige to ECS. Only a handful failed to complete their courses. Oxford and Cambridge remained the pinnacle, the latter taking 21, the former nearly four times that number, St Hilda's alone offering 27 places. London was the obvious choice, 170 at 11 different colleges; others ventured further from home.

Perhaps a list of the 57 courses studied might inspire: Agricultural Economics, American Studies, Ancient History and Archaeology, Anthropology (one pursuing her studies on an island in the Indian Ocean), Architecture, Bacteriology, Biochemistry, Botany, Chemical Physics, Chemistry, Classics, Combined/Comparative/General and Hispanic Studies, Dentistry, Drama and Theatre Arts, Economics, Economic History, English and French (the two most popular), French with German/ Spanish/ Latin, General Science, Geography, German alone or with Dutch, History alone or with Political Economics, Law, Mathematics alone or with Philosophy, Medicine, Microbiology, Music alone or with Drama, Natural Science, Pharmacy, Physiology, Physics, Psychology alone or with Sociology or Statistics (one gaining a First), Political Economics, Spanish alone or with Portuguese, Social Geography, Science, Social Administration/Studies, Sociology, Theology, Town Planning and Zoology.

Girls followed virtually no scientific careers before the mid-Twenties. Subsequently, they disprove the notion that girls are poor at Sciences; they gained brilliant honours in various disciplines. Over 100 also worked in laboratories.

Of the 22 doctors, the first qualified before the Great War; some had to graduate via Trinity College, Dublin, where one was the only woman to get a First. The first of 16 dentists qualified in the Twenties. Nursing was expectedly popular throughout the decades. It is hard now to believe that, such was the competition in the Thirties, one worthy candidate failed to secure a place. Over 150 qualified at 26 different hospitals.

Many, generally from the Thirties onwards and especially since the War, have found satisfaction in various caring professions: speech therapists, pharmacists, almoners, masseuses, occupational therapists, psychologists, psychiatrists, chiropodists, orthoptists, radiographers, even a psychotherapist. Individuals have worked in schools for the deaf, for the Distressed Gentlefolks's Association, for the Manic Depressive Fellowship. Others specialised in remedial work and counselling.

ECS was proud of them all and of its eight recipients of the MBE and one OBE, its two Mayors, six Deputy Mayoresses and the two who became 'Lady' by virtue of their husbands' elevation. It was also delighted with those who refuse to be categorised, the pioneers, whether because they have succeeded as women or in their own spheres, such as the first woman to be in charge of a Public Health Authority, one of the first women eligible for membership of the Stock Exchange or the world-renowned horticulturalist. One even achieved posthumous fame as the address at her memorial service was given by a Chaplain to the Queen.

5. Parental Occupations

a) Fathers

Here again, most numbers quoted are approximate. Details, requested on acceptance of a girl, may be duplicated, wrongly recorded, ambiguous, refused, over-modest or over-boastful, non-existent or even destroyed. Two wars further distort the picture as men left jobs to serve in factories or Forces, some taking different work on demobilisation. Others changed or lost work or gained promotion. For the last 5-6 years, only 17 are available. Jobs number 4,926, not necessarily the number of fathers, but enough to allows some generalisations, although a true statistician may be unsatisfied with the groupings.

Although before the Second War, the family was a more stable unit than it was by 1967, many early students had a troubled background, 19 fathers having died before 1914. Altogether, 220 fathers died before or during their daughters' schooldays, 57 during the Great War, which also left 7 men disabled. Eight more were disabled in the Second War, one was a Japanese POW, more than a dozen were killed. Ten more fathers were invalids, which meant that one daughter had to leave. Nine were widowers.

One was in prison, another forbidden access and at least two had simply disappeared. Thirty-five had retired, a quarter of them in the first five years, a few through ill-health or disablement, most because of age.

Divorce (3 during the Second War) and separation are more recent phenomena, 25 in all having been notified; 5 re-marriages (one to the mother of another pupil, one girl having to leave home as a result) are recorded, together with 54 stepfathers (and 5 stepmothers), nearly all after 1945. These men's varied jobs have been included.

Thirty-four girls were looked after by guardians. As 23 of these were before 1914, Prospectus and first Rules were addressed to Parents and Guardians. Several girls were in an institution, even when father was alive and working. In the Sixties, one was adopted, one in care. Before 1919, 3 fathers had independent means; after 1946, 12 were known to be unemployed. Before 1939, 3 had 2 part-time jobs, fewer than might be expected during the slump.

Unemployed, dead, disabled, retired, unknown for whatever reason, number 343, or almost 7%.

From the outset, at least 17 (excluding Service Personnel) worked abroad, holding positions as diverse as foreman blacksmith, farmer, hotel assistant and Civil Servant.

The term OA (Ordinary Artisan) covered more than half of the country's working population up to the Thirties; Enfield was no exception.

Most fathers, overall 18·8%, were in trade, wholesale but mainly retail, which dominated throughout, although numbers decreased after 1945. Surprisingly many owned their own shops and small businesses or were directors, managers, or partners of larger ones (over 200), although the majority were, of course, assistants with a similar number of specialists in their own spheres; 110 were commercial travellers and representatives, many were warehousemen, buyers, fitters, cashiers, clerks, credit controller, collectors and 2 inspectors.

Most dealt in comestibles: 40 butchers included at least 4 masters, 39 were bakers of different products, 40 were grocers (one devoted exclusively to tea and coffee), 34 licensed victuallers, 14 were in catering (one in a Kosher kitchen) and hotel work, 9 worked with fish, 8 with fruit and vegetables.

Seventy-five were involved with outfitting, tailoring and ancillary trades; the boot and shoe trade supported 28 and included one disabled engineer, 24 were drapers whilst one man made handbags. In various capacities, household furniture trade employed another 27, 16 were in jewellery (an OA before 1914 in ivory and tortoiseshell), 15 were barbers/hairdressers, 15 sold newspapers etc. No other group reached double figures: in coal and iron (before 1939), film renters, booksellers (one secondhand), oilmen, in china and glass, antique dealers, and florists. Individuals ran general and domestic stores, sold bicycles, sports goods, 'foreign produce', industrial goods, soap (wholesale) and postage stamps. A grand total of over 900.

White collar men came second with 15·8%, some 780 men, specification being mostly vague: 'clerical'. Whereas numbers remained steady, men too enjoyed an ever wider range of posts and greater levels of responsibility. Finance took the largest share with a minimum of 56 in banks, 52 in both accountancy and insurance; typists, consultants, registrars just rose to double figures. Secretaries, 28, worked for individuals and corporate institutions. Well over 100 were Civil Servants, some with high ranking posts at home and abroad, most after the Second War. Forty-eight were officials in local government.

Not far behind came the manual workers, almost 12%, with 591 men, at at least 17 different levels; they held third place throughout ECS' story. At least half were unskilled labourers until the mid-Thirties, rising as bench or charge hands, gangers, mates to foremen, supervisors, and inspectors. Just over 100 trades are mentioned, the more exotic ones ceasing with the Thirties, and several subdivided: – makers of bedding, boilers, boxes, brief cases, brushes, cables, filaments, flexible metallic tubes, gauges, heating apparatus, industrial goods, lamp bulbs, lead shot, packing cases, patterns, scales, sweets, synthetic resins, textiles, tubes: finishers: turners of ebonite, fountain pens: filers: fitters of hot water, laboratories, tubing and maintenance: gas blower, collector, apparatus benchhand, engine driver, meter maker, salesman: glass blowers, glaziers, experimental worker, makers, moulders: iron makers, turners, moulders; machine minders, operators, wood and spindle workers: metal hardeners, refiners, sheet and precious metal men: toolmen, contractors, sharpeners: wire workers, drawers, weaver: cutters of marble, measures and stock: advertising sign fixer, ash hopper, asphalt driver: blacksmiths; capstan setter, chemical plant operator, cleaner, coin meter collector, cokemaster, compressor driver, consort case worker, coppersmith, cordite worker: dye carter: electroplater and gilder: felt mill operator, fibrous plasterer, furnacemen: goldblockers: jute goods supervisor: lamp maintenance man, laundryman, locksmith: manual instructor, masons, mechanics, metropolitan water board men, millwrights, moulders(plastic, rubber); packers, paper workers, photometric men, plant assistant, press driver, printers, progress chaser and estimator: riggers, rollermen: setters, silencer (!), sprayers, stampers, stokers, storekeepers and warehousemen (the largest single group), strander, stripper: telephonists, thread grinder, ticket writer, timekeepers, tinners, turbine greaser: ventilation fitter, viewers: welders, wheelwrights. Nor must the plastic designer, plater and power station attendant be forgotten.

A sharp drop to 6·94% with those in transport, 180+ on the roads, with, again, a wide variety: owners, inspectors, makers, drivers and conductors of all imaginable vehicles including trams and trolleybuses, even of a stage coach. The railways, especially the LNER for Enfield, regarded as providing safe jobs in the Twenties and Thirties, supported 153; some of their jobs belong to earlier days – coal porter, crossing sweeper, doorman farrier, shunter. Numbers dropped significantly after the Second War; the pre-war proportion had been 9·4%. Nine only were connected with the sea, from bargee to ocean cable operator.

In sixth place, close behind with 6·8%, 335, come construction workers, general and domestic, a flourishing sphere, and 312 estate agents. Men dealing with wood, not forgetting a Saw Doctor, predominate, 102. Next come the actual builders (one doubling as funeral director) 74 and painters, paperhangers (one doubling as a window cleaner) 53. Also reaching double figures were plumbers of all grades, 25+. There were stonemasons, plasterers, rate fixers and collectors, auctioneers, scaffolder.

Engineering increased enormously during and after the Second War as scope widened: 170 before 1939 rose to 323, or 6·55%. From labourers to the Chief Bill clerk of the City Engineering Department, men were of all grades and skills. Twenty-six spheres are noted from aeronautics and bakelite to sanitation, television, ventilation and water works.

Close behind come professionals, 6·53%. The largest number was in finance: 86 accountants, 2 company directors, 11 stockbrokers, 5 underwriters, a statistician and the Director of Economic Affairs. Forty worked in the legal domain, one a student (retired police officer from Sierra Leone), as, for example, bailiffs, barristers and Notarys Public. Next comes music with 18 performers, 3 organists (one in a cinema in the Thirties), 10 publishers, various instrument makers, together with the Assistant Chorus Master at Covent Garden and a member of the Grenadier Guards Band. Close on their heels are the 32 in the Art world, mainly as commercial artists, draughtsmen (19) and designers. Thirteen journalists worked, for example, at the News Desk of the *Daily Express,* as assistant editor of *Shipping*; there were publishers, readers, an early editor of the local *Gazette* and the literary advisor to Selfridges. Only six were librarians. Twenty-two were analytical and works chemists, 9 were architects, 6 were in the theatre, films, broadcasting. They worked as metallurgists, photographers, physicists, scientists; individuals were quantity surveyor, computer programmer, examiner of patents. An overall total of 322.

Ninth come those in Service careers or in uniform, 217 or 4·4%, closely followed by those in factories, 180 or 3·65%. The number of servicemen more than doubled in the Second War before declining rapidly. The figure is inflated with temporary involvement. Five were in the peacetime army up to 1939. During the Great War, at least 28 joined the army, two the Navy which, in peacetime, employed 12 including a chief stoker and a member of the Royal Marine Light Infantry. Two served in the Merchant Navy, one a Master Mariner, a sergeant and an officer in the RAF. Between 1939 and 1946, the War directly took 41 from a variety of civilian employment; 18 are known to have enlisted in the Air Force, 7 in the Navy, others in Civil Defence. Post-war saw officers and soldiers in Occupied Germany.

About 50 served in the Police, of whom 23 are known to have been constables and 5 inspectors. Eighteen were caretakers, commissionaires, lift attendants, nightwatchmen and, more recently, in Security, 11 were in the Fire Service. Not all of the 95 in the Post Office wore uniform; there was even one in the Postal and Telegraph Office of the Royal Household. A mixed bag included a hotel superintendent, a waiter in the Great Eastern hotel, a pre-1914 butler, prison officer and a Conservative Club steward.

War work was dominated by Royal Small Arms Factory, founded in 1815 and at one time employing more than 5,000. Until the Great War, it was a male preserve, but many women were then drafted in. Over 100 fathers were Lockies in E.R.B's time, over 30 being pulled in during the Great War and another 40 just before and during the Second War. Numbers declined rapidly after 1946 and hardship was caused to Enfield by its closure in 1988 – so possibly 145 altogether. Thirty plus worked in other Gunpowder and Explosives Works, another 7 were 'in munitions'. It was in this community that there was the most marked distinction between clerks (a handful), artisans (the majority) and the Bosses. Twenty-four skilled jobs were named from armourer and artificer to tool sharpeners and barrel drillers.

Education took the modest total of 167, almost 3·4%, from caretakers to two professors and 8 university lecturers; 120 taught, mostly in elementary schools, more than half before 1939. Only 11 were known to be Heads, one receiving the OBE for National Savings work. Others served in administration; individuals were Supervisor of Poor Law Schools, a correspondence school manager, an educational representative and, in the Sixties, two mature students.

Numbers working on the land show the biggest change over the years, decreasing markedly from the Thirties. There were 53 pre-1914. Overall, 163 derived their living from it, a modest 3·3%, in farming and horticulture; 12 worked specifically with horses, two with greyhounds and one each with pigs and chickens. There was one vet and one working with the Animal Health Trust and the RSPCA. Fourteen were gardeners, 11 of them before 1939. Miscellaneous jobs included a cemetery supervisor, a crop sprayer and Clerk of the Royal Agricultural Society.

The caring jobs, in the widest sense, appealed to 2·53% of the total, to more as the years went by, for the percentage pre-1939 was a modest 1·3%, distorted during the War to 5%. They included, for example, 12 doctors, a professor of medical science, five opticians (one combining it with watchmaking), 31 chemists and a number making medical aids and surgical appliances, and one selling health foods. Among ancillary carers were relieving officers, and ambulance men.

It seems appropriate to add those in religion: 18 were ministers of five denominations plus Church and Salvation Armies (the latter both parents) with 4 missionaries (one divorced by his wife), nearly all before the Second War.

Two small groups remain: 1·5% were in printing and ·73% were electricians. Skills again were many, 20 being listed from lithographic overseer to packer of *The Illustrated Evening News*. The 36 electricians included makers of bulbs and instruments, maintenance and laboratory men and Controller of Public Lighting.

A few remain, the unique ones who became fewer as the years went by: Enquiry Agent: Golf Course Supervisor (with his wife): handyman: Lawn Tennis Bat Maker and Bender: managers of a Dance Hall and of a Children's Boating Pool: oysterman (Labourer): gypsy (in the Sixties): Ventriloquist (retired): Gold and Silver Stick Mounter (Proprietor): two Members of Parliament; finally, Gentleman (Deceased).

What greater mixture could any sociologist dream?

b) Mothers

Of the 26 widows before 1939 (5 before the Great War), 8 were independent (one dying shortly herself), 8 remarried and one withdrew her child. Nine mothers are recorded as in charge of their daughters in cooperation with another person, a figure which rose to 33 during the war; 69 were totally on their own for a variety of reasons – desertion, divorce (no alimony), separation, husbands' temporary war service , even choice. Another died, causing another premature leaver. One was permanently in hospital, one left home, one was abroad with her husband, more than one required her daughter's companionship. Apart from 4 widows (2 dressmakers, a ladies' cloakroom attendant, a cook), only 2 admitted to gainful employment: – hairdresser (Proprietor) and organiser of a crèche on behalf of working mothers.

During the Second War, many had to find work, which was readily available, when their husbands were called up or killed. Others simply wanted to. Post-war, despite competition from men demobilised, well over 120 had jobs, again sometimes for personal reasons, but often in the new spirit of equality. Some still felt guilty of admitting it, others wished to conceal their extra personal income from Authority, even from husbands. Records are therefore statistically unsound, but the spread is probably fairly representative. Those who did not go out to work now said 'Housewife'. One, uniquely, was pregnant.

Twenty-four are known to have remarried, but there must have been more. One was a foster mother, 5 were stepmothers, which, for one girl, created a very unhappy situation.

Part-time employment, although sometimes in the evenings, was obviously more convenient. If sessions could coincide with school hours, days and terms, so much the better. Ninety-four stated specifically that they were part-timers, but it is impossible to differentiate; 290 are known to have been in paid work.

At least 7 were carers, 18 in hospitals (matron, nurses, cleaners), 11 as home helps, 8 looked after children, more were in Social Services, with pensioners or as welfare assistants; a few were doctors, physiotherapist, chiropodist, pharmacist. One was a Guide for Physically Handicapped, one Head of a Remand Home.

Almost as many, over 60, are known to have worked in schools: 15 teachers (nursery, infants, ECS, maladjusted, dance, Keep-Fit, Head of a Private School): lecturers, Education Officer: 4 brave souls were mature students. Others were cleaners 5, dinner ladies 11, school cooks, laboratory technicians, playground supervisors and 5 housekeepers.

Secretarial work absorbed more than 45, in private and public offices. They were also auditors, a dictaphone typist, a comptometer operator, telephonist and receptionist.

Not far behind, 42 were in shops and similar establishments which often had flexible hours, as general assistants, hairdressers, barmaids, in canteens, cafés and in markets. Others were cashiers, a florist, a corsetier.

Thirty plus laboured in factories, although little, apart from a scarf and apron checker, laundry workers and cleaners, has been vouchsafed of actual trades.

Working at home proved sensible for a handful: 6 dressmakers, 2 milliners, a toymaker, a landlady.

A few do not fit these categories: a company and 2 deputy directors, 2 librarians, draughtswoman, journalist, nursery gardener, agent, water agriculturalist, driving instructor, singer and iceskater (both professionally), Golf Club Stewardess.

One became an ECS Governor.

An ever-increasing number – 170 are known – had been ECS pupils themselves; 11 sent their daughters in 1963 alone.

INDEX

a) Girls   m = married, name unknown: † = dead

Saunders B. (Macleod) 362-3 428 504
    E. 253
Scholl N. 200
Schollick J. (Hill) 228 354
Schwarzloh C. 534
Scopes J. 174 176 232 253
    N. 174 177
Score M. 70 77
Scott P. (1935-1993) 476-7
Scutcher J. 488
Sellick S. (Parker) 538
Shadbolt S. 548
Shafford K. 304
Sharman B. 475
Sharp P. 455
Sharpe H.M. 362
Shearman E. (Macleod) 445
Shelley M. 485
Shepherd G. 442 447 465
Shimmins B. 485
Shimwell M. 485
Simmonds S. 463
Simmons M. (Curtis) 474
Singleton E. 70
Sledge B. 387 441
Smart H. 526
Smith E. 119 503 F. 541
    Meryl 398 513 541
    Molly 494
Sommerard A. (1930-1966) 460
Sowter J. 476
Spenceley G. 475
Spencer I (m) 90 120
    N. (m) 89 120
Spratley E.M. 121
Spriggs J. (Walles, 1929-1993) 476
Spurge G. (Hindaugh, 1936-1990) 474 521
Spurgeon J. 521
Stableton D. (Coker) 301 319 362
Staines G. 506 538

Stearns M. 460
Steel J. (Fisher) 543
Steer J. 387 476
Stephens H. 397 483
    O. (Jay, 1926-1988) 361
Stephenson M. 462
Stevens M. 534
Stewart D.C. (Waller) 301
Stiff J. (Green) 534
Stobo M. 480
Stone B. E. 362 E. 442 L. 440
    Margaret (Conan) 361
    Mary 361
Strangleman B. (m) 456
Stubbs C. 387 494
Stuchbury B. 488
Styles L. 119
Swainson M. 441
Swallow J. 491
Sykes C. 513
Syrett J. 547
Talbot E. 539
Tanner L. (Westbrooke) 534
    M.E. 199
Tarring S. 483
Tattersall A. 456 L. 521
Taylor A. 399 439
    B. (Doyle, 1934-†) 406 439
    J. 447 513 538,9 R. 468
Telling C.P. 71
Theobald M. 320
Thickett S. 475
Thomas M. and W. 476 P. 460
Thompson J. (1948-1976?) 521 537
    N.J. (Bower) 281 287,8
    P. 534
Thornton S. 491
Tingley I. 494
Tippett A. 543
Todd A. (Braybrook) 363
Townshend W. 253

b) Staff, Clergy, Education Officers, Governors.

Tavener Mrs (née Crook) 493
Taylor Mrs G. (1907-1992) 554
   Miss Maria (b 1889) 105
   Mrs Marjorie 390 512
Thomas Miss (Pollard) 332 389 440 481
Miss Thompson (Spalding) 354
   Mrs (1925-1998) 471
Thurston Miss (b 1904) 421
Tibbs Miss (m) 476
Tomlinson Miss (1912-199?) 308 356 396 471
Twine Mrs 538

Vear Mrs 546
de Vinney Miss (b 1906) 162

Walles Miss (b 1908) 428
Webb Mr (†) 542 Miss S. (†) 494

Westaway Miss 162
Westwood Mrs (née Murrant) 350 354
Wheatley Miss (b 1895) 162
Whelan Miss (Gull, b 1906) 227
Whitehead Mr (Charlie) 267-8 273 380 382 390-1 403 418 426 438 444 451 512 516-7 531 537 564 574
Wicks Miss (b 1893) 159
Wilson Miss (Atkins) 484
Woods Miss (b 1887) 42 102-3 170-2 185-7 235 271 275 289 293 306 332 354-5 416 418 456
Wooldridge Mrs (Steve, 1908-1993) 455 487 504 535
Woolmer Miss (b 1888) 45 52 110
Wormell Miss (b 1901) 158
Wright Miss (b 1907) 162
Wynne Miss 428

Yeoman Miss (b 1891) 159 162